THE INFORMATION SOCIETY

THE INFORMATION SOCIETY

Critical Concepts in Sociology

Edited by
Robin Mansell

Volume III
Democracy, Governance and Regulation

LONDON AND NEW YORK

First published 2009
by Routledge
2 Park Square, Milton Park, Abingdon, Oxon, OX14 4RN, UK

Simultaneously published in the USA and Canada
by Routledge
270 Madison Avenue, New York, NY 10016

Routledge is an imprint of the Taylor & Francis Group, an informa business

Editorial material and selection © 2009, Robin Mansell; individual owners retain copyright in their own material

Typeset in 10/12pt Times NR MT by Graphicraft Limited, Hong Kong
Printed and bound in Great Britain by
the MPG Books Group

All rights reserved. No part of this book may be reprinted or reproduced or utilised in any form or by any electronic, mechanical, or other means, now known or hereafter invented, including photocopying and recording, or in any information storage or retrieval system, without permission in writing from the publishers.

British Library Cataloguing in Publication Data
A catalogue record for this book is available from the British Library

Library of Congress Cataloging in Publication Data
The information society : critical concepts in sociology / edited by Robin Mansell.
p. cm. — (Critical concepts in sociology)
Includes bibliographical references and index.
ISBN 978-0-415-44308-1 (set, hardback) — ISBN 978-0-415-44309-8 (volume 1, hardback) — ISBN 978-0-415-44310-4 (volume 2, hardback) — ISBN 978-0-415-44311-1 (volume 3, hardback) — ISBN 978-0-415-44312-8 (volume 4, hardback) 1. Information society. I. Mansell, Robin.
HM851.I5324 2009
303.48′33—dc22
2008042128

ISBN 10: 0-415-44308-3 (Set)
ISBN 10: 0-415-44311-3 (Volume III)

ISBN 13: 978-0-415-44308-1 (Set)
ISBN 13: 978-0-415-44311-1 (Volume III)

Publisher's Note

References within each chapter are as they appear in the original complete work.

CONTENTS

VOLUME III   DEMOCRACY, GOVERNANCE AND REGULATION

Acknowledgements vii

Introduction to Volume III 1
ROBIN MANSELL

PART 7
Democracy, networks and power 13

49 **Information poverty and political inequality: citizenship in the age of privatized communications** 15
GRAHAM MURDOCK AND PETER GOLDING

50 **Political science research on teledemocracy** 32
WILLIAM H. DUTTON

51 **Democratic rationalization: technology, power, and freedom** 50
ANDREW FEENBERG

52 **The media and the public sphere** 73
NICHOLAS GARNHAM

53 **New mediation and direct representation: reconceptualizing representation in the digital age** 86
STEPHEN COLEMAN

54 **Real-time politics: the Internet and the political process** 109
PHILIP E. AGRE

55 **Political authority in a mediated age** 149
SUSAN HERBST

CONTENTS

56 The Internet, public spheres, and political communication: dispersion and deliberation 170
PETER DAHLGREN

57 Rethinking ICTs: ICTs on a human scale 190
CEES J. HAMELINK

PART 8
Governing networks 197

58 Communication policy in the global information economy: whither the public interest? 199
WILLIAM H. MELODY

59 Law and borders: the rise of law in cyberspace 222
DAVID R. JOHNSON AND DAVID POST

60 The zones of cyberspace 266
LAWRENCE LESSIG

61 The Internet and U.S. communication policy-making in historical and critical perspective 276
ROBERT W. McCHESNEY

62 The second enclosure movement and the construction of the public domain 305
JAMES BOYLE

63 The telecom crisis and beyond: restructuring of the global telecommunications system 353
DAL YONG JIN

64 Internet co-governance: towards a Multilayer Multiplayer Mechanism of Consultation, Coordination and Cooperation (M_3C_3) 371
WOLFGANG KLEINWÄCHTER

65 Commons-based peer production and virtue 391
YOCHAI BENKLER AND HELEN NISSENBAUM

ACKNOWLEDGEMENTS

The publishers would like to thank the following for permission to reprint their material:

Blackwell Publishing for permission to reprint Graham Murdock and Peter Golding (1989). Information Poverty and Political Inequality: Citizenship in the Age of Privatized Communications. *Journal of Communication*, 39(3): 180–195.

Sage Publications and William H. Dutton for permission to reprint William H. Dutton (1992). Political Science Research on Teledemocracy. *Social Science Computer Review*, 10(4): 505–522.

Sage Publications for permission to reprint Stephen Coleman (2005). New Mediation and Direct Representation: Reconceptualizing Representation in the Digital Age. *New Media & Society*, 7(2): 177–198.

Taylor & Francis for permission to reprint Philip E. Agre (2002). Real-time Politics: The Internet and the Political Process. *The Information Society*, 18(5): 311–331.

Springer Science and Business Media for permission to reprint Susan Herbst (2003). Political Authority in a Mediated Age. *Theory and Society*, 32(4): 481–503.

Taylor & Francis for permission to reprint Peter Dahlgren (2005). The Internet, Public Spheres, and Political Communication: Dispersion and Deliberation. *Political Communication*, 22(2): 147–162.

Sage Publications for permission to reprint Cees J. Hamelink (2006). Rethinking ICTs: ICTs on a Human Scale. *European Journal of Communication*, 21(3): 389–396.

Sage Publications and William H. Melody for permission to reprint William H. Melody (1989). Communication Policy in the Global Information Economy: Whither the Public Interest? In Marjorie Ferguson (ed.), *Public*

ACKNOWLEDGEMENTS

Communication – The New Imperatives: Future Directions for Media Research (pp. 16–38). London: Sage.

Stanford Law Review for permission to reprint David R. Johnson and David Post (1996). Law and Borders: The Rise of Law in Cyberspace. *Stanford Law Review*, 48(5): 1367–1402.

Stanford Law Review for permission to reprint Lawrence Lessig (1996). The Zones of Cyberspace. *Stanford Law Review*, 48(5): 1403–1411.

Blackwell Publishing for permission to reprint Robert W. McChesney (1996). The Internet and U.S. Communication Policy-making in Historical and Critical Perspective. *Journal of Communication*, 46(1): 98–124.

Sage Publications for permission to reprint Dal Y. Jin (2005). The Telecom Crisis and Beyond. *Gazette: The International Journal for Communication Studies*, 67(3): 289–304.

Blackwell Publishing for permission to reprint Yochai Benkler and Helen Nissenbaum (2006). Commons-based Peer Production and Virtue. *Journal of Political Philosophy*, 14(4): 394–419.

Disclaimer

The publishers have made every effort to contact authors/copyright holders of works reprinted in *The Information Society (Critical Concepts in Sociology)*. This has not been possible in every case, however, and we would welcome correspondence from those individuals/companies whom we have been unable to trace.

INTRODUCTION TO VOLUME III

Robin Mansell

> Ideally, the role of the media should precisely be to contribute to the creation of an agonistic public space in which there is the possibility for dissensus to be expressed or different alternatives to be put forward.
> (Interview with Chantal Mouffe in Carpentier and Cammaerts 2006: 11)

Democracy, networks, and power

The literature on the relationship between democratic processes, governance and regulatory practice – both formal and informal – is enormous. It is informed by those more persuaded by a pluralist approach and those whose orientation gives more emphasis to enduring conflict. In the context of 'the Information Society' vision, the former tends to predominate, while those who argue in support of diverse information societies are more likely to undertake research from a critical perspective and to focus on conflict and the ways in which it may or may not be resolved.

James Danziger and William Dutton's (1977) early analysis of the use of computers to support local government services showed the importance of empirical research to understand the functional needs of government, the limitations of technology, and the values and interests that might be served politically – both those of service providers within government and those of citizens. This research was an example of efforts to develop an understanding of the social shaping of technology, which was in contrast to work that assumed that technology provides solutions and is inherently democratic, prominent in much of the literature on 'teledemocracy' in the United States in the 1970s and 1980s, such as Becker (1981).

Voice and decision making

Dutton's (1992) analysis of the literature on teledemocracy demonstrated how speculative these early idealistic claims had been. The introduction of information and communication technologies (ICT) provided no guarantees that citizens would have a voice that would be listened to by political authorities. Dutton argued that 'the technical features and normative frameworks tied to computer-based communication networks could have a systematic influence on the content of interpersonal and group communication, which therefore might merit unique regulatory approaches' (1996: 270). His case studies indicated that the normative framework would inevitably include very different political views – ranging from civil libertarian to communitarian, to the views of those advocating protection of property rights.

This work, nevertheless, contains an optimism that 'real world' democracy could translate into online democracy: 'the public should be able to conduct meetings in cyberspace in ways that are as civil and democratic as in the real world' (Dutton 1996: 288). To achieve this, Dutton suggested that there might be a need for moderated public discussion accompanied by the imposition of norms and regulations to enable citizen's voices to be heard. Dutton's perspective on the democratizing potential of ICT was echoed in Lawrence Lessig's (1999, 2006) argument that software code, embedded in networks, sets limits and constrains the norms established for information exchange and communication.

A more cautious and limited set of expectations about the implications of the Information Society is evident in Graham Murdock and Peter Golding's (1989) work. In the case of Britain, they pointed out that more market-oriented communication and information systems were being developed, with the promise to the public that this would enlarge the space for people to make choices about their lives and to exercise control in ways that would be both liberating and empowering. Murdock and Golding's critical perspective was grounded in political economy and they provided convincing evidence that the information and communication system was unlikely to be liberating or empowering unless commercial forces could be held at bay. Similarly, in the context of the United States, Andrew Feenberg (1992) suggested that these technologies embodied a 'subversive rationalization', a view reached by drawing on constructivist and hermeneutic theories of technology.

Public spheres of participation

Much of the debate over the implications of digital technologies for democracy is informed by an understanding of the conditions required for rational debate in the 'public sphere', as represented by Jürgen Habermas (1962) as an elite space for dialogue, and developed by other scholars in modified form. In Britain, Nicholas Garnham (1993) analysed the role of the media in creating an informed citizenry, while acknowledging the limits to this aspiration within a capitalist economy. Feenberg argued that:

> individuals who are incorporated into new types of technical networks have learned to resist through the net itself in order to influence the powers that control it. This is not a contest for wealth or administrative power, but a struggle to subvert the technical practices, procedures, and designs structuring everyday life.
> (Feenberg 1992: 319)

Phil Agre's (2002) synthesis of research on the contribution of network technologies to participation in democratic decision making suggests that they are more likely to amplify existing tendencies and opportunities for political action and participation than to give rise to wholly new ones.

Some contributors to debates about e-democracy emphasize the potential of online deliberation. For example, Stephen Coleman's concern has been to seek ways in which 'digitally-mediated direct representation could provide a basis for a more dialogical and deliberative democracy in place of the dialogue of the deaf which tends to characterize contemporary political representation' (2005: 177). And Peter Dahlgren's (2001, 2005) work on the public sphere suggests that while the Internet is destabilizing for some aspects of democratic practice, it opens up new opportunities for public debate because it encourages diversity in the viewpoints expressed. This is particularly evident with the growth in online communities such as Facebook, MySpace and many others. Although some have claimed that online networking may undermine the authoritative status of professional journalism, my work with Charlie Beckett (Beckett and Mansell 2008) suggests that this is not necessarily so. Dahlgren distances himself from idealist searches for deliberative democracy, suggesting that it is much more important to understand the new forms of online civic cultures. Susan Herbst's (2003) work attends to the implications of technologically mediated discourse for the authoritative status of political actors, while another line of research developed by Maria Bakardjieva and Andrew Feenberg (2002) focuses on the possibilities for dialogue at the local community level and the implications for democracy.

Dialogue and political action

Cees Hamelink locates the debates about ICT and democracy in the context of a concern for the human condition: 'In the spirit of a discursive process, all stakeholders should design visions for possible futures that either enlarge dependence, increase vulnerability and expand uncertainty or *diminish these human features and strengthen human autonomy, integrity and security*' (Hamelink 2006: 394, emphasis added).

Contributors to debates about the need for multiple stakeholders to envisage new online spaces for democratic dialogue and to act to ensure that they develop, vacillate between optimism and pessimism. Optimism about the potential of ICT to be used to reduce poverty by enabling new online forms of entrepreneurial wealth creation in ways that respect human rights led to the World Summit on the Information Society (WSIS) in 2003 and 2005. Following initial hope that this United Nations-sponsored forum might result in action to alleviate human suffering and inequality, after its first phase in 2003 scholars such as Hamelink (2004) warned that exclusion of civil society representatives and critical scholars meant that the processes and spaces for dialogue that had been created were unlikely to achieve such action. Other scholars, such as Andrew Calabrese (1997, 2005), were more optimistic, but many are sceptical about the democratic potential of online sites as suggested by the work of Slavko Splichal (2006) and Chris Ogbondah (1997). The history of the debates in intergovernmental fora, and especially UNESCO, is not represented in this collection. Interested readers could refer to Mansell and Nordenstreng (2006) for an account of the political tensions which were resolved mainly in the interests of those promoting the Information Society vision.

Academic discussion about whether the democratic potential of the Information Society, that is, a society envisaged and promoted within the wealthy countries, is consistent with a Habermasian or a quasi-Habermasian view of the public sphere as the venue for rational debate and consensus formation is challenged by the work of Chantal Mouffe (2005). She understands democracy as an agonistic, conflictual process. Apart from the quotation at the beginning of this introduction, she has not specifically discussed the Information Society or analysed the role of media or ICT in detail. Nevertheless, her understanding of the workings of democracy offers a rich theoretical framework that is helpful in making sense of the mediated environment. Phil Graham's (2000) work also challenges the idealism of much research in this area.

Governing information societies

Information societies are malleable insofar as their characteristics are established by human choices. As a result, the governance of their networks (technical and social) is crucial to their future shape. Governance is concerned with formal and informal norms and practices. A substantial amount of scholarship focuses specifically on Internet governance – in terms of the control, structure and functioning of the electronic spaces that the Internet protocol enables.

Internet governance

Following the 2005 WSIS, an Internet Governance Forum (IGF) was established to support the United Nations mandate for action resulting from the Summit.[1] The IGF is intended to offer an opportunity for multi-stakeholder dialogue on governance issues related to fostering sustainability of the Internet and a range of other issues concerning its security, robustness and future development, which are very controversial. All these issues affect the costs of access and control over the Internet in different geographical locations, and many are related to whether the right to communicate should be enshrined in international laws and conventions.[2]

Controversies at global level are replicated within countries. These partly reflect ongoing debate, such as David Johnson and David Post's (1996) argument that the Internet should not be regulated, in order to give free rein to innovators and the suggestions of Lawrence Lessig (1996) and others that the architecture of the Internet governs how it can be used and biases its future development. Insofar as values are embedded in the technological design of the Internet, there is a need for governance to enable the generative, open features of the Internet to remain in place as its protocol develops. Jonathan Zittrain takes this argument further, suggesting that we need to rely mainly on 'technically skilled people of goodwill to keep them going ... as true alternatives to a centralized, industrialized information economy' (2008: 246). Others, such as Wolfgang Kleinwächter (2006), are more favourable to the idea that multiple stakeholders should participate in the regime of global governance for the Internet.

Governance issues involving the Internet are also central to discussions about the ownership and rights associated with digital information (from scientific papers to digital music). This is a major area of tension even among proponents of the singular vision of the Information Society. There are those who are committed to the view that information is a commodity, which, to secure incentives for creative expression, is best bought and sold in the market. For instance, Stan Liebowitz and Stephen Margolis (2005) argue that, while economists do not have the full information necessary to definitively comment on the continuing expansion of copyright reach, there is good reason to enforce and extend it in the information age. Their position contrasts with those of scholars, such as Paul A. David (1993, 2004), who argue that incentives for creative expression are also fostered by an open environment. Ronald Bettig (1992, 1997) envisages a progressive narrowing of the open spaces of the Internet through the extension of the intellectual property rights regime encompassing increasing amounts of digital culture. James Boyle (1992) provides an overview of the position of the liberal state on these issues, pointing out that those who seek to extend the protections available to creators through copyright often assume that authors are always writing as independent individuals rather than under contracts with corporations.

Lawrence Lessig (2001, 2004) has championed the need for an open information commons to promote innovative activities, and Yochai Benkler and Helen Nissenbaum support what has come to be known as 'commons-based peer production', suggesting that this serves both as a medium for producing information goods which is very effective, and as 'a context for positive character formation' consistent with an ethical position (Benkler and Nissenbaum 2006: 394–5).[3] Christopher May (2002) examines the way the intellectual property regime governs the global division of labour in information production markets, and in Mansell and Steinmueller (1998,

2000) Edward Steinmueller and I examined the competing interests in traditional and new means of protecting intellectual property. The ethical issues have been addressed by Gian Greco and Luciano Floridi (2004), who raise concerns about the decline of the digital commons in the absence of countermeasures to prevent its overuse.

Regulatory challenges

Liberalization of the markets for telecommunication and broadcasting has been a major site of controversy, beginning with debates in the United States about how best to limit monopoly power and to ensure that public interest considerations are not neglected in the face of corporate interest in profits.[4] The spread of legal and regulatory initiatives designed to introduce competition in the telecommunication and broadcasting industries has had different outcomes in Europe and in other regions, especially with respect to the consequences of commercialization for the build-out of infrastructure networks and for the sustainability of public service broadcasting. Jill Hills (1990, 1998) and Heather Hudson (1997)[5] documented global developments, and Hills and Maria Michalis (2000) examined liberalization pressures in the light of Internet developments.

With the move towards market liberalization and privatization, William Melody raised a crucial question about what would become of 'public interest' considerations in information societies governed principally by market forces, saying that 'to begin the process of redefining the public interest in the information society, it is necessary to return to the essential functions of information and communication in modern participatory democracy, that is, to provide opportunities for citizens to be informed and to be heard' (Melody 1989: 29).

The results of his analysis of regulation in the United States, Canada, South Africa and various European and Asian countries suggested to him that many regulatory regimes, however constituted within political structures, were becoming too detached from citizens' concerns. His more recent work (Melody 2005) provides a framework for analysing regulation in the network environment of the twentieth-century. In market-driven environments, he argues, regulators are likely to favour corporate interests. Nicholas Garnham (1997) turned to the economist Amartya Sen's (1999) work on people's capabilities and the choices they exercise in their lives, as the basis for decisions about whether to intervene in the marketplace. He suggested that as connectivity to networks and equitable access are becoming more essential to individuals' abilities to conduct their lives there will often be a requirement for regulatory intervention in the interest of fairness and equity. This argument was developed with respect to telecommunication networks, not to the question of whether the Internet should be regulated.

The possibility of formal regulation of the Internet in Western countries is rarely seen as attractive because of the view that development of the Internet requires that it should flourish in an unrestricted way. The regulatory literature in this area is dominated by claims about the importance of 'Net neutrality', rather than by a concern for the public's interest, discussed by François Bar *et al.* (2000) and by Bruce Owen (2007) in the context of the United States. Net neutrality refers to the idea that the Internet should be available to all on a uniform, non-discriminatory basis without differentiation in terms of quality of service; that is, it should remain a transparent, end-to-end network. Owen takes issue with this view, observing that it is reminiscent of the argument that telecommunication companies should serve as common carriers without interest in content. Robert McChesney (1996) has argued that the Internet is not neutral and that indeed there is a need for regulatory intervention to ensure it is not overly commercialized. Robert Horwitz and William Currie (2007) focus on the less than salutary results of liberalization in South Africa, and Dal Jin (2005) demonstrates the varying implications of the last few decades of liberalization measures, on a global scale.

A major development since the World Wide Web was launched for public use in 1991 has been the growth of the search engine market, where Google and other popular search engines, such as Baidu in China, dominate. As Lucas Introna and Helen Nissenbaum argue:

> search engines raise not merely technical issues but also political ones. Our study of search engines suggests that they systematically exclude (in some cases by design and in some, accidentally) certain sites and certain types of sites in favor of others, systematically giving prominence to some at the expense of others.
> (Introna and Nissenbaum 2000: 169)

The economic models leading to the promotion of new online applications through 3-D and mobile advertising and advergames, and netvertising images, as well as banner ads and pop-ups, are increasingly sophisticated (Stafford and Faber 2005) and may also give rise to distortions in information markets that create the need for protection of the public interest. As in the case of search engines, however, there are few supporters of formal regulation to mitigate potential abuses of market power in these areas. There is interest in self-regulation by Internet service providers, such as those encouraged by the United Kingdom's Internet Watch Foundation,[6] which aims to reduce illegal child abuse images and other threats.[7] There also is research on the powers of states to control the Internet, as in a study by Shanthi Kalathil and Taylor Boas (2003), and the geographical reach and effectiveness of the law with respect to free speech and security online are addressed in Mathias Klang and Andrew Murray's (2005) work on human rights protection in the information age.

Conclusion

This volume includes papers that offer assessments of the way information societies are implicated in changing power relationships with respect to individuals in their roles as citizens and consumers. It also includes papers that address the governance and regulatory measures that are being devised to create incentives to ensure that various conceptions of the public interest are upheld.

For some, a major goal is the creation and maintenance of a public sphere or spheres for rational discourse and democratic decision making. For others, the goal is to extend the spaces for the negotiation of conflictual issues that have a substantial bearing on the way people experience their lives in mediated societies. Included in this section are papers illustrating research advancing the claim that information societies are underpinned by technologies that empower social movements and papers providing critical assessments of these claims.

Notes

1 See http://www.intgovforum.org/ (accessed 22 August 2008).
2 Information on this topic is available at: http://www.waccglobal.org/wacc/programmes/recognising_and_building_communication_rights (accessed 22 August 2008).
3 See also Benkler (2003, 2004).
4 The contribution of the academic community to US policy making in the communication field is reviewed by Braman (2003).
5 Hudson also examined the application of ICT in rural contexts in developing countries.
6 See http://www.iwf.org.uk/ (accessed 22 August 2008).
7 See also results of a study on Internet self-regulation conducted by the Programme in Comparative Media Law and Policy at Oxford University, funded by the European Commission (EC) under the Internet Action Plan, which examined self-regulatory codes of conduct across national, European Union and international boundaries covering a wide range of media, including Internet, film, video games, digital television, mobile communications, at http://pcmlp.socleg.ox.ac.uk/selfregulation/iapcoda/030329-selfreg-global-report.htm (accessed 22 August 2008). In 2008 the EC adopted a proposal continuing its Safer Internet Programme (2009–13), which addresses communications services from Web 2.0 such as social networking, and is aimed at fighting illegal content and harmful conduct such as grooming and bullying, at http://ec.europa.eu/information_society/activities/sip/programme/index_en.htm, (accessed 22 August 2008).

References

Agre, P. E. (2002). 'Real-time politics: The Internet and the Political Process'. *The Information Society*, 18(5): 311–31.
Bakardjieva, M. and Feenberg, A. (2002). 'Community Technology and Democratic Rationalization'. *The Information Society*, 18(3): 181–92.

Bar, F., Cohen, S., Cowhey, P., Delong, B., Kleeman, M. and Zysman, J. (2000). 'Access and Innovation Policy for the Third Generation Internet'. *Telecommunications Policy*, 24(6–7): 489–518.

Becker, T. (1981). 'Teledemocracy: Bringing Power Back to the People'. *The Futurist*, 15(6): 6–9.

Beckett, C. and Mansell, R. (2008). 'Crossing Boundaries: New Media and Networked Journalism'. *Communication, Culture & Critique*, 1(1): 90–102.

Benkler, Y. (2003). 'Freedom in the Commons: Towards a Political Economy of Information'. *Duke Law Journal*, 52(6): 1,245–76.

—— (2004). 'Sharing Nicely: On Shareable Goods and the Emergence of Sharing as a Modality of Economic Production'. *Yale Law Journal*, 114(2): 273–358.

—— and Nissenbaum, H. (2006). 'Commons-based Peer Production and Virtue'. *Journal of Political Philosophy*, 14(4): 394–419.

Bettig, R. V. (1992). 'Critical Perspectives on the History and Philosophy of Copyright'. *Critical Studies in Mass Communication*, 9(2): 131–55.

—— (1997). 'The Enclosure of Cyberspace'. *Critical Studies in Mass Communication*, 14(2): 138–57.

Boyle, J. (1992). 'A Theory of Law and Information: Copyright, Spleens, Blackmail, and Insider Trading'. *California Law Review*, 80(6): 1,413–540.

Braman, S. (ed.) (2003). *Communication Researchers and Policy-making*. Cambridge, MA: MIT Press.

Calabrese, A. (1997). 'Creative Destruction? From the Welfare State to the Global Information Society'. *Javnost – The Public*, 4(4): 7–24.

—— (2005). 'Global Activism, Global Media'. *European Journal of Communication*, 20(4): 555–9.

Carpentier, N. and Cammaerts, B. (2006). 'Hegemony, Democracy, Agonism and Journalism: An Interview with Chantal Mouffe'. *Journalism Studies*, 7(6): 964–75.

Coleman, S. (2005). 'New Mediation and Direct Representation: Reconceptualizing Representation in the Digital Age'. *New Media & Society*, 7(2): 177–98.

Dahlberg, L. (2001). 'Democracy via Cyberspace: Mapping the Rhetorics and Practices of Three Prominent Camps'. *New Media & Society*, 3(2): 157–77.

Dahlgren, P. (2001). 'The Public Sphere and the Net: Structure, Space, and Communication'. In W. L. Bennett and R. M. Entman (eds), *Mediated Politics: Communication in the Future of Democracy* (pp. 33–55). Cambridge: Cambridge University Press.

—— (2005). 'The Internet, Public Spheres, and Political Communication: Dispersion and Deliberation'. *Political Communication*, 22(2): 147–62.

Danziger, J. N. and Dutton, W. H. (1977). 'Technological Innovation in Local-Government – Case of Computers'. *Policy and Politics*, 6(1): 27–49.

David, P. A. (1993). 'Intellectual Property Institutions and the Panda's Thumb: Patents, Copyrights, Trade Secrets in Economic Theory and History'. In M. B. Wallerstein, M. E. Mogee and R. A. Schoen (eds), *Global Dimensions of Intellectual Property Rights in Science and Technology* (pp. 19–61). Washington, DC: National Academy Press.

—— (2004). 'Can "Open Science" Be Protected from the Evolving Regime of IPR Protections?' *Journal of Institutional and Theoretical Economics*, 160(1): 9–34.

Dutton, W. H. (1992). 'Political Science Research on Teledemocracy'. *Social Science Computer Review*, 10: 505–23.

—— (1996). 'Network Rules of Order: Regulating Speech in Public Electronic Fora'. *Media Culture & Society*, 18(2): 269–90.
Feenberg, A. (1992). 'Subversive Rationalization, Technology, Power, and Democracy'. *Inquiry – An Interdisciplinary Journal of Philosophy*, 35(3–4): 301–22.
Garnham, N. (1993). 'The Media and the Public Sphere'. In C. Calhoun (ed.), *Habermas and the Public Sphere* (pp. 359–76). Cambridge, MA: MIT Press.
—— (1997). 'Amartya Sen's "Capabilities" Approach to the Evaluation of Welfare: Its Application to Communications'. *Javnost – The Public*, 4(4): 25–34.
Graham, P. (2000). 'Hypercapitalism: A Political Economy of Informational Idealism'. *New Media & Society*, 2(2): 131–56.
Greco, G. M. and Floridi, L. (2004). 'The Tragedy of the Digital Commons'. *Ethics and Information Technology*, 6(2): 73–81.
Habermas, J. (1962). *The Structural Transformation of the Public Sphere: An Inquiry into a Category of Bourgeois Society*. Cambridge, MA: MIT Press (republished 1989).
Hamelink, C. (2004). 'Did the WSIS Achieve Anything at All?' *Gazette: The International Journal for Communication Studies*, 66(3–4): 281–90.
—— (2006). 'Rethinking ICTs: ICTs on a Human Scale'. *European Journal of Communication*, 21(3): 389–96.
Herbst, S. (2003). 'Political Authority in a Mediated Age'. *Theory and Society*, 32(4): 481–504.
Hills, J. (1990). 'The Telecommunications Rich and Poor'. *Third World Quarterly*, 12(2): 71–90.
—— (1998). 'Liberalization, Regulation and Development: Telecommunications'. *International Communication Gazette*, 60(6): 459–76.
—— and Michalis, M. (2000). 'The Internet: A Challenge to Public Service Broadcasting?' *International Communication Gazette*, 62(6): 477–93.
Horwitz, R. B. and Currie, W. (2007). 'Another Instance Where Privatization Trumped Liberalization: The Politics of Telecommunications Reform in South Africa – A Ten Year Retrospective'. *Telecommunications Policy*, 31(8–9): 445–62.
Hudson, H. E. (1997). *Global Connections: International Telecommunications Infrastructure and Policy*. New York: Van Nostrand Reinhold.
Introna, L. D. and Nissenbaum, H. (2000). 'Shaping the Web: Why the Politics of Search Engines Matters'. *The Information Society*, 16(3): 169–85.
Jin, D. Y. (2005). 'The Telecom Crisis and Beyond'. *Gazette: The International Journal for Communication Studies*, 67(3): 289–304.
Johnson, D. R. and Post, D. (1996). 'Law and Borders: The Rise of Law in Cyberspace'. *Stanford Law Review*, 48(5): 1,367–402.
Kalathil, S. and Boas, T. C. (2003). *Open Networks, Closed Regimes: The Impact of the Internet on Authoritarian Rule*. Washington, DC: Carnegie Endowment for International Peace.
Klang, M. and Murray, A. (eds) (2005). *Human Rights in the Digital Age*. London: Glasshouse Press/Cavendish Publishing.
Kleinwächter, W. (2006). 'Internet Co-Governance: Towards a Multilayer Multiplayer Mechanism of Consultation, Coordination and Cooperation'. *E-Learning*, 3(3): 473–87.
Lessig, L. (1996). 'The Zones of Cyberspace'. *Stanford Law Review*, 48(5): 1,403–11.
—— (1999). *Code and Other Laws of Cyberspace*. New York: Basic Books.

—— (2001). *The Future of Ideas: The Fate of the Commons in a Connected World*. New York: Random House.

—— (2004). *Free Culture: How Big Media Uses Technology and the Law to Lock Down Culture*, New York: Penguin.

—— (2006). *Code: Version 2.0*. New York: Basic Books.

Liebowitz, S. J. and Margolis, S. E. (2005). 'Seventeen Famous Economists Weigh in on Copyright: The Role of Theory, Empirics, and Network Effects'. *Harvard Journal of Law and Technology*, 18(2): 435–57.

McChesney, R. W. (1996). 'The Internet and US Communication Policy-Making in Historical and Critical Perspective'. *Journal of Communication*, 46(1): 98–124.

Mansell, R. and Nordenstreng, K. (2006). 'Great Media and Communications Debates – An Assessment of the MacBride Report after 25 Years'. *Information Technologies and International Development*, 3(4): 15–36.

—— and Steinmueller, W. E. (1998). 'Intellectual Property Rights: Competing Interests on the Internet'. *Communications & Strategies*, 30(2): 173–97.

—— and Steinmueller, W. E. (2000). *Mobilizing the Information Society: Strategies for Growth and Opportunity*. Oxford: Oxford University Press.

May, C. (2002). 'The Political Economy of Proximity: Intellectual Property and the Global Division of Information Labour'. *New Political Economy*, 7(3): 317–43.

Melody, W. H. (1989). 'Communication Policy in the Global Information Economy: Whither the Public Interest?' In M. Ferguson (ed.), *Public Communication: The New Imperatives: Future Directions for Media Research* (pp. 16–38). London: Sage.

—— (2005). 'Regulation and Network Investment: A Framework for Analysis'. In A. K. Mahan and W. H. Melody (eds), *Stimulating Investment in Network Development: Roles for Regulators* (pp. 19–37). Lyngby: Technical University of Denmark for IDRC, infoDev and LIRNE.net.

Mouffe, C. (2005). *The Return of the Political*. London: Verso.

Murdock, G. and Golding, P. (1989). 'Information Poverty and Political Inequality – Citizenship in the Age of Privatized Communications'. *Journal of Communication*, 39(3): 180–94.

Ogbondah, C. W. (1997). 'Communication and Democratization in Africa'. *International Communication Gazette*, 59(4): 271–94.

Owen, B. M. (2007). *The Net Neutrality Debate: Twenty Five Years after United States v. AT&T and 120 Years after the Act to Regulate Commerce*. SIEPR Discussion Papers, 06-15 Stanford, CA: Stanford Institute for Economic Policy Research, n.p.

Sen, A. (1999). *Development as Freedom*. Oxford: Oxford University Press.

Splichal, S. (2006). 'In Search of a Strong European Public Sphere: Some Critical Observations on Conceptualizations of Publicness and the (European) Public Sphere'. *Media Culture and Society*, 28(5): 695–715.

Stafford, M. R. and Faber, R. J. (2005). *Advertising, Promotion and New Media*. New York: M. E. Sharpe.

Zittrain, J. (2008). *The Future of the Internet and How to Stop It*. London: Allen Lane.

Part 7

DEMOCRACY, NETWORKS AND POWER

49

INFORMATION POVERTY AND POLITICAL INEQUALITY

Citizenship in the age of privatized communications

Graham Murdock and Peter Golding

Source: *Journal of Communication* 39(3) (1989): 180–95.

"Where material inequality massively differentiates people's access to goods and services, and those goods and services are themselves a necessary resource for citizenship, then political rights are the victim of the vicissitudes of the marketplace and its inegalitarian structure."

The new market-oriented communications and information system that is currently gaining ground within liberal democracies is being sold to the general public on the promise that it will enlarge people's choices and increase their control over their lives, that it will be both liberating and empowering. This emerging order is the product of two major processes: technological innovation and convergence, and "privatization." The first is creating a range of new kinds of communications and information services and restructuring established media industries; the second is providing the essential social and ideological context in which these changes are being developed and promoted.

"Privatization," with which we are primarily concerned in this article, operates on two main levels. Economically it involves moving the production and provision of communications and information services from the public sector to the market, both by transferring ownership of key facilities to private investors and by making success in the marketplace the major criterion for judging the performance of all communications and information organizations (including those that remain in the public sector). This reconstitution of production is accompanied by a parallel restructuring of consumption. First, nonwork activity becomes ever more securely rooted in the home. Second, the new market-oriented system of provision addresses people predominantly through their identity as consumers, both of the communications and information products they buy and of the products promoted in the expanded advertising system that finances many of the new services. In the process, the system marginalizes or displaces other identities, in particular the identity of citizen.

Although a number of commentators have attacked the "privatization" of communications and information services and challenged the claim that the new communications technologies are, in Ithiel de Sola Pool's phrase, "technologies of freedom," very few have linked these critiques to current debates on the nature of citizenship in complex democracies or asked what role communications plays in sustaining and extending it. Taking contemporary Britain as a particular case of a liberal democracy in the process of change, this article discusses the connections between the organization of communications and information facilities and the constitution of citizenship, arguing two basic points. First, we draw attention to debates on the nature of citizenship in political sociology and political philosophy that assign a central and complex role to communications, debates that media researchers need to explore both conceptually and empirically. We then go on to demonstrate that policies in the areas of communications, taxation, and welfare being pursued by the Thatcher administrations in Britain, and in varying degrees by a number of other liberal democratic governments, are combining to comprehensively undermine the resources required for full and effective citizenship.

We begin with a brief exploration of current debates on the nature of citizenship. The starting point for most modern discussions in this area is T. H. Marshall's essay, *Citizenship and Social Class*, written in 1949 (17). Marshall distinguishes three basic dimensions of citizenship—civil, political, and social—and traces the development of the rights associated with them together with the institutions that promote and guarantee them.

Civil rights are centrally concerned with an individual's freedom of action within the sphere of "civil society." They include freedom of speech, freedom of thought and religion, freedom of movement and association, and, centrally, the freedom to own and dispose of property. Property rights are assigned a pivotal role in classical liberal theory as the major guarantor of individual choice. In this conception the market is unambiguously the sphere of liberty that the state threatens to erode whenever it goes beyond its assigned "nightwatchman" role of regulating the use of force and overseeing the legal system that guarantees individual rights. In the words of British Home Secretary Douglas Hurd, for Conservatives "private property is the natural bulwark of liberty" (13).

The second set of rights, political rights, is concerned with the conditions under which people participate in the exercise of political power—by holding public office, electing members of the national and local bodies that formulate policies and pass laws, and involving themselves in the exercise of those laws through jury membership. The image of the citizen as a participant in the political process is of course at the center of the classical conceptions dating back to ancient Greece. It is what separates citizens from subjects. The latter may have the right to protection under the law, but only citizens can take part in determining the nature of the laws by which they will consent to be governed (33).

Marshall sees the third set of citizenship rights, social rights, as the distinctive product of the twentieth century. His presentation of them centers on the struggle to secure a basic standard of life and well-being for all through the institutionalization of the welfare state. For our purposes, however, we need to add the rights of universal access to communications and information facilities, which emerged at the same time and were underwritten by public provision funded out of local and national taxes and institutionalized through the organizations responsible for continuing education, public libraries, and, later, public broadcasting. Although Marshall does not stress the importance of communications rights, they are presupposed by his general definition of the social rights of citizenship, which cover "the whole range from the right to a modicum of economic welfare and security to the right to share to the full in the social heritage and to live the life of a civilised being according to the standards prevailing in the society" (17, p. 11). This definition involves a substantial widening of the traditional conception of citizenship. It is no longer simply about participation in the political process; it is also about the conditions that allow people to become full members of the society at every level (15).

Although Marshall's schema has done much to advance and broaden the discussion of citizenship, it is open to a number of criticisms. Conceptually, he presents the three dimensions of citizenship as a simple list without arranging them in order of priority. Yet it is clear from the overall thrust of his argument that he sees social rights as the essential precondition for the meaningful exercise both of political participation and of full social membership. Or, put another way, poverty is a powerful mechanism for excluding people from these entitlements (7).

Marshall was writing in 1949, after the Labour Government elected in 1945 had pushed through the reforms that completed the creation of the modern British welfare state, and he had good reason to think that this restructuring was an irreversible step toward securing the basic resources for citizenship. Forty years later, with the experience of a decade of radical conservative administrations headed by Thatcher to assimilate, it is clear that this optimism was premature and that these resources have been progressively eroded in ways that we shall detail presently.

With the benefit of hindsight it is also clear that Marshall's argument suffers from a somewhat uncritical definition of the "social heritage" that provides the cultural and psychological glue binding citizens together in common membership of the society. Part of the problem is that the development of citizenship in its present form has been coterminous with the formation of the modern nation-state (32). As a result, membership is identified with participation in the national culture as defined by authoritative political and cultural institutions. This ignores the extent to which the formation and maintenance of these definitions entailed the marginalization and suppression of other identities.

As the fissures and cracks in this edifice have become more evident, with the resurgence of regional nationalisms and Britain's transition to a multiracial society, so it has become more than ever necessary to recognize diversity and difference and to move toward "a new definition of solidarity and coexistence centred on mutual respect" (19, p. 178). This, in turn, implies a more pluralistic conception of social membership, one that makes room for particularity and difference and recognizes that the "reconciliation of rival claims and conflicting interests can only be partial and provisional" (21, p. 30). In the present situation, then, the social component of citizenship can no longer be defined in Marshall's terms as "the right to share in full in the social heritage." Rather, it must be thought of as the right of "individuals and social groups to affirm themselves and to be recognized for what they are or wish to be" (18, p. 258).

In this light, it is clear that communications and information are central to the exercise of full and effective citizenship in the contemporary era (29). This is not in itself a new insight. Liberal democrats have long recognized that access to adequate information and to a diversity of debate and representations is a basic precondition for the effective functioning of a democratic polity and for the full exercise of citizenship rights (1). Accordingly, they have seen the communications system as an essentially public set of institutions charged with a duty to provide the necessary resources for effective citizenship. And they have applied this injunction equally to all organizations, whether publicly managed or privately owned.

We can identify three main kinds of relations between communications and citizenship. First, people must have access to the information, advice, and analysis that will enable them to know what their rights are in other spheres and allow them to pursue these rights effectively. Second, they must have access to the broadest possible range of information, interpretation, and debate on areas that involve political choices, and they must be able to use communications facilities in order to register criticism, mobilize opposition, and propose alternative courses of action. And third, they must be able to recognize themselves and their aspirations in the range of representations offered within the central communications sectors and be able to contribute to developing those representations.

These rights in turn imply that the communications and information system should have two essential features. At the level of production, it should offer the maximum possible diversity of provision and provide mechanisms for user feedback and participation. At the level of consumption, it should guarantee universal access to the services that can ensure the exercise of citizenship regardless of income or area of residence. The central question is, "Can these essential communicative resources for citizenship be guaranteed by a production and distribution system that is increasingly organized around market mechanisms?" Our answer has to be "no," at least not given the present organizations of the relevant markets and the distribution of income.

Whenever access to the communications and information resources required for full citizenship depends upon purchasing power (as expressed directly through customer payments or indirectly through the unequal distribution of advertising subsidies to production), substantial inequalities are generated that undermine the nominal universality of citizenship. As we shall show, income differentials have widened considerably under the three Thatcher governments at the same time as the communications and information system has been progressively "privatized" and the public sector eroded and commercialized. As a result, the poor suffer from a double disadvantage. They are priced out of the markets for new services and left with an infrastructure of public provision that is either unable or unwilling to provide the full range of resources for citizenship (22).

The next section looks in more detail at the main political and economic dynamics that are currently restructuring the provision of information and communications services. We then chart the pattern of income differentials and indicate their consequences for access to communications and information goods in the new "privatized" marketplace.

"Privatization" is most usefully employed as a general description of economic initiatives that aim to increase the reach of market institutions and philosophies at the expense of the public sphere. Within this process we can identify four main movements: denationalization, which involves selling shares in public companies to private investors; liberalization, which introduces competition into areas that were previously public or private monopolies; the regearing of the regulatory regime to allow corporations more flexibility to maneuver; and the commercialization of those organizations that remain in the public sector, through the introduction of market mechanisms and commercial criteria of evaluation.

From the outset of the Thatcher administrations, communications and information industries have been at the forefront of these shifts. Although a full survey would take us well beyond the scope of this article, privatization's general impact on access to information and communications resources is well illustrated by recent changes in two central areas: telecommunications and television services.

The telephone is the hub of most people's interpersonal information system. Not only does it connect them with the informal networks offered by friends, neighbors, and relatives, it also provides a major point of access to the professional information services of organizations like Citizens' Advice Bureaus, voluntary and community groups, and welfare rights agencies. Indeed, as public funding for these organizations has been steadily whittled away, forcing some to close branches or limit their hours, telephone access has become more important than ever. However, as Table 1 clearly shows, some of the groups most in need of information and advice on their rights are among those least likely to have access to a domestic telephone. And even those who do may find their use curtailed by the relatively high cost of making calls.

When the Post Office administered the telephone network, its policy was to keep down the cost of local calls (which make up the bulk of poor households' use) by cross-subsidizing losses out of the profits generated by trunk and international traffic (most of which was accounted for by business users). In the early 1970s, however, concerted pressure from the corporate community, coupled with the high costs of modernizing the network, led to a relaxation of this policy. Between 1973 and 1978 the price of long-distance calls covering a distance of more than 35 miles dropped by 13 percent, while the real price of local calls at peak times rose by a massive 183 percent (30, pp. 121–146). This rebalancing of the tariff structure in favor of business users has been reinforced by the twin impact of liberalization and denationalization.

In February 1982, the Mercury consortium was granted a license to compete with British Telecom (the renamed telecommunications sector of the old Post Office, hived off from the mail sector by the British Telecommunications Act of 1981). Mercury's main aim was to gain a slice of BT's lucrative business custom; BT responded by cutting the price of trunk and

Table 1 Percent of households in selected income groups in 1986 that own communications and information facilities.

Weekly income	TV %	Telephone %	Video recorder %	Home computer %
£60–80	96.9	67.4	12.6	3.3
£100–125	98.1	76.7	21.2	7.6
£150–175	97.7	76.3	31.6	9.6
£225–250	97.5	87.3	43.5	21.2
£325–375	98.0	94.1	56.5	26.5
£550 and over	98.4	98.2	64.8	28.8

Source: *Family Expenditure Survey 1986* (37, Table 3).

transatlantic calls and moving toward charging customers the full economic costs of local calls. This shift was further accelerated when the majority (50.2 percent) of BT's shares were sold to private investors in November 1984, transforming it from a public utility to a commercial corporation dedicated to maximizing its profits. A 1989 survey revealed that, regulatory limits on pricing notwithstanding, Britain has the second most expensive local calls of any advanced country (25).

Although those without ready access to a domestic telephone have the network of public call boxes to fall back on, here again recent changes have worked to the disadvantage of the poor. BT is in the process of replacing its old stock of coin-operated boxes with metal and glass booths, many of which will accept only a major credit card or a special phone card that has to be purchased beforehand. Although this conversion will undoubtedly reduce vandalism from attempts to break open coin collection boxes, it further restricts access among those who do not have a credit card and are unable to tie up their discretionary spending in advance of making a call. Their problems are compounded by the fact that under the current regulatory arrangements, unlike domestic tariffs, rises in the cost of calls from public boxes are not subject to set limits but are free to respond to judgments of what the market will bear.

The difficulties that low-income groups experience in gaining convenient and affordable access to basic telephone services are further compounded in the case of value-added services. Many of those most able to benefit from these facilities are least able to obtain them.

Home shopping provides a case in point. The poor are already disadvantaged in regard to shopping. Since most do not have access to a car, they are unable to take maximum advantage of the choice and price advantages offered by supermarkets in city centers or hypermarkets on the edge of towns. Instead they are confined to the relatively limited choice and high prices of local shops. This problem is particularly acute for the elderly and the disabled, who have mobility problems. The ability to order goods from a central store and have them delivered to the home would do much to compensate for this situation. Yet the British experience to date clearly shows that such schemes will reach those most in need only if there is extensive public subsidy. Run on a straightforward commercial basis, these programs are invariably geared to servicing the better off, thereby extending the advantages they already enjoy. In this case, poverty not only excludes people from the information and communications resources they need for full citizenship, it also inhibits them from exercising their full rights as consumers (22).

A parallel situation obtains in the area of television services. Historically, television services in Britain have been seen as a public resource that should speak for and to the full range of social experiences and interests and should be available equally to everyone, regardless of level of income or area of residence. This ideal was guaranteed financially by noncompetitive funding, whereby the British Broadcasting Corporation received the whole of the compulsory license fee levied on the possession of a television set, and the Independent Television companies had exclusive rights to sell advertising on ITV and Channel 4 in their franchise areas. A comprehensive system of regulation obliged both the BBC and ITV to maintain a diverse production base capable of addressing a plurality of interests.

This public service duopoly will be dismantled when the plans announced in the government's 1988 White Paper on broadcasting are implemented (41). The government will allocate the two remaining channels on Britain's five-channel national direct broadcast satellite (DBS) system, operated by British Satellite Broadcasting. It also proposes to license a new national terrestrial service and a number of local multipoint video distribution systems. All of these initiatives would be financed out of varying combinations of spot advertising, sponsorship, and viewer subscriptions and would be regulated by a new body, the Independent Television Commission, which would oversee all commercial television services, including cable. Unlike the present Independent Broadcasting Authority, which supervises the ITV system, the new commission would operate with a 'light touch," prioritizing the growth of television services as a business rather than defending and extending broadcasting as a public service in pursuit of diversity. Last, and most significant, the present license fee would be phased out and the BBC's funding switched to a predominantly subscription basis to bring the Corporation into line with the general movement toward a "pay-per" communications system (20).

As the present cable services demonstrate, however, subscription systems operate against the poor by making people's range of choice directly dependent on their ability to pay. In mid-1988, it cost an average of £17.86 a month to buy into cable services (34). This represented a virtual doubling of the average household's expenditure on basic broadcast services. It will cost at least that much again to obtain the full range of new DBS services, over and above the initial outlay on equipment.

Nor is a videocassette recorder necessarily a cheap way to extend the uses of the basic television set. Table 1 shows that there is a strong linear relation between VCR possession and income. Moreover, the more affluent can use their VCRs with greater versatility, for two reasons. First, they are more likely to be able to afford to subscribe to cable or DBS channels and so have access to a greater range of movies and other programs for time-shifting. Second, the recent shake-out in the videotape rental sector resulting in the disappearance of a number of smaller, local outlets has reduced the choices available to many poorer households.

However, even if the effective threat to established broadcast services is less than the more pessimistic commentators are forecasting, the arrival of new services and competition for subscription and advertising income is still likely to have an effect on the range of program production. And as the Report of the Committee on Financing the BBC recognized, those programs that are arguably most central to the provision of resources for citizenship are most at risk in the new commercial environment (40, pp. 127–128). They include investigative documentaries, innovative contemporary drama, and programs for minorities who have low spending power.

One response to this new marketplace is to commercialize public institutions from within. This entails exploiting resources to the maximum by generating spin-off products and merchandising opportunities based on programs and by leasing out spare capacity (23). The BBC is currently pursuing this strategy with considerable vigor. It has purchased a publishing house to boost its growing stable of magazines based on programs. It also leases parts of its available spectrum space to companies wishing to advertise to clients and to a commercial consortium that downloads a regular medical program, supported by the large pharmaceutical companies, to VCRs in doctors' homes and offices.

The rationale for these activities is that the revenue they generate can be plowed back into general program making. But there is a distinct danger that the tail will end up wagging the dog, so that production ideas come to be evaluated for their merchandising potential and the requirements of commercial clients come to shape the distribution of scarce resources, transferring some from the public to the corporate sector. At the same time, in a period when the real value of the income derived from the public purse is being reduced, there are considerable incentives to look for other ways to make money. Nor is this trend confined to broadcasting. It is evident across the range of public information services, including museums (where entry charges are now being reintroduced) and libraries.

Public library services in Britain are provided and supervised by local government but are governed by legislation and policy set by the Minister of Arts within the Department of Education and Science. In early 1988 the government set out proposals "to enlarge the scope for library authorities to generate increased revenues by joint ventures with the private sector and charging for specialised services" (42, p. 1). These proposals were in line with a number of other initiatives requiring local authorities to put many of their services out to tender to private contractors, including leisure facilities, refuse collection, and school catering. Compared to many of these services, public libraries are small in scale. In 1985–1986 the public library stock was 114 million books, and the service cost only £386 million per year. Nonetheless, it was with an eye toward increasing the minuscule £21.6 million income generated by library services that the proposals were ventured.

In fact, the reception given to this policy was almost uniformly hostile, and in a ministerial announcement in February 1989 (39) most of the proposals were rejected, including suggestions for charging for more popular or recent books. Nonetheless, the door was left open to some of the more significant shifts in the commercialization of public library information services, including new powers to charge users for borrowing nonprint materials, using facilities such as computers, and getting assistance from library staff.

The argument that citizens need extensive access to information about policy initiatives and government activities takes on added urgency at a time when the balance between state and citizen is shifting to the disadvantage of the latter. A number of observers see the growth of state power as an inevitable outcome of the development of capitalist democracies in the last two or three decades. As the role of the state in steering economic and social activities grows, so do the problems it faces in sustaining both the revenues and the legitimacy (cf. 10, 26) to perform this role.

Paradoxically, as neoconservative governments have taken office in many advanced industrial societies, this crisis of state function has produced a rhetoric of reduced state activity coupled with strengthened statutory agencies and legislation to secure social and economic stability (cf. 4, 14). Not the least of the manifestations of this neoliberal strong state, particularly in the United Kingdom, has been a series of actions designed to control the flow of information from government to public. This takes two forms: the positive promotion of some government action, coupled with selective prevention of public access to information about other activities.

All governments engage in public relations. Keeping the public informed of what they are doing while tacitly gilding the lily is far from sinister thought control. However, the scale and professionalism of public relations have very rapidly increased in the United Kingdom over the past decade (6).

The most familiar mechanism of direct government public relations is the Lobby, a privileged and accredited group of journalists regularly briefed by senior politicians on a non-attributable basis. The system has both detractors and defenders, but it had become so increasingly and assertively exploited by 1986 that two national newspapers withdrew from the Lobby entirely. The substantial advance in government public relations has suggested to some that we are entering a new phase in what Oscar Gandy has referred to as "information subsidies" (5). A weekly meeting in the Cabinet Office, chaired by the Prime Minister's Press Secretary, coordinates and supervises the work of departmental information officers, ensuring the proper "processing" of information (11). The British government's expenditure on publicity has grown from £20 million a decade ago to £120 million in 1988–1989. Concern about the scale of the increase and the uses to which these funds are being put had become so great by early 1989 that the National Audit Office launched a parliamentary investigation on behalf of the influential all-party Public Accounts Committee.

The corollary of positive promotion is the secretive retention of embarrassing or inconvenient information. Pressure on the media has been sustained and occasionally virulent in recent years, ranging from the faintly ludicrous attempt to suppress the memoirs of a former senior intelligence agent recorded in Peter Wright's *Spycatcher* to the (ultimately unsuccessful) banning of a BBC documentary on the zircon spy satellite, a lengthy battle over a radio series dealing with security matters (only eventually broadcast after substantial vetting), and the implementation of the Home Secretary's ban on broadcasting interviews with members of named terrorist organizations in Northern Ireland. Although checkered and in many ways limited as a program of censorship, this sequence of events is widely regarded as having had a major inhibiting effect on the adventurousness of critical and independent journalism. Continuing demands for a Bill of Rights or major liberalization of secrecy legislation have merely resulted in an Official Secrets Bill that features "a presumption of secrecy in favour of the government; no provision for freedom of information. . . . In short the Government has put forward a carefully modulated deal which amounts to more secrecy and less information" (31, pp. 17, 20).

At a less elevated level much concern has been aroused by the apparent cooption of government statistical resources into the service of state public relations (28). From the abstract view of Habermas this is a structural necessity: "The public realm, set up for effective legitimation, has above all the function of directing attention to topical areas—that is, of pushing other themes, problems, and arguments below the threshold of attention and, thereby, of witholding [sic] them from opinion-formation" (10, p. 70). Statistics describing the level and distribution of unemployment have been subject to well over twenty official redefinitions of terms and categories, making monitoring of data series well-nigh impossible. Regular publication of figures on the number of people living in poverty was discontinued in 1988 to be replaced by a new set of figures that the House of Commons Social Services Committee described in alarm as "likely to lead to an underestimate of the numbers on low income and distort any analysis of this group's standard of living" (16, p. 8).

Clearly, if governments are in the business of positively promoting their own perceptions and interpretations of policy developments while increasingly engaged in a war of attrition with independent media and research, the accessibility of a range of information sources becomes socially and politically vital for citizens. What opportunities exist, then, for people to have access to a range and diversity of communications and information resources?

If the provision of information is increasingly entrusted to the market, then access to that information becomes dependent on economic as well as political and technological constraints. "Tradeable information" is available to those individuals or groups who have the disposable spending power to make discretionary decisions about purchasing information goods and who may forego them without the opportunity costs being too high.

The widening gap in disposable incomes in Britain raises concern about the social effects of this development. In 1988 average gross weekly earnings were £218. However, 7.1 percent earned less than £100 per week and 99 percent earned more than £350 per week. Two million men and 2.8 million women earned less than £150, while .7 million people earned more than £450 weekly (38, Part A, Table 1; Part B, Table X5). In the period 1981–1987 the real weekly earnings of the lowest paid decile rose by 11.5 percent, but for the top decile the rise was 24.8 percent (36, Table 5.14). Independent calculations that allow for all taxes suggest a wider differential, with the poorest fifth only 1 percent better off and the best-paid fifth 24 percent better off (2). Not surprisingly, wealth differentials remain vast, the top 5 percent owning 40 percent of wealth in 1985 and the bottom 50 percent owning just 7 percent (36, Table 5.23). At the lower end, the number of people living on or below social security levels of income increased from 9.38 million in 1985 to roughly 11 million in 1988 (16, p. 35; 27).

The consequence of these movements in income differentials is a growing gap between different groups' expenditure choices and patterns. Table 2, which shows the levels of spending on services by income groups, illustrates the markedly higher spending power of better-off groups in this sector. In all wealthier societies, spending on services has been growing as a proportion of consumer expenditure. But lower-income groups have a lower consumption elasticity for service goods than higher-income groups; their income is substantially committed to the necessities of food, clothing, fuel, and housing.

In terms of aggregate demand this may not matter. After all, of the £274,318 million of disposable income available to the economy in 1986, the bottom fifth of households commanded only 5.9 percent, while the pockets of the top fifth were burning with 42.2 percent of the total (35, Table 5.18). However, for individual households the implications, not least

Table 2 Average 1986 weekly expenditure on services by households in selected income groups (in pounds).

Weekly income	Expenditure on services
£60–80	8.70
£100–125	11.35
£150–175	19.80
£225–250	19.86
£325–375	32.08
£550 and over	68.14
All households	22.67

Source: *Family Expenditure Survey 1986* (37, Table 5).

Table 3 Average 1986 weekly expenditure on communications goods and services by households in selected income groups (in pounds).

Weekly income	TV/video/ audio equipment	Books/ newspapers/ magazines	Cinema	TV/video rental/ license
£60–80	0.57	1.51	0.03	1.73
£100–125	0.91	2.00	0.02	1.72
£150–175	2.73	2.48	0.09	2.16
£225–250	4.51	2.98	0.11	2.08
£325–375	5.33	3.50	0.15	2.31
£550 and over	10.19	5.54	0.28	2.50

Source: Family Expenditure Survey 1986 (37, Table 1).

for their access to information goods and services, are significant in the extreme.

Communications and information goods and services consume a growing proportion of expenditure on services in general. Expenditure on video and television, for example, doubled between 1976 and 1987. (The differentiated pattern of this expenditure is highlighted by Table 3.) Expenditure on communications and information resources increased very rapidly up the income scale, with the partial exception of cinema admissions (which are of very limited importance at all income levels and are just as much differentiated by age and household type) and television (where the flat-rate BBC license fee has a leveling effect on the expenditure gradient).

The outcome of this expenditure pattern displayed in Table 1 shows that the ownership of even traditional hardware like the telephone is severely limited among lower-income groups (and is actually at its lowest among single-parent and pensioner groups, arguably those in greatest need of such a communications resource). For video and home computers the differential is even more marked. As we have suggested elsewhere (9), this is unlikely to be relieved by the general tendency to "trickle down," familiar in the diffusion history of previous generations of new technologies and household durables. By their very nature, these goods cumulatively advantage their owners and provide access to expensive and extensive value-added facilities, so that poorer groups are chasing a moving and fast-receding target.

This emerged particularly clearly in a 1989 survey of home computer penetration in the English Midlands (24). Not only were households in lower-income groups less likely to have a computer, but those who did own one were much more likely to have a relatively low-powered and unsophisticated model. They were also much less likely to possess additional hardware such as printers and modems that are essential for a wide range of applications, including horizontal communications with other users.

These economic barriers to developing computer competence were often reinforced by social dynamics. Because there were fewer users in their neighborhoods and they generally worked in jobs that did not involve using computers, the less-well-off computer owners had only limited access to the kinds of advice and support networks enjoyed by more affluent users and therefore experienced more difficulty in sustaining commitment and developing skills.

The general pattern of socioeconomic change, then, suggests that the shift to a more market-oriented provision of information and communications goods is emerging at a time when the ability of different groups in the population to dispose of their income on these goods is being markedly distinguished by widening gaps in income and wealth. Information poverty of society as a whole, generated by the growing power over information held by both state and corporate sectors, is complemented by the information poverty of lower-income groups directly resulting from their material deprivation.

Questions raised by the concept of citizenship are of crucial interest to researchers concerned with the communications media. The argument and evidence we have presented here are intended to point up the need to reestablish links between the concerns of communications scholars, especially those narrowly confined by an interest in novel technologies, and broader issues in social and political philosophy.

The tension between the actual operations of capitalist markets and the promise of full and equal citizenship has been a prominent feature of social and political criticism since the beginning of the modern era (12, 33). Markets address people primarily in their role as consumers rather than as citizens. Indeed, they present the freedom to choose among competing products as the central and defining liberty of the modern age. As a consequence, "citizenship becomes less a collective, political activity than an individual, economic activity—the right to pursue one's interests, without hindrance, in the marketplace" (3, p. 5). Clearly, people's economic rights as both producers and consumers are an essential component of their rights as citizens, but they certainly do not exhaust those rights as we have defined them here.

Nor can the right to purchase or not to purchase be equated with the right to participate in determining the rules that regulate market transactions. Moreover, as we have shown, for many people in contemporary Britain choices in the marketplace are purely nominal, since they lack the economic means to translate their needs and desires into purchases. This is the second major point of tension between the promise of citizenship and market dynamics. Where material inequality massively differentiates people's access to goods and services, and those goods and services are themselves a necessary resource for citizenship, then political rights are the victim of the vicissitudes of the marketplace and its inegalitarian structure.

These concerns have been brought into sharp relief in recent years because of the rapid shift in social policy in countries like Britain as the underlying difficulties of the postwar social democratic welfare states have surfaced into radical political innovation and debate. As a consequence, many people are experiencing dislocation in their immediate life situation and uncertainty about their rights. Consequently, there is a greater need than ever for adequate and accessible information and communications resources. Yet people most adversely affected by these changes are the ones with least access to these resources within the new privatized system of communications.

This argument has implications, too, for our approach to research in the field of communications. At the very least we would wish to signal again (8) the dangers in allowing communications research to become too self-enclosed. The most powerful and significant issues to be addressed remain those questions of power, inequality, and social order that have been at the core of social philosophy and research throughout the modern period. We have argued here that the links between citizenship and the newly emerging communications order should occupy a central place in addressing those questions. Otherwise communications research risks betraying not only its own intellectual pedigree and promise but the community and society it serves.

References

1 Carey, J. W. "Reconceiving 'Mass' and 'Media.'" In *Communication as Culture: Essays on Media and Society.* London: Unwin Hyman, 1989.
2 Cox, G. *The Pay Divide.* Low Pay Briefing Paper, Number 10. Manchester: Greater Manchester Low Pay Unit, 1988.
3 Dietz, M. G. "Context Is All: Feminism and Theories of Citizenship." *Daedalus*, Fall 1987, pp. 1–24.
4 Gamble, A. *The Free Economy and the Strong State: The Politics of Thatcherism.* London: Macmillan, 1988.
5 Gandy, O. *Beyond Agenda Setting: Information Subsidies and Public Policy.* Norwood, N.J.: Ablex, 1982.
6 Golding, P. "Citizenship and Political Communications: The Media and Democracy in an Inegalitarian Social Order." In M. Ferguson (Ed.), *Public Communications: The New Imperatives.* Newbury Park, Cal. and London: Sage, forthcoming.
7 Golding, P. (Ed.). *Excluding the Poor.* London: Child Poverty Action Group, 1986.
8 Golding, P. and G. Murdock. "Theories of Communication and Theories of Society." *Communication Research* 5(3), 1978, pp. 339–356.
9 Golding, P. and G. Murdock. "Unequal Information: Access and Exclusion in the New Communications Market-Place." In M. Ferguson (Ed.), *New Communication Technologies and the Public Interest.* Newbury Park, Cal. and London: Sage, 1986, pp. 71–83.

10. Habermas, J. *Legitimation Crisis.* London: Heinemann, 1976.
11. Hillyard, P. and J. Percy-Smith. *The Coercive State: The Decline of Democracy in Britain.* London: Fontana, 1988.
12. Hont, I. and M. Ignatieff (Eds.). *Wealth and Virtue: The Shaping of Political Economy in the Scottish Enlightenment.* Cambridge: Cambridge University Press, 1983.
13. Hurd, D. "Citizenship in the Tory Democracy." *New Statesman,* April 29, 1988, p. 14.
14. Keane, J. *Democracy and Civil Society: On the Predicaments of European Socialism, the Prospects for Democracy, and the Problem of Controlling Social and Political Power.* London: Verso, 1988.
15. King, D. S. and J. Waldron. "Citizenship, Social Citizenship and the Defence of Welfare Provision." *British Journal of Political Science* 18(4), 1988, pp. 415–443.
16. Low Pay Unit. *Low Pay Review* 33, Spring 1988.
17. Marshall, T. H. *Citizenship and Social Class.* Cambridge: Cambridge University Press, 1950.
18. Melucci, A. "Social Movements and the Democratisation of Everyday Life." In J. Keane (Ed.), *Civil Society and the State.* London: Verso, 1988, pp. 245–260.
19. Melucci, A. *Nomads of the Present: Social Movements and Individual Needs in Contemporary Society.* London: Hutchinson Radius, 1989.
20. Mosco, V. "Introduction: Information in the Pay-Per Society." In V. Mosco and J. Wasko (Eds.), *The Political Economy of Information.* Madison: University of Wisconsin Press, 1988, pp. 3–26.
21. Mouffe, C. "The Civics Lesson." *New Statesman and Society,* October 7, 1988, pp. 28–31.
22. Murdock, G. "Poor Connections: Income Inequality and the 'Information Society.'" In P. Golding (Ed.), *Excluding the Poor.* London: Child Poverty Action Group, 1986, pp. 70–83.
23. Murdock, G. "Television and Citizenship: In Defence of Public Broadcasting." In A. Tomlinson (Ed.), *Consumption, Identity and Style.* London: Routledge, forthcoming.
24. Murdock, G., P. Hartmann, and P. Gray. "Home Computers: The Social Construction of a Complex Commodity." *International Review of Sociology,* in press.
25. National Utilities Services. *International Telecommunications Survey.* London: National Utilities Services, 1989.
26. Offe, C. *Contradictions of the Welfare State.* London: Hutchinson, 1984.
27. Oppenheim, C. *Poverty: The Facts.* London: Child Poverty Action Group, 1988.
28. Ponting, C. *Whitehall: Tragedy and Farce.* London: Sphere, 1986.
29. Roche, M. "Citizenship, Social Theory, and Social Change." *Theory and Society* 16, 1987, pp. 363–399.
30. Summerscale, J. and C. Wells. *British Telecom.* London: DeZoete and Bevan, 1984.
31. Thornton, P. *Decade of Decline: Civil Liberties in the Thatcher Years.* London: National Council for Civil Liberties, 1988.
32. Turner, B. S. *Citizenship and Capitalism: The Debate Over Reformism.* London: Allen & Unwin, 1986.
33. Vincent, A. and R. Plant. *Philosophy, Politics and Citizenship: The Life and Thought of the British Idealists.* Oxford: Basil Blackwell, 1984.

34 United Kingdom. Cable Authority. *Annual Report and Accounts 1987–88.* London: Cable Authority, 1988.
35 United Kingdom. Central Statistical Office. *Financial Statistics*, No. 322. London: Her Majesty's Stationery Office, 1989.
36 United Kingdom. Central Statistical Office. *Social Trends*, Volume 19. London: Her Majesty's Stationery Office, 1989.
37 United Kingdom. Department of Employment. *Family Expenditure Survey 1986.* London: Her Majesty's Stationery Office, 1988.
38 United Kingdom. Department of Employment. *New Earnings Survey.* London: Her Majesty's Stationery Office, 1988.
39 United Kingdom. *Hansard Parliamentary Debates (Commons)* 146, February 8, 1989, col. 988.
40 United Kingdom. Home Office. *Report of the Committee on Financing the BBC.* Cmnd. 9824. London: Her Majesty's Stationery Office, 1986.
41 United Kingdom. Home Office. *Broadcasting in the Nineties: Competition, Choice, and Quality.* Cmnd. 517. London: Her Majesty's Stationery Office, 1988.
42 United Kingdom. Office of Arts and Libraries. *Financing Our Public Library Service: Four Subjects for Debate.* Cmnd. 324. London: Her Majesty's Stationery Office, 1988.

50
POLITICAL SCIENCE RESEARCH ON TELEDEMOCRACY

William H. Dutton

Source: *Social Science Computer Review* 10(4) (1992): 505–22.

Whatever consequences flow from the November 1992 elections, H. Ross Perot's independent campaign for President of the United States has already lent an unprecedented measure of legitimacy to discussions of teledemocracy. Perot's advancement of interactive TV as a means for discovering and marshaling public opinion on national issues generated innovative uses of the media by other candidates and renewed debate over the wisdom of electronic plebiscites as well as other forms of electronic political participation. The press approached Perot's proposals with skepticism, but journalists have nevertheless devoted considerable attention to Perot's electronic forums, ways in which they might be organized, and what effect they could have on American politics.

Teledemocracy is not new. It is a general concept covering a variety of visions of how electronic media could be used to facilitate more direct and equitable participation in politics. In the United States, discussion of the role of computers and telecommunications in facilitating public political participation began in earnest during the late 1960s. At that time, stimulated by the promises surrounding two-way, interactive cable television systems, proponents saw the convergence of computing and telecommunications as offering a technological fix to the many pragmatic constraints on more direct participation in governance. Proponents argued that the electronic media with their increasing capacity for interactive communications would permit urban America to emulate and thereby recapture the virtues of the New England town meeting.

These utopian visions of voting and polling from the home were soon countered by dystopian forecasts that the new media could be used by government officials to manipulate and control public opinion, what Kenneth Laudon (1977) would label "managed democracy." Most social and political scientists agreed with Anthony Smith (1977), who saw the electronic media as more likely to usher in an age of "telocracy" than teledemocracy.

In these early debates about the political implications of electronic media, political scientists were central. They joined with computer scientists and other social scientists to assess the problems, opportunities, and prospects of this technological scenario (Sackman & Nie, 1970; Sackman & Boehm, 1972). Unfortunately, in my view, this debate as well as the research it spawned was prematurely muted by the economic malaise of the cable industry in the early 1970s and the huge gulf that became evident between expectations and reality. Field trails of two-way, interactive cable television in the 1970s demonstrated that such systems were feasible technically, but also that the benefits of interactive cable fell far short of the added cost of installing two-way capability (Dutton, Blumler, & Kraemer, 1987). As a result of this market failure of interactive cable, political scientists dropped out of the debates on teledemocracy.

Since the 1970s, political science research on teledemocracy has been so limited that journalists tracking Ross Perot's proposals were more likely to turn toward social psychologists than to political scientists for insights about electronic forums. With few exceptions, which are described below, the political science discipline had dismissed this technology. Political scientists neglected the study of computers and telecommunications even in their own domain of political campaigns and elections (Meadow, 1984). When journalists did turn to political scientists, they were often treated to utopian or dystopian conjectures, unsupported by empirical research. One stark example is provided by the chairman of the Department of Government at the University of Texas, James Fishkin, when asked about the wisdom of Ross Perot's electronic forums. Fishkin claimed that:

> Electronic town meetings are just a device to step outside established political mechanisms—to abandon traditional forms of representation and elections—in order to acquire a mantle of higher legitimacy. And in the very worst case, it could be invoked toward extraconstitutional ends.
>
> (*Time*, May 25, 1992, p. 28)

Fishkin's rather Orwellian perspective on Ross Perot and electronic forums underscores the degree to which political scientists continue to view teledemocracy from the same utopian-dystopian, proversus antitechnology stances that were taken in the 1960s.

My review of political science research on teledemocracy reinforces this conclusion. Since teledemocracy was first promoted, political scientists have marginalized its study, even if they frequently rehearse the opportunities and threats embodied by such proposals. In the following section, I describe the focuses of the literature on teledemocracy, which demonstrates the marginal role of research on this topic within the political science discipline. I argue that a higher status should be accorded to research on teledemocracy. Computing and telecommunications are readily available and are quite likely to be used to do everything from holding public forums to paying for parking, whether political scientists study this phenomenon or not. Increasingly, the decision to use electronic media to facilitate political participation will be a political choice rather than an electronic dream or "nightmare" (Wicklein, 1981). These choices should be informed by research on the factors shaping these developments and their impacts.

Streams of literature on teledemocracy

Scholarly research on teledemocracy is virtually absent from the mainstream journals in political science, but it finds its way into print through more specialized journals dealing with information technology. Discussions of teledemocracy are more common within more popular magazines and trade journals. From a computer-based keyword search of literature over more than 2 decades, I was able to identify only 33 books or articles that focused on teledemocracy or the more general use of computers and telecommunications for facilitating public participation in politics, excluding textbooks, book reviews, purely journalistic accounts, and editorials. In order not to overweight a single study, I grouped articles or books together when I knew them to be reports from a single project.

Tables 1 and 2 list the 33 works that form the basis of my generalizations about political science research on teledemocracy. Table 1 lists work completed by the early 1980s, primarily in the era of interactive cable and mainframe computing. Table 2 lists work completed since the rapid advance and application of microcomputing and digital telecommunication networks and services.

It is apparent from Tables 1 and 2 that the literature on teledemocracy is not large and that it is scattered across a wide variety of trade and professional journals.[1] The major streams of this literature can be captured by about seven themes represented as columns in these tables. The work listed in both tables is rated by the degree to which it focuses on one or more of these seven themes. These categories are not mutually exclusive or exhaustive, but they are adequate to cover the work reviewed for this essay.

Fully two-thirds of the articles focus on presenting a case for or against the idea of teledemocracy. Early work within this category is dominated by treatments of cable television, such as Ithiel de Sola Pool's discussion of how interactive cable television might improve the feedback politicians receive from the public (Pool & Alexander, 1973), but also Kenneth Laudon's (1977) argument about interactive cable as a threat to democratic control. Some treatments, such as Harold Sackman's books (Sackman & Nie, 1970; Sackman & Boehm, 1972), strive to be more disinterested and present both

Table 1 Early work on computers and telecommunications in politics and governance.

Study	(+) Teledemocracy (−)	Speculative Assessment	Designs, Systems, Schemes	Review & Synthesis of Literature	Educational or Policy Initiatives	Research on Impacts	Cases/Research Political Shaping
Sackman, et al. '70 & '72	+/−	×	×				
Eberlein '71	+		×		×		
Pool & Alexander '73	+	×	×		×		
Lowi '75 (81)	−	×					
Laudon '77	−	×		×		×	
Flood '78	+		×				
Abdu Ho '79	+		×				
Frantzich '82						×	×
Kraemer et al. '81; Danziger et al. '82		−				×	×

Table 2 Later work on computers and telecommunications in politics and governance.

Study	(+) Teledemocracy (−)	Speculative Assessment	Designs, Systems, Schemes	Review & Synthesis of Literature	Educational or Policy Initiatives	Research on Impacts	Cases/Research Political Shaping
Rubens '83	+						
Smith '83	+	×	×				
Barber '84	+	×	×				
Becker & Scarce '84	+	×	×	×			
Duten et al. '84							×
Metayer '84	+/−	×		×			
Cleveland '85	+	×					
Mitropoulos '85	−			×			
Whicker '86					×	×	
Arterton '87				×	×	×	
Davidge '87	+					×	
White '87	+	×			×		
Abramson et al. '88	+/−	×	×	×			
Downing '89	+		×	×			
Halal '89	+	×					
Henningsen '89	−	×					
Smith-Grotto '89					×		
Sussman '89	+		×		×		
Glenn '90					×		
Pitta '90	+/−						
Dutton & Guthrie '91; Dutton et al, '91, '92						×	×
Ganley '91	+/−	×	×	×			
Varley '91	+					×	×
Guthrie '91				×			×
Dutton et al. '92						×	
Total[1]	67% (22)	42% (14)	39% (13)	33% (11)	27% (9)	27% (8)	18% (6)

Simple count over all studies coded in both Tables 1 and 2.

positive and negative aspects of teledemocracy. Nevertheless, the dominant theme of most work in this area is argument for or against the idea of electronic democracy.

A second, closely related stream of work speculates about the political implications of teledemocracy. These speculative assessments capture nearly half (42%) of the works reviewed. I defined speculative assessments by a focus on rational versus empirical analysis of the likely outcomes of technological change. Speculations are based on a rational extension of features perceived to be inherently determined by characteristics built into the technology or the groups that control its introduction and use. Theodore Lowi's analysis of the political impact of information technology fits in this category, as does Cleveland's (1985) treatment of the democratic bias of the new media. Empirical research on the actual impacts of electronic forms of political participation falls in a separate category, since it distinguishes only about a fourth (27%) of the work on teledemocracy.

Another type of work focuses on how teledemocracy systems should be designed or constructed—prescriptions for the design of systems to support teledemocracy. They range from proponents of interactive cable television, such as Pool and Alexander (1973), to proponents of specific techniques for voting and polling, such as Abdu Ho (1979). Nearly 40 percent of the work prescribes particular designs for electronic systems.

A related category, which also has a prescriptive element, is work that argues for particular educational or policy initiatives as a response to teledemocracy. The most common theme here is a concern for educating the public to be capable of fully participating in a more technologically sophisticated political process. Some identify the skills required for effective participation, such as how to be selective in processing information, how to deal with information overload, and how to access the quality of online information. Computer literacy is a dominant thrust of this recent work.

As noted above, empirical research on teledemocracy is relatively rare. Only about one-fourth (27%) of the 33 studies reported original research on the impacts of electronic forms of participation. Less than a fifth (18%) report empirical research on the political shaping of teledemocracy, that is, the politics of designing, adopting, or implementing electronic media for facilitating political participation.

Of course, the lack of empirical research is understandable, as few experiments with teledemocracy have been sustained over time; the use of electronic systems designed to facilitate political participation has only recently been possible to observe. Indeed, a large proportion of the empirical research on the political shaping and impacts of teledemocracy has been anchored in some of the first systems successfully implemented by American local governments, such as Santa Monica's Public Electronic Network (PEN), described below (Dutton & Guthrie, 1991).

Given this dearth of empirical research, there has been a surprisingly large number of reviews and syntheses of work on teledemocracy (even excluding the present attempt). Many reviews of a limited body of research have led many to rediscover and repeat many of the same general themes and issues, such as the well-practiced dialectic among the utopian and dystopian treatments of teledemocracy.

Therefore, the literature on teledemocracy is limited. There is much rehashing of old arguments. Also, the topic has been dominated by personal assessments of teledemocracy as opposed to more scholarly analysis and empirical research. Despite these weaknesses, there are reasons why a more sustained program of research could develop around teledemocracy.

First, there is a small but growing number of political scientists interested in science and technology studies, including research on communication and information technologies. Studies of technology have become increasingly sophisticated in defining frameworks for study of the social shaping and impacts of technological change. Ironically, compared with the 1960s, when political scientists were more engaged by debates over teledemocracy, there might now be a more substantial group of political scientists with an interest in technology studies per se and the conceptual tools to move beyond debates over whether teledemocracy is good or bad. Studies of the politics *in* and *of* technology are addressing issues of: Who is shaping the technology? In what ways? With what effect? Whose interests are served?

Second, and most important, teledemocracy is no longer futuristic. As Perot's proposals assume, it can be done. Electronic systems are already being put into place that will affect the relationships between government officials, agencies, and the lay public. I will turn now to these developments, which point toward the opportunity as well as the need for launching an empirical research program.

Emerging applications of information technology[2]

A small but increasingly visible number of state and local governments are applying communication and information technology in ways designed to facilitate public access to government agencies and services. These innovations find expression in a variety of applications across a range of functional areas. While there is no master plan shaping these individual initiatives, they are connected by a focus on using new communication and information technology to catch up with the private sector; increase the speed, accuracy, and efficiency of public services; and bring government closer to the public. Whatever the intentions behind these initiatives might be, the long-term, indirect consequences of these developments need to be explored, since they promise to go beyond improving the efficiency of existing practices, to altering the way we do things—such as voting, polling, lobbying, and obtaining services.

Generally, innovative applications of communication and information technology fall within five general types of applications, described in Table 3, which my colleagues and I have labeled as broadcasting; transactions; access to public records; interpersonal communications; and surveying and monitoring (Dutton, Guthrie, O'Connell, & Wyer, 1991).

Broadcasting

The most prominent uses of new communication and information technologies are aimed at broadcasting information for the general public. As cable systems have diffused, public agencies have more frequently used these channels for distributing governmental and other public information, such as by scrolling textual information or cablecasting live events, such as council meetings. Cablecasting governmental affairs is becoming a common practice. Localities like West Hartford, Connecticut, have advanced the state of the art in this area by producing more sophisticated local news and public affairs programming, which they refer to as "neighborhood TV" (Dutton et al., 1991). Rather than simply pointing a camera at live events, these producers and growing ranks of volunteers seek to translate lengthy meetings into bite-sized programs that capture the interest of the local audience. The old vision of community programming over cable is only now beginning to be fully realized in a few localities.

Beyond the local level, the success of the Congressional-Satellite Public Affairs Network (C-SPAN) has prompted state officials to emulate their programming (Weston & Givens, 1989). The state of California has launched a system, which it calls the California-Satellite Public Affairs Network: The California Channel (CAL-SPAN).

State and local governments are also experimenting with using information kiosks, multimedia personal computer platforms for distributing information to the public. These kiosks generally combine laser disk storage devices and microcomputers with a touch screen to allow people to access government and other public service information. They are being placed in libraries, shopping malls, recreation centers, and grocery stores to provide public information in the form of text, video, graphics, or sound, all in multiple languages to adapt to a more multicultural society. They are promoted as a means for bringing information closer to people, not expecting them to travel to city hall and speak English. In this area, Public Technology, Inc., in partnership with IBM has supported a "24-hour City Hall" project, which has placed kiosks in over a dozen local jurisdictions. In 1992, immediately after the Los Angeles protests and riots, North Communications, a Los Angeles firm that has worked with IBM in developing kiosk systems, launched what it called the LA Project. North distributed a small number of kiosks throughout Los Angeles, designed to support South Central and neighboring Los Angeles residents in seeking phone numbers,

Table 3 Governmental applications of computing and telecommunications emerging in the 1990s.

Communication Task:	Selected Examples:	Early Applications:	Systems Employed:
Broadcasting	Satellite-linked cable TV systems Local cable TV Touch screen, multi-media PC	Cablecasting of public meetings, hearings Neighborhood TV Multi-lingual kiosks	C-SPAN, California Channel (Cal-SPAN) West Hartford, Connecticut 24-hour City Hall, Hawaii Access, LA Project
Transactions	Touch screen, multi-media PC Magnetic strips & smart cards Voice processing Automated teller machines Automatic vehicle identification systems	Apply for social services Renew/ up-date driver's license Electronic benefit transfers Schedule inspections Welfare and medicaid transactions Automated assignment of tolls for use of roads	Tulare Touch California DMV's Info/California New York City food stamp benefits Arlington County Proposals at the state and federal levels Under discussion in California
Access to Public Records	Audiotext, recorded messages Dial-up electronic bulletin boards Dial-up access to public databases	Answers to routine public inquiries Public, government, community information Access to land records by title companies	Hillsborough County's Fact Finder; Phone Phoenix PARIS/PALS Pasadena; Santa Monica's PEN; New York City Board of Education's NYCENET Proposed in Arlington County, Virginia
Interpersonal Communication	Voice mail, asynchronous voice communication Facsimile Electronic mail Computer conferencing & bulletin boards Audio and video conferencing	Parent-teacher exchanges Inquires about teacher certification Application for building permits Citizen complaints, inquiries, requests Electronic forums on public issues Arraignment; bond reviews; and other pretrial meetings	City of New York State of Connecticut City of Spokane Santa Monica's PEN Santa Monica's PEN; NYCENET San Bernardino, CA; Dade County, Florida....
Surveying and Monitoring	Computer-assisted dialing & interviewing Audience response systems Video & electronic surveillance	Opinion polling Voting and polling from the home Automatic vehicle identification systems	Political campaigns QUBE system in Columbus, Ohio Caltrans experiments with toll collections

Note: This chart adapted from William Dutton, Kendall Guthrie, Jacqueline O'Connell, and Joanne Wyer (1991).

public information, business loans, employment, and other assistance of possible value in recovering from the disturbances.

Transactions

The Department of Social Services in Tulare County, California, has developed a kiosk system called "Tulare Touch." Tulare Touch uses a multilingual video and audio touch screen connected to an expert system. The department has 35 kiosks with a touch screen at each district office. Welfare clients step up to a kiosk, choose which language they wish to use, and then are walked through a welfare application. Fraud screens provide checks of income or other information by linking with other files to verify the client's eligibility. The system approves or rejects the applicant at the time of application or gives the applicant a list of information needed for any future application. The project was aimed at reducing costs by using the capabilities of an expert system to minimize errors in determining eligibility and calculating payments.

In late October 1991, California's Department of Motor Vehicles (DMV) launched a 9-month pilot project called "Info/California" (Hanson, 1991). Information kiosks are available in Sacramento and San Diego and permit citizens to conduct a variety of transactions, such as registering an out-of-state vehicle. This system is modeled after an automated teller machine. Other state and local governments are using similar electronic systems for distributing benefits, such as food stamps, hoping to provide recipients with benefit cards that could be used much like a credit card in local groceries and supermarkets. Other government agencies are experimenting with "smart cards" as another approach to automated payment and billing.

Arlington County, Virginia, has implemented what is called the "parkulater," a device about the size of a pocket calculator. It uses a small computer chip and acts as "electronic dollars" for commuters parked at meters. The user keys in the type of meter and places the parkulater by his or her front windshield, and the time runs until the driver leaves and turns it off. So the parker is billed only for actual time and does not need correct change. By 1992, as many as a half-dozen other jurisdictions were using this technology.

Access to public records

New technologies are being employed to provide an additional means for public access to records, using specialized computer bulletin boards, videotext and other online access, videodisc kiosks, audiotext, and the facsimile distribution of forms and records.

Voice mail systems are being used to answer routine citizen inquiries. "Phone Phoenix" is one system offering prerecorded messages over the telephone as a means for answering many common, repeated questions and disseminating information, such as a schedule of current events. The system also monitors calls, enabling the city to determine what topics are of interest to citizens. Some cities are using these systems to handle more specialized information needs. Dallas, Texas, uses audiotext to communicate with people requesting information about the status of building permits. Arlington County, Virginia, has implemented a form of audiotext that provides building contractors with dial-up access for scheduling a building inspection.

A number of jurisdictions have experimented with electronic bulletin boards and other online systems for offering dial-up online access to databases. From 1987 to 1988, a committee of the California State Legislature developed "The Capitol Connection," a dial-in bulletin board for individuals wishing to keep up with the committee and the legislature's agenda. Libraries have been among the most likely agencies to develop online services, allowing computer users to access the library's card catalog from their home or office. The Pasadena, California, Public Library expanded on this concept to develop a database of civic organizations, city commissions, and social service agencies as well as a community calendar listing everything from performing arts programs to garden club meetings (Guthrie, 1991).

A few other cities are using computer bulletin boards to provide information. The city of Santa Monica, California, has led the way with its public Electronic Network (PEN). PEN contains community events, the council's agenda, and other information on city departments, officials, and services. It is accessible from personal computers or any of 18 public terminals distributed throughout the city (Dutton & Guthrie, 1991). The New York City Board of Education has also developed a computer bulletin board called NYCENET, used by both educators and students.

Specialized databases

A number of government agencies are considering the provision of online access to specialized databases, both as a means for improving services and as a way to generate new revenues. For example, an Arlington County, Virginia, agency has considered providing online access to land records, believing that some title companies might be willing to pay for this convenience. If land records are automated for other reasons, this kind of service is increasingly practical at only a marginal cost. Hampton, Virginia, has provided 25 incoming lines to its computer; people who subscribe can access information such as the sales history of property, the owner, city tax assessments, school assignments, and permits. Geographically based information systems that integrate census, housing, and other information are another specialized database that is potentially valuable to telemarketing firms.

Online access to records, increasingly stored on optical disk imaging systems and integrated with facsimile equipment, provides an attractive alternative to private firms and a new revenue source for the public sector. Information can be retrieved for on-screen viewing or directly faxed to the user.

Interpersonal communications

Government officials and personnel have long communicated with the public in person, over the counter, by mail, and by telephone. Increasingly they are using voice mail, facsimile, electronic mail, and computer conferencing systems.

Voice mail is viewed as a means to reduce the staff time required to handle routine telephone calls. It is also being used to enhance rather than replace interpersonal communication, for example, by supporting parent-teacher communication, allowing the teachers to leave a message at the end of each day and providing the working parents with a means to hear the teacher's message or leave a message for the teacher. Other state and local agencies are using voice mail for answering inquiries about teacher certification, filing insurance claims, and inquiring about the status of claims.

Cities are also using facsimile machines to receive and, more recently, to distribute forms. Cities can send and receive applications for permits via facsimile. Optical disk storage systems can be used in conjunction with facsimile machines to distribute records identified through an online search.

A potentially more dramatic departure is the use of electronic mail. This technology has been adopted since the 1970s by government agencies for internal, organizational communications, but a few governments have begun to apply this technology as a means to support dialogue with the public.

Santa Monica's Public Electronic Network (PEN) stands out in this area. PEN allows citizens to send electronic messages to city hall, council members, any city department, and the library's reference desk. City staff can then reply to the request electronically. It received 5,000 messages in the first 2 years of PEN's operation. Sixty percent of the individuals described their messages to city hall as inquiries. About one-fourth sent either comments, complaints, or other kinds of messages to city officials. Some city department heads and supervisors have been relutcant to implement electronic mail between citizens and city hall for fear it would open a floodgate for complaints. In PEN's case, it does seem to have increased the number of complaints and requests coming to the city. Therefore, this facility is perceived to have increased the workload on city staff but also the responsiveness of the city to the general public (Dutton, O'Connell, & Wyer, 1992).

PEN is also innovative in that it allows citizens to send electronic messages to one another. This electronic mail feature facilitates PEN's use for electronic meetings and conferencing about public affairs. In Santa Monica and elsewhere, electronic mail and conferencing software are being used to support public forums on policy issues. In contrast to the electronic voting and polling systems proposed in the 1970s, these forums are designed to foster dialogue to set agenda and explore options rather than facilitate voting and polling from the home (Dutton *et al.*, 1991). While Santa Monica's PEN system is the only municipally funded project that has extensively developed a conferencing capability, political forums have been developed on FreeNet, a nonprofit operation in Cleveland, Ohio, and by Berkeley's Community Memory project. The New York City Board of Education's NYCENET system also features discussions.

Finally, government agencies are using audio and video teleconferencing in creative ways to reduce travel and increase communication with remote locations. One instance is in the criminal justice area, where a number of jurisdictions are trying to reduce their costs for transporting inmates by providing a two-way video link between their jails and courts. People arrested for misdemeanors, and in some jurisdictions for felonies, can be arraigned and receive a bond review from the jail location rather than being transported to the courts.

Surveying and monitoring

A variety of other applications of electronic media are increasingly moving citizens in more direct, albeit mediated, interaction with government agencies. Advances in computer-assisted dialing and interviewing systems are being used by public opinion polling firms and could be used by governments in similar ways to gather information about the public. The entertainment media are experimenting with new versions of interactive television that utilize over-the-air broadcasting, in home terminals, and the telephone network to poll viewers as they play along with televised game shows. The same technology could be used by government agencies to interact with the audiences of public or governmental affairs programming, as was done for a time over interactive cable TV on the QUBE system in Columbus, Ohio (Davidge, 1987). Such systems could resurrect and have resurrected interest in voting and polling from the home, even if it is unlikely that they will ever diffuse to a large proportion of the public.

Also, the ordinary push-button telephone could be used increasingly for polling citizens on a variety of issues—either alone or in conjunction with televised speeches or debates. The introduction of screen phones, initially designed to facilitate voice processing by presenting options over a liquid crystal display device mounted on the phone, will undoubtedly encourage such applications.

Finally, the use of video and other electronic systems for monitoring the public will increasingly bring more direct linkages with governments. For example, transportation agencies plan to employ video more routinely to monitor traffic conditions in realtime. Caltrans, the California Department of Transportation, is developing an automatic vehicle identification system

(AVI), much like that developed in Singapore, to automatically collect tolls. Singapore uses its system to control traffic by charging additional fees for the use of streets within the central business district during peak rush hours.

Summary and conclusion

Candidates such as Ross Perot as well as federal, state, and local government officials and personnel are pushing electronic systems to serve a variety of public objectives. Since the 1980s, governments have begun to emulate the use of computing and telecommunications systems in the banking and retail service industries to support information, communication, and other governmental transactions with the public. Some focus on providing information services, such as information kiosks, whereas others, such as computer-based forums, are more focused on communication among people. Some projects, such as PEN, combine both of these objectives. Many projects are aimed at the general public, but increasingly agencies are targeting more specific audiences. Whether political scientists view teledemocracy as desirable or not, the technological infrastructure to support electronic forms of political participation and governance is being put in place.

The implications of computing and telecommunications in the public sector have been discussed for decades, but debate about teledemocracy and related developments has seldom been grounded in empirical research. Many of the more innovative projects discussed above provide an opportunity to redress this imbalance. These projects depart significantly from the way computing and telecommunications have been employed by American state and local governments since the 1950s. They employ new communication and information technologies in ways that might be both efficient and more capital intensive than labor intensive. Most important, they are intended as a means to bring government closer to the general public as well as to specialized clients of the public sector. Most of them focus on service delivery more than on teledemocracy, narrowly defined, but nevertheless hold the potential for changing the way the public interacts with candidates, officials, and public agencies by developing a new technological infrastructure that can be used for other purposes.

The political implications of these applications of communication and information technology extend far beyond their immediate technical benefits. They are relevant to the relative equity of participation in politics and the equity of services delivered to the public. These applications might affect the privacy of individuals if more information about public opinions, beliefs, and activities migrates into the files of public bureaucracies. As the new media create new spaces for public discourse and debate, they become an arena for political speech that is as relevant to first amendment concerns as are the more traditional media. The application of computers and telecommunications in the public sector is indeed relevant to democratic values.

Political scientists are a logical source for more in-depth descriptions and comparative analysis of the full range of projects identified above. At minimum, there is a need for more systematic evaluations of these early projects. Political scientists are best equipped to understand the political implications of these developments, since they should have a relatively sophisticated understanding of political participation and policy-making processes. Finally, they should easily view these technological choices as equivalent to major public policy choices facing national, state, and local governments.

A great deal of hype surrounds the new media. Some hype is forgivable if not necessary. One can hardly expect state and local government officials to spend time and money on a project that is not vigorously and enthusiastically promoted. Some of this hype, however, can be dysfunctional, if not debilitating. It can undermine valid arguments based on the actual potential of new communication and information technology. Also, the hype is sometimes so outlandish, such as that found in early visions of teledemocracy, that real developments are too easily dismissed as utopian or dystopian misadventures. Hype also tends to confuse the technically unsophisticated—that is, most of us—about what is "state of the art" versus "state of the practice" versus "wishful thinking." Information technology can mystify managers who do not fully understand it. As a consequence, valuable time is often spent pursuing approaches that cannot be achieved with off-the-shelf technology. Systematic, disinterested evaluations of these projects might anchor more realistic perspectives on the actual operation, cost, and implications of these electronic services.

In thinking about who should study the consequences of these developments —computer scientists, the developers, political scientists, or whomever— I'm reminded of a refrain from Tom Lehrer's (1965) "Wernher von Braun" from the musical titled "Tom Foolery," which goes:

> "Once the rockets are up,
> who cares where they come down?
> That's not my department,"
> says Wernher von Braun.

Once political scientists recognize that the application of new communication and information technologies is no longer futuristic—that it is already happening in ways that might affect the character of politics and governance—then the responsibility falls squarely in their laps as well as on those who are developing these applications. It is their department, so to speak, and developments launched in the early 1990s provide ample opportunities to study technological innovations that have the potential to change American politics and governance.

Notes

The author thanks G. David Garson for his comments and the computer search of the social science literature on which this review is based. The author also wishes to acknowledge the work of several former students and colleagues, Kendall Guthrie, Jacqueline O'Connell, and Joanne Wyer, for their assistance in conducting the field research on innovations in state and local government computing and telecommunications. Finally, thanks go to Rachel Osborn for tracking down some lyrics and to Cherilyn Parsons for her comments and advice during the final stages of editing.

1. The literature for the review was selected from articles uncovered by a computer search of the social science literature, using the following keywords: teledemocracy, computers or information technology or communication technology and democracy, government, public sector, public services, public administration, political participation, or politics.
2. The findings discussed in this section are adapted from a survey conducted by the author along with Kendall Guthrie, Jacqueline O'Connell, and Joanne Wyer (Dutton *et al.*, 1991).

References

Abdu Ho, A. 1979. Citizen participation through modified delphi technique. Ph.D. diss., University of Missouri, Columbia, MO.

Abramson, J. B., Arterton, F. C., & Orren, G. R. 1988. *The electronic commonwealth*. New York: Basic Books. Arterton, F. C. 1987. *Teledemocracy*. Beverly Hills: Sage.

Barber, B. 1984. *Strong democracy: Participatory politics for a new age*. Los Angeles: University of California Press.

Becker, T., & Scarce, R. 1984. Teledemocracy emergent: State of the art and science. Paper delivered to the Annual Meeting of the American Political Science Association, 30 August–2 September.

Benjamin, G., ed. 1982. *The communication revolution in politics* (pp. 13–23). New York: American Academy of Political Science.

Cleveland, H. 1985. The twilight of hierarchy. *Public Administration Review* (January/February): 185–95.

Danziger, J. N. 1986. Computing and the political world. *Computers and the Social Sciences* 2 (4): 183–200.

Danziger, J. N., Dutton, W. H., Kling, R., & Kraemer K. 1982. *Computers and politics*. New York: Columbia University Press.

Davidge, C. 1987. America's talk-back television experiment: QUBE. In W. Dutton, J. Blumler, & Kenneth Kraemer (eds.), *Wired cities: Shaping the future of communications* (pp. 75–101). Boston: G. K. Hall.

Downing, J. D. 1989. Computers for political change. *Journal of Communication* 39 (3): 154–62.

Downs, A. 1967. A realistic look at the payoffs from urban data systems. *Public Administration Review* 27 (3): 204–10.

Dutton, W. 1989. Looking beyond teledemocracy: The politics of communications and information technology. In A. A. Berger (ed.), *Political culture and public opinion* (pp. 79–96). New Brunswick, NJ: Transaction Publishers.

Dutton, W. H., Blumler, J. G., & Kraemer, K. L. eds. 1987. *Wired cities*. Boston: G. K. Hall.

Dutton, W. H., & Guthrie, K. K. 1991. The political construction of an information utility. *Informatics and the Public Sector*, (forthcoming).

Dutton, W. H., Guthrie, K., O'Connell, J., & Wyer, J. 1992. The strategic value of an information utility. Working paper. Los Angeles: Annenberg School for Communication, University of Southern California.

Dutton, W. H., O'Connell, J., & Wyer, J. 1991. State and local government innovations in electronic services. Report prepared for the Office of Technology Assessment, U.S. Congress. Los Angeles: Annenberg School for Communication, University of Southern California.

Dutton, W., Steckenrider, J., Ross-Christensen, D., Lynch, L., Goldfarb, B., Hirschberg, L., Barcroft, T., & Williams, R. 1984. Electronic participation by citizens in U.S. local government. *Information Age* 6 (April): 78–97.

Eberlein, G. 1971. Conditions and consequences of a social-economic-technological model of the future. *Soziologenkorrespondenz* 2 (3–4): 295–308.

Flood, M. M. 1978. Let's redesign democracy. *Behavioral Science* 23 (6): 429–40.

Frantzich, S. E. 1982. *Computers in congress*. Beverly Hills: Sage.

Ganley, G. D. 1991. Power to the people via personal electronic media. *Washington Quarterly* 14 (2): 5–22.

Glenn, A. D. 1990. Democracy and technology. *Social Studies* 81 (5): 215–17.

Guthrie, K. 1991. The politics of citizen access technology: The development of communication and information utilities in four cities. Ph.D. diss., Annenberg School for Communication, University of Southern California.

Guthrie, K., & Dutton, W. H. 1991. The politics of citizen access technology. Paper presented at the 87th Annual Meeting of the American Political Science Association, Washington DC, 29 August–1 September.

Guthrie, K., Schmitz, J., Ryu, D., Harris, J., Rogers, E., & Dutton, W. 1990. Communication technology and democratic participation: PENers in Santa Monica. Paper presented at the Association of Computer Machinery's (ACM) Conference on Computers and the Quality of Life, Washington DC, September.

Hala, W. E. 1989. One world. In *The future: Opportunity not destiny* (pp. 36–51). Bethesda, Maryland. Edited by the World Futures Society.

Hanson, W. 1991. Info/California launched. *Government Technology* (December).

Henningsen, M. 1989. The future of a western political formation. *Alternatives* 14 (3): 327–42.

Kraemer, K. L., Dutton, W. H., & Northrop, A. 1981. *The management of information systems*. New York: Columbia University Press.

Kraemer, K. L., King, J. L., Dunkle, D. E., Lane, J. P., & George, J. F. 1985. Official microcomputer use and policy in larger U.S. cities. *Baseline Data Report* 17 (1). Washington, DC: ICMA.

Kraemer, K. L., King, J. L., Dunkle, D. E., & Lane, J. P. 1986. Trends in municipal information systems. *Baseline Data Report* 18 (2). Washington, DC: ICMA.

——. 1986. Trends in municipal information systems, 1975–1985. Public Policy Research Organization: Irvine, CA.

Kraemer, K., King, J., & Schetter, D. 1985. Innovative uses of information technology in facilitating public access to agency decision-making: An assessment of the experience in state and local governments. Report prepared for the U.S. Congress Office of Technology Assessment.

Laudon, K. C. 1977. *Communications technology and democratic participation.* New York: Praeger.

Lowi, T. 1981. The political impact of information technology. In T. Forester (ed.) *The microelectronics revolution* (453–72). Cambridge, MA: MIT Press. Reprinted from IEEE *Transactions on Communications,* COM-*23* (10), October 1975.

Maciuszko, K. 1990. A quiet revolution: Community online systems. *Online* (November): 24–32.

Meadow, R., ed. 1984. *New communications technology in politics.* Washington, DC: Annenberg School of Communication.

Metayer, G. 1984. From the ancient agora to the high-tech marketplace: Transformations in democracy. *Sociologie et Societes* 16 (1): 103–14.

Mitropoulos, M. 1985. Implications of cable TV for participatory democracy. *Cities* 2 (2): 178–79.

Norris, D. F. 1989. High tech in city hall: Uses and effects of microcomputers in United States local governments. *Social Science Computer Review* 7 (2): 137–46.

Pine, E. 1990. The rise of the electronic city hall. *Western City* (July): 8–11.

Pitta, J. 1990. Electronic democracy. *Forbes,* 1 October, 132.

Rubens, J. 1983. Retooling American democracy, *The Futurist* 17 (1): 59–64.

Sackman, H., & Nie, N., eds. 1970. *The information utility and social choice.* Montvale, NJ: A^{5}PS Press.

Sackman, H., & Boehm, B. 1972. *Planning community information utilities.* Montvale, NJ: AFIPS Press.

Smith, A. 1978. *The politics of information.* London: Macmillan.

Smith-Grotto, K. 1989. Computer literacy and citizenship in a democracy. *Louisiana Social Studies Journal* 16 (1): 30–33.

Sola Pool, I. de, & Alexander, H. E. 1973. Politics in a wired nation. In I. de Sola Pool (ed.), *Talking back: Citizen feedback and cable technology.* Cambridge, MA: MIT Press.

Sussman, L. 1989. *Power, the press and the technology of freedom: The coming age of ISDN.* New York: Freedom House.

Varley, P. 1991. Electronic democracy. *Technology Review* 94 (8): 42–52.

Westen, T., & Givens, B. 1989. *The California channel: A new public affairs television network for the state.* Los Angeles: Center for Responsive Government.

Whicker, M. L. 1986. Direct democracy devices. *Journal of Policy Modeling* 82: 255–71.

White, C. S. 1987. Information technology and participative government: Educating an informed and participative citizenry. Paper presented at the Annual Meeting of the National Council for the Social Studies, Dallas, TX, 15 November.

Wicklein, J. 1981. *Electronic nightmare.* Boston: Beacon Press.

Wilkinson, T. 1989. Santa Monica gets wired: Computer link to citizens. *Los Angeles Times* (12 February).

51

DEMOCRATIC RATIONALIZATION: TECHNOLOGY, POWER, AND FREEDOM

Andrew Feenberg

Source: D. M. Kaplan (ed.) (2004) *Readings in the Philosophy of Technology*, Lanham, NJ: Rowman & Littlefield, pp. 209–26.

The limits of democratic theory

Technology is one of the major sources of public power in modern societies. So far as decisions affecting our daily lives are concerned, political democracy is largely overshadowed by the enormous power wielded by the masters of technical systems: corporate and military leaders, and professional associations of groups such as physicians and engineers. They have far more to do with control over patterns of urban growth, the design of dwellings and transportation systems, the selection of innovations, and our experience as employees, patients, and consumers than all the governmental institutions of our society put together.

Marx saw this situation coming in the middle of the nineteenth century. He argued that traditional democratic theory erred in treating the economy as an extrapolitical domain ruled by natural laws such as the law of supply and demand. He claimed that we will remain disenfranchised and alienated so long as we have no say in industrial decision making. Democracy must be extended from the political domain into the world of work. This is the underlying demand behind the idea of socialism.

Modern societies have been challenged by this demand for over a century. Democratic political theory offers no persuasive reason of principle to reject it. Indeed, many democratic theorists endorse it.[1] What is more, in a number of countries, socialist parliamentary victories or revolutions have brought parties to power dedicated to achieving it. Yet today we do not appear to be much closer to democratizing industrialism than in Marx's time.

This state of affairs is usually explained in one of the following two ways.

On the one hand, the common sense view argues that modern technology is incompatible with workplace democracy. Democratic theory cannot reasonably press for reforms that would destroy the economic foundations of society. For evidence, consider the Soviet case: although they were socialists, the communists did not democratize industry, and the current democratization of Soviet society extends only to the factory gate. At least regarding the ex–Soviet Union, everyone can agree on the need for authoritarian industrial management.

On the other hand, a minority of radical theorists claims that technology is not responsible for the concentration of industrial power. That is a political matter, due to the victory of capitalist and communist elites in struggles with the underlying population. No doubt modern technology lends itself to authoritarian administration, but in a different social context it could just as well be operated democratically.

In what follows, I will argue for a qualified version of this second position, somewhat different from both the usual Marxist and democratic formulations. The qualification concerns the role of technology, which I see as *neither* determining nor neutral. I will argue that modern forms of hegemony are based on the technical mediation of a variety of social activities, whether it be production or medicine, education or the military, and that, consequently, the democratization of our society requires radical technical as well as political change.

This is a controversial position. The common sense view of technology limits democracy to the state. By contrast, I believe that unless democracy can be extended beyond its traditional bounds into the technically mediated domains of social life, its use value will continue to decline, participation will wither, and the institutions we identify with a free society will gradually disappear.

Let me turn now to the background to my argument. I will begin by presenting an overview of various theories that claim that insofar as modern societies depend on technology, they require authoritarian hierarchy. These theories presuppose a form of technological determinism that is refuted by historical and sociological arguments I will briefly summarize. I will then present a sketch of a nondeterministic theory of modern society I call *critical theory of technology*. This alternative approach emphasizes contextual aspects of technology ignored by the dominant view. I will argue that technology is not just the rational control of nature; both its development and impact are also intrinsically social. I will then show that this view undermines the customary reliance on efficiency as a criterion of technological development. That conclusion, in turn, opens broad possibilities of change foreclosed by the usual understanding of technology.

Dystopian modernity

Max Weber's famous theory of rationalization is the original argument against industrial democracy. The title of this chapter implies a provocative reversal of Weber's conclusions. He defined rationalization as the increasing role of calculation and control in social life, a trend leading to what he called the "iron cage" of bureaucrac.[2] "Democratic" rationalization is thus a contradiction in terms.

Once traditionalist struggle against rationalization has been defeated, further resistance in a Weberian universe can only reaffirm irrational life forces against routine and drab predictability. This is not a democratic program but a romantic antidystopian one, the sort of thing that is already foreshadowed in Dostoyevsky's *Notes from Underground* and various back-to-nature ideologies.

My title is meant to reject the dichotomy between rational hierarchy and irrational protest implicit in Weber's position. If authoritarian social hierarchy is truly a contingent dimension of technical progress, as I believe, and not a technical necessity, then there must be an alternative way of rationalizing society that democratizes rather than centralizes control. We need not go underground or native to preserve threatened values such as freedom and individuality.

But the most powerful critiques of modern technological society follow directly in Weber's footsteps in rejecting this possibility. I am thinking of Heidegger's formulation of "the question of technology" and Ellul's theory of "the technical phenomenon."[3] According to these theories, we have become little more than objects of technique, incorporated into the mechanism we have created. As Marshall McLuhan once put it, technology has reduced us to the "sex organs of machines." The only hope is a vaguely evoked spiritual renewal that is too abstract to inform a new technical practice.

These are interesting theories, important for their contribution to opening a space of reflection on modern technology. I will return to Heidegger's argument in the conclusion to this chapter. But first, to advance my own argument, I will concentrate on the principal flaw of *dystopianism*, the identification of technology in general with the specific technologies that have developed in the last century in the West. These are technologies of conquest that pretend to an unprecedented autonomy; their social sources and impacts are hidden. I will argue that this type of technology is a particular feature of our society and not a universal dimension of "modernity" as such.

Technological determinism

Determinism rests on the assumption that technologies have an autonomous functional logic that can be explained without reference to society. *Technology* is presumably social only through the purpose it serves, and purposes are in the mind of the beholder. Technology would thus resemble science and mathematics by its intrinsic independence of the social world.

Yet unlike science and mathematics, technology has immediate and powerful social impacts. It would seem that society's fate is at least partially dependent on a nonsocial factor that influences it without suffering a reciprocal influence. This is what is meant by *technological determinism*. Such a deterministic view of technology is commonplace in business and government, where it is often assumed that progress is an exogenous force influencing society rather than an expression of changes in culture and values.

The dystopian visions of modernity I have been describing are also deterministic. If we want to affirm the democratic potentialities of modern industrialism, we will therefore have to challenge their deterministic premises. These I will call the *thesis of unilinear progress* and the *thesis of determination by the base*. Here is a brief summary of these two positions.

1   Technical progress appears to follow a unilinear course, a fixed track, from less to more advanced configurations. Although this conclusion seems obvious from a backward glance at the development of any familiar technical object, in fact it is based on two claims of unequal plausibility: first, that technical progress proceeds from lower to higher levels of development; and second, that that development follows a single sequence of necessary stages. As we will see, the first claim is independent of the second and is not necessarily deterministic.
2   Technological determinism also affirms that social institutions must adapt to the "imperatives" of the technological base. This view, which no doubt has its source in a certain reading of Marx, is now part of the common sense of the social sciences.[4] Below, I will discuss one of its implications in detail: the supposed "trade-off" between prosperity and environmental values.

These two theses of technological determinism present decontextualized, self-generating technology as the unique foundation of modern society. Determinism thus implies that our technology and its corresponding institutional structures are universal, indeed, planetary in scope. There may be many forms of tribal society, many feudalisms, and even many forms of early capitalism, but there is only one modernity and it is exemplified in our society for good or ill. Developing societies should take note: as Marx once said, calling the attention of his backward German compatriots to British advances: *De te fabula narratur*—of you the tale is told.[5]

Constructivism

The implications of determinism appear so obvious that it is surprising to discover that neither of its two theses can withstand close scrutiny. Yet contemporary sociology of technology undermines the first thesis of unilinear progress, whereas historical precedents are unkind to the second thesis of determination by the base.

Recent constructivist sociology of technology grows out of new social studies of science. These studies challenge our tendency to exempt scientific theories from the sort of sociological examination to which we submit nonscientific beliefs. They affirm the *principle of symmetry,* according to which all contending beliefs are subject to the same type of social explanation regardless of their truth or falsity.[6] A similar approach to technology rejects the usual assumption that technologies succeed on purely functional grounds.

Constructivism argues that theories and technologies are underdetermined by scientific and technical criteria. Concretely, this means two things: first, there is generally a surplus of workable solutions to any given problem, and social actors make the final choice among a batch of technically viable options; and second, the problem–definition often changes in the course of solution. The latter point is the more conclusive but also more difficult of the two.

Two sociologists of technology, Pinch and Bijker, illustrate it with the early history of the bicycle.[7] The object we take to be a self-evident "black box" actually started out as two very different devices: a sportsman's racer and a utilitarian transportation vehicle. The high front wheel of the sportsman's bike was necessary at the time to attain high speeds, but it also caused instability. Equal-sized wheels made for a safer but less exciting ride. These two designs met different needs and were in fact different technologies with many shared elements. Pinch and Bijker call this original ambiguity (of the object designated as a "bicycle") "interpretative flexibility."

Eventually the "safety" design won out. and it benefited from all the later advances that occurred in the field. In retrospect, it seems as though the high wheelers were a clumsy and less efficient stage in a progressive development leading through the old "safety" bicycle to current designs. In fact, the high wheeler and the safety shared the field for years, and neither was a stage in the other's development. The high wheeler represents a possible alternative path of bicycle development that addressed different problems at the origin.

Determinism is a species of Whig history that makes it seem as though the end of the story was inevitable from the very beginning by projecting the abstract technical logic of the finished object back into the past as a cause of development. That approach confuses our understanding of the past and stifles the imagination of a different future. Constructivism can open up that future, although its practitioners have hesitated so far to engage the larger social issues implied in their method.[8]

Indeterminism

If the thesis of unilinear progress falls, the collapse of the notion of determination by the technological base cannot be far behind. Yet it is still frequently invoked in contemporary political debates.

I shall return to these debates later in this chapter. For now, let us consider the remarkable anticipation of current attitudes in the struggle over the length of the workday and over child labor in mid-nineteenth-century England. The debate on the Factory Bill of 1844 was entirely structured around the deterministic opposition of technological imperatives and ideology. Lord Ashley, the chief advocate of regulation, protested in the name of familial ideology that

> the tendency of the various improvements in machinery is to supersede the employment of adult males, and substitute in its place, the labour of children and females. What will be the effect on future generations, if their tender frames be subjected, without limitation or control, to such destructive agencies.[9]

He went on to deplore the decline of the family consequent upon the employment of women, which "disturbs the order of nature" and deprives children of proper upbringing. "It matters not whether it be prince or peasant, all that is best, all that is lasting in the character of a man, he has learnt at his mother's knees." Lord Ashley was outraged to find that

> females not only perform the labour, but occupy the places of men; they are forming various clubs and associations, and gradually acquiring all those privileges which are held to be the proper portion of the male sex. . . . They meet together to drink, sing, and smoke; they use, it is stated, the lowest, most brutal, and most disgusting language imaginable.

Proposals to abolish child labor met with consternation on the part of factory owners, who regarded the little (child) worker as an "imperative" of the technologies created to employ him. They denounced the "inefficiency" of using full-grown workers to accomplish tasks done as well or better by children, and they predicted all the usual catastrophic economic consequences—increased poverty, unemployment, loss of international competitiveness—from the substitution of more costly adult labor. Their eloquent representative, Sir J. Graham, therefore urged caution:

> We have arrived at a state of society when without commerce and manufactures this great community cannot be maintained. Let us, as far as we can, mitigate the evils arising out of this highly artificial

state of society; but let us take care to adopt no step that may be fatal to commerce and manufactures.

He further explained that a reduction in the workday for women and children would conflict with the depreciation cycle of machinery and lead to lower wages and trade problems. He concluded that "in the close race of competition which our manufacturers are now running with foreign competitors . . . such a step would be fatal." Regulation, he and his fellows maintained in words that echo still, is based on a "false principle of humanity, which in the end is certain to defeat itself." One might almost believe that Ludd had risen again in the person of Lord Ashley: the issue is not really the length of the workday, "but it is in principle an argument to get rid of the whole system of factory labour." Similar protestations are heard today on behalf of industries threatened with what they call environmental "Luddism."

Yet what actually happened once the regulators succeeded in imposing limitations on the workday and expelling children from the factory? Did the violated imperatives of technology come back to haunt them? Not at all. Regulation led to an intensification of factory labor that was incompatible with the earlier conditions in any case. Children ceased to be workers and were redefined socially as learners and consumers. Consequently, they entered the labor market with higher levels of skill and discipline that were soon presupposed by technological design. As a result, no one is nostalgic for a return to the good old days when inflation was held down by child labor. That is simply not an option (at least not in the developed capitalist world).

This example shows the tremendous flexibility of the technical system. It is not rigidly constraining but on the contrary can adapt to a variety of social demands. This conclusion should not be surprising given the responsiveness of technology to social redefinition discussed previously. It means that technology is just another dependent social variable, albeit an increasingly important one, and not the key to the riddle of history.

Determinism, I have argued, is characterized by the principles of unilinear progress and determination by the base; if determinism is wrong, then technology research must be guided by the following two contrary principles. In the first place, technological development is not unilinear but branches in many directions, and it could reach generally higher levels along more than one different track. And, secondly, technological development is not determining for society but is overdetermined by both technical and social factors.

The political significance of this position should also be clear by now. In a society where determinism stands guard on the frontiers of democracy, indeterminism cannot but be political. If technology has many unexplored potentialities, no technological imperatives dictate the current social hierarchy. Rather, technology is a scene of social struggle, a *parliament of things* on which civilizational alternatives contend.

Interpreting technology

In the next sections of this chapter, I would like to present several major themes of a nondeterminist approach to technology. The picture sketched so far implies a significant change in our definition of technology. It can no longer be considered as a collection of devices, nor, more generally, as the sum of rational means. These are tendentious definitions that make technology seem more functional and less social than in fact it is.

As a social object, technology ought to be subject to interpretation like any other cultural artifact, but it is generally excluded from humanistic study. We are assured that its essence lies in a technically explainable function rather than a hermeneutically interpretable meaning. At most, humanistic methods might illuminate extrinsic aspects of technology, such as packaging and advertising, or popular reactions to controversial innovations such as nuclear power or surrogate motherhood. Technological determinism draws its force from this attitude. If one ignores most of the connections between technology and society, it is no wonder that technology then appears to be self-generating.

Technical objects have two hermeneutic dimensions that I call their *social meaning* and their *cultural horizon*.[10] The role of social meaning is clear in the case of the bicycle introduced above. We have seen that the construction of the bicycle was controlled in the first instance by a contest of interpretations: was it to be a sportsman's toy or a means of transportation? Design features such as wheel size also served to signify it as one or another type of object.[11]

It might be objected that this is merely an initial disagreement over goals with no hermeneutic significance. Once the object is stabilized, the engineer has the last word on its nature, and the humanist interpreter is out of luck. This is the view of most engineers and managers; they readily grasp the concept of *goal* but they have no place for *meaning*.

In fact, the dichotomy of goal and meaning is a product of functionalist professional culture, which is itself rooted in the structure of the modern economy. The concept of a goal strips technology bare of social contexts, focusing engineers and managers on just what they need to know to do their job.

A fuller picture is conveyed, however, by studying the social role of the technical object and the lifestyles it makes possible. That picture places the abstract notion of a goal in its concrete social context. It makes technology's contextual causes and consequences visible rather than obscuring them behind an impoverished functionalism.

The functionalist point of view yields a decontextualized temporal cross-section in the life of the object. As we have seen, determinism claims implausibly to be able to get from one such momentary configuration of the object to the next on purely technical terms. But in the real world, all sorts of unpredictable attitudes crystallize around technical objects and influence later design changes. The engineer may think these are extrinsic to the device he or she is working on, but they are its very substance as a historically evolving phenomenon.

These facts are recognized to a certain extent in the technical fields themselves, especially in computers. Here we have a contemporary version of the dilemma of the bicycle discussed above. Progress of a generalized sort in speed, power, and memory goes on apace while corporate planners struggle with the question of what it is all for. Technical development does not point definitively toward any particular path. Instead, it opens branches, and the final determination of the "right" branch is not within the competence of engineering because it is simply not inscribed in the nature of the technology.

I have studied a particularly clear example of the complexity of the relation between the technical function and meaning of the computer in the case of French videotext.[12] Called *Teletel,* this system was designed to bring France into the Information Age by giving telephone subscribers access to databases. Fearing that consumers would reject anything resembling office equipment, the telephone company attempted to redefine the computer's social image; it was no longer to appear as a calculating device for professionals but was to become an informational network for all.

The telephone company designed a new type of terminal, the *Minitel,* to look and feel like an adjunct to the domestic telephone. The telephonic disguise suggested to some users that they ought to be able to talk to each other on the network. Soon the *Minitel* underwent a further redefinition at the hands of these users, many of whom employed it primarily for anonymous online chatting with other users in the search for amusement, companionship, and sex.

Thus, the design of the *Minitel* invited communications applications that the company's engineers had not intended when they set about improving the flow of information in French society. Those applications, in turn, connoted the *Minitel* as a means of personal encounter, the very opposite of the rationalistic project for which it was originally created. The "cold" computer became a "hot" new medium.

At issue in the transformation is not only the computer's narrowly conceived technical function but also the very nature of the advanced society it makes possible. Does networking open the doors to the Information Age in which, as rational consumers hungry for data, we pursue strategies of optimization? Or is it a postmodern technology that emerges from the breakdown of institutional and sentimental stability, reflecting, in Lyotard's words, the "atomisation of society into flexible networks of language games?"[13] In this case, technology is not merely the servant of some predefined social purpose; it is an environment within which a way of life is elaborated.

In sum, differences in the way social groups interpret and use technical objects are not merely extrinsic but also make a difference in the nature of the objects themselves. *What* the object *is* for the groups that ultimately decide its fate determines what it *becomes* as it is redesigned and improved over time. If this is true, then we can only understand technological development by studying the sociopolitical situation of the various groups involved in it.

Technological hegemony

In addition to the sort of assumptions about individual technical objects that we have been discussing so far, that situation also includes broader assumptions about social values. This is where the study of the cultural horizon of technology comes in. This second hermeneutic dimension of technology is the basis of modern forms of social hegemony; it is particularly relevant to our original question concerning the inevitability of hierarchy in technological society.

As I will use the term, *hegemony* is a form of domination so deeply rooted in social life that it seems natural to those it dominates. One might also define it as that aspect of the distribution of social power that has the force of culture behind it.

The term *horizon* refers to culturally general assumptions that form the unquestioned background to every aspect of life.[14] Some of these support the prevailing hegemony. For example, in feudal societies, the *chain of being* established hierarchy in the fabric of God's universe and protected the caste relations of the society from challenge. Under this horizon, peasants revolted in the name of the king, the only imaginable source of power. Rationalization is our modern horizon, and technological design is the key to its effectiveness as the basis of modern hegemonies.

Technological development is constrained by cultural norms originating in economics, ideology, religion, and tradition. We discussed earlier how assumptions about the age composition of the labor force entered into the design of nineteenth-century production technology. Such assumptions seem so natural and obvious that they often lie below the threshold of conscious awareness.

This is the point of Herbert Marcuse's important critique of Weber.[15] Marcuse shows that the concept of rationalization confounds the control of labor by management with control of nature by technology. The search for control of nature is generic, but management only arises against a specific social background, the capitalist wage system. Workers have no immediate interest in output in this system, unlike earlier forms of farm and craft labor, since their wage is not essentially linked to the income of the firm. Control of human beings becomes all-important in this context.

Through mechanization, some of the control functions are eventually transferred from human overseers and parcelized work practices to machines. Machine design is thus socially relative in a way that Weber never recognized, and the "technological rationality" it embodies is not universal but particular to capitalism. In fact, it is the horizon of all the existing industrial societies, communist as well as capitalist, insofar as they are managed from above. (In a later section, I discuss a generalized application of this approach in terms of what I call the *technical code*.)

If Marcuse is right, it ought to be possible to trace the impress of class relations in the very design of production technology as has indeed been shown by such Marxist students of the labor process as Harry Braverman and David Noble.[16] The assembly line offers a particularly clear instance because it achieves traditional management goals, such as deskilling and pacing work, through technical design. Its technologically enforced labor discipline increases productivity and profits by increasing control. However, the assembly line only appears as technical progress in a specific social context. It would not be perceived as an advance in an economy based on workers' cooperatives in which labor discipline was more self-imposed than imposed from above. In such a society, a different technological rationality would dictate different ways of increasing productivity.[17]

This example shows that technological rationality is not merely a belief, an ideology, but is also effectively incorporated into the structure of machines. Machine design mirrors back the social factors operative in the prevailing rationality. The fact that the argument for the social relativity of modern technology originated in a Marxist context has obscured its most radical implications. We are not dealing here with a mere critique of the property system, but have extended the force of that critique down into the technical "base." This approach goes well beyond the old economic distinction between capitalism and socialism, market and plan. Instead, one arrives at a very different distinction between societies in which power rests on the technical mediation of social activities and those that democratize technical control and, correspondingly, technological design.

Double aspect theory

The argument to this point might be summarized as a claim that social meaning and functional rationality are inextricably intertwined dimensions of technology. They are not ontologically distinct, for example, with meaning in the observer's mind and rationality in the technology proper. Rather they are *double aspects* of the same underlying technical object, each aspect revealed by a specific contextualization.

Functional rationality, like scientific-technical rationality in general, isolates objects from their original context in order to incorporate them into theoretical or functional systems. The institutions that support this procedure, such as laboratories and research centers, themselves form a special context with their own practices and links to various social agencies and powers. The notion of "pure" rationality arises when the work of decontextualization is not itself grasped as a social activity reflecting social interests.

Technologies are selected by these interests from among many possible configurations. Guiding the selection process are social codes established by the cultural and political struggles that define the horizon under which the technology will fall. Once introduced, technology offers a material validation of the cultural horizon to which it has been preformed. I call this the *bias* of technology: apparently neutral, functional rationality is enlisted in support of a hegemony. The more technology society employs, the more significant is this support.

As Foucault argues in his theory of "power/knowledge," modern forms of oppression are not so much based on false ideologies as on the specific technical "truths" that form the basis of the dominant hegemony and that reproduce it.[18] So long as the contingency of the choice of "truth" remains hidden, the deterministic image of a technically justified social order is projected.

The legitimating effectiveness of technology depends on unconsciousness of the cultural-political horizon under which it was designed. A recontextualizing critique of technology can uncover that horizon, demystify the illusion of technical necessity, and expose the relativity of the prevailing technical choices.

The social relativity of efficiency

These issues appear with particular force in the environmental movement today. Many environmentalists argue for technical changes that would protect nature and in the process improve human life as well. Such changes would enhance efficiency in broad terms by reducing harmful and costly side effects of technology. However, this program is very difficult to impose in a capitalist society. There is a tendency to deflect criticism from technological processes to products and people, from a priori prevention to a posteriori cleanup. These preferred strategies are generally costly and reduce efficiency under the horizon of the given technology. This situation has political consequences.

Restoring the environment after it has been damaged is a form of collective consumption, financed by taxes or higher prices. These approaches dominate public awareness. This is why environmentalism is generally perceived as a cost involving trade-offs, and not as a rationalization increasing overall efficiency. But in a modern society obsessed by economic well-being, that perception is damning. Economists and businesspeople are fond of explaining the price we must pay in inflation and unemployment for worshipping at Nature's shrine instead of Mammon's. Poverty awaits those who will not adjust their social and political expectations to technology.

This trade-off model has environmentalists grasping at straws for a strategy. Some hold out the pious hope that people will turn from economic to spiritual values in the face of the mounting problems of industrial society. Others expect enlightened dictators to impose technological reform even if a greedy populace shirks its duty. It is difficult to decide which of these solutions is more improbable, but both are incompatible with basic democratic values.[19]

The trade-off model confronts us with dilemmas—environmentally sound technology versus prosperity, workers' satisfaction and control versus productivity, and so on—when what we need are syntheses. Unless the problems of modern industrialism can be solved in ways that both enhance public welfare and win public support, there is little reason to hope that they will ever be solved. But how can technological reform be reconciled with prosperity when it places a variety of new limits on the economy?

The child labor case shows how apparent dilemmas arise on the boundaries of cultural change, specifically, where the social definition of major technologies is in transition. In such situations, social groups excluded from the original design network articulate their unrepresented interests politically. New values the outsiders believe would enhance their welfare appear as mere ideology to insiders who are adequately represented by the existing designs.

This is a difference of perspective, not of nature. Yet the illusion of essential conflict is renewed whenever major social changes affect technology. At first, satisfying the demands of new groups after the fact has visible costs and, if it is done clumsily, will indeed reduce efficiency until better designs are found. But usually better designs can be found and what appeared to be an insuperable barrier to growth dissolves in the face of technological change.

This situation indicates the essential difference between economic exchange and technique. Exchange is all about trade-offs: more of A means less of B. But the aim of technical advance is precisely to avoid such dilemmas by elegant designs that optimize several variables at once. A single cleverly conceived mechanism may correspond to many different social demands, one structure to many functions.[20] Design is not a zero-sum economic game but an ambivalent cultural process that serves a multiplicity of values and social groups without necessarily sacrificing efficiency.

The technical code

That these conflicts over social control of technology are not new can be seen from the interesting case of the "bursting boilers."[21] Steamboat boilers were the first technology regulated in the United States. In the early nineteenth century, the steamboat was a major form of transportation similar to the automobile or airlines today. Steamboats were necessary in a big country without paved roads and lots of rivers and canals. But steamboats frequently blew up when the boilers weakened with age or were pushed too hard. After several particularly murderous accidents in 1816, the city of Philadelphia consulted with experts on how to design safer boilers, the first time an American governmental institution interested itself in the problem. In 1837, at the request of Congress, the Franklin Institute issued a detailed report and recommendations based on rigorous study of boiler construction. Congress was tempted to impose a safe boiler code on the industry, but boilermakers and steamboat owners resisted and government hesitated to interfere with private property.

It took from that first inquiry in 1816 to 1852 for Congress to pass effective laws regulating the construction of boilers. In that time, 5,000 people were killed in accidents on steamboats. Is this many casualties or few? Consumers evidently were not too alarmed to continue traveling by riverboat in ever increasing numbers. Understandably, the ship owners interpreted this as a vote of confidence and protested the excessive cost of safer designs. Yet politicians also won votes demanding safety.

The accident rate fell dramatically once technical changes such as thicker walls and safety valves were mandated. Legislation would hardly have been necessary to achieve this outcome had it been technically determined. But, in fact, boiler design was relative to a social judgment about safety. That judgment could have been made on strictly market grounds, as the shippers wished, or politically, with differing technical results. In either case, those results *constitute* a proper boiler. What a boiler *is* was thus defined through a long process of political struggle culminating finally in uniform codes issued by the American Society of Mechanical Engineers.

This example shows just how technology adapts to social change. What I call the *technical code* of the object mediates the process. That code responds to the cultural horizon of the society at the level of technical design. Quite down-to-earth technical parameters such as the choice and processing of materials are *socially* specified by the code. The illusion of technical necessity arises from the fact that the code is thus literally "cast in iron," at least in the case of boilers.[22]

Conservative antiregulatory social philosophies are based on this illusion. They forget that the design process always already incorporates standards of safety and environmental compatibility; similarly, all technologies support some basic level of user or worker initiative. A properly made technical object simply *must* meet these standards to be recognized as such. We do not treat conformity as an expensive add-on, but regard it as an intrinsic production cost. Raising the standards means altering the definition of the object, not paying a price for an alternative good or ideological value as the trade-off model holds.

But what of the much discussed cost–benefit ratio of design changes such as those mandated by environmental or other similar legislation? These calculations have some application to transitional situations, before technological advances responding to new values fundamentally alter the terms of the problem. But, all too often, the results depend on economists' very rough estimates of the monetary value of such things as a day of trout fishing or an asthma attack. If made without prejudice, these estimates may well help to prioritize policy alternatives. But one cannot legitimately generalize from such policy applications to a universal theory of the costs of regulation.

Such fetishism of efficiency ignores our ordinary understanding of the concept that alone is relevant to social decision making. In that everyday sense, efficiency concerns the narrow range of values that economic actors routinely affect by their decisions. Unproblematic aspects of technology are not included. In theory, one can decompose any technical object and account for each of its elements in terms of the goals it meets, whether it be safety, speed, reliability, and the like, but in practice no one is interested in opening the "black box" to see what is inside.

For example, once the boiler code is established, such things as the thickness of a wall or the design of a safety valve appear as essential to the object. The cost of these features is not broken out as the specific "price" of safety and compared unfavorably with a more efficient but less secure version of the technology. Violating the code in order to lower costs is a crime, not a trade-off. And since all further progress takes place on the basis of the new safety standard, soon no one looks back to the good old days of cheaper, insecure designs.

Design standards are only controversial while they are in flux. Resolved conflicts over technology are quickly forgotten. Their outcomes, a welter of taken-for-granted technical and legal standards, are embodied in a stable code and form the background against which economic actors manipulate the unstable portions of the environment in the pursuit of efficiency. The code is not varied in real world economic calculations but treated as a fixed input.

Anticipating the stabilization of a new code, one can often ignore contemporary arguments that will soon be silenced by the emergence of a new horizon of efficiency calculations. This is what happened with boiler design and child labor; presumably, the current debates on environmentalism will have a similar history, and we will someday mock those who object to cleaner air as a "false principle of humanity" that violates technological imperatives.

Noneconomic values intersect the economy in the technical code. The examples we are dealing with illustrate this point clearly. The legal standards that regulate workers' economic activity have a significant impact on every aspect of their lives. In the child labor case, regulation helped to widen educational opportunities with consequences that are not primarily economic in character. In the riverboat case, Americans gradually chose high levels of security, and boiler design came to reflect that choice. Ultimately, this was no trade-off of one good for another, but a noneconomic decision about the value of human life and the responsibilities of government.

Technology is thus not merely a means to an end; technical design standards define major portions of the social environment, such as urban and built spaces, workplaces, medical activities and expectations, life patterns, and so on. The economic significance of technical change often pales beside its wider human implications in framing a way of life. In such cases, regulation defines the cultural framework *of* the economy; it is not an act *in* the economy.

Heidegger's "essence" of technology

The theory sketched here suggests the possibility of a general reform of technology. But dystopian critics object that the mere fact of pursuing efficiency or technical effectiveness already does inadmissible violence to human beings and nature. Universal functionalization destroys the integrity of all that is. As Heidegger argues, an "objectless" world of mere resources replaces a world of "things" treated with respect for their own sake as the gathering places of our manifold engagements with "being."[23]

This critique gains force from the actual perils with which modern technology threatens the world today. But my suspicions are aroused by Heidegger's famous contrast between a dam on the Rhine and a Greek chalice. It would be difficult to find a more tendentious comparison. No doubt, modern technology is immensely more destructive than any other. And Heidegger is right to argue that means are not truly neutral, and that their substantive content affects society independent of the goals they serve. But I have argued here that this content is not *essentially* destructive; rather, it is a matter of design and social insertion.

However, Heidegger rejects any merely social diagnosis of the ills of technological societies and claims that the source of their problems dates back at least to Plato, that modern societies merely realize a *telos* immanent in Western metaphysics from the beginning. His originality consists in pointing out that the ambition to control being is itself a way of being and hence subordinate at some deeper level to an ontological dispensation beyond human control. But the overall effect of his critique is to condemn human agency, at least in modern times, and to confuse essential differences between types of technological development.

Heidegger distinguishes between the *ontological* problem of technology, which can only be addressed by achieving what he calls "a free relation" to technology, and the merely *ontic* solutions proposed by reformers who wish to change technology itself. This distinction may have seemed more interesting in years gone by than it does today. In effect, Heidegger is asking for nothing more than a change in attitude toward the selfsame technical world.

65

But that is an idealistic solution in the bad sense, and one that a generation of environmental action would seem decisively to refute.

Confronted with this argument, Heidegger's defenders usually point out that his critique of technology is not merely concerned with human attitudes but also with the way being reveals itself. Roughly translated out of Heidegger's language, this means that the modern world has a technological form in something like the sense in which, for example, the medieval world had a religious form. *Form* is no mere question of attitude but takes on a material life of its own: power plants are the gothic cathedrals of our time. But this interpretation of Heidegger's thought raises the expectation that he will offer criteria for a reform of technology. For example, his analysis of the tendency of modern technology to accumulate and store up nature's powers suggests the superiority of another technology that would not challenge nature in Promethean fashion.

Unfortunately, Heidegger's argument is developed at such a high level of abstraction he literally cannot discriminate between electricity and atom bombs, agricultural techniques and the Holocaust. In a 1949 lecture, he asserted: "Agriculture is now the mechanized food industry, in essence the same as the manufacturing of corpses in gas chambers and extermination camps, the same as the blockade and starvation of nations, the same as the production of hydrogen bombs."[24] All are merely different expressions of the identical enframing that we are called to transcend through the recovery of a deeper relation to being. And since Heidegger rejects technical regression while leaving no room for a better technological future, it is difficult to see in what that relation would consist beyond a mere change of attitude.

History or metaphysics

Heidegger is perfectly aware that technical activity was not "metaphysical" in his sense until recently. He must therefore sharply distinguish modern technology from all earlier forms of technique, obscuring the many real connections and continuities. I would argue, on the contrary, that what is new about modern technology can only be understood against the background of the traditional technical world from which it developed. Furthermore, the saving potential of modern technology can only be realized by recapturing certain traditional features of technique. Perhaps this is why theories that treat modern technology as a unique phenomenon lead to such pessimistic conclusions.

Modern technology differs from earlier technical practices through significant shifts in emphasis rather than generically. There is nothing unprecedented in its chief features, such as the reduction of objects to raw materials, the use of precise measurement and plans, and the technical control of some human beings by others, large scales of operation. It is the centrality of these features that is new, and of course the consequences of that are truly without precedent.

What does a broader historical picture of technology show? The privileged dimensions of modern technology appear in a larger context that includes many currently subordinated features that were defining for it in former times. For example, until the generalization of Taylorism, technical life was essentially about the choice of a vocation. Technology was associated with a way of life, with specific forms of personal development, virtues, and so on. Only the success of capitalist deskilling finally reduced these human dimensions of technique to marginal phenomena.

Similarly, modern management has replaced the traditional collegiality of the guilds with new forms of technical control. Just as vocational investment in work continues in certain exceptional settings, so collegiality survives in a few professional or cooperative workplaces. Numerous historical studies show that these older forms are not so much incompatible with the *essence* of technology as with capitalist economics. Given a different social context and a different path of technical development, it might be possible to recover these traditional technical values and organizational forms in new ways in a future evolution of modern technological society.

Technology is an elaborate complex of related activities that crystallizes around tool making and using in every society. Matters such as the transmission of techniques or the management of its natural consequences are not extrinsic to technology per se but are dimensions of it. When, in modern societies, it becomes advantageous to minimize these aspects of technology, that too is a way of accommodating it to a certain social demand, not the revelation of its preexisting essence. In so far as it makes sense to talk about an essence of technology at all, it must embrace the whole field revealed by historical study, and not only a few traits ethnocentrically privileged by our society.

There is an interesting text in which Heidegger shows us a jug "gathering" the contexts in which it was created and functions. This image could be applied to technology as well, and in fact there is one brief passage in which Heidegger so interprets a highway bridge. Indeed, there is no reason why modern technology cannot also gather its multiple contexts, albeit with less romantic pathos than jugs and chalices. This is in fact one way of interpreting contemporary demands for such things as environmentally sound technology, applications of medical technology that respect human freedom and dignity, urban designs that create humane living spaces, production methods that protect workers' health and offer scope for their intelligence, and so on. What are these demands if not a call to reconstruct modern technology so that it gathers a wider range of contexts to itself rather than reducing its natural, human, and social environment to mere resources?

Heidegger would not take these alternatives very seriously because he reifies modern technology as something separate from society, as an inherently contextless force aiming at pure power. If this is the essence of technology, reform would be merely extrinsic. But at this point, Heidegger's position converges with the very Prometheanism he rejects. Both depend on the narrow definition of technology that, at least since Bacon and Descartes, has emphasized its destiny to control the world to the exclusion of its equally essential contextual embeddedness. I believe that this definition reflects the capitalist environment in which modern technology first developed.

The exemplary modern master of technology is the entrepreneur, single-mindedly focused on production and profit. The enterprise is a radically decontextualized platform for action, without the traditional responsibilities for persons and places that went with technical power in the past. It is the autonomy of the enterprise that makes it possible to distinguish so sharply between intended and unintended consequences, between goals and contextual effects, and to ignore the latter.

The narrow focus of modern technology meets the needs of a particular hegemony; it is not a metaphysical condition. Under that hegemony, technological design is unusually decontextualized and destructive. It is that hegemony that is called to account, not technology per se, when we point out that today technical means form an increasingly threatening life environment. It is that hegemony, as it has embodied itself in technology, that must be challenged in the struggle for technological reform.

Democratic rationalization

For generations, faith in progress was supported by two widely held beliefs: that technical necessity dictates the path of development, and that the pursuit of efficiency provides a basis for identifying that path. I have argued here that both these beliefs are false and that, furthermore, they are ideologies employed to justify restrictions on opportunities to participate in the institutions of industrial society. I conclude that we can achieve a new type of technological society that can support a broader range of values. Democracy is one of the chief values a redesigned industrialism could better serve.

What does it mean to democratize technology? The problem is not primarily one of legal rights but of initiative and participation. Legal forms may eventually routinize claims that are asserted informally at first, but the forms will remain hollow unless they emerge from the experience and needs of individuals resisting a specifically technological hegemony.

That resistance takes many forms, from union struggles over health and safety in nuclear power plants to community struggles over toxic waste disposal to political demands for regulation of reproductive technologies. These movements alert us to the need to take technological externalities into account and demand design changes responsive to the enlarged context revealed in that accounting.

Such technological controversies have become an inescapable feature of contemporary political life, laying out the parameters for official "technology assessment."[25] They prefigure the creation of a new public sphere embracing the technical background of social life, and a new style of rationalization that internalizes unaccounted costs born by "nature," in other words, something or somebody exploitable in the pursuit of profit. Here, respect for nature is not antagonistic to technology but enhances efficiency in broad terms.

As these controversies become commonplace, surprising new forms of resistance and new types of demands emerge alongside them. Networking has given rise to one among many such innovative public reactions to technology. Individuals who are incorporated into new types of technical networks have learned to resist through the net itself in order to influence the powers that control it. This is not a contest for wealth or administrative power, but a struggle to subvert the technical practices, procedures, and designs structuring everyday life.

The example of the *Minitel* can serve as a model of this new approach. In France, the computer was politicized as soon as the government attempted to introduce a highly rationalistic information system to the general public. Users "hacked" the network in which they were inserted and altered its functioning, introducing human communication on a vast scale where only the centralized distribution of information had been planned.

It is instructive to compare this case to the movements of AIDS patients.[26] Just as a rationalistic conception of the computer tends to occlude its communicative potentialities, so in medicine, caring functions have become mere side effects of treatment, which is itself understood in exclusively technical terms. Patients become objects of this technique, more or less "compliant" to management by physicians. The incorporation of thousands of incurably ill AIDS patients into this system destabilized it and exposed it to new challenges.

The key issue was access to experimental treatment. In effect, clinical research is one way in which a highly technologized medical system can care for those it cannot yet cure. But until quite recently, access to medical experiments has been severely restricted by paternalistic concern for patients' welfare. AIDS patients were able to open up access because the networks of contagion in which they were caught were paralleled by social networks that were already mobilized around gay rights at the time the disease was first diagnosed.

Instead of participating in medicine individually as objects of a technical practice, they challenged it collectively and politically. They "hacked" the medical system and turned it to new purposes. Their struggle represents a counter tendency to the technocratic organization of medicine, an attempt at a recovery of its symbolic dimension and caring functions.

As in the case of the *Minitel,* it is not obvious how to evaluate this challenge in terms of the customary concept of politics. Nor do these subtle struggles against the growth of silence in technological societies appear significant from the standpoint of the reactionary ideologies that contend noisily with capitalist modernism today. Yet the demand for communication these movements represent is so fundamental that it can serve as a touchstone for the adequacy of our concept of politics to the technological age.

These resistances, like the environmental movement, challenge the horizon of rationality under which technology is currently designed. Rationalization in our society responds to a particular definition of technology as a means to the goal of profit and power. A broader understanding of technology suggests a very different notion of rationalization based on responsibility for the human and natural contexts of technical action. I call this *democratic rationalization* because it requires technological advances that can only be made in opposition to the dominant hegemony. It represents an alternative to both the ongoing celebration of technocracy triumphant and the gloomy Heideggerian counterclaim that "only a God can save us" from techno-cultural disaster.[27]

Is democratic rationalization in this sense socialist? There is certainly room for discussion of the connection between this new technological agenda and the old idea of socialism. I believe there is significant continuity. In socialist theory, workers' lives and dignity stood for the larger contexts that modern technology ignores. The destruction of their minds and bodies on the workplace was viewed as a contingent consequence of capitalist technical design. The implication that socialist societies might design a very different technology under a different cultural horizon was perhaps given only lip service, but at least it was formulated as a goal.

We can make a similar argument today over a wider range of contexts in a broader variety of institutional settings with considerably more urgency. I am inclined to call such a position socialist and to hope that, in time, it can replace the image of socialism projected by the failed communist experiment.

More important than this terminological question is the substantive point I have been trying to make. Why has democracy not been extended to technically mediated domains of social life despite a century of struggles? Is it because technology excludes democracy, or because it has been used to suppress it? The weight of the argument supports the second conclusion. Technology can support more than one type of technological civilization, and may someday be incorporated into a more democratic society than ours.

Notes

This chapter expands a presentation of my book *Critical Theory of Technology* (New York: Oxford University Press, 1991), delivered at the American Philosophical

Association, December 28, 1991, and first published in an earlier version in *Inquiry* 35, nos. 3–4 (1992): 301–22.

1. See, for example, Joshua Cohen and Joel Rogers, *On Democracy: Toward a Transformation of American Society* (Harmondsworth, UK: Penguin, 1983); and Frank Cunningham, *Democratic Theory and Socialism* (Cambridge: Cambridge University Press, 1987).
2. Max Weber, *The Protestant Ethic and the Spirit of Capitalism*, trans. T. Parsons (New York: Scribners, 1958), 181–82.
3. Martin Heidegger, *The Question Concerning Technology*, trans. W. Lovitt (New York: Harper & Row, 1977); and Jacques Ellul, *The Technological Society*, trans. J. Wilkinson (New York: Vintage, 1964).
4. Richard W. Miller, *Analyzing Marx: Morality, Power and History* (Princeton, N.J.: Princeton University Press, 1984), 188–95.
5. Karl Marx, *Capital* (New York: Modern Library, 1906), 13.
6. See, for example, David Bloor, *Knowledge and Social Imagery* (Chicago: University of Chicago Press, 1991), 175–79. For a general presentation of constructivism, see Bruno Latour, *Science in Action* (Cambridge, Mass.: Harvard University Press, 1987).
7. Trevor Pinch and Wiebe Bijker, "The Social Construction of Facts and Artefacts: or How the Sociology of Science and the Sociology of Technology Might Benefit Each Other," *Social Studies of Science*, no. 14 (1984).
8. See Langdon Winner's blistering critique of the characteristic limitations of the position, entitled, "Upon Opening the Black Box and Finding It Empty: Social Constructivism and the Philosophy of Technology," in *The Technology of Discovery and the Discovery of Technology: Proceedings of the Sixth International Conference of the Society for Philosophy and Technology* (Blacksburg, Va.: The Society for Philosophy and Technology, 1991).
9. *Hansard's Debates, Third Series: Parliamentary Debates 1830–1891* 73 (February 22–April 22, 1844). The quoted passages are found between 1088 and 1123.
10. A useful starting point for the development of a hermeneutics of technology is offered by Paul Ricoeur in "The Model of the Text: Meaningful Action Considered as a Text," in P. Rabinow and W. Sullivan, eds., *Interpretive Social Science: A Reader* (Berkeley: University of California Press, 1979).
11. Michel de Certeau used the phrase "rhetorics of technology" to refer to the representations and practices that contextualize technologies and assign them a social meaning. De Certeau chose the term "rhetoric" because that meaning is not simply present at hand but communicates a content that can be articulated by studying the connotations that technology evokes. See the special issue of *Traverse*, no. 26 (October 1982), entitled *Les Rhetoriques de la Technologie*, and, in that issue, especially, Marc Guillaume's article, "Telespectres": 22–23.
12. See chapter 7, "From Information to Communication: The French Experience with Videotext," in Andrew Feenberg, *Alternative Modernity* (Berkeley: University of California Press, 1995).
13. Jean-François Lyotard, *La Condition Postmoderne* (Paris: Editions de Minuit, 1979), 34.
14. For an approach to social theory based on this notion (called, however, *doxa*, by the author), see Pierre Bourdieu, *Outline of a Theory of Practice*, trans. R. Nice (Cambridge: Cambridge University Press, 1977), 164–70.
15. Herbert Marcuse, "Industrialization and Capitalism in the Work of Max Weber," in *Negations*, trans. J. Shapiro (Boston: Beacon, 1968).

16 Harry Braverman, *Labor and Monopoly Capital* (New York: Monthly Review, 1974); and David Noble, *Forces of Production* (New York: Oxford University Press, 1984).
17 Bernard Gendron and Nancy Holstrom, "Marx, Machinery and Alienation," *Research in Philosophy and Technology* 2 (1979).
18 Foucault's most persuasive presentation of this view is *Surveiller et Punir* (Paris: Gallimard, 1975).
19 See, for example, Robert Heilbroner, *An Inquiry into the Human Prospect* (New York: W. W. Norton, 1975). For a review of these issues in some of their earliest formulations, see Andrew Feenberg, "Beyond the Politics of Survival," *Theory and Society*, no. 7 (1979).
20 This aspect of technology, called *concretization*, is explained in Gilbert Simondon, *Du Mode d'Existence des Objets Techniques* (Paris: Aubier, 1958), ch. 1.
21 John G. Burke, "Bursting Boilers and the Federal Power," in M. Kranzberg and W. Davenport, eds., *Technology and Culture* (New York: New American Library, 1972).
22 The technical code expresses the "standpoint" of the dominant social groups at the level of design and engineering. It is thus relative to a social position without, for that matter, being a mere ideology or psychological disposition. As I will argue in the last section of this chapter, struggle for sociotechnical change can emerge from the subordinated standpoints of those dominated within technological systems. For more on the concept of standpoint epistemology, see Sandra Harding, *Whose Science? Whose Knowledge?* (Ithaca, N.Y.: Cornell University Press, 1991).
23 The texts by Heidegger discussed here are, in order, "The Question Concerning Technology," "The Thing," and "Building Dwelling Thinking," all in *Poetry, Language, Thought*, trans. A. Hofstadter (New York: Harper & Row, 1971).
24 Quoted in T. Rockmore, *On Heidegger's Nazism and Philosophy* (Berkeley: University of California Press, 1992), 241.
25 Alberto Cambrosio and Camille Limoges, "Controversies as Governing Processes in Technology Assessment," in *Technology Analysis & Strategic Management* 3, no. 4 (1991).
26 For more on the problem of AIDS in this context, see Andrew Feenberg, "On Being a Human Subject: Interest and Obligation in the Experimental Treatment of Incurable Disease," *The Philosophical Forum* 23, no. 3 (spring 1992).
27 "Only a God Can Save Us Now," Martin Heidegger interviewed in *Der Spiegel*, translated by D. Schendler, *Graduate Philosophy Journal* 6, no. 1 (winter 1977).

52

THE MEDIA AND THE PUBLIC SPHERE

Nicholas Garnham

Source: Craig Calhoun (ed.) (1993) *Habermas and the Public Sphere*, Cambridge, MA: MIT Press, pp. 359–76.

We have had to wait over a quarter of a century for an English language edition of Habermas's *Structural Transformation of the Public Sphere*. Such a long time is a rigorous test of the work's continuing relevance.

Since its original appearance in German it has been subjected to vigorous criticism, and Habermas has himself pursued an intellectual path that has taken him far from the book's central concerns. Since I want to argue here for the continuing and indeed increased relevance of those concerns, it is best to get the criticisms out of the way first. While those criticisms are, in my view, broadly justified, they do not undermine the book's continuing claim to our attention as a fruitful starting point for work on urgent contemporary issues in the study of the mass media and democratic politics.

The criticisms have been these:

- That he neglects the importance of the contemporaneous development of a plebeian public sphere alongside and in opposition to the bourgeois public sphere, a sphere built upon different institutional forms, e.g., trade unions, and with different values, e.g., solidarity rather than competitive individualism.
- That he idealizes the bourgeois public sphere. Recent historical research, that of Robert Darnton for instance, has revealed the viciously competitive structure of the early print market controlled not by freely discoursing intellectuals in search of public enlightenment but by booty capitalists in search of a quick profit.
- That by excluding the household and the economy from the public sphere, he systematically suppressed the question of democratic accountability within both gender relations and relations of production.

- That his rationalist model of public discourse leaves him unable to theorize a pluralist public sphere and it leads him to neglect the continuing need for compromise between bitterly divisive and irreconcilable political positions. This in its turn leads him to lament the entry of political parties into the public sphere.
- That the last part of the book remains too dependent upon Adorno's model of the cultural industries with its elitist cultural tendencies, its exaggeration of the manipulative powers of the controllers of those industries, and its neglect of the possibilities of public-service models of state intervention within the informational sphere.
- That Habermas's model of communicative action, developed as the norm for public discourse, neglects, when faced by distorted communication, all those other forms of communicative action not directed toward consensus.
- That therefore he neglects both the rhetorical and playful aspects of communicative action, which leads to too sharp a distinction between information and entertainment and to a neglect of the link, in for instance Rousseau's notion of public festivals, between citizenship and theatricality. This last point is of particular importance in thinking about the role of the mass media in contemporary democracies.

These criticisms are all cogent and serve as a necessary basis for the development and refinement of Habermas's original approach. In my view, however, they do not detract from the continuing virtues of the central thrust of that approach.

Its first virtue is to focus upon the indissoluble link between the institutions and practices of mass public communication and the institutions and practices of democratic politics. Most study of the mass media is simply too media-centric. In recent years, research and debate has largely taken for granted the existing structure of both the media and politics, the one articulated around the relationship between a so-called free press and a state-regulated broadcasting system, the other around political parties and some form of representative parliamentary or congressional government.

The overwhelming focus of concern has been the problem of representation in the mediative sense of that word, that is, the question posed has been how well or badly do the various media reflect the existing balance of political forces and the existing political agenda, and with what effect upon political action, in particular, on voting patterns. Important as these questions are, they miss the central and most urgent question now raised by the developing relationship between the media and politics because they fail to start from the position that the institutions and processes of public communication are themselves a central and integral part of the political structure and process.

The second virtue of Habermas's approach is to focus on the necessary material resource base for any public sphere. Debate on the relationship between public communication and democracy is still dominated by the free press model. This model remains an essentially idealist transposition of the model of face-to-face communication to that of mediated communication. It occludes the problem raised by all forms of mediated communication, namely, how are the material resources necessary for that communication made available, and to whom?

Its third virtue is to escape from the simple dichotomy of free market versus state control that dominates so much thinking about media policy. Habermas, on the contrary, distinguishes the public sphere from both state and market and can thus pose the question of the threats to democracy and the public discourses upon which it depends coming both from the development of an oligopolistic capitalist market and from the development of the modern interventionist welfare state.

These virtues are perhaps of even greater relevance now than when the book originally appeared for two reasons. First, because the development of an increasingly integrated global market and centers of private economic power with global reach are steadily undermining the nation-state, and it is within the political structure of the nation-state that the question of citizenship and of the relationship between communication and politics has been traditionally posed. We are thus being forced to rethink this relationship and the nature of citizenship in the modern world. What new political institutions and new public sphere might be necessary for the democratic control of a global economy and polity? These questions have been given a new urgency by the development of a single European market and by the rapid breakup of the Soviet empire with its associated need to rebuild a civil society and public sphere from the ashes of Stalinism.

Second, because our inherited structures of public communication, those institutions within which we construct, distribute, and consume symbolic forms, are themselves undergoing a profound change. This change is characterized by a reinforcement of the market and the progressive destruction, at least in western Europe, of public service as the preferred mode for the allocation of cultural resources; by a focus on the TV set as the locus for an increasingly privatized, domestic mode of consumption; by the creation of a two-tier market divided between the information-rich (provided with high-cost specialized information and cultural services) and the information-poor (provided with increasingly homogenized entertainment services on a mass scale); by a shift from largely national to largely international markets in the informational and cultural spheres. Symptoms of this shift are the expansion of the new TV delivery services, such as video cassettes, cable, and direct-broadcasting satellites, under market control and on an international basis; the progressive deregulation and privatization of national telecommunication monopolies; the increased penetration of sponsorship into the financing of both sport and the arts; the move of education and research institutes, such as universities, toward the private sector under the pressure of public spending cuts; the growing tendency to make profitability the criteria for the provision of public information, whether via such government bodies as the U.S. Government Printing Office or the U.K. Stationary Office or increasingly via private agencies. All these are examples of a trend to what has been dubbed, usually by those in favor of these developments, the information society or information economy. The result of this trend will be to shift the balance in the cultural sector between the market and public service decisively in favor of the market and to shift the dominant definition of public information from that of a public good to that of a privately appropriable commodity.[1]

Responses to these problems are still largely posed within the terms of a debate that has traditionally understood the political function and effect of modes of public communication within the terms of the Hegelian state versus civil society dichotomy. The dominant theory within that debate has been the liberal theory of the free press, which has either simply assumed that the market will provide appropriate institutions and processes of public communication to support a democratic polity or, in its stronger form, argues that only the market can ensure the necessary freedom from stale control and coercion. The critique of this position has been able to collect impressive evidence of the way in which market forces produce results, in terms of oligopoly control and the depoliticization of content, that are far from the liberal ideal of a free market place of ideas. But the strength of the hold that liberal theory still exercises can be judged by the inadequacy of proposals for press reform generated by the left and the weakness with which such proposals have been pursued. For the left itself remains trapped within a free-press model inherited from the nineteenth century. The hold of this model is also illustrated by the way in which no equally legitimated theory has been developed to handle the dominant form of public communication, broadcasting. The public service, state-regulated model, whether publicly or privately funded, has in effect always been seen not as a positive good but as an unfortunate necessity imposed by the technical limitations of frequency scarcity. Those on the left who are opposed to market forces in the press nonetheless have in general given no more than mealymouthed support to public-service broadcasting. They have concentrated their critique on the question of the coercive or hegemonic nature of state power. Seeing the public service form as either a smokescreen for such power or as occupied from within by commercial forces, they have concentrated on criticizing the inadequacy and repressive nature of the rules of balance and objectivity within which public service broadcasting is forced to operate. The left has, therefore, tended to fall back either on idealist formulations of free communications with no organizational substance or material support or on technical utopianism that sees the expansion of channels of communication as inherently desirable because pluralistic. Both positions are linked to some version, both political and artistic, of free expression, for example, in Britain, the long debate and campaign around the creation of channel 4, the touching faith in cable access, the support for "free" or "community" radio, and so on.[2]

In light of the inadequacy of these approaches I want to argue that Habermas's concept of the public sphere offers a sounder basis for the critical analysis of current developments both in the media and democratic politics and for the analysis and political action necessary to rebuild systems of both communication and representative democracy adequate to the contemporary world.

Let me now briefly outline the basic argument that I wish to make with regard to the relationship between the institutionalized practices of mass communication and democratic politics. First, I take it as axiomatic that some version of communicative action lies at the heart of both the theory and practice of democracy. The rights and duties of a citizen are in large part defined in terms of freedom of assembly and freedom to impart and receive information. Without such freedoms it would be impossible for citizens to possess the knowledge of the views of others necessary to reach agreements between themselves, whether consensual or majoritarian, as to either social means or ends; to possess knowledge of the actions of those to whom executive responsibilities are delegated so as to make them accountable; to possess knowledge of the external environment necessary to arrive at appropriate judgment of both personal and societal interests.

It then follows, I believe, that the key problem we face is the adaption of this basic theory, and of the ideological formations associated with it, to the conditions of large-scale societies in which both social and communicative relations are inevitably mediated through both time and space.

This mediation raises two distinct problems. First, so far as the media of communication themselves are concerned, both the initial theory and subsequent related ideologies were based upon face-to-face communication in a single physical space. Thus freedom of assembly guaranteed access to the channel of communication, while the natural human attributes of speech and gesture ensured universal, equal access to the means of communication. Once communication is mediated, these universal equalities can no longer be guaranteed. Even in a situation of face-to-face communication it was early recognized that unequal access to the learned manipulative skills of rhetoric could and did influence the outcome of democratic debate. But in a situation of mediated communication, access to both channel and means depends upon the mobilization of scarce material resources, the distribution of which is dependent upon the very structures of economic and political power that democratic processes of debate were intended to control.

Second, what also became mediated is the content of communication and the subject of debate, or to use Habermas's terminology, the experience of the lifeworld. This indeed is the core of the Marxist theory of ideology.

The existence of ideology rests not upon the stupidity and manipulability of human agents, as some simplistic current media and cultural studies critics, in their claims for pluralist, postmodern freedoms and their disdainful dismissal of boring old class politics, would have it. On the contrary, it rests on the nontransparency of the lifeworld, a nontransparency that makes interpretation always both difficult and provisional and the possibility of error ever present. Our everyday social relations, our very individual social identities, are constructed in a complex process of mediations. We see ourselves as husbands, wives, lovers, fathers, mothers, friends, neighbors, workers, and consumers increasingly in terms of ways of seeing those identities that are constructed in and through mediated communication: soap operas, novels, films, songs, etc. And we often act out those roles using objects of consumption provided and in large part determined by the system of economic production and exchange.

Third, a mismatch has developed between our theories and practices of democratic politics and our theories and practices of communication. Politics has in part adapted to large-scale societies through structures of representation: political parties, elected representatives, and full-time bureaucratic state officials. This development has, of course, always been fought, as in some sense inauthentic, by the advocates of forms of direct democracy. A suspicion of representation as a form of alienation and thus the adoption of the goal of the supersession of politics and of the "withering away of the state" have occupied an important place in the Marxist tradition. This links, of course—and this is important for my discussion in relation to Habermas's intellectual project—to a romantic opposition to the processes of modernist rationalization. But in general, for better or worse, representative forms have been established. To make my position clear, it is for me axiomatic both that representative structures cannot be bypassed and that the processes of rationalization and alienation involved in the modernizing process are a liberating gain rather than any sort of loss of supposed preexisting authenticity. The arguments against direct democracy bear repetition if only because visions of direct democracy are used as an escape from the problems that the concept of the public sphere raises. As Bobbio has argued, direct democracy works best with simple either/or choices (e.g., whether or not to have nuclear power) but cannot deal with the multiple variables that are more typical of political decisions in a complex and pluralistic modern society. The sifting of options necessary for such decision making can only be done by representatives. Moreover, these representatives then require space for free thought; they cannot be mandated. A further powerful argument against forms of direct democracy is that they overpoliticize life and turn into tyrannies that leave little if any time for the leading of private, autonomous personal lives.

These problems were in a sense sidestepped in classic Enlightenment thought, for instance, in the writings of Tom Paine, because at that period the market was simply assumed to be a benign mediator between private individuals, an anonymous system within which no one ruled.

The operation of the media of communication, however, has never really confronted this problem of representation. Our thinking about communications still remains largely trapped within a paradigm of direct individual face-to-face communication. This takes three forms. First, it is argued that the media, through the market, are driven by the satisfaction of individual consumer choice. This individualistic rational-choice model of economic interaction has been widely criticized within economics for its unreality and, in particular, for neglecting the realities of unequally distributed economic power, for concentrating upon distribution at the expense of production, for being static and thus ahistorical, for neglecting externalities, and for making assumptions of perfect information that neglect the costs to the individual or group of information acquisition.

Second, mediated symbolic forms are seen either as the expression of a single author (we see this for instance in the left demonology of the press baron) or as the objective, and therefore unmediated, reflection of an external reality—the journalist is seen as the witness of an event, a stand-in therefore for the individual reader's or viewer's direct, unmediated experience. Here the problem is that the complex institutional processes of mediation are ignored and along with them the problem of the existence of media workers as a distinct socioeconomic group with its own interests.

Third, current technical developments in communication (based upon the convergence of computing and switched telecommunications) are legitimated in terms of a desirable move away from mass communication and back toward forms of interpersonal communication that are seen as inherently more desirable and liberating. A classic and symptomatic text in this regard is Ithiel de Sola Pool's *Technologies of Freedom* and its notion of constant electronic referenda.

Fourth, this last point underlines the fact that while the rights to free expression inherent in democratic theory have been continually stressed, what has been lost is any sense of the reciprocal duties inherent in a communicative space that is physically shared. I think two crucial duties follow from this. First, there is the duty to listen to the views of others and to alternative versions of events. Second, participation in debate is closely linked to responsibility for the effects of the actions that result. A crucial effect of mediated communication in a context of mediated social relations is to favor irresponsible communication. In a sense, this is the idea covered by Habermas's notion of the appropriateness of a speech act, but it tends, I think, to be lost in the rationalist stress of Habermas's general theory. That is, it is not just that communicative action in the lifeworld is directed toward agreement, a questionable proposition. It is that the speaker cannot dissociate him- or herself from the possible effects of his or her discourse.

This question of responsibility brings us to perhaps the central question I wish to raise, namely that of universality. There are two different concepts of universality at stake. The first is procedural and refers to the minimum set of shared discourse rules that must constitute a public sphere. Here the question is whether the rationality claimed for discourse within the public sphere is universal in the sense that neither the normative nor the validity claims made are culturally specific, but the debate on both ends and means is potentially capable of producing consensus among all human beings. The second refers to the size and nature of the political entity of which we are citizens and with which, I want to argue, the public sphere must be coterminous. How widely are we to conceive of the writ of the consensus decisions arrived at among citizens in the public sphere? Are we to conceive of ourselves as citizens of the world or of a nation-state or of a community or of what? Finally, what is the relationship, and what could or should be the relationship, between the particularisms of the lifeworld and the generalized rationalizations of the systems world? My argument here leads me to argue against the politics of what Habermas, giving altogether too much, in my view, to the postmodernists, has called a pluralist decentered postmodern world and against the parallel validation of those developments in media technology and media markets that are moving us toward interpersonal systems of communication at the expense of mass communication and toward a highly segmented media market place made up of interest-specific market niches at the expense of more generalized media. In brief, I would want to argue against the pluralists that it is impossible to conceive of a viable democratic polity without at the same time conceiving of at least some common normative dimension. What the elements of that common normative dimension should be and what room it should leave for personal and group autonomy within it are, of course, at the center of this debate. To put it more strongly, I want to argue that at some level cultural relativism and a democratic polity are simply incompatible. If we wish to preserve the notion of cultural relativism, we must at the same time conceive of a universe of plural but mutually isolated polities. In my view, that is no longer a realistic option.

As regards the question of universality and cultural relativism, there are, I think, two issues. First, is discourse either actually or at least potentially universal; can all human beings, as a species characteristic, arrive at a common view as to both the nature and the truth of a proposition? Second, are there universal interests? For me, the answer to the second question determines the first. I would argue that historically both the economic and political aspects of system rationality have not only become global but are also understood as global by a growing proportion of the world's population, in part precisely because of the growth and spread of global systems of mediated communication. As recent events in China have shown, all political actors are now playing on a world stage and employing, in spite of the problems of linguistic and cultural translation, a world language of symbols. To claim the Enlightenment project, out of misplaced ethnocentric guilts, as exclusively (and detrimentally) Western, for instance, or to claim rationality as exclusively (and detrimentally) male seems to me to condescend to those of other cultures or subordinated social groups who are fighting our common struggle to understand and control the world in pursuit of human liberty. In Britain it has been interesting, for instance, to see how shallow the political and intellectual positions based on cultural relativism have looked in the light of the Salman Rushdie affair. But I would go further. If we accept that the economic system is indeed global in scope and at the same time crucially determining over large areas of social action, the Enlightenment project of democracy requires us to make a Pascalian bet on universal rationality. For without it the project is unrealizable, and we will remain in large part enslaved to a system outside our control.

This brings me back to the question of the desirability of a pluralist decentered politics. I should stress for an American audience that my general approach is placed firmly within a European political and intellectual context. In particular, it focuses upon the characteristically Western European institutional form of public service broadcasting and current threats to that form's survival.

It is also set, as Habermas himself sets his more recent work on the public sphere, against the background of a crisis in the welfare-state form and in the modes and institutions of social-democratic politics that created and sustained that form in Western Europe since 1945. This crisis has, of course, been deepened by recent developments in the Soviet Union and Eastern Europe into a more general critique of the socialist vision and the historical model of social progress that underpinned that vision, at both the intellectual and popular levels. In particular, problems of bureaucratic power have loomed larger for a significant majority of citizens than those of economic power, and this, allied to the experience of economic slowdown and the impact of global economic restructuring, has led to a revalidation of market mechanisms allied to the rise of forms of populist neoconservatism.

In short, the problems posed are, first, What might be the conditions for democracy in societies such as those of Western Europe; indeed, is democracy in the classic form thinkable at all outside the problematic of the Enlightenment? Second, what is the desirable or realizable relationship between the economic system and the political system and between, to use Habermas's terminology, lifeworld and systems world?

One of the left's characteristic responses to this situation, at least in Britain, has been, at the level of economic policy, to embrace consumerism, underpinned in production by theories of post-Fordist flexible specialization and of the service or information economy, and, at the level of politics, to argue for a version of the rainbow coalition, that is, for a neo-Gramscian, postmodernist politics based not on a working class party but on a shifting coalition of a range of those fragmented social-interest groups produced, it is argued, by the "decentered pluralism" (to use Habermas's description) of our new consumer society.

The mirror image of this position on the right is that of Hayek, who argues that so complex are the interactions within an economic system that the project of rational politics is doomed to founder and who thus advocates the dissolution of politics as such in favor of the universal pursuit of self-interest within a market.

But the fact remains that we should not exaggerate economic systematicity. While total control is clearly impossible, it is possible to envisage interventions that limit the randomly determining impact of the economic system. Indeed, political and corporate actors are every day making willed interventions in what they see as their calculated interest, and this system of interventions is underpinned by systems of information gathering, assessment, and communication. The problem is to open up both the actions and the related informational exchanges to processes of democratic accountability.

In short, the problem is to construct systems of democratic accountability integrated with media systems of matching scale that occupy the same social space as that over which economic or political decisions will impact. If the impact is universal, then both the political and media systems must be universal. In this sense, a series of autonomous public spheres is not sufficient. There must be a single public sphere, even if we might want to conceive of this single public sphere as made up of a series of subsidiary public spheres, each organized around its own political structure, media system, and set of norms and interests. Thus even if we accept that debate within the public sphere is riven with controversy and in many instances may be directed at agreeing to disagree rather than toward consensus, we are still faced with the unavoidable problem of translating debate into action. If, whether we like it or not, the problem faced has a general impact upon us all, then there can only be one rationally determined course of interventionist political action. This course of action either has to be agreed to consensually or has to be imposed, whether by a majority or a minority. If market forces are global in scope, any effective political response has to be global. The individual citizen or group cannot, except in very rare circumstances, simply opt out and refuse to play whatever game has been decided upon. The same applies equally strongly to issues of nuclear weapons or the environment.

In particular, we cannot ignore the continuing role of the nation-state as both an economic actor and as a "power container," in Giddens's phrase, as the structure at the political level within which democratic political action, allegiance, and identity is still largely organized. It is no accident, in my view, that such states are associated with a dominant linguistic group, and thus discourse space, and with national media systems. We are witnessing at present parallel developments that both undermine the powers of the nation-state, especially economically, and internationalize media, both its systems of distribution and its content. How, therefore, should we envisage the construction of a new international public sphere and parallel system of democratic political accountability?

In my view, our attitude to this pluralist political project is crucial to our discussion of the media and the public sphere, because those social groups identified as potential elements in this shifting coalition largely exist in terms of group identities created via the forms and institutions of mediated communication (magazines, radio stations, record labels) or via consumer-taste publics that themselves use, as their badges of identity, symbols created and circulated in the sphere of advertising.

The issues this raises for us are, I believe, twofold. First, are these group identities and the individual identities that subtend them the "authentic" expression of the lifeworld erupting into the systems world and using the products and systems of that world for their own plural purposes, or on the contrary, are they a determined symptom of that systems world? We are, in short, here presented with the old linguistic conundrum of the relation between *langue* and *parole*. While accepting the relative autonomy of the meaning-creating agent and the possibilities of cultural bricolage, they are at present much exaggerated by media and cultural analysts. We have to raise the question of how much room for maneuver agents actually have within a symbolic system within which both the power to create symbols and access to the channels of their circulation is heirarchically structured and intimately integrated into a system of economic production and exchange, which is itself heirarchically structured. There is a left cultural romanticism, increasingly prevalent in media and cultural studies, that sees all forms of grassroots cultural expression as "resistance," although resistance to what is not at all clear. The problem here is twofold. To accept them as resistance does not avoid the problem that both the forms and the potential success of resistance can be determined by the system being resisted. Second, it fails to take account of that element of misrecognition that Bourdieu, for instance, has in my view rightly identified as essential to the relatively smooth reproduction of a system of social relations by interacting intelligent agents. Here we confront a major problem with Habermas's approach to the problem via the theory of universal pragmatics. That is, his notion of communicative rationality does not allow for the possibility of the rational acceptance of misrecognition within the terms of the limited material resources and time boundedness of actions in the lifeworld. Nor does it allow for what I can only describe as the rational cynicism, identified, for instance, by Abercrombie and his colleagues in *The Dominant Ideology Thesis,* which recognizes very clearly the realities of domination but calculates that the risks of change are greater than those of the status quo.

This brings me to the problem of rationality in another form. My position on the public sphere and on public service broadcasting has been criticized on the grounds that I overvalue politics and a particular model of rationalist discourse at the expense of disregarding the modes and functions of most mediated communication, which is nonrationalist and is concerned with psychological and imaginative satisfactions that have little to do with politics. Such an approach, it is argued, tends to concentrate analysis on news, current affairs, and documentaries and on the model of the so-called quality press, while neglecting all forms of popular entertainment. There is a lot of truth in this criticism, or rather, it points to a real problem to which I have no satisfactory answer. This is the problem I have posed in terms of the relation between the lifeworld and the systems world and the role of the media in mediating between them. In short, it is part of the problem posed by Habermas in *The Structural Transformation of the Public Sphere*, a problem that was always part of the Frankfurt School problematic, namely the relation between psychology, politics, and economics. Habermas posed it originally in terms of the relation of the creation of a private sphere and private sentiments to the creation of the public sphere. I would certainly want to stress that I am not claiming that the properly political debates in the public sphere are only carried by forms of media content overtly labeled as being concerned with politics. On the contrary, what I shall call as shorthand the entertainment content of the media is clearly the primary tool we use to handle the relationship between the systems world and the lifeworld. It is on the basis of understandings drawn from those communicative experiences and of identities formed around them that we arrive at more overtly rational and political opinions and actions. The dynamics of this process and the relative weight within it of rationalized systems determinants and of the nonrationalized experiences of the lifeworld are a crucial and neglected area for media and cultural-studies research. If pursued, they may enable us to chart the limits of both politics and economics and at the same time to discover the media forms and structures most likely to foster the development of citizens, rather than mere consumers.

In conclusion, I want to raise the question, central to Habermas's project, of the validation of the Enlightenment project. Habermas has sought an ontological validation in universal pragmatics. This approach has been widely and, in my view, correctly criticized on linguistic grounds. But I do not believe that such a grounding is necessary. For me, the grounding can only be in history itself. That is, the evidence for the possibility of the Enlightenment project is that large numbers of human beings from different cultures have actually believed in it and fought to realize it. Only history will show whether the project is in fact realizable. The possibility of arriving at a rationally grounded consensus can only be demonstrated in practice by entering into a concrete and historically specific process of rational debate with other human beings on the assumption that the system world is at least partially subjectable to rational control, that it is in the ultimate interest of most human beings so to control it, that other human beings can be led both to a rational recognition of that interest within a common discourse space and to a consensual agreement as to the appropriate cooperative courses of action to follow. On the basis of those assumptions the task is to cooperate in building the political, economic, and communicational institutions conducive to that end. This will be no easy task. There is no guarantee of success. But in my view the only alternative is to accept the impossibility of liberation either in an irrational Hobbesian world dominated by war of all against all or in a totally rationalized world in which our actions are determined by a structure beyond our control. If that is the only truth, our own deliberations are reduced to the merest trivia.

In the face of postmodernist critiques of this whole tradition of thought and these critics' rejection of rationality in favor of a utopian and romantic pursuit of difference for its own sake, it is necessary to stress that the strand of the Enlightenment project, of which Habermas's work on the public sphere is a part, expresses a tragic, not a utopian, vision. It is a preromantic, classical vision that in constant awareness of human limitation recognizes the extreme fragility of human civilization and the need, but at the same time the difficulty, of sustaining the social bonds of mutual obligation upon which that civilization depends in the face of the manifold forces that threaten it, forces that are internal and psychological as well as external. It sets out to save a small portion of our existence from the rule of fate. Its rationalist and universalist vision must thus be distinguished from that other strand in the dialectic of the Enlightenment, that of scientific rationality and the hubris of human power that accompanied it. The model of the public sphere and of the democratic polity of which it is a part is thus that of the classical garden, a small tamed patch within a sea of untamed nature (fate) ever ready to rake over if the attention of the gardeners slackens for an instant. Its ruling virtue is stoicism rather than the untrammeled pursuit of happiness.

Acknowledgment

In revising this paper for publication I have benefited immeasurably from the critical comments of my colleague John Keane.

Notes

1 For a fuller treatment of these problems, see my "Public Service versus the Market," *Screen* 24, no. 1 (1983).
2 For a fuller treatment of these problems and, in particular, of the relation between the concept of the public sphere and the tradition of public service broadcasting, see my "Media and the Public Sphere" in P. Golding *et al.*, eds., *Communicating Politics* (Leicester: Leicester University Press, 1986).

53

NEW MEDIATION AND DIRECT REPRESENTATION

Reconceptualizing representation in the digital age

Stephen Coleman

Source: *New Media & Society* 7(2) (2005): 177–98.

Abstract

This article explores three responses to the emergence of digitally mediated political representation. The first regards disintermediation as a basis for direct democracy, transcending the traditional arrangements and institutions of political representation. The second model institutionalizes digital information and communication technology (ICT) within the rational–bureacratic framework of existing governance. The third model is based upon a reconceptualization of democratic representation, based upon new notions of accountability, plurality and authentic reality. It is argued that virtual deliberation and indirect representation are under severe political strain and that digitally-mediated direct representation could provide a basis for a more dialogical and deliberative democracy in place of the dialogue of the deaf which tends to characterize contemporary political representation.

An extensive literature, both speculative and empirical, now exists examining the likely effects of new, digital media, such as the internet, upon the theory and practice of political representation. These accounts have often been characterized by crude dichtomies: technology as a utopian liberator versus technocratic dystopianism; direct democracy versus politics as normal; determinism versus choice. The aim of this article is to move beyond such dichotomized accounts and set out a more dialectical analysis, embracing the tense connections between the relationships of representation and mediation. Stated simply, the argument is that mediation does not simply affect representation, but is an essential element of representation. In a complex, mass society indirect social interaction is the norm and political representations tend to be vertically and indirectly mediated. The argument of this article is that new, digital technologies of mediation make possible more direct techniques of representation which do not transcend the necessity for representing or being represented in a political democracy, but serve to democratize representation by making it a more direct relationship.

Representation, information and communication

To represent is to mediate between the absent and the present. Representation is an essentially communicative activity, entailing the symbolic embodiment of a previously absent entity. Photography is perhaps the most vivid and spectral manifestation of this dialectical process; the photographic image depends for its success upon identically reflecting an absent presence, while having to be disconnected from its subject in space and time in order to guarantee its authenticity as a representation rather than an original. The tense conflation of disconnection and reconnection is central to the meaning and function of representation. A map presents a symbolic depiction of the London Underground and yet is decidedly *not* the London Underground. It is authentic insofar as it tells us what we need to know about the London Underground. Representation both replicates its subject and leaves it untouched: 'the thing remains, imparting information to the representation but not at the expense of any of its own matter or energy' (Nichols, 1991: 149). Representation performs an indexical, informational function; it renders an account which must be read, decoded, interpreted and evaluated for its authenticity.

The problem of *political* representation is rather more complex, particularly democratically accountable representation, where the information provided must accord (at least to some extent) with the wishes of those who are represented. Whereas a photograph, map, portrait or sketch represents without direct accountability to the represented subject, the democratic representation of public interests entails an intimate relationship between the wishes of the represented and the actions of representatives. As Pitkin has argued, this relationship has tended to be depicted in contrasting ways: that representatives should be controlled by the mandates of the represented and that the role of representatives is to act in accordance with their own views, regardless of the wishes of the represented:

> The mandate theorist says: if the situation is such that we can no longer see the constituents as present then there is no representation,

and if the man habitually votes the opposite of their wishes we
can no longer see them as present in his voting... The independence theorist says: if the situation is such that we can no longer see
the rep acting, but rather we see the constituents acting directly for
themselves, then there is no representation.

(Pitkin, 1967: 153)

The perspicacious originality of Pitkin's analysis of political representation is her rejection of this dichotomy. She argues that:

[I]t is not enough to choose between the representative's judgment
and the constituents' wishes; and there is no rational basis for choosing between them *tout court*. Representation as an idea implies that
normally they will coincide, and that when they fail to coincide
there is a reason.

(Pitkin, 1967: 165)

Pitkin's final definition of the substantive act of representing serves to illuminate the perpetual communicative tension that characterizes all representative democracies:

[R]epresenting... means acting in the interest of the represented, in
a manner responsive to them. The representative must act independently; his action must involve discretion and judgment; he must
be the one who acts. The represented must also be (conceived as)
capable of independent action and judgment, not merely being taken
care of. And, despite the resulting potential for conflict between
representative and represented about what is to be done, the conflict must not normally take place. The representative must act in
such a way that there is no conflict, or if it occurs an explanation is
called for. He must not be found persistently at odds with the wishes
of the represented without good reason in terms of their interest,
without a good explanation of why their wishes are not in accord
with their interest.

(Pitkin, 1967: 210)

This definition allows us to make qualitative judgements about representation. Rather than succumbing to the populist lament that political representatives fail because they do not mirror or mimic public opinion – or vociferous opinion, media opinion or my opinion, as the case may be – it is possible to evaluate the act of representing in terms of its independence, recognition of the views of the represented, avoidance of conflict with the represented and capacity to explain apparently unrepresentative actions to the represented. Democratic representing involves the effective communication of meanings and intentions. This is an inherently problematic task, for the production of meanings is itself a mediated process. As Silverstone persuasively argues:

> We need to understand this process of mediation, to understand how meanings emerge, where and with what consequences. We need to be able to identify those moments where the process appears to break down. Where it is distorted by technology or intention. We need to understand its politics: its vulnerability to the exercise of power; its dependence on the work of institutions as well as individuals; and its own power to persuade and to claim attention and response.
>
> (Silverstone, 1999: 18)

To represent is to mediate between experience, voice and action; to mediate is to represent the absent in the present. Within the dialectic between representation and mediation lies an acute tension, for the quality of representing depends upon a complex interaction between two relationships: the expressed wishes of the represented and the representative's informed apprehension of the interests of the represented; and the mediated flow of meanings and intentions between representative and represented. It follows from this that the nature of political representation is always likely to be intimately related to available means and methods of communication.

Discourses of mediation and representation

The megaphone is the metaphorical medium of demagogic politics. Megaphones transmit, but do not receive; they amplify the voices of the leaders above those of the led; they are territorial, reaching a geographically-defined public in a specific space; they are authoritarian: it is hard to heckle a speaker with a megaphone. Television is the quintessential megaphone medium. Since the late 1950s, the professionalization of political message-management has coincided with the rise of television as the principal medium of communication between the political elite and those they represent. In the spirit of megaphone communication, television is a national (or regional) transmission medium dedicated to a monological narrative directed at a non-interacting audience.

By contrast, radar is a more appropriate technological metaphor for an inclusive, collaborative and interactive conception of representation. The function of radar is to detect distant objects and determine their characteristics by analysis of high-frequency radiowaves reflected from their surfaces. In short, it is about sensitive listening. Analogue communication technologies, such as radio and television, are poorly suited for radar activity; digital technologies, such as the internet, make for effecive radar devices precisely because they are interactive, diminishing the significance of the old dichotomy between sender and receiver, producer and audience.

Simultaneous with transformative changes in the realm of mediation, from analogue–megaphone to digital–radar technologies, have been dramatic changes in the conception and nature of political representation. Traditionally, the legitimating force in representative democracies has been contractual. Candidates for representation have offered promises to voters who have evaluated them in terms of the quality of the benefits on display and the probity of the candidates as likely promise-keepers. The candidate who is elected as representative enters into a contract with voters to deliver the promised benefits. Failure to deliver is likely to result in non-re-election of the representative. In this model of representation, election campaigns are the key political moment for communication between representatives and citizens.

Political scientists have observed a recent trend from contractual to permanent representation. The so-called permanent campaign, whereby governing and campaigning are fused within a perpetual relationship, has come to characterize representative politics. Whereas contractual representatives entered into a relationship with voters based upon offers and obligations, permanent representatives tend to be reactive and reflexive, dependent upon monitoring and adapting to public opinion. In the words of the British Prime Minister, Tony Blair, after his 1997 election victory, 'We are not the masters, but the servants of the people'. According to Mann and Ornstein:

> The permanent campaign can be described as our unwritten Anti-Constitution. The written Constitution would keep the citizenry at arm's length from the governing process. The Anti-Constitution sees all efforts at deliberation outside the public eye as conspiratorial. The Constitution would normally consider the people as a sum of localities linked to government through representatives who take counsel with each other. The Anti-Constitution sees a largely undifferentiated public where one representative is interchangeable with another as long as he or she takes instructions. The Constitution would submit the results of governing to the people at regular intervals in many different election venues. The Anti-Constitution prescribes instant responsiveness to the continuous monitoring of the people's mass opinion and mood.
>
> (2000: 17–18)

At a more theoretical level of argument, Mansbridge (1998: 6) argues that 'representation by promising' is giving way to 'anticipatory democracy' in which 'the voter's power works backward and the representative's attention forward'. The electorate becomes more like a standing jury, reviewing the ongoing performance of government; and representatives become more like advocates, seeking to connect with citizens via a range of tools, including polls, focus groups, media management and interest-group networking. Mansbridge suggests that:

> Rather than treating opinion polls as mindless and interest groups as no more than the tool of 'special interests', an empirical analysis driven by appropriate normative concerns should ask how well these institutions serve the purposes of mutual communication and education.
>
> (1998: 6)

In short, the problem might not be permanent representation per se, but the weak and inappropriate modes of mediation that support it.

Mansbridge's emphasis upon 'mutual communication and education' suggests a more publically deliberative approach to policy formation and decision-making. Whereas contractual representation required little deliberative input from citizen-voters, permanent representation creates strong incentives for citizen-jurors to deliberate on questions of public policy. Electorates aggregate; juries deliberate. When representation becomes permanent, citizens become more like standing juries than occasional electorates.

Rather than regard transformations of mediation (from analogue to digital) and representation (from contractual to permanent) as isolated phenomena, as commentators have tended to do, this article seeks to explore the dialectical, although not deterministic, connections between these paradigmatic shifts. Three main responses to these linked developments can be traced. First, some enthusiasts for the new media have regarded interactive communication technologies as a source of potential liberation from the artificialities and inherent ambiguities of political representation. Often regarded as idealistic, futuristic or technocratic, these thinkers were among the first to develop notions of 'electronic democracy'. Second, there are political practitioners, including elected representatives and parliamentary officials, who have tended to regard new forms of mediation as pragmatic techniques which can be adapted to the procedures and cultures of institutional representation. Their outlook is supported theoretically by Schumpeterian political scientists who, in the name of political realism, resist excessive claims made for digital media. Third, a synthesis is to be identified between developments in the spheres of mediation and representation, which could result in a reconceptualization of democratic representation.

Transcending representation

Dreams of disintermediation and direct democracy are not new. Traditionally, visions of prelapsarian and millenarian harmony have been rooted in notions of perfect mutual understanding based upon a normative notion of unadulterated communication (Passmore, 1970; Simonson, 1996). Peters, a critic of such normative claims, argues that:

> 'Communication' is a registry of modern longings. The term evokes a utopia where nothing is misunderstood, hearts are open, and expression is uninhibited.
>
> (Peters, 1999: 2)

For those who regard representation as a consequence of miscommunication, the use of interactive technology as a tool for transparency and trancendence through disintermediation has been an alluring prospect. Advocates of democratic reform have pointed to the connection between interactive communication technologies and direct democracy. Toffler (1981: 431) argues that 'spectacular advances in communications technology' have undermined old political assumptions: 'the old objections to direct democracy are growing weaker at precisely the same time that the objections to representative democracy are growing stronger.' Becker and Slaton contend that:

> New forms of electronically based democratic political organization will emerge [which] will transform representative government into a system much less responsive to traditionally organized pressure groups and more responsive to a broad base of its citizenry.
>
> (2000: 81)

Grossman observes that:

> In kitchens, living rooms, dens, bedrooms, and workplaces throughout the nation, citizens have begun to apply ... electronic devices to political purposes, giving those who use them a degree of empowerment they never had before ... By pushing a button, typing on-line, or talking to a computer, they will be able to tell their president, senators, members of Congress, and local leaders what they want them to do and in what priority order.
>
> (1995: 146)

President Bill Clinton's former strategic adviser, Dick Morris, argues that:

> The internet offers a potential for direct democracy so profound that it may well transform not only our system of politics but our very form of government ... Bypassing national representatives and speaking directly to one another, the people of the world will use the internet increasingly to form a political unit for the future.
>
> (2001: 1033)

These proposals for citizen empowerment facilitated by interactive communication technologies offer support to republican and communitarian conceptions of democracy (Barber, 1998; Burnheim, 1989; Etzioni, 1992).

Critics of theories of digital transformation argue that they fail to take account of perennial problems of scale, complexity and design. These are formidable barriers to participatory democracy of any kind.

Scale

Political representation is often presented as a solution to the intractable problem of communities being too large to assemble in one place and deliberate collectively. Because most contemporary political units are national or regional in scale, face-to-face models of deliberation and decision-making which worked well for New England town meetings or Swiss canton assemblies are inappropriate. Even in the oft-cited Greek *agora*, the size of the eligible citizenry was so large that policies had to be made by a smaller council and discussions addressed by leading orators, rather than the give-and-take of participatory discourse. By electing representatives, whose principal tasks are to aggregate public preferences and deliberate on behalf of the public, the problem of scale is overcome.

In the view of some democratic theorists, the function of political representation is to produce a microcosmic reflection of the public. In accordance with this view, representatives should look like the public demographically and think like the public politically. John Adams, one of the Founding Fathers of the US, argued that a representative assembly 'should be in miniature an exact portrait of the people at large. It should think, feel, reason and act like them' (Adams, 1854: 195). John Stuart Mill considered that the British parliament, as a representative assembly, had a more important role in reflecting the interests and perspectives of diverse groups and classes than in actually governing or even influencing policy. Indeed, Mill's vigorous support for Hare's scheme for proportional representation was based upon a greater concern that parliament should be an inclusive coalition of minorities rather than a legislative powerhouse (Mill, 1861).

An extension of the microcosmic conception of representation is the claim that 'the politics of presence' is as important, if not more so, than 'the politics of ideas' (Phillips, 1995: 5). The argument of 'presence' democrats is that representatives' capacity to mirror the experiences of the represented is a key source of authentic legitimacy. This approach weakens the notion of a single public entrusting its welfare to a single representative entity; both citizenship and representation become more fragmented, pluralized and decentred, opening up the possibility that political representation can operate on the level and scale of human experience rather than state or institutional formations. In practice, however, as 'presence' democrats accept, attempts to overcome problems of scale through various forms of proportional representation can result in two problems: the absence of clearly aggregated majorities, leading to rule by minorities who hold the balance of power; and the balkanization of politics, whereby every preference becomes a 'special interest' and representation reflects consumerist demands rather than more enduring and coherent social values.

Complexity

A second defence of political representation against direct democracy concerns complexity. The rejection of the public's intellectual capacity for policy and decision-making is prevalent amongst early theorists of public opinion and democratic representation. Lippmann famously argued that:

> The private citizen has come to feel rather like a deaf spectator in the back row, who ought to keep his mind on the mystery off there, but cannot quite manage to stay awake. He knows he is somehow affected by what is going on. Rules and regulations continually, taxes annually, and wars occasionally remind him that he is being swept along by great drifts of circumstance. Yet these public affairs are in no convincing way his affairs. They are for the most part invisible. They are managed, if they are managed at all, in distant centers, from behind the scenes by unnamed powers. As a private person he does not know for certain what is going on, or who is doing it, or where he is being carried. No newspaper reports his environment so that he can grasp it; no school has taught him how to imagine it; his ideals, often, do not fit with it; listening to speeches, uttering opinions, and voting do not, he finds, enable him to govern it. He lives in a world in which he cannot see, does not understand, and is unable to direct. In the cold light of experience, he knows that his sovereignty is a fiction. He reigns in theory, but in fact he does not govern.
>
> (1925: 10)

Schumpeter made clear the consequences of this position:

> Democracy does not mean and cannot mean that the people actually rule in any obvious sense of the terms 'people' and 'rule'. Democracy means only that the people have the opportunity of accepting or refusing the men who are to rule them. But since they might decide this also in entirely undemocratic ways, we have had to narrow our definition by adding a further criterion identifying the democratic method, *viz.*, free competition among would-be leaders for the vote of the electorate.
>
> (1976: 269)

A variation of this theme relates political complexity to the perennial conundra of rational choice. Reference to trade-offs, prisoners' dilemmas and Pareto curves suggests that none but the most professionally and calculatingly organized factions could hope to influence policy formation or decision-making in accordance with their predetermined intentions (Arrow, 1951; Dunleavy, 1992; Riker, 1982). Given that individual actors are concerned to optimize their own preferences, in a condition of political complexity where consequences are often unpredictable and information resources are unequally spread, there is a strong possibility of collective choices running counter to majority preferences. As most citizens lack the skills to influence aggregate decisions, direct democracy could result in their systemic disempowerment.

Direct democracy is often associated with forms of populism that disregard complexity. Frequently, populist politics is driven more by values than knowledge. Levels of public knowledge about policy issues are notoriously low. Instant voting on questions of national policy via interactive communication technologies could result in uninformed 'technopopulism', with all the weaknesses of 'mobocracy', compounded by the speed of message flows.

Technocracy

A third defence of political representation against digitally-based direct democracy concerns the often uncritical view of new information and communication technologies (ICT). Technologies are never neutral: they are designed, shaped and socially modified in accordance with discourses that are often profoundly political and hegemonic (Lessig, 1999). For example, Introna and Nissembaum have studied the design and practices of search engines and express concern about:

> the ways that developers, designers and producers of search engines will direct these technological limitations, the influences that may come into play in determining any systematic inclusions and exclusions, the wide-ranging factors that dictate systematic prominence for some sites, dictating systematic invisibility for others.
> (2000: 170)

Search engines confer web existence upon otherwise isolated sites; the ways in which these are compiled and ranked determines the power of the medium. Similar critiques have been offered in relation to the linguistic nature of the web: where most users are non-American, but the overwhelming majority of websites are produced in the US for American-English speakers (Lebert, 1999).

The prospect of the internet enabling direct, plebiscitary democracy generates anxiety among political theorists and citizens alike. Whatever the deficiencies of representation (and, for most people, these apply to politicians rather than institutions or principles), until problems of scale, complexity and design are adequately addressed by direct democrats, their proposals are likely to remain within the realm of unrealised, technocratic prophecy.

Re-presenting representation

While direct democrats and technocrats have wanted to technologize democracy, it can be argued that the traditional bodies of representative democracy have sought to institutionalize the technology, using ICT to replicate existing practices rather than adapt to new ways of communicating. This is consistent with the Schumpeterian trilogy of invention–innovation–diffusion, according to which organizations respond to new technologies in three stages: first, they use them to automate existing processes; then they begin to recognize opportunities for more efficient working; and finally, they re-engineer themselves around the benefits of the technology (Schumpeter, 1976).

As the central representative institutions in democratic nation-states, parliaments have tended to exemplify the Schumpeterian trilogy. Taking the British parliament as an example, it was slow to adopt the use of ICT, resisting central procurement of technological equipment and providing limited access to ICT for MPs. A 1994 survey of parliamentary use of ICT in several countries found that only Turkey, apart from the UK, lacked a parliamentary data network, and only Denmark, Finland, Spain and the German Bundesrat shared the British Parliament's lack of a video network providing live feeds of proceedings to members' offices. In the two years after that survey parliament created a data network for members (the PDVN), an online daily record of its proceedings and a website (Coleman, 2000).

The gradual progress of the British parliament from stage one to two of the Schumpeterian trilogy can be seen in relation to two main areas of its work: MPs' communication with their constituents and parliament's provision of information to the public.

As elected representatives, MPs have a problem: the executive often acts as if it does not need them, and the public often acts as if it does not want them. MPs are uncertain of their role, insecure about their legitimacy and eager to 'reconnect' with 'ordinary people'. Frustrated by the traditional media, which politicians feel represents them unfairly, the prospect of unmediated (or self-mediated) communication with the public has considerable appeal to some MPs. Most MPs now have email addresses at which they can be contacted by constituents and are receiving an increasing proportion of their correspondence electronically. This presents them with a number of problems. First, using the technology requires new skills and extra resources which put pressure on already overburdened offices.

Second, there is a danger of email overload or emailers having expectations of speedy response that cannot be met by MPs' working practices. Some MPs have decided on principle that responses to emails will be no faster than to paper letters. Third, it is not always clear that email correspondence comes from a citizen in their own constituency and MPs, by tradition, only communicate about the problems of their own constituents. The process of filtering emails to authenticate the senders is relatively simple, but so far this has been slow to be adopted. So, MPs are caught in a dilemma of desperately wanting to be more in touch with those they represent, but not to be reached by constituents to the extent that they are overwhelmed. Several MPs have responded to this problem by making their email addresses inactive – a 'solution' that no significant business would dare to adopt.

MPs' websites are classic examples of automating bad practices. Whereas it used to be the case that politicians would produce self-advertising paper leaflets, usually destined for their constituents' waste paper bins, now they are putting their family photographs, soundbites and stories of successful campaigning on personal websites. Members of the US Congress were the first to establish websites, but, 'most members of Congress did not discuss legislation [on their websites], even legislation they had sponsored or co-sponsored. Also, most avoided discussing policy issues' (Davis, 1999: 133). A 1999 Office of Management and Budgets (OMB) Watch study found that almost one-fifth of all material on congressional members' websites was over six months old and concluded that it is

> difficult for a citizen to use the web to find information about their members' stances, as the site may not be updated, or may not contain the information that they are looking for. Even if the site is later updated, the user may not return.
>
> (Carter, 2000: 102)

In the case of the British parliament, even though there is evidence to suggest that web-based access to MPs is the preferred medium for internet users, only one in 20 UK internet users report visiting political websites of any kind, including MPs' sites (Coleman, 2001; Gibson *et al.*, 2002).

The use of ICT to provide public information largely replicates offline services. *Hansard* online looks and feels much like the printed version; those unfamiliar with parliamentary proceedings are likely to find it no easier to use. The parliamentary website (http://www.parliament.uk) provides in electronic form the kind of information that interested members of the public might have asked for by letter or telephone. There has been a failure to use ICT to build connections between parliament and the public, such as by encouraging citizens to personalize information, discuss policy or legislative issues online or raise questions.

ICT has been used to support the ongoing process of making parliament more transparent. In 1989 cameras were allowed into the House of Commons for the first time. Then, broadcasters and politicians were sanguine about the potential of televising parliament, but two decades of live and recorded parliamentary broadcasting have tempered media enthusiasm (Coleman, 1999; Negrine, 1998). The rise of webcasting is a response to the demise of parliamentary broadcasting on universally accessible channels. The migration of parliament from television to the web is less a reflection of digital innovation than media marginalization.

The former leader of the House of Commons, Robin Cook, has argued that:

> There is a connection waiting to be made between the decline in democratic participation and the explosion in new ways of communicating ... The new technologies can strengthen our democracy, by giving us greater opportunities than ever before for better transparency and a more responsive relationship between government and electors.
>
> (Cook, 2002)

This is suggestive, but it would be a mistake to assume a deterministic relationship between 'new technologies' and a more direct form of representation. The latter calls for institutional adaptation of a procedural, political and cultural nature.

The House of Commons Information Committee, in its recent report, *Digital Technology: Working for Parliament and the Public*, argued that:

> There is concern amongst the public – and indeed amongst Members – that the House appears remote, that it does not respond as well as it might to the public, and that it could do more to hold the executive to account. Public perceptions and expectations of Parliament appear to be changing and there is authoritative evidence to indicate that public participation in the political process appears to be in decline ... Information and Communications Technologies (ICT) can play an important role in influencing perceptions and helping to meet public expectations. Indeed, they cannot be ignored.
>
> (2002: 6)

The question for representative institutions is whether new mediation is simply a means of creating access to existing practices (Schumpeter's first stage), or whether these new processes of interactive mediation necessitate institutional adaptation to new ways of representing.

Reconceptualizing representation

The rationale for politicians' interest in digital mediation is a profound sense of disconnection from the public. Reconnection is their goal. Political connectedness (or connectivity) is an under-theorized concept. What does it mean for representatives and the public to be connected? For politicians, connectedness is a route to consent and legitimacy, both of which they regard as being distorted by distracting, biased and uncontrollable mediations of the public agenda. To connect is to have unmediated and undistorted access to the represented, to be better understood, to nurture public consent. The role of the represented in this conception of connectivity remains as spectators before the screen, locked into an unequal communicative relationship with an untrusted elite.

One-sided connectivity, rather like Postman's (1986) 'one-way conversation' of broadcasting, has more the characteristic of an assault than a partnership. Being connected, in a democratic sense, requires communicative collaboration between representatives and the represented, and a prospect of mutual gain for both. This entails representatives not just being in touch with the public, but being touched by them, in the sense of an intimate and mutually communicative relationship.

Reconceptualizing democratic representation in this way augments the significance of mediation. As a mediated process, representation is inextricably bound up with problems of signification and discourse. What do we expect political representatives to be like? What do representatives expect those they represent to be like? How well does the media present representatives and represented to one another? What rhythms, idioms and metaphors are appropriate when we speak of being represented? What do political speeches represent, and does it matter if most people fail to understand them? What is it like to *feel* represented? What are the available resources and strategies for political self-representation? If the represented are 'capable of independent action and judgment' and are 'not merely being taken care of' (as Pitkin insists), what sort of actions and judgements should we expect from 'ordinary' people – and if they do not show such signs of independence, what might this mean for the notion of democratic citizenship? Representing representation is a far from simple matter.

There are three ways in which digitally-mediated representation might stimulate and facilitate such mutually beneficial communicative collaboration. First, by enabling a more expansive and interactive kind of accountability to take place. Second, by accommodating a pluralistic network of representations, in contrast to the singular, linear conception of political representation characteristic of analogue mediation. Third, by creating new spaces of public self-representation and experiential reflexivity which might nurture what Young (2000: 138–9) refers to as 'the sensibility of group-positioned experience'.

Accountability

Apart from authorization, via elections or other plebiscitary mechanisms, accountability of representatives to the represented is the most fundamental requirement of democratic governance. By holding representatives to account the public can sit in permanent judgement, with a view to rewarding or punishing politicians at the next election. But citizens are dependent upon highly mediated accounts of the political process, often leaving them bewildered and elected representatives frustrated.

In problematizing accountability, the absence of certain elements becomes apparent. The first of these concerns interactivity. Norms of accountability require representatives' interests and actions to be open to public scrutiny. This is, in its weakest sense, an essentially protective measure, intended to guard against corruption and incompetence. A fuller and more positive notion of accountability entails giving accounts which, in an inclusive democracy, should not be confined to representatives. Account-giving involves much more than transparency: it calls for views, policies and actions to be explained, contextualized and related to social experience. Giving an account is to enter into a relationship with the account's recipient. Such a relationship need not be that of leader and led or expert and lay public, but can be more complex, such as in accounts drawn from unique experiences or communities of practice (Wenger, 1998).

Democratic account-giving can take many forms, including those that are not typically political, rationalistic or linear. Levinas's distinction between 'saying' and 'said' (which Young outlines in her work) is highly relevant here. Levinas argues that the form and cultural framing of communicative encounters (what he calls 'saying') is just as important as their content (the 'said'). If, for example, the environment of an encounter is designed to confer high status upon one speaker and lesser status upon others, this will be just as damaging to meaningful accountability as mendacious content would be. The significance of accounting lies not only in what is said but in how it is said and the assumptions about those who are receiving it (Levinas, 1981).

By conceiving of accountability as an interactive process, as made possible by digital modes of communication, the credibility of normative claims for a more deliberative democracy where citizens' preferences are not simply calculated and aggregated, but exposed to public reason and the possibility of transformation, is enhanced.

An example of such a process, where the experience and expertise of the public was recruited in order to inform and broaden political debate, is a series of recent online policy consultations organized on behalf of the

British parliament. These have been shown to provide a space for more inclusive public deliberation; generate and connect networks of interest or practice; lead to greater than usual interaction between representatives and represented; and avoid the uninformed and poor quality which characterizes much online discussion. Although such consultations are still in an experimental phase, the evidence from them suggests that citizens like being invited to think and make recommendations about policy issues that concern them (Coleman, 2003).

A second gap in the traditional conception of accountability relates to the time and place for account-giving. By contrast with democratic authorization, which takes place in regular, well-publicized elections preceded by regulated, relatively bounded campaigns periods, accountability has neither a time nor a place for its enactment. In its negative sense, accounting takes place when politicians are caught out; they are open to scrutiny because they were not cunning enough to evade it. A more positive notion of accountability conceives it as a permanent relationship of open communication.

If, as was argued above, representatives are now permanently in campaign mode, citizens are in ongoing judgement and scrutiny has become anticipatory, democratic accountability cannot afford to be occasional, ad hoc or governed by journalistic hunches. Traditional barriers to accountability, such as the speed of decision-making and the physical distance between representatives and their constituents, are becoming obsolete. Public networks of digital mediation, with their capacity for synchronous communication and asynchronous storage and retrieval of information, are well suited to permanent communicative relationships.

The print and broadcast media have not adapted well to the age of the permanent news cycle. Broadcast news inhabits a world of routinized time and ritualized space. The Greenwich time signal. *The World at One.* The shipping forecast. The BBC. If democratic representation is to be inclusive and responsive, it must mediate a range of temporal and spatial moments, both reflecting and enacting history. Representation is a site of permanent discursive dialectic, requiring channels of mediation that are both permanent and historically-rooted, live and archived, account-giving and account-collecting. The historically transcendent and geographically unbounded character of digital networks renders them appropriate for the kind of ongoing accountability required for permanent representation.

Plurality

The traditional conception of political representation is bilateral and linear. The representative sits in the house of representation (parliament, Congress) and the represented live in their geographically bounded constituencies. The rise of devolved and supranational regions of representation have recently inspired arcane debates between sovereignty and subsidiarity but, even in these cases, the nodal points of representation are defined territorially, in ways that would have made sense to 18th-century villagers.

Traditional liberal pluralism, as reflected in most European and North-American constitutional arrangements, is open to challenge on at least three fronts. First, it is based upon a rigid and narrow conception of identity. Social identity is complex, comprising a variety of demographic, cultural and personal factors. To represent people on the basis of territorial residence can be constraining. Other kinds of constraints and diminutions are associated with the aggregative packaging of policies by political parties. A pluralistic notion of representation accepts that people experience the world from multiple perspectives, each of which is (or may be) valid. For example, a black British European who votes Labour but opposes Blair on the war in Iraq has a range of positions, each of which can only be represented fairly if all of the others are as well.

Second, not all democratic representation needs to be in the formal political sphere. There is a need for spaces of informal representation, reflecting aspects of the personal that are intimately associated with power, but not with formal governance. The informal realm of democratic self-representation, often associated with gender, sexuality, ethnicity, culture and morality, is as popular with the public as formal politics is unpopular, but formidable problems are encountered in trying to connect these to institutional representation.

Third, and closely related to the discussion of account-giving, there is the challenge of pluralistic styles of engagement. The tendency to see politics, representation and democracy as suit-and-tie affairs, pervaded by what Nichols calls 'discourses of sobriety' (1991: 3), has a gatekeeping effect, limiting the entry to representation to those who speak its language. Difference democrats are concerned to promote processes of political mediation that do not exclude the less confident or articulate, the marginalized and the informal. They argue that a fundamental problem of representation is not simply the exclusion of the public from policy deliberation, but the discourse of deliberation itself, as an exclusive, rationally-bounded process of mediating politics (Benhabib, 1996; Young, 2000). Sanders argues that the kind of public reason advocated by deliberative democrats is exclusive, and therefore that:

> [T]aking deliberation as a signal of democratic practice paradoxically works undemocratically, discrediting on seemingly democratic grounds the views of those who are less likely to present their arguments in ways that we recognize as characteristically deliberative. In our political culture, these citizens are likely to be those who are already underrepresented in formal political institutions and who are systematically disadvantaged.
>
> (1996: 349)

The absence of social cues and the flattening of hierarchies within online environments accord with the demands of democratic theorists for a more differentiated, but less prejudiced or stigmatizing form of democratic representation. Miller (1995) has applied Goffmanesque analysis to online environments, exploring the range of 'expressive resources' used by people to 'give off' a sense of virtual presence. From weblogs to homepages to chat groups to email-based networks, the scope for digital self-representation is considerable. Digital self-representation is often 'desperately burdened by the lack of the other familiar markers of identity' (Crystal, 2001: 62), but this has the benefit of accommodating the complex, fluid and often multiple aspects of identity that characterize real (as opposed to institutionally represented) social life.

In practice, how might digitally-based communication contribute to the more pluralistic mediation of representation? While analogue media operate on the basis of singular conceptions of the public, the audience and the readership, digital media are embedded within a constellation of heterogeneous networks. When people communicate digitally their identities are more fluid; they can have more than one address, draw upon diverse sources of information and belong to a range of social networks. Although the debate between 'mobilization' and 'reinforcement' theories of online politics is far from being resolved, Norris has concluded, on the basis of her empirical study of civil society groups online, that:

> [T]he existence of 'flash' movements triggered by particular issues or events, like anti-globalization protests in the streets of Seattle, Washington DC and Prague, and the anti-fuel tax coalition shutting down motorways from London to Oslo, suggests that this digital information environment has the capacity to alter the structure of opportunities for communication and information in civic society, providing a culture that that is particularly conducive for alternative social movements, fringe parties from the libertarians to the Greens, and transnational advocacy networks seeking to organize and mobilize dispersed groups for collective action.
>
> (2001: 210)

As well as protest and marginal political movements, the internet facilitates a degree of informal, self-directed, dialogical communication which has tended to fall outside the remit of the pre-digital media. From virtual communities to loose networks of practice or passion, digitally-based communication tends to broaden the range and depth of what might be called non-politicized democratic activity.

Reality

Late modern politics is characterized by the demise of deference and the celebration of experience. Arguably, it has been the transparency and instantaneity of televised politics which ultimately undermined public deference. New media, particularly video technologies such as camcorders and closed-circuit television (CCTV), have provided an impetus to the sharing of mediated experience in seemingly live and untreated ways. In reality TV, the great multimedia phenomenon of the early 21st century, technologies of surveillance meet cultures of everyday experience to construct images (and sometimes illusions) of unadulterated self-representation.

Elsewhere I have identified a conspicuous gap between the forms of representation witnessed in two tele-mediated houses: the House of Commons and the *Big Brother* house (Coleman, 2003). The sense in which the public feels represented by each of these reveals radically contrasting conceptions of representation. Whereas MPs in the House of Commons are judged on the basis of how well they speak for us, the housemates in *Big Brother* are evaluated in terms of their authentic claims to be like us: to present the public to itself.

The authenticity of representation can be conceived in terms of resemblance and trust. According to the first, a representation is authentic because it seems to be like its subject. So, the *Big Brother* housemates derive authentication from speaking, thinking and acting in ways that resemble the public who are watching them. According to the trust-based conception, it is precisely the inevitable absence of obvious identity between representation and represented that necessitates an ongoing process of testing and judgement about discrepant claims and assurances of authenticity. As Silverstone (1999: 180) puts it, 'For trust to be relevant, there must be a possibility for others to betray us'. The debate about authenticity in politics is in reality about the alleged betrayal of the public through misrepresentation. This pervasive problem of authentication concerns citizens' sense of not being recognized, respected or understood by their representatives. The phenomenon of 'blogging' can be seen as a direct response to this sense of being lost, ignored and outside the sphere of public communication. The growing number of political weblogs are, in this sense, a grass roots attempt to authenticate deeper and more expansive accounts and narratives than traditional political discourse permits. Weblogs are indicative of a struggle to become meaningfully present in a world where private words often go unacknowledged.

The representation of political reality entails more than the cultivation of credibility. Authenticity arises in conditions of accessibility that transcend mere institutional transparency. Instead of politicians seeking to be more 'in touch' with the public, accessibility requires that they inhabit mutual communicative spaces with the public. These we might call spaces of touchability, where realities can be tested in the common realm of experience and emotion as well as opinion and persuasion. Spaces of political representation are perceived by the public to be exclusive, unwelcoming and unfeeling. Until recently, in the British parliament, visiting members of the public were described as 'strangers'. To be governed by, or as, strangers is to be politically alienated.

Conclusion – towards direct representation?

No matter how often the notion of direct democracy is dismissed, discussions of digital politics keep drifting back to it. There is a good reason for this: although the arguments for direct, plebiscitory decision-making are unsophisticated and normatively unattractive, the associated promise of direct information and communication flows is appealing and accords with both democratic norms of discursive autonomy and technological possibilities of relatively disintermediated interactivity. Extricating arguments for more direct forms of communication between representatives and represented from proposals for push-button democracy resists the lure of technopopulism and lays the foundation for a contemporary argument for direct representation.

In the 18th century politics was characterized by the notion of virtual representation, whereby the rich and privileged voted on behalf of the disenfranchised majority. This disappeared in the 20th century (after women finally won the right not to be represented by the votes of men), but in the age of mass media a form of virtual deliberation arose, whereby professional politicians and journalists tended to dominate political discussion on behalf of the public. Virtual deliberation is a product of indirect representation, itself a pragmatic response to Lippmanesque and Schumpeterian notions of democracy as paternalistic representation.

An atmosphere of crisis surrounds virtual deliberation and indirect representation in the early 21st century. There is widespread distrust of paternalistic representation (manifested by seemingly remote politicians, parties and political institutions); public disenchantment with virtual deliberation (primarily, the political coverage provided by television and the press); and a post-deferential desire by citizens to be heard and respected more. A response to this crisis is suggested by two innovations: the shift in democratic theory from aggregative to deliberative democratic norms; and the rise of digital ICT, with their inherent capacity for many-to-many interactivity. In combination, these five factors make the notion of direct representation seem both practical and appealing.

Direct representation entails an adherence to Pitkin's agent–principal model of democratic representation, with three of its elements strengthened. First, communication between citizens and representative is conceived as a two-way process, situated in shared spaces of collaborative interaction. Second, the obligation of representatives to account to, and hear accounts from, citizens becomes central to the act of representing. Third, with the growth of the permanent campaign and anticipatory accountability, representation becomes a more ongoing, deliberative process, rather than an ad hoc aggregation of private preferences. Direct representation amounts to more than a stylistic change in the mode of political communication, although there is a strong stylistic element, rooted in a cultural discourse of authenticity and shared reality. More significantly, direct representation offers a basis for a more dialogical and deliberative democracy in place of the dialogue of the deaf which tends to characterize contemporary political representation.

Acknowledgements

Thanks to Jay Blumler, Matthew Taylor, Ian Kearns and two anonymous reviewers for very helpful comments on the ideas presented here. Thanks to my research assistant, Shachar Nativ, for technical support.

References

Adams, C. F. (1854) *The Works of John Adams, Second President of the United States. Vol. IV.* Boston, MA: Little, Brown & Co.

Arrow, K. J. (1951) *Social Choice and Individual Values.* New York and London: Wiley/Chapman & Hall.

Barber, B. R. (1998) *A Place for Us: How to Make Society Civil and Democracy Strong.* New York: Hill and Wang.

Becker, T. L. and C. D. Slaton (2000) *The Future of Teledemocracy.* Westport, CT: Praeger.

Benhabib, S. (1996) *Democracy and Difference: Contesting the Boundaries of the Political.* Princeton, NJ: Princeton University Press.

Burnheim, J. (1989) *Is Democracy Possible? The Alternative to Electoral Politics.* Berkeley, CA: University of California Press.

Carter, M. (2000) 'Speaking Up in the Internet Age: Use and Value of Constituent Email and Congressional Websites', in S. Coleman, J. A. Taylor and W. B. H. J. van de Donk (eds) *Parliament in the Age of the Internet*, pp. 102–18. Oxford: Oxford University Press/Hansard Society for Parliamentary Government.

Coleman, S. (1999) *The Electronic Media, Parliament and the Public.* London: Hansard Society for Parliamentary Government.

Coleman, S. (2000) 'Westminster in the Information Age', in S. Coleman, J. A. Taylor and W. B. H. J. van de Donk (eds) *Parliament in the Age of the Internet*, pp. 9–26. Oxford: Oxford University Press/Hansard Society.

Coleman, S. (2001) *Democracy Online: What Do We Want from MPs' Websites?* London: Hansard Society for Parliamentary Government.

Coleman, S. (2003) *A Tale of Two Houses: the House of Commons, the Big Brother House and the People at Home.* London: Channel 4/Hansard Society for Parliamentary Government.

Cook, R. (2002) 'Speech to Yougov Conference', Queen Elizabeth Conference Centre, London, 10 April.

Crystal, D. (2001) *Language and the Internet*. Cambridge: Cambridge University Press.
Davis, R. (1999) *The Web of Politics: the Internet's Impact on the American Political System*. New York: Oxford University Press.
Dunleavy, P. (1992) *Democracy, Bureaucracy, and Public Choice: Economic Explanations in Political Science*. New York: Prentice Hall.
Etzioni, A. (1992) 'Teledemocracy', *The Atlantic* 270(4): 36–9.
Gibson, R., W. Lusoli and S. Ward (2002) 'UK Political Participation Online – the Public Response: a Survey of Citizens' Activity via the Internet', URL (consulted 23 February 2004): http://www.esri.salford.ac.uk/ESRCResearchproject/papers/UK_public_response.pdf.
Grossman, L. K. (1995) *The Electronic Republic: Reshaping Democracy in the Information Age*. New York: Viking.
House of Commons Information Committee (2002) *Digital Technology: Working for Parliament and the Public*. London: House of Commons Information Committee.
Introna, L. D. and H. Nissenbaum (2000) 'Shaping the Web: Why the Politics of Search Engines Matters', *The Information Society* 16(3): 169–86.
Lebert, M. (1999) 'Multilingualism on the Web', URL (consulted 23 February 2004): http://www.cefrio.qc.ca/projets/Documents/multieng0.htm.
Lessig, L. (1999) *Code and Other Laws of Cyberspace*. New York: Basic Books.
Levinas, E. (1981) *Otherwise Than Being: or Beyond Essence* (Martinus Nijhoff Philosophy Texts, Vol. 3). Hingham, MA: Kluwer Boston.
Lippmann, W. (1925) *The Phantom Public*. New York: Harcourt.
Mann, T. E. and N. J. Ornstein (2000) *The Permanent Campaign and its Future*. Washington, DC: American Enterprise Institute.
Mansbridge, J. (1998) 'The Many Faces of Representation'. Kennedy School of Government Politics Research Group Working Paper. Cambridge, MA: John F. Kennedy School of Government.
Mill, J. S. (1861) *Considerations on Representative Government*. London: Parker & Son/Bourn.
Miller, H. (1995) 'The Presentation of Self in Electronic Life: Goffman on the Internet', paper presented at the Embodied Knowledge and Virtual Space Conference, available at: http://www.ntu.ac.uk/soc/psych/miller/goffman.htm.
Morris, D. (2001) 'Direct Democracy and the Internet', *Loyola of Los Angeles Law Review* 34(3): 1033–53.
Negrine, R. M. (1998) *Parliament and the Media: a Study of Britain, Germany, and France*. London: Royal Institute of International Affairs.
Nichols, B. (1991) *Representing Reality: Issues and Concepts in Documentary*. Bloomington, IN: Indiana University Press.
Norris, P. (2001) *Digital Divide: Civic Engagement, Information Poverty, and the Internet Worldwide, Communication, Society, and Politics*. New York: Cambridge University Press.
Passmore, J. A. (1970) *The Perfectibility of Man*. London: Duckworth.
Peters, J. D. (1999) *Speaking Into the Air: a History of the Idea of Communication*. Chicago, IL: University of Chicago Press.
Phillips, A. (1995) *The Politics of Presence*, Oxford Political Theory. Oxford: Clarendon Press.
Pitkin, H. F. (1967) *The Concept of Representation*. Berkeley, CA: University of California Press.

Postman, N. (1986) *Amusing Ourselves to Death: Public Discourse in the Age of Show Business*. New York: Penguin Books.

Riker, W. H. (1982) *Liberalism Against Populism: a Confrontation Between the Theory of Democracy and the Theory of Social Choice*. San Francisco, CA: W.H. Freeman.

Sanders, L. (1996) 'Against Deliberation', *Political Theory* 25(3): 347–76.

Schumpeter, J. A. (1976) *Capitalism, Socialism, and Democracy* (5th edn). London: Allen and Unwin.

Silverstone, R. (1999) *Why Study the Media?* London: Sage.

Simonson, P. (1996) 'Dreams of Democratic Togetherness: Communication Hope from Cooley to Katz', *Critical Studies in Mass Communication* 13: 324–42.

Toffler, A. (1981) *The Third Wave*. London: Pan/Collins.

Wenger, E. (1998) *Communities of Practice: Learning, Meaning, and Identity*, *Learning in Doing*. Cambridge: Cambridge University Press.

Young, I. M. (2000) *Inclusion and Democracy*, *Oxford Political Theory*. Oxford: Oxford University Press.

54

REAL-TIME POLITICS
The Internet and the Political Process*

Philip E. Agre

Source: *The Information Society* 18(5) (2002): 311–31.

> Research on the Internet's role in politics has struggled to transcend technological determinism—the assumption, often inadvertent, that the technology simply imprints its own logic on social relationships. An alternative approach traces the ways, often numerous, in which an institution's participants appropriate the technology in the service of goals, strategies, and relationships that the institution has already organized. This *amplification model* can be applied in analyzing the Internet's role in politics. After critically surveying a list of widely held views on the matter, this article illustrates how the amplification model might be applied to concrete problems. These include the development of social networks and ways that technology is used to bind people together into a polity.

The Internet's promise of ubiquitous information makes it a perfect screen for projecting the hopes and fears of a society. Nowhere are these projected hopes and fears more elaborate than with regard to politics. Closely bound to national and thus personal identity, yet also by its nature a permanent source of disappointment, the political process is being intensively reimagined in the context of new information and communications technologies. By considering the most prominent ways in which American culture, at least, has imagined the wired political process, and by subjecting the various forms of imagination to the somewhat harsher light of social analysis, it will be possible to sketch a structural theory of the Internet's actual and potential role in the political life of democratic societies.[1]

Let us begin with brief discussions of 10 common (and loosely interrelated) proposals. My purpose is not to debunk or dismiss these proposals, at least not entirely, but to gather materials toward a more robust analysis.[2]

1 Many theorists, explicitly or not, have equated wired democracy with online discussion fora, for example, on Usenet, the Well, or the Web.[3] Some proceed to focus on promising cases of virtual deliberation (e.g., Coleman, 1999; Ranerup, 2001), while others criticize the quality of discussion in particular online forums (e.g., Wilhelm, 1999). In each case the online forum is evaluated relative to an idealized model of the public sphere with its norms of rational debate (Brants, Huizenga, & van Meerten, 1996; Ess, 1996; Walker & Akdeniz, 1998, p. 492; cf. Dean, 2001). The Internet gets credit for its ability to support a pluralistic diversity of intersecting public spheres (Becker & Wehner, 2001, pp. 78–80; cf. Lievrouw, 2001), and it is criticized as a force for fragmentation (Buchstein, 1997, p. 251; Sunstein, 2001) or as yet another site for the silencing of voices through various forms of psychological terrorism (e.g., Herring, 1993). While some studies of online discussion fora have usefully described the phenomenology of a new medium (e.g., Reid, 1999; Rheingold, 1993), the optimistic and pessimistic theories alike have generally framed the questions inadequately. The problem in either case is that the public sphere is, and always will be, a much larger phenomenon than an Internet discussion forum. This is true in several ways. First, the debates in online fora interact with goings-on in other media, for example, television (Bimber, 2000; cf. Bolter & Grusin, 1998). Second, different online fora are embedded in various ways in larger social structures such as professions and social movements, and their dynamics are hard to understand except in terms of this embedding (Friedland, 1996; Miller & Slater, 2000; Slevin, 2000; Wynn & Katz, 1997). In particular, a forum's embedding shapes it as an institution—for example, in its ground rules and legal status (Docter & Dutton, 1999). And third, online discussion fora comprise only a small proportion of the uses of the Internet and other convergent digital media in politics. When the Internet is used to distribute talking points to partisans, press releases to reporters, or administrative memos to the staff of a political organization, that too is a potentially significant "impact" of the Internet on politics (Davis, 1999, pp. 70–74; Stromer-Galley, 2000; Wayne, 2000a).
2. A related strand of thought judges the Internet by its ability to bring about a condition of unmediated intimacy often known as political community (e.g., Galson, 1999; Sassi, 2001). Again different estimates of this criterion are optimistic or pessimistic, and again the criterion is misguided (cf. Jones, 1995). The norm of intimacy has different sources in different national political cultures, but in each case it is a form of

nostalgia, whether for the religious-communitarian city on a hill (Agre, 2002; Shain, 1996) or for the village community that supposedly predated the upheavals of modernism or capitalism (Wellman, 1999, pp. 1–15). Unmediated intimacy may be feasible in a small group; it may even be necessary and beneficial in the ways that advocates of "strong democracy" (Barber, 1984) and participatory localism (Sclove, 1995) recommend. But modern society, particularly in an era when everything can be connected to everything else, is too big for that (Calhoun, 1992, 1998). Intimacy is particularistic; it requires an investment of time and effort. Modern societies operate because they have learned to operate, at least for many purposes, in the opposite extreme mode of impersonality (North, 1990). The rule of law will not function if judges are deeply embedded in the relational webs of the litigants; that is why judges rotate on circuits. Markets likewise require a taken-for-granted framework of law and custom in order for large numbers of buyers and sellers to transact business with tolerably low overhead. And large-scale political associations require impersonal procedures for choosing leaders, organizing debates, and handling money. Norms of intimacy may have their place—lurching entirely to the impersonal opposite extreme is not warranted either. But the hard analytical problem is to understand how the intimate and the impersonal interact.

3. The Internet is often held to make intermediaries redundant, and this has suggested to many authors that the future of politics lies in referenda (e.g., Grossman, 1995; Hollander, 1985; Slaton, 1992; Toffler & Toffler, 1995). This is the system called "direct democracy" by its promoters and "plebiscitary democracy" by its detractors. The argument has some merit: To the extent that political parties, legislative representatives, and other political intermediaries serve as communications channels, networking with their constituents and with one another, the spread of ubiquitous digital networks should be able to automate them and undermine their gatekeeping power. In a sophisticated polity the increased use of referenda may well be justified (Budge, 1996). Direct democracy can also be feasible in small groups. But experience in politics and markets alike has shown that simple disintermediation scenarios are rarely accurate, and that computer networking more often brings a reshuffling of the many functions of intermediaries (Brown, Duguid, & Haviland, 1994; Sarkar, Butler, & Steinfield, 1995; Spulber, 1999). New information and communication technologies are helpful not least because they compel analysis of such things, thereby making visible phenomena that might have been taken for granted (Casson, 1997). Political parties and legislatures, for example, do not simply transmit information; they actively process it, especially by synthesizing political opinions and interests into ideologically coherent platforms. They also engage in the discovery process of negotiation. Proposals for

direct democracy inevitably misconstrue or neglect these intermediary functions, and political functions that become invisible are likely to be manipulated (e.g., Arterton, 1987, p. 191; Clark, 1998; McLean, 1989). New information technologies will not automate these functions, but they might support them and change their dynamics in ways that can be investigated once their survival is acknowledged.[4]

4. Debates over information technology in politics are hardly new, and a common, almost taken-for-granted proposal during the 1970s has been called *managerial democracy:* the intensified use of computer decision-making tools by government staffs to rationalize, professionalize, and ultimately depoliticize many of the functions of government (Laudon, 1977, pp. 19–24). Once the administration of public services was reduced to an operations research problem, it was held, the problematic aspects of the political process would become redundant—an end to ideology and its irrational conflicts. The reality, as scholars such as the UC Irvine school made clear, is that rational public administration did not live up to the promises that have been made for it (Danziger, Dutton, Kling, & Kraemer, 1982).[5] For one thing, the politics largely went underground, with the dominant political coalitions manipulating the technology for their own ends under the guise of rational methods. For another, the technology was simply incapable of living up to its promises. Real-world public management problems are more complex than the models admit, and one is often condemned to guessing the values of hundreds of largely subjective and inevitably political parameters. Of course, rationality and professionalization do have their place in government. But computerized decision-support tools do not eliminate the tension between politics and expertise that is central to all modern government.

5. Many proposals focus on the voting process. Voting is a central ritual of democracy, as well as a process of information capture and aggregation, so it seems natural to use digital networks to facilitate the voting process (e.g., Becker & Slaton, 2000; Mohen & Glidden, 2001; Motluk, 1997). The idea is reasonable enough in the abstract, but the devil is in the details (Philips & Spakovsky, 2001; Grossman, 2001; Valenty & Brent, 2000; Weber, 2001). In particular, proposals to bring voting to the home over the Internet are problematic (Alexander, 2001). Low voter turnout may well be alleviated to a degree by easier voting, but the requirements for a sound voting process are complex. Even supposing that the injustice caused by the unequal distribution of the technology is overcome with time, problems of vote fraud are more serious. Any voting method that can be overseen by others is susceptible to vote buying and intimidation. Physical isolation of the voter—for example, in a voting booth—is the only sure answer, and the rapid growth of absentee voting in the United States is a matter of great concern, as are

vote-by-mail systems such as Oregon's. Despite these difficulties, proposals for electronic voting continue to inspire great passion, and some proponents (e.g., Becker & Phillips, 2001) have been willing to make harsh ad hominem accusations toward critics. Other voting proposals are constitutional in nature; they argue that more advanced technology will support more complex voting methods that allocate representatives or decide referenda in mathematically more advanced ways. The problems here are numerous: the challenges to legitimacy posed by any attempt to revise anything so central to a constitution as its voting methods, the narrowly formalistic concern with mechanisms that only treat the symptoms of a troubled political culture, the mathematical problems that can make optimal voting schemes literally impossible,[6] and the cognitive and information-design problems that complex voting systems entail. Although modified voting systems might be part of a larger picture, they are a small part of the picture and therefore inadvisable until that picture becomes clear.

6. The Internet allows every host to originate its own packets, for example, by serving Web pages or broadcasting electronic messages to a mailing list. This qualitative symmetry between big and small Internet users, together with exponential declines in the underlying cost of computing, has led many authors, such as Gilder (1992), to speculate that advanced digital networks will transfer power from large hierarchical organizations to the multitude of dispersed individuals. The Internet certainly harbors significant potential for individual initiative, but the idea that it equalizes power between the great and small needs careful attention. The analysis will proceed along very different lines, for example, according to whether "power" is understood in economic or political terms, and neither understanding of "power" should be confused with the technical notion of computational "power." Even though the Internet's architecture treats all hosts equally in qualitative terms, little follows about the quantitative consequences of that equality, for the simple reason that power in society depends on other factors besides the ability to exchange data on a network. In the economic realm, for example, an organization with an established brand name will, other things being equal, achieve greater market share, and thus greater economies of scale in production, than lesser known players. Many information-intensive markets have a winner-take-all character and entry costs that make established players nearly impossible to dislodge, regardless of one's technical capacity for exchanging packets with others. In the political realm, a technology that democratizes the technical capacity to speak and organize is certainly to be welcomed. But "brand names" play an important role in politics as well, as do long-cultivated networks of personal acquaintance. In politics and markets alike, the Internet helps both the incumbents and the challengers,

and both the big and small players. The actual redistribution of power—assuming one knows what "power" even means—will require detailed more analysis, and cannot be inferred from the technical workings of the machinery.

7. One libertarian school holds that the Internet largely dictates the direction of public policy by creating the conditions for a decentralized global market. By facilitating capital flight and making operations mobile, for example, the Internet is held to promote regulatory competition among the world's jurisdictions, inasmuch as "capital goes where it is wanted, and stays where it is well treated" (Wriston, 1999, p. 342). Starved of taxes, regulation-minded governments will therefore be compelled to adopt neoliberal policies (Cairncross, 1997; Friedman, 1999; Wriston, 1992). This theory has its elements of truth, but it is far from completely accurate. Information exhibits vast economies of scale, which promote economic concentration. Economies of scale, moreover, require many companies to operate globally, thus subjecting them to the law of every major jurisdiction—the opposite of the idealized picture of migratory capital. Many business activities require geographic proximity, and the use of computer networks to loosen some geographic bonds only increases the forces of agglomeration that cause other functions to centralize in world cities like New York or regional innovation centers like Silicon Valley (Krugman, 1991; Mitchell, 2000; Sassen, 1991). Furthermore, the conception of market and government as intrinsically opposed to one another has always been wrong (Hodgson, 1988); the conditions of the modern market were largely brought about by robust intervention by governments (Polanyi, 1944), and governments to this day are deeply allied with their domestic industries in using their diplomatic leverage to promote exports (Melody, 1985). This process has developed for centuries, and has now been internalized beneath a veneer of neoliberal ideology in mechanisms such as the World Trade Organization. The growth of government has historically played a major role in the development of institutions for capturing and circulating information (Hewson, 1999), and computer networking increases the potential for governments to exert control, for example, over their constituent jurisdictions, without regard for geography (Frissen, 1997, pp. 114–115). These dynamics are only intensifying as new information technologies make it possible to coordinate industrial and political activities over wide geographical areas.

8. An opposed school of thought, for example, among the followers of Innis (1951), sees new communications technologies as inevitably centralizing because they allow peripheral regions to be integrated more tightly into the systems of economic and political centers (Gillespie & Robins, 1989).[7] When the emperor is far away, a degree of de facto regional autonomy remains; but the Internet makes the emperor

ubiquitous in the same manner as other technologies of control (Beniger, 1986; Lyon, 2001; Scott, 1998). This, too, is a partial truth that becomes disastrous when treated as the whole. New information and communication technologies are not inherently technologies of control; after all, privacy-enhancing technologies such as cryptography stand available as one social choice among many (Agre & Rotenberg, 1997). The new technologies also afford great flexibility in the construction and reconstruction of associations and networks; they facilitate the many forces of disembedding (Carrier & Miller, 1998; Giddens, 1990; Polanyi, 1957) that pull individuals loose from close-knit orders of communitarian social control. The picture is complex, and social structures are centralizing and decentralizing, both, in different and interacting ways.

9. E-mail and chat-room interactions arrive tagged not with visible faces but with cryptic addresses, so many scholars have argued, if tentatively, that the Internet is a force for social equality (e.g., Graddol & Swann, 1989, pp. 175–178; Poster, 1997). In the words of a much-reprinted New Yorker cartoon (e.g., Mitchell, 1996, p. 6), "On the Internet, nobody knows you're a dog."[8] Conventional markers of social difference (gender, ethnicity, age, rank) are likewise held to be invisible, and consequently it is contended that the ideas in an online message are evaluated without the prejudices that afflict face-to-face interaction. This argument exemplifies the dangers of overgeneralizing from particular uses of the technology. Different forums construct identity in a great variety of ways. Some forums, such as role-playing MUDs, do permit the construction of entirely "virtual" make-believe identities, although even in those forums "true names" are often the norm (Baym, 1998, p. 55; Schiano, 1999). Other forums authenticate their participants to prevent abuse, or else real-world social identities are implicated in the content and process of the discussion (e.g., Burkhalter, 1999; Donath, 1999). In many institutional contexts, such as academia and business, it is normal for individuals to construct elaborate public personae; an institutional participant who receives a message from a stranger can research that person's background much more readily than might be possible in the pre-Internet world. So it is not true, as a broad generalization, that the Internet decouples communications from identity. The reverse is often the case. Depending on how the Internet is used, it can even reinforce the conventional constructions of identity, or impose even finer gradations of status.

10. Finally, it has often been argued that the Internet is a democratizing force because it facilitates open information (e.g., Cairncross, 1997). There can be no doubt that the Internet and related technologies have played a positive role in opposition movements in several countries (Ferdinand, 2000, pp. 14–15), but the picture is more complex. First of all, the Internet has no power to make information open on its own;

the political culture has to want it, and in many societies authoritarian habits beyond a narrow stratum of intellectuals run deep. Nor is the association between the Internet and open information at all inevitable; companies such as IBM build Internet-based systems for their business and government customers whose purpose is precisely to keep information from becoming open. In the public sphere, new technologies also serve as instruments of surveillance, commercialization, and propaganda, all of which are entirely capable of negating the benefits of open information in practice (Buchstein, 1997). More factors have to be taken into account.

Institutions

The picture that emerges from these analyses has many elements, but some broad patterns are clear. Political activities on the Internet are embedded in larger social processes, and the Internet itself is only one element of an ecology of media. The Internet does not create an entirely new political order; to the contrary, to understand its role requires that we understand much else about the social processes that surround it. Single factors do not suffice; nor do one-sided generalizations. Instead there emerges a pattern of tensions: between centralization and decentralization, between intimacy and impersonality, and between politics and professionalism (cf. Calhoun, 1998, p. 383; Frissen, 1997, p. 111).[9] Faced, for example, with the tension between the potentially antidemocratic implications of technology-enhanced government surveillance and the potentially prodemocratic implications of increased public access to information, it is not enough to declare blandly (as does Cairncross, 1997, p. 257) that one force is more important than the other. Both forces are real and substantial, and a serious theory requires an understanding of the many and various ways in which the forces interact (van de Donk & Tops, 1995).[10] Above all one finds complexity: If the Internet has "effects," it has many effects scattered throughout the structures of society, so that it is difficult if not impossible to compute a resultant of the vectors along which the various effects run.

To make sense of these phenomena, it helps to take an institutional approach (Agre & Schuler, 1997; Avgerou, 2002; Bud-Frierman, 1994; Ducatel, Webster & Herrmann, 2000; Dutton, 1999; Gandy, 1993; Kling & Iacono, 1989; Laudon, 1985; Mansell & Steinmuller, 2000; Orlikowski, 2000; van Dijk, 1999; for theoretical background, see Commons, 1970 [1950]; Goodin, 1996; Knight, 1992; March & Olsen, 1989; North, 1990; Powell & DiMaggio, 1991). Society is organized by a diversity of institutions, each of which defines social roles and identities, rules and enforcement mechanisms, situations and strategies. Banking is an institution, and so is the newspaper business. The family is an institution, as are the church, the university, and contract law. The political system comprises several institutions—political parties, legislatures, aspects of the legal system, various types of associations, the customary forms of debate and other communicative interactions, the rules of parliamentary order, the methods of interest group organizing, the profession and practice of news management, and many more. These institutions are centrally concerned with information, but they are also concerned with power and identity and many other aspects of social life.

Institutions persist, and their ways of ordering human relationships can remain relatively unchanged for decades and centuries. The recalcitrance of institutions may be masked during a period of rapid change in information and communications technologies, when a swarm of specific innovations focuses attention on novelty and its opportunities, but even these developments cannot be well understood except against the background of the many dynamics that tend to keep institutions functioning in the way they already do. Institutions shape thought and language, among other things, and alternative institutional forms can be hard to imagine—even at a time when such imagining is fashionable. Because participants in an institution must coordinate their activities, it is often rational for purposes of compatibility to do things in the ways that others are doing them. Institutions must likewise continue to complement one another, and the transition of several interlocking institutions to new forms is almost impossible to coordinate. Institutions persist in part because of the bodies of skill that have built up within them; another institutional form might be preferable after a long learning period, but in the short term it is the existing forms that people are good at. Above all, institutions persist because they provide a terrain upon which individuals and groups can pursue their goals—goals that the institution itself has taught them, to be sure, but goals that inspire people to forgo substantial opportunity costs anyway.

To say that institutions coordinate activity is not to say that they are wholly cooperative; more often the institution provides a relatively stable and predictable framework for a segmentary politics whose participants cooperate and compete in shifting ways. The framework that the institution provides is itself largely political, and it is well understood as a routinized accommodation among the stakeholder groups that comprise it.

When institutions change, it is not because a technology such as the Internet descends and, deus ex machina, reorganizes the institution's constitutive order in its own image. Institutions do often change as a result of the opportunities that a new technology makes available, but it is only through the workings of the institution that the dynamics of the change can be found. As Calhoun (1998, p. 382) puts it, "the main impact [of the Internet], especially in the short to medium term, will be to allow us to do more of the things we were already organized and oriented to do." Nor is the point restricted to the Internet; Fischer (1992) concluded that Americans in the early 20th century used the telephone "to pursue their [existing] ends . . . more aggressively and fully" (p. 28) and "to widen and deepen existing social patterns rather than to alter them" (p. 262). People in a given institutional setting use a new technology to pursue the goals that the institution provides, using the strategies that the institution suggests, organized by the cognitive and associative forms that the institution instills. If the technology is incomprehensible within the thought forms of the institution then it will probably go unused (Orlikowski, 1993). If nobody can devise an action pattern for deploying the technology in ways that mesh with the existing gears of the institution, then no significant effects of the technology's adoption are likely to be found. It follows that the Internet creates little that is qualitatively new; instead, for the most part, it amplifies existing forces (Agre, 1998a). Social forces are nothing but coordinated human will, and institutions channel human will in some directions more than others. To the extent that institutional actors can pursue existing goals by reinterpreting existing action patterns in terms of a newly available technology, the forces that their massed actions create will be amplified.

To predict the consequences of widespread Internet use, therefore, it is necessary to survey the forces at work in the existing institutions. This may be difficult if the institutional forms have long remained in equilibrium; the exact nature of the forces might only become evident as the equilibrium begins to move. The Internet will not amplify all forces equally, and not all of the forces will be headed in the same direction. The Internet is amplifying hundreds if not thousands of forces in scores of institutional fields, each with its own logic and resources, and many of those forces conflict. If we ask what effect the Internet will have on the political process, for example, then the question is ill-posed: The Internet has its effect only in the ways that it is appropriated, and it is appropriated in so many different ways that nobody has enough information to add them up. Some of the changes will take the form of "the same, only more so"; others will be qualitative, as the existing accommodations become untenable. Institutions may implode, or they may fragment and reconfigure, or their functions may be absorbed by rivals. Some of the amplifications will be consciously intended by their participations; others will be unanticipated; and in either case the newly amplified forces and their consequences will create a new status quo for the institution's participants to interpret and respond to within the framework of cognition and action that the institution provides (Orlikowski, 2001). Each case needs to be evaluated on its own. In an older vocabulary we can safely say that the contradictions are heightened, but for the most part the dialectic must be sought in its particulars.[11]

This perspective on the Internet's place in society aligns itself neither with the optimists nor the pessimists but with the realists (Kling, 1997); it is a story neither of continuity or discontinuity alone but of measured components of both. It is sensitive to the dual roles of institutions as both constraints and enablements, and it is tuned equally to the real workings of the technology and to the workings of the social mechanisms with which the technology interacts. It concerns phenomena that are localized not simply in organizational centers but in the distributed sites of practice where institutions shape action and are thereby reshaped in turn. It seeks neither to escape this enmeshment in social process nor to enclose it. It is impressed by the Internet, but it sees the Internet as a small part of the story. It lives with tension; it is neither conservative nor revolutionary.

Before discussing the relationship between the amplification model and other models, it will be helpful to illustrate the concept of amplification with a few brief examples.

1. Among relatively simple cases of amplification is the finding that the people who make extensive use of online political information tend to be the same people who are already strongly interested in politics (Bimber, 1999; Davis, 1999, pp. 23–25; Neuman, 1991, p. 109; Norris, 1999). This sort of finding has disappointed many who have placed naive hopes in the Internet as a force for increased civic involvement. Some have denounced the Internet and Internet hype by the same logic. But such findings are altogether natural from the perspective of the amplification model. They do not logically imply that the Internet does not promote civic involvement, since the Internet might promote civic involvement in many other ways than by providing political information, and we will not know the bottom line until a fuller model of the forces influencing civic involvement in politics becomes available (Norris, 2001; Skocpol & Fiorina, 1999). In any event, the Internet's role in intensifying the political activities of the already involved is significant in itself, and its consequences for the dynamics of political life ought to be explored as well.
2. One of the handful of people who can claim to have invented the personal computer is Lee Felsenstein (Freiberger & Swaine, 1984, p. 100). A red-diaper activist from Berkeley as well as an electrical engineer, Felsenstein wanted to automate the work of volunteers who ran bulletin boards for political movements. Activists would call the volunteer on the phone to report an upcoming event or inquire about events, and the events would be recorded on slips of paper on an actual bulletin board. The job was generally too much for any individual, and volunteers would often burn out by the time they became well enough known to be useful. Mainframe computers were far too large and costly for this job, so Felsenstein invented personal computers and bulletin board systems to amplify the existing force toward the centralized posting of notices of events. The technology was then appropriated by others for other purposes.
3. The Internet also amplifies the routine of issue politics whereby temporary coalitions are pulled together dynamically according to how the various interests sort out (Laumann & Knoke, 1989). This process has

long been conducted with face-to-face meetings, telephone calls, and other media, but the Web and electronic mail are exceptionally useful for coordinating moderate numbers of parties with established relationships in moderately complex but largely routinized ways (cf. Tomita, 1980). The incentives to create such alliances are still present, but now the competitive imperative to do so quickly is even greater.

4. The political process became much more informationally intensive during the open-government revolution of the 1970s, when legislatures and bureaucrats found themselves increasingly compelled to provide rational-sounding justifications for their decisions (Greider, 1992, p. 46). There arose in response a substantial industry producing justifications to order—the so-called think tanks (Ricci, 1993; Smith, 1991). While think tanks are not simply libraries or dispassionate research organizations, nonetheless a history waits to be written of the exploding information infrastructure of politics, particularly at that time and since. The forces encouraging information-intensive politics have only increased, motivated by competitive pressures and the epochal innovation of 24-hour news with CNN. By 1992, then, a substantial tactical research apparatus had arisen, and the Clinton era consisted largely of a day-by-day war of information—not just on the part of government and political parties, but also on the part of privately funded organizations that did nothing but research and publicize alleged scandals (Lieberman, 1994). The 24-hour news cycle constantly required these organizations to come up with facts that served specific rhetorical purposes, such as defusing an opponent's accusation by unearthing examples of comparable actions by others (cf. Lewis, 2000). More recently, digital video editing has allowed political campaigns to produce television advertisements on several hours' notice, thus accelerating the back-and-forth of dueling campaign ads.

5. In any electoral campaign, candidates will try to assemble a coalition that captures a majority of votes without stretching itself so thinly that it invites defection. If all goes as expected, the candidates will end up competing for a few percent of voters in the precise middle of the ideological spectrum. Of course, the precision of these campaign strategies is limited by the accuracy of research on public opinion. The decreasing cost of advanced information and communication technologies, however, allows campaigns to research public opinion in greater depth. The natural consequence is to amplify a tendency toward close elections, to the point where, in the American presidential election of 2000, the error margins of antiquated voting systems gave rise to a serious political crisis. Yet because political parties develop their ideologies and platforms on a national basis, this whole analysis assumes that electoral districts are roughly representative of the electorate as a whole. In reality, redistricting is often driven by the same political strategists.

When one party controls the redistricting process, as in the American states, the outcome is generally quite the opposite: electoral jurisdictions that are so ideologically homogenous that elections are rarely competitive. And as the technologies of public opinion research become more sophisticated, political segregation through strategic redistricting has become amplified as well, to the point where only a small proportion of Congressional districts are seriously competitive (Brownstein, 2002; The Economist, 2002). In such cases, the amplified tendency toward close elections is swamped by another, larger effect. In other cases, closer elections might well be found, assuming that yet other effects do not change the picture in other ways.

Comparing models

As these examples make clear, the Internet can amplify political processes in numerous ways. The political process comprises a complicated institutional circuitry of routinized information flows (Agre, 1995), and information technology accelerates many of this circuitry's constituent activities. A question that naturally arises is this: In what sense can the Internet change anything? The amplification model gives a clear answer to this question: The Internet changes nothing on its own, but it can amplify existing forces, and those amplified forces might change something. But are those changes qualitative, or are they merely quantitative?[12] Does the Internet really bring anything new? And what does "new" even mean? After all, few political phenomena are completely unprecedented. Do only constitutional changes count as "new?" Is "change" a codeword for a political revolution? The Internet is not old enough to have changed political institutions in such major, qualitative ways. But the invention of writing had profound social consequences through the way that institutions appropriated it (e.g., Giddens, 1985; Goody, 1986), and the Internet certainly has a great potential to amplify institutional forces. The a priori case is clear enough. Before the question can even be usefully asked, however, a more refined analysis is required.

It will help to contrast the amplification model with a relatively sophisticated model that is prevalent in the literature, which I call the *reinforcement model*. The reinforcement model is driven by a political question: It identifies a problematic structural aspect of the polity, and it asks whether the Internet (or whatever information technology is being introduced at the time) corrects the problem.[13] Most often, the author endorses a "participatory" vision of democracy and therefore asks whether the new technology enables a wider range of citizens to become involved in the political process. The conclusions of this inquiry are negative, so information technology is viewed as reinforcing the system rather than repairing it.[14]

Although the amplification and reinforcement models will often make similar predictions, they differ in several ways. The amplification model is not based on a normative theory of politics; it recognizes that different normative theories are likely to drive different empirical inquiries (Bellamy, 2000; van Dijk, 2001), but it takes no normative position. The reinforcement model reckons "change" in coarse terms: It asks whether a new technology has altered the polity in a particular fundamental way. The amplification model is more fine-grained: It takes for granted that "changes" large and small, quantitative and qualitative, will be found throughout the system, and it seeks to describe those changes and lay the groundwork for the longer, harder task of determining their consequences. The reinforcement model predicts that no qualitative change will be found; the amplification model regards the question as open and urges that it be investigated concretely.

A basic difference is analytical. The amplification model is predicated on "forces," which are the aggregate effects of the actions that institutions organize people to perform. Modern institutions evolve through the interaction of numerous forces, and the amplification model asks how the interaction among forces might be changing. The reinforcement model is predicated on outcomes rather than causes. Particular theories of reinforcement might employ a concept of "forces" to describe the social processes set in motion through the use of new information technologies, or they might use other concepts instead. What matters is the prediction: that the social processes being described will leave certain structural aspects of society unchanged. My own concern is not to refute the reinforcement model, or even necessarily to demonstrate that the amplification model makes better predictions, but instead to contribute new analytical resources.

Let us consider some examples of the reinforcement model. An important early study by Danziger, Dutton, Kling, and Kraemer (1982) considered the role of computing in the organizational politics of American local governments. These authors wished to determine the impact of information technology on the distribution of power among organizational groups such as politicians, administrators, financial experts, and urban planners. To this end, they conducted a large-scale study, using both survey and ethnographic methods. In doing so, they discovered that political contests shape the design and configuration of computers, which then have consequences for the distribution of power. The result that emerged through their analysis is that, statistically, the politics of local governments shaped computers in a way that left the existing distribution of power in place. They referred to this result as "reinforcement politics" (p. 18),[15] and they concluded that computing is a "conservative technology" (1982, p. 231). The solution, they suggested, was to equalize power relations by increasing the scope of public participation in decisions affecting local government computing (pp. 232-244).

Even without these envisaged reforms, however, theirs is not a simple tale of stasis. They do not claim that nothing changes; organizational coalitions will adopt new technologies that promise to enhance their power, and along with new technologies come new organizational forms. In this sense, existing forces can be amplified, and even lead to structural changes, while still reinforcing the power relations of the organization. The point is especially clear in cases where different forces are chronically in tension. In their historical account, for example, changing computer architectures shifted the balance of forces in political conflicts over centralization and decentralization.[16] Although computing in the mainframe era could only be bought in large blocks (1982, p. 117), minicomputers promised decentralized computing (p. 125). Yet at the same time, the rise of information management software "seemed to suggest that the government might be managed as an integrated whole, rather than as a series of departmental baronies" (p. 125). Technology on their analysis is to some degree an independent variable, in that basic architectural changes take place on a larger stage than local government, but the adoption and configuration of computing in a given setting are mediated by local politics, which are mediated in turn by the uses of computing in practice.

In a recent study of the Internet's place in politics, Davis (1999) argued that

> rather than acting as a revolutionary tool rearranging political power and instigating direct democracy, the Internet is destined to become dominated by the same actors in American politics who currently utilize other mediums. Undoubtedly, public expression will become more common and policy makers will be expected to respond hastily. But the mobilization of public expression will still largely be the creation of groups and individuals who currently dominate the political landscape.... Today, the production of political news and information is the result of the interaction among official entities, interest group representatives, and the news media. Such interaction will also govern the Internet's presentation of news and information.... The current forces dominating political news delivery, who dwarf the independent efforts, also will overshadow them on the Internet.
>
> (1999, p. 5)[17]

While these assertions are entirely plausible, especially in the short run, they are also quite coarse-grained. Davis' argument is organized as a rebuttal to a certain foil: the widespread notion that the Internet will bring about an unmediated political system dominated by the initiatives of unorganized individuals. And indeed, little evidence suggests that any such system is emerging. In that sense, nothing is likely to change. Notice, however, the types of changes that the Davis argument treats as insignificant, or else merely as confirmation that existing structures have remained unchanged[18]:

- The introduction of new players in the existing categories, such as the additional news networks on cable.
- The shifts in relative magnitudes among the various subcategories of players, such as the great expansion of museums and public radio or the retrenchment of newspapers.
- The competitive consequences of the increased number of media, which for competitive reasons compel media organizations to seek economies of scope by producing content in most or all of them.
- The emergence of new genres of political communication (e.g., the mixing of political and celebrity formats) and the evolution of existing genres (e.g., the influence of Web design on television).
- The changes in the ethos of journalism (e.g., increased orientation to entertainment) and in patterns of sourcing (e.g., the ability to canvass experts' and advocates' opinions in larger numbers by broadcasting identical e-mail queries to them rather than calling them individually on the phone).
- The acceleration of ongoing dynamics within the existing institutions (e.g., the news cycle and the legislative process).
- The greater ease with which well-funded political movements can construct their own independent media systems (e.g., political parties' video studios, which can produce their own cable programming as well as training materials and advice on issues for their activists and candidates).
- The quantitative shifts in independent political organizations' spending on mass-media advertising versus one-to-one forms of interaction.

It may be argued that these changes are not produced by the Internet, which is merely one contributing factor among many. But for the amplification model, that is just the point. The Internet is appropriated within the framework of existing institutions, and it contributes to the forces that those institutions have already organized. The same people who appropriate the Internet in the service of particular strategies are also likely to appropriate other media as well: cable television, telemarketing, direct mail, and so on, most of which are facilitated by emerging information technologies in several ways. In analyzing new uses of information technology, the forces are analytically prior to the tools.

As a final example of the reinforcement model, let us consider Hagen (2001). Hagen describes with some acuity how "digital democracy" projects in the United States, United Kingdom, and Germany have been shaped by the political cultures of each country, and especially the deficiencies that each political culture perceives in itself. He judges these projects as failures, however, essentially because the root problem in each case is citizen disillusionment resulting from globalization (2001, p. 65). He is skeptical, therefore, about the Internet's ability to "save" democracy, and he explains his skepticism using the word "amplify":

> ICT do not change political institutions and processes by virtue of their mere existence. Rather, their use may amplify existing social behaviours and trends. This can be [attributed] to the fact that the development of technological applications is controlled by specific dominant factors. With its instrumental character. ICT becomes a trend-amplifier in a given area of application.
>
> (Hagen, 2001, p. 55)[19]

Despite his vocabulary, however, a close reading makes clear that he is using the reinforcement model. Like Danziger, Dutton, Kling, and Kraemer (but unlike Davis), Hager attributes the amplifying effects of the Internet to the ability of dominant social powers to shape the technology itself, and not to the uses to which a very general-purpose technology is likely to be put. And his argument as a whole, like the others', is structured around the question of whether the Internet will reverse these established power relations. What is crucial for Hagen, following Arterton (1987), is the model of the political process that is embodied in the technology:

> Computer technology is not an independent force working for the better or worse of democracy, but it is amplifying other trends at work or reinforces existing institutions. This explains why on the whole, . . . those projects . . . have aimed to support traditional, well-established structures [rather] than those which have tried to employ new, transformative democratic ways and means.
>
> (Hagen, 2001, p. 56)

This passage reflects a curious tension in Hagen's argument (and in much of the reinforcement literature). On the one hand, computer technology is characterized as an amplifier of existing trends. On the other hand, amplification is treated as a wholly conservative force. It follows that computer-based political initiatives can produce true change only if they refuse to amplify, but instead stand outside the terrain of contending forces. Yet he has just asserted that computer technology is not an exogenous force but something internal to the institutional system. This makes it hard to understand how any change is possible, even in principle. Hagen's analysis might be contrasted (for example) with dialectical theories that hold that institutions are intrinsically dynamic, that they generate the conditions of their transformation through their own internal contradictions, that those contradictions suffuse all aspects of a society including its technology, and that social practice is necessarily a matter of selectively amplifying one endogenous force or another.

The underlying problem with Hagen's analysis lies in his diffuse model of "amplification." His notion that the Internet "amplifies" social trends is very broad. Because he does not explain what sorts of things these "trends" are, he cannot explain which specific technologies amplify which specific trends. He also places too much weight on the question of which model of democracy is embodied by a particular technology. Although specific technologies can be tailored to quite specific models of use, in practice the economics of software militate in favor of generalized functionalities that are compatible with a wide range of institutional forms. Other factors are equally important, such as the intrinsic cost of the machinery, technical training and support, and training and support in the practical skills of politics. What matters, in Danziger, Dutton, Kling, and Kraemer's (1982) terms, is the "computer package" as a whole. Political changes through the adoption of information technology, therefore, are unlikely to take the form of stand-alone "digital democracy projects," but will more likely involve a diversity of institutional players appropriating relatively generic technology in a diversity of institutional locations.

Digital embedding

The reinforcement model, I have suggested, is concerned with a question that cannot now be answered, assuming it is well posed at all: whether the Internet's use in politics will lead to qualitative changes in the constitution of the political system. A better starting place, I want to argue, is with a different question that is closer to the ground of everyday political practice: What role does the Internet play in the evolution of the very category of the person? This phrase, "the category of the person," refers to the way in which people are conceptualized and interwoven by a society's institutions.[20] A polity is ultimately a maze of practical arrangements by which people live together, and the Internet is ubiquitous in the sense that it changes the detailed workings of nearly every one of those arrangements.[21] The sheer ubiquity of the Internet, however, does not automatically imply that its use will have any particular type or magnitude of aggregate consequences. Only by analyzing that ubiquity will its actual consequences become apparent. I consider two aspects of the Internet's ubiquity, one relatively familiar and the other less so, and then I draw tentative conclusions about the sense in which the Internet, by amplifying existing social forces, might change things.

Lateral relationships

The Internet can connect anyone and anyone else, but the patterns of connection are not random. One pattern is that people exchange information with others with whom they have something in common (Agre, 1998b). Choose any condition that people find important, and it is nearly certain that a far-flung community will have arisen of people who share that condition. These communities of practice include professions, interest groups, extended families, and people who live with the same illness or share a recreational interest.[22] Most of the functioning online fora on the Internet are organized around these commonalities, but communities of practice should not be identified analytically with the technologies that support them. Few communities are strictly "virtual." Most communities employ several media, and most of them have some degree of formal organizational existence that is defined in technology-independent terms.

It helps to understand communities of practice in institutional terms: What a community's members share before anything else is a location in some institution. For example, cardiologists are a community of practice because they are all members of the same profession with its shared training, vocabulary, publications, meetings, rules, career paths, and so on. Not every institutional location, however, defines a community of practice. For example, the students in a school may form a community of practice, but only if their dealings with one another are intensive enough. Universities whose students mainly commute to classes typically lament their lack of community. Likewise, the patients of a given medical system, who might initially lack any knowledge of one another despite their structural commonalities, might form themselves into a community of practice, for example, through support groups or activist movements.

In addition to their common structural location, the members of a community of practice generally also share a common practical and epistemic world: certain places, activities, and recurring practical dilemmas within which questions arise and answers make sense. The community's members will experience incentives to share information, although the mechanisms of information sharing will depend on the workings of the institution: The institution might induce its participants to study one another's work products, or journalists might circulate among them gathering information for trade journals. By reducing some of the costs of some kinds of information sharing, the Internet amplifies the forces that bring communities of practice together (Brown, Duguid, & Haviland, 1994). It bears repeating that those forces must already exist; if information sharing is unimaginable without the Internet, it may still be unimaginable with it (Orlikowski, 1993). But where the forces are present and the resources are sufficient, the Internet is generally adopted furiously once a critical mass of community members signs on. The effects on society will depend on the specifics; for example, diaspora communities can more effectively support their brethren in civil wars if that is what they wish, and human rights campaigners can more easily spread news of the atrocities that result (Kaldor, 1999, pp. 208–209; cf. Zhang & Hao, 1999).

The pooling of knowledge in communities of practice serves many purposes in politics. Some are relatively obvious: using the Internet and other emerging communications technologies, for example, the participants in activist groups can more easily coordinate their political tactics (Frederick,

1993). But the main significance of the ubiquitous lateral comparing of notes might be more fundamental: It amplifies what might be called the collective cognition of the society. This cognitive background noise, which occurs in any society but is especially developed in the networked democracies, covers a spectrum from mundane chatter through the coordination of practical activities to the sharing of news on current issues to the overt work of political coalition building. The entire spectrum is necessary: Without the hum of everyday information sharing, it is unlikely that a community's members will be on the same page when a political issue emerges. The dividing line between "political" and "nonpolitical" communication is, for this reason, nonexistent. When legislators and administrators monitor the thinking and experience of their counterparts in other jurisdictions, for example, they are laying the cognitive groundwork for harmonizing their governance activities more profoundly than any treaty could do, and this effect will surely only intensify with the spread of the Internet and the globalization of English.[23] It is possible, therefore, that researchers who fail to discover "political participation" on the Internet are looking in the wrong place.

Knowledge pooling is generally considered a good thing, but its consequences can be mixed. When communications are weak, local communities are relatively isolated, and mutual isolation has advantages. Best practices may not be transferred, but neither are worst delusions. Evolutionary theories of institutional change depend on the existence of these cognitive islands, so that institutional experiments can proceed relatively uncorrupted by the example of others.[24] Global networking does not necessarily bring about global homogeneity if other forces exist to keep subcommunities apart, but arbitrage is a powerful force.

These concerns arise, for example, in the development of law. The common law tradition requires appeals courts to discern patterns in decisions that emerge from individual cases. This assumes that comparable cases can be tried somewhat independently of one another, so that the appeals courts can credibly claim to have discovered that order in establishing their precedents. The danger is that the appeals court is actually ratifying a conventional wisdom that influenced each individual decision along similar lines when alternative analyses might otherwise have been found. Because lawyers have strong incentives to communicate among themselves, this danger has always been present. The spread of highly developed legal information systems, however, has certainly amplified it.

Similar concerns arise in the evolution of federalism and in the globalization of the policy process (Bennett, 1997). When the policy-formation processes of different jurisdictions are tightly intertwined by social networks, news reporting, Web monitoring, and the coordinated strategies of supranational interest groups, it becomes less likely that a variety of approaches can be tried separately and compared.

Spacing

A final example of amplification is found in the reconstruction of human relationships. Every individual has a social network, and the Internet makes it possible for everyone to stay in touch more continually with everyone they know. Extended families, for example, can organize mailing lists to broadcast news updates that might otherwise have spread more slowly through dyadic phone calls or annual reunions. Buyers and sellers in a marketplace can interconnect their computers to track availability and prices, or to monitor ongoing compliance with a complex contract. Professors report spending additional time each day, on top of their usual teaching duties, answering their students' electronic mail (Rhoades, 2000, p. 39). In some cases no particular force impels this increased regularity of contact. But technical limits are no longer a great barrier when, for reasons of sentiment or self-interest, those forces do exist. Spouses can talk 10 times a day on their cell phones; friends can exchange a steady patter of text messages. Holiday card lists need no longer be pruned on account of the costs of postage; people who fall out of touch can more easily find one another again. Software enables salespeople to keep track of their relationships with a multitude of clients. The result, Wellman (2001) argues, is to amplify a sort of networked individualism: individuals embedded in continual, electronically mediated engagement with their entire social networks.[25]

A larger phenomenon might be called "spacing": drawing out the logic of institutionally organized relationships and making that logic explicit in the configurations of technology. Before discussing the concept of spacing theoretically, let us consider some examples. One example might be found in commonly observed patterns among relatively affluent families in the West. As television sets and telephone lines become cheap, the family home tends to break apart into separate media spheres for each individual—what Bovill and Livingstone (2001) calls "bedroom culture." Families that are dispersed into these separate spheres need not fall out of touch; on the contrary, new communications technologies such as cellular telephones and electronic mail make everyone constantly reachable, a development that children in particular do not always welcome (English-Lueck, 1998). Something important has happened here: Each individual inhabits a discrete world, yet the worlds are interconnected, and the interconnections are negotiated within a framework organized by the prevailing rules of the institution—in this case, the institution of the nuclear family. The institution might give some individuals the authority to initiate contact with others, or it might provide others with the right to render themselves unreachable, and these aspects of the relationship are reinvented in the new technical context (Dutton, 1999). The phenomenon is called "spacing" because it gives technological form to the institutionally organized spaces between people, inscribing in technology and its uses their separate individuality and the protocols through which they interact.

Another example of spacing is found in academic research. To participate in the research community is to construct an elaborate public persona through research papers and presentations. A research library is, among other things, a warehouse of the public personae of professional researchers, and researchers commonly monitor one another's careers by reading articles, attending talks at conferences, taking note of participation on editorial boards, and so on. New researchers are socialized into an array of rituals for developing relationships with others based on their personae, including the ritual of defining precisely and publicly the intellectual relationships between their own research projects and those of others.[26] The resulting professional network is a central fact of life for numerous purposes, from job hunting to conference organizing to tenure and promotion.

New information and communication technologies draw out these relationships more explicitly, so that each member of an individual's network can be a more continual presence. In addition to the letters employed by 17th-century researchers and the conference interactions of the 20th century, contemporary researchers can exchange a steady stream of electronic messages with everyone in their network (Koku, Nazer, & Wellman, 2001). Home pages on the Web make a researcher's vita public and searchable. As research publications become available electronically, the researcher's persona becomes instantly and universally available. Networks of relationships become visible in the bibliographies of these online publications, and are also reified in the alias files that map network members' names to their electronic mail addresses.

In each case—family and research community—the institution defines a set of roles and relationships with their attendant rules, representations, incentives, expectations, and strategies. The individual is embedded not simply in a social network, as in Wellman's theory of networked individualism, but in a network of institutional locations. Information and communications technologies do not revolutionize these institutional facts; rather, the technologies are used in ways that clarify and amplify their logic. To some degree, as in conferencing systems and digital libraries, the institutional roles and relationships may be inscribed into the architecture of the technology. In any event, as in the use of cellular telephones, the technology is inserted into the communication practices of a relatively stable institutional field. The technologies connect the individuals, the connection patterns map the institution, and the principal basis of communication shifts increasingly from geographical locality to structural relationships (Simmel, 1955 [1922]). The various parties become continual presences for one another, but their interactions have an architecture that is defined by the institution and made explicit in the workings and usage patterns of the technology.[27] The parties are not atomized, but neither are they merged. Rather, the technology reflects and amplifies the spacing among them—the institutionally structured middle distances that define them each as distinct persons in the social order.

The relevance of this story to the political process is straightforward. Liberal political institutions are organized around the individual, and the secret ballot and voting booth shift voting from community and party to individual (Barber, 1984, pp. 187–188). Likewise, the scale, dynamism, and relatively loose integration of mass society shift the organizational basis of politics away from neighborhood hierarchies and toward the individual as a statistic. Information technologies have further transformed the individual (at least from a large political organization's point of view) into a database entry. Mass political communications retain their economies of scale, but they are increasingly integrated with political strategies on other levels. Political organizations become able to gather data on individual voters (Hunter, 2002; McLean, 1989, pp. 61–76; Mintz & O'Harrow, 2000; Wayne, 2000b), and as more attributes of each voter are stored, it becomes possible to generate scripts tailored to each voter's interests, for example, in get-out-the-vote campaigns (Stepanek, 2000) or in day-to-day tactical campaigns of telephoning voters (Jameson, Glaze, & Teal, 1999). Although such databases existed before the Internet became widespread, the Internet can distribute tactical messages much more cheaply than can fax machines (Kerber, 2000). As technology improves and information-gathering intensifies, and as political information gathered for one purpose (e.g., polling) becomes available for other purposes (e.g., fund raising), the information infrastructure of the political system is growing rapidly.

As Poster (1990) observes, database entries do not just passively describe people. On the contrary, the database is part and parcel of a discourse in Foucault's sense of the term—a complex of linguistic forms and practical arrangements that organize both the individual's own subjectivity and the institutions in which the individual participates.[28] The point is not that database entries are always accurate, or that database entries completely define the people they represent. The point is simply that the data and the person are woven together into a system, with all of the complexity, contingency, and internal tension that that implies. In this sense, political databases help to reify a particular sort of political subject.[29] The particular conception of voters that the databases embody certainly has its precedents: in marketing, the science of public opinion measurement, earlier methods of political campaigning, and the research of academic political scientists. By embodying this conception, however, the technology helps give the relationships a fixed and routinized character. Voters can now expect to receive programmed, targeted communications that address them with some precision, enclosing them in a permanent, real-time system of political surveillance and tactical campaigning.[30]

The point generalizes to the full range of institutionally organized roles and relationships that make up a complex modern polity. Large companies, for example, have long used computers to track and tactically mobilize organizational "stakeholders" who maintain relationships with particular legislators (e.g., Cox, 1984, pp. 18–19), and the Internet makes this practice cheaper and faster, encouraging its use on a larger scale. In fact, political intermediaries of all types use the Internet to indoctrinate and mobilize their constituents, for example through e-mailed newsletters. Given that the Internet has disappointed many democratic theorists by failing to create extensive "participation" by ordinary citizens, one's evaluation of the Internet's place in politics will rest largely on its role in amplifying the role of political intermediaries. The consequences of this role depend, in turn, on whose agency is emphasized. Do intermediaries use the Internet to mold their passive followers, or do citizens use the Internet to shop among intermediaries, maintaining only shallow and transient relations with any of them? The answer presumably lies between these extremes.[31] Perhaps intermediaries will even fall apart as the Internet's ubiquitous, low-cost communication mechanisms take over much of their infrastructural role. For present purposes, the point is simply that the Internet is helping to give a more explicit shape to a set of structural relationships that already existed. Citizens are developing their own private media spheres, in which they receive and exchange political messages increasingly fitted to themselves as individuals.

Considered from one perspective, this development in the category of the person is conservative. Oakeshott (1991 [1975]), for example, distinguished between two conceptions of the person as a political being: a merger of the Many into the One expressing the unifying purposes of the state, versus an individuation of personae in the social forms of civil association, each of them contracting their own relationships as they see fit. Civil association, in particular, is not a simple or natural condition of negative freedom. It is institutional; it is constituted by an authority; it must be instilled and legitimated. It does not discover distinct individuals and introduce them to one another; quite the contrary, it simultaneously produces individuals and organizes the spaces between them. This view of the person contrasts with the view that is implicit in calls for intimacy or solidarity as the basis of politics. Because Oakeshott viewed political order as flowing from the state, he believed that collapsing the boundaries among individuals would submerge their individual judgement in a collective mind that the state would control. He saw this as an invitation to tyranny, and he saw the individualism of civil association as the foundation of a conservative order.

Oakeshott's is an especially strong endorsement of spacing as a precondition of a virtuous political order. But even if associational orders flow from more diverse sources than Oakeshott allows, the larger point is clear enough. By drawing out and reifying the informational architecture of relationships, and by making all of a person's relations to others continually present, the Internet amplifies a particular type of social order. This effect, once again, is not intrinsic to the Internet; it arises through the incentives that existing institutions create to take hold of the Internet in familiar ways, along familiar lines. Nor does it follow that the Internet's impact on society is essentially conservative; the tendency toward increasingly explicit spacing among individuals is only one of the many forces that the Internet amplifies, and many of these forces conflict.

Nonetheless, the implications for the political process would also seem clear. Civil association is a system of interlocking institutions, not a shapeless meeting of unformed minds, and the Internet allows the relational order of those institutions to be inscribed in the finest details of daily life. For those who are interpellated into the political process, the relationships of political combat are increasingly pervasive, increasingly constant. It may be too strong to say, with Buchstein (1997, p. 260), that "the Internet is less applicable [to] the creation of new forms of democratic public spheres than [to] the support of already existing ones." But new political forms will emerge only by counterbalancing or transcending a regime of political integration, and a category of the political subject, that the Internet is rapidly amplifying.

Assessment

Among the many dynamics that interacts with spacing is the intensification of lateral communication that I described earlier in this section. The steady background hum of information sharing within communities of practice, though measureable on the level of Internet message traffic, will be harder to evaluate in political terms. Even so, some of the consequences are clear enough: the strengthening (to whatever degree) of interest groups that have formerly lacked an infrastructure for lateral communications, the occasions for networking and cross-fertilization (at whatever rate) across borders, and the growth (however tentative) of a global civil society. In fact, we would appear to confront a tension between two forces: a radical force arising from the increased ability of institutional stakeholder groups to organize across organizational and political boundaries, and a conservative force arising from the increased reification of existing institutional orders in the usage patterns of digital communications media.

Appearances, though, are misleading. The relationship between lateral relationships and spacing is more complicated than a crudely defined tension between stasis and change. Consider, for example, the political organizations that might arise within a given stakeholder group: consumer advocates, medical activists, union members, shareholders, industry executives, and so on. To be effective, those organizations need formal structures: decision-making mechanisms, divisions of labor, accounting systems, communications channels, and other institutional arrangements, each of which defines a repertoire of roles and relationships. A political organization that adopts

Internet tools to support these structures—whether conferencing, spreadsheets, voting mechanisms, membership databases, or other functions—will thereby reify that existing system of relationships. The Internet might help the organization to expand its membership, respond more quickly to its environment, cooperate more effectively with similar organizations in other jurisdictions, and ultimately exert greater power in the political process. The consequences for the substance of policy, and even for the qualitative organization of political institutions on a larger scale, might be significant, but these effects will come about because of spacing, not in spite it.

Of course, these developments will surely create opportunities and stresses that lead to organizational changes of other types—changes that arise through the same combination of entrepreneurship, economics, and accident that drive organizational changes in any setting. The technology might inhibit some changes through the inertia of institutionalization (Kling & Iacono, 1989), or it might promote them by providing new tools to the changes' proponents. Or it might do both. The matter will have to be assessed in each case. And that is perhaps the most important recommendation of the amplification model: the need to take each case on its own terms, analyzing the full range of interacting forces that might exert a long-term effect on the substance and process of politics.

Notes

* I presented earlier versions of the article at Santa Clara University and the University of Arizona, and I appreciate the helpful comments of the audiences at those places. I also appreciate helpful comments from Chris Hunter, Richard Nimijean, Harmeet Sawhney, and the anonymous referees.

1 For convenience I allow the meaning of "the Internet" to shift as needed across the whole universe of convergent digital technologies. The term preferred in Europe, information and communication technologies (ICTs), is more accurate, but it carries too many connotations of bureaucracy and not enough connotations of digital convergence.

2 The list of theoretical proposals that I will present is hardly complete. For broader surveys of the literature, see Arterton (1987), Axford and Huggins (2001), Dutton (1992), Harrison, Stephen, and Falvey (1999), Malina (1999), and van de Donk and Tops (1995). Neuman (1991, pp. 5–6) provides a concise bulleted list of the conventional claims about the political effects of new media. Friedland (1996) situates the early history of the community networking movement in the context of theories of civic life. Practical guides to the Internet's role in politics include Bennett and Fielding (1999), Browning (1996), Kush (2000), Maxwell (2000), Schwartz (1996), and Walch (1999). See also Alexander and Pal (1998), Barney (2000), Gibson and Ward (2000), Gutstein (1999), Kakabadse and Kakabadse (2000), Rash (1997), Selnow (1998), and Sunstein (2001). Works that have appeared as this article is going to press include Kamarck and Nye (2002), McIver and Elmagarmid (2002), Rosenau and Singh (2002), and Saco (2002).

3 See, for example, Kitchin (1998), Mitchell (1996), Toulouse and Luke (1998), and Vandenberg (2000), or the "cyberdemocratic" model advocated in Hoff,

Horrocks, and Tops (2000), which is otherwise quite sophisticated. For a historical perspective see Grosswiler (1998), and for an extensive skeptical analysis see Netanel (2000). An early speculation about the online polity is Toffler (1970, pp. 423–428).

4 On the use of the Internet by legislatures, see Coleman, Taylor, and van de Donk (1999).

5 See also Hoos (1983) and Lilienfeld (1978).

6 The problem, briefly, is that when more than two options are available, voters cannot always meaningfully rank-order them, for example because they differ along multiple dimensions. Arrow (1951) proved a set of theorems to the effect that no rational voting scheme is possible in some such situations. For further discussion and the implications for electronic referenda, see McLean (1989).

7 It should be said that Innis's own thought was more discerning and less deterministic than this implies, particularly about the ambivalent nature of economic and power relations between centers and peripheries.

8 The cartoon, by Peter Steiner, appeared on page 61 of the 5 July 1993 issue of *The New Yorker*.

9 Likewise, Fischer (1992, p. 265) resolves the question of whether the telephone increased Americans' local or long-distance relationships by concluding that it increased both, and that it intensified existing involvements rather than creating new ones. His point is not that nothing changed; he also concluded that the telephone contributed to what he calls "privatism": conducting social activities in the home rather than in public places (p. 266). On the whole, though, he concludes that "we might consider a technology, such as the telephone, not as a force impelling 'modernity,' but as a tool modern people have used to various ends, including perhaps the maintenance, even enhancement, of past practices" (p. 272).

10 In contrast to "monist" theories that emphasize a single factor in explaining the social consequences of new media technologies, Neuman (1991, pp. 15–20) argues for "balance theories" based on the search for "interaction effects" among explanatory factors on different levels of analysis. In particular, he suggests (1991, pp. 41–43, 165) that the forces of the communications revolution, which tend toward democratic pluralism, are in conflict with the forces of audience psychology and political economy of the mass media, which tend toward totalitarianism, leading to a balance at an uncertain point in the middle. Winston's (1998) argument is broadly similar.

11 Ranerup (1999) enumerates some of the "contradictions" involved in the design of a system for online deliberation, using the term to refer to the trade-offs that arise in designing an online forum that is embedded in a contradictory institutional field.

12 In the case of print culture in early modern England, by way of comparison, Zaret (2000, p. 13) observed that

> printing's relevance for the birth of the public sphere goes beyond change in the *scope* and extends to the *content* of political communication. Competition among stationers is important for explaining changes in *scope*, when a flood of cheap texts and simple prose enlarged public access to political debates and discussion. For explaining changes in the *content* of political communication, the heightened capacity of printing, relative to scribal culture, for reproducing texts is crucial for understanding how political discourse became oriented to the constitution and invocation of public opinion.

Zaret argued that this led to the "imposition of a dialogical order on conflict" (2000, p. 13). He continued:

> Printing's technical capacity to reproduce texts led to the production of broadsides and pamphlets that referred to other texts, often accompanied by partial and, less often, full reproduction of the referenced texts. Readers thus confronted political texts that responded to prior texts, simultaneously referring to, excerpting from, and commenting on them.
> (2000, pp. 13–14)

13 The comments of an anonymous referee clarified my thinking on this point.
14 A notable exception to the pattern is Arterton (1987). For Arterton, the political problem to be overcome is low levels of voter participation, especially as manifested in low voter turnout. But in reviewing early experiments with two types of technological fix for this problem, online discussion groups and electronic plebiscites, he is cautiously optimistic. He is aware of (what he calls) "the co-optation hypothesis," but holds that the experiments he studied did not prove it (1987, pp. 199–200).
More representative (though not centrally concerned with the political system) are Morrison, Svennevig, and Firmstone (1999), who counterpose the exaggerated rhetoric of a "communications revolution" to (what they call) "functional amplification." Their project is clearly frustrated by the difficulty of turning the language of "revolution" into a hypothesis that is sufficiently well-defined to test.

> We take it that the term "communications revolution" must mean one or all of the following: a radical change in social organization; a radical change in how people view the world; and/or a radical change in the way people lead their lives. Our findings do not point to a communications revolution having taken place, nor do they indicate that such a revolution is about to happen. What they do suggest is functional amplification rather than any displacement of existing communications.
> (pp. 58–59)

Their notion of functional amplification, however, draws its substance from a polemical opposition to the idea of revolution. That is why, as with much of the literature on the reinforcement model, the term "amplification" strangely loses its normal connotations of dangerous, unbounded increase, and instead suggests inertia or homeostasis: "E-mail is, in functional terms, essentially an amplification of the physical mail system. It makes life easier (or at least faster, which is not necessarily the same thing), but not radically different" (p. 59). They assert, reasonably enough, that "At this time we simply cannot say, for example, whether the substitution of e-mail for posted letters will change the relationship between individuals and to institutions at large" (p. 59). But observe how the superficial nature of the "revolutionary" hypothesis of a generalized change between individuals and institutions threatens to condemn rebuttals such as Morrison, Svennevig, and Firmstone's to a similar superficiality. Later, in rebutting the "revolutionary" hypothesis that the cellular telephone cause a more mobile society, they do say this:

> It has been the increased mobility of both business and social life that has guaranteed the mobile phone a place in contemporary life. The success of the mobile phone offers a particularly close fit between social

> factors and technological possibilities, and a good instance of the dialectical relationship of the social and the technological.
>
> (p. 72)

But they proceed to explain this dialectic purely in terms of the network effects that give rise to the familiar S-shaped technology adoption curve, and not in terms of any coevolution between the workings of the technology and the workings of the society that both produces and appropriates it.

15. The various chapters of Danziger, Dutton, Kling, and Kraemer (1982) were authored by different pairs of the authors, but for simplicity I have cited the book as a whole. On the idea of reinforcement politics see also Laudon (1974) and Pratchett (1995). Ferdinand (2000, p. 9) observes that "Existing parliaments in democracies . . . have tended to be more interested in applying the new technologies to help them become more effective, rather than adopting innovations that might undermine their traditional status and authority."

16. As this example illustrates, "forces" in the amplification model should not be confused with "interests," "coalitions," or other political groupings in studies such as Danziger, Dutton, Kling, and Kraemer (1982).

17. Hill and Hughes (1998, p. 182) and Norris (1999) have drawn similar conclusions. Graham, a conservative opponent of democracy, argues that "the Internet . . . by its very nature . . . has a tendency to promote reinforcement of interest and opinion among the like-minded" (1999, p. 83).

18. This list of phenomena is obviously drawn from experience in the United States, although the larger point probably generalizes. In earlier work with Owen (Davis & Owen, 1998), Davis gives some of these factors greater weight (for a summary see pp. 255–256) and also emphasizes the distinctive features of the new media. Still, Davis and Owen's argument is organized around the question of whether new media are significantly enhancing political participation. Their conclusion is essentially negative: "The realization of a truly democratic vision of public discourse facilitated via the new media . . . will require a large-scale societal commitment to change" (Davis & Owen, 1998, p. 257).

19. He attributes this idea to Reese *et al.* (1979). Also, note that Hagen uses the terms "ICT" (i.e., information and communication technologies) and "Internet" interchangeably. As I mentioned in note 1, this is my own practice as well. In addition, I have corrected an apparent English usage problem in the quoted passage: In place of "attributed," Hagen actually says "contributed."

20. See Carrithers, Collins, and Lukes (1985). A more precise phrasing would be: the way—no doubt complex and contradictory—that the individual is *constituted* by a society's institutions.

21. I am using the word "ubiquitous" in a nonstandard way. For Weiser (1991), ubiquitous computing is woven transparently into everyday life; I want to suggest that Weiser's concept of ubiquity can be productively developed by analyzing everyday life into the overlapping zones of activity that different institutions organize. Computing, on this analysis, is not just ubiquitous in a literal, geographic sense ("everywhere"); it is also ubiquitous in a structural sense ("everything").

22. The term "communities of practice" is due to Lave and Wenger (1991). For a systematic analysis see Wenger (1998). Organizational theorists have long emphasized the theme of lateral communication; it is often attributed to Fayol (1949 [1916]), who despite his prevailing rationalism and conservatism argued that strict hierarchical control was insufficient and advocated a "gang-plank" system whereby subordinates on a given organizational level have structured

opportunities to interact. Only with more recent work, however, have these lateral relations been interpreted as spontaneous organisms with complex physiologies. The notion that Internet discussion groups constitute what Rheingold (1993, p. 110) called "grassroots groupminds" has been part of the culture of the medium from its earliest days.

23 An especially striking example of this phenomenon is worth quoting at length:

> The most informal and passive level of transnational judicial interaction is the cross-fertilization of ideas through increased knowledge of both foreign and international judicial decisions and a corresponding willingness actually to cite those decisions as persuasive authority. The Israeli Supreme Court, the German Constitutional Court, and the Canadian Supreme Court have long researched US Supreme Court precedents in preparing their own conclusions on constitutional issues such as freedom of speech, privacy rights or fair process. Young constitutional courts in Eastern and Central Europe and the former Soviet Union are now eagerly following suit. The paradigm case in this regard is a recent decision by the South African Supreme Court. In finding the death penalty unconstitutional under the South African Constitution, the Court cited decisions from national and supranational courts all over the world, including Hungary, India, Tanzania, Canada, Germany, and the European Court of Human Rights.
> (Slaughter, 2000, pp. 204–205, footnote omitted)

On the general phenomenon of governance networks, see also Marin and Mayntz (1991) and Riles (2000).

24 On evolutionary theories of institutional change, see Hodgson (1993, 1999).
25 See also Bellamy (2000, pp. 49–50). Fischer (1992, p. 268) observes that the telephone "expanded a dimension of social life, the realm of frequent checking-in, rapid updates, easy scheduling of appointments, and quick exchanges of casual confidences, as well as the sphere of long-distance conversation."
26 I have codified a great deal of this practical networking knowledge in a how-to article for doctoral students entitled "Networking on the Network" that is available on the Web at http://dlis.gseis.ucla.edu/people/pagre/network.html.
27 Akrich (1992) makes a similar point in describing how social roles are inscribed into the workings of designed artefacts.
28 In fact, Poster says that the database is itself a discourse, but it is more accurate to say that the database is one of the constituents of the larger discourse that binds numerous parties together into a polity.
29 The Foucauldian analysis of the liberal subject has been developed in a large literature; see for example Barry, Osborne, and Rose (1996). My purpose here, however, is not to evaluate this literature, which in my view fails to provide an adequate account of political agency or of institutions generally, but simply to draw on certain elements of Poster's Foucauldian analysis of databases.
30 On origins the "permanent campaign" and the profession that administers it, see Blumenthal (1980). For an update, see Johnson (2001).
31 For a brief discussion, see Horrocks, Hoff, and Topps (2000).

References

Agre, Philip E. 1995. Institutional circuitry: Thinking about the forms and uses of information. *Information Technology and Libraries* 14(4):225–230.

Agre, Philip E. 1998a. Yesterday's tomorrow. *Times Literary Supplement* 3 July: 3–4.
Agre, Philip E. 1998b. Designing genres for new media. In *Cyber Society 2.0: Revisiting CMC and community*, ed. S. G. Jones, pp. 69–99. Newbury Park, CA: Sage.
Agre, Philip E. 2002. Cyberspace as American culture. *Science as Culture* 11(2): 171–189.
Agre, Philip E., and Schuler, Douglas, eds. 1997. *Reinventing technology, rediscovering community: Critical explorations of computing as a social practice.* Greenwich, CT: Ablex.
Agre, Philip E., and Rotenberg, Marc, eds. 1997. *Technology and privacy: The new landscape.* Cambridge, MA: MIT Press.
Akrich, Madeleine. 1992. Beyond social construction of technology: The shaping of people and things in the innovation process. In *New technology at the outset: Social forces in the shaping of technological innovations*, eds. M. Dierkes and Ute Hoffman, pp. 173–190. Frankfurt: Campus.
Alexander, Cynthia J., and Pal, Leslie A., eds. 1998. *Digital democracy: Policy and politics in the wired world.* Toronto: Oxford University Press.
Alexander, Kim. 2001. Ten things I want people to know about voting technology. Paper presented at Computerized Voting: A New Solution for a New Generation of Voters, January. <http://democracyonline.org/taskforce/conferences/debate/alexander.pdf>
Arrow, Kenneth. 1951. *Social choice and individual values.* New York: Wiley.
Arterton, F. Christopher. 1987. *Teledemocracy. Can technology protect democracy?* Newbury Park, CA: Sage.
Avgerou, Chrisanthi. 2002. *Information systems and global diversity.* Oxford: Oxford University Press.
Axford, Barrie, and Huggins, Richard, eds. 2001. *New media and politics.* London: Sage.
Barber, Benjamin R. 1984. *Strong democracy: Participatory politics for a new age.* Berkeley: University of California Press.
Barney, Darin. 2000. *Prometheus wired: The hope for democracy in the age of network technology.* Chicago: University of Chicago Press.
Barry, Andrew, Osborne, Thomas, and Rose, Nikolas, eds. 1996. *Foucault and political reason: Liberalism, neo-liberalism, and rationalities of government.* Chicago: University of Chicago Press.
Baym, Nancy K. 1998. The emergence of on-line community. In *CyberSociety 2.0: Revisiting CMC and community*, ed. S. G. Jones, pp. 35–68. Newbury Park, CA: Sage.
Becker, Barbara, and Wehner, Josef. 2001. Electronic networks and civil society: Reflections on structural changes in the public sphere. In *Culture, technology, communication: Towards an intercultural global village*, ed. C. Ess, pp. 67–85. Albany: State University of New York Press.
Becker, Ted, and Phillips, Deborah M. 2001. Symposium. *Insight on the News* 17(24):40.
Becker, Ted, and Slaton, Christa Daryl. 2000. *The future of teledemocracy.* Westport, CT: Praeger.
Bellamy, Christine. 2000. Modelling electronic democracy: Towards democratic discourses for an information age. In *Democratic governance and new technology:*

Technologically mediated innovations in political practice in Western Europe, eds. J. Hoff, I. Horrocks, and P. Tops, pp. 33–53. London: Routledge.

Beniger, James R. 1986. *The control revolution: Technological and economic origins of the information society*. Cambridge, MA: Harvard University Press.

Bennett, Colin J. 1997. Convergence revisited: Toward a global policy for the protection of personal data? In *Technology and privacy: The new landscape*, eds. P. E. Agre and M. Rotenberg, pp. 99–123. Cambridge, MA: MIT Press.

Bennett, Daniel, and Fielding, Pam. 1999. *The Net effect: How cyberadvocacy is changing the political landscape*. Washington, DC: Capitol Advantage.

Bimber, Bruce. 1999. The Internet and citizen communication with government: Does the medium matter? *Political Communication* 16(4):409–428.

Bimber, Bruce. 2000. The study of information technology and civic engagement, *Political Communication* 17(4):329–333.

Blumenthal, Sidney. 1980. *The permanent campaign: Inside the world of elite political operatives*. Boston: Beacon Press.

Bolter, Jay David, and Grusin, Richard. 1998. *Remediation: Understanding new media*. Cambridge, MA: MIT Press.

Bovill, Moira, and Livingstone, Sonia. 2001. Bedroom culture and the privatization of media use. In *Children and their changing media environment: A European comparative study*, eds. S. Livingstone and M. Bovill, pp. 179–200. Mahwah, NJ: Lawrence Erlbaum Associates.

Brants, Kees, Huizenga, Martine, and van Meerten, Reineke. 1996. The new canals of Amsterdam: An exercise in local electronic democracy. *Media, Culture and Society* 18(2):233–247.

Brown, John Seely. 1994. Paul Duguid, and Susan Haviland, Toward informed participation: Six scenarios in search of democracy in the information age. *Aspen Institute Quarterly* 6(4):49–73.

Browning, Graeme. 1996. *Electronic democracy: Using the Internet to influence American politics*, ed. D. J. Weitzner. Wilton, CT: Pemberton Press.

Brownstein, Ronald. 2002. Close house races go the way of rotary phones, Newt Gingrich. *Los Angeles Times* 15 April:A13.

Buchstein, Hubertus. 1997. Bytes that bite: The Internet and deliberative democracy. *Constellations* 4(2):248–263.

Bud-Frierman, Lisa, ed. 1994. *Information acumen: The understanding and use of knowledge in modern business*. London: Routledge.

Budge, Ian. 1996. *The new challenge of direct democracy*. Cambridge: Polity Press.

Burkhalter, Byron. 1999. Reading race online: Discovering racial identity in Usenet discussions. In *Communities in cyberspace*, eds. M. A. Smith and P. Kollock, pp. 60–75. London: Routledge.

Cairncross, Frances. 1997. *The death of distance: How the communications revolution will change our lives*. Boston: Harvard Business School Press.

Calhoun, Craig. 1992. The infrastructure of modernity: Indirect social relationships, information technology, and social integration. In *Social change and modernity*, eds. H. Haferkamp and N. J. Smelser, pp. 205–236. Berkeley: University of California Press.

Calhoun, Craig. 1998. Community without propinquity revisited: Communications technology and the transformation of the urban public sphere. *Sociological Inquiry* 68(3):373–397.

Carrier, James G., and Miller, Daniel, eds. 1998. *Virtualism: A new political economy.* Oxford: Berg.

Carrithers, Michael, Collins, Steven, and Lukes, Steven, eds. 1985. *The category of the person: Anthropology, philosophy, history.* Cambridge: Cambridge University Press.

Casson, Mark. 1997. *Information and organization: A new perspective on the theory of the firm.* New York: Clarendon Press.

Clark, Sherman J. 1998. A populist critique of direct democracy. *Harvard Law Review* 112(2):434–482.

Coleman, Stephen. 1999. Cutting out the middle man: From virtual representation to direct democracy. In *Digital democracy: Discourse and decision making in the information age*, eds. B. N. Hague and B. Loader, pp. 195–210. London: Routledge.

Coleman, Stephen, Taylor, John, and van de Donk, Wim, eds. 1999. *Parliament in the age of the Internet.* Oxford: Oxford University Press.

Commons, John R. 1970. *The economics of collective action.* Madison: University of Wisconsin Press. Originally published in 1950.

Cox, William R. 1984. Government relations. In *Experts in action: Inside public relations*, ed. B. Cantor, pp. 7–30. New York: Longman.

Danziger, James N. Dutton, William H., Kling, Rob, and Kraemer, Kenneth L. 1982. *Computers and politics: High technology in American local governments.* New York: Columbia University Press.

Davis, Richard, and Owen, Diana. 1998. *New media and American politics.* New York: Oxford University Press.

Davis, Richard. 1999. *The web of politics: The Internet's impact on the American political system.* Oxford: Oxford University Press.

Dean, Jodi. 2001. Cybersalons and civil society: Rethinking the public sphere in transnational technoculture. *Public Culture* 13(2):243–265.

Docter, Sharon, and Dutton, William H. 1998. The First Amendment online: Santa Monica's public electronic network. In *Cyberdemocracy: Technology, cities and civic networks*, eds. R. Tsagarousianou, D. Tambini, and C. Bryan, pp. 125–151. London: Routledge.

Donath, Judith S. 1999. Identity and deception in the virtual community. In *Communities in cyberspace*, eds. M. A. Smith and P. Kollock, pp. 29–59. London: Routledge.

Ducatel, Ken, Webster, Juliet, and Herrmann, Werner, eds. 2000. *The information society in Europe: Work and life in an age of globalization.* Lanham, MD: Rowman and Littlefield.

Dutton, William H. 1992. Political science research on teledemocracy. *Social Science Computer Review* 10(4):55–61.

Dutton, William H. 1999. *Society on the line: Information politics in the digital age.* Oxford: Oxford University Press.

The Economist. 2002. How to rig an election. *The Economist.* 25 April: 47–48. <http://www.economist.com/world/na/displaystory.cfm?story_id=1099030>

English-Lueck, Jan A. 1998. Technology and social change: The effects on family and community, COSSA Congressional Seminar, June. <http://www.sjsu.edu/depts/anthropology/svcp/SVCPcosa.html>

Ess, Charles. 1996. The political computer: Democracy, CMC, and Habermas. In *Philosophical perspectives on computer-mediated communication*, ed. C. Ess, pp. 197–230. Albany: State University of New York Press.

Fayol, Henri. 1949. *General and industrial management*, trans. C. Storrs. London: Pitman. Originally published in French in 1916.

Ferdinand, Peter, ed. 2000. *The Internet, democracy and democratization*. London: Cass.

Fischer, Claude S. 1992. *America calling: A social history of the telephone to 1940*. Berkeley: University of California Press.

Frederick, Howard. 1993. Computer networks and the emergence of global civil society. In *Global networks: Computers and international communication*, ed. L. M. Harasim, pp. 283–295. Cambridge: MIT Press.

Freiberger, Paul, and Swaine, Michael. 1984. *Fire in the valley: The making of the personal Computer*. Berkeley, CA: Osborne/McGraw-Hill.

Friedland, Lewis A. 1996. Electronic democracy and the new citizenship. *Media, Culture and Society* 18(2): 185–212.

Friedman, Thomas L. 1999. *The Lexus and the olive tree*. New York: Farrar, Straus, Giroux.

Frissen, Paul. 1997. The virtual state: Postmodernisation, informatisation and public administration. In *The governance of cyberspace: Politics, technology and global restructuring*, ed. B. D. Loader, pp. 111–125. London: Routledge.

Galston, William A. 1999. (How) does the Internet affect community? Some speculation in search of evidence. In *Democracy.com? Governance in a networked world*, eds. E. C. Kamarck and J. S. Nye, Jr., pp. 45–59. Hollis, NH: Hollis.

Gandy, Jr., Oscar H. 1993. *The panoptic sort: A political economy of personal information*. Boulder: Westview Press.

Gibson, Rachel, and Ward, Stephen, eds. 2000. *Reinvigorating democracy? UK politics and the Internet*. Aldershot, UK: Ashgate.

Giddens, Anthony. 1985. *The nation-state and violence*. Berkeley: University of California Press.

Giddens, Anthony. 1990. *The consequences of modernity*. Stanford, CA: Stanford University Press.

Gilder, George. 1992. *Life after television*. New York: Norton.

Gillespie, Andrew, and Robins, Kevin. 1989. Geographical inequalities: The spatial bias of the new communications technologies. *Journal of Communication* 39(3): 7–18.

Goodin, Robert E., ed. 1996. *The theory of institutional design*. Cambridge: Cambridge University Press.

Goody, Jack. 1986. *The logic of writing and the organization of society*. Cambridge: Cambridge University Press.

Graddol, David, and Swann, Joan. 1989. *Gender voices*. Oxford: Blackwell.

Graham, Gordon. 1999. *The Internet: A philosophicalinquiry*. London: Routledge.

Greider, William. 1992. *Who will tell the people? The betrayal of American democracy*. New York: Simon and Schuster.

Grossman, Lawrence K. 1995. *The electronic republic: Reshaping democracy in the information age*. New York: Viking.

Grossman, Wendy M. 2001. No e(asy) cure: Electronic voting won't fix butterfly ballots, dimpled chads or W.'s presidency. *Scientific American* 284(2):36.

Grosswiler, Paul. 1998. Historical hopes, media fears, and the electronic town meeting concept: Where technology meets democracy or demagogy? *Journal of Communication Inquiry* 22(2):133–151.

Gutstein, Donald. 1999. *E.con: How the Internet undermines democracy.* Toronto: Stoddart.
Hagen, Martin. 2001. Digital democracy and political systems. In *Digital democracy: Issues of theory and practice*, eds. K. L. Hacker and J. van Dijk, pp. 54–69. London: Sage.
Harrison, Teresa M. Stephen, Timothy, and Falvey, Lisa. 1999. Democracy and new communication technologies. Paper presented at the Annual Conference of the International Communication Association, San Francisco. <http://www.llc.rpi.edu/research_details2.cfm?Research_ID=13>
Herring, Susan C. 1993. Gender and democracy in computer-mediated communication. *Electronic Journal of Communication* 3(2).
Hewson, Martin. 1999. Did global governance create informational globalism? In *Approaches to global governance theory*, eds. M. Hewson and T. J. Sinclair, pp. 97–115. Albany: State University of New York Press.
Hill, Kevin A., and Hughes, John E. 1998. *Cyberpolitics: Citizen activism in the age of the Internet.* Lanham, MD: Rowman and Littlefield.
Hodgson, Geoffrey M. 1993. *Economics and evolution: Bringing life back into economics.* Cambridge: Polity Press.
Hodgson, Geoffrey M. 1999. *Evolution and institutions: On evolutionary economics and the evolution of economics.* Cheltenham, UK: Elgar.
Hoff, Jens, Horrocks, Ivan, and Tops, Pieter, eds. 2000. *Democratic governance and new technology: Technologically mediated innovations in political practice in Western Europe.* London: Routledge.
Hollander, Richard S. 1985. *Video democracy: The vote-from-home revolution.* Mt. Airy, MD: Lomond.
Hoos, Ida R. 1983. *Systems analysis in public policy: A critique*, rev. ed. Berkeley: University of California Press.
Horrocks, Ivan, Hoff, Jens, and Tops, Pieter. 2000. Reflections on the models of democracy: Cyberdemocracy? In *Democratic governance and new technology: Technologically mediated innovations in political practice in Western Europe*, eds. J. Hoff, I. Horrocks, and P. Tops, pp. 185–187. London: Routledge.
Hunter, Christopher D. 2002. Political privacy and online politics: How e-campaigning threatens voter privacy. *First Monday* 7(2). <http://www.firstmonday.org/issues/issue7_2/hunter/>
Innis, Harold. 1951. *The bias of communication.* Toronto: University of Toronto Press.
Jameson, John, Glaze, Chris, and Teal, Gary. 1999. Effective phone contact programs and the importance of good data. *Campaigns and Elections* 20(6):64–69.
Johnson, Dennis W. 2001. *No place for amateurs: How political consultants are reshaping American democracy.* New York: Routledge.
Jones, Steven G. 1995. Understanding community in the information age. In *CyberSociety: Computer-mediated communication and community*, ed. S. G. Jones, pp. 10–35. Thousand Oaks, CA: Sage.
Kakabadse, Nada K., and Kakabadse, Andrew K. 2000. *Creating futures: Leading change through information systems.* Aldershot, UK: Ashgate.
Kaldor, Mary. 1999. Transnational civil society. In *Human rights in global politics*, eds. T. Dunne and N. J. Wheeler, pp. 195–213. Cambridge: Cambridge University Press.

Kamarck, Elaine Ciulla, and Nye, Jr., Joseph S., eds. 2002. *Governance.com: Democracy in the information age.* Washington, DC: Brookings Institution Press.

Kitchin, Rob. 1998. *Cyberspace: The world in the wires.* Chichester, UK: Wiley.

Kling, Rob, and Iacono, Suzanne. 1989. The institutional character of computerized information systems. *Office: Technology and People* 5(1):7–28.

Kling, Rob. 1997. Reading "all about" computerization: How genre conventions shape nonfiction social analysis. In *Reinventing technology, rediscovering community: Critical explorations of computing as a social practice*, eds. P. E. Agre and D. Schuler, pp. 19–46. Greenwich, CT: Ablex.

Knight, Jack. 1992. *Institutions and social conflict.* Cambridge: Cambridge University Press.

Koku, Emmanuel, Nazer, Nancy, and Wellman, Barry. 2001. Netting scholars: Online and offline. *American Behavioral Scientist* 44(10):1752–1774.

Krugman, Paul. 1991. *Geography and trade.* Cambridge, MA: MIT Press.

Kush, Christopher. 2000. *Cybercitizen: How to use your computer to fight for all the issues you care about.* New York: St. Martin's Press.

Laudon, Kenneth C. 1974. *Computers and bureaucratic reform: The political functions of urban information systems.* New York: Wiley.

Laudon, Kenneth C. 1977. *Communications technology and democratic participation.* New York: Praeger.

Laudon, Kenneth C. 1985. Environmental and institutional models of system development: A national criminal history system. *Communications of the ACM* 28(7):728–740.

Laumann, Edward O., and Knoke, David. 1989. Policy networks of the organizational state: Collective action in the national energy and health domains. In *Networks of power: Organizational actors at the national, corporate, and community levels*, eds. R. Perrucci and H. R. Potter, pp. 17–55. New York: Aldine de Gruyter.

Lave, Jean, and Wenger, Etienne. 1991. *Situated learning: Legitimate peripheral participation.* Cambridge: Cambridge University Press.

Lewis, Martin. 2000. This may be a pre-mortem of the 2000 campaign. Time.com 3 November. <http://www.time.com/time/nation/article/0,8599,59665,00.html>

Lieberman, Trudy. 1994. Churning Whitewater. *Columbia Journalism Review* 33(1): 26–30.

Lievrouw, Leah A. 2001. New media and the "pluralization of life-worlds": A role for information in social differentiation. *New Media and Society* 3(1):7–28.

Lilienfeld, Robert. 1978. *The rise of systems theory: An ideological analysis.* New York: Wiley.

Lyon, David. 2001. *Surveillance society: Monitoring everyday life.* Buckingham, UK: Open University.

Malina, Anna. 1999. Perspectives on citizen democratisation and alienation in the virtual public sphere. In *Digital democracy: Discourse and decision making in the Information Age*, eds. B. N. Hague and B. Loader, pp. 23–38. London: Routledge.

Mansell, Robin, and Steinmueller, W. Edward. 2000. *Mobilizing the information society: Strategies for growth and opportunity.* Oxford: Oxford University Press.

March, James G., and Olsen, Johan P. 1989. *Rediscovering institutions: The organizational basis of politics.* New York: Free Press.

Marin, Bernd, and Mayntz, Renate, eds. 1991. *Policy networks: Empirical evidence and theoretical considerations.* Frankfurt: Campus.

Maxwell, Bruce. 2000. *How to track politics on the Internet.* Washington, DC: Congressional Quarterly Press.

McIver, Jr., William J., and Elmagarmid, Ahmed K., eds. 2002. *Advances in digital government: Technology, human factors, and policy.* Boston: Kluwer.

McLean, Iain. 1989. *Democracy and new technology.* Cambridge: Polity Press.

Melody, William H. 1985. The information society: Implications for economic institutions and market theory. *Journal of Economic Issues* 19(2):523–539.

Miller, Daniel, and Slater, Don. 2000. *The Internet: An ethnographic approach.* New York: New York University Press.

Mintz, John, and O'Harrow, Robert. 2000. Software digs deep into lives of voters. *Washington Post.* 10 October:A1.

Mitchell, William J. 1995. *City of bits: Space, place, and the Infobahn.* Cambridge, MA: MIT Press.

Mitchell, William J. 2000. Designing the digital city. In *Digital cities: Technologies, experiences, and future perspectives*, eds. T. Ishida and K. Isbister, pp. 1–6. Berlin: Springer.

Mohen, Joe, and Glidden, Julia. 2001. The case for Internet voting. *Communications of the ACM* 44(1):72, 74–85.

Morrison, David, Svennevig, Michael, and Firmstone, Julie. 1999. The social consequences of communications technologies in the United Kingdom. In *The communications revolution at work: The social, economic and political impacts of technological change*, ed. Robert Boyce, pp. 57–82. Montreal: McGill-Queen's University Press.

Motluk, Alison. 1997. Click on the candidate. *New Scientist*, 26 April:26–27.

Netanel, Neil. 2000. Cyberspace self-governance: A skeptical view from democratic theory. *California Law Review* 88(2):395–498.

Neuman, W. Russell. 1991. *The future of the mass audience.* Cambridge: Cambridge University Press.

Norris, Pippa. 1999. Who surfs? New technology, old voters and virtual democracy. In *Democracy.com? Governance in a networked world*, eds. E. C. Kamarck and J. S. Nye, Jr., pp. 71–94. Hollis, NH: Hollis.

Norris, Pippa. 2001. *Digital divide: Civic engagement, information poverty, and the Internet worldwide.* Cambridge: Cambridge University Press.

North, Douglass C. 1990. *Institutions, institutional change, and economic performance.* Cambridge: Cambridge University Press.

Oakeshott, Michael. 1975. Talking politics. *National Review* 5 December:1345–1347, 1423–1428. Reprinted (1991) in *Rationalism in politics and other essays*, 2nd ed., pp. 438–461. Indianapolis: Liberty Fund.

Orlikowski, Wanda J. 1993. Learning from Notes: Organizational issues in groupware implementation. *The Information Society* 9(3):237–250.

Orlikowski, Wanda J. 2000. Using technology and constituting structures: A practice lens for studying technology in organizations, *Organization Science* 11(4):404–428.

Orlikowski, Wanda J. 2001. Improvising organizational transformation over time: A situated change perspective. In *Information technology and organizational transformation: History, rhetoric, and practice*, eds. J. Yates and J. Van Maanen, pp. 223–274. Thousand Oaks, CA: Sage.

Philips, Deborah M., and von Spakovsky, Hans A. 2001. Gauging the risks of Internet elections. *Communications of the ACM* 44(1):73–85.

Polanyi, Karl. 1944. *The great transformation.* Boston: Beacon Press.
Polanyi, Karl. 1957. Aristotle discovers the economy. In *Trade and market in the early empires: Economies in history and theory,* eds. K. Polanyi, C. M. Arensberg, and H. W. Pearson, pp. 64–96. Glencoe, IL: Free Press.
Poster, Mark. 1990. Foucault and databases: Participatory surveillance. In *The mode of information: Post structuralism and social context,* pp. 69–98. Cambridge: Polity Press.
Poster, Mark. 1997. Cyberdemocracy: Internet and the public sphere. In *Internet culture,* ed. D. Porter, pp. 201–217. London: Routledge.
Powell, Walter W., and DiMaggio, Paul J., eds. 1991. *The new institutionalism in organizational analysis.* Chicago: University of Chicago Press.
Pratchett, Lawrence. 1995. Democracy denied: The political consequences of ICTs in UK local government. In *Orwell in Athens: A perspective on informatization and democracy,* eds. W. B. H. J. van de Donk, I. T. M. Snellen, and P. W. Tops, pp. 127–142. Amsterdam: IOS Press.
Ranerup, Agneta. 1999. Internet-enabled applications for local government democratisation: Contradictions of the Swedish experience. In *Reinventing government in the information age: International practice in IT-enabled public sector reform,* ed. Richard Heeks, pp. 177–193. London: Routledge.
Ranerup, Agneta. 2001. Online forums as a tool for people-centered governance. In *Community informatics: Shaping computer-mediated socialnetworks,* eds. L. Keeble and B. Loader, pp. 205–219. London: Routledge.
Rash, Wayne, Jr. 1997. *Politics on the Nets: Wiring the political process.* San Francisco: Freeman.
Reese, Jurgen, Kubicek, Herbert, Lange, Bernd P., Lutterbeck, Bernd, and Reese, Uwe. 1979. *Gefahren der Informations technologischen Entwicklung.* Frankfurt: Campus.
Reid, Elizabeth. 1999. Hierarchy and power: Social control in cyberspace. In *Communities in cyberspace,* eds. M. A. Smith and P. Kollock, pp. 107–133. London: Routledge.
Rheingold, Howard. 1993. *The virtual community: Homesteading on the electronic frontier.* Reading, MA: Addison-Wesley.
Rhoades, Gary. 2000. The changing role of faculty. In *Higher education in transition: The challenges of the new millennium,* eds. J. Losco and B. L. Fife, pp. 29–49. Westport, CT: Bergin and Garvey.
Ricci, David M. 1993. *The transformation of American politics: The new Washington and the rise of think tanks.* New Haven, CT: Yale University Press.
Riles, Annelise. 2000. *The network inside out.* Ann Arbor: University of Michigan Press.
Saco, Diana. 2002. *Cybering democracy: Public space and the Internet.* Minneapolis: University of Minnesota Press.
Sarkar, Mitra Barun, Butler, Brian, and Steinfield, Charles. 1995. Intermediaries and cybermediaries: A continuing role for mediating players in the electronic marketplace. *Journal of Computer-Mediated Communication* 1(3).
Sassen, Saskia. 1991. *The global city: New York, London, Tokyo.* Princeton, NJ: Princeton University Press.
Sassi, Sinikka. 2001. The controversies of the Internet and the revitalization of local political life. In *Digital democracy: Issues of theory and practice,* eds. K. L. Hacker and J. van Dijk, pp. 90–104. London: Sage.

Schiano, Diane J. 1999. Lessons from LambdaMOO: A social, text-based virtual environment, *Presence* 8(2):127–139.

Schwartz, Edward. 1996. *Netactivism: How citizens use the Internet.* Sebastopol, CA: Songline Studios.

Sclove, Richard E. 1995. *Democracy and technology.* New York: Guilford Press.

Scott, James C., 1998. *Seeing like a state: How certain schemes to improve the human condition have failed.* New Haven, CT: Yale University Press.

Selnow, Gary W. 1998. *Electronic whistle-stops: The impact of the Internet on American politics.* Westport, CT: Praeger.

Shain, Barry. 1996. *The myth of American individualism.* Princeton, NJ: Princeton University Press.

Simmel, Georg. 1955. *The web of group-affiliations*, trans. Reinhard Bendix. Glencoe, IL: Free Press. Originally Published in 1922.

Skocpol, Theda, and Fiorina, Morris P., eds. 1999. *Civic engagement in American democracy.* Washington, DC: Brookings Institution Press.

Slaton, Christa Daryl. 1992. *Televote: Expanding citizen participation in the quantum age.* New York: Praeger.

Slaughter, Anne-Marie. 2000. Government networks: The heart of the liberal democratic order. In *Democratic governance and international law*, eds. G. H. Fox and B. R. Roth, pp. 199–235. Cambridge: Cambridge University Press.

Slevin, James. 2000. *Internet and society.* Cambridge, UK: Polity Press.

Smith, James Allen. 1991. *The idea brokers: Think tanks and the rise of the new policy elite.* New York: Free Press.

Stepanek, Marcia. 2000. How the data-miners want to influence your vote. *Business Week Online* 26 October. <http://www.businessweek.com/bwdaily/dnflash/oct2000/nf20001026_969.htm>

Stromer-Galley, Jennifer. 2000. Democratizing democracy: Strong democracy, US political campaigns and the Internet. In *The Internet, democracy and democratization*, ed. P. Ferdinand, pp. 36–58. London: Cass.

Sunstein, Cass R. 2001. *Republic.com.* Princeton, NJ: Princeton University Press.

Toffler, Alvin. 1970. *Future shock.* New York: Random House.

Toffler, Alvin, and Toffler, Heidi. 1995. *Creating a new civilization: The politics of the third wave.* Atlanta, GA: Turner.

Tomita, Tetsuro. 1980. The new electronic media and their place in the information market. In *Newspapers and democracy: International essays on a changing medium*, ed. A. Smith, pp. 49–62. Cambridge, MA: MIT Press.

Toulouse, Chris, and Luke, Timothy W., eds. 1998. *The politics of cyberspace.* London: Routledge.

Valenty, Linda O., and Brent, James C. 2000. Online voting: Calculating risks and benefits to the community and the individual. In *The Internet upheaval: Raising questions, seeking answers in communications policy*, eds. I. Vogelsang and B. M. Compaine, pp. 99–126. Cambridge, MA: MIT Press.

van de Donk, Wim B. H. J., and Tops, Pieter W. 1995. Orwell or Athens? Informatization and the future of democracy: A review of the literature. In *Orwell in Athens: A perspective on informatization and democracy*, eds. W. B. H. J. van de Donk, I. T. M. Snellen, and P. W. Tops, pp. 13–32. Amsterdam: IOS Press.

Vandenberg, Andrew. 2000. Cybercitizenship and digital democracy. In *Citizenship and democracy in a global era*, ed. A. Vandenberg, pp. 289–306. New York: St. Martin's Press.

van Dijk, Jan. 1999. *The network society: Social aspects of new media*, trans. Leontine Spooreberg. London: Sage.

van Dijk, Jan. 2001. Models of democracy and concepts of communication. In *Digital democracy: Issues of theory and practice*, eds. K. L. Hacker and J. van Dijk, pp. 1–47. London: Sage.

Walch, Jim. 1999. *In the Net: An Internet guide for activists*. London: Zed.

Walker, Clive, and Akdeniz, Yaman. 1998. Virtual democracy. *Public Law* Autumn:489–506.

Wayne, Leslie. 2000a. E-mail part of the effort to turn out the voters. *New York Times* 6 November:C6.

Wayne, Leslie. 2000b. Voter profiles selling briskly as privacy issues are raised. *New York Times* 9 September:A1.

Weber, Thomas E. 2001. "Scalable" ballot fraud: Why one tech maven fears computer voting. *Wall Street Journal* 19 March:B1.

Weiser, Mark. 1991. The computer for the 21st century. *Scientific American* 265(3): 94–104.

Wellman, Barry. 1999. The network community: An introduction. In *Networks in the global village: Life in contemporary communities*, ed. Barry Wellman, pp. 1–47. Boulder, CO: Westview.

Wellman, Barry. 2001. Physical place and cyberplace: The rise of personalized networking. *International Journal of Urban and Regional Research* 25(2):227–252.

Wenger, Etienne. 1998. *Communities of practice: Learning, meaning, and identity*. Cambridge: Cambridge University Press.

Wilhelm, Anthony G. 1999. Virtual sounding boards: How deliberative is online political discussion? In *Digital democracy: Discourse and decision making in the information age*, eds. B. N. Hague and B. Loader, pp. 154–178. London: Routledge.

Winston, Brian. 1998. *Media technology and society: A history from the telegraph to the Internet*. London: Routledge.

Wriston, Walter B. 1992. *The twilight of sovereignty: How the information revolution is transforming our world*. New York: Scribner.

Wriston, Walter B. 1999. Dumb networks and smart capital. *Cato Journal* 17(3):333–344. <http://www.cato.org/pubs/journal/cj17n3-12.html>

Wynn, Eleanor, and Katz, James E. 1997. Hyperbole over cyberspace: Self-presentation and social boundaries in Internet home pages and discourse. *The Information Society* 13(4):297–327.

Zhang, Kewen, and Xiaoming, Hao. 1999. The Internet and ethnic press: A study of electronic Chinese publications, *The Information Society* 15(1):21–30.

55

POLITICAL AUTHORITY IN A MEDIATED AGE

Susan Herbst

Source: *Theory and Society* 32(4) (2003): 481–503.

Abstract

The nature and impact of authority have been central to social theory since antiquity, and most students of politics, culture and organizations have – in one manner or another – visited the topic. Theorists recognize that the exercise of authority is conditioned by the environment, but their work has not always integrated fundamental changes in communication infrastructure, and in particular the diffusion of mass media. With the daily evolution of telecommunications, this is a good historical moment to reevaluate the notion of authority. My goal is to assess ways to both preserve extraordinarily useful categories from the past, and at the same time, make those typologies more sensitive to contemporary mediated communication. Here I synthesize American research on media and political communication with recent theoretical approaches to authority, expanding current views of coercion and submission.

Whether authority is of personal or institutional origin it is created and maintained by public opinion, which in its turn is conditioned by sentiment, affection, reverence or fatalism.... For submission to authority may result either from a deliberate recognition of it as a good or from an acquiescence in it as inevitable, to be endured permanently or temporarily with skepticism, indifference or scorn, with fists clenched but in the pockets.

Roberto Michels, 1930

One of the most interesting phenomena of our time is the way news and entertainment media seem able to imbue particular individuals and institutions with apparent great import and authority. Examples abound: Newt Gingrich, in his early days as Speaker of the U.S. House of Representatives, appeared to have more authority than Dennis Hastert did, authors who appear frequently in the media seem to have more clout than those who are reclusive, and the same holds true for our clergy, some of whom seek the media spotlight and undoubtedly gain great recognition and influence as a result. We recognize that these public figures hold differential status positions in the public sphere, and that media have much to do with the creation of this hierarchy. But until this point, scholars of American politics and social life have yet to theorize rigorously, study or try to understand this murky but pervasive process. My goal in this article is to do just that, integrating political theory and the study of communication in order to advance our knowledge of this unexpected and powerful result of media penetration.

For centuries political scientists, sociologists, anthropologists, philosophers, literary critics and many others have struggled with the nature of political authority: what it is and why it matters. The literature is voluminous, covering nearly all the ground one might have hoped for during previous eras, with focused attention to the concerns of those eras. There are well-known writings on authority from antiquity, the Renaissance, the Enlightenment, and other periods, with a proliferation of interest in the United States during the mid- to late twentieth century.[1] This recent acceleration of interest in authority was due in part to the maturation of disciplines, political science and sociology in particular. But interest likely peaked with the rise of authoritarian governments, reflections on the horrors of the world wars, and American angst about governance, dissent, urbanization, and cultural change.[2] These debates were and are productive ones, underscoring the troubling gray areas one invariably finds in attempts to understand social control. There is a sense throughout the literature that authority is the mortar that holds the moving parts of a society together, and so it is no wonder that it has been a preoccupation of many insightful students of politics and social life.

Despite the sustained attention that the exercise of authority has received, there are some significant gaps in the literature and aspects of the concept that need radical reassessment, if the notion is to be useful as a guide to theorizing and empirical research in our own times. For example, much of the twentieth century literature, while it often makes vague gestures to the concerns of class and social stratification, seems to assume a homogeneous society. This problem went hand-in-hand with a generalized lack of attention to social diversity during the mid-century, years before this issue prompted both theoretical work about the public sphere and rigorous study of gender, race, and ethnicity.[3] My concern here is not with diversity, though, but with the structural and cultural changes in our system of political communication that have wreaked serious havoc with the conventional meanings of authority.

The diffusion of communication technologies, such as television and the Internet, paired with trends in both the economics and marketing of media and telecommunications have wrought overwhelming challenges in understanding our communication infrastructure.[4] Indeed, scholars in political sociology and communication have tracked these changes in media with imagination and vigor, puzzling over what they mean for democratic theory and practice.[5] It is in this spirit that I – with some trepidation – approach the chronic and daunting problem of authority, trying to bring to both social theory and American politics insights from the study of political communication. I argue here for a new category of authority – *media-derived authority* – that should take a secure place alongside de jure authority and other traditional meanings of the term. I review some of the more important writings on authority, the relevant communication notions, and extract some vivid examples from the contemporary media to underscore the pressing need for a new definition of authority in public life. A central question for us, as it was for Michels and his contemporaries writing over seventy years ago, revolves around the repressive or oppressive nature of authority – Michels's "clenched fists." Citizens still regularly clench fists in their pockets, no doubt, in the face of authority of all kinds. But it is often done in the comfort and security of their own homes, under the perpetual gaze of the mass media.

The nature of authority

Sociologists, political scientists, and many other scholars seek an understanding of authority, as it is a force to be reckoned with, regardless of governmental structure and political culture. In democracies, totalitarian regimes, post-communist societies, and even states deep in the violent throes of civil war, authority looms as a phantom hovering over both leadership and citizenry. In any political setting, authority is exercised, blocked, debated, accepted, and most of all, noticed with passion. Like many nebulous phenomena in the social world, most famously perhaps pornography, it is difficult to define authority precisely, though people tend to think they "know" it when they see it. And like so many political actions, the exercise of authority tends to be noted cognitively (especially by those on the receiving end), but also *felt*. Authority and its exercise evoke emotion as it typically involves either submission or challenge that can be either harrowing or simply annoying, depending on the case. Most people have known and felt authority in their individual lives, from the oversight of parents and teachers, to that of bosses, deans, or government agencies. Authority is one of the busy intersections where social control and freedom clash, and it makes people recognize that life is based in community, with social networks both omnipresent and inescapable.

Authority is not negative, of course, as prominent thinkers have noted, Max Weber among them. Weber struggled with most aspects of authority throughout his troubled life, as he wrestled with demons both intellectual and personal.[6] In his darker moments, Weber recognized that the iron cage of rationalization was one inhabited by many authority figures, whom we – ironically – elect and support through our own institutions and practices. There is widespread resentment to bureaucracies, as those who have tried to correct a billing error or lost a driver's license recognize. But people tolerate these structures and institutions, not quite certain that they work, but not knowing what the alternative could be.

I do not review here the vast social scientific and humanistic literatures on authority.[7] Instead, this article takes guidance from the philosopher Raymond Geuss, who recently provided one of the more succinct and comprehensive syntheses of the literature on political authority. Geuss argues that there are five overlapping forms of authority, all of which this article draws upon: epistemic, natural, de facto, de jure, and moral.[8]

Epistemic authority is the authority derived through expertise in a bounded domain: Milton Friedman is *an* (although certainly not *the*) authority in economics, Stephen Hawking is an authority on the universe, and people hope that their local medical specialists are authorities in such areas as cardiology and oncology. Natural authority, by contrast, is most akin to leadership: the person with natural authority has no particular legal right to demand action, but by nature of his or her charisma, encourages voluntary submission. People tend to obey those with natural authority, as in a dangerous situation, because those who possess it are somehow perceived as able to coordinate human efforts and avoid disaster.

It is worth pausing for a moment on this category of natural charismatic authority, as it is one of the more nebulous ones, and could be confused with attractiveness or any other number of magnetic characteristics a leader might exhibit. There is indeed an element of simple attractiveness (physical, rhetorical, etc.) within this form of authority. Yet one must have a bit more than just attractiveness to hold natural authority: It somehow generates compliance, even with no legal warrant or formal position, and can – most importantly – overtake de jure authority in real circumstances. And there is undoubtedly overlap of natural authority with both moral authority and epistemic authority. On a troubled airplane flight, for example, passengers might well follow the lead of a fellow passenger with some flying experience, medical experience or even great charisma over the flight attendant, who is the only one in the cabin with true legal warrant to command passengers. Although the concept of charismatic authority is still fuzzy, it can in most contexts be distinguished from simple persuasiveness and appeal. As Guess puts it: "... '[N]atural authority' is an interesting phenomenon precisely because I may not be able to say exactly why I think I have reason to take seriously what a person with natural authority says."[9]

Those with de facto authority rule by force, as in an occupying army. As Geuss puts it, "[C]ertain people actually control a certain area; they monopolize the use of violence and succeed in getting their commands obeyed."[10] We follow those in de facto authority primarily out of fear. Those with de jure authority, in contrast, are elected to, appointed to, or inherit specific legitimate roles within organizations, wielding their authority in a legal manner, enforceable through officially sanctioned violence or imprisonment. Finally, moral authority is present, Geuss argues, when "[Force] X has a warrant which will stand up to some further moral scrutiny that could be brought to bear on it and on the whole system of accepted rules from which it derives."[11] People obey those with moral authority because they should: There are normative undergirdings to these statements and commands.

The overlapping nature of the categories makes them a bit cumbersome, but necessarily so, as authority is one of the murkier human behavioral dynamics found in the empirical world. It might be better, in the end, to think of people or institutions as holding one or more of the forms of authority simultaneously. Forms of authority often seem *clustered*, as though they ride together in many circumstances.

Fuzziness notwithstanding, these five categories of Geuss quite neatly cover the massive, diverse literature on authority. Among the advantages of his scheme is that instead of trying to distinguish authority from power, influence, competence, and the like (as in Bierstedt's essay on the subject), and then trying to set them aside for the purposes of cleanly defining authority (to date an extraordinarily unproductive endeavor), Geuss *incorporates* what we know about those phenomena and recognizes how they contribute to building a theory of authority. Geuss's categories are not always connected or clustered however, as one can have isolated forms of authority. To use an academic example: Professors know that their dean has de jure authority to promote them, raise their salary, or approve their request for sabbatical. But despite these many powers, legally supported by the college or university, the dean may clearly lack epistemic authority (has produced poor scholarship), may lack natural authority (is unpersuasive and without charisma), and may lack moral authority (has a flawed vision of higher education). De facto authority is the trickiest use of the term, as it involves non-legal but enormously powerful threats of force that are difficult to ignore. One way to ease the complexities associated with this form of authority is to keep in mind that it is entirely domain-specific, and indeed often geographic in its warrant. It is about controlling bodies and minds in physical space of some sort. One can in theory escape de facto authority, by fleeing the territory in question, but may not want to, for compelling economic, cultural, safety or familial reasons.

What is missing from most accounts of authority, in all categories, is a focus on communication. It is typically assumed that authority is communicated or expressed *somehow* but it is hard to visualize exactly how that transmission process works – through what sort of rhetoric, or most important in this essay, what channel of communication. In the literature, one either does or does not have authority in the eyes of a community, but how this is discerned as a rather complicated and heretofore ignored story. Michels, as in the opening quotation above, is clearly cognizant of communication as are all the better theorists. They know it matters immensely, particularly in the cases of epistemic, natural and moral authority, where the manner in which a command or proscriptive statement is expressed can make all the difference. I may be an expert on welfare policy, for example, but if I cannot frame my concerns or ideas in a persuasive manner, my writings and my speeches will fail to move even the most sympathetic audience. Among the closest that theorists have come to acknowledging communication directly is the attempt of Carl Friedrich to link authority to both reason and public expression. He noted that:

> [A]uthority is a *quality* of communication, rather than of persons, and when we speak of the authority of a person, we are using a short-hand expression to indicate that he possesses the capacity to issue authoritative communications.... What matters is that this capacity to issue communications which may be elaborated by reasoning is a decisive phenomenon in a great many social and more particularly political relationships.[12]

These insights are helpful, as they begin to explore the underpinnings the exercise of authority can have in communicative rationality. Friedrich believes that rationality gets "hinted at" or as he puts it, authority claims reflect "the potentiality of reasoned elaboration."[13] But also instructive is that authority must be *located* somewhere. People have it, institutions have it, but how does one know they have it and how does one know which type of authority they possess? These facts are discovered by observations: how they act, the information they disseminate, how they speak – in general, what we can see and hear of them. Authority is embedded in the forms, channels, and signals associated with communication and most often, with speech. Whether one heeds these expressions is another matter entirely, but the channels through which one comes to understand authority are essential and too often overlooked.

Media, public opinion, and authority

Lines of authority within organizations tend to be among the easiest cases of authority to discuss: People have roles, responsibilities and powers, and although there are individuals in many organizations who exercise unusual forms of natural authority due to their talents or attractiveness, these cases often pale in contrast to de jure ones, which make the organization run. My concern here is not so much with authority as exercised in the narrow confines of an organization or company, but in the more nebulous realm of the public sphere, one arena where legitimacy has been debated fiercely over the last two decadesorso.[14] Scholars of communication have studied legitimacy, power and authority (sometimes without realizing it) in a variety of eras and guises, often with a keen eye toward persuasive impacts on citizens. Some have asked how media set legitimated agendas, how television provides authoritative issue frames, or how journalists themselves gain authority.[15] There are studies of presidents' attempts to stretch their authority as best they can, of candidates' interests in controlling campaign agendas, and textured studies of how citizens themselves navigate among the legitimated "frames" provided by the media. There is also now an extensive literature on the uses of opinion polls in public discourse, as an authoritative tool in argumentation.[16] All of this research has illuminated conditions under which expertise, authority and power are exercised. Yet at this point there are few general theories or concepts that explain how media can smooth the way for the exercise of authority and where it fails. In fact, we lack basic language to discuss authority, as understood by political theorists or sociologists, in its relation to political communication.

There is, however, one exception to the latter observation, well known to communication scholars yet a concept largely underdeveloped since the 1940s, when it first appeared during the glory days of the Columbia School (the Bureau of Applied Social Research). It is of course the notion of "status conferral." Paul Lazarsfeld and Robert Merton argued that the media – newspapers, film and radio in their day – have the power to tell us which behaviors are normative, the tendency to dampen citizenship ("narcotizing dysfunction"), and the ability to confer legitimacy on people and institutions:

> The mass media bestow prestige and enhance the authority of individuals and groups by *legitimizing their status*. Recognition by the press or radio or magazines or newsreels testifies that one has arrived, that one is important enough to have been singled out from the large anonymous masses, that one's behavior and opinions are significant enough to require public notice.... The audiences of mass media apparently subscribe to the circular belief: "If you really matter, you will be at the focus of mass attention and, if you *are* at the focus of mass attention, then surely you must really matter"[17]

This is a powerful observation, but one of the reasons it has not been as useful as it might be in empirical media research is that Merton and Lazarsfeld did not specify the mechanisms by which status conferral occurs. Are media able to confer status because we see journalists as having expertise to choose what is important (epistemic authority)? Or do we attend to their citations because it is cognitively efficient, because they are our agents, and we have no other means of knowing? (It is in fact the journalist's role to conduct a surveillance of the world and single items out for the reader, something they can do because they represent major, international news organizations with arms extending across the globe). Or is status conferral more likely a simple and indeed superficial statistical artifact, whereby the sheer probability of being portrayed in the local or national media is so low that one gains status simply by being plucked from the masses? The primary difficulty with status conferral, for the purposes here, is that it is not strong enough to denote real power in the public sphere: Status here is not quite charismatic authority, but more a form of attractiveness. For example, status conferral is enormously useful in thinking about how engaging actors or ballplayers can lend their charms to automobiles, coffeemakers and cellular telephones in television advertisements. While Merton and Lazarsfeld were certainly working toward the general problem of authority, they were not quite there. Authority has a much bigger punch than status conferral, and is decidedly political.

It is in the general spirit of Merton and Lazarsfeld, but also with an eye to the extensive literature on authority, that I argue for new terminology and a new approach to studying authority. The centerpiece of this approach is the concept of *media-derived authority*, a particular sort of legitimation one receives through mediated channels. It would be a sixth sense of authority to add to Geuss's scheme above, and although it too has overlap with the other forms, it is unique enough and important enough to deserve its own place at this moment. Many and varied other institutions – other than media – grant authority of course. But the media are not a bounded institution, and this is what makes their influence so profound: They are, for better or worse, the very fabric of the public sphere itself. Therefore, it makes sense to discuss media-derived authority in trying to understand how individuals and institutions gain authority in public life.

But to specifics, media-derived authority is the legitimation one garners through communication channels and media texts (e.g., appearance on news programs, in political campaign advertisements, images in news montage, reference in the monologues of late night television program hosts, etc.). It is a matter of amount of coverage one receives and to some extent, the style of the coverage. Friedrich is again helpful here: Media-derived authority is very much about text and channel, about the communications of the person or institution in authority. One recent quantitative attempt to understand part of this phenomenon is Richard Posner's ranking of public intellectuals. He counts the number of mentions certain academics, authors, and thinkers receive, in the media, to determine who is prominent in public discourse.

This is a worthwhile exercise, but lacks theoretical justification and placement in the larger scheme of political authority.[18]

I want to clarify and underscore this key analytic point: Like the five forms of authority Guess outlines, media-derived authority can pair with others. Many leaders, for example hold three or four sources of authority simultaneously, while others have only one. And, although this complicates things further, media-derived authority is both a sixth form of authority to supplement Guess, and communication itself is *embedded* in other forms of authority. So, for example, charismatic authority has rhetorical/communicative components, but (following Friedrich) a charismatic leader may also have media-derived authority, giving his ideas even more force than he might have without access to the mass media audience.

But how exactly do we recognize when someone has achieved some or a considerable degree of media-derived authority? It is not simply a matter of someone's name, ideas, or countenance appearing in the media, although those can be critical dimensions of the phenomenon. Four central dimensions of media-derived authority, in the case of an individual, organization, or institution X might be:

A. *Volume:* X receives high volume of coverage relative to others;
B. *Tone:* X receives, on balance, decidedly deferential attention of journalists and media gatekeepers, relative to others (e.g., has longer sound bites, or has his or her language/issue frames accepted or valorized);
C. *Public Opinion Signal:* There are implicit or explicit assumptions that X either represents or can move public opinion;
D. *Reasoned Elaboration:* X is portrayed as having the capacity to provide logic and persuasive evidence, should that be necessary.

These are some initial dimensions of media-derived authority and I provide anecdotes about these below from print sources. All four dimensions can be operationalized, although a bit differently depending on the authority figures (person or institution) and media source in question. It is the case, as with Geuss's five categories above, that authority is in the eye of the beholder – it is something that is *felt* by those who submit, either readily or against their (in this case, cognitive) will. So it is clear that audience or "effects" studies as we call them in media research are helpful, if not vital in understanding the complete picture of media-derived authority. But the first step is to be sure we have a rigorous idea of what we mean by the phenomenon, how it fits with existing theory, and generate hypotheses about where it might be found. My main interest here is (using the language of experimental design) in thinking about the "stimulus material" or the authority markers in media.

There is another concept that media-derived authority may but should not be confused with: the social psychological notion of "source credibility."[19]

Source credibility, a phenomenon investigators have explored rigorously in laboratory settings, is typically defined as "cue-based" communication: It specifies the conditions under which experimental subjects will attend to characteristics of the source (attractiveness, gender, humor) in evaluating a message. Authoritative figures undoubtedly often have source credibility, but they have much more than that: *They have a right to power*, either through legality, rationality, moral force, or expertise. Source credibility comes closest to epistemic authority, but is not quite the same: Those with epistemic authority tend to have cultural sway because they have mastered a body of knowledge. Unlike source credibility, which has indeed been useful in some forms of research, media-derived authority is a culturally and historically situated formation, not one that can be easily manipulated in a laboratory. This is in part because authority evolves over time, in the reality of the American public sphere, within particular sets of institutions and configurations of social forces. Having "credibility," in other words, is a sociological (not psychological) question of legitimacy, in the first instance at least.

Media-derived authority can be found in any mass communicated artifact – television programs, newspaper articles, popular magazines, radio broadcasts, Internet sites, and the like. It can be located through large-scale content analytic schemes, using the framework above, or through more qualitative and textual analyses as in the anecdotal evidence below. Dimensions of media-derived authority can be operationalized in a variety of ways, depending upon the nature of the entity in question as well as the nature of the medium. For example, say that one derives more authority in media the more deferential the coverage is (i.e., tone, above). In analyzing how a public figure is covered in the editorial pages of *The New York Times*, this is a fairly straightforward analytic exercise, evaluating semantics, and might be done through any number of methodologies, qualitative or quantitative. Web sites, on the other hand, present more complicated challenges. Some web sites, for news organizations for example, are closely edited and adhere to the standard journalistic norms used by the print or broadcast arms of those news organizations. But there are a multitude of other web sites, with varying standards for what constitutes proper coverage of public affairs, and so a different tack might be needed to understand how authority is derived when there are unusual standards for news coverage used in a web site. One must consider the particular function of those sites, the sponsoring organization's goals, the intended and actual audiences, and how the text is likely to be used by consumers. These are complicated issues, no doubt, but empirically manageable ones if we are seeking to understand how authority can be gained through Internet sites as well as the conventional print and broadcast media. There is, in any case, no avoiding the Internet in studying political communication, so theorists and researchers will need to continue to develop increasingly sophisticated tools and rules of thumb to study it.

As Michels points out in the opening quotation, "whether authority is of personal or institutional origin it is created and maintained by public opinion." This is, to be sure, one of the most important notions to keep in mind as we re-consider authority in a mediated age. At this moment, the study of American public opinion and the study of authority are entirely unconnected: Public opinion analysts and survey researchers are interested in a large variety of important matters, but the communication of authority is not one of them. Analysts certainly know the percentage of Americans who support this or that policy, and sometimes, with what intensity or propensity for action. They have a good sense of why particular socio-cultural or economic characteristics, on the part of an individual voter, correspond with particular preferences. But all of this is quite far from what Michels asks us to ponder: how citizens end up supporting authority. Again, in a bounded organization – say, a classroom – it is clear how and why students might submit to the authority of the teacher. But in the larger realm of civil society, the process by which people ascribe authority to particular issues, individuals or institutions has been studied less well. Media-derived authority may be one good conceptual and terminological point of departure, opening up new ways to study persuasion and the movements of public opinion.

At the end of the day we must always ask: how does a new concept – media-derived authority in this case – add value to our theorizing and our research? There are many contributions, but two are perhaps most apparent. For one, media-derived authority is an efficient way to pull together a variety of somewhat limited (e.g., "agenda-setting"), undeveloped ("status conferral") and experimentally-based ("source credibility") concepts, while forcing all of them out into the public sphere for sociological and political exploration. Media-derived authority, in other words, demands a dialogue among philosophers of political authority, political scientists interested in persuasion and popular opinion in the public sphere, and scholars intent on understanding media effects. Second, and less selfishly academic, media-derived authority begins to illuminate the sort of power and influence we recognize so well, yet have no name for. It can – with proper empirical documentation – explain why media figures with no discernable conventional grounds for authority seem to have it nonetheless, and why those with great de jure authority seem so non-authoritative, or somehow unworthy of their roles. Media can and do make both phenomena possible: They can pump up those without conventional authority, and demote those who already hold it. In the public sphere – a world of attitudes, ideas, and feelings – how individuals and institutions *appear* is extraordinarily important. No figures viewed on television can directly, at that moment, exercise authority over the viewers. But their authority is, over time, either bolstered or diminished by media attention, and this process undoubtedly has real effects as these individuals try to pass legislation, start wars, or mobilize public opinion.

Does media-derived authority deserve its own new category, given the already existing ones? Apparently so: It is clearly not de facto authority or de jure authority, as there is no immediate physical force behind it per se and no legal-rational basis. Media-derived authority is not moral authority, as it does not necessarily speak to issues of how one should live. It is not epistemic authority: Viewers and readers do not automatically believe media or think journalists, for example, always know more than they do. Figures who derive authority through media are not necessarily charming or attractive or with particular leadership qualities. So natural authority and charisma are not the basis of their legitimacy. The basis is in the technological and rhetorical power of the media themselves; the way they single out and listen to certain individuals and institutions, signaling to viewers that they should as well – that it behooves them to pay attention to those on the airwaves. To put it dramatically: One of the most compelling powers of the media is to bestow influence of a particular sort, that deserves deference, has unclear but certain rational underpinnings, and has potential impacts on public opinion.

Instructive examples of media-derived authority

Two sorts of cases are useful, initially, in trying to clarify the importance and problematic nature of media-derived authority. One set of cases is that of public figures who hold de jure authority, for example, presidents or senators. The other set are those who may have authority within their organizations, but have somehow parlayed that influence and position into public sphere authority through the mass media. I start with the first set, utilizing the multiple genres of news, editorial, and commentary. They are difficult to distinguish among, but all are useful.

Although the case obviously demands extended analysis, and will receive it over the coming years, President George W. Bush's run for the presidency in 2000 is a useful one in underscoring the existence and possible effects of media-derived authority. Debate about whether Bush had won the office legitimately was abundant in the media during the re-counts and into the post-election months. But at this writing, there is still struggle over the question of his authority, a struggle of a sort not seen in recent presidencies. Some presidents lost their ability to mobilize public opinion, during particular periods of their presidencies or in a linear fashion over the course of their terms, but Bush's capture of the White House remains unique. He still endures questions about his way into the office, as in this sardonic editorial remark in the *Pittsburgh Post-Gazette* from November 25, 2001 (reproduced from *The New Republic*):

> So Bush is now a legitimate president, right? Well, it depends on how you define the term. Legally, of course, he is. The [*New York*]

Times seems to be referring to this kind of legitimacy when it maintains that the recount strengthens Bush's "legal claim" to the presidency.[20]

Here we see an unusually blunt interest on the part of the writer in the authority of the President, how much he has, and whether colleagues in the newspaper business (the *Wall Street Journal* is also mentioned in this editorial) appreciate the problematic nature of Bush's claim to legitimate rule. In the text, the writer Johnathan Chait makes the argument that Bush lacks de jure authority, since the re-count and Supreme Court decisions were either murky or faulty. But most important here is how Chait gets enmeshed in the debate about media-derived authority as well. It is a sophisticated piece of journalism, whether that was clear to readers or not, in that it brings the questions of de jure and media-derived authority into direct sunlight. These sorts of meta-level struggles that media have – often about their own ability to fight authority, to grant it, or to claim it – are common but need explication and systematic study if one is to understand the conditions under which authority is obtained in public sphere debate.

A simpler example, also about the Bush presidency, comes from a news story – not an editorial – in the *Houston Chronicle* of December 28, 2001. The journalist, in seeking to understand how the events of September 11th changed the nature of the Bush presidency, unknowingly walks right into the academic debates about authority. In arguing that "September 11th transformed Bush from a domestic-oriented politician trying to overcome the contentiousness of a disputed election into a powerful and popular commander in chief," the journalist bestows authority on the president. It is charismatic authority, in part: The president made fine speeches and acted the part of leader. But he could not do this alone, because both the technological capability to broadcast this charisma and the surrounding commentary on his speeches and actions are the domain of the mass communication system. The journalist, Bennett Roth, even quotes historian David Kennedy who notes about Bush: "It does seem to me he had an aura of insubstantiality and illegitimacy. . . . And both of those have disappeared." In this case, Bush derives authority directly from the media text: The *Chronicle*, in this front-page news story (dateline Washington), helps to bolster the authority and legitimacy of the Bush presidency. Whether readers, upon processing this story, were convinced by the premise is of course a question for empirical research. But the "stimulus material" – the attempt of media to bestow authority – is quite clearly there. From a normative perspective, has the journalist overstepped, with regard to objective assessment of the Bush presidency? Again, it is hard to say and it depends on one's expectations of media, but the important aspect of this case is that the journalist had no compunction about judgments of authority, wrote in the professional manner of conventional American journalism, citing sources on both sides (including prominent academic ones), and included a thoughtful review of major events of the fall of 2001.

President Bush receives substantial media coverage in all outlets, but so do other figures with de jure authority, and it is intriguing to note how they are treated by media with regard to their status. Women office-holders are a particularly interesting subset of authoritative figures, as they face special challenges in the world of American journalism. In an inappropriately gendered analysis, but one that clearly served the purpose of the journalist, the women senators from California were described thusly in a 1997 article from *The Washingtonian* magazine:

> "Barbara [Boxer] is much more of a schmoozer, the high-school cheerleader, your good friend, somebody who's fun whether you agree with her or not," a congressional Democrat from California says. By contrast, [Diane] Feinstein is "definite, direct. She has this authority about her. She is in charge of every meeting . . . runs the meetings even when she doesn't know what she is talking about."[21]

This text bestows authority, beyond the sort she already holds, to Feinstein (it is not clear, in contrast, whether the journalist finds it in Boxer or not). It may not quite be the sort of coverage a U.S. senator would hope for, but does underscore legitimacy that she has (her "aura") beyond what she accrued through the legal election apparatus of the state of California.

As mentioned above, those without legal, de jure authority can achieve media-derived authority, and indeed do so often in both the news and entertainment media. Pundits and columnists are often propelled into legitimate public roles, via the apertures provided by their news organizations. For example, William Safire of *The New York Times* is regarded as a commentator with great authority by politicians and other media. The latter is absolutely critical, as seen above, because media sources so often cite each other as influential: They are all, in fact, entangled in a rather intricate web of authority bestowal. This often involves an interesting and very common journalistic trope, the subtext of which is "Our news outlet is objective and reports the facts, other media outlets actually have power/authority." Since the earliest days of radio, media organizations have denied their power in the political sphere, preferring to see themselves as conduits and analysts.[22] Admitting to power or authority is bad form, because it might give the appearance of partisanship or bias. In any case, media cite media, and help to create or sustain media-derived authority. A good case in point is this opening paragraph from a 1994 *U.S. News and World Report* article on the *Report's* very own profession:

> Pundit power. William Safire may be at the top of America's modern punditocracy. But when Bobby Inman withdrew his nomination as

defense secretary last week . . . he blamed the *New York Times* columnist for bringing him down after a decade-long vendetta. Safire has indeed complained about Inman's alleged anti-Israel leanings and business dealings, but in a column following Inman's announcement, Safire countered: "No pundit is that powerful."[23]

The two journalists go on to note "Safire is probably right," arguing that journalists of *previous* decades, particularly Walter Lippmann or Joseph Alsop, had real power. This is a typical example of media confusion about their own authority – whether they have it or not, whether they want it, and whether they should admit to thinking about either. In any case, it is illuminating to scrutinize these moments, in the larger attempt to understand media-derived authority.

One last example goes beyond journalists themselves as authority figures and into the world of industry, where leaders of major corporations and minor firms can achieve power and influence via the mass media. Whether they are labeled as influential or powerful, there is no question that sustained media commentary and attention to particular figures are staples of contemporary American journalism. In one interesting 1998 editorial from *The San Francisco Chronicle*, there is speculation about whether or not at least one captain of industry has even more authority than the president:

> Many Americans are watching the Justice Department's antitrust suit against Microsoft, but not because they're fascinated by Internet browsers. Their real question is whether Bill Gates is more powerful than our government. . . . Gates has created an unprecedented system for collecting data on consumers who use his products and constructed an elaborate media campaign to neutralize the growing suspicions we harbor about . . . Gates.[24]

Again, this is not just about power and authority, but about journalistic willingness to declare who holds it and why. It has long been a function of the mass media to describe the activities of world and local leaders – whether they are in government or business. But in understanding the influence of media, and how it intersects with current theories about authority structures, it is instructive to scrutinize just how and where authority is bestowed in the public sphere. Microsoft's Gates is very often the source of media commentary about influence, authority and power, and importantly, his authority is sustained and evolving. Hence this opening to a news analysis article that vividly underscores the deferential tone often used by media in dealing with anointed authority figures:

> For the most part, the Bill Gates on the witness stand at the company's antitrust trial last week was a public relations dream. Gone

was the uncooperative persona displayed on a videotaped deposition earlier in the case. This time, arguing in the company's defense against the sanctions sought by a coalition of state prosecutors, Mr. Gates played by turns his familiar roles as high-technology visionary and brilliant businessman.[25]

Are journalists simply reporting on his charisma (natural authority), his epistemic authority (expertise) and market dominance (de facto authority)? Or do they themselves, as the public's channel of communication in learning about Gates and others, also offer him *another* form of authority, perhaps even more compelling than the rest? It is the case that media are conduits for existing, conventional authority: Those holding this authority get it broadcasted through the media. But those who hold it and those who do not can achieve even greater authority through media attention *independent* of their existing status. It is exactly the sort of deferential coverage, hinting at command of public opinion as well as the capacity for elaboration, that one needs to look for in developing the concept of media-derived authority.

Political communication in our time

There are a multitude of possible approaches to understanding the role and power of the mass media in politics. But to this point, there has been a lack of theoretical tools to help us in discerning what it is exactly that the media do, when it comes to shaping the public sphere. The media do highlight particular issues (agenda-setting or priming), they commit sins of omission, thereby leaving out particular perspectives or candidates, and on the more positive side, try to tell the public what is going on in Washington and why they should care. The power of the media has always been a vital topic, since the earliest days of media research now nearly a century ago, but it seems that the more researchers study the effects of newspapers, television, and the Internet, the more they know about *particular* attitudinal and institutional change, and the less they see the general nature of media power. Research on how the media cover specific issues, individuals, and institutions is essential. But it is necessary to step back and figure out *how* media power connects with and differs from the influence of other institutions, and link that research back to political theory. Building on Timothy Cook, I want to underscore that the media – taken together, despite their many points of heterogeneity – are indeed an institution with unique effects: The media, as discussed in this article, have the ability to bestow a particular kind of authority that few other institutions can.

The sheer reach and rhetorical power of media are entirely unique, and recognition of this fact has been uneven in contemporary social science. Political communication scholars are themselves to blame in part, for their sometimes narrow focus inability to dismiss epistemological dead-ends quickly (e.g., minimal effects theories such as Joesphy Klapper's in the 1960s), and lack of sustained attempts to integrate communications theory and findings with those of American politics, social theory, and philosophy. But scholars now know enough about basic media organization, practices, and mechanisms that they can come back to political theory with tremendous contributions, those to the theory of authority being just one of many. Communications technologies keep changing, and changing rapidly, which is a burden that many scholars outside of political communication need not confront: Few other institutions change with such rapidity. The courts, legislatures, the presidency, and bureaucracies evolve very slowly, in contrast, and give scholars the chance to keep up. No such luxury exists in communications.

For many years, scholars tended to see the mass media as one of many institutions competing for the ability to shape the public sphere and socialize citizens. Media were viewed as existing alongside of the classic institutions designated by sociologists as authoritative – the schools, family, government, and religion.[26] In the zero-sum game of shaping American minds, media were thought to be in the fight, taking up slack wherever possible as other institutions falter. From the most high-profile cases (media providing issue information where political candidates should have) to the most mundane cases (children coming home from school, entertained by television as both parents work), media fill empty voids. It is then a good moment, in part because of Internet penetration, to re-group and recognize that media are best seen as a meta-institution. They certainly compete with other institutions to some extent, in some important circumstances: The struggle between the Pentagon and journalists over coverage of the Persian Gulf War or Iraq wars are outstanding examples. But it makes more sense, theoretically and empirically, to try to understand how media – in addition to competing with other institutions – oversee the configuration of social forces and institutions in place. How do media boost or demean those already in power, and what are their motives in doing so? How do the unique technological powers of media – to provide moving, vivid imagery and catch the greatness and gaffes of political life – fit with the rest of politics and authority relations?

It may not make complete theoretical or empirical sense at this point to think of media – given the diversity of outlets and proliferation of information through the Internet – as a conventional institution. With each major news event, the recent pedophilia scandals within the Catholic Church being a good example, it becomes clear that media conduct a surveillance of all institutions and are in fact the *environment* within which our conventional institutions fight to maintain authority, dignity, and effectiveness.

One of the more important questions that looms is the relationship between authority and attention of audiences. Above I argue that the study of effects (broadly defined) must come after determining what authority is and where to find it. True enough, but this skirts the more general issue of empirical research possibilities that researchers might pursue with new knowledge about the properties of authority. This article offers no new methodology for studying media audiences directly, primarily because I find the existing arsenal of tools – ethnography, field observation, archival work, surveys, and laboratory experimentation to be perfectly adequate for studying authority and its impacts (Stanley Milgram's classic work notwithstanding, I am least optimistic about laboratory work on this particular topic, because coercion and authority, as they are politically manifest, tend to be rather difficult to simulate in experimental settings). That said, and using current methods, one can start to think about how to isolate forms of authority, how they cluster at times, and effects these clusters have in everyday political persuasion. Concepts like "source credibility" seem to dilute the notion of authority, disconnecting it both from real contexts of power and from the history of political theory.

The goal of this article is not to argue that there is only one way to study media power, that scholars have been on the wrong track, or that I have definitively located the place of media within the constellation of institutional networks in the United States. The tasks suggested will allow many different approaches. But this article aims to strengthen the link between political communication studies and more traditional conceptions and approaches to authority in social theory. As the field of communication comes of age – under the pressure and anxiety of keeping up with a volatile and constantly changing media – authority is among its central concerns. And in a way, regardless of which institutions or sets of political actors are to be studied, everyone needs to be a scholar of communication to some degree: Media have become the central means by which citizens come to know the social world but also how they come to know authority, in all its forms.

Acknowledgments

I want to express gratitude to the *Theory and Society* Editors and reviewers, and to colleagues who gave me valuable feedback on this article: Sarah Maza, Gary Saul Morson, and David Zarefsky. Inspiration for this article comes from Robert Merton, whom I never met, and who still is, to my mind, the premier theorist of public communication.

Notes

1 For early work on authority, see: Aristotle, *The Politics*, trans. E. Barker (Oxford: Oxford University Press, 1946); Thucydides, *History of the Peloponnesian War*, trans. Rex Warner (Baltimore: Penguin Books, 1970); Niccolo Machiavelli, *The Prince*, trans. N. H. Thompson (Buffalo, NY: Prometheus Books, 1986); Jean-Jacques Rousseau, *The Social Contract and the Discourse on the Origin of*

Inequality, editor, Lester G. Croker (New York: Washington Square Press, 1967). The more recent works include: Robert Bierstedt, "The Problem With Authority," in Monroe Berger, Theodore Abel, and Charles Page, editors, *Freedom and Control in Modern Society* (New York: D. Van Nostrand Company, 1954); Peter M. Blau, "Critical Remarks on Weber's Theory of Authority," *American Political Science Review* 57 (1963): 305–316; Sebastian De Grazia, "What Authority is Not," *American Political Science* 53 (1959) 321–331; Carl J. Friedrich, "Authority, Reason, and Discretion," in Carl J. Friedrich, editor, *Authority* (Cambridge, MA: Harvard University Press, 1958): 28–48; H. L. A. Hart, "Commands and Authoritative Legal Reasons," in Joesph Raz, editor, *Authority* (New York: New York University Press, 1990): 92–114; and Steven Lukes, "Perspectives on Authority" also in Raz, *Authority*; 203–217. Also see R. Nisbet and R. Perrin, *The Social Bond* (New York: Alfred A. Knopf, 1970); Robert Peabody, "Authority," in David Sills, editor, *International Encyclopedia of the Social Sciences* (New York: The Macmillan Company and the Free Press, 1968): 473–477; and Judith Sklar "Rousseau's Images of Authority," *American Political Science Review* 58 (1964): 919–932.

2 See T. W. Adorno, *The Authoritarian Personality* (New York: Harper, 1950); Walter Lippmann, *The Phantom Public* (New York: Harcourt, Brace, 1925); David Riesman, *The Lonely Crowd: A Study of the Changing American Character* (New Haven: Yale University Press, 1950); and Joseph Schumpeter, *Capitalism, Socialism, and Democracy* (New York: Harper and Row, 1950).

3 See Nancy Fraser, *Unruly Practices: Power, Discourse and Gender in Contemporary Social Theory* (Minneapolois, MN: University of Minnesota Press, 1989).

4 This is a rather extensive literature, but two strong starting points are Bruce Owen and Steven Wildman, *Video Economics* (Cambridge, MA: Harvard University Press, 1992), and Joesph Turrow, *Breaking Up America: Advertisers and the New Media World* (Chicago: University of Chicago Press, 1997).

5 See W. Lance Bennett and Robert M. Entman, editors, *Mediated Politics: Communication In the Future of Democracy* (Cambridge, U.K.: Cambridge University Press, 2001); Bernard Berelson, Paul F. Lazarsfeld, and William N. McPhee, *Voting* (Chicago: University of Chicago Press, 1954); Timothy Cook, *Governing With the News: The News Media as a Political Institution* (Chicago: University of Chicago Press, 1998); Robert Entman, *Democracy Without Citizens: Media and the Decay of American Politics* (New York: Oxford University Press, 1989); Todd Gitlin, *The Whole World is Watching* (Berkeley: University of California Press, 1980); Doris Graber, *Mass Media and American Politics*, 4th edition (Washington, DC Congressional Quarterly Press, 1993); Roderick Hart, *Seducing America: How Television Charms the Modern Voter* (Thousand Oaks, CA: Sage, 1999); Shanto Iyengar, *Is Anyone Responsible?* (Chicago: University of Chicago Press, 1991); Shanto Iyengar and Donald R. Kinder, *News That Matters* (Chicago: University of Chicago Press, 1987); Joseph Klapper, *The Effects of Mass Communication* (Glencoe, IL: The Free Press, 1960); Paul F. Lazarsfeld, Bernard R. Berelson, and Hazel Gaudet, *The Peoples' Choice: How The Voter Makes Up His Mind in a Presidential Campaign* (New York: Duell, Sloan, and Pearce, 1948); Pippa Norris, *A Virtuous Circle: Political Communications in Postindustrial Societies* (New York: Cambridge University Press, 2002). Thomas E. Patterson, *Out of Order* (New York: Vintage, 1994); Ithiel de Sola Pool, *Technologies of Freedom* (Cambridge, MA: Belknap, 1983); and John Zaller, *The Nature and Origins of Mass Opinion* (New York: Cambridge University Press, 1992).

6 See Reinhard Bendix, *Max Weber: An Intellectual Portrait* (Berkeley: University of California Press, 1977); Dirk Kasler, *Max Weber: An Introduction to His Life*

      and Work (Chicago: University of Chicago Press, 1988); Wolfgang Mommsen, *Max Weber and German Politics* (Chicago: University of Chicago Press, 1984); and Max Weber, *Economy and Society: An Outline of Interpretive Sociology*, editors, Guenther Roth and Claus Wittich (Berkeley: University of California, 1978).
7. See Steven Lukes, "Perspectives on Authority," in *Authority*, Joesph Raz, editor, and Hart, "Commands and Authoritative Legal Reasons," in the same volume.
8. Raymond Geuss, *History and Illusion in Politics* (Cambridge: Cambridge University Press, 2001).
9. Ibid, 40.
10. Ibid.
11. Ibid, 41.
12. Friedrich, "Authority, Reason, and Discretion," 36.
13. Ibid, 37.
14. See Craig Calhoun, editor, *Habermas and the Public Sphere* (Cambridge, MA: MIT Press, 1992) and Jurgen Habermas, *The Structural Transformation of the Public Sphere: An Inquiry into a Category of Bourgeois Society* (Cambridge, MA: MIT Press, 1989).
15. See Maxwell McCombs and Donald Shaw, "Agenda-Setting Re-Visited" (symposium) *Journal of Communication* 43 (1993): 58–128; Shanto Iyengar and Donald Kinder, *News That Matters*, Entman, *Democracy Without Citizens: Media and the Decay of American Politics*; Herbert Gans, *Deciding What's News: A Study of the CBS Evening News, The NBC Nightly News, Newsweek and Time* (New York: Pantheon, 1979); Barbie Zelizer, *Covering the Body: The Kennedy Assassination, the Media And the Shaping of Collective Memory* (Chicago: University of Chicago Press, 1992).
16. On presidential authority and candidates, see Roderick Hart, *The Sound of Leadership: Presidential Communication in the Modern Age* (Chicago: University of Chicago Press, 1987) or Hart's *Campaign Talk: Why Elections are Good For Us* (Princeton: Princeton University Press, 2000); and also Joshua Meyrowitz, *No Sense of Place: The Impact of Electronic Media on Social Behavior* (New York: Oxford University Press, 1985). For works on citizens' use frames, see Wilaim Gamson, *Talking Politics* (New York: Cambridge University Press, 1992), and Nina Eliasoph, *Avoiding Politics: How Americans Produce Apathy in Everyday Life* (New York: Cambridge University Press, 1998). On polls as authoritative public discourse, see Benjamin Ginsberg, *The Captive Public: How Mass Opinion Promotes State Power* (New York: Basic, 1986); Susan Herbst, *Numbered Voices: How Opinion Polls Have Shaped American Politics* (Chicago: University of Chicago Press, 1993); Herbst, *Reading Public Opinion: How Political Actors View the Democratic Process* (Chicago: University of Chicago Press, 1998); and Lawrence Jacobs and Robert Shapiro, *Politicians Don't Pander: Political Manipulation and the Loss of Democratic Responsiveness* (Chicago: University of Chicago Press, 2000).
17. Lazarsfeld and Merton, "Mass Communication, Popular Taste and Organized Social Action," in Lyman Bryson, editor, *The Communication of Ideas* (New York: Harper and Brothers, 1948): 101–2.
18. Richard Posner, *Public Intellectuals: A Study in Decline* (Cambridge, MA: Harvard University Press, 2002). Although it is dated, I much prefer, for its comprehensiveness and cautious mapping of social networks, Charles Kadushin's study, *The American Intellectual Elite* (Boston: Little, Brown, 1974). Although the study was completed before the rapid diffusion of cable television, the Internet and other advances in telecommunication, Kadushin keys his explorations of

intellectual prestige to the media. He is eloquent on the topic of how espistemic authority (Geuss's terminology) and periodicals of mid-century (*Commentary, Dissent, The New York Review of Books, The Partisan Review,* and others) were closely linked and mutually reinforcing.

19 See Shanto Iyengar and Nicholas A. Valentino, "Who Says What? Source Credibility as a Mediator of Campaign Advertising," in A. Lupia, M. McCubbins and S. Popkin, editors, *Elements of Reason: Cognition, Choice and the Bounds of Rationality* (Cambridge: Cambridge University, 2002); 108–129; Richard Petty and John Cacioppo. *Attitudes and Persuasion: Classic and Contemporary Approaches* (Dubuque, IA: W.C. Brown, 1981).
20 Johnathan Chait, "Gore Beats Bush," *Pittsburgh Post-Gazette,* November 25, 2001, p. B-1.
21 Gregg Zoroya, "Fire and Ice," *Washingtonian,* October, 1997, p. 45.
22 Willard Rowland, *The Politics of TV Violence: Policy Uses of Communication Research* (Newbury Park: Sage, 1983).
23 Amy Bernstein and Lynn Rosellini, "Pundit Power," *U.S. News and World Report,* January 31, 1994, p. 15.
24 Jeffrey Klein, "Bill Gates' Brave New World." *The San Francisco Chronicle,* 1998, p. A19.
25 Amy Harmon, "Why Gates Has Trouble Saying He's Sorry," *The New York Times,* April 29, 2002, p. C1.
26 This is the position James R. Beniger and I took in "Mass Media and Public Opinion: Emergence of an Institution," in M. Hallinan, D. Klein, and J. Glass, editors, *Change in Societal Institutions* (New York: Plenum, 1990).

56

THE INTERNET, PUBLIC SPHERES, AND POLITICAL COMMUNICATION

Dispersion and deliberation

Peter Dahlgren

Source: *Political Communication* 22(2) (2005): 147–62.

The theme of the Internet and the public sphere now has a permanent place on research agendas and in intellectual inquiry; it is entering the mainstream of political communication studies. The first part of this presentation briefly pulls together key elements in the public sphere perspective, underscoring three main analytic dimensions: the structural, the representational, and the interactional. Then the discussion addresses some central themes in the current difficulties facing democracy, refracted through the lens of the public sphere perspective. In particular, the destabilization of political communication systems is seen as a context for understanding the role of the Internet: It enters into, as well as contributes to, this destabilization. At the same time, the notion of destabilization can also embody a positive sense, pointing to dispersions of older patterns that may have outlived their utility. Further, the discussion takes up obvious positive consequences that follow from the Internet, for example that it extends and pluralizes the public sphere in a number of ways. Thereafter the focus moves on to the interactional dimension of the public sphere, specifically in regard to recent research on how deliberation proceeds in the online public sphere in the contemporary environment of political communication. Finally, the analytic category of deliberative democracy is critically examined; while useful, some of its rationalist biases, particularly in the context of extra-parliamentarian politics, limit its utility. It is suggested that the concept of civic cultures offers an alternative way to understand the significance of online political discussion.

For about a decade now, many researchers and other observers have been asking whether the Internet will have—or is already having—an impact on the public sphere and, if so, the attributes of this impact. Such discussions become unavoidably framed by the general international consensus, emerging since the early 1990s, that democracy has hit upon hard times; more specifically, the hope is often expressed that the Internet will somehow have a positive impact on democracy and help to alleviate its ills.

Yet, given the variations in democratic systems and cultures around the world, and given the pace of change—social, political, and technological—we should not expect to soon arrive at some simple, definitive answer to these questions. Indeed, thus far the evidence seems equivocal; moreover, the conclusions one might derive are inexorably tied to the assumptions one has about the character of democracy. Rather than yielding any fast answers, we should acknowledge that the theme of the Internet and the public sphere has a permanent place on research agendas and in intellectual inquiry for the foreseeable future. It is now entering the mainstream of concern for the study of political communication and taking its place alongside the established research on the traditional mass media. We may occasionally still ask if the traditional mass media enhance or hamper democracy, but most research on that theme today focuses its questions on more specific features within the overall complexity of the landscape. So too can we expect the research on Internet to evolve—not least in highlighting the increasing technical convergences between mass and interactive media.

In the first part of the presentation that follows, I briefly pull together key elements in the public sphere perspective. I underscore three main analytic dimensions: the structural, the representational, and the interactional. Then I address central themes in the current difficulties facing democracy, refracted through the lens of the public sphere perspective. In particular, the current destabilization of political communication systems must be seen as a context for understanding the Internet: It enters into, as well as contributes to, this destabilization. At the same time, the notion of destabilization can also embody a positive sense, pointing to dispersions of older patterns that may have outlived their utility and possibilities for reconfiguration. We can note, for example, the obvious positive consequences that the Internet extends and pluralizes the public sphere in a number of ways. It is this kind of tension that I would accentuate, rather than any cheery optimism, dour pessimism, or cavalier dismissal.

Thereafter I focus my attention on the interactional dimension of the public sphere. Specifically, I take up some of the recent research findings in how deliberation proceeds in the online public sphere in the current destabilized environment of political communication. I find the notion of deliberative democracy useful, though its rationalist biases, particularly in the context of extra-parliamentarian politics, do limit its utility. I suggest that what I call civic cultures offer an enhanced way to understand the significance of online political discussion.

Democracy's communication spaces: three dimensions

In schematic terms, a functioning public sphere is understood as a constellation of communicative spaces in society that permit the circulation of information, ideas, debates—ideally in an unfettered manner—and also the formation of political will (i.e., public opinion). These spaces, in which the mass media and now, more recently, the newer interactive media figure prominently, also serve to facilitate communicative links between citizens and the power holders of society. The key text here is, of course, Habermas's (1989). There are problems and ambiguities in his book, as many have pointed out (see, for example, the collection by Calhoun, 1992), yet, for many committed to a democratic society, the concept itself remains compelling, both empirically and normatively. Habermas himself has returned to the concept, revising and updating it (cf. Habermas, 1996). The term "public sphere" is most often used in the singular form, but sociological realism points to the plural. In large-scale, differentiated late modern societies, not least in the context of nation states permeated by globalization, we have to understand the public sphere as constituting many different spaces.

As a starting point, I find it helpful to conceptualize the public sphere as consisting of three constitutive dimensions: structures, representation, and interaction (I discussed this in more detail in Dahlgren, 1995). The structural dimension has to do with the formal institutional features. Most obviously, this includes media organizations, their political economy, ownership, control, regulation, and issues of their financing, as well as the legal frameworks defining the freedoms of—and constraints on—communication. The structural dimension thus directs our attention to such classic democratic issues as freedom of speech, access, and the dynamic of inclusion/exclusion. Beyond the organization of the media themselves, the structural dimension also points to society's political institutions, which serve as a sort of "political ecology" for the media and set boundaries for the nature of the information and forms of expression that circulate. A society where democratic tendencies are weak is not going to give rise to healthy institutional structures for the public sphere, which in turn means that the representational dimension will be inadequate.

In regard to the Internet, the structural dimension directs our attention to the way in which the communicative spaces relevant for democracy are broadly configured. This has to do with such things as the manner in which cyber-geography is organized in terms of legal, social, economic, cultural, technical, and even Web-architectural features. Such factors have an impact on the ways in which the Net is accessible (or not) for civic use.

The representational dimension refers to the output of the media, the mass media as well as "minimedia" that target specific small groups via, for example, newsletters or campaign promotion materials. And given the increasing "massification" of communication on the Internet, representation becomes highly relevant for online contexts of the public sphere as well. In this dimension, one can raise all of the familiar questions and criteria about media output for political communication, including fairness, accuracy, completeness, pluralism of views, agenda setting, ideological tendencies, modes of address, and so forth.

In terms of the dimension of interaction, it may be useful to recall Habermas as well as other writers, such as Dewey (1954), who argue that a "public" should be conceptualized as something other than just a media audience. Publics, according to Habermas and Dewey, exist as discursive interactional processes; atomized individuals, consuming media in their homes, do not comprise a public. With the advent of the public opinion industry (cf. Splichal, 1999; Lewis, 2001), the focus on aggregate statistics of individual views became established. While such approaches do have their uses, it is imperative not to lose sight of the classic idea that democracy resides, ultimately, with citizens who engage in talk with each other. This is certainly the basic premise of those versions of democratic theory that see deliberation as fundamental.

Interaction actually consists of two aspects. First, it has to do with the citizens' encounters with the media—the communicative processes of making sense, interpreting, and using the output. The second aspect of interaction is that between citizens themselves, which can include anything from two-person conversations to large meetings. To point to the interaction among citizens—whether or not it is formalized as deliberation—is to take a step into the social contexts of everyday life. Interaction has its sites and spaces, its discursive practices, it psychocultural aspects; in this sense, the public sphere has a very fluid, sprawling quality, a view that correlates with what Alasuutari (1999) and others call the third generation of reception research on the mass media, where studies move beyond the actual sites of media reception and probe the circulation of meaning in broader micro-contexts of everyday life.

With the advent of the Net, civic interaction takes a major historical step by going online, and the sprawling character of the public sphere becomes all the more accentuated. We should also recognize that, empirically, the categories of representation and interaction on the Net often blur into each other. We tend to think in terms of either "one to many" forms of communication, as typified by the mass media, or "one to one communication" that is paradigmatic of interaction. This neat distinction unravels on the Internet, where, for example, group communication can have attributes of both mass communication and interaction.

These three dimensions—the structural, the representational, and the interactional—provide an analytical starting point for examining the public sphere of any given society or analyzing the contribution of any given communication technology.

Destabilized political communication

That contemporary democracies are facing difficult times has become an established topic in both the public debate and the research literature, and the evidence translates readily into issues in regard to the public sphere's structures, representations, and modes of interaction. The discussions about the poor health of democracy intensified during the 1990s, at about the same time that the Internet was rapidly leading a media revolution. It did not take long for many observers to connect the two phenomena in an optimistic way. That new information and communication technologies are affecting all spheres of life in late modern society is of course not news, but there remains ambiguity as to the extent to which they are enhancing democracy (cf. Anderson & Cornfield, 2003; Jenkins & Thornburn, 2003). One's understanding—and perhaps even appreciation—of this ambiguity grows as one's insight into the complexity of democracy's difficulties deepens.

In a recent overview, Blumler and Gurevitch (2000) summarized the ways that the traditional systems of political communication in Western democracies are being destabilized by changes in late modern society (see also the collection by Bennett & Entman, 2001, for an extensive overview of this landscape). They took up a number of by now familiar themes:

- increased sociocultural heterogeneity and the impact that this has on the audiences/actors within political communication.
- the massive growth in media outlets and channels, along with changes in the formats of media output, the blurring and hybridization of genres, and the erosion of the distinction between journalism and nonjournalism.
- today's increased number of political advocates and "political mediators," including the massive growth in the professionalization of political communication, with experts, consultants, spin doctors, and so forth sometimes playing a more decisive role than journalists
- the changing geography of political communication as the significance of traditional national borders becomes weakened
- the cacophony that emerges with this media abundance and so many political actors and mediators
- the growing cynicism and disengagement among citizens

One can also add that deregulated, conglomerate media industries driven by market forces push increasingly to the margins all normative considerations (e.g., journalistic values) that do not enhance short-term profits (cf. Baker,

2002). The consequences of these transformations run deep, and the coherence of the political communication system comes into question. This destabilization encompasses several at times antithetical tendencies. On the negative side, we can list chaos, inefficiency, unpredictability, and so forth. Also, the centripetal forces of private capital are coalescing under the prevailing neoliberal order, drawing power away from the formal political arena via a variety of mechanisms and thereby constricting and weakening democracy. On the positive side, we would certainly place such trends as the increase in political voices, new modes of political engagement, and definitions of what constitutes politics. Further, cultural heterogeneity may suggest dispersions and openings that can be developed for democratic gains. Destabilization can thus extend political communication through horizontal civic communication, as well as through vertical communication between citizens. Yet, again, it must be acknowledged that from a systems perspective, too much dispersion and polyvocality undercut political effectiveness and hamper governance.

To consider the role of the public sphere in general requires us to insert it into the force fields of this historical setting. The public sphere is an expression of and a contribution to these force fields, and this is all the more true as we consider its manifestations on the Net. It is there that we find the real "vanguard" of the public sphere, the domain where the most intense developments are taking place—what we might call the cyber transformation of the public sphere. Though we cannot be fully unequivocal here, we can still sketch some of the main vectors using the three dimensions I presented above. From the standpoint of structures, the Internet's political economy suggests that its development is quickly veering toward the intensified commercialization that characterizes the traditional media model (Patekis, 2000). The Internet has by now also become an integrated element in the dynamics of global capitalism (Schiller, 1999). Market logic, together with emerging legal frameworks and the impetus toward political restrictions, serves to constrain the extent and forms of representation for civic purposes in ways quite familiar from the mass media, diminishing its potential as a properly civic communicative space (Lessig, 1999, 2001).

Moreover, the use of the Net for political purposes is clearly minor compared with other purposes to which it is put. The kinds of interaction taking place can only to a small degree be considered manifestations of the public sphere; democratic deliberation is completely overshadowed by consumerism, entertainment, nonpolitical networking and chat, and so forth. Further, the communicative character of the political discussion does not always promote the civic ideal; much of it is isolated (and at times unpleasant), and its contributions to democratic will formation cannot always be assumed (Wilhelm, 2000).

At the same time, we note that the present architecture of the Net does still offer available space for many forms of civic initiatives. The criteria for access and use are such that the "digital divide" in the Western democracies has been diminishing, even if it would be unrealistic to assume that it will disappear (at the global level the prospects are quite remote, as is well known). The Internet is becoming integrated with the established system of political communication, yet it is also being used to challenge established power structures. Even the efforts of some more overtly authoritarian regimes around the world to curtail the democratic uses of the Net have not been fully successful, though inventories of the mechanisms of control are sobering. The progressive and subversive role of the Net should not be overestimated (Kalathil & Boas, 2003); "closed systems" can short-circuit the potential gains to be had by online political conversation (Fung, 2002). The sketchy evidence gives us some general impressions, but we obviously need a good deal more research before we can make specific claims about the political potential of the Net in different kinds of political contexts. At this stage, however, it does seem to be the case that, for those who have access and the political motivation, and who are living within open, democratic societies, the Internet offers very viable possibilities for civic interaction but clearly cannot promise a quick fix for democracy, a position that Blumler and Gurevitch (2001) affirmed in another recent article.

Multisector online public spheres

If the vision of a singular, integrated public sphere has faded in the face of the social realities of late modern society, so has much of the normative impetus that may have previously seen this as an ideal. The goal of ushering all citizens into one unitary public sphere, with one specific set of communicative and cultural traditions, is usually rejected on the grounds of pluralism and difference. There must exist spaces in which citizens belonging to different groups and cultures, or speaking in registers or even languages, will find participation meaningful. Differences of all kinds, including political orientation and interests, gender, ethnicity, cultural capital, and geography, can warrant specialized communicative spaces. At some points, certain groups may require a separate space where they can work out internal issues and/or cultivate a collective identity. Not least we must take into account alternative or counter public spheres (cf. Fenton & Downey, 2003; Asen & Brouwer, 2001), where political currents oppositional to the dominant mainstream can find support and expression. These were first formulated in terms of class ("the proletarian public sphere"; see Negt & Kluge, 1993) as a direct response to Habermas's emphasis on the bourgeois public sphere. Later, Fraser (1992) further developed the idea, not least with feminist horizons.

It is here where the Internet most obviously makes a contribution to the public sphere. There are literally thousands of Web sites having to do with the political realm at the local, national, and global levels; some are partisan, most are not. We can find discussion groups, chat rooms, alternative journalism, civic organizations, NGOs, grass roots issue-advocacy sites (cf. Berman & Mulligan, 2003; Bennett, 2003b), and voter education sites (see Levine, 2003). One can see an expansion in terms of available communicative spaces for politics, as well as ideological breadth, compared to the mass media. Structurally, this pluralization not only extends but also disperses the relatively clustered public sphere of the mass media.

If the Internet facilitates an impressive communicative heterogeneity, the negative side of this development is of course fragmentation, with public spheres veering toward disparate islands of political communication, as Galston (2003) had argued. Here opens up yet another important research theme, one that must encompass an overarching systemic perspective. That various groups may feel they must first coalesce internally before they venture out into the larger public sphere is understandable; however, cyber ghettos threaten to undercut a shared public culture and the integrative societal function of the public sphere, and they may well even help foster intolerance where such communities have little contact with—or understanding of—one another. Fragmentation also derives simply from the mushrooming of advocacy groups and the array of issues available. While traditional online party politics and forms of e-government may serve as centripetal forces to such fragmentation, the trend is clearly in the direction of increasing dispersion.

The question of multi-public spheres glides readily into the issue of the links between the different spheres to the centers of decision making. The public sphere per se is no guarantee for democracy: There can be all kinds of political information and debate in circulation, but there must be structural connections—formalized institutional procedures—between these communicative spaces and the processes of decision making, as Sparks (2001) argued. There can obviously be no automatic, lock-step connection here, not without degeneration into a chaotic populism. Yet, there must be some semblance of impact, some indication that the political talk of citizens has consequences, or else disengagement and cynicism can set in—as is precisely what many observers claim has been a pattern for a decade or so in the mainstream, mass mediated systems of political communication of the Western liberal democracies.

Today the most notable gap between communication in the public sphere and institutional structures for binding decisions is found in the global arena. Transnational forums, global networking, and opinion mobilization are very much evident on the Net, yet the mechanisms for transforming opinion at the global level into decisions and policies are highly limited, to say the least. There are simply few established mechanisms for democratically based and binding transnational decision making. While we might see the embryonic outlines of a global civil society (cf. Keane, 2003), its full realization is not on the horizon, even if the idea is a powerful and progressive element of the social imaginary.

In terms of the structural dimension, we can specify a number of different sectors of Net-based public spheres, including:

1. Versions of *e-government*, usually with a top-down character, where government representatives interact with citizens and where information about governmental administration and services is made available. While interaction may be relatively constricted, it can still at times serve as a sector of the public sphere. This sector is sometimes distinguished from *e-governance*, which emphasizes horizontal civic communication and input for government policy (Malina, 2003).
2. The *advocacy/activist domain*, where discussion is framed by organizations with generally shared perceptions, values, and goals—and geared for forms of political intervention. These include traditional parliamentarian politics, established corporate and other organized interest group politics (e.g., unions), and the new politics of social movements and other activists.
3. The vast array of diverse *civic forums* where views are exchanged among citizens and deliberation can take place. This is generally understood as the paradigmatic version of the public sphere on the Net, but it would be quite erroneous to neglect the others.
4. The prepolitical or *parapolitical domain*, which airs social and cultural topics having to do with common interests and/or collective identities. Here politics is not explicit but always remains a potential. Clearly, there is no absolute way in which the boundary between the nonpolitical and the parapolitical can be drawn, since it is always in part discursively negotiated and changeable.
5. The *journalism domain*, which includes everything from major news organizations that have gone online (e.g., newspapers and CNN) to Net-based news organizations (usually without much or any original reporting) such as Yahoo! News, alternative news organizations such as Indymedia and Mediachannel, as well as one-person weblog sites (also known as "bloggers"). Interestingly, the research literature has tended to focus mainly on deliberative interaction in terms of online public spheres and/or mass media journalism. We should not forget that the online journalism sector is a core element of the public sphere on the Internet.

This list can of course be made more elaborate; for example, one could divide civic forums into those which originate from journalistic initiatives and those with other origins. The point is simply to highlight a bit more specifically the sprawling character of the multisector online public sphere.

Two perspectives

Two contending perspectives are emerging in regard to the role of the Internet in the public sphere. One view posits that while there have been some interesting changes in the way democracy works, on the whole, the import of the Internet is modest; the Net is not deemed yet to be a factor of transformation. Margolis and Resnick (2000, p. 14) concluded that "there is an extensive political life on the Net, but it is mostly an extension of political life off the Net." So while the major political actors may engage in online campaigning, lobbying, policy advocacy, organizing, and so forth, this perspective underscores that there does not seem to be any major political change in sight. The argument is that the Internet has not made much of a difference in the ideological political landscape, it has not helped mobilize more citizens to participate, nor has it altered the ways that politics gets done. Even the consequences of modest experiments to formally incorporate the Internet into the political system with "e-democracy" have not been overwhelming (cf. Clift, 2003). E-government efforts to incorporate citizens into discussions and policy formulations usually have a decisive top-down character (see Malina, 2003, for a discussion of the UK circumstances), with discursive constraints deriving from the elite control of the contexts.

This evidence cannot be lightly dismissed, but what should be emphasized is that this perspective is anchored in sets of assumptions that largely do not see beyond the formal political system and the traditional role of the media in that system. Indeed, much of the evidence is based on electoral politics in the U.S. (cf. the collections by Jenkins & Thornburn, 2003, and Anderson & Cornfield, 2003). While the problems of democracy are acknowledged, the view is that the solutions lie in revitalizing the traditional models of political participation and patterns of political communication.

Other scholars alternatively take as their point of departure the understanding that we are moving into a new, transitional era in which the certitudes of the past in regard to how democracy works have become problematic. Democracy is seen to be, precariously, at a new historical juncture. Few observers would dismiss the central importance of electoral politics: A more robust democracy will not emerge by blithely sidestepping traditional, formal structures and procedures. However, certitudes of the traditionalist view of a "return to normalcy" are challenged, not least by some of the kinds of developments that Blumler and Gurevitch (2000) mentioned (see above), such as increased sociocultural heterogeneity and the changing position of the nation state. In terms of the Internet, however, the argument is that they become particularly salient precisely in the domain of informal, extra-parliamentarian politics. There has been massive growth in what we can call advocacy or issue politics, often in the form of ongoing campaigns. Some of the advocates are large and powerful interest groups; others take the form of social movements or have a more grass roots character. Many represent versions of "new" politics (called "life politics" by Giddens, 1991, and "sub-politics" by Beck, 1997; Bennett, 2003b, spoke of "lifestyle" politics); such politics can materialize all over the social terrain in many different contexts.

This "infinite" view of politics is increasingly in confrontation with the more traditional "bounded" notion, to use the terms of Blumler and Gurevitch (2000). Common for most is that electoral politics is often sidestepped, signaling a growing bifurcation between traditional parties and single-issue advocacy groups. There is not that much research available yet on these new forms of engagement, but initial findings suggest a variety of different organizational forms, usually very loose and horizontal in character, with fluid memberships (cf. Bennett, 2003a; Cammaerts & van Audenhove, 2003). This suggests a very different kind of organizational structure, as well as view of membership, relative to traditional parties.

It is often commented that the ostensible political apathy and disaffiliation from the established political system for many citizens may not necessarily signal a disinterest in politics per se. Rather, many citizens have refocused their political attention outside the parliamentary system, or they are in the process of redefining just what constitutes the political, often within the context of social movements. Among such groups, the boundaries between politics, cultural values, identity processes, and local self-reliance measures become fluid (Beck, 1997). Politics becomes not only an instrumental activity for achieving specific goals, but also an expressive activity, a way of asserting, within the public sphere, group values, ideals, and belonging. The evidence for such views makes good qualitative sense; however, it is almost impossible to get a quantitative grip on these developments. The fluid—and virtual—character of the organizations involved, the ease of joining and withdrawing, prevent us from getting a sense of the numbers involved. We can't know how many people any given Web site actually represents.

In the arena of new politics, the Internet becomes not only relevant but central: It is especially the capacity for the "horizontal communication" of civic interaction that is paramount. Both technologically and economically, access to the Net (and other new technologies, such as mobile phones) has helped facilitate the growth of large digital networks of activists. At present, it is in the tension-filled crevices deriving from the changes in the media industries, in sociocultural patterns, and in modes of political engagement that we can begin to glimpse new public sphere trends where the Internet clearly makes a difference. In their recent survey of the available research from political science, Graber *et al.* (2002, pp. 3–4) noted:

> The literature on interest networks and global activism seems particularly rich in examples of how various uses of the Internet and the Web have transformed activism, political pressure, and public communication strategies. . . . Research on civic organizations and

political mobilization is characterized by findings showing potentially large effects of new media and for the breadth of directly applicable theory.

Set in relation to the population as a whole, the numbers involved here may not seem overwhelming, but the embryonic patterns taking shape in the public sphere now may, with historical hindsight in the future, prove to have been quite significant.

Interaction: limits of deliberative democracy

In the discussions about democracy and the public sphere in recent years, the theme of deliberative democracy is often aired. In the final sections of this presentation, I wish to address this topic by looking at some findings from recent research on online forums, as well as considering the concept itself. In particular, I see limitations in the notion of deliberative democracy as an analytic horizon for understanding the democratic impact of political discussion in online public spheres. While useful, my view is that this notion only takes us part of the way in analyzing and understanding political discussion on the Internet, especially if we focus on new, extra-parliamentarian politics. The rational biases of the deliberative democracy perspective need to be complemented with what I call civic cultures.

Theories of democracy have generally posited that the communicative interaction among citizens is of prime importance. Civic discussion is seen as constitutive of publics, which are both morally and functionally vital for democracy. The specific notion of deliberative democracy integrates elements of political theory with perspectives on communication (I developed these points in more detail in Dahlgren, 2002). Habermas and those working within his theoretical tradition have had a major impact in shaping the idea of deliberative democracy. The idea of deliberation points to the procedures of open discussion aimed at achieving rationally motivated consensus. Certainly dialogue is preferable to violence, and good dialogue is preferable to poor dialogue, but with the referent of the Habermasian ideal speech situation, demanding criteria are placed on the nature of political discussion. High standards are useful and necessary to define directions, even if we realize that reality often falls short of the ideals. There is a growing literature, largely normative and theoretic, addressing the concept of deliberative democracy (see, for example, Chambers & Costain, 2000; Elster, 1998; Sanders, 1997; Benhabib, S., 1996; Bohman, 1996; Fishkin, 1991; Dryzek, 1990).

Not surprisingly, recent research has shown that online discussions do not always follow the high ideals set for deliberative democracy. Speech is not always so rational, tolerance toward those who hold opposing views is at times wanting, and the forms of interaction are not always so civil (Wilhelm, 2000). Hagemann (2002) found in his analysis of political party discussion lists in the Netherlands that, the communicative rationality of the contributions was not impressive, in that they were often typified by the assertion of opinion without supporting arguments. Fung (2002) noticed that in the Hong Kong situation, journalists might sometimes debate under the false guise of ordinary citizens. Certainly political life offline can often be like that, so there is no particular reason to expect an ontological transformation merely because discussion shifts to cyberspace. Yet, it is important that current research is showing the particular character of some of these communicative shortcomings on the Net.

There are also sociological shortcomings in regard to deliberative democracy, the most basic being the familiar low level of participation, awareness of which in turn seems to further reduce the motivation to engage via the Net (Schultz, 2000; Heikkilä & Lehtonen, 2003). (It might be useful, however, to reflect more on the theoretic issue that Schultz (2000) raises: While we might bemoan low participation on the Internet, given that attention is a scarce resource and with increasing participation, there is less time for participants to listen to each other, what would be the consequences of very high participation be? The issue of "optimal" levels of participation in specific contexts, based on discursive feasibility, is in need of investigation.) In any case, there is also good news from this research. Tsaliki (2002) found a very satisfactory level of public deliberation in her comparative study of online forums in Greece, the Netherlands, and Britain. Also, the Internet seems to offer opportunities to participate for many people who otherwise find that there are too many taboos and too much discomfiture in talking about politics in their own face-to-face environments (Stromer-Galley, 2002).

In regard to such aspects as these, the vision of deliberative democracy provides a useful compass for envisioning what enhanced online public spheres could be. Yet, there are two basic conceptual difficulties in the discursive rationalism in Habermas's (1989) original position regarding the public sphere, and this is amplified by his later work on pragmatics and the ideal speech situation (Habermas, 1984, 1987). The first is by now familiar, and I will just mention it without further development: The rationalist bias tends to discount a wide array of communicative modes that can be of importance for democracy, including the affective, the poetic, the humorous, the ironic, and so forth. The second problem has received less attention. Basically, the argument is that adherence to the perspective of deliberative democracy risks downplaying relations of power that are built into communicative situations. Kohn (2000, p. 409) approaches this issue by saying that "reasonableness is itself a social construction which usually benefits those already in power.... Democratic theory must consider how critical perspectives capable of challenging the dominant definition of rationality are generated, contested, and institutionalized." While she underscores the important role that deliberative democracy has, she makes the point that it tends to privilege the modes of communication among the elites. She argues that, historically, the expansion of the democratic character of society has been prompted by mobilization, the generation of collective identities, and concerted action, not by the attainment of deliberative consensus.

Arguing in a parallel, if a bit more abstract manner, Mouffe (1999) makes the case that the political is an irreducible dimension of all social relations and that conflict—she uses the term antagonism—is always present in the ever-shifting relations between various interests, between changing groupings of "us" and "them" in plural societies. The task is not to strive for consensus, which is ultimately temporary, or to eradicate power from democratic politics, but rather to formulate forms of power that are in keeping with democratic values and a democratic system. Instead of trying to remove passions from politics, replacing them with rational consensus, the aim should be to "mobilize those passions towards the promotion of democratic designs" (Mouffe, 1999, p. 756). While she does not have so much to say about the specifics of political discussion, she too sees the vision of Habermasian deliberative democracy suppressing the reality of power relations.

These critical reflections can be linked to the point noted above that the Internet has a more compelling role to play in the advocacy/activist sector of the online public sphere, in the context of new extra-parliamentarian politics. Political discussion within these organizations strives for internal consensus (or at least compromise), often to some degree of collective identity, and for political mobilization. Externally, however, the thrust of their political address toward power holders in the political or economic realm is not to attain consensus, but rather to affect on policy. Toward political society at large, they seek to stimulate public opinion. Those working in the alter-globalization movement, as well as those in, for instance, environmental, human rights, feminist, and peace organizations, are striving to make a political difference in settings that are characterized by highly unequal relations of power. While rational consensus may at times be a suitable strategy, deliberation is not always the best overall frame for describing or analyzing the political interaction that takes place.

Civic cultures and political discussion

As a complementary way to analyze and understand political interaction in online public spheres, I propose that we treat political discussion not just in terms of its rational communicative qualities, but also as a form of practice integrated within more encompassing civic cultures. I have been developing the notion of civic culture (Dahlgren, 2000a, 2000b, 2003) as a way to conceptualize the factors that can enhance or impede political participation—the enactment of citizenship understood as forms of social agency. Space only permits a brief overview of this notion here, and then I will return to the question of political discussion, framing it as part of civic cultures.

The idea of civic culture takes as its starting point the notion of citizens as social agents, and it asks what the *cultural* factors are behind such agency (or its absence). Civic cultures point to both the conditions and the manifestations of such participation; they are anchored in the mind-sets and symbolic milieu of everyday life. Civic cultures are potentially both strong and vulnerable: They help to promote the functioning of democracy, they can serve to empower or disempower citizens, yet like all domains of culture, they can easily be affected by political and economic power. A key assumption here is that a viable democracy must have an anchoring at the level of citizens' lived experiences, personal resources, and subjective dispositions. The notion of civic cultures grafts some fruitful elements from cultural theory onto some more familiar themes from political communication. This highlights that such dimensions as meaning, identity, and subjectivity are important elements of political communication.

We can point to public spheres, to their representations and possible forms of interaction, yet questions remain about why people participate in them or not. The framework of civic cultures seeks to address these questions and provide empirical starting points for analysis. Given that the foundation of the civic culture frame is the citizen-agent, this frame is thus interested in the processes of becoming—how people develop into citizens, how they come to see themselves as members of and potential participants in societal development. Civic culture is an analytic construct that seeks to identify the possibilities of people acting in the role of citizens. This is a role which can have non- or pre-political aspects, but which may develop toward politics and indeed evolve into formalized politics. The key here is to underscore the processual and contextual dimension: The political and politics are not simply given, but are constructed via word and deed.

The civic culture concept does not presuppose homogeneity among its citizens; it in fact assumes that there are many ways in which citizenship and democracy can be enacted. It does, however, suggest the need for minimal shared commitments to the vision and procedures of democracy, which in turn entails a capacity to see beyond the immediate interests of one's own group. Needless to say, this is a challenging balance to maintain. However, different social and cultural groups can express civic culture in different ways, theoretically enhancing democracy's possibilities. To facilitate the use of this materialist and constructionist concept, I treat it as comprising a number of dynamically interrelated parameters: values, affinity, knowledge, identities, and practices.

Values: It should be underscored that values must have their anchoring in everyday life; a political system will never achieve a democratic character if the world of the everyday reflects antidemocratic normative dispositions.

Affinity: This points to a minimal sense of commonality among citizens in heterogeneous late modern societies, a sense that they belong to the same social and political entities, despite all other differences. They have to deal with each other to make their common entities work, whether at the level of neighborhood, nation state, or the global arena. This commonality is grounded in a realization among all groups of the mutual need to maintain democracy and adhere to its rules. Without this affinity, there can be no progress in communicating with adversaries, or even cooperation and networking among like-minded.

Knowledge: Referential cognizance of the world is indispensable for the life of democracy. A subset of knowledge is competencies and, in particular, communicative skills, which points to some degree of literacy and the relevance of education for democracy. Modes of knowledge are evolving, however, especially among the young, in keeping with cultural changes and new media technologies that can promote new modalities of thought and expression, new ways of knowing and forms of communicative competencies.

Identities: Citizenship is a formal status, with rights and obligations. However, it also has a subjective side: People must be able to see themselves as members and potential participants with efficacy in social and political entities; this must be a part of people's multidimensional identities. Citizenship is central to the issues of social belonging and social participation. Identities of membership are not just subjectively produced by individuals, but evolve in relation to social milieus and institutional mechanisms.

Practices: Democracy must be enacted in concrete, recurring practices—individual, group, and collective—relevant for diverse situations. Such practices help generate personal and social meaning to the ideals of democracy. They must have some element of the routine, of the taken for granted about them (e.g., elections), if they are to be a part of a civic culture, yet the potential for spontaneous interventions, one-off, novel forms of practice, needs to be kept alive. Civic cultures require many other practices, pertinent to many other circumstances in everyday life. Across time, practices become traditions, and experience becomes collective memory. Today's democracy needs to be able to refer to a past without being locked in it. New practices and traditions can and must evolve to ensure that democracy does not stagnate.

The most fundamental and most ubiquitous practice is precisely civic interaction, and discussion. Interaction is one of the dimensions of the public sphere, and as I noted, one can empirically investigate civic discussion by examining, for instance, its various discursive modes, its spatial and contextual sites and settings, and its social circumstances, both on- and offline.

From this vantage point, discussion in the context of the extra-parliamentarian new politics within the advocacy/activist domain of online public spheres can be seen in a different light. In the context of destabilized political communication systems, the discussions generated in these settings by these actors hold out the modest potential for making a contribution to the renewal, growth, and strengthening of civic cultures among many citizens who feel distanced from the arenas of formal party politics. This view must of course be nuanced. For example, there are a wide variety of political colors in this sector, and not all of them may be considered democratic and progressive. Also, we are no doubt talking about relatively small numbers of seriously engaged citizens. The general situation here can be compared with the protest movements of the 1960s and 1970s, where rather small but determined groups could have a significant impact on political agendas. One of the differences is that today the groups are generally much more sophisticated and effective, not least thanks to their access to the new media and their skills with them.

Discussion here may or may not always take the form of Habermasian deliberation, but what is more important is the reciprocal dynamics that it can generate, reinforcing the parameters of civic culture and the impact this may have on the larger political situation. The values and commitments espoused by these groups are largely very democratic, and can be seen as a counter to some of the very undemocratic values associated with the prevailing neo-liberal order. They are able to diffuse their knowledge through the Net to each other, and on occasion their efforts are picked up by journalists on the Net or in the traditional mass media and become disseminated further to wider publics (Bennett, 2003a). The affinities demonstrated by many of these groups foster a spirit of cooperation between various organizations and their loosely defined memberships, contributing to the formation of a broader counter political culture (see the Cammaerts and van Audenhove article, in this issue). Via the identities that are developed by participation, people are exploring new ways of being citizens and doing politics. Among the other notable practices are the sharing of information and experience, often transnationally, maintaining permanent campaigns to try to influence on public opinion on particular issues, and in some cases organizing political anti-consumption (i.e., boycotts), which can serve to concretely link the politically abstract with people's everyday lives.

While it is important to keep a clear perspective and not exaggerate the extent of the activities or their impact, it would also be foolish to underestimate what seems to be a major development in the contemporary history of Western democracy. The Internet is at the forefront of the evolving public sphere, and if the dispersion of public spheres generally is contributing to the already destabilized political communication system, specific counter public spheres on the Internet are also allowing engaged citizens to play a role in the development of new democratic politics. Discussion here may take the form of deliberation, with various degrees of success, but what is more important in this context is that talk among citizens is the catalyst for the civic cultures that are fuelling this engagement. The jury is still out on what the verdict will be regarding the impact of these developments on the larger democratic systems—and I suspect that it will be out for quite some time—but in the meantime important developments in political communication are in motion.

References

Alasuutari, P. (Ed.) (1999). *Rethinking the media audience*. London: Sage.
Anderson, D. M., & Cornfield, M. (Eds.) (2003). *The civic web: Online politics and democratic values*. Lanham, MD: Rowman & Littlefield.
Asen, R., & Brouwer, D. C. (Eds.) (2001). *Counterpublics and the state*. Albany: State University of New York Press.
Baker, C. E. (2002). *Media, markets, and democracy*. New York: Cambridge University Press.
Beck, U. (1997). *The reinvention of politics*. Cambridge: Polity Press.
Benhabib, S. (Ed.). (1996). *Democracy and difference*. Princeton, NJ: Princeton University Press.
Bennett, W. L. (2003a). New media power: The Internet and global activism. In N. Couldry & J. Currans (Eds.), *Contesting media power* (pp. 17–37). Lanham, MD: Rowman & Littlefield.
Bennett, W. L. (2003b). Lifestyle politics and citizen-consumers: Identity, communication and political action in late modern society. In J. Corner & D. Pels (Eds.), *Media and political style: Essays on representation and civic culture* (pp. 137–150). London: Sage.
Bennett, W. L., & Entman, R. (Eds.) (2001). *Mediated politics in the future of democracy*. Cambridge: Cambridge University Press.
Berman, J., & Mulligan, D. K. (2003). Issue advocacy in the age of the Internet. In D. M. Anderson & M. Cornfield (Eds.), *The civic web: Online politics and democratic values* (pp. 77–83). Lanham, MD: Rowman & Littlefield.
Blumler, J. G., & Gurevitch, M. (2000). Rethinking the study of political communication. In J. Curran & M. Gurevitch (Eds.), *Mass media and society* (3rd ed., pp. 155–172). London: Arnold.
Blumler, J. G., & Gurevitch, M. (2001). The new media and our political communication discontents: Democratizing cyberspace. *Information, Communication & Society*, 4, 1–14.
Bohman, J. (1996). *Public deliberation: Pluralism, complexity and democracy*. Cambridge, MA: MIT Press.
Cammaerts, B., & Van Audenhove, L. (2003). *ICT-usage among transnational social movements in the networked society: To organize, to mediate, to influence*. Amsterdam: ASCoR, University of Amsterdam.
Chambers, S., & Costain, A. (Eds.) (2000). *Deliberation, democracy and the media*. Lanham, MD: Rowmann & Littlefield.
Clift, J. (2003). E-democracy: Lessons from Minnesota. In D. M. Anderson & M. Cornfield (Eds.), *The civic web: Online politics and democratic values* (pp. 157–165). Lanham, MD: Rowman & Littlefield.
Dahlgren, P. (2000a). The Internet and the democratization of civic culture. *Political Communication*, 17, 335–340.
Dahlgren, P. (2000b). Media, citizens and civic culture. In M. Gurevitch & J. Curran (Eds.), *Mass media and society* (3rd ed., pp. 310–328). London: Edward Arnold.
Dahlgren, P. (2002). In search of the talkative public: Media, deliberative democracy and civic culture. *Javnost/The Public*, 9(3), 5–26.

Dahlgren, P. (2003). Reconfiguring civic culture in the new media milieu. In J. Corner & D. Pels (Eds.), *Media and political style: Essays on representation and civic culture* (pp. 151–170). London: Sage.

Dewey, J. (1954). *The public and its problems.* Chicago: Swallow Press.

Dryzek, J. (1990). *Discursive democracy: Politics, policy and political science.* Cambridge: Cambridge University Press.

Elster, J. (Ed.). (1998). *Deliberative democracy.* Cambridge: Cambridge University Press.

Fenton, N., & Downey, J. (2003). Counter public spheres and global modernity. *Javnost/The Public, 10(1)*, 15–32.

Fishkin, J. (1991). *Democracy and deliberation.* New Haven, CT: Yale University Press.

Fraser, N. (1992). Rethinking the public sphere: A contribution to the critique of actually existing democracy. In C. Calhoun (Ed.), *Habermas and the public sphere* (pp. 109–142). Boston: MIT Press.

Fung, A. (2002). One city, two systems: Democracy in an electronic chat room in Hong Kong. *Javnost/The Public, 9(2)*, 77–94.

Galston, W. A. (2003). If political fragmentation is the problem, is the Internet the solution? In D. M. Anderson & M. Cornfield (Eds.), *The civic web: Online politics and democratic values* (pp. 35–44). Lanham, MD: Rowman & Littlefield.

Giddens, A. (1991). *The consequences of modernity.* Cambridge: Polity Press.

Graber, D., Bimber, B., Bennett, W. L., Davis, R., & Norris, P. (2003). The Internet and politics: Emerging perspectives. In H. Nissenbaum, M. Price, & S. B. Bernstein (Eds.), *The academy and Internet.* New York: Peter Lang.

Habermas, J. (1984, 1987). *Theory of communicative action* (2 vols.). Cambridge: Polity Press.

Habermas, J. (1989). *The structural transformation of the public sphere.* Boston: MIT Press.

Hagemann, C. (2002). Participants in and contents of two Dutch political party discussion lists on the Internet. *Javnost/The Public, 9(2)*, 61–76.

Heikkilä, H., & Lehtonen, P. (2003). Between a rock and a hard place: Boundaries of public spaces for citizen deliberation. *Communications: The European Journal of Communication Research, 28*, 157–172.

Jenkins, H., & Thornburn, D. (Eds.) (2003). *Democracy and new media.* Cambridge, MA: MIT Press.

Kalathil, S., & Boas, T. C. (Eds.) (2003). *Open networks, closed regimes.* Washington, DC: Carnegie Endowment for International Peace.

Keane, J. (2003). *Global civil society?* Cambridge: Cambrige University Press.

Kohn, M. (2000). Language, power, and persuasion: Towards a critique of deliberative democracy. *Constellations, 7*, 408–429.

Lessig, L. (1999). *Code and other laws of cyberspace.* New York: Basic Books.

Lessig, L. (2001). *The future of ideas: The fate of the commons in a connected world.* New York: Random House.

Levine, P. (2003). Online campaigning and the public interest. In D. M. Anderson & M. Cornfield (Eds.), *The civic web: Online politics and democratic values* (pp. 47–62). Lanham, MD: Rowman & Littlefield.

Lewis, J. (2001). *Constructing public opinion.* New York: Columbia University Press.

Malina, A. (2003). e-Transforming democracy in the UK: Considerations of developments and suggestions for empirical research. *Communications: The European Journal of Communication Research, 28*, 135–155.

Margolis, M., & Resnick, D. (2000). *Politics as usual: The cyberspace "revolution."* London: Sage.

Mouffe, C. (1999). Deliberative democracy or agonistic pluralism? *Social Research, 66*, 745–758.

Negt, O., & Kluge, A. (1993). *The public sphere and experience.* Minneapolis: University of Minnesota Press.

Patekis, K. (2000). The political economy of the Internet. In J. Curran (Ed.), *Media organizations in society* (pp. 84–106). London: Arnold.

Sanders, L. (1997). Against deliberation. *Political Theory, 25*, 347–376.

Schiller, D. (1999). *Digital capitalism: Networking the global marketing system.* Cambridge, MA: MIT Press.

Schultz, T. (2000). Mass media and the concept of interactivity: An exploratory study of online forums and reader e-mail. *Media, Culture & Society, 22*, 205–221.

Sparks, C. (2001). The Internet and the global public sphere. In W. L. Bennett & R. M. Entman (Eds.), *Mediated politics: Communication in the future of democracy* (pp. 75–95). New York: Cambridge University Press.

Splichal, S. (1999). *Public opinion: Developments and controversies in the twentieth century.* Lanham, MD: Rowman & Littlefield.

Stromer-Galley, J. (2002). New voices in the public sphere: A comparative analysis of interpersonal and online political talk. *Javnost/The Public, 9(2)*, 23–42.

Tsaliki, L. (2002). Online forums and the enlargement of the public sphere: Research from a European project. *Javnost/The Public, 9(2)*, 95–112.

Wilhelm, A. G. (2000). *Democracy in the digital age.* London: Routledge.

57

RETHINKING ICTS
ICTs on a human scale

Cees J. Hamelink

Source: *European Journal of Communication* 21(3) (2006): 389–96.

Abstract

Developments in the field of information and communication technologies (ICTs) may in the near future increasingly lose sight of the human scale. The assessment of emerging technologies and their application in terms of the human condition seems urgently needed, therefore. A useful field for such an assessment is the digitalization of health care.

Modern ICTs operate increasingly on a grand scale: in surveillance, intelligence, warfare, transport and finance systems. Technology represents the human capacity to invent, innovate and develop tools. Human beings may not be very well equipped for their survival, but they are adept at designing constructs (such as languages, technologies) that compensate for innate inadequacies. Amid the impressive array of human cultural constructs the question arises whether they may wander too far away from human nature. Could it be that the distance between construct and nature grows so huge that what seemed a solution turns out to be a danger? The development of advanced, sophisticated armaments may be a case in point. Modern arms (such as computer-guided fighter planes) no longer match the human capacity to understand what we are doing and what the consequences may be. The fighter pilot is morally so distant from his targets, he may as well be playing a computer game rather than destroying human lives. But even if he tried to understand and reason morally about his acts, he could not possibly begin to imagine what the effects of his actions are. Whereas our minds live still in the age of horse-drawn carriages and spears, our bodies travel in super-fast cars and have the devastating power of nuclear arms at their disposal. Can minds catch up with bodies? The astonishing developments in science and technology began to inspire the belief that the rational, conscious and free human mind that the Enlightenment projected, was capable of dealing with these developments in a humanitarian way. This belief was fundamentally challenged by the 20th-century horrors of Auschwitz and Hiroshima. Science and technology have made it possible to realize very destructive projects of ever-larger dimensions. The human mind, however, seems rather ill-prepared for large-scale operations. Health services, schools, cities, transport systems can, beyond a certain scale, no longer guarantee human well-being.

If we find this undesirable, we have to confront the question of whether technological development should be restricted. Should we, as Bill Joy contemplates, limit 'our pursuit of certain kinds of knowledge' (Joy, 2000)? In a modern world that is largely inspired by the Enlightenment ideals of human improvement through science and technology, this is difficult to imagine. The holy mantra seems to be that knowledge in itself is good and that acquiring more knowledge, even better. And, indeed, the search for knowledge satisfies a fundamental human desire to 'fly away from ignorance' as William Shakespeare elegantly put it. As we acquire more knowledge, we should also become aware of the dark side to an uncritical reverence for scientific and technological development. In recent decades, science and technology have brought humankind close to the destruction of the planet, and the imminent technological developments and their convergence make the extinction of humanity a very real possibility.

One may object that humans as individuals have a strong desire to survive. This may be true, but it does not guarantee that the collective of humans as a species will not be guided by an equally strong negligence with regard to its future. The nuclear arms race of recent history does not provide a very reassuring picture. The collective has a great capacity for irresponsible, destructive action. Technology has rarely ever been invented, developed and applied under the guidance of normative, moral principles. The ability to engineer was and is – often in combination with commercial or military interest – the essential driving force. Can we afford this in the 21st century?

Should not the development of ICTs be measured against a normative yardstick that incorporates the features of the human condition and that would assist in the definition of a human scale for science and technology development?

Characteristic of humans are their dependence, vulnerability and uncertainty

Dependence

Human beings are fundamentally dependent upon fellow humans since as social animals they cannot – with few exceptions – survive in isolation. They are equally dependent upon all sorts of technical tools for their survival and well-being. Against this basic dependence upon the outside world, there is a strong desire to be free from the constraints this imposes upon human life. There is a history-long struggle to dominate the forces of nature and escape dependence upon the unpredictable and often catastrophic ways in which these forces affect human lives. There is also throughout history an emancipatory drive towards the definition of human identity and autonomy. At the core of universal human rights, the world community has posited the moral claim to the autonomy of all human beings.

The human scale can be found in the equilibrium between the factual state of dependence and the moral claim to autonomy.

Vulnerability

The common experience of humanity is vulnerability. Humans have only limited control over their physical environment, have little understanding of their own emotions and actions, and live with levels of aggression that are hardly restricted by the kind of instincts that serve the non-human species so much better. Humans are easily vulnerable to the machinations of others and equally threaten the vulnerability of others by their actions.

Against the experience of vulnerability, there is a strong desire towards the protection of human integrity against harm. To protect human physical, mental and moral integrity, an impressive array of instruments has been developed ranging from accident-proof cars and insurance policies, to medical treatments, psychotherapeutic techniques and religious codes and rites. In its formulation of universal rights, the world community has placed important emphasis on the right to the protection of human integrity.

The human scale can be found in the equilibrium between the factual state of vulnerability and the moral claim to integrity.

Uncertainty

Human beings live in a chaotic, confusing and complex reality. The unexpected and unwanted things that happen much of the time are out of their control. They try to order their lives and social systems, but are again and again confronted with the unpredictable outcomes of their own actions. They live in chaotic environments in which minute causes can have enormous consequences. They would like to foresee and control such consequences, but the human capacity to forecast is flawed and the future remains fundamentally uncertain.

Against the experience of uncertainty, humans have tried throughout the ages to find a level of security in belief systems, legal institutions and moral conventions. The search for a basic predictability in the ways humans treat each other was a basic inspiration for the universal declaration of human rights that was adopted by the world community in 1948.

The human scale can be found in the equilibrium between the factual state of uncertainty and the moral claim to security.

The question that now poses itself is what does seeking balances between dependence vs autonomy, vulnerability vs integrity and uncertainty vs security mean and imply for the human scale in ICT development, innovation and application?

Dependence/autonomy

As a result of technological development, there is an ever-increasing number of tools and instruments that are ill-understood by their human users. Throughout our daily routines, we use pieces of electrical and electronic equipment (varying from ATMs, cellphones, cars, self check-in systems at airports, to microwave ovens) that function on the basis of complex hardware – and software technologies that few of us master. As a matter of fact, increasingly today's advanced technologies exceed the knowledge and skills of even well-trained specialists. Whereas people could fairly easily learn how to repair their bikes, with cars loaded with digital gadgets there is almost complete dependence upon the expert. Next, the expert is increasingly dependent upon computerized data-systems that 'think and decide' for the expert. Advancements in artificial intelligence, nanotechnology, biotechnology and robotics reinforce a process of knowledge 'extensification' that places the processing and understanding of knowledge increasingly under the control of intelligent tools and instruments. In this process, human beings may begin to lose their autonomy over the acquisition of knowledge and become dependent upon digital copies and electronic searches.

This may ultimately imply the total loss of human autonomy to dependence upon a new generation of cyborgs.

Vulnerability/integrity

With the increasing dependence upon advanced technology, we become more vulnerable to its malfunctioning as a result of systemic flaws or deliberate misuse.

An inescapable part of living in modernity is that – as Ulrich Beck (1992) has proposed – we live in a 'risk society'. Human integrity is threatened by warfare (nuclear, biological and chemical), terrorism, organized crime, changes in the environment (increasing ultraviolet radiation, rising temperatures, disappearance of rain forests, shortage of drinking water, desertification, depletion of fossil fuels, decreasing biodiversity), carcinogenic ingredients in food supplies, pollution by poisonous materials (acid rain, chemical products from insecticides to deodorants), series of natural disasters (asteroids, comets, volcanoes, floods, tornados) and genetic experiments. To this discouraging list we have to add the observation that also the deployment of ICT systems implies enormous risks. Through its many different applications – ranging from electronic mail to e-commerce – ICTs pervade a wide range of social domains and have a serious impact on national economies and private lives.

As more and more social domains (like banking, telecommunications, air traffic or energy supply) become dependent upon cyberspace technology, society's vulnerability to the malfunctioning of the technological infrastructure raises the possibility of serious destabilization. Among the possible causes are software failures and deliberate destruction of computer systems.

Uncertainty/security

Technological innovations are often presented with the pretence of creating more certainty: modern meteo-systems, earthquake warning systems, medical life-support systems, their assurances notwithstanding, offer interesting calculations and equations, but no irrefutable certainty. In a way, the rapid accumulation and expansion of human knowledge demonstrate that there is more we do not know than we do know. Modern science and technology – which are in a way organized uncertainty – have made us aware in unprecedented ways of all we do not understand. Advanced ICTs add considerably to human uncertainty by providing increasing volumes of information that are too much to process and order, by facilitating the permanent surveillance of people in their daily activities and by leaving people uncertain as to how much information is being collected about them, by whom and for what purposes.

Choices

Human decision-making takes place against the background of the characteristics of dependence, vulnerability and uncertainty. The space within which human choices are made is limited. When it comes to such essential choices as the times of birth and death, the type of gender and race or the quality of health and intelligence, there is little freedom to choose. Yet, there remain many situations where we can take different routes and can say 'Yes' or 'No'.

Implicit in the realization that we make choices – and often choices that critically affect others – is the responsibility to account for them! Therefore, we may be asked to defend our moral choices and expose the mental map that guides our choices to public scrutiny. This holds equally for the designers, developers and manufacturers of ICTs, as for the policy-makers and regulators and also the corporate and private users.

Following the argument about the human condition, it can be claimed that morally defensible choices related to ICTs are those that take into account human dependence, vulnerability and uncertainty. This means that we question whether inventions, developments and innovations in ICTs enlarge the dependent, vulnerable and uncertain state of their users. In other words: are choices inspired by empathy with the fragility of the human condition? There can hardly ever be the guarantee that a given choice is optimal but at least choices can be accounted for beyond the common arguments of profit, greed or selfish interest.

In the spirit of a discursive process, all stakeholders should design visions for possible futures that either enlarge dependence, increase vulnerability and expand uncertainty or diminish these human features and strengthen human autonomy, integrity and security.

The field of medical technology can be used as a concrete illustration of the assessment of emerging technologies in the light of the human scale. Increasingly, health care institutions are going digital and apply ICTs to electronic patient records, decision support systems, telediagnostics, virtual surgery, online gene data banks or computerized diagnosis and prescription. It seems that the future of health care will be largely shaped by developments in artificial intelligence, robotics, informatics and telecommunication technology. In many hospitals, a choice will have to be made about the acquisition of a computational system called APACHE. The acronym APACHE stands for acute physiology, age, chronic health evaluation. The system processes vital medical information on the basis of inference from data in a database and computes the probability of mortality and thus the futility of prolonged treatment. The costs of acquiring such a computational futility metric (CFM) system are approximately US$300,000. The system will assist in the deployment of scarce financial resources and facilitate the efficient allocation of finances. Its introduction raises fundamental questions about issues of accountability in the case of machine error in judgement, of expert dependence upon machine reasoning, of reliability in data processing based upon inference and of the role of patient consent.

What should the key considerations be in the choice about digital medical technology? Patients' well-being? Mortality rates in the digital hospital? The informed consent of patients? The risks of technical fallibility? The level of productivity in health care services?

An assessment in terms of human scale would measure the introduction of a system like APACHE against the following questions.

- Does the CFM system increase patient and doctor dependence upon digital technology or will it strengthen their autonomy in vital decision-making about human life?
- Does the CFM system increase patient vulnerability or will it guarantee more patient integrity?
- Does the CFM system improve the balance between uncertainty and security?

The procedure for a human rights assessment of advanced digital technology would only make sense if all those affected by the choices that will be made can partake. The stakeholders would include patients' associations, medical doctors, nurses, hospital management, public health policy-makers and ICT professionals. Such a procedure could begin with an experimental status and after several trial runs be upgraded to a more formal, institutional status. Whatever the outcome, the assessment would certainly be a crucial contribution to the rethinking of ICTs.

References

Beck, U. (1992) *Risk Society: Towards a New Modernity*. London: Sage.
Joy, B. (2000) 'Why the Future Doesn't Need Us'. *Wired* No. 8.04.10.

Part 8

GOVERNING NETWORKS

58

COMMUNICATION POLICY IN THE GLOBAL INFORMATION ECONOMY

Whither the public interest?

William H. Melody

Source: Marjorie Ferguson (ed.) (1989) *Public Communication – The New Imperatives: Future Directions for Media Research*, London: Sage, pp. 16–39.

Information and communication developments have tended to erode heretofore separable areas of public policy, and to increase the probability of unforeseen implications arising in areas outside the purview of traditional policy analysis. Industrial policy, social policy and cultural policy are more integrated than they have been in the past. Each has significant implications for the others. The press, print, broadcast, library, telecommunication and computer industries are becoming more interrelated and interdependent, so that government policies toward one industry cannot help but have significant implications for others.

The difficulty to date has been understanding the many important dimensions of information and communication policy issues, particularly when it comes to assessing the long-term implications. There has been a tendency for governments to recognize only those immediate issues that have been thrust before them, generally in fragmented fashion, outside either a long-term or a systemic context. The great challenge for policy research is to explain the complex set of interrelations among policy areas that were previously thought to be reasonably discrete and separable, and thereby to provide a better understanding of the environment in which informed policy decisions must be made (Melody, 1989a).

The successful development of new information and communication markets for the benefit of all sectors of society will require major adaptations by both private and public institutions. If markets in tradeable information are going to work efficiently and equitably, they must be developed upon a foundation of public information that provides the education and training necessary for citizens to function effectively as workers, managers, consumers and responsible citizens. Determining the appropriate adaptations, both by the public and the private sectors, to the new information and communication environment is a crucial task for public policy.

Many individuals and organizations can benefit substantially from the rapid expansion of the information and communication sector, but at least some are likely to be disadvantaged, in both relative and absolute terms, especially if traditional public and social services are displaced, downgraded or made more expensive. To illustrate, a considerable portion of the information now accessible through public libraries is subject to commoditization and sale in private markets, where it would be accessible only through telecommunication-based information services. In recent years, many libraries have expanded access to a variety of bibliographic databases. But they have cut back their physical holdings of government reports and statistics, general research reports and studies, periodicals and even books. This has greatly facilitated research projects with the funding support to pay for computer searches and acquisition of the desired material. But most academic researchers, students, and the lay public can rarely afford to use computer searches, and are increasingly frustrated by the more limited access to hard-copy resources.

The telephone system is being upgraded to the technical standards of an integrated services digital network (ISDN) that is more efficient for the plethora of new information services required by sophisticated high-volume users. But it may be significantly more costly for small-volume users and users with only local telephone service requirements. This could make it more difficult to achieve, and for some countries to maintain, a universal basic telephone service (Melody, 1989b).

The characteristics of information markets create special problems associated with the transfer of computer and telecommunication technologies to developing countries. The market incentives are to sell new technology facility systems in developing countries to establish the infrastructure for both the domestic and international communication of information services. Given the established base of information in the technologically advanced countries, and their lead in establishing new information services, the information flows are predictable. Final consumer information, such as television programmes (often accompanied by advertising), is likely to dominate the flow from developed to developing countries. Specialized information markets that create value as a result of the monopoly of information are likely to generate a dominant flow of information about developing countries to developed countries and transnational corporations. These conditions may place developing country firms and agencies at an increased competitive disadvantage in their own countries because of an information deficiency about conditions there (Melody, 1985).

A major challenge for public policy is to find methods to ensure that developments in the information and communication sector do not exacerbate class divisions in society and that the benefits are spread across all classes. This requires new conceptions and operational definitions of the 'public interest' and of public services. It requires new interpretations of the requirements of social policy, and the design of new institutional structures for its effective implementation. It also requires a re-evaluation of the role of information and communication in participatory democracy and the public policies necessary to encourage its diffusion across all segments of society.

An increase in the quantity and diversity of information sources and communication opportunities seems to be upon us, as markets in this field have grown rapidly from national to global. The economy of the future has already been dubbed 'the information society'. But what of the public interest in the age of information overload and new communication opportunities? Is there still an important or even essential role for public interest policies, if the gap between theory and practice along the uncertain path to participatory democracy is to be reduced in the information age? This chapter explores these issues and suggests an updated interpretation of the public interest that is adapted to the changing information/communication environment.

Information, communication and participatory democracy

Participatory democracy requires a citizenry that is both informed and has a continuing opportunity to be heard in the market-place of ideas. For most of history, dictators and even democratically elected governments have attempted to bias and restrict the information made available to the public, while limiting and controlling access to the market-place of ideas. Indeed, this is perhaps the essential contradiction of democratic theory versus practice. For those in power, the practice inevitably falls far short of the requirements of theory. *Spycatcher* and Irangate are examples in two nations that have done much to further the cause of participatory democracy in the world today.

In democratic countries, the rights of citizens to be informed and have access to the market-place of ideas have been accepted as an obligation of national governments. These rights have been enshrined in a variety of laws, policies and regulations. The right to be informed has been reflected primarily in programmes in three areas: (1) opportunities for universal education of the population, ostensibly to promote learning and the ability to assess critically the changing world; (2) the widespread availability of public libraries as repositories of both historical and current information, and public access to information about the policies and practices of government and other dominant institutions in society; and (3) independent and widespread reporting and interpretation of changing local, national and international events by the mass media – primarily the press, radio and television.

Recognizing that it is technologically, economically and physically impossible for everyone to be read, heard and seen via the mass media, on an equal access basis, public policy has been directed to ensuring terms of mass media access that reflect the broad interests of the general public. These include: (a) requiring 'responsible' presentations and fair dealing by those in privileged positions of power who control access to the general public through the media; (b) safeguarding rights of reply and legal protection from libel for individuals and organizations that feel unfairly treated; and (c) taking positive steps to maintain a diversity of information sources and a variety of content from the mass media.

To facilitate direct intercommunication among the citizenry, interpersonal and interorganization communication networks have been encouraged through national public postal and telecommunication systems with a fundamental policy objective to provide universal service. Both the mass media and the post-telegraph-telephone (PTT) sectors of the economy have been recognized as being significantly different from other industries because of their importance to the preservation of citizen's rights to be informed and to communicate freely, conditions essential to political democracy. For the most part, these industries have been treated as 'business affected with a public interest', and subjected to special treatment under law and government policy.

The institutional mechanisms for implementing and enforcing the public interest in the mass media and PTT sectors have differed among countries and among industries within the same country, and have changed over time. When new technologies have led to fundamental changes in the structure of communication industries, a reassessment of public interest requirements in the light of the changed conditions is almost always necessary (Melody, 1973). In recent years, both major communication sectors have applied a number of new information and communication technologies and have undergone substantial structural change, challenging traditional public interest notions and the established mechanisms for implementing them.

The press

With the help of the Gutenberg press, the virtual monopoly over public information was wrested from the authorities (church and state) and the professional class (monks) in the late fifteenth and sixteenth centuries. Since then, a continuing struggle has taken place between the state and the 'independent' press with respect to the freedom of the press from state restrictions in providing information to the public. It was such a contentious issue in democratic Britain in the eighteenth century that the American revolutionaries established freedom of the press as a fundamental constitutional protection from government. The historic concern with the press has been government monopoly and control of information, not private monopoly and control. Given the technological and institutional conditions of the day, a diversity of private supply (even at the local level) was the expected result that was borne out in reality.

In more recent times, such mechanisms as press councils and libel laws have provided a token of social responsibility and accountability of an increasingly powerful and concentrated private press to the citizenry it serves. But for most other purposes the press has been treated as any other industry. A diversity of supply has been assumed. Moreover, this diversity has been presumed to be protected in most democratic countries under the anti-monopoly laws governing economic activity in general.

It has only been in recent times, with the rapidly diminishing number of newspapers and sources of news, that the problem of private monopoly and control of the press has arisen in an increasing number of countries. Diversity has been reduced substantially. Yet for most observers, the public interest has been seen essentially as preserving conditions of 'independent' reporting, not a diversity of information services and viewpoints. In fact, the line of analysis coming into fashion in recent years is that ownership domination is not the crucial issue. As long as there is editorial independence then common ownership involving the press with printing, distribution outlets, other media companies or major transnational corporations in other industries may provide economies of scale and scope. According to this view of information, quasi-monopoly of the private press may be efficient and effective as long as it is responsible and fair. Moreover, it is argued, there is ample competition with other media and other sources of information.

Helped considerably by the new computer and telecommunication technologies, the march to international oligopolization of the press as part of enormous multi-media transnational corporations is proceeding rapidly. National anti-monopoly laws seem inadequate to the task of addressing the broader public interest implications, or of fashioning appropriate policies to ensure that the public interest is served. It would seem inevitable that public policy soon will have to address the issue of public interest implications of the continued private monopolization of the press. If diversity is going to be sharply reduced, and barriers to access thereby increased, then the public interest responsibilities of the press must increase, and stronger mechanisms of accountability be established (Melody, 1976; Owen, 1975). But this can only be done in the context of the changing information and communication sectors of the economy, of which the press is an important part.

Radio and television

Radio and television were introduced long after the press had won freedom from direct government control in democratic societies. Radio and television required use of a public resource, the radio spectrum. Effective communication required at least a system of licensing and technical regulation that specified frequency, power and other characteristics of broadcast signals, and restricted entry to the industry. The underlying technological conditions meant that government had to be involved, either as supplier of the service or regulator of the private suppliers.

Different countries, each following its own traditions, adopted different institutional models for implementing the public interest. In many countries, government owned and operated 'public service' broadcasting entities were established. In the United States a model of government licensing and regulation of private broadcasters was adopted. Specific requirements for programming in the public interest were established. In other countries a mixed system was adopted. Under both the 'public service' models and the 'regulated private programming in the public interest' models of broadcasting, a policy of diversity of programme types in response to the diversity of interests in society (for example, news, public affairs, children's, religious programmes, etc.) was adopted as the responsibility of broadcasters. Under both systems a balanced programme schedule was required to be responsive to the diversity of interests in society and the broader public interest.

Research has demonstrated how the characteristics of media content are heavily influenced by the structure of the institutions that make up the total broadcasting system.[1] The major differences in programme content produced by competitive commercial and monopoly public service broadcasting are well known. But there is great variation within both the commercial and public service models. In the past, commercial broadcasting has not been totally ruled by profit maximization and often has provided some public service programming. Historically there have been limits on the extent to which commercialization is permitted to penetrate programme content. For example, there normally (but not necessarily on children's shows) has been an observable separation between the programmes and the advertisements.

Similarly, public service objectives are defined differently in different countries, and are constrained in varying degrees by cost and audience criteria. Some public service broadcast organizations emphasize a national public service while others emphasize a regional or local public service. Among those emphasizing a national public service, the BBC historically has interpreted its public service mandate, in the Reithian tradition,[2] as a paternalistic educational uplifting of the masses. In more recent times this view has been under assessment both within and without the BBC. The Canadian Broadcasting Corporation (CBC) mandate is to promote national unity, to develop a national consciousness and to interpret Canada for Canadians. The US Public Broadcasting Service's (PBS) primary purpose is to promote artistic, cultural, public affairs and related programming as a supplement to the United States commercial broadcasting system. Other countries have different models of public service broadcasting (Melody, 1987a).

In addition, the system of finance, the structural relations with production houses, the standards of accountability employed and other factors all affect programme content. These institutional constraints do not deny creativity and discretion so much as channel it in particular directions. Some of the most creative programming is channelled into advertisements.

New communication technologies, including CATV, direct broadcast satellites and VCRs are opening a variety of new options for delivering broadcast content and for implementing new methods of payment such as subscription and pay-per-view. In radio, new radio frequency and station allocations and pirate radio are expanding listener choice. International television broadcasting is expanding viewer choice. In the past, international broadcasting primarily involved exchanges among countries of national programmes produced for domestic consumption. This is now being superseded by programme production specifically created for global markets, often involving co-production among multiple countries and sometimes bringing together public service and private commercial broadcasters in co-productions (Collins *et al.*, 1988).

Clearly the traditional distinctions between public service and private commercial broadcasting are being eroded. The former positions of privilege and power enjoyed by the dominant institutions in both systems are diminishing. For example, the BBC has a new potentially lucrative opportunity to enter global broadcast markets which will soon engulf the UK. But it would have to shift part of its programming away from traditional UK public service broadcasting. The CBC has been instructed by the Canadian government to direct its programming to global markets as a means of reducing its government subsidy. National governments everywhere are paying particular attention to the export potential of their public service institutions, including both education and mass media content.[3]

This apparent surfeit of new opportunity and choice that seems to be arising in the broadcast media could be interpreted as justification for a major relaxation, if not complete elimination, of public service and public interest obligations. However, greater choice does not necessarily mean greater diversity, adequate service to minority interests, or improved conditions of access to audiences for those desiring it. Clearly, the traditional conception of a quasi-monopoly public service broadcaster playing media den mother to the nation has been superseded by events. But the public interest responsibilities historically assumed by the national public service broadcaster remain. The challenge to future public policy is to establish workable institutional arrangements that will ensure that those responsibilities are met by the system as a whole.

Post–telecommunication networks

The communication systems that have provided the greatest opportunity for the population at large to participate as initiators of information exchange have been the postal and telecommunication networks. The opportunity to influence a mass audience is not present, but as media that permit, indeed require, active participation in the communication of ideas, they can provide – and historically have provided – a major stimulus toward participatory democracy. Monitoring the postal and telephone activities of particular individuals and organizations is a major concern of totalitarian governments, and a not insignificant one in many democracies.

Communication via post-telecommunication systems sometimes is viewed as not really important in affecting people's knowledge, beliefs and actions. The vast majority of messages are classified as commercial or social. But the vast majority of messages over the mass media are also commercial or social, and much less personal. Moreover, advertisers continue to find post-telecommunication effective vehicles for reaching markets of significant size. Winning the hearts and minds of people one at a time may be more effective than mass conversions–modern television advertising and the church of the airwaves notwithstanding. Even more important, participatory democracy is enhanced by increasing the numbers of people actively participating, and capable of applying their own critical assessments of mass media messages. It is enriched by an increase in the number actively initiating communication in the market-place of ideas, and by a reduced effectiveness of mass media propaganda of all kinds.

In almost all countries, the post was recognized early on as an important public service. Although the motives of national governments in extending the post were not the purest – for example, to facilitate taxation and military recruitment – the concept of a universal public service, accessible to all at a reasonable cost, was accepted in principle and implemented broadly in practice. It provided a major stimulus in the desire of many people to learn to read and particularly to write.

With the introduction of the telegraph (1844) and later the telephone (1878), most countries absorbed these new technologies into the national public service postal monopoly. In the United States, where they were invented and initially patented, private companies were established. After periods of vigorous – some would say destructive – competition, government regulation of territorial monopoly telephone companies was established at the state level (*circa* 1910), and was followed by creeping Federal regulation, culminating in the Federal Communications Act of 1934. It is debatable whether monopolization led to regulation, or whether the Bell System was successful in its campaign to get itself regulated as a means of eliminating its competitors by law rather than superior efficiency. Canada elected to follow the US, rather than the British model of telephone development, after a very intense debate in the House of Commons in the early 1900s.

The gap between theory and practice in the spread of universal telephone service has been significant. In North America, regulators were uniformly ineffective in getting the telephone companies to extend service to small towns and rural areas within their enfranchised territories. Near-universal service was eventually obtained by the establishment of municipal companies, co-operatives, small private companies, and in Canada, provincial companies. These developments were uniformly opposed by the private monopoly telephone companies, and sometimes by the regulators (Melody, 1989b).

Among countries adopting the public service model for telecommunication, Sweden was unique in that it established a telecommunication administration separate from its postal authority, and with very limited monopoly privileges. Sweden achieved universal service coverage some time ago. Those countries that incorporated telecommunication into the postal administration generally failed miserably in their attempts to achieve universal telephone service. Until a decade ago, household penetration rates in European PTT countries ranged from 10 to 70 per cent, with a general inferior quality of service and usually long waiting lists for basic connections. The most common explanations are: the inefficiency of long-standing bureaucracies; the use of telecommunication as a profit-maximizing money-spinner to subsidize the post, and general government coffers; and political resistance to committing funds for extending public service responsibilities beyond the post.

The ubiquitous telephone is an essential component of building and maintaining widespread political, economic, social and cultural networks in many democratic countries. In others, its absence is a significant barrier to participation by major segments of the population. According to the International Telecommunication Union, a majority of the world's population lives more than two hours away from the nearest telephone.

The renewed interest in telecommunication shown by national policy-makers in virtually all developed and many developing countries does not arise from a sudden recognition that universal service will facilitate participatory democracy and economic efficiency at the local and national levels. Rather, it is a recognition that the telecommunication infrastructure is becoming a crucial building block affecting the competitiveness and efficiency of the entire national economy in the evolving global information economy. This is prompting a fundamental institutional restructuring of the telecommunication sector in many countries (Melody, 1986a).

In many countries, progress toward the achievement of universal telephone service is being achieved by removing the dead hand of bureaucracy, exposing inadequacies of service coverage and adopting commercial efficiency standards. In only a few years after privatization, British Telecom (BT) has increased its household penetration rate from about 65 to 80 per cent. However, charges for connection and local use have increased significantly and the overall quality of service outside the major central business districts has declined. Whether BT will push its household penetration rate beyond the point of profit maximization, and whether the new regulatory agency, Oftel, is capable of enforcing social policy objectives such as universal service in the new telecommunication environment, remain to be seen. Given the pressures upon the telecommunication network as a cornerstone of national industrial policy in many countries, the public interest in a social policy of universal telephone service may be difficult to achieve. Yet in the 'information society', increasingly dependent on the telecommunication system, the need for universal service is likely to become even more important. The historic models of public service or regulated private telecommunication monopolies have generally been ineffective, and clearly are not applicable for the future. But the public interest needs are increasing in importance.

The information society

The growing significance of new electronic information and communication networks has brought to the foreground a recognition of the overwhelming importance of information and communication in society. The characteristics of information generation and dissemination affect the nature of markets and the structure of industry, as well as the competitiveness of firms, and the prosperity of regions and nations. They affect the internal structure of organizations, ranging from corporations to government agencies, political parties, universities, trade unions, libraries and volunteer groups. The implications of the changes now taking place in the information and communication sector are made all-pervasive precisely because they affect the characteristics of essential information and communication networks both for individuals and organizations.[4]

Because of its pervasive penetration of economic and social institutions, the newly forming information and communication sector is not easily separated from other sectors. Essentially it consists of microelectronics; computer hardware, software and services; telecommunication equipment and services; the mass media and a plethora of new database and information services, as well as the more traditional forms of information and communication such as print, library and postal services. Stimulated by continuing major technological change, this sector has experienced a rapid rate of economic growth in recent years. Moreover, the direct economic effects are compounded by the fact that major parts of this sector provide important infrastructure services, or facilitate functions that affect the operation and efficiency of almost all other industries, as well as government agencies and most other institutions.

Information gathering, processing, storage and transmission over efficient telecommunication networks is the foundation upon which technologically advanced nations will close the twentieth century as so-called 'information economies' or 'information societies', that is, societies that have become dependent upon complex electronic information and communication networks, and which allocate a major portion of their resources to information and communication activities. This sector may become even more significant to the development of national and international economic growth than any of the major transport expansion eras of the past, including canal, rail or highway.

Moreover, the implications go much beyond national considerations. The expansion of the information and communication sector serves to integrate the domestic economy more easily into the international economy by means of efficient international information and communication networks. As international economic integration is expanded, the impact of domestic public policies is reduced. Control over the domestic economy by national governments is weakened. These developments are forcing governments to recognize the need for a full range of international trade policies, addressed not only to direct trade in information and communication equipment and services, but also to acknowledge the implications of global information and communication networks and services for other industries. For example, these considerations are central to current discussions at the International Telecommunication Union (ITU) as well as GATT (ITU, 1989).

The international banking and finance industries have already been restructuring their organizations, and methods of operation, in the light of enhanced opportunities for transferring money and data instantaneously around the world. Many transnational corporations have been able to improve their organizational efficiency and control by centralizing more decisions at their world headquarters, while maintaining flexibility in decentralized production. This has raised the possibility that significant decision-making power, as well as research and development and information services activities, will be removed from 'national' subsidiaries that in some cases have been reduced to the status of branch plants.

Medical, tax, credit and other detailed information relating to citizens and institutions of one country is being stored with increasing frequency in another. This raises important public policy questions in a number of areas, including for example, the terms of conditions of access to information, privacy of personal information, and the scope and limitations of national and regional sovereignty. It raises questions as to the vulnerability of a country's economic and political decision-making systems to losses of essential information because of breakdowns in crucial information and communication networks that occur outside the country.

Significant changes in information and communication networks require a reinterpretation of traditional notions of public information (for example, news, libraries, government reports and statistics), private information (for example, strategic corporate plans and forecasts) and the terms and conditions for access to such information. In more and more circumstances, information itself is becoming a marketable commodity. There are now many thousands of databases in the world selling a variety of information to clients over modern telecommunication networks, and the number is growing rapidly. Proposed changes in copyright laws now under discussion in several countries would permit a further expansion by strengthening legal property rights to information.

Continuing growth in the information and communication sector is opening opportunities in a wide variety of information and communication markets, trading in both public and private information. Although these markets are adding value to international trade they are very imperfect markets. Their growth raises important questions, both of government regulation of monopoly power in national and international markets, and of government policy with respect to access by the public to traditional types of public information.

The public interest in the information society

Over thirty-five years ago the Canadian economist and communication scholar Harold A. Innis observed, 'enormous improvements in communication have made understanding more difficult' (Innis, 1951: 31). We would be hard put to demonstrate that the quantum leap in communication technologies, and the vast increase in communication and information transfer that now takes place using these technologies, have led to an increased understanding of human and social affairs. Communication opportunities have increased significantly for most organizations and many individuals. The volume and variety of communication over these new systems has increased dramatically. But these improvements in communication have also contributed to an increase in the complexity of economic and social relations, introduced new elements of uncertainty, had negative effects for some people, increased class disparities and in certain instances debased our information and communication currency.

Adjustments to a society in which new information and communication systems will play a more central role will require changes to existing laws, policies and regulations. These changes can either promote or retard adjustment patterns and can have very differential effects across sectors of society. It is not a simple matter of removing regulatory barriers and restrictions. It is a matter of assessing the implications of existing laws, policies and regulation, developing new policy options and assessing their short- and long-term implications. In the information society, policy direction will become more important. Therefore, it is essential that it be informed and that it encompass the broad public interest.

To begin the process of redefining the public interest in the information society, it is necessary to return to the essential functions of information and communication in modern participatory democracy, that us, to provide opportunities for citizens to be informed and to be heard. One might expect that in an information society, an increasing percentage of the population would be more informed and exercise more opportunities to initiate communication. An extrapolation of trends examined in this chapter indicates that, barring public policy intervention, the opposite may be true.

The diversity of sources, both within the different media and across the media, is being significantly reduced. The diversity in broadcast programming that now arises from a variety of different national industry structures, ranging from national public service to commercial, is gravitating towards a much more homogeneous international structure responding primarily to the interests of global mass-market advertising. For public service broadcasters, the increasing absolute costs of programming (which will be driven up further by high-definition television), the increasing opportunity costs of foregone commercial revenue, and the pressures for international co-production for global markets are already directing them ever closer to commercial programming standards. This is a privatization of purpose, if not ownership. Indeed, without public policy intervention, the television broadcast media could become little more than a global electronic billboard (Melody, 1988).

The decline in the quality of postal services throughout most of the world in recent years is expected to continue. In many countries important communication cannot be left to the post. The telecommunication system is being converted to Rolls-Royce Integrated Services Digital Network standards, but it may also require Rolls-Royce costs for the basic telephone service needed by everyone. For the most part, new global information and communication services will only be used by the better trained, educated, informed and economically comfortable segment of society. These people will not be affected by the reduced public services noted above. They will have better alternatives.

An overriding issue of social policy, it would seem, is to ensure the maintenance of existing public information and communication services to those dependent upon them during the transition to the electronic information society. An even more important requirement will be to enhance education and training programmes, so that an increasing portion of society obtains the skills and income necessary to benefit from the new opportunities. The public interest requires that the diffusion of the new opportunities be planned and implemented at a pace which minimizes the losses imposed on those who cannot benefit from them, and is accompanied by programmes to help the potential victims of change become beneficiaries of it.

Yet, on the basis of current trends, it would appear that neither national public service suppliers nor national regulatory authorities are likely to be very effective in implementing public interest objectives. Both are likely to lose sight of domestic public interest requirements in the wake of national concerns about international competitiveness and new export opportunities in expanding global markets.

Information/communication as a public utility

Historically, certain industries have been recognized both in custom and law as 'business affected with a public interest'. These are businesses that supply services under conditions where the public is dependent upon reasonable and non-exploitative treatment by a business monopoly. Inns, wharves, bridges, canals, grain warehouses, railways, electricity, gas, water, telephone and other services have all qualified in the past or do so at present. Each supplier was or is in a position of monopoly dominance in supplying an essential service to the general public. Because of this monopoly of an essential service, the businesses are 'affected with a public interest'. They are required by law to make their services equally available to the public under fair, reasonable and non-discriminatory prices and conditions.

Although the concept of business affected with a public interest was initially developed in English common law, its application over the last century is generally traced to a landmark decision of the US Supreme Court in the case of *Munn* v. *Illinois* (1877):

> When, therefore, one devotes his property to use in which the public has an interest, he in effect grants to the public an interest in that use, and must submit to be controlled by the public far the common good, to the extent of the interest he has thus created.[5]

The concept of business affected with a public interest has found its way into various codes of law in many countries. It provides the direct basis for public utility regulation and government public service provision (including telecommunication and post) in most countries. It is an indirect basis for regulating broadcasting.

Perhaps the most distinguishing characteristic of the information society is the increasing dependence of institutions and people on particular kinds of information and communication in order to function effectively in their economic, political, social and cultural activities. Although one could easily demonstrate that this always has been so – even in Greek city states and aboriginal communities – it is clear that the very different and more complex economic and social relations in the information society create a very different set of information and communication dependencies. In the information society this is governed increasingly by electronic communication networks which determine both access to information and the range of actual communication networks to which people and organizations have access. The types, structures, timing, selection and interpretation of information are unique, as are the needs to initiate communication in a timely and skilled manner in a variety of circumstances.

In the information society, access to information and communication would appear to be the most essentially public utility. It would be a logical extension of national law and policy to declare the international media and telecommunication conglomerates to be international public utilities subject to international regulation. But this would overlap with the jurisdiction of national authorities as well as some existing international agencies, for example, the ITU. It would require new international law to be effective. Given experience in other areas, including the interminable debates over devising international law for the oceans and for space, this does not appear to be a promising option for the foreseeable future.

It would seem that the global information and communication industries may have outgrown the national institutional mechanisms for ensuring that the public interest is seriously considered in their policies and practices. Could this mean that in the information society, the volume of information directed at passive recipients will increase substantially (especially entertainment and advertising), but that the population as a whole will be less informed and less capable of participating in the conduct of their own societies?

Public interest research

Perhaps the major deficiencies of public policy formulation generally are an inadequacy of substantive research and analysis on the public interest implications of policy options, and an absence of effective advocacy of concrete policy actions that would reflect the public interest. In the market-place of competing evidence, analysis and ideas, public interest advocacy has suffered. Regulatory authorities and national public service suppliers all too quickly become 'judges' and 'authorities'. Rather than seek out evidence on public interest implications, and give it great weight in the face of advocacy from powerful vested interests, they have tended to wait for public interest implications to be thrust before them under conditions where they cannot be avoided. This is illustrated well by a comment from a former chair of the Independent Broadcasting Authority, who explained that 'The public interest is what I say it is. And I was appointed because I know.'[6]

Whatever the institutional form by which public interest considerations are brought into the policy process, it will be ineffective unless there is a solid base in public interest research. It then must be followed up by advocacy of the practical implications for action. From where might this come?

In a democratic society, public policy should be responsive to the quality and quantity of evidence and argument advocated for particular positions put forward by various interests. In these debates, there are two primary perspectives that require representation, but which in most cases are absent.

One is the perspective of those groups in society that may be significantly affected by the policies adopted, but which do not have a sufficiently organized financial vested interest to mount a representation, for example, disabled users of the public telephone service, children's interests in television or probable victims of technological change. This perspective is necessary to ensure that in the final balancing of interests that underlies most policy decisions, consideration of the interests of important segments of the public are not omitted.

The second perspective is that of society as a whole, focusing directly on the overall structure of benefits, costs and consequences for society. This perspective would examine those consequences that lie outside the normal realm of special interest decisionmakers, and would include an evaluation of economic externality, and social and cultural consequences of policy options (Ferguson, 1986).

Public interest groups exist in many areas of society to advocate the special interests of neglected publics, for example, consumer associations, environmental groups, children's television advocates, etc. However, with severely restricted funding and inadequate research, effectiveness is limited. To the best of this author's knowledge, there is no public interest group advocating the information rights of the uninformed, or the right to have effective communication access to those denied it. Part of the problem, of course, is that it is very unclear what precisely should be advocated, given the underlying lack of research, evidence and policy analysis.

Perhaps more than any other policy area, information and communication policies require an overall systemic analysis. They have enormous external consequences for the viability of political democracy as well as economic and social relations of all kinds. But what institution in society is likely to be in a position to undertake continuing research, policy analysis and effective advocacy of the public interest in information and communication?

Academia and the public interest

Academic researchers are in a unique position to provide a substantial contribution to policy deliberations from a systemic perspective in at least two important respects. First, the absence of a close connection with particular institutions that have a direct vested interest in the immediate results of policy considerations provides an essential detachment. This permits academic researchers to address the long-term societal implications of the issues more thoroughly, independently and continuously even than the policy making agencies. Second, by training and vocational practice, the perspective of academics should be more compatible with the exercise of research on long-run implications for society than that provided by any other institutional environment. For many aspects of policy issues, independent academic research can provide an assessment of issues which examines aspects of reality that elude special interest research and the normal analytical horizons of policy-makers.

Due in part to the absence of a significant body of such research, at the present time there is no conceptual or descriptive map by which one can assess; the size, structure and implications of information and communication in the information society. Without this essential background information, neither policy decisions by government nor market decisions by corporations are as informed as they should be, or could be.

Academic research has much more to contribute to policy issues than might at first appear. Across the social sciences in particular, there is a substantial amount of fragmented research on a variety of information and communication issues. An assessment of its significance for policy requires that it be pulled together, integrated and examined from a systemic perspective. This knowledge then needs to be interpreted in the light of the major policy issues under debate. For the future, if more effective research co-ordination is established, the knowledge gained can be cumulative rather than fragmentary.

Moreover, if the scope of this interdisciplinary research enterprise is extended to include implications for policy, and supported by strong programmes of dissemination to policy maker and lay audiences (as well as the research community), the benefits will begin to penetrate the social system more effectively.[7] Within the framework of this new model of policy research, it should be possible to develop a much clearer understanding of the role of information and communication processes in the information society and their implications for policy.

The areas that require priority research attention are fundamental ones. The current state of knowledge on information availability and use by different sectors of society is extremely weak. Basic descriptive and statistical data are fragmented. Considered assessments of the public information needs of different sectors of society, and the terms and conditions of access necessary to meet these needs are required as benchmarks for public policy. Information indicators could be developed to measure, for example, relations between citizen needs, availability and uses of public information; the accessibility and use of public information by major segments of the population; and the rate of diffusion of essential public information throughout the population. Indeed we know from existing research that only a small proportion of minority cultures, and the poor of all cultures know their rights as citizens in democratic countries. If all the sick and elderly knew enough to claim all the benefits to which they are entitled, public health systems would be swamped and bankrupted in a few months.

In certain respects, the function of post-industrial economies in their present form depends upon major sections of society not having sufficient information, skill and knowledge to exercise their rights fully. As society becomes more information- and communication-intensive, these class distinctions based upon information disparities are likely to increase. But research on information processes, disseminated widely and advocated in policy arenas, could do much to promote both information and social equity in society. A corollary of this line of research is the documentation of public information deficiencies and their economic and social implications.

Parallel types of research are needed in respect of communication processes, especially those communication processes necessary to obtain access to essential information. This goes much beyond such questions as the availability of a universal telephone service, which is a precondition to electronic communication. It addresses questions of actual use, knowledge about how to acquire relevant information via the telecommunication system, and the extent to which useful information is actually obtained. If 20 per cent of the population is barely literate, does this indicate anything about their ability to find their way through a government bureaucracy using the telephone? The research needed here is neither on physical network connections, nor on idealistic rights to communicate. Rather, it is on the benefits obtained from actual communication, the barriers to access and the policies that encourage or prevent effective communication and the realities of information transfer.

Research is also needed on guidelines for making sense out of an environment of information overload. Effective understanding, followed by rational action requires an ability to filter, synthesize and interpret information. For many in society, including all business and political leaders, effective comprehension requires that information be screened, assessed and summarized before it is even examined. In a society of information overload, this new role of information interpreter is becoming ever more essential to rational decision making. Research is needed, to understand the processes at work; to define the most appropriate ways for interpreting public information for the public; and to devise operational programmes for implementing public information interpretation services.

It may well be that in future the new role of interpreting important information to the public could best be filled by public libraries. Given the trend of the public press, its interpretive role for the future is more likely to decline than expand for the public at large. Libraries could become advice centres on public information, including not only the location of relevant information and how to access it, but also what the information means and what action might be considered by citizens exercising their rights. (This, of course, would be vigorously opposed by the legal profession.) An extension of this role could be an information ombudsman. The primary functions would be to break down barriers to public information, and to advocate the public's information needs in relevant policy debates.

Several countries have established an information commissioner to deal with specific complaints by citizens that government agencies are withholding information from them that should be accessible. This is primarily the role of an *ad hoc* ombudsman and is concerned with the release of information by national government agencies to specific individuals and organizations. An unfortunate effect of U.S. 'sunshine' laws, which require open access to discussions by government policy makers, has been to make bureaucrats more, not less, protective of their information.

What is being suggested here is a much more proactive ombudsman role that examines in a systematic manner the information needs of the general public and the best ways of ensuring that they will be met. It is a step toward stimulating national governments to develop a national public information policy that would apply not just to government agencies, but also to major corporations and other influential institutions in society. The standard for judgement would be, what does the public need to know in order to function most effectively as a responsible citizenry in a participatory democracy?

A research strategy on information and communication policy is likely to find that such questions arise as important components of policy issues in many areas. Policy makers in seemingly unrelated areas may be unaware of the information and communication implications of the policy options they are considering. For certain kinds of policies, for example, the introduction of major new communication technologies such as ISDN or high-definition television, an information/communication impact statement might be a required consideration in the policy formulation. For other policies, for example, the environment, public health and so on, information reporting and communication requirements are likely to be an important aspect of effective policy implementation.

A key factor influencing the actual information/communication implications of policy decisions of all kinds will be the information/communication diffusion processes throughout society. This is a subject about which academic research already has something to say. But much more is known from the far more extensive research on the diffusion of material technologies, than about the diffusion of information, or of communication opportunities.

It is comforting to believe that there is a single policy authority and a carefully specified policy issue to which one's research and analysis can be directed. It is the policy authority's responsibility to seek out and consider the public interest in its policy processes. But when an authority is designated, for example, the FCC, IBA or Oftel, it represents only one of several loci where important policy decisions in the field are made. In the United States, for example, the Congress, executive branch, courts, state governments, one or more industries, foreign firms and governments, international agencies and potentially other institutions may exercise influence in the dynamic mosaic of policy development and implementation. Moreover, the formal policy-making authorities tend to have quite narrow remits defined by industry or technological boundaries, in comparison to the much broader agenda of information and communication processes in society. In addition, as indicated above, the authorities seldom go looking for public interest considerations. To a significant degree, only the research itself will expose the breadth of key policy decisions that affect public information and communication opportunities and uses.

Just as the model of the paternalistic national public service operator is becoming less relevant in the information society, so also is the model of beneficent national public interest regulation. Both were imperfect mechanisms acquiring increasing imperfections as time passed and society changed. Policy formulation in the information/communication sector is becoming more diffused. The structure of the policy-making process is not easily identified, assessed or influenced. Indeed, the policy process, access to it and diffusion of policy information is itself an important area for research. It could assist greatly in keeping the doors of the policy arena open, and the public more aware of its rights in the policy formulation process.

The policy research being suggested here would find its way into policy at local, state, national, regional and global levels in a variety of ways. Researchers would not be alone in seeking to place the knowledge gained from their research before policy-makers. Such knowledge will almost always find institutional support somewhere, ranging from public interest groups and government agency staff to specific firms and industries. Virtually all important policy issues are contested by several very different interests reflecting a variety of perspectives. In most instances, at least one of these is likely to find a common interest on any particular issue with the policy implications of knowledge gained from independent academic research. For academic researchers, there is a challenge to interpret the policy implications of their research in light of the policy issues being examined, and to disseminate their research results in a form that will be most easily understood by those involved in the policy debates.

It should not, of course, be expected that academic research is going to yield magic answers to the formidable issues of public policy in the information society. In fact, there are likely to be few issues in which all the research will clearly point to a specific policy solution. The contribution of the research is to inform the policymaking debates, to raise the knowledge level of the discussion, to ensure that information and analysis relating to the long-term, systemic and public interest implications are included in the debates, and to attempt to guide the policy debates in the direction of the most relevant issues. A major contribution of this research is likely to be the elimination of policy options that could have negative consequences for the general public, but substantial beneficial consequences for a large vested interest. Rarely will it point unequivocally to a precise optimum policy. Moreover, the greatest influence of the policy research is more likely to come from its integration into the on-going activities of the many organizations involved in the policy process, than from occasional injections of purportedly definitive policy research studies.

Some researchers may be concerned that on-going interaction with organizations involved in the policy process runs the risk of biasing the research. Indeed, it does. But probably less so than the risk of bias that arises from a much lower level of information and knowledge about the real issues and problems, a very superficial understanding of the policy-making processes and a naïve belief that detachment, innocence (and sometimes ignorance) avoid biases. More direct involvement is likely to force the exposure of judgements and hidden valuations so that their consequences can be assessed. The independence of policy research, and indeed all social science research, must ultimately be preserved by awareness and sensitivity of the problem of bias, which always exists in one form or another.

Researchers must have sufficient confidence that they can maintain their intellectual independence when they bring their contributions into the market-place of ideas on public policy. The knowledgeable, independent views that have merit for application in public policy must be those that have stood the test of critical review of the evidence and analysis by those who disagree. Is this test any different from the test that academic research has always used in seeking the truth (that is, a critical review by knowledgeable peers), except perhaps that the public policy arena may provide a more rigorous application of it? Certainly a claim of independence arising from limited knowledge about the issues and non-involvement in the process cannot expect to carry much weight in a participatory democracy.

The academic social science research community is a major institution in modern society. One of its fundamental purposes is to develop information and knowledge about the changing structure of society. This academic research community is uniquely placed to extend its activities to policy research from a public interest perspective, particularly on the implications of changing information and communication structures in society. It is uniquely placed to be the best advocate of the policy implications of its public interest research. No other institution in society is so well structured to research and advocate for the public interest. Should the research community take this responsibility seriously, the contributions of research can more directly influence the course of events in the world. The public interest can become a major, rather than a fringe, force in policy-making, and the academic research community can fulfil its own potential in participatory democracies.

Notes

1 For a comparative perspective see Noll *et al.* (1973); Owen *et al.* (1974); Cave and Melody (1989).
2 The classic statement attributed to Lord Reith was 'few members of the broadcast audience know what they want, and fewer still want what they need', reflecting the ethos of the BBC under his leadership.

3 For comparative perspectives on these issues, see Mattelart *et al.* (1984); Wedell (1983) and Commission of the European Communities (1984).
4 For an examination of social science research and training developments in this area in the UK, see Melody and Mansell (1986b).
5 See *Munn* v. *Illinois* 94 US 113, 126. For discussion of related issues, see Melody (1971).
6 Personal interview with the author.
7 Indeed, this new model for social science research in the field is being adopted by major new academically based research programmes in several countries. Examples are the Programme on Information and Communication Technologies (PICT) in the UK, and the Centre for International Research on Communication and Information Technologies (CIRCIT) in Australia; see Melody (1987b).

References

Cave, M. and Melody, W. H. (1989) 'Models of Broadcast Regulation: The UK and North American Experience', pp. 224–43 in C. Veljanovski (ed.), *Freedom in Broadcasting*. London: Institute of Economic Affairs.

Collins, R., Garnham, N. and Locksley, G. (1988) *The Economics of Television*. London: Sage.

Commission of the European Communities (1984) *Television without Frontiers*. Brussels: EEC.

Ferguson, M. (ed.) (1986) *New Communication Technologies and the Public Interest: Comparative Perspectives on Policy and Research*. London: Sage.

Innis, H. A. (1951) *The Bias of Communication*. Toronto: University of Toronto Press.

International Telecommunications Union (ITU) (1989) *The Changing Telecommunications Environment: Policy Considerations for the Members of the ITU*. Geneva: ITU.

Mattelart, A., Delacourt, X. and Mattelart, M. (1984) *International Image Markets*. London: Comedia.

Melody, W. H. (1973) 'The Role of Advocacy in Public Policy Planning', pp. 165–81 in G. Gerbner, L. Gross and W. Melody (eds), *Communications Technology and Social Policy*. New York: Wiley.

Melody, W. H. (1976) 'Mass Media: The Economics of Access to the Marketplace of Ideas', pp. 216–36 in O. Aronoff (ed.), *Business and the Media*. Santa Monica, CA: Goodyear.

Melody, W. H. (1986) 'Telecommunication: Policy Directions for the Technology and Information Services', pp. 77–106 in *Oxford Surveys in Information Technology*, vol 3. Oxford: Oxford University Press.

Melody, W. H. (1987a) 'The Canadian Broadcasting Corporation's Contribution to Canadian Culture' *The Royal Society of Arts Journal*, 125: 286–97.

Melody, W. H. (1987b) 'Examining the Implications of Changing Information and Communication Structures: The UK PICT', *Prometheus*, 5 (2) (Dec.): 221–36.

Melody, W. H. (1988) 'Pan European Television: Commercial and Cultural Implications of European Satellites', pp. 267–81 in R. Paterson and P. Drummond (eds), *Television and its Audience: International Research Perspectives*. London: British Film Institute.

Melody, W. H. (1989a) 'The Changing Role of Public Policy in the Information Economy', *Papers in Science, Technology and Public Policy*. London: Imperial College and Science Policy Research Unit, University of Sussex.

Melody, W. H. (1989b) 'Policy Issues in the Evolution of ISDN', pp. 53–60 in J. Arnbak (ed.), *ISDN in Europe: Innovative Services or Innovative Technology?* Amsterdam: Elsevier Science Publishers.

Melody, W. H. and Mansell, R. (1986) *Information and Communication Technologies: Social Science Research and Training*, vols 1 and 2. London: Economic and Social Research Council.

Noll, R. G., Peck, M. J. and McGowan, J. J. (1973) *Economic Aspects of Television Regulation*. Washington, DC: Brookings Institution.

Owen, B. M. (1975) *Economics and Freedom of Expression*. Lexington, MA: D.C. Heath.

Owen, B. M., Beebe, J. H. and Manning, W. G., Jr. (1974) *Television Economics*. Lexington, MA: D.C. Heath.

Wedell, G. (1983) 'The End of Media Nationalism in Europe', *Intermedia*, 2 (4/5).

59

LAW AND BORDERS
The rise of law in Cyberspace

David R. Johnson and David Post*

Source: *Stanford Law Review* 48(5) (1996): 1367–402.

> David Johnson and David Post argue that Cyberspace requires a system of rules quite distinct from the laws that regulate physical, geo graphically-defined territories. Cyberspace challenges the law's traditional reliance on territorial borders; it is a "space" bounded by screens and passwords rather than physical markers. Professors Johnson and Post illustrate how "taking Cyberspace seriously" as a unique place can lead to the development of both clear rules for online transactions and effective legal institutions.

Introduction

Global computer-based communications cut across territorial borders, creating a new realm of human activity and undermining the feasibility —and legitimacy—of laws based on geographic boundaries. While these electronic communications play havoc with geographic boundaries, a new boundary, made up of the screens and passwords that separate the virtual world from the "real world" of atoms, emerges. This new boundary defines a distinct Cyberspace that needs and can create its own law and legal institutions. Territorially based law-makers and law-enforcers find this new environment deeply threatening. But established territorial authorities may yet learn to defer to the self-regulatory efforts of Cyberspace participants who care most deeply about this new digital trade in ideas, information, and services. Separated from doctrine tied to territorial jurisdictions, new rules will emerge to govern a wide range of new phenomena that have no clear parallel in the nonvirtual world. These new rules will play the role of law by defining legal personhood and property, resolving disputes, and crystallizing a collective conversation about online participants' core values.

LAW AND BORDERS: THE RISE OF LAW IN CYBERSPACE

I. Breaking down territorial borders

A. *Territorial borders in the "real world"*

We take for granted a world in which geographical borders—lines separating physical spaces—are of primary importance in determining legal rights and responsibilities.[1] Territorial borders, generally speaking, delineate areas within which different sets of legal rules apply. There has until now been a general correspondence between borders drawn in physical space (between nation states or other political entities) and borders in "law space." For example, if we were to superimpose a "law map" (delineating areas where different rules apply to particular behaviors) onto a political map of the world, the two maps would overlap to a significant degree, with clusters of homogeneous applicable law and legal institutions fitting within existing physical borders.

1. The trademark example

Consider a specific example to which we will refer throughout this article: trademark law—schemes for the protection of the associations between words or images and particular commercial enterprises. Trademark law is distinctly based on geographical separations.[2] Trademark rights typically arise within a given country, usually on the basis of a mark on physical goods or in connection with the provision of services in specific locations within that country. Different countries have different trademark laws, with important differences on matters as central as whether the same name can be used in different lines of business. In the United States, similar businesses can even use the same name, provided there is sufficient geographic separation of use to avoid confusion.[3] In fact, there are many local stores, restaurants, and businesses with identical names that do not interfere with each other because their customers do not overlap. The physical cues provided by different lines of business allow a mark to be used by one line of business without diluting its value in others.[4] There is no global registration scheme;[5] protection of a particularly famous mark on a global basis requires registration in each country. A trademark owner must therefore also be constantly alert to territorially based claims of abandonment, and to dilution arising from uses of confusingly similar marks, and must master each country's different procedural and jurisdictional laws.

2. When geographic boundaries for law make sense

Physical borders are not, of course, simply arbitrary creations. Although they may be based on historical accident, geographic borders for law make sense in the real world. Their logical relationship to the development and enforcement of legal rules is based on a number of related considerations.

POWER

Control over physical space, and the people and things located in that space, is a defining attribute of sovereignty and statehood.[6] Law-making requires some mechanism for law enforcement, which in turn depends on the ability to exercise physical control over, and impose coercive sanctions on, law-violators. For example, the U.S. government does not impose its trademark law on a Brazilian business operating in Brazil, at least in part because imposing sanctions on the Brazilian business would require assertion of physical control over business owners. Such an assertion of control would conflict with the Brazilian government's recognized monopoly on the use of force over its citizens.[7]

EFFECTS

The correspondence between physical boundaries and "law space" boundaries also reflects a deeply rooted relationship between physical proximity and the effects of any particular behavior. That is, Brazilian trademark law governs the use of marks in Brazil because that use has a more direct impact on persons and assets within Brazil than anywhere else. For example, a large sign over "Jones' Restaurant" in Rio de Janeiro is unlikely to have an impact on the operation of "Jones' Restaurant" in Oslo, Norway, for we may assume that there is no substantial overlap between the customers, or competitors, of these two entities. Protection of the former's trademark does not—and probably should not—affect the protection afforded the latter's.

LEGITIMACY

We generally accept the notion that the persons within a geographically defined border are the ultimate source of law-making authority for activities within that border.[8] The "consent of the governed" implies that those subject to a set of laws must have a role in their formulation. By virtue of the preceding considerations, those people subject to a sovereign's laws, and most deeply affected by those laws, are the individuals who are located in particular physical spaces. Similarly, allocation of responsibility among levels of government proceeds on the assumption that, for many legal problems, physical proximity between the responsible authority and those most directly affected by the law will improve the quality of decision making, and that it is easier to determine the will of those individuals in physical proximity to one another.

NOTICE

Physical boundaries are also appropriate for the delineation of "law space" in the physical world because they can give notice that the rules change when the boundaries are crossed. Proper boundaries have signposts that provide warning that we will be required, after crossing, to abide by different rules, and physical boundaries—lines on the geographical map—are generally well-equipped to serve this signpost function.[9]

B. The absence of territorial borders in Cyberspace

Cyberspace radically undermines the relationship between legally significant (online) phenomena and physical location. The rise of the global computer network is destroying the link between geographical location and: (1) the *power* of local governments to assert control over online behavior; (2) the *effects* of online behavior on individuals or things; (3) the *legitimacy* of a local sovereign's efforts to regulate global phenomena; and (4) the ability of physical location to give *notice* of which sets of rules apply. The Net thus radically subverts the system of rule-making based on borders between physical spaces, at least with respect to the claim that Cyberspace should naturally be governed by territorially defined rules.

Cyberspace has no territorially based boundaries, because the cost and speed of message transmission on the Net is almost entirely independent of physical location. Messages can be transmitted from one physical location to any other location without degradation, decay, or substantial delay, and without any physical cues or barriers that might otherwise keep certain geographically remote places and people separate from one another.[10] The Net enables transactions between people who do not know, and in many cases cannot know, each other's physical location. Location remains vitally important, but only location within a *virtual* space consisting of the "addresses" of the machines between which messages and information are routed. The system is indifferent to the *physical* location of those machines, and there is no necessary connection between an Internet address and a physical jurisdiction. Although the domain name initially assigned to a given machine may be associated with an Internet Protocol address that corresponds to that machine's physical location (for example, a ".uk" domain name extension), the machine may be physically moved without affecting its domain name. Alternatively, the owner of the domain name might request that the name become associated with an entirely different machine, in a different physical location.[11] Thus, a server with a ".uk" domain name need not be located in the United Kingdom, a server with a ".com" domain name may be anywhere, and users, generally speaking, are not even aware of the location of the server that stores the content that they read.

The power to control activity in Cyberspace has only the most tenuous connections to physical location. Nonetheless, many governments' first response to electronic communications crossing their territorial borders is to try to stop or regulate that flow of information.[12] Rather than permitting self-regulation by participants in online transactions, many governments establish trade barriers, attempt to tax border-crossing cargo, and respond especially sympathetically to claims that information coming into the jurisdiction might prove harmful to local residents. As online information becomes more important to local citizens, these efforts increase. In particular, resistance to "transborder data flow" (TDF) reflects the concerns of sovereign nations that the development and use of TDF's will undermine their "informational sovereignty,"[13] will impinge upon the privacy of local citizens,[14] and will upset private property interests in information.[15] Even local governments in the United States have expressed concern about their loss of control over information and transactions flowing across their borders.[16]

But efforts to control the flow of electronic information across physical borders—to map local regulation and physical boundaries onto Cyberspace— are likely to prove futile, at least in countries that hope to participate in global commerce.[17] Individual electrons can easily, and without any realistic prospect of detection, "enter" any sovereign's territory. The volume of electronic communications crossing territorial boundaries is just too great in relation to the resources available to government authorities. United States Customs officials have generally given up. They assert jurisdiction only over the physical goods that cross the geographic borders they guard and claim no right to force declarations of the value of materials transmitted by modem.[18] Banking and securities regulators seem likely to lose their battle to impose local regulations on a global financial marketplace.[19] And state attorneys general face serious challenges in seeking to intercept the electrons that transmit the kinds of consumer fraud that, if conducted physically within the local jurisdiction, would be easier to shut down.

Faced with their inability to control the flow of electrons across physical borders, some authorities strive to inject their boundaries into the new electronic medium through filtering mechanisms and the establishment of electronic barriers.[20] Others have been quick to assert the right to regulate all online trade insofar as it might adversely affect local citizens. The Attorney General of Minnesota, for example, has asserted the right to regulate gambling that occurs on a foreign web page that a local resident accessed and "brought into" the state.[21] The New Jersey securities regulatory agency has similarly asserted the right to shut down any offending Web page accessible from within the state.[22]

But such protective schemes will likely fail as well. First, the determined seeker of prohibited communications can simply reconfigure his connection so as to appear to reside in a location outside the particular locality, state, or country. Because the Net is engineered to work on the basis of "logical," not geographical, locations, any attempt to defeat the independence of messages from physical locations would be as futile as an effort to tie an atom and a bit together. And, moreover, assertions of law-making authority over Net activities on the ground that those activities constitute "entry into" the physical jurisdiction can just as easily be made by any territorially-based authority. If Minnesota law applies to gambling operations conducted on the World Wide Web because such operations foreseeably affect Minnesota residents, so, too, must the law of any physical jurisdiction from which those operations can be accessed. By asserting a right to regulate whatever its citizens may access on the Net, these local authorities are laying the predicate for an argument that Singapore or Iraq or any other sovereign can regulate the activities of U.S. companies operating in Cyberspace from a location physically within the United States. All such Web-based activity, in this view, must be subject simultaneously to the laws of all territorial sovereigns.

Nor are the effects of online activities tied to geographically proximate locations. Information available on the World Wide Web is available simultaneously to anyone with a connection to the global network. The notion that the effects of an activity taking place on that Web site radiate from a physical location over a geographic map in concentric circles of decreasing intensity, however sensible that may be in the nonvirtual world, is incoherent when applied to Cyberspace. A Web site physically located in Brazil, to continue with that example, has no more of an effect on individuals in Brazil than does a Web site physically located in Belgium or Belize that is accessible in Brazil. Usenet discussion groups, to take another example, consist of continuously changing collections of messages that are routed from one network to another, with no centralized location at all. They exist, in effect, everywhere, nowhere in particular, and only on the Net.[23]

Territorial regulation of online activities serves neither the legitimacy nor the notice justifications. There is no geographically localized set of constituents with a stronger and more legitimate claim to regulate it than any other local group. The strongest claim to control comes from the participants themselves, and they could be anywhere. And in Cyberspace, physical borders no longer function as signposts informing individuals of the obligations assumed by entering into a new, legally significant, place. Individuals are unaware of the existence of those borders as they move through virtual space.

The rise of an electronic medium that disregards geographical boundaries throws the law into disarray by creating entirely new phenomena that need to become the subject of clear legal rules but that cannot be governed, satisfactorily, by any current territorially based sovereign. For example, although privacy on the Net may be a familiar concept, analogous to privacy doctrine for mail systems, telephone calls, and print publications, electronic communications create serious questions regarding the nature and adequacy of geographically based privacy protections. Communications that create vast new transactional records may pass through or even simultaneously exist in many different territorial jurisdictions.[24] What substantive law should we apply to protect this new, vulnerable body of transactional data?[25] May a French policeman lawfully access the records of communications traveling across the Net from the United States to Japan? Similarly, whether it is permissible for a commercial entity to publish a record of all of any given individual's postings to Usenet newsgroups, or whether it is permissible to implement an interactive Web page application that inspects a user's "bookmarks" to determine which other pages that user has visited, are questions not readily addressed by existing legal regimes—both because the phenomena are novel and because any given local territorial sovereign cannot readily control the relevant, globally dispersed, actors and actions.[26]

Because events on the Net occur everywhere but nowhere in particular, are engaged in by online personae who are both "real" (possessing reputations, able to perform services, and deploy intellectual assets) and "intangible" (not necessarily or traceably tied to any particular person in the physical sense), and concern "things" (messages, databases, standing relationships) that are not necessarily separated from one another by any physical boundaries, no physical jurisdiction has a more compelling claim than any other to subject these events exclusively to its laws.

1. The trademark example

The question of who should regulate or control Net domain names presents an illustration of the difficulties faced by territorially based law-making. The engineers who created the Net devised a "domain name system" that associates numerical machine addresses with easier-to-remember names. Thus, an Internet Protocol machine address like "36.21.0.69" can be derived, by means of a lookup table, from "leland.stanford.edu." Certain letter extensions (".com," ".edu," ".org," and ".net") have developed as global domains with no association to any particular geographic area.[27] Although the Net creators designed this system as a convenience, it rapidly developed commercial value, because it allows customers to learn and remember the location of particular Web pages or e-mail addresses. Currently, domain names are registered with specific parties who echo the information to "domain name servers" around the world. Registration generally occurs on a "first come, first served" basis, generating a new type of property akin to trademark rights, but without inherent ties to the trademark law of any individual country.[28] Defining rights in this new, valuable property presents many questions, including those relating to transferability, conditions for ownership (such as payment of registration fees), duration of ownership rights, and forfeiture in the event of abandonment, however defined. Who should make these rules?

Consider the placement of a "traditional" trademark on the face of a World Wide Web page. This page can be accessed instantly from any location connected to the Net. It is not clear that any given country's trademark authorities possess, or should possess, jurisdiction over such placements. Otherwise, any use of a trademark on the Net would be subject simultaneously to the jurisdiction of every country. Should a Web page advertising a local business in Illinois be deemed to infringe a trademark in Brazil just because the page can be accessed freely from Brazil? Large U.S. companies may be upset by the appearance on the Web of names and symbols that overlap with their valid U.S.-registered trademarks. But these same names and symbols could also be validly registered by another party in Mexico whose "infringing" marks are now, suddenly, accessible from within the United States. Upholding a claim of infringement or dilution launched by the holder of a U.S.-registered trademark, solely on the basis of a conflicting mark on the Net, exposes that same trademark holder to claims from other countries when the use of their U.S.-registered mark on the Web would allegedly infringe a similar mark in those foreign jurisdictions.

2. *Migration of other regulated conduct to the net*

Almost everything involving the transfer of information can be done online: education, health care, banking, the provision of intangible services, all forms of publishing, and the practice of law. The laws regulating many of these activities have developed as distinctly local and territorial. Local authorities certify teachers, charter banks with authorized "branches," and license doctors and lawyers. The law has in essence presumed that the activities conducted by these regulated persons cannot be performed without being tied to a physical body or building subject to regulation by the territorial sovereign authority, and that the effects of those activities are most distinctly felt in geographically circumscribed areas. These distinctly local regulations cannot be preserved once these activities are conducted by globally dispersed parties through the Net. When many trades can be practiced in a manner that is unrelated to the physical location of the participants, these local regulatory structures will either delay the development of the new medium or, more likely, be superseded by new structures that better fit online phenomena.[29]

Any insistence on "reducing" all online transactions to a legal analysis based in geographic terms presents, in effect, a new "mind-body" problem on a global scale. We know that the activities that have traditionally been the subject of regulation must still be engaged in by real people who are, after all, at distinct physical locations. But the interactions of these people now somehow transcend those physical locations. The Net enables forms of interaction in which the shipment of tangible items across geographic boundaries is irrelevant and in which the location of the participants does not matter. Efforts to determine "where" the events in question occur are decidedly misguided, if not altogether futile.

II. A new boundary for Cyberspace

Traditional legal doctrine treats the Net as a mere transmission medium that facilitates the exchange of messages sent from one legally significant geographical location to another, each of which has its own applicable laws. But trying to tie the laws of any particular territorial sovereign to transactions on the Net, or even trying to analyze the legal consequences of Net-based commerce as if each transaction occurred geographically somewhere in particular, is most unsatisfying. A more legally significant, and satisfying, border for the "law space" of the Net consists of the screens and passwords that separate the tangible from the virtual world.

A. Cyberspace as a place

Many of the jurisdictional and substantive quandaries raised by border-crossing electronic communications could be resolved by one simple principle: conceiving of Cyberspace as a distinct "place" for purposes of legal analysis by recognizing a legally significant border between Cyberspace and the "real world." Using this new approach, we would no longer ask the unanswerable question "where" in the geographical world a Net-based transaction occurred. Instead, the more salient questions become: What procedures are best suited to the often unique characteristics of this new place and the expectations of those who are engaged in various activities there? What mechanisms exist or need to be developed to determine the content of those rules and the mechanisms by which they can enforced? Answers to these questions will permit the development of rules better suited to the new phenomena in question, more likely to be made by those who understand and participate in those phenomena, and more likely to be enforced by means that the new global communications media make available and effective.

1. The new boundary is real

Treating Cyberspace as a separate "space" to which distinct laws apply should come naturally. There is a "placeness" to Cyberspace because the messages accessed there are persistent and accessible to many people.[30] Furthermore, because entry into this world of stored online communications occurs through a screen and (usually) a password boundary, you know when you are "there." No one accidentally strays across the border into Cyberspace.[31] To be sure, Cyberspace is not a homogenous, place; groups and activities found at various online locations possess their own unique characteristics and distinctions, and each area will likely develop its own

LAW AND BORDERS: THE RISE OF LAW IN CYBERSPACE

set of distinct rules.[32] But the line that separates online transactions from our dealings in the real world is just as distinct as the physical boundaries between our territorial governments—perhaps more so.

Crossing into Cyberspace is a meaningful act that would make application of a distinct "law of Cyberspace" fair to those who pass over the electronic boundary. As noted, a primary function and characteristic of a border or boundary is its ability to be perceived by the one who crosses it.[33] As regulatory structures evolve to govern Cyberspace-based transactions, it will be much easier to be certain which of those rules apply to your activities online than to determine which territorial-based authority might apply its laws to your conduct. For example, you would know to abide by the "terms of service" established by CompuServe or America Online when you are in their online territory, rather than guess whether Germany, or Tennessee, or the SEC will succeed in asserting their right to regulate your activities and those of the "placeless" online personae with whom you communicate.

2. The trademark example

The ultimate question of who should set the rules for uses of names on the Net presents an apt microcosm for examining the relationship between the Net and territorial-based legal systems. There is nothing more fundamental, legally, than a name or identity—the right to legally recognized personhood is a predicate for the amassing of capital, including the reputational and financial capital, that arises from sustained interactions. The domain name system, and other online uses of names and symbols tied to reputations and virtual locations, exist operationally only on the Net. These names can, of course, be printed on paper or embodied in physical form and shipped across geographic borders. But such physical uses should be distinguished from electronic use of such names in Cyberspace, because publishing a name or symbol on the Net is not the same as intentional distribution to any particular jurisdiction. Instead, use of a name or symbol on the Net is like distribution to all jurisdictions simultaneously. Recall that the non-country-specific domain names like ".com" and ".edu" lead to the establishment of online addresses on a global basis. And through such widespread use, the global domain names gained proprietary value. In this context, assertion by any local jurisdiction of the right to set the rules applicable to the "domain name space" is an illegitimate extraterritorial power grab.

Conceiving of the Net as a separate place for purposes of legal analysis will have great simplifying effects. For example, a global registration system for all domain names and reputationally significant names and symbols used on the Net would become possible. Such a Net-based regime could take account of the special claims of owners of strong global marks (as used on physical goods) and "grandfather" these owners' rights to the use of their strong marks in the newly opened online territory. But a Net-based global registration system could also fully account for the true nature of the Net by treating the use of marks on Web pages as a global phenomena, by assessing the likelihood of confusion and dilution in the online context, and by harmonizing any rules with applicable engineering criteria, such as optimizing the overall size of the domain name space.

A distinct set of rules applicable to trademarks in Cyberspace would greatly simplify matters by providing a basis to resist the inconsistent and conflicting assertions of geographically local prerogatives. If one country objects to the use of a mark on the Web that conflicts with a locally registered mark, the rebuttal would be that the mark has not been used inside the country at all, but only on the Web. If a company wants to know where to register its use of a symbol on the Net, or to check for conflicting prior uses of its mark, the answer will be obvious and cost effective: the designated registration authority for the relevant portion of the Net itself. If we need to develop rules governing abandonment, dilution, and conditions on uses of particular types of domain names and addresses, those rules —applicable specifically to Cyberspace—will be able to reflect the special characteristics of this new electronic medium.[34]

B. Other Cyberspace regimes

Once we take Cyberspace seriously as a distinct place for purposes of legal analysis, many opportunities to clarify and simplify the rules applicable to online transactions become available.

1. Defamation law

Treating messages on the Net as transmissions from one place to another has created a quandary for those concerned about liability for defamation: Messages may be transmitted between countries with very different laws, and liability may be imposed on the basis of "publication" in multiple jurisdictions with varying standards.[35] In contrast, the approach that treats the global network as a separate place would consider any allegedly defamatory message to have been published only "on the Net" (or in some distinct subsidiary area thereof)—at least until such time as distribution on paper occurs.[36] This recharacterization makes more sense. A person who uploads a potentially defamatory statement would be more able to determine the rules applicable to his own actions. Moreover, because the Net has distinct characteristics, including an enhanced ability of the allegedly defamed person to reply, the rules of defamation developed for the Net could take into account these technological capabilities—perhaps by requiring that the opportunity for reply be taken advantage of in lieu of monetary compensation.[37] The distinct characteristics of the Net could also be taken into account when applying and adapting the "public figure" doctrine in a context that is both global and highly compartmentalized and that blurs the distinction between private and public spaces.

2. Regulation of net-based professional activities

The simplifying effect of "taking Cyberspace seriously" likewise arises in the context of regimes for regulating professional activities. As noted, traditional regulation insists that each professional be licensed by every territorial jurisdiction where she provides services.[38] This requirement is infeasible when professionals dispense services over the Net and potentially provided in numerous jurisdictions. Establishing certification regimes that apply only to such activities on the Net would greatly simplify matters. Such regulations would take into account the special features of Net-based professional activities like telemedicine or global law practice. For example, they would take into account special risks caused by giving online medical advice in the absence of direct physical contact with a patient or by answering a question regarding geographically local law from a remote location.[39] Using this new approach, we could override the efforts of local school boards to license online educational institutions, treating attendance by students at online institutions as a form of "leaving home for school" rather than characterizing the offering of education online as prosecutable distribution of disfavored materials into a potentially unwelcoming community that asserts local licensing authority.

3. Fraud and antitrust

Even an example that might otherwise be thought to favor the assertion of jurisdiction by a local sovereign—protection of local citizens from fraud and antitrust violations—shows the beneficial effects of a Cyberspace legal regime. How should we analyze "markets" for antitrust and consumer protection purposes when the companies at issue do business only through the World Wide Web? Cyberspace could be treated as a distinct marketplace for purposes of assessing concentration and market power. Concentration in geographic markets would only be relevant in the rare cases in which such market power could be inappropriately leveraged to obtain power in online markets—for example by conditioning access to the Net by local citizens on their buying services from the same company (such as a phone company) online. Claims regarding a right to access to particular online services, as distinct from claims to access particular physical pipelines, would remain tenuous as long as it is possible to create a new online service instantly in any corner of an expanding online space.[40]

Consumer protection doctrines could also develop differently online—to take into account the fact that anyone reading an online ad is only a mouse click away from guidance from consumer protection agencies and discussions with other consumers. Can Minnesota prohibit the establishment of a Ponzi scheme on a Web page physically based in the Cayman islands but accessed by Minnesota citizens through the Net? Under the proposed new approach to regulation of online activities, the answer is clearly no. Minnesota has no special right to prohibit such activities. The state lacks enforcement power, cannot show specially targeted effects, and does not speak for the community with the most legitimate claim to self-governance. But that does not mean that fraud might not be made "illegal" in at least large areas of Cyberspace. Those who establish and use online systems have a interest in preserving the safety of their electronic territory and preventing crime. They are more likely to be able to enforce their own rules. And, as more fully discussed below, insofar as a consensually based "law of the Net" needs to obtain respect and deference from local sovereigns, new Net-based law-making institutions have an incentive to avoid fostering activities that threaten the vital interests of territorial governments.

4. Copyright law

We suggest, not without some trepidation, that "taking Cyberspace seriously" could clarify the current intense debate about how to apply copyright law principles in the digital age. In the absence of global agreement on applicable copyright principles, the jurisdictional problems inherent in any attempt to apply territorially based copyright regimes to electronic works simultaneously available everywhere around the globe are profound. As Jane Ginsburg has noted:

> A key feature of the GII [Global Information Infrastructure] is its ability to render works of authorship pervasively and simultaneously accessible throughout the world. The principle of territoriality becomes problematic if it means that posting a work on the GII calls into play the laws of every country in which the work may be received when ... these laws may differ substantively. Should the rights in a work be determined by a multiplicity of inconsistent legal regimes when the work is simultaneously communicated to scores of countries? Simply taking into account one country's laws, the complexity of placing works in a digital network is already daunting: should the task be further burdened by an obligation to assess the impact of the laws of every country where the work might be received? Put more bluntly, for works on the GII, there will be no physical territoriality.... Without physical territoriality, can legal territoriality persist?[41]

But treating Cyberspace as a distinct place for purposes of legal analysis does more than resolve the conflicting claims of different jurisdictions: It also allows the development of new doctrines that take into account the special characteristics of the online "place."

The basic justification for copyright protection is that bestowing an exclusive property right to control the reproduction and distribution of works on authors will increase the supply of such works by offering authors a financial incentive to engage in the effort required for their creation.[42] But even in the "real world," much creative expression is entirely independent of this incentive structure, because the author's primary reward has more to do with acceptance in a community and the accumulation of reputational capital through wide dissemination than it does with the licensing and sale of individual copies of works.[43] And that may be more generally true of authorship in Cyberspace. Because authors can now, for the first time in history, deliver copies of their creations instantaneously and at virtually no cost anywhere in the world, one might expect authors to devise new modes of operation that take advantage of, rather than work counter to, this fundamental characteristic of the new environment.[44] One such strategy has already begun to emerge: giving away information at no charge—what might be called the "Netscape strategy"[45]—as a means of building up reputational capital that can subsequently be converted into income (for example, by means of the sale of services). As Esther Dyson has written:

> Controlling copies (once created by the author or by a third party) becomes a complex challenge. You can either control something very tightly, limiting distribution to a small, trusted group, or you can rest assured that eventually your product will find its way to a large nonpaying audience—if anyone cares to have it in the first place. . . . The trick is to control not the copies of your work but instead a *relationship* with the customers—subscriptions or membership. And that's often what the customers want, because they see it as an assurance of a continuing supply of reliable, timely content.
>
> Much chargeable value will be in certification of authenticity and reliability, not in the content. Brand name, identity, and other marks of value will be important; so will security of supply. Customers will pay for a stream of information and content from a trusted source. For example, the umbrella of *The New York Times* sanctifies the words of its reporters. The content churned out by *Times* reporters is valuable because the reporters undergo quality-control, and because others believe them.[46]

A profound shift of this kind in regard to authorial incentives fundamentally alters the applicable balance between the costs and benefits of copyright protection in Cyberspace, calling for a reappraisal of long-standing principles.[47] So, too, do other unique characteristics of Cyberspace severely challenge traditional copyright concepts.[48] The very ubiquity of file "copying"—the fact that one cannot access any information whatsoever in a computer-mediated environment without making a "copy" of that information[49]—implies that any simple-minded attempt to map traditional notions of "copying" onto Cyberspace transactions will have perverse results.[50] Application of the "first sale" doctrine (allowing the purchaser of a copyrighted work to freely resell the copy she purchased) is problematic when the transfer of a lawfully owned copy technically involves the making of a new copy before the old one is eliminated,[51] as is defining "fair use" when a work's size is indeterminate, ranging from (1) an individual paragraph sold separately on demand in response to searches to (2) the entire database from which the paragraph originates, something never sold as a whole unit.[52]

Treating Cyberspace as a distinct location allows for the development of new forms of intellectual property law, applicable only on the Net, that would properly focus attention on these unique characteristics of this new, distinct place while preserving doctrines that apply to works embodied in physical collections (like books) or displayed in legally significant physical places (like theaters). Current debates about applying copyright law to the Net often do, implicitly, treat it as a distinct space, at least insofar as commercial copyright owners somewhat inaccurately refer to it as a "lawless" place.[53] The civility of the debate might improve if everyone assumed the Net should have an appropriately different law, including a special law for unauthorized transfers of works from one realm to the other. We could, in other words, regulate the smuggling of works created in the physical world by treating the unauthorized uploading of a copy of such works to the Net as infringement. This new approach would help promoters of electronic commerce focus on developing incentive-producing rules to encourage authorized transfers into Cyberspace of works not available now, while also reassuring owners of existing copyrights that changes in the copyright law for the Net would not require changing laws applicable to distributing physical works. It would also permit the development of new doctrines of implied license and fair use that, as to works first created on the Net or imported with the author's permission, appropriately allow the transmission and copying necessary to facilitate their use within the electronic realm.[54]

III. Will responsible self-regulatory structures emerge on the net?

Even if we agree that new rules should apply to online phenomena, questions remain about who sets the rules and how they are enforced. We believe the Net can develop its own effective legal institutions.

In order for the domain name space to be administered by a legal authority that is not territorially based, new law-making institutions will have to develop. Many questions that arise in setting up this system will need answers: Should a new top level domain be created?[55] Do online addresses belong to users or service providers? Does one name impermissibly interfere with another, thus confusing the public and diluting the value of the pre-existing name?[56] The new system must also include procedures to give notice in conflicting claims, to resolve these claims, and to assess appropriate remedies (including, possibly, compensation) in cases of wrongful use. If the Cyberspace equivalent of eminent domain develops, questions may arise over how to compensate individuals when certain domain names are destroyed or redeployed for the public good of the Net community.[57] Someone must also decide threshold membership issues for Cyberspace citizens, including how much users must disclose (and to whom) about their real-world identities to use e-mail addresses and domain names for commercial purposes. Implied throughout this discussion is the recognition that these rules will be meaningful and enforceable only if Cyberspace citizens view whoever makes these decisions as a legitimate governing body.

Experience suggests that the community of online users and service providers is up to the task of developing a self-governance system.[58] For example, the current domain name system evolved from decisions made by engineers and the practices of Internet service providers.[59] Now that trademark owners are threatening the company that administers the registration system, the same engineers who established the original domain name standards are again deliberating whether to alter the domain name system to take these new policy issues into account.[60]

Every system operator who dispenses a password imposes at least some requirements as conditions of continuing access, including paying bills on time or remaining a member of a group entitled to access (for example, students at a university).[61] System operators (sysops) have an extremely powerful enforcement tool at their disposal to enforce such rules—banishment.[62] Moreover, communities of users have marshaled plenty of enforcement weapons to induce wrongdoers to comply with local conventions, such as rules against flaming,[63] shunning,[64] mailbombs,[65] and more. And both sysops and users have begun explicitly to recognize that formulating and enforcing such rules should be a matter for principled discussion, not an act of will by whoever has control of the power switch.[66]

While many of these new rules and customs apply only to specific, local areas of the global network, some standards apply through technical protocols on a nearly universal basis. And widespread agreement already exists about core principles of "netiquette" in mailing lists and discussion groups[67]—although, admittedly, new users have a slow learning curve and the Net offers little formal "public education" regarding applicable norms.[68] Moreover, dispute resolution mechanisms suited to this new environment also seem certain to prosper.[69] Cyberspace is anything but anarchic; its distinct rule sets are becoming more robust every day.

Perhaps the most apt analogy to the rise of a separate law of Cyberspace is the origin of the Law Merchant—a distinct set of rules that developed with the new, rapid boundary-crossing trade of the Middle Ages.[70] Merchants could not resolve their disputes by taking them to the local noble, whose established feudal law mainly concerned land claims. Nor could the local lord easily establish meaningful rules for a sphere of activity that he barely understood and that was executed in locations beyond his control. The result of this jurisdictional confusion was the development of a new legal system—*Lex Mercatoria*.[71] The people who cared most about and best understood their new creation formed and championed this new law, which did not destroy or replace existing law regarding more territorially based transactions (e.g., transferring land ownership). Arguably, exactly the same type of phenomenon is developing in Cyberspace right now.[72]

Governments cannot stop electronic communications from coming across their borders, even if they want to do so. Nor can they credibly claim a right to regulate the Net based on supposed local harms caused by activities that originate outside their borders and that travel electronically to many different nations. One nation's legal institutions should not monopolize rule-making for the entire Net. Even so, established authorities will likely continue to claim that they must analyze and regulate the new online phenomena in terms of some physical locations. After all, they argue, the people engaged in online communications still inhabit the material world, and local legal authorities must have authority to remedy the problems created in the physical world by those acting on the Net. The rise of responsible law-making institutions within Cyberspace, however, will weigh heavily against arguments that describe the Net as "lawless" and thus connect regulation of online trade to physical jurisdictions. As noted, sysops, acting alone or collectively, have the power to banish those who commit wrongful acts online.[73] Thus, for online activities that minimally affect the vital interests of sovereigns, the self-regulating structures of Cyberspace seem better suited to dealing with the Net's legal issues.[74]

IV. Local authorities, foreign rules: reconciling conflicts

What should happen when conflicts arise between the local territorial law (applicable to persons or entities by virtue of their location in a particular area of physical space) and the law applicable to particular activities on the Net? The doctrine of "comity," as well as principles applied when delegating authority to self-regulatory organizations, provide us with guidance for reconciling such disputes.

The doctrine of comity, in the Supreme Court's classic formulation, is "the recognition which one nation allows within its territory to the legislative, executive or judicial acts of another nation, having due regard both to international duty and convenience, and to the rights of its own citizens or of other persons who are under the protections of its law."[75] It is incorporated into the principles set forth in the Restatement (Third) of Foreign Relations Law of the United States, in particular Section 403, which provides that "a state may not exercise jurisdiction to prescribe law with respect to a person or activity having connections with another state when the exercise of such jurisdiction is unreasonable,"[76] and that when a conflict between the laws of two states arises, "each state has an obligation to evaluate its own as well as the other state's interest in exercising jurisdiction ... [and] should defer to the other state if that state's interest is clearly greater."[77] Comity arose as an attempt to mitigate some of the harsher features of a world in which lawmaking is an attribute of control over physical space but in which persons, things, and actions may move across physical boundaries. It functions as a constraint on the strict application of territorial principles that attempts to reconcile "the principle of absolute territorial sovereignty [with] the fact that intercourse between nations often demand[s] the recognition of one sovereign's lawmaking acts in the forum of another."[78] In general, comity reflects the view that those who care more deeply about and better understand the disputed activity should determine the outcome. Accordingly, it may be ideally suited to handle, by extension, the new conflicts between the nonterritorial nature of cyberspace activities and the legitimate needs of territorial sovereigns and of those whose interests they protect on the other side of the cyberspace border. This doctrine does not prevent territorial sovereigns from protecting the interests of those individuals located within their spheres of control, but it calls upon them to exercise a significant degree of restraint when doing so.

Local officials handling conflicts can also learn from many examples of delegating authority to self-regulatory organizations.[79] Churches are allowed to make religious law.[80] Clubs and social organizations can define rules that govern activities within their spheres of interest.[81] Securities exchanges can establish commercial rules, so long as they protect the vital interests of the surrounding communities. In these situations, government has seen the wisdom of allocating rule-making functions to those who best understand a complex phenomenon and who have an interest in assuring the growth and health of their shared enterprise.

Cyberspace represents a new permutation of the underlying issue: How much should local authorities defer to a new, self-regulating activity arising independently of local control and reaching beyond the limited physical boundaries of the sovereign? This mixing of both tangible and intangible boundaries leads to a convergence of the intellectual categories of comity in international relations and the local delegation by a sovereign to self-regulatory groups. In applying both the doctrine of "comity" and the idea of "delegation"[82] to Cyberspace, a local sovereign is called upon to defer to the self-regulatory judgments of a population partly, but not wholly, composed of its own subjects.[83]

Despite the seeming contradiction of a sovereign deferring to the authority of those who are not its own subjects, such a policy makes sense, especially in light of the underlying purposes of both doctrines. Comity and delegation represent the wise conservation of governmental resources and allocate decisions to those who most fully understand the special needs and characteristics of a particular "sphere" of being. Although Cyberspace represents a new sphere that cuts across national boundaries, the fundamental principle remains. If the sysops and users who collectively inhabit and control a particular area of the Net want to establish special rules to govern conduct there, and if that rule set does not fundamentally impinge upon the vital interests of others who never visit this new space, then the law of sovereigns in the physical world should defer to this new form of self-government.

Consider, once again, the trademark example. A U.S. government representative has stated that, since the government paid for the initial development and administration of the domain name system, it "owns" the right to control policy decisions regarding the creation and use of such names.[84] Obviously, government funds, in addition to individual efforts on a global scale, created this valuable and finite new asset. But the government's claim based on its investment is not particularly convincing. In fact, the United States may be asserting its right to control the policies governing the domain name space primarily because it fears that any other authority over the Net might force it to pay again for the ".gov" and ".mil" domain names used by governmental entities.[85] To assuage these concerns, a Net-based authority should concede to the government on this point. For example, it should accommodate the military's strong interest in remaining free to regulate and use its ".mil" addresses.[86] A new Net-based standards-making authority should also accommodate the government's interests in retaining its own untaxed domain names and prohibiting counterfeiting. Given responsible restraint by the Net-based authority and the development of an effective self-regulatory scheme, the government might well then decide that it should not spend its finite resources trying to wrest effective control of non-governmental domain names away from those who care most about facilitating the growth of online trade.

Because controlling the flow of electrons across physical boundaries is so difficult, a local jurisdiction that seeks to prevent its citizens from accessing specific materials must either outlaw all access to the Net—thereby cutting itself off from the new global trade—or seek to impose its will on the Net as a whole. This would be the modern equivalent of a local lord in medieval times either trying to prevent the silk trade from passing through his boundaries (to the dismay of local customers and merchants) or purporting to assert jurisdiction over the entire known world. It may be most difficult to envision local territorial sovereigns deferring to the law of the Net when the perceived threat to local interests arises from the very free flow of information that is the Net's most fundamental characteristic—when, for example, local sovereigns assert an interest in seeing that their citizens are not adversely affected by information that the local jurisdiction deems harmful but that is freely (and lawfully) available elsewhere. Examples include the German government's attempts to prevent its citizens from accessing prohibited materials,[87] or the prosecution of a California bulletin board operator for making material offensive to local "community standards" available for downloading in Tennessee.[88] Local sovereigns may insist that their interest (in protecting their citizens from harm) is paramount and easily outweighs any purported interest in making this kind of material freely available. But the opposing interest is not simply the interest in seeing that individuals have access to ostensibly obscene material, it is the "meta-interest" of Net citizens in preserving the global free flow of information. If there is one central principle on which all local authorities *within* the Net should agree, it must be that territorially local claims to a right to restrict online transactions (in ways unrelated to vital and localized interests of a territorial government) should be resisted. This is the Net equivalent of the First Amendment, a principle already recognized in the form of the international human rights doctrine protecting the right to communicate.[89] Participants in the new online trade must oppose external regulation designed to obstruct this flow. This central principle of online law is important to the "comity" analysis, because it makes clear that the need to preserve a free flow of information across the Net is just as vital to the interests of the Net as the need to protect local citizens against unwelcome information may appear to a local territorial sovereign.[90] For the Net to realize its full promise, online rule-making authorities must not respect the claims of territorial sovereigns to restrict online communications when unrelated to vital and localized governmental interests.

V. Internal diversity

One of a border's key characteristics is that it slows the interchange of people, things, and information across its divide. Arguably, distinct sets of legal rules can only develop and persist where effective boundaries exist. The development of a true "law of Cyberspace," therefore, depends upon a dividing line between this new online territory and the nonvirtual world. Our argument so far has been that the new online sphere is cut off, at least to some extent, from rule-making institutions in the material world and requires the creation of a distinct law applicable just to the online sphere.

But we hasten to add that Cyberspace is not a homogeneous or uniform territory behind that border, where information flows without further impediment. Although it is meaningless to speak of a French or Armenian portion of Cyberspace, because the physical borders dividing French or Armenian territory from their neighbors cannot generally be mapped onto the flow of information in Cyberspace, the Net has other kinds of internal borders delineating many distinct internal locations that slow or block the flow of information. Distinct names and (virtual) addresses, special passwords, entry fees, and visual cues—software boundaries—can distinguish subsidiary areas from one another. The Usenet newsgroup "alt.religion.scientology" is distinct from "alt.misc.legal," each of which is distinct from a chat room on Compuserve or America Online which, in turn, are distinct from the Cyberspace Law Institute listserver or Counsel Connect. Users can only access these different forums through distinct addresses or phone numbers, often navigating through login screens, the use of passwords, or the payment of fees. Indeed, the ease with which internal borders, consisting entirely of software protocols, can be constructed is one of Cyberspace's most remarkable and salient characteristics; setting up a new Usenet newsgroup, or a "listserver" discussion group, requires little more than a few lines of code.[91]

The separation of subsidiary "territories" or spheres of activity within Cyberspace and the barriers to exchanging information across these internal borders allow for the development of distinct rule sets and for the divergence of those rule sets over time.[92] The processes underlying biological evolution provide a useful analogy.[93] Speciation—the emergence over time of multiple, distinct constellations of genetic information from a single, original group—cannot occur when the original population freely exchanges information (in the form of genetic material) among its members. In other words, a single, freely interbreeding population of organisms cannot divide into genetically distinct populations. While the genetic material in the population changes over time, it does so more or less uniformly—for example, the population of the species *Homo erectus* becomes a population of *Homo sapiens*—and cannot give rise to more than one contemporaneous, distinct genetic set. Speciation requires, at a minimum, some barrier to the interchange of genetic material between subsets of the original homogeneous population. Ordinarily, a physical barrier suffices to prevent one subgroup from exchanging genetic data with another. Once this "border" is in place, divergence within the "gene pool"—the aggregate of the underlying genetic information—in each of the two subpopulations may occur.[94] Over time, this divergence may be substantial enough that even when the physical barrier disappears, the two subgroups can no longer exchange genetic material—i.e., they have become separate species.

Rules, like genetic material, are self-replicating information.[95] The internal borders within Cyberspace will thus allow for differentiation among distinct constellations of such information—in this case rule-sets rather than species. Content or conduct acceptable in one "area" of the Net may be banned in another. Institutions that resolve disputes in one "area" of Cyberspace may not gain support or legitimacy in others. Local sysops can, by contract, impose differing default rules regarding who has the right, under certain conditions, to replicate and redistribute materials that originate with others. While Cyberspace's reliance on bits instead of atoms may make *physical* boundaries more permeable, the boundaries delineating digital online "spheres of being" may become *less* permeable. Securing online systems from unauthorized intruders may prove an easier task than sealing physical borders from unwanted immigration.[96] Groups can establish online corporate entities or membership clubs that tightly control participation in, or even public knowledge of, their own affairs. Such groups can reach agreement on or modify these rules more rapidly via online communications. Accordingly, the rule sets applicable to the online world may quickly evolve away from those applicable to more traditional spheres and develop greater variation among the sets.

How this process of differentiation and evolution will proceed is one of the more complex and fascinating questions about law in Cyberspace—and a subject beyond the scope of this article. We should point out, however, an important normative dimension to the proliferation of these internal boundaries between distinct communities and rule-sets. Cyberspace may be an important forum for the development of new connections between individuals and mechanisms of self-governance by which individuals attain a sense of community. Commenting on the erosion of national sovereignty in the modern world and the failure of the existing system of nation-states to cultivate a moral connection between the individual and the community (or communities) in which she is embedded, Sandel has written:

> The hope for self-government today lies not in relocating sovereignty but in dispersing it. The most promising alternative to the sovereign state is not a cosmopolitan community based on the solidarity of humankind but *a multiplicity of communities and political bodies—some more extensive than nations and some less—among which sovereignty is diffused.* Only a politics that disperses sovereignty both upward [to transnational institutions] and downward can combine the power required to rival global market forces with the differentiation required of a public life that hopes to inspire the allegiance of its citizens. . . .
>
> If the nation cannot summon more than a minimal commonality, it is unlikely that the global community can do better, at least on its own. A more promising basis for a democratic politics that reaches beyond nations is a revitalized civic life nourished in the more particular communities we inhabit. In the age of NAFTA the politics of neighborhood matters more, not less.[97]

Furthermore, the ease with which individuals can move between different rule sets in Cyberspace has important implications for any contractarian political philosophy deriving a justification of the State's exercise of coercive power over its citizens from their consent to the exercise of that power. In the nonvirtual world, this consent has a strong fictional element: "State reliance on consent inferred from someone merely remaining in the state is particularly unrealistic. An individual's unwillingness to incur the extraordinary costs of leaving his or her birthplace should not be treated as a consensual undertaking to obey state authority."[98] To be sure, citizens of France, dissatisfied with French law and preferring, say, Armenian rules, can try to persuade their compatriots and local decision-makers of the superiority of the Armenian rule-set.[99] However, their "exit" option, in Albert Hirschman's terms,[100] is limited by the need to physically relocate to Armenia to take advantage of that rule set.[101] In Cyberspace, though, any given user has a more accessible exit option, in terms of moving from one virtual environment's rule set to another's, thus providing a more legitimate "selection mechanism" by which differing rule sets will evolve over time.[102]

The ability of inhabitants of Cyberspace to cross borders at will between legally significant territories, many times in a single day, is unsettling. This power seems to undercut the validity of developing distinct laws for online culture and commerce: How can these rules be "law" if participants can literally turn them on and off with a switch? Frequent online travel might subject relatively mobile human beings to a far larger number of rule sets than they would encounter traveling through the physical world over the same period. Established authorities, contemplating the rise of a new law applicable to online activities, might object that we cannot easily live in a world with too many different sources and types of law, particularly those made by private (nongovernmental) parties, without breeding confusion and allowing anti-social actors to escape effective regulation.

But the speed with which we can cross legally meaningful borders or adopt and then shed legally significant roles should not reduce our willingness to recognize multiple rule sets. Rapid travel between spheres of being does not detract from the distinctiveness of the boundaries, as long as participants realize the rules are changing. It also does not detract from the appropriateness of rules applying within any given place, any more than changing commercial or organizational roles in the physical world detracts from a person's ability to obey and distinguish rules as a member of many different institutional affiliations.[103] Nor does rapid travel lower the enforceability of any given rule set within its appropriate boundaries, as long as groups can control unauthorized boundary crossing of groups or messages. Alternating between different legal identities many times during a day may confuse those for whom Cyberspace remains an alien territory, but for those for whom Cyberspace is a more natural habitat in which they spend increasing amounts of time it may become second nature. Legal systems must learn to accommodate a more mobile kind of legal person.[104]

VI. Conclusion

Global electronic communications have created new spaces in which distinct rule sets will evolve. We can reconcile the new law created in this space with current territorially based legal systems by treating it as a distinct doctrine, applicable to a clearly demarcated sphere, created primarily by legitimate, self-regulatory processes, and entitled to appropriate deference—but also subject to limitations when it oversteps its appropriate sphere.

The law of any given place must take into account the special characteristics of the space it regulates and the types of persons, places, and things found there. Just as a country's jurisprudence reflects its unique historical experience and culture, the law of Cyberspace will reflect its special character, which differs markedly from anything found in the physical world. For example, the law of the Net must deal with persons who "exist" in Cyberspace only in the form of an e-mail address and whose purported identity may or may not accurately correspond to physical characteristics in the real world. In fact, an e-mail address might not even belong to a single person. Accordingly, if Cyberspace law is to recognize the nature of its "subjects," it cannot rest on the same doctrines that give geographically based sovereigns jurisdiction over "whole," locatable, physical persons. The law of the Net must be prepared to deal with persons who manifest themselves only by means of a particular ID, user account, or domain name.

Moreover, if rights and duties attach to an account itself, rather than to an underlying real world person, traditional concepts such as "equality," "discrimination," or even "rights and duties" may not work as we normally understand them. For example, when AOL users joined the Net in large numbers, other Cyberspace users often ridiculed them based on the ".aol" tag on their email addresses—a form of "domainism" that might be discouraged by new forms of Netiquette. If a doctrine of Cyberspace law accords rights to users, we will need to decide whether those rights adhere only to particular types of online appearances, as distinct from those attaching to particular individuals in the real world.

Similarly, the types of "properties" that can become the subject of legal discussion in Cyberspace will differ from real world real estate or tangible objects. For example, in the real world the physical covers of a book delineate the boundaries of a "work" for purposes of copyright law;[105] those limits may disappear entirely when the same materials are part of a large electronic database. Thus, we may have to change the "fair use" doctrine in copyright law that previously depended on calculating what portion of the physical work was copied.[106] Similarly, a web page's "location" in Cyberspace may take on a value unrelated to the physical place where the disk holding that Web page resides, and efforts to regulate web pages by attempting to control physical objects may only cause the relevant bits to move from one place to another. On the other hand, the boundaries set by "URLs" (Uniform Resource Locators, the location of a document on the World Wide Web) may need special protection against confiscation or confusingly similar addresses. And, because these online "places" may contain offensive material, we may need rules requiring (or allowing) groups to post certain signs or markings at these places' outer borders.

The boundaries that separate persons and things behave differently in the virtual world but are nonetheless legally significant. Messages posted under one e-mail name will not affect the reputation of another e-mail address, even if the same physical person authors both messages. Materials separated by a password will be accessible to different sets of users, even if those materials physically exist on the very same hard drive. A user's claim to a right to a particular online identity or to redress when that identity's reputation suffers harm, may be valid even if that identity does not correspond exactly to that of any single person in the real world.[107]

Clear boundaries make law possible, encouraging rapid differentiation between rule sets and defining the subjects of legal discussion. New abilities to travel or exchange information rapidly across old borders may change the legal frame of reference and require fundamental changes in legal institutions. Fundamental activities of lawmaking—accommodating conflicting claims, defining property rights, establishing rules to guide conduct, enforcing those rules, and resolving disputes—remain very much alive within the newly defined, intangible territory of Cyberspace. At the same time, the newly emerging law challenges the core idea of a current law-making authority—the territorial nation state, with substantial but legally restrained powers.

If the rules of Cyberspace thus emerge from consensually based rule sets, and the subjects of such laws remain free to move among many differing online spaces, then considering the actions of Cyberspace's system administrators as the exercise of a power akin to "sovereignty" may be inappropriate. Under a legal framework where the top level imposes physical order on those below it and depends for its continued effectiveness on the inability of its citizens to fight back or leave the territory, the legal and political doctrines we have evolved over the centuries are essential to constrain such power. In that situation, where exit is impossible, costly, or painful, then a right to a voice for the people is essential. But when the "persons" in question are not whole people, when their "property" is intangible and portable, and when all concerned may readily escape a jurisdiction they do not find empowering, the relationship between the "citizen" and the "state" changes radically. Law, defined as a thoughtful group conversation about core values, will persist. But it will not, could not, and should not be the same law as that applicable to physical, geographically-defined territories.

Notes

* The authors wish to thank Becky Burr, Larry Downes, Henry J. Perritt, Jr., and Ron Plesser, as well as the other Fellows of the Cyberspace Law Institute (Jerry Berman, John Brown, Bill Burrington, Esther Dyson, David Farber, Ken Freeling, A. Michael Froomkin, Robert Gell-man, I. Trotter Hardy, Ethan Katsh, Lawrence Lessig, Bill Marmon, Lance Rose, Marc Rotenberg, Pamela Samuelson, and Eugene Volokh), CLI Co-Directors Carey Heckman, John Podesta, and Peggy Radin, and Jim Campbell, for their assistance in the formulation of these ideas. The usual disclaimer, of course, applies: the authors alone are responsible for errors, omissions, misstatements, and misunderstandings set forth in the following.

1 See EEOC v. Arabian American Oil Co., 499 U.S. 244, 248 (1991) ("It is a longstanding principle of American law 'that legislation of Congress, unless a contrary intent appears, is meant to apply only within the territorial jurisdiction of the United States.'") (quoting Foley Bros. v. Filardo, 336 U.S. 281, 285 (1949)).

2 See la JEROME GILSON, TRADEMARK PROTECTION AND PRACTICE § 9.01 (1991); Dan L. Burk, *Trademarks Along the Infobahn: A First Look at the Emerging Law of Cybermarks*, 1 U. RICH. J. L. & TECH. 1 (1995), *available at* http://www.urich.edu/jolt/vlil/burk.html; Jeffrey M. Samuels & Linda B. Samuels, *The Changing Landscape of International Trademark Law*, 27 GEO. WASH. J. INT'L L. & ECON. 433, 433 (1993–94).

3 Dawn Donut Co. v. Hart's Food Stores, 267 F.2d 358, 365 (2d. Cir. 1959) (holding that the owner of a registered trademark may not enjoin another's use of that mark in a geographically separate market if the holder of the registered mark does not intend to expand into that market).

4 *See, e.g.*, California Fruit Growers Exch. v. Sunkist Baking Co., 166 F.2d 971 (7th Cir. 1947) (finding that the sale of "Sunkist" fruits and "Sunkist" bakery products in the same market would not cause consumer confusion); Restaurant Lutece Inc. v. Houbigant, Inc., 593 F. Supp. 588 (D.N.J. 1984) (denying a preliminary injunction by the restaurant "Lutece" against a company wishing to sell "Lutece" perfume and cosmetics).

5 Clark W. Lackert, *International Efforts Against Trademark Counterfeiting*, COLUM. BUS. L. REV. 161 (1988); Samuels & Samuels, *supra* note 2, at 433.

6 RESTATEMENT (THIRD) OF FOREIGN RELATIONS LAW OF THE UNITED STATES § 201 (1987) ("Under international law, a state is an entity that has a defined territory and a permanent population, under the control of its own government...."); *id.* § 402 ("[A] state has jurisdiction to prescribe law with respect to (1)(a) conduct that, wholly or in substantial part, takes place within its territory; (b) the status of persons, or interests in things, present within its territory; (c) conduct outside its territory that has or is intended to have substantial effect within its territory...."); *see also* Lea Brilmayer, *Consent, Contract, and Territory*, 74 MINN. L. REV. 1, 10–17 (arguing that a consent theory of statehood relies on prior assumptions of territorial sovereignty).

7 The sovereign's ability to claim personal jurisdiction over a particular party turns importantly on the party's relationship to the physical jurisdiction over which the sovereign has control, e.g., the presence of the party or the party's assets, within the jurisdiction, or activities of the party that are directed to persons or things within the jurisdiction. Similarly, the law chosen to apply to a contract, tort, or criminal action has historically been influenced primarily by the physical location of the parties or the deed in question. *See generally* HENRY

H. Perritt Jr., *Jurisdiction in Cyberspace*, in Law and the Information Superhighway (forthcoming 1996) (discussing the "conventional doctrines" of personal jurisdiction and choice of law and the shortcomings of these geographically-based concepts as applied to Cyberspace).

8 *Declaration on Principles of International Law Concerning Friendly Relations and Co-operation Among States in Accordance with the Charter of the United Nations*, G. A. Res. 2625, U.N. GAOR 6th Comm., 25th Sess., Agenda Item 85, at 121 (1970); *Declaration of the Inadmissibility of Intervention in the Domestic Affairs of States and the Protection of their Independence and Sovereignty*, G. A. Res. 2131, U.N GAOR 1st Comm., 20th Sess., Agenda Item 107, at 11 (1965); *see generally* Brilmayer, *supra* note 6 (arguing that a state's power cannot be explained solely by consent theory since territorial sovereignty must also be presumed).

9 The exception that proves this rule is the outrage we feel when a journalist who crosses a territorial boundary without any signs is imprisoned for a supposed offense against the local state. Some "signposts" are culturally understood conventions that accompany entry into specialized places, such as courtrooms, office buildings, and churches. But not all signposts and boundaries dividing different rule sets are geographically or physically based. Sets of different rules may apply when the affected parties play particular roles, such as members of self-regulatory organizations, agents of corporate entities, and so forth. Henry H. Perritt, Jr., Selfgoverning Electronic Communities 36–49, 59–60 (Apr. 2, 1995) (unpublished manuscript, on file with the *Stanford Law Review*). But even these roles are most often clearly marked by cues of dress, or formal signatures that give warning of the applicable rules.

10 As Woody Allen once quipped: "Space is nature's way of keeping everything from happening to you." Although there is distance in online space, it behaves differently from distance in real space. *See* M. Ethan Katsh, The Electronic Media and the Transformation of Law 92–94 (1989) (discussing the benefits of moving data over great distances at high speeds and the potential risks of transforming that data in the process); M. Ethan Katsh, Law in a Digital World 57–64, 218 (1995) (noting that although physical distance is becoming less of an obstacle in the age of computers, electronic communication may create informational distance).

11 For a general description of the Domain Name System, see Burk, *supra* note 2, at para. 12–14; *see also* R. Bush, B. Carpenter & J. Postel, *Delegation of International Top Level Domains* (Jan. 1996), *available at* ftp://ds.internic.net/internet-drafts/draft-ymbk-itld-admin-00.txt (describing how to ensure an open and competitive international market for domain names); P. Mockapetris, *RFC 882, Domain Names—Concepts and Facilities* (Nov. 1983), *available at* ftp://ds.internic.net/rfc/rfc882.txt (discussing the basic principles of domain names); P. Mockapetris, *RFC 883, Domain Names—Implementation and Specifications* (Nov. 1983), *available at* ftp://ds.internic.net/rfc/rfc883.txt (discussing the use of domain names in mail systems and other network software).

12 *See* Jon Auerbach, *Fences in Cyberspace: Governments Move to Limit Free Flow of the Internet*, Boston Globe, Feb. 1, 1996, at 1 (describing how government censorship and filtration has caused "digital Balkanization" of the Internet); Seth Faison, *Chinese Cruise Internet, Wary of Watchdogs*, N.Y. Times, Feb. 5, 1996, at A1 (describing the Chinese government's regulatory attempts to steer "the flow of electronic information through officially controlled parts"); *see generally* Anne Wells Branscomb, *Jurisdictional Quandaries for Global Networks*, *in* Global Networks: Computers and International Communication 83,

103 (Linda M. Harasim ed., 1993) (exploring efforts to exercise jurisdictional control over electronic information services).

13 Anthony Paul Miller, *Teleinformatics, Transborder Data Flows and the Emerging Struggle for Information: An Introduction to the Arrival of the New Information Age*, 20 COLUM. J. L. & SOC. PROBS. 89, 107–08 (1986). Miller discusses the willingness of some national governments to forgo the benefits of unregulated TDF's so as to protect their political, social, and cultural interests. *Id.* at 107–08, 127–35.

14 *Id.* at 105–07, 111–18 (suggesting that the perceived threat of the exploitative use of computerized personal data has prompted the Organization for Economic Cooperation and Development (OCED) and governments throughout Western Europe to restrict the content of TDF's so as to protect individual and corporate privacy).

15 *Id.* at 109–11 (noting the attempt, particularly among computer software developers, to curb the threat that TDF's pose to intellectual property rights); *see also* Doreen Carvajal, *Book Publishers Worry About Threat of Internet*, N.Y. TIMES, Mar. 18, 1996, at A1 (describing the appearance on the Internet of *Le Grand Secret*, a book about former French President Francois Mitterand, despite France's banning of the book and discussing the book publishers' general concern about unauthorized Internet distributions).

16 For example, A. Jared Silverman, former chief of the New Jersey Bureau of Securities, expressed concern about the ability of the State to protect its residents against fraudulent schemes if it does not assert the right to regulate every online securities offering accessible, via the net, from within the State. A. Jared Silverman, Online Offerings: Is Cyberspace a Medium for Capital Formation, or a Jurisdiction Unto Itself? 2–3 (Jan. 1996) (unpublished manuscript, on file with the *Stanford Law Review*); *see also* Gregory Spears, *Cops and Robbers on the Net*, KIPLINGER'S PERS. FIN. MAG., Feb. 1995, at 56 (surveying state securities regulators' responses to online investment scams). Moreover, various state attorneys general have expressed concern about gambling and consumer fraud reaching their state's residents over the net. *See* note 21 *infra*.

17 The difficulty of policing an electronic border may have something to do with its relative length. *See* Professor Peter Martin, Comment at the NewJuris Electronic Conference (Sept. 22, 1993) (discussing cyberspace's "near infinite boundary" as compared with territorial jurisdictions). Physical roads and ports linking sovereign territories are few in number, and geographical boundaries can be fenced and policed. In contrast, the number of starting points for an electronic "trip" out of a given country is staggering, consisting of every telephone capable of connecting outside the territory. Even if electronic communications are concentrated into high volume connections, a customs house on an electronic border would cause a massive traffic jam, threatening the very electronic commerce such facilities were constructed to encourage.

18 *Cf.* INFORMATION INFRASTRUCTURE TASK FORCE, INTELLECTUAL PROPERTY AND THE NATIONAL INFORMATION INFRASTRUCTURE: THE REPORT OF THE WORKING GROUP ON INTELLECTUAL PROPERTY RIGHTS 221 (1995) (hereinafter "White Paper") ("Although we recognize that the U.S. Customs Service cannot, for all practical purposes, enforce a prohibition on importation by transmission, given the global dimensions of the information infrastructure of the future, it is important that copyright owners have the other remedies for infringements of this type available to them."). Ironically, the Voice of America cannot prevent the information it places on the Net from doubling back into the United States, even though this domestic dissemination violates the 1948 Smith-Mundt Act.

John Schwartz, *Over the Net and Around the Law*, WASH. POST, Jan. 14, 1995, at C1.

19 *See* WALTER B. WRISTON, THE TWILIGHT OF SOVEREIGNTY: HOW THE INFORMATION REVOLUTION IS TRANFORMING OUR WORLD 61 (1992) (noting that the new financial market "is not a geographic location to be found on a map but rather more than two hundred thousand electronic monitors all over the world that are linked together" and that "no one is in control"). Wriston adds:

> Technology has made us a "global" community in the literal sense of the word. Whether we are ready or not, mankind now has a completely integrated international financial and information marketplace capable of moving money and ideas to any place on this planet in minutes. Capital will go where it is wanted and stay where it is well treated. It will flee from manipulation or onerous regulation of its value or use, and no government power can restrain it for long.

Id. at 61–62. The Securities and Exchange Commission has taken the position that securities offerings "that occur outside the United States" are not subject to the registration requirements of Section 5 of the Securities Act of 1933, even if United States residents are the purchasers in the overseas market. 17 C.F.R. § 230.901 (1995); *see also* 17 C.F.R. § 230.903 (1995) (saying that in order for offers and sales to be deemed to "occur outside the United States," there must be, *inter alia*, "no directed selling efforts . . . made in the United States"); 17 C.F.R. § 230.902(b)(1) (1995) (defining "directed selling efforts" as "any activity undertaken for the purpose of, or that could reasonably be expected to have the effect of, conditioning the market in the United States" for the securities in question). If, as many predict, trading on physical exchanges increasingly gives way to computerized trading, *see, e.g.*, Therese H. Maynard, *What is an "Exchange"—Proprietary Electronic Securities Trading Systems and the Statutory Definition of an Exchange*, 49 WASH. & LEE L. REV. 833, 862–63 (1992), Lewis D. Solomon & Louise Corso, *The Impact of Technology on the Trading of Securities: The Emerging Global Market and the Implications for Regulation*, 24 J. MARSHALL L. REV. 299, 318–19 (1991), this rule will inevitably become increasingly difficult to apply on a coherent basis; where, in such a market, does the offer "occur"? Can information about the offering placed on the World Wide Web "reasonably be expected to have the effect of conditioning the market in the United States" for the securities in question? *See id.* at 330 (noting that "[c]hoice of law questions take on a new dimension in the electronic global market"). The authors wish to thank Professor Merritt Fox for drawing our attention to these issues in the securities context. Merritt Fox, The Political Economy of Statutory Reach: U.S. Disclosure Rules for a Globalizing Market for Securities, Address at Georgetown University Law Center (Mar. 6, 1996).

20 For example, the German government, seeking to enforce its laws against distribution of pornographic material, ordered CompuServe to disable access by German residents to certain global Usenet newsgroups. Karen Kaplan, *Germany Forces Online Service to Censor Internet*, L. A. TIMES, Dec. 29, 1995, at A1; Ruth Walker, *Why Free-Wheeling Internet Hits Teutonic Wall Over Porn*, CHRISTIAN SCI. MONITOR, Jan. 4, 1996, at 1; *Cyberporn Debate Goes International*; *see also* Kara Swisher, *Germany Pulls the Shade On CompuServe, Internet*, WASH. POST, Jan. 1, 1996, at F13. Anyone inside Germany with an Internet connection could easily find a way to access the prohibited news groups during

the ban, for instance by linking up through another country. Auerbach, *supra* note 12, at 15. Although initially compliant, CompuServe subsequently rescinded the ban on most of the files by sending parents a new program to choose for themselves what items to restrict. *CompuServe Ends Access Suspension: It Reopens All But Five Adult-Oriented Newsgroups*, L. A. TIMES, Feb. 14, 1996, at D1.

Similarly, Tennessee may insist (indirectly, through enforcement of a federal law that defers to local community standards) that an electronic bulletin board operated in California install filters that prevent offensive screens from being displayed to users in Tennessee if the operators are to avoid liability under Tennessee's local obscenity standards. *See* United States v. Thomas, 74 F.3d 701 (6th Cir. 1996) (affirming a California couple's convictions under federal obscenity laws for postings made in California to an electronic bulletin board that was accessible from and offensive to the community standards of Tennessee; *see also* Electronic Frontier Foundation, *A Virtual Amicus Brief in the Amateur Action Appeal, available at* http://www.eff.org/pub/Legal/Cases/AABBS —Thomases—Memphis/Old/aa—eff—vbrief.html. The bulletin board in this case had very clear warnings and password protection. This intangible boundary limited entrance to only those who freely chose to see the materials and accepted the system operator's rules. *Id.* It is our contention that posting offensive materials in areas where unwilling readers may come across them inadvertently raises problems that are best addressed by those who understand the technology involved, rather than by extrapolating from the conflicting laws of multiple geographic jurisdictions.

21 The Minnesota Attorney General's Office posted a warning statement stating that "[p]ersons outside of Minnesota who transmit information via the Internet knowing that information will be disseminated in Minnesota are subject to jurisdiction in Minnesota courts for violations of state criminal and civil laws." *Warning to all Internet Users and Providers, available at* http://www.state.mn.us/ebranch/ag/memo.txt. (emphasis omitted). The assertion of jurisdiction rested on the Minnesota general criminal jurisdiction statute, which provides that "[a] person may be convicted and sentenced under the law of this State if the person . . . (3) Being without the state, intentionally causes a result within the state prohibited by the criminal laws of this state." MINN. STAT. ANN. § 609.025 (West 1987). Minnesota also began civil proceedings against Wagernet, a Nevada gambling business which posted an Internet advertisement for online gambling services. *See* Complaint, Minnesota v. Granite Gate Resorts, Inc., No. 9507227 (1995), *available at* http://www.state.mn.us/ebranch/ag/ggcom.txt. The Florida Attorney General, by contrast, contends that it is illegal to use the Web to gamble from within Florida but concedes that the Attorney General's office should not waste time trying to enforce the unenforceable. 95-70 Op. Fla. Att'y Gen. (1995), *available at* http://legal.firn.edu/units/opinions/95-70.html. For a general discussion of these pronouncements, see Mark Eckenwiler, *States Get Entangled in the Web*, LEGAL TIMES, Jan. 22. 1996, at S35.

22 *See State Regulators Crack Down on "Information Highway" Scams*, DAILY REP. FOR EXEC. (BNA), July 1, 1994, *available in* Westlaw, BNA-DER database, 1994 DER 125, at d16.

23 *See* David G. Post, *The State of Nature and the First Internet War*, REASON, Apr. 1996, at 30–31 (describing the operation of the alt.religion.scientology Usenet group). Groups like alt.religion.scientology

> come into existence when someone . . . sends a proposal to establish the group to the specific newsgroup (named "alt.config") set up for

> receiving such proposals. The operators of each of the thousands of computer networks hooked up to the Internet are then free to carry, or to ignore, the proposed group. If a network chooses to carry the newsgroup, its computers will be instructed to make the alt.religion.scientology "feed," i.e., the stream of messages posted to alt.religion.scientology arriving from other participating networks, accessible to its users, who can read—and, if they wish, add to—this stream before it is passed along to the next network in the worldwide chain. It's a completely decentralized organism—in technical terms, a "distributed database"—whose content is constantly changing as it moves silently around the globe from network to network and machine to machine, never settling down in any one legal jurisdiction, or on any one computer.

Id.; see generally What is Usenet?, available at http://www.smartpages.com/bngfaqs/news/announce/newusers/top.html; Answers to Frequently Asked Questions about Usenet, available at http://www.smartpages.com/bngfaqs/news/announce/newusers/top.html.

24 European countries try to protect data about their citizens by banning the export of information to countries that do not afford sufficient protections. *See* Peter Blume, *An EEC Policy for Data Protection*, 11 COMPUTER/L. J. 399 (1992); Joseph I. Rosenbaum, *The European Commission's Draft Directive on Data Protection*, 33 JURIMETRICS J. 1, 4–12 (1992); Symposium, *Data Protection and the European Union's Directive: The Challenge for the United States*, 80 IOWA L. REV. 431 (1995). But the data regarding their citizens' activities may not be subject to the countries' control—the data may originate as a result of actions recorded on outside servers.

25 *See* Joel R. Reidenberg, *The Privacy Obstacle Course: Hurdling Barriers to Transnational Financial Services*, 60 FORDHAM L. REV. S137 (1992); David Post, *Hansel & Gretel in Cyberspace*, AM. LAW., Oct. 1995, at 110.

26 Many new issues posed by phenomena unique to the Net are even less familiar than the privacy issue. For example, because electronic communications are not necessarily tied to real world identities, new questions about the rights to continued existence, or to protection of the reputation, of a pseudonym arise. Also, there are new forms of offensive behavior that the Net makes possible. The potential to launch a computer virus or to "spam the net" by sending multiple offpoint messages to newsgroups, for example, creates a need to define rules governing online behavior. And the increased communication that the Net offers has brought together people that otherwise would not have met. When large numbers of people collaborate across the Net to create services or works of value, we face questions of whether they have formed a corporate entity or partnership with rights and duties of its own that are distinct from those of the individual participants. This new entity may have been created in a context in which there was no "registration" with any particular geographic authority and in which the rights of any such authority to regulate that new "legal person" remain unsettled.

27 *See* text accompanying note 11 *supra*.

28 Conflicts between domain names and registered trademarks have caused Network Solutions, Inc. (NSI), the agent for registration of domain names in the United States, to require that registrants "represent and warrant" that they have the right to a requested domain name and promise to "defend, indemnify and hold harmless" NSI for any claims stemming from use or registration of

the requested name. Network Solution Inc., *NSI Domain Name Dispute Policy Statement* (Revision 01, effective November 23, 1995), *available at* ftp://rs.internic.net/policy/internic/internic-domain-4.txt. For a useful overview of the domain name registration system and of the tensions between trademark rights and domain names, see Gary W. Hamilton, *Trademarks on the Internet: Confusion, Collusion or Dilution?*, 4 TEX. INTELL. PROP. L. J. 1 (1995); *see also* Proceedings of the NSF/DNCEI & Harvard Information Infrastructure Project, *Internet Names, Numbers, and Beyond: Issues in the Coordination, Privatization, and Internationalization of the Internet* (Nov. 20, 1995), *available at* http://ksgwww.harvard.edu/iip/nsfmin1.html (discussing protection of the "trademark community" on the Net).

29 *See* David R. Johnson, *The Internet vs. the Local Character of the Law: The Electronic Web Ties Iowa and New York into One Big System*, LEGAL TIMES, Dec. 5, 1994, at S32 (predicting the "natural selection of local regulatory regimes that favor the Net").

30 Indeed, the persistence and accessibility of electronic messages create such a sense of "placeness" that meetings in Cyberspace may become a viable alternative to meetings in physical space. *See* I. Trotter Hardy, *Electronic Conferences: The Report of an Experiment*, 6 HARV. J. L. & TECH. 213, 232–34 (1993) (discussing the advantages of e-mail conferences). In contrast, there is no "Telespace" because the conversations we conduct by telephone disappear when the parties hang up. Voicemail creates an aural version of electronic mail, but it is not part of an interconnected system that you can travel through, by hypertext links or otherwise, to a range of public and semi-public locations.

31 *See* David R. Johnson, *Traveling in Cyberspace*, LEGAL TIMES, Apr. 3, 1995, at 26 (noting that because an online user must usually go past a password and a warning label to access a newsgroup, it is unlikely that person will accidentally be exposed to an offensive posing). Some information products combine a local CD-ROM with online access to provide updated information. But even these products typically provide some on-screen indication when the user is going online. Failure to provide notice might well be deemed fraudulent, particularly if the service imposes additional charges for use of the online system. In any event, a product that brings information to the screen, from an online location, without disclosing the online connection to the user, has not created a legally significant "visit" to online space. "Visiting" a space implies some knowledge that you are there.

32 *See* text accompanying notes 92–96 *infra* (discussing internal differentiation among rule-sets in different online areas).

33 Having a noticeable border may be a prerequisite to the establishment of any legal regime that can claim to be separate from pre-existing regimes. If someone acting in any given space has no warning that the rules have changed, the legitimacy of any attempt to enforce a distinctive system of law is fatally weakened. No geographically-based sovereign could plausibly claim to have jurisdiction over a territory with secret boundaries. And no self-regulatory organization could assert its prerogatives while making it hard for members and nonmembers to tell each other apart or disguising when they are (or are not) playing their membership-related roles.

34 For example, we will have to take into account the desire of participants in online communications for pseudonymity. This will affect the extent to which information about the applicant's identity must be disclosed in order to obtain a valid address registration. *See* A. Michael Froomkin, *Anonymity and Its Enmities*, 1995 J. of Online Law art. 4, *available at* http://www.law.cornell.

edu/jol/jol.table.html (discussing the mechanics of anonymity and how it affects the creation of pseudonymous personalities and communication on the Net); A. Michael Froomkin, *Flood Control on the Information Ocean: Living With Anonymity, Digital Cash, and Distributed Databases*—U. PITT. J. L. COM., *available at* http://www.law.miami.edu/froomkin (forthcoming 1996) (exploring the use and possible regulation of computer-aided anonymity); David G. Post, *Pooling Intellectual Capital: Thoughts on Anonymity, Pseudonymity, and Limited Liability in Cyberspace*, U. Chi. Legal Forum (forthcoming), *available at* http://www-law.lib.uchicago.edu/forum/ (discussing the value of pseudonymous communications). And any registration and conflict-resolution scheme will have to take into account the particular ways in which Internet addresses and names are viewed in the marketplace. If shorter names are valued more highly (jones.com being more valuable than jones isp.members.directory.com), this new form of "domain envy" should be considered in developing applicable policy.

35 *See* Michael Smyth and Nick Braithwaite, *First U.K. Bulletin Board Defamation Suit Brought*, NAT'L L. J., Sept. 19, 1994, at C10 (noting that English courts may be a more attractive forum for plaintiffs charging defamation in cyberspace).

36 Subsequent distribution of printed versions might be characterized as publiction, without undermining the benefits of this new doctrine, because it would much easier to determine who has taken such action and where (in physical space) it occurred, and the party who engages in physical distribution of defamatory works has much clearer warning regarding the nature of the act and the applicability of a particular territorial state's laws.

37 Edward A. Cavazos, *Computer Bulletin Board Systems and the Right of Reply: Redefining Defamation Liability for a New Technology*, 12 REV. LITIG. 231, 243–47 (1992). This "right of reply" doctrine might apply differently to different areas of the Net, depending on whether these areas do in fact offer a meaningful opportunity to respond to defamatory messages.

38 Early efforts to avoid this result in the "telemedicine" seem to take the form of allowing doctors to interact with other doctors in consultations, requiring compliance with local regulations only when the doctor deals directly with a patient. *See* Howard J. Young & Robert J. Waters, *Licensure Barriers to the Interstate Use of Telemedicine* (1995), *available at* http://www.arentfox.com/newslett/tele1b.htm. The regulation of lawyers is muddled: Regulations are sometimes based on the location of the lawyer's office (as in the case of Texas' regulation of advertising), sometimes based on the content of legal advice, and sometimes based on the nature and location of the client.

39 Indeed, practicing the "law of the Net" itself presumably requires qualifications unrelated to those imposed by local bars.

40 In this, as in other matters, it is critical to distinguish the different layers of the "protocol stack." It may be possible to establish power with regard to physical connections. It is much harder to do so with respect to the logical connections that exist at the "applications" layer.

41 Jane C. Ginsburg, *Global Use/Territorial Rights: Private International Law Questions of the Global Information Infrastructure*, 42 J. COPYRIGHT SOC'Y U.S.A. 318, 319–320 (1995) (footnotes omitted).

42 *See generally* William Landes & Richard Posner, *An Economic Analysis of Copyright Law*, 18 J. LEG. STUD. 325 (1989) (examining the extent to which copyright law supports efficient allocation of resources).

43 For example, the creative output of lawyers and law professors—law review articles, briefs and other pleadings, and the like—may well be determined largely by factors completely unrelated to the availability of copyright protection for

those works. That category of authors, generally speaking, obtains reputational benefits from wide dissemination that far outweigh the benefits that could be obtained from licensing individual copies. For an analysis of the incentive structure in the publishing market, see Stephen Breyer, *The Uneasy Case for Copyright: A Study of Copyright in Books, Photocopies, and Computer Programs*, 84 HARV. L. REV. 281, 293–309 (1970); *see also* Howard P. Tuckman & Jack Leahey, *What is an Article Worth?*, 83 J. POL. ECON. 951 (1975) (suggesting a method for calculating the monetary value of an academic article).

44 There is a large and diverse literature on the new kinds of authorship that are likely to emerge in cyberspace as a function of the medium's interactive nature, the ease with which digital information can be manipulated, and new searching and linking capabilities. Among the more insightful pieces in this vein are KATSH, LAW IN A DIGITAL WORLD, *supra* note 10, at 92–113, 195–236; SHERRY TURKLE, THE SECOND SELF: COMPUTERS AND THE HUMAN SPIRIT (1984); Pamela Samuelson, *Digital Media and the Changing Face of Intellectual Property Law*, 16 RUTGERS COMPUTER & TECH. L. J. 323 (1990); Eugene Volokh, *Cheap Speech*, 104 YALE L. J. 1805 (1994).

45 Netscape Corporation gave away, at no charge, over four million copies of their Web browser; it is estimated that they now control over 70% of the Web browser market, which they have managed to leverage into dominance in the Web *server* software market, sufficient to enable them to launch one of the most successful Initial Public Offering in the history of the United States. *See* Beppi Crosario, *Netscape IPO booted up: Debut of Hot Stock Stuns Wall Street Veterans*, BOSTON GLOBE, Aug. 10, 1995, at 37; Laurence Zuckerman, *With Internet Cachet, Not Profit, A New Stock Is Wall St.'s Darling*, N.Y. TIMES, Aug. 10, 1995, at 1. Other companies are following Netscape's lead; for example, RealAudio, Inc. is distributing software designed to allow Web browsers to play sound files in real time over the Internet, presumably in the hopes of similarly establishing a dominant market position in the server market. *See* http://www.realaudio.com.

46 Esther Dyson, *Intellectual Value*, WIRED, July 1995, at 138–39, 183.

47 David G. Post, Who Owns the Copy Right? Opportunities and Opportunism on the Global Network 2–3 (Oct. 29, 1995) (unpublished manuscript, on file with the *Stanford Law Review*).

48 *See* Jane C. Ginsburg, *Putting Cars on the "Information Superhighway": Authors, Exploiters, and Copyright in Cyberspace*, 95 COLUM. L. REV. 1466, 1488 (1995) (concluding that it is very difficult for authors to "discover and combat infringements" of their works in Cyberspace); David G. Post, *New Wine, Old Bottles: The Evanescent Copy*, AM. LAW., May 1995, at 103 (discussing the choices that legal authorities face in developing copyright law in Cyberspace) [hereinafter *New Wine*].

49 It is virtually impossible to browse the Net without copying:

> "Browsing" on the World Wide Web, for example, necessarily involves the creation of numerous "copies" of information. First, a message is transmitted from Computer A to (remote) Computer B, requesting that Computer B send a copy of a particular file (for example, the "home page" stored on Computer B) back to Computer A. When the request is received by Computer B, a copy of the requested file is made and transmitted back to Computer A (where it is copied again —"loaded" into memory—and displayed). And the manner in which messages travel across the Internet to reach their intended recipient(s) —via intermediary computers known as "routers," at each of which

the message is "read" by means of "copying" the message into the computer's memory—[involve] ... innumerable separate acts of ... "reproduction."

File copying is not merely inexpensive in cyberspace, it is ubiquitous. And it is not merely ubiquitous, it is indispensable. ...

Thus, if you equipped your computer with a "copy lock"—an imaginary device that would prevent the reproduction of any and all information now stored in the computer in any form—the computer essentially would stop functioning.

David Post, *Leaping Before Looking: Proposals Would Make Unsettling Changes*, LEGAL TIMES, Apr. 8, 1996, (Special Report), at 39, 44.

50 *See* Jessica Litman, *The Exclusive Right to Read*, 13 CARDOZO ARTS & ENT. L. J. 29, 40–42 (noting that under a view that "one reproduces a work every time one reads it into a computer's random access memory ... any act of reading or viewing [a digital] work would require the use of a computer and would, under this interpretation, involve an actionable reproduction"); *New Wine*, *supra* note 48, at 104 ("If the very act of getting a document to your screen is considered the 'making of a copy' within the meaning of the Copyright Act, then a high proportion of the millions of messages traveling over the Internet each day potentially infringes on the right of some file creator ... to control the making of copies."); Pamela Samuelson, *The Copyright Grab*, WIRED, Jan. 1996, at 137 (same); Pamela Samuelson, *Legally Speaking: Intellectual Property Rights and the Global Information Economy*, 39 COMMUN. A.C.M. 23, 24 (1996) [hereinafter LEGALLY SPEAKING] (describing the view that browsing of digital works is infringing if "temporary copying" must occur "in a computer's memory to enable users to read documents").

51 Neel Chatterjee, *Imperishable Intellectual Creations: The Limits of the First Sale Doctrine*, 5 FORDHAM INTELL. PROP. MEDIA & ENT. L. J. 383, 416–19 (1995) (discussing Information Infrastructure Task Force proposal to exclude transmissions from the first sale doctrine).

52 *See, e.g.*, Telerate Sys. v. Caro, 689 F. Supp. 221, 228–30 (S.D.N.Y. 1988) (finding that copying a "few pages" of a 20,000 page database was substantial enough to weigh against fair use).

53 *See, e.g.*, Benjamin Wittes, *A (Nearly) Lawless Frontier: The Rapid Pace of Change in 1994 Left the Law Chasing Technology on the Information Superhighway*, THE RECORDER, Jan. 3, 1995, at 1.

54 For example, we could adopt rules that make the "caching" of web pages presumptively permissible, absent an explicit agreement, rather than adopting the standard copyright doctrine. (Caching involves copying Web pages to a hard drive so that future trips to the site take less time to complete). Because making "cached" copies in computer memory is essential to speed up the operation of the Web, and because respecting express limits or retractions on any implied license allowing caching would clog up the free flow of information, we should adopt a rule favoring browsing. *See* CYBERSPACE LAW INSTITUTE, *Copyright Law on the Internet: The Special Problem of Caching and Copyright Protection* (Sept. 1, 1995), *available at* http://www.II.georgetown.edu:80/cli.html (arguing for such an approach); *New Wine*, *supra* note 47 (proposing a new rule for caching Web pages); Samuelson, *Legally Speaking*, *supra* note 50, at 26–27 (discussing copyright issues raised by file caching).

55 See text accompanying note 11 *supra* for an explanation of the domain name system.

56 This danger of confusion exists whether the name conflicts with "real world" trademark uses or only other online uses. To be sure, whoever decides these questions must consider the views of geographically based authorities when online names interfere with the existing trademarks of physical goods. But they must also decide ownership questions about online identities with addresses, names, and logos having no application offline. The views of territorially based authorities would appear to have less bearing in this context.

57 Newly discovered public needs, such as using a particular domain or eliminating it to establish a new system, could interfere with "investment backed expectations." To keep geographically based trademark authorities at bay, Net authorities may need a responsible "foreign policy" to ward off over-regulation by local sovereigns, such as "grandfathering in" strong global trademarks and preventing those who acquired certain domain names on a "first-come, first-served" basis from engaging in holdups.

58 *See* David G. Post, *Anarchy, State, and the Internet: An Essay on Law-Making in Cyberspace*, 1995 J. ONLINE L. art. 3, par. 7–8, *available at* http://www.law.cornell.edu/jol/jol.table.html.

59 *See* A. M. Rutkowski, Internet Names, Numbers and Beyond: Issues in the Coordination, Privatization, and Internationalization of the Internet (Nov. 20, 1995) (unpublished manuscript, on file with the *Stanford Law Review*) (identifying issues associated with the administration of Internet names and numbers).

60 David W. Maher, *Trademarks on the Internet: Who's in Charge?*, (1996) *available at* http://www.aldea.com/cix/maher.html (arguing that trademark owners have a stake in the Net that must be taken into account).

61 Other rules require refraining from actions that threaten the value of the online space or increase the risk that the system operator will face legal trouble in the real world. Many coherent online communities also have rules that: preserve the special character of their online spaces; govern posted messages; discourage "flaming" (sending an insulting message) or "spamming" (sending the same message to multiple newsgroups); and mandate certain professional qualifications for participants.

62 *See* Robert L. Dunne, *Deterring Unauthorized Access to Computers: Controlling Behavior in Cyberspace Through a Contract Law Paradigm*, 35 JURIMETRICS J. 1, 12–14 (1994) (suggesting that system operator agreements to banish offenders would deter unauthorized computer access more effectively than current criminal sanctions).

63 *See* John Seabrook, *My First Flame*, NEW YORKER, June 16, 1994, at 70 (describing the online phenomenon of flaming, where a user loses "self control and write[s] a message that uses derogatory, obscene, or inappropriate language").

64 A computer user "shuns" another by refusing to receive messages from that person (or, more generally, by employing a software program known as a "kill file" to automatically deflect any e-mail messages from a specified address).

65 Computer users "mailbomb" a victim by sending a large number of junk electronic mail messages with the goal of overloading the receiving computer, or at least inconveniencing the receiver.

66 Jennifer Mnookin, Virtual(ly) Law: A Case Study of the Emergence of Law on LambdaMOO (May 15, 1995) (unpublished manuscript, on file with the *Stanford Law Review*) (describing the emergence of a legal system in the LambdaMOO virtual community, "an interactive, real-time conferencing program based in physical spatial metaphors").

67 Joanne Goode and Maggie Johnson, *Putting Out the Flames: The Etiquette and Law of E-Mail*, ONLINE, Nov. 1991, at 61 (suggesting guidelines for using

electronic mail and networking); S. Hambridge, *Netiquette Guidelines* (Oct. 1995), *available at* ftp://ds.internic.net/rfc/rfc1855.txt (same).
68 *See* James Barron, *It's Time to Mind your E-Manners*, N.Y. TIMES, Jan. 11, 1995, at C1, C6 (discussing how new users learn "netiquette").
69 *See* I. Trotter Hardy, *The Proper Legal Regime for "Cyberspace,"* 55 U. PITT. L. REV. 993, 1051–1053 (1994) (suggesting that Cyberspace users should form their own "virtual courts" for international torts); Henry H. Perritt, Jr., *Dispute Resolution in Electronic Network Communities*, 38 VILL. L. REV. 349, 398–400 (1993) (proposing an alternative dispute resolution mechanism for tort claims that could be implemented by a computer network service provider); Henry H. Perritt, Jr., *President Clinton's National Information Infrastructure Initiative: Community Regained?*, 69 CHI.-KENT L. REV. 991, 1011–16 (1994) (advocating the use of new information technology to facilitate dispute resolution). One such dispute resolution service, the "Virtual Magistrate," has already arisen on the Net. *See* http://vmag.law.vill.edu:8080.
70 *See* LEON E. TRAKMAN, THE LAW MERCHANT: THE EVOLUTION OF COMMERCIAL LAW 11–12 (1983) (Law Merchant was "'a system of law that did not rest exclusively on the institutions and local customs of any particular country, but consisted of certain principles of equity and usages of trade which general convenience and a common sense of justice have established to regulate the dealings of merchants and mariners in all the commercial countries of the civilized world'") (quoting Bank of Conway v. Starry, 200 N.W. 505, 508 (N.D. 1924) (alterations omitted); Hardy, *supra* note 69, at 1020 (Law Merchant was "simply an enforceable set of customary practices that inured to the benefit of merchants, and that was reasonably uniform across all the jurisdictions involved in the [medieval] trade fairs"); Perritt, *supra* note 9, at 48 ("[U]ntil the seventeenth century, the law merchant was an independent legal system with its own normative rules, its own institutions, and its own coercive measures."). Bruce Benson describes the development of the Law Merchant as follows:

> With the fall of the Roman Empire, commercial activities in Europe were almost nonexistent relative to what had occurred before and what would come after. Things began to change in the eleventh and twelfth centuries [with the] emergence of a class of professional merchants. There were significant barriers to overcome before substantial interregional and international trade could develop, however. Merchants spoke different languages and had different cultural backgrounds. Beyond that, geographic distances frequently prevented direct communication, let alone the building of strong interpersonal bonds that would facilitate trust. Numerous middlemen were often required to bring about an exchange. . . . All of this, in the face of localized, often contradictory laws and business practices, produced hostility towards foreign commercial customs and led to mercantile confrontations. There was a clear need for Law as a "language of interaction."

Bruce L. Benson, *The Spontaneous Evolution of Commercial Law*, 55 Southern Econ. J. 644, 646–47 (1989).
71 Benson describes the development of the Law Merchant:

> [D]uring this period, because of the need for uniform laws of commerce to facilitate international trade, "the basic concepts and institutions of modern Western mercantile law—lex mercatoria . . . —

> were formed, and, even more important, it was then that mercantile law in the West first came to be viewed as an integrated, developing system, a body of law." Virtually every aspect of commercial transactions in all of Europe (and in cases even outside Europe) were "governed" by this body of law after the eleventh century.... This body of law was voluntarily produced, voluntarily adjudicated and voluntarily enforced. In fact, it had to be. There was no other potential source of such law, including state coercion.

Id. at 647 (quoting HAROLD J. BERMAN, LAW AND REVOLUTION: THE FORMATION OF WESTERN LEGAL TRADITION 333 (1983).

72 I. Trotter Hardy strongly supports this view:

> The parallels [between the development of the Law Merchant and] cyberspace are strong. Many people interact frequently over networks, but not always with the same people each time so that advance contractual relations are not always practical. Commercial transactions will more and more take place in cyberspace, and more and more those transactions will cross national boundaries and implicate different bodies of law. Speedy resolution of disputes will be as desirable as it was in the Middle Ages! The means of an informal court system are in place in the form of on-line discussion groups and electronic mail. A "Law Cyberspace" coexisting with existing laws would be an eminently practical and efficient way of handling commerce in the networked world.

Hardy, *supra* note 69, at 1021; *see also* Perritt, *supra* note 9, at 49 (arguing that the *lex mercatoria* system is analogous to the framework that the electronic community should apply); Post, *supra* note 58, at n. 15 (noting that, like Law Merchant, Cyberspace could be "an example of unregulated and unconstrained rule-making in the absence of state control.").

73 This enforcement tool is not perfect—any more than the tool of banishing merchants from the medieval trade fairs was perfect for the development of the Law Merchant. *See* Paul R. Milgrom, Douglass C. North & Barry R. Weingast, *The Role of Institutions in the Revival of Trade: The Law Merchant, Private Judges, and the Champagne Fairs*, 2 ECON. & POL. 1 (1990) (describing the use of banishment and other enforcement mechanisms prior to the rise of the state). Individuals intent on wrongdoing may be able to sneak back on the Net or into a particular online area with a new identity. But the enforcement tools used by legal authorities in the real world also have limits. We do not refrain from recognizing the sovereignty of our territorial governments just because they cannot fully control their physical borders or all of the actions of their citizens.

74 Social philosopher Michael Sandel has made a similar point in writing that new transnational law-making institutions are needed if the "loss of mastery and the erosion of community that lie at the heart of democracy's discontent" is to be alleviated:

> In a world where capital and goods, information and images, pollution and people, flow across national boundaries with unprecedented ease, politics must assume transnational, even global, forms, if only to keep up. Otherwise, *economic power will go unchecked by democratically sanctioned political power.* . . . .

... We cannot hope to govern the global economy without transnational political institutions. . . .

Michael J. Sandel, *America's Search for a New Public Philosophy*, ATLANTIC MONTHLY, Mar. 1996, at 57, 72–73 (emphasis added); *see also* text accompanying notes 96–97 *infra*, for additional parallels between our arguments and Sandel's.

75 Hilton v. Guyot, 159 U.S. 113, 164 (1895); *see also* Mitsubishi Motors v. Soler Chrysler-Plymouth, 473 U.S. 614 (1985) (holding that concerns of international comity require enforcement of an arbitration clause); The Bremen v. Zapata Off-Shore Co., 407 U.S. 1, 15 (1972) (upholding a forum selection clause "in light of present-day commercial realities and expanding international trade"); Lauritzen v. Larsen, 345 U.S. 571, 582 (1953) ("International or maritime law . . . aims at stability and order through usages which considerations of comity, reciprocity and long-range interest have developed to define the domain which each nation will claim as its own."). Good general treatments of the comity doctrine can be found in LEA BRILMAYER, CONFLICT OF LAWS: FOUNDATIONS AND FUTURE DIRECTIONS 145–89 (1991); MARK W. JANIS, AN INTRODUCTION TO INTERNATIONAL LAW 330–38 (1988); Joel R. Paul, *Comity in International Law*, 32 HARV. INT'L L. J. 1 (1991); Steven R. Swanson, *Comity, International Dispute Resolution Agreements, and the Supreme Court*, 21 LAW & POL'Y INT'L BUS. (1990); Hessel E. Yntema, *The Comity Doctrine*, 65 MICH. L. REV. 9 (1966); James S. Campbell, New Law For New International Trade (Dec. 3, 1993), at 5–6 (unpublished manuscript, on file with the *Stanford Law Review*).

76 RESTATEMENT (THIRD) OF FOREIGN RELATIONS LAW OF THE UNITED STATES § 403(1) (1987).

77 *Id* § 403(3).

78 Harold G. Maier, *Remarks*, 84 PROC. AM. SOC. INT'L L. 339, 339 (1990); *see also id.* at 340 (arguing that the principle of comity informs the interest-balancing choice of law principles in the Restatement); Paul, *supra* note 75, at 12–13 (comity arose out of "[t]he need for a more sophisticated system of conflicts . . . in connection with the emergence of the nation state and the rise of commerce that brought different nationalities into more frequent contact and conflict with one another"); *id.* at 45–48 (noting that although the relationship between the "classical doctrine of comity" and the Restatement's principle of "reasonableness" is uncertain, the former "retains a significant function in the Restatement"); *id.* at 54 (comity principle "mitigates the inherent tension between principles of territorial exclusivity and sovereign equality"); *cf.* Campbell, *supra* note 75, at 6 (The Supreme Court's comity jurisprudence "inquires, in cases involving international trade, what values facilitate that trade. Trading nations have a common interest in supporting these values, and therefore national agencies—courts, legislators, administrators—should seek to respect, and thereby strengthen, these values as they engage in the processes of law formation").

79 Perritt, *supra* note 9, at 1–2, 36–49.

80 *Cf.* Gopnik, *The Virtual Bishop*, NEW YORKER, Mar. 18, 1996, at 63 ("Of course, the primitive Church was a kind of Internet itself, which was one of the reasons it was so difficult for the Roman Empire to combat it. The early Christians understood that what was most important was not to claim physical power in a physical place but to establish a network of believers—to be on line.") (quoting French Bishop Jacques Gaillot).

81 Perritt, *supra* note 9, at 42–43; *cf.* MICHAEL WALZER, SPHERES OF JUSTICE: A DEFENSE OF PLURALISM AND EQUALITY 281–83 (1983) (discussing differences among various spheres of power and authority).

82 The idea of "delegation" is something of a fiction. But legal fictions have a way of becoming persuasive and, therefore, real. *See, e.g.*, LON L. FULLER, LEGAL FICTIONS 55 (1967). Self-regulatory bodies evolve independently of the State and derive their authority from the sovereign only insofar as the sovereign, after the fact, claims and exercises a monopoly over the use of force.

83 *See* Henry H. Perritt, Jr., Computer Crimes and Torts in the Global Information Infrastructure: Intermediaries and Jurisdiction 20–22 (Oct. 12, 1995) (unpublished manuscript, on file with the *Stanford Law Review*) (arguing that under the self-regulatory approach "communities of suppliers and consumers of information would adopt their own rules for defamation, intellectual property infringement, misrepresentation, and indecency, and would apply these rules through arbitration machinery agreed to through the community").

84 *See* Maher, *supra* note 60 (noting the "arrogance" of the Federal Networking Council's position on this issue).

85 *Cf. id.* (noting that while other groups faced fees for new domain names, "[s]pecial arrangements are made for users of '.gov' and 'edu'").

86 *See id.* (noting "[t]he .mil domain is excluded" from the jurisdiction of the private corporation that administers the registration of domain names).

87 *See* note 20 *supra.*

88 *See id.*

89 *See* Jonathan Graubert, *What's News: A Progressive Framework for Evaluating the International Debate Over the News*, 77 CAL. L. REV. 629, 631 (1989) ("The guiding principle in international communications since World War II has been the U.S.-inspired goal of a 'free flow of information.' According to this principle, '[f]reedom of information implies the right to gather, transmit and publish news anywhere and everywhere without fetters.'") (citing G. A. Res. 59 U.N. Doc. A/64/Add. 1, at 95 (1947)) (alterations in original). The free-flow-of-information principle has been defined as a necessary part of freedom of opinion and expression. *See* Article 19 of the Universal Declaration of Human Rights, G. A. Res. 217(III)A, U.N. Doc. A/810, at 74–75 (1948) (stating that freedom of expression includes "freedom to hold opinions without interference and to seek, receive and impart information and ideas through any media and regardless of frontiers").

90 Moreover, the right of individuals to participate in various online realms depends critically on their obtaining information about those realms. Insofar as any territorial government merely claims that its laws and values are morally superior, it is not well situated to oppose a free flow of information that might lead its citizens to disagree. This would be the equivalent of defending ignorance as a necessary ingredient for preservation of the local state's values.

91 Listservers, for example, can be set up on any network (or Internet) server by means of simple instructions given to one of several widely available software programs (listproc or majordomo). A Usenet discussion group in the "alt." hierarchy can be established by sending a simple request to the "alt.config" newsgroup. *See* What is Usenet & Answers to Frequently Asked Questions About Usenet, *supra* note 23.

Cyberspace not only permits the effective delineation of internal boundaries between different online spaces, but it also allows for effective delineation of distinct online roles within different spheres of activity. In the nonvirtual world, we slip in and out of such roles frequently. The rules applicable to the behavior of a single individual, in a single territorial jurisdiction, may change as he moves between different legally significant persona (acting as an employee, a member of a church, a parent, or the officer of a corporation, for example). Cyberspace may make the boundaries between these different roles easier to maintain, insofar as explicit "tags," distinct "signature files," or screen names—can relatively easily be attached to messages originating from the author's different roles.

92 Post, *supra* note 58, at para. 26 (asserting that the individual network "organizations" will probably determine the substantive rule-making for Cyberspace); *see also* David R. Johnson & Kevin A. Marks, *Mapping Electronic Data Communications onto Existing Legal Metaphors: Should We Let Our Conscience (and Our Contracts) Be Our Guide?*, 38 VILL. L. REV. 487, 488–89 (1993) (explaining that communication service providers, owners of disks carrying centralized databases, and people presiding over electronic discussion groups have the power to select applicable rules).

93 For illuminating discussions of the many parallels between biological evolution and social evolution in Cyberspace, see KEVIN KELLY, OUT OF CONTROL: THE LAW OF NEO-BIOLOGICAL CIVILIZATION (1994); John Lienhard, *Reflections on Information, Biology, and Community*, 32 HOUS. L. REV. 303 (1995); Michael Schrage, *Revolutionary Evolutionist*, WIRED, July 1995, at 120.

94 This geographic barrier merely permits divergence to occur; it does not guarantee it. Speciation will only occur, for example, if the two divided subpopulations are subject to different selection pressures or at least one of them is small enough to accrue significant random changes in its gene pool ("genetic drift"). For good, nontechnical descriptions of evolutionary theory, see DANIEL C. DENNETT, DARWIN'S DANGEROUS IDEA: EVOLUTION AND THE MEANINGS OF LIFE (1995); JOHN MAYNARD SMITH, ESSAYS ON GAMES, SEX, AND EVOLUTION (1988); JOHN MAYNARD SMITH, ON EVOLUTION (1972); GEORGE C. WILLIAMS, ADAPTATION AND NATURAL SELECTION: A CRITIQUE OF SOME CURRENT EVOLUTIONARY THOUGHT (1966).

95 To survive, rules must be passed on somehow, whether in the form of "case reports" or other inter-individual or inter-generational methods. *See* RICHARD DAWKINS, THE SELFISH GENE (new ed. 1989). General parallels between biological evolution and the evolution of legal rules are discussed in FRIEDRICH HAYEK, I LAW, LEGISLATION, AND LIBERTY 44–49 (1973); FRIEDRICH HAYEK, THE CONSTITUTION OF LIBERTY 56–61 (1960); *see generally* Tom W. Bell, *Polycentric Law*, 7 HUMANE STUD. REV. 1 (Winter 1991/92), *available at* http://osf1.gmu.edu/ihs/w91issues.html.

96 Cyberspace, as M. Ethan Katsh has written, is a "software world" where "code is the Law." M. Ethan Katsh, *Software Worlds and the First Amendment: Virtual Doorkeepers in Cyberspace*, 1996 U. CHI. LEGAL FORUM (forthcoming), *available at* http://www.law.lib.uchicago.edu/forum (quoting WILLIAM MITCHELL, CITY OF BITS (1995)). Katsh adds:

> To a considerable extent, networks really are what software allows them to be. The Internet is not a network but a set of communications protocols. . . . [T]he Internet is software. Similarly, the World Wide Web is not anything tangible. It is client-server software that permits machines linked on a network to share and work with information on any of the connected machines.

Id.; see also Post, *supra* note 58, at para. 16 ("[N]etworks are not merely governed by substantive rules of conduct, they have no existence apart from such rules."). And software specifications can be unforgiving (as anyone who has tried to send an e-mail message to an incorrectly spelled network recipient can attest):

> Entry of messages into, and routing of messages across, digitally-based electronic networks . . . are controlled by more effective protocols [than

generally govern non-electronic communications networks in the "real world"]: *each network's technical specifications (typically embodied in software or switching mechanisms) constitute rules that precisely distinguish between compliant and non-compliant messages. This boundary [is not an] artificial construct because the rules are effectively self-enforcing. To put the matter simply, you can't 'almost' be on the Georgetown University LAN or America Online—you are either transmitting LAN- or AOL-compliant messages or you are not.*

Id. at para. 20 (emphasis added). Thus, individual network communities can be configured, by means of unique specifications of this kind, to bar all (or some specified portion of) inter-network traffic with relative ease.

97 Sandel, *supra* note 74, at 73–74 (emphasis added).
98 Brilmayer, *supra* note 6, at 5.
99 In Albert Hirschman's terms, they have a "voice" in the development of French law, at least to the extent that French law-making institutions represent and are affected by citizen participation. ALBERT O. HIRSCHMAN, EXIT, VOICE AND LOYALTY 106–19 (1970).
100 *See id.* at 106–09; *cf.* Richard A. Epstein, *Exit Rights under Federalism*, LAW & CONTEMP. PROBS., Winter 1992, at 147, 151–165 (discussing the ability of exit rights to constrain governmental power and the limitations of such rights).
101 The idea that citizens can easily exit physical jurisdictions is, of course, unrealistic:

There has always been a strong fictional element to using this notion of a social contract as a rationale for a sovereign's legitimacy. When exactly did you or I consent to be bound by the U.S. Constitution? At best, that consent can only be inferred indirectly, from our continued presence within the U.S. borders—the love-it-or-leave-it, vote-with-your-feet theory of political legitimacy. But by that token, is Saddam Hussein's rule legitimate, as least as to those Iraqis who have 'consented' in this fashion? Have the Zairois consented to Mobutu's rule? In the world of atoms, we simply cannot ignore the fact that real movement of real people is not always so easy, and that most people can hardly be charged with having chosen the jurisdiction in which they live or the laws that they are made to obey. But in cyberspace, there is an infinite amount of space, and movement between online communities is entirely frictionless. Here, there really is the opportunity to obtain consent to a social contract. Virtual communities can be established with their own particular rule-sets; power to maintain a degree of order and to banish wrongdoers can be lodged, or not, in particular individuals or groups; and those who find the rules oppressive or unfair may simply leave and join another community (or start their own).

Post, *supra* note 23, at 33.
102 The ease with which individuals may move between communities (or inhabit multiple communities simultaneous through a fractionation of their own individual identities) also implies that Cyberspace may provide conditions necessary and sufficient for something more closely resembling the optimal collective production of a particular set of goods—namely, "laws"—than can be achieved in the real world. Cyberspace may closely approximate the idealized model for the allocation of local goods and services set forth by Charles Tiebout, in which optimal allocation of locally produced public goods is provided by small

jurisdictions competing for mobile residents. *See* Charles Tiebout, *A Pure Theory of Local Expenditures*, 64 J. POL. ECON. 416 (1956). The Tiebout model of intergovernmental competition has four components: (1) a perfectly elastic supply of jurisdictions, (2) costless mobility of individuals among jurisdictions, (3) full information about the attributes of all jurisdictions, and (4) no interjurisdictional externalities. *See* Robert P. Inman & Daniel L. Rubinfeld, *The Political Economy of Federalism*, Working Paper No. 94-15, Boalt Hall Program in Law and Economics (1994), at 11–16, *reprinted in Developments in Public Choice* (D. Mueller ed., 1995). (As Inman and Rubinfeld demonstrate, a fifth assumption of the Tiebout model—the provision of public goods with a "congestible technology" such that the per capita cost of providing each level of a public good first decreases and then increases as more individuals move into the jurisdiction—is not necessary for the model. *Id.* at 13.) In a Tieboutian world,

> ... each locality provides a package of local public goods consistent with the preferences of its residents (consumer-voters). Residents whose preferences remain unsatisfied by a particular locality's package of goods and services would (costlessly) move.... Escape from undesirable packages of goods and services is feasible as a result of two explicit characteristics of the Tiebout model: absence of externalities and mobility of residents.

Clayton P. Gillette, *In Partial Praise of Dillon's Rule, or, Can Public Choice Theory Justify Local Government Law*, 67 CHI-KENT L. REV. 959, 969 (1991). We suggest that Cyberspace may be a closer approximation to ideal Tieboutian competition between rule-sets than exists in the nonvirtual world. This is a consequence of (1) the low cost of establishing an online "jurisdiction," *see* text accompanying note 91 *supra*, (2) the ease of exit from online communities, (3) the relative ease of acquiring information about the practices of online communities, and (4) the greater impermeability of the internal, software-mediated boundaries between online communities in Cyberspace, *see* note 96 *supra*, which may mitigate (at least to some extent) the problem of inter-community externalities.

103 The Net may need new meta-rules for transporting information across these borders. For example, the members of the LamdaMOO multi-user domain debated at length whether to permit the use of information obtained from the virtual discussion group out in the "real world." Mnookin, *supra* note 66, at 21–23. Various online systems have rules about copying or reposting materials from one online area to another. For example, the terms of service for Counsel Connect contains the following rules for acceptable copying:

> [M]embers who submit material shall be deemed to (i) grant to ... subscribers to the system a paid up, perpetual, world-wide irrevocable license to use, copy, and redistribute such materials and any portions thereof and any derivative works therefrom ... Each member agrees, as a condition of such license, (i) not to remove identifying source information from verbatim copies of member-supplied materials ... and (ii) not to reproduce portions thereof in any way that identifies the source but fails to describe accurately the nature and source of any modification, alteration thereto or selection therefrom.
>
> B. Notwithstanding the licenses granted by members and information suppliers, subscribers ... shall not engage in systematic, substantial

> and regular replication of materials supplied to the system by a commercial publisher ... where the effect of such actions is to provide another person who is not an authorized subscriber to such materials with a substantial substitute for such a subscription.

Terms and Conditions for Use of Counsel Connect (on file with the *Stanford Law Review*). America Online's Terms of Service Agreement contain a somewhat similar clause:

> [Members] acknowledge that (i) AOL contains information, software, photos, video, graphics, music, sounds and other material and services (collectively, "Content"). ... AOL permits access to Content that is protected by copyrights, trademarks, and other proprietary (including intellectual property) rights. ... [Members'] use of Content shall be governed by applicable copyright and other intellectual property laws. ... By submitting Content to a "Public Area" ... [members] automatically grant ... AOL Inc. the royalty-free, perpetual, irrevocable, nonexclusive right and license to use, reproduce, modify, adapt, publish, translate, create derivative works from, distribute, perform and display such Content (in whole or part) worldwide. ...

AOL Inc.'s Terms of Service Agreement (on file with the *Stanford Law Review*).

104 *See* Sandel, *supra* note 74, at 74 ("Self-government today ... requires a politics that plays itself out in a multiplicity of settings, from neighborhoods to nations to the world as a whole. Such a politics requires citizens who can abide the ambiguity associated with divided sovereignty, who can think and act as multiply situated selves."); *see also* SHERRY TURKLE, LIFE ON THE SCREEN: IDENTITY IN THE AGE OF THE INTERNET (1995); TURKLE, *supra* note 44. To be sure, sophisticated analysis even of traditional legal doctrines suggests that we appear before the law only in certain partial, conditional roles. JOSEPH VINING, LEGAL IDENTITY: THE COMING OF AGE OF PUBLIC LAW 139–69 (1978). But this partial and conditional nature of "persons" who hold rights and duties is more pronounced in Cyberspace.

105 *See* Chatterjee, *supra* note 51, at 406 n. 142 (noting that "[o]riginal copyright paradigms were created to protect only [physical] books").

106 Electronic information can be dispensed in any sized serving, ranging from a few words to an entire database. If we use the database as a whole as our measure, then any user's selection will be an insignificant portion. In contrast, if we tried to use the traditional boundaries of the book's cover, the user cannot observe this standard. In some cases it is an entirely theoretical boundary, with respect to material only dispensed from the database. This case demonstrates again that the absence of physical borders between "works" in Cyberspace undermines the utility of doctrines, like copyright law, that are based on the existence of such physical boundaries.

107 Whether the law should consider that interest to be a "property" right or a right on behalf of the "persona" in question remains in doubt.

60

THE ZONES OF CYBERSPACE

Lawrence Lessig

Source: *Stanford Law Review* 48(5) (1996): 1403–11.

Cyberspace is a place. People live there. They experience all the sorts of things that they experience in real space, there. For some, they experience more. They experience this not as isolated individuals, playing some high tech computer game; they experience it in groups, in communities, among strangers, among people they come to know, and sometimes like.[1]

While they are in that place, cyberspace, they are also here. They are at a terminal screen, eating chips, ignoring the phone. They are downstairs on the computer, late at night, while their husbands are asleep. They are at work, or at cyber cafes, or in a computer lab. They live this life there, while here. And then at some point in the day, they jack out, and are only here. They step up from the machine, in a bit of a daze; they turn around. They have returned.

David Johnson and David Post want us to take this life in cyberspace seriously. They want the law to understand it as elsewhere. So far elsewhere is it that it deserves, they argue, a special respect from real space law. Cyberspace will "create" new law and legal institutions of its own,[2] and this new law should free this space from at least some of the claims of real space law. A separateness will emerge. Not quite a sovereignty, but something close will develop.

This is a small and quirky field, cyberlaw; these are two of its most important thinkers, and this is a paper that will be at the center of much thought in cyberlaw to come. I have no doubt that in large measure, Johnson and Post will be right: A new law will emerge here, and a certain comity will follow it around. But Johnson and Post want to argue for a separation between real space law and cyberspace law that I don't believe can yet be sustained, nor do I believe that it should. The effects of that place will never be far removed from this. And our understanding of what that place will become is just beginning. We, here, in this world, will keep a control on the development there. As well we should.

The closeness that cyberspace is

There is an interesting link between Dan Farber's paper and this. Farber offered three perspectives on legislative jurisdiction—a localist, a globalist, and an evolutionary.[3] The link is to the first two. A localist looks for strong links with stuff that happens in local space before she claims an authority to regulate beyond her borders. A globalist is far less picky. Everything affects everything, the globalist insists, and our regulation should reach anything that affects us.

Johnson and Post mix these two perspectives. They present a picture of cyberspace that is both global and local. They first establish the separateness of cyberspace by arguing that since it is everywhere if anywhere, and hence no place in particular, it is therefore a space no where here—separate, removed. Its globalness establishes its separateness; no locale can make any special claim upon it.

But in the very next breath, they are insistent localists: Cyberspace, separate from real space, has little effect over real space; hence should real space have little control over cyberspace. When real space jurisdictions assert control over cyberspace life, this is an "illegitimate extra-territorial power grab"[4]—unjustified,[5] and unwise. As they write: "[Governments cannot] credibly claim a right to regulate the net based on supposed local harms caused by activities that originate outside their borders and that travel electronically to many different nations."[6]

This argument they support with positive as well as normative arguments, but I confess I don't find the positive points very persuasive. The first is a kind of is-ism—the real world is made of atoms, cyberspace of bits; the rules of the atoms don't work very well when applied to bits. Bits don't respect borders, they can't be cabined by borders. They go wherever the net goes, and the net goes everywhere without much limit. Hence rules that would contain atoms can't be applied well to bits.

This feels more like slogan than argument. I don't care really whether it is atoms, or bits; the legitimacy of regulation turns upon effects. If the net has an effect on that half of the cybercitizen that is in real space, if it has an effect on third parties who are only in real space, then the claim of a real space sovereign to regulate it will be as strong as any equivalent atom induced effect. If a state has the power to regulate the importation of obscenity, it can't make any difference whether that importation is via atoms or bits,[7] at least from the perspective of the justifiability of the regulation.[8] Its justification rests here in effects.

If this localism, in Farber's terms, is to be defended, something other than physics must be appealed to. Johnson and Post have a second argument, grounded in futility: The example here is the German threat against CompuServe. In January, 1996, Bavarian officials threatened CompuServe with prosecution if it continued to carry sexually explicitly newsgroups from

USENET. In response, CompuServe removed these newsgroups from its service worldwide.

Schemes like this to regulate local access don't work, Johnson and Post argue, because "the determined seeker of prohibited communications can simply reconfigure his connection so as to appear to reside in a [different] location."[9] True enough—Germans determined enough can (even now) use CompuServe to gain access to the prohibited material.[10] But this forgets my colleague Coase. A regulation need not be absolutely effective to be sufficiently effective. It need not raise the cost of the prohibited activity to infinity in order to reduce the level of that activity quite substantially. If regulation increases the cost of access to this kind of information, it will reduce access to this information, even if it doesn't reduce it to zero. That is enough to justify the regulation. If government regulation had to show that it was perfect before it was justified, then indeed there would be little regulation of cyberspace, or of real space either. But regulation, whether for the good or the bad, has a lower burden to meet.

There is something to the futility argument. This is David Post's piece, *Anarchy, State and the Internet*.[11] Post's argument there, echoed in the piece in this review, is that the architecture of cyberspace compels a different kind of regulation. The internet, he argues, is a network of networks; each network is its own law, each carries its own rule-set. Because these "rule-sets" are not tied to any particular geographical space, they can exit whenever the geographical space becomes hostile. It matters not at all, the argument goes, whether the server supporting one network is located in Germany, or France, or Russia.[12] So long as the networks are interconnected, if the laws of Germany become hostile, the network can simply move to Russia. From the standpoint of the users, this move is invisible. And so any effort by Germany to control what exists on German servers will be defeated by this structural plasticity.

But what follows from this is not that no regulation is possible; what follows is that successful regulation will be different. There is a competition among rule-sets; cyberspace creates a market among these rule-sets. But there are still ways to regulate a market, so long as the regulator has some market power. Germany's effort at silencing sex-speech on Compuserve may be thought pathetic, since so easily evaded; nonetheless, it did have the effect of pushing Compuserve to implement a technology that would allow the company to censor material based on the location of the reader. A pathetic, but successful, regulation by Germany. Or the same could be said about America's regulation of cryptography.[13] No doubt any effort directly to ban encryption technologies will, in the end, fail; but efforts to subsidize particular technologies will not so obviously fail. Regulation is possible, but through different means.

The insight that Post, and Johnson and Post, have is that because the transactions costs of exit are so low, the power of government to regulate this space is futile. But the conclusion doesn't follow from the premise. Transactions costs are low; but so long as they are not zero, there is space for regulation. The regulation will be of a different form; its techniques will have to become quite different. But if well designed, they will not be futile.

There will be a law of cyberspace, but Johnson and Post have not shown enough to show just why it will be in any special way immune from real space regulations. It will be regulated by real space regulation to the extent that it affects real space life, and it will quite dramatically affect real space life. That is the amazing thing about this space—that this virtual place has such power over what we call the nonvirtual. This effect must be at the core of any argument about cyberspace's difference, not its absence.

The question of what cyberspace will be

To argue that real space law should leave cyberspace alone one needs a normative argument—an argument about why it is good or right to leave cyberspace alone. This depends upon consequences, and consequences depend upon what cyberspace will become. Johnson and Post push the first half of this quite well; but it is the second half that is the more important. And more troubling.

The argument focusing on consequences is simple pragmatism. Cyberlaw will evolve to the extent that it is easier to develop this separate law than to work out the endless conflicts that the cross-border existences here will generate.[14] Some fields will be easier to regulate with this cyber common law, and as this cyber common law of cyberspace develops, and earns the respect of other jurisdictions, it will be easier for these other jurisdictions simply to defer to this law.[15] The alternative is a revival of conflicts of law; but conflicts of law is dead—killed by a realism intended to save it. And without a usable body of law to deploy against it, a law of cyberspace will emerge as the simpler way to resolve the inevitable, and repeated, conflicts that cyberspace will raise.

But this pragmatism must say something about what cyberspace will become, and it is here that I think Johnson and Post are most ambitious, one might say romantic, while I am firmly skeptical. Their picture is of a democracy in cyberspace—of a world of cybercitizens deciding on the laws that will apply to them, and a claim that this more perfect democracy deserves respect.[16] The separation that they argue for comes then from the respect that we owe this autonomy.

This is a hope built on a picture of cyberspace as it is just now. As it is just now, cyberspace is such a place of relative freedom. The technologies of control are relatively crude. Not that there is no control. Cyberspace is not anarchy. But that control is exercised through the ordinary tools of human regulation—through social norms, and social stigma; through peer pressure, and reward. How this happens is an amazing question—how people who need never meet can establish and enforce a rich set of social norms is a question that will push theories of social norm development far. But no one who has lived any part of her life in this space as it is just now can doubt that this is a space filled with community, and with the freedom that the imperfections of community allows.

This is changing. Cyberspace is changing. And to understand what this change could be, we must think again about the very nature of cyberspace itself—more particularly, about the nature of how cyberspace regulates itself.

Think of how a community regulates itself in real space. In real space, when the state wants to regulate something—say littering—the state threatens, or cajoles, through prisons or fines or furry little animals on TV, to induce people to internalize this norm against littering. If the state succeeds, behavior changes. But its success depends upon individuals internalizing what the state requires. Between the norm and the behavior sought is a human being, mediating whether to conform or not. Lots of times, for lots of laws, the choice is not to conform. Regardless of what the law says, it is an individual who decides whether to conform.

Regulation in cyberspace is, or can be, different. If the regulator wants to induce a certain behavior, she need not threaten, or cajole, to inspire the change. She need only change the code—the software that defines the terms upon which the individual gains access to the system, or uses assets on the system. If she wants to limit trespass on a system, she need not rely simply on a law against trespass; she can implement a system of passwords. If she wants to limit the illegal use of copyrighted material, she need not rely on the threat of copyright law; she can encrypt the copyrighted material so only those intended to have access will have access. Always in principle, and increasingly in practice, there is a code (as in software) to assure what the code (as in law) demands, which means always in principle and increasingly in practice, law is inscribed in the code.

Code is an efficient means of regulation. But its perfection makes it something different. One obeys these laws as code not because one should; one obeys these laws as code because one can do nothing else. There is no choice about whether to yield to the demand for a password; one complies if one wants to enter the system.[17] In the well implemented system, there is no civil disobedience. Law as code is a start to the perfect technology of justice.

It is not this just now. Just now the architecture of cyberspace is quite imperfect. Indeed, what is central about its present architecture is the anarchy that it preserves. Some see this anarchy as inherent in the space, as unavoidable.[18] But this anarchy is just a consequence of the present design. In its present design, cyberspace is open, and uncontrolled; regulation is achieved through social forces much like the social forms that regulate real space. It is now unzoned: Borders are not boundaries; they divide one system from another just as Pennsylvania is divided from Ohio. The essence of cyberspace today is the search engine—tools with which one crosses an infinite space, to locate, and go to, the stuff one wants. The space today is open, but only because it is made that way. Or because we made it that way. (For whatever is true about society, at least cyberspace is socially constructed.)

It could be made to be different, and my sense is that it is. The present architecture of cyberspace is changing. If there is one animating idea behind the kinds of reforms pursued both in the social and economic spheres in cyberspace, it is the idea to increase the sophistication of the architecture in cyberspace, to facilitate boundaries rather than borders. It is the movement to bring to zoning to cyberspace. From this perspective, the Communications Decency Act of 1996, and the Nil White Paper on Copyright are the very same thing: Neither aims at eliminating material in cyberspace; both aim instead at inducing a technology for zoning. The Communications Decency Act does this by granting wide defenses to individuals who take steps to block access by minors, while threatening huge penalties to those who don't.[19] The White paper does this by giving broad support to technologies that control access to copyrighted material, while narrowing the scope for fair use of material otherwise available on the net. The aim of both is to subsidize technologies of control—to increase the ability to select who gets access to what—and the medium cyberspace is perfectly designed for that control.

We are just at the beginning of this change. Zoning will replace the present wilderness of cyberspace, and this zoning will be achieved through code—a tool, as Johnson and Post suggest, more perfect than any equivalent tool of zoning in real space. The architecture of cyberspace will in principle allow for perfect zoning—a way perfectly to exclude those who would cross boundaries. It is the perfection of the architecture that Jerry Frug's contribution to this symposium speaks of; and the movement that I am describing from open to closed is just the movement that he, and Richard Ford, have described (and criticized) in real space law.[20] Indeed, if there is one clear return from the mixing of the perspectives that this symposium has done, it is the lessons that the first panel can offer the last: For in the rich descriptions offered there—of movements in real space from open to closed, and in the structures of incentives that might yield this move, even though individuals in the end might regret it,[21]—we can draw parallels to the movement that we might see here. Movements from what, speaking of free-speech terrains, Monroe Price calls an open terrain to a closed;[22] but more generally, from a world where boundaries are borders, to a world where boundaries are walls.

One might well say that this movement to more perfect zoning is just what "the people want." But want here is complex. They want control over what their kids get access to; they want control over who "takes" their intellectual "property." They want to control what their citizens read. All these "theys" have lots to gain from the architecture that cyberspace is becoming, and we are a lot of these "theys." Commerce is built on property, and property depends upon boundaries. What possible reason could there be to question the value of clear borders?[23]

But we might nonetheless find reason to be skeptical, or at least reason to raise doubts. And it is upon two such doubts that I want to end this essay. First, a doubt about the design: As important as the nature of these newly zoned spaces is, more important is who is designing them. They are the construction, as Johnson and Post describe, of "engineers."[24] Engineers write the code; the code defines the architectures, and the architectures define what is possible within a certain social space. No process of democracy defines this social space, save if the market is a process of democracy.[25]

This might not be so bad, assuming that there are enough places to choose from, and given that it is cyberspace, the places to choose from could be many, and the costs of exit are quite low.[26] Even so, note the trend: the progression away from democratic control. We will stand in relation to these places of cyberspace as we stand in relation to the commodities of the market: one more place of unending choice; but one less place where we, collectively, have a role in constructing the choices that we have.

Which brings us back to the question that I began with above, and the second doubt that I want to raise in the end. This next generation of cyberspace will provide individuals with the perfect technology of choice; it will empower individuals to select into the world that they want to see, to select out of the world that they don't.[27] But the they who check out also live here; when not in cworld, they must participate in the making, and regulating, of the life that is here. And so the question: Just how will this life in cworld affect their ability to connect to this life in the real world? Will this power of exit enhance or undermine their ability to engage as citizens in the world from which they can't easily disengage? Will the many communities of that world make it more or less possible to function well in the communities of this world? These are questions, the answers to which turn on the architecture that cyberspace will become. But what the architecture of cyberspace will become is a choice we make here. So again we are back to the question how this space may regulate that space, if that space affects life here.

These questions point to a choice, about what cyberspace will become. One alternative is an open space; the other closed. I don't mean these are the only choices. Architectures don't come in natural kinds. My point instead is the choice—that there is a decision to be made about the architecture that cyberspace will become, and the question is how that decision will be made.

Or better, *where* will that decision be made. For this change has a very predictable progress. It is the same progress that explains the move to zoning in cities. It is the result of a collection of choices made at an individual level, but no collective choice made at a collective level. It is the product of a market. But individual choice might aggregate in a way that individuals collectively do not want. Individual choices are made within a particular architecture; but they may yield an architecture different from what the collective might want.

Might, not will. The point is not about pessimism, it is about possibility. But the possibility suggests a question about how quickly we liberate that space from regulation by the real space. For if there are choices to be made about how this space will evolve, it is not quite clear where in cyberspace these choices can be made. If cyberspace were to become this perfect technology of technology *and* democracy, then there would be little reason to worry. But a perfect technology of control does not entail a perfect technology of justice, and it is this that commends a continued check.

It is not clear where that leaves the law of cyberspace, or what strategy this recommends. But if the argument for deference that Johnson and Post here beg is a normative argument, we must say something more about the normative attractiveness of the world that cyberspace will be. If it is a world that facilitates our isolation, if it is an even better technology for constructing this isolation, if it is an even more efficient way to undermine the citizenship of this world, then one might question it. At a minimum, one might question whether we know what we must do to avoid these as outcomes. And we might want to preserve the possibility to avoid them.

Notes

1 For descriptions, see HOWARD RHEINGOLD, THE VIRTUAL COMMUNITY 38–65 (1995); SHERRY TURKLE, LIFE ON THE SCREEN: IDENTITY IN THE AGE OF THE INTERNET (1995).
2 David R. Johnson & David Post, *Law and Borders—The Rise of Law in Cyberspace*, 48 STAN L. REV. 1367, 1387–91 (1996).
3 Daniel A. Farber, *Stretching the Margins: The Geographic Nexus in Environmental Law*, 48 STAN. L. REV. 1247, 1248 (1996).
4 Johnson & Post, *supra* note 2, at 1380.
5 So, of a net-based Ponzi scheme from the Cayman Islands over which Mionesota has tried to assert juridiction, Johnson and Post would argue that "clearly" Minnesota would not have any jurisdiction over the scheme. *Id.* at 1383.
6 *Id.* at 1390.
7 Pointing to the recent *Amateur Action* case, United States v. Thomas, 74 F.3d 701 (6th Cir. 1996), Johnson and Post argue that the standard for obscenity should not be the local physical community where the material is consumed, but rather the online community within which the material is delivered. But in that case, where the postmaster downloaded some material online, and received other material through the mail, this rule would require that one community govern the online access, and another govern the mail access. This is a difference I don't understand. Whatever the mode of transmission, whether the Internet or UPS, the test should be the same. And in both cases, the relevant question would seem to be what effect this has on them in the jurisdiction where they live, when they step away from the video machine or computer terminal. Maybe the effect is so insignificant that it ought in neither case be regulated. But if it is regulated in the

one, the fact that the medium in the other is bits shouldn't change the matter. Except according to a quite different argument, which I sketch below.

8 Or at least, if it did make a difference, the difference would turn on the greater, not lesser, ability of bits to be regulated than atoms. If the only interest that obscenity laws advanced were a zoning interest—assuring that only those who want to view the material viewed it—then one might argue that because bytes are so much better regulated than atoms, the justification for obscenity regulation is reduced. Because, that is, the technology can better assure that only the intended recipient receives the regulated material, the regulations of that material in cyberspace should be less absolute than in real space. But the Court has never precisely defined for us the real interests advanced by obscenity regulation. In Stanley v. Georgia, 394 U.S. 557(1969), it sounded as if the interest were purely a zoning interest; but the Court rejected this notion in Paris Adult Theater I v. Slaton, 413 U.S. 49 (1973).

9 Johnson & Post, *supra* note 2, at 1374.

10 *See* Jon Auerbach, *Fences in Cyberspace: Governments Move to Limit Free Flaw of the Internet*, BOSTON GLOBE, Feb. 1, 1996, at 1, 15.

11 David G. Post, *Anarchy, State, and the Internet: An Essay on Law-Making in Cyberspace*, 1995 J. ONLINE L. art. 3, *available at* http://www.law.cornell.edu/jol/post.html.

12 Of course claims like this are always exaggeration. To an American user today, it matters quite a bit whether the server she is accessing is located in Ohio or Oslo, for access to Oslo, or any European location, can be quite slow. While in theory it doesn't matter where the server is, if the U.S. government succeeded in getting all material of a certain kind (say, obscenity) moved to nonAmerican servers, it would have a significantly reduce consumption of that material

13 *See generally* A. Michael Froomkin, *The Metaphor is the Key: Cryptography, The Clipper Chip, and the Constitution*, 143 U. PENN. L. REV. 709 (1995) (examining the constitutional and policy questions that underlie governmental regulation of consumer cryptography).

14 Johnson & Post, *supra* note 2, at 1391–95.

15 *Id.*

16 *See, e.g., id.* at 1389–91.

17 Hackers don't. But what hackers do doesn't define what the effect of law as code is on the balance of the non-hacker public.

18 Hackers for example—the civil disobedients of cyberspace. Hackers define for themselves a certain anarchy, by devoting themselves to finding the holes in the existing code. Some believe that the complexity of the code means these holes will always exist, and hence this anarchy will always exist. But I don't think one need believe hacking impossible to believe it will become less and less significant. People escaped from concentration camps, but that hardly undermines the significance of the evil in concentration camps.

19 The Act has two defenses. The first gives a substantive defense to prosecution if a user "has taken, in good faith, reasonable, effective, and appropriate actions under the circumstances to restrict or prevent access by minors." § 501(2). The second directs that "no cause of action may be brought . . . against any person [where that person] has taken in good faith to implement a defense authorized under this section." § 501(2). These defenses together mark out an extraordinarily large scope for protection. Recently the Justice Department has outlined what it considers to be adequate steps to satisfy these defenses. These include simply registering an "indecent" site with one of the services that helps users screen "indecent" sites. The act is presently being challenged, and will most likely

be held unconstitutional because of the overbreadth of the "indecency" provisions. But that is independent of the structure of its defenses. *See* American Civil Liberties Union v. Reno, 929 F. Supp. 824 (E.D. Pa. 1996).

20 Jerry Frug, *The Geography of Community*, 48 STAN. L. REV. 1047 (1996); Richard Thompsom Ford, *The Boundaries of Race: Political Geography in Legal Analysis*, 107 HARV. L. REV. 1841, 1860–78 (1994).

21 *See* Vicki Been, *Comment on Professor Jerry Frug's* The Geography of Community, 48 STAN. L. REV. 1109 (1996).

22 Monroe E. Price, *Free Expression and Digital Dreams: The Open and Closed Terrain of Speech*, 22 CRITICAL INQUIRY 64 (1995).

23 *See* William Ian Miller, *Sanctuary, Red Light Districts, and Washington, D.C.: Some Observations on Neuman's Anomalous Zones*, 48 STAN. L. REV. 1235 (describing the costs of clear lines).

24 *See* Johnson & Post, *supra* note 2, at 1388.

25 *See* CASS SUNSTEIN, DEMOCRACY AND THE PROBLEM OF FREE SPEECH (1994); Cass R. Sunstein, *The First Amendment in Cyberspace*, 104 YALE L.J. 1757 (1995).

26 Not zero, mind you. Given the anonymity of this space, one must build a certain social capital to function well. Exit, or banishment, is the forfeiting of that social capital. As in real life, this is a teal loss, and this loss is what makes communities somewhat sticky.

27 See the world Eugene Volokh describes in *Cheap Speech and What It Will Do*, 104 YALE L.J. 1805 (1995).

61
THE INTERNET AND U.S. COMMUNICATION POLICY-MAKING IN HISTORICAL AND CRITICAL PERSPECTIVE

Robert W. McChesney[1]

Source: *Journal of Communication* 46(1) (1996): 98–124, and *Journal of Computer-Mediated Communication* 1(4): n.p.

Two oppositional and epoch-defining trends dominate U.S. and global media and communication. On one hand, there have been both rapid corporate concentration and commercialization of media industries. The proposed 1995 mergers of Disney with Capital Cities/ABC and Time Warner with Turner Broadcasting, as well as the sale of CBS to Westinghouse, highlight this trend. Most business analysts expect even more merger and buyout activity, leading to as few as six to ten colossal conglomerates dominating global communication before the market stabilizes (Stille, 1995). According to some political theorists, this rampant commercialization of communication poses a severe challenge to the social capacity to generate a democratic political culture and public sphere (Habermas, 1989). Virtually all known theories of political democracy would suggest that such a concentration of media and communication in a handful of mostly unaccountable interests is little short of an unmitigated disaster.

On the other hand, newly developed computer and digital communication technologies can undermine the ability to control communication in a traditionally hierarchal manner. The most dramatic development along these lines has been the Internet, which permits inexpensive, global, interactive, and mass computer communication, as well as access to a previously unimaginable range of information. The Internet has been alternately described as a "functioning anarchy" that is virtually impossible to control from a centralized command post (Lipson, 1995) and "a grass-roots, bottom-up system" (Flowers, 1995, p. 24). Kapor (1994) notes the historical significance of what is now termed cyberspace: "Instead of a small number of groups having privileged positions as speakers-broadcast networks and powerful newspapers—we are entering an era of communication of the many to the many ... the nature of the technology itself has opened up a space of much greater democratic possibility." The executive director of the Internet Society characterizes the Internet as "a profound turning point in the evolution of human communication—of much greater significance than the creation of the printing press" (Flowers, 1995, p. 26).

The long-term trend toward corporate concentration derives from the core logic of capitalism and is presently the dominant force of the two. My fundamental question, then, is to what extent can the emerging communication technological revolution, particularly the Internet, override the antidemocratic implications of the media marketplace and foster more democratic media and a more democratic political culture? This issue is addressed here as a matter of communication policy-making, concentrating upon the U.S. experience. In the first section I locate the current communication policy debates in the broad tradition of U.S. political history and discuss how corporate control of communication has been effectively removed from these debates. This is especially true in the 1990s, as Congress, the White House, and the Federal Communications Commission (FCC) address how best to develop the information highway. This presupposition of corporate, for—profit control reduces the range of legitimate policy debates to tangential issues. According to this premise, corporate control of communication should be maximized and the technological possibilities for decentralized, citizen communication should remain minimized, except where profitable. I argue for genuine, democratic, public participation in communication policy-making, with the aim of establishing nonmarket mechanisms to achieve socially determined goals. In the second section I take up the claim that the traditional policy concerns outlined in the first section are irrelevant for the new computer communication technologies, because these technologies have such a powerful intrinsic democratic bias that the traditional issue over who should control them is essentially moot. To address this contention, I locate the rise of the new technologies in the emergence of global corporate capitalism and the tensions between democracy and capitalism. I argue that the new communication technologies are, in fact, the product and a defining feature of a global capitalism that greatly enhances social inequality. For the Internet and the eventual information highway to approach their full democratic potential will require the types of policy measures now being broached only marginally.

Although I compare Internet and contemporary communication policy-making to the historical case of broadcasting, the differences in the technologies suggest it highly unlikely that they will develop along similar lines. The Internet has vastly more potential as an engine of democratic communication, and the real issue before us is how much of that potential will be fulfilled. I conclude that the policy issues surrounding the emerging communication revolution must be accompanied by a nearly unprecedented degree of politicalization in the United States, if we are to approach the democratic potential of these technologies. The communication revolution also presents a special challenge to the discipline of communication in the United States and globally. Just as the global economy and the communication system are in the throes of a turbulent transformation, communication research and education in the United States are at a crossroads. The stance communication scholars assume toward communication policy-making in the coming years may determine the status of the field for generations.

The Internet and U.S. communication policy-making

Two sets of fundamental political questions emerge when discussing the development of any major communication technology. The first set asks, who will control the technology and for what purpose? The corollary to this question is, who will not control the new technology and what purposes will not be privileged? In the case of U.S. television, for example, a few enormous corporations were permitted to control the medium for the purpose of maximizing profits, which would be realized by selling advertising time. Thus the United States put the development of television on a very distinct trajectory, a path rather unlike that which was adopted in most parts of Europe.

The second set of questions deals with the social, cultural, economic, and political impact of the new communication technology on the overall society and explores why the new communication technology is important. The institutional structures created to answer the first set of policy questions will generally determine the answers to the second set. In fact, much of communication policy-making at this second level consists of trying to coerce the communication system—its owners and operators—into behavior they ordinarily would not pursue. The classic case in point would be the constant discussion about reducing the level of television violence. At the same time, however, the second set of policy questions cannot be limited entirely to structural issues, or it would not need to be considered fundamental. Regardless of how a communication technology is owned and operated, it will have consequences that are often unintended and unanticipated, and related only in varying degrees to its structural basis. Thus television dramatically altered the domestic culture of U.S. households in the postwar years (Spigel, 1992), and it has arguably had a strong effect upon the nature of journalism (Baughman, 1992) and public discourse (Postman, 1985).

The process by which society answers these questions can be regarded as policy-making. The more a society is genuinely democratic, the more that society's policy debates concerning the application and development of paramount communication technologies will be open, informed, thoughtful, and passionate. Regardless of how democratic the policy-making process may be, however, these questions still emerge and will be answered in one form or another. As a rule of thumb, if certain forces thoroughly dominate a society's political economy, they will thoroughly dominate its communication system, and the first set of policy questions will not even be subject to debate. So it is and so it has been with the Communist Party in various "people's republics," and, for the most part, with big business interests in this country.

The United States is in the midst of a fundamental reconfiguration of communication media, often characterized as the information superhighway, or the era of the interactive telecomputer. This is a truly revolutionary era not because of the awesome and bedazzling developments in technology, but because these new digital and computer technologies are likely to break down the traditional communication media industries and call forth a reconstitution of the communicationinfrastructure across the board. In short, the first set of policy-making questions have re-emerged, and the answers we find to them may well set the course of development for generations.

Moreover, the current communication revolution continues, rather dramatically, the historical process whereby mediated communication has become increasingly central to the political economies and cultures of the world's peoples. Global capitalism, politics, culture, and education, to mention a few examples, are being reconstructed in this new era of the information highway. The entire manner in which individuals interact with the world is in the process of being transformed. Hence, the second set of policy issues concerning the social implications of the new communication technologies are of the utmost importance.

The current communication revolution is not unprecedented. It corresponds most closely to the 1920s, when the emergence of radio broadcasting forced society to address the two sets of political questions mentioned above. As with the Internet in the 1990s, radio broadcasting was a radically new development, and there was great confusion throughout the 1920s concerning who should control this powerful new technology and for what purposes. There was little sense of how radio could be made a profitable enterprise, and there was considerable discussion of how liberating and democratic it could be. Much of the impetus for radio broadcasting in the first decade came first from amateurs (Douglas, 1987) and then from nonprofit and noncommercial groups that immediately grasped the public service potential of the new technology (Feldman, 1996; Frost, 1937; Godfried, 1996). It was only in the late 1920s that capitalists began to sense that through network operation and commercial advertising, radio broadcasting could generate substantial profits. Through their immense power in Washington, DC, these commercial broadcasters were able to dominate the Federal Radio Commission such that the scarce number of air channels were effectively turned over to them with no public and little congressional deliberation on the matter. In the aftermath of this commercialization of the airwaves, elements of U.S.

society coalesced into a broadcast reform movement that attempted to establish a dominant role for the nonprofit and noncommercial sector in U.S. broadcasting (McChesney, 1993). These opponents of commercialism came from education, religion, labor, civic organizations, women's groups, journalism, farmers' groups, civil libertarians, and intellectuals. They recognized quickly that their task was doubly difficult, as they had squandered their opportunity to establish a nonprofit system in the 1920s, when the commercial interests were still wrestling with the question of how to capitalize on radio. They looked to Canada and Britain, where nonprofit interests were able to direct policy before the commercial interests had become entrenched, thus providing the groundwork for workable public service broadcasting models for the United States. The reformers attempted to tap into the intense public dislike for radio commercialism in the years before 1934, when Congress annually considered legislation for the permanent regulation of radio broadcasting (Smulyan, 1994). These reformers were explicitly and nonnegotiably radical; they argued that if private interests controlled the medium and their goal was profit, no amount of regulation or self-regulation could overcome the bias built into the system. Commercial broadcasting, the reformers argued, would downplay controversial and provocative public affairs programming and emphasize whatever fare would sell the most products for advertisers. Theirs was a sophisticated critique of the limitations of capitalist communication systems for a democratic society, which foreshadowed much of the best media criticism and scholarship of recent years.

The reform movement disintegrated after the passage of the Communications Act of 1934, which established the FCC (and which will be substantially altered for the first time by the Communications Act of 1995, as explained below). The 1930s reformers did not lose to the commercial interests, however, in any fair debate on a level playing field. The radio lobby dominated because it was able to keep most Americans ignorant or confused about the communication policy matters then under discussion in Congress through their control of key elements of the news media and their sophisticated public relations aimed at the remainder of the press and the public. In addition, the commercial broadcasters became a force that few politicians wished to antagonize; almost all of the congressional leaders of broadcast reform in 1931–32 were defeated in their reelection attempts, a fate not lost on those who entered the next Congress. With the defeat of the reformers, the industry claims that commercial broadcasting was inherently democratic and American went without challenge and became internalized in the political culture. Thereafter the only legitimate manner by which to criticize U.S. broadcasting was to assert that it was uncompetitive and, therefore, needed aggressive regulation. The basis for the "liberal" claim for regulation was that the scarce number of channels necessitated regulation, not that the capitalist basis of the industry was fundamentally flawed. This was a far cry from the criticism of the 1930s broadcast reformers, who argued that the problem was not simply one of lack of competition in the marketplace, as much as it was the rule of the marketplace per se. It also means today that, with the vast expansion in the number of channels in the current communication revolution, the scarcity argument has lost its power and liberals are at a loss to withstand the deregulatory juggernaut (Avery, 1993).

This constricted range of policy debate was the context for the development of subsequent communication technologies, including facsimile, FM radio, and television in the 1940s. That the communication corporations had first claim to these technologies was unchallenged, even to such public-service-minded New Dealers as James Lawrence Fly, Clifford Durr, and Frieda Hennock. In comparison to the public debate over radio in the 1930s, there was almost no public debate concerning alternative ways to develop these technologies. By the 1940s and thereafter, liberals knew the commercial basis of the system was inviolate, and they merely tried to carve out a nonprofit sector on the margins. This was problematic, because whenever these nonprofit niches were seen as blocking profitable expansion, their future was on thin ice. Thus the primary function of the nonprofit sector in U.S. communications has been to pioneer the new technologies when they were not yet seen as profitable-for example, AM radio in the 1920s and FM radio and UHF television in the 1950s-and then to be pushed aside once they have shown the commercial interests the potential of the new media (McChesney, 1995a). This has already been the fate of the Internet's computer networks, which, after substantial public subsidy, were turned over to private operators (Kanaley, 1994; Shapiro, 1995).

Policy and the profit motive

The emergence of the Internet and related technologies is forcing a reconsideration of media policy unlike, say, television or FM radio, because the nature of digital communication renders moot the traditional distinctions between various media and communication sectors. It is clear that the broadcasters and newspaper chains that have ruled for generations will not necessarily rule, or even survive, in the coming age, although the companies that own them will fare better if they move strategically into the new digital world. This theme dominates the business pages of the press and the business-oriented media. The key question, then, is to identify which firms and which sectors will dominate and capitalize on the communication revolution, and which firms and which sectors will fall by the wayside. This is the tale being told in our business press, and, by prevailing wisdom, this is the key policy battle concerning the Internet and the information highway.

Consistent with the pattern set in the middle 1930s, the primacy of corporate control and the profit motive is a given. All sectors of the federal government repeatedly emphasize that the information superhighway "will be built, owned, and operated by the private sector" (Newslink, 1995, p. 1). The range of legitimate debate extends from those like Newt Gingrich, who argue that profits are synonymous with public service, to those like Vice-President Al Gore, who argue that there are public interest concerns the marketplace cannot resolve, but can only address once the profitability of the dominant corporate sector has been assured (New York Times, 1995). The historical record of communication regulation indicates that although the Gore position can be dressed up, once the needs of corporations are given primacy, the public interest will invariably be pushed to the margins. Nowadays, liberal politicians rarely invoke the rhetoric of public interest regulation that, though mostly hollow, typified the middle 20th century. In fact, the debate is so truncated that the preferred (some would argue, the only) means of regulating communication firms is to create incentives for them, that is, to pay them to act differently such that their profits do not fall (National Telecommunications and Information Administration, 1991).

This situation exists for many of the same reasons broadcast reformers were demolished in the 1930s. Politicians may favor one sector over another in the battle to cash in on the highway, but they cannot oppose the cashing-in process without placing their political careers in jeopardy. Both the Democratic and Republican parties have strong ties to the large communication firms and industries (Auletta, 1995a), and the communication lobbies are perhaps the most feared, respected, and well endowed of all who seek favors on Capitol Hill (Andrews, 1995; Mills, 1995). The only grounds for political courage in this case would be if there were an informed and mobilized citizenry ready to do battle for alternative policies. Where would citizens get informed, though, if not through the news media, where news coverage is minimal and restricted to the range of legitimate debate, which, in this case, means no debate at all? That is why the information superhighway is covered as a business story, not a public policy story. Perhaps it is only coincidental that the firms that control U.S. journalism are almost all major players in the corporate jockeying for the inside lane on the information highway. This is not a public policy issue to them, and they have no desire for it to become one (Hickey, 1995). It is a stunning conflict of interest that goes without comment.

These factors all crystallized with the passage by the Senate and the House of Representatives of the Communications Act of 1995. Perhaps one of the most corrupt pieces of legislation in U.S. history, the bill was effectively written by and for business. Much is made of the new law's commitment to competitive markets. This is, in fact, a euphemism for a deregulation that almost certainly will lead to increased concentration, if the historical record provides any insight (Du Boff, 1984; Stille, 1995). As Aufderheide (1995b) notes, the law "proposes, in essence, to let the big get bigger, and more vertically integrated" (p. 3), placing complete trust in the communication corporations. The limited opposition to the legislation has come primarily from those firms that thought they did not see enough benefits thrown their way, or that felt that their competitors got too many (Aufderheide, 1995a). "In all these years of walking the halls of Congress, I have never seen anything like the Telecommunications Bill," one career lobbyist noted. "The silence of public debate is deafening. A bill with such astonishing impact on all of us is not even being discussed" (Bien, 1995, p. 1). In sum, the debate over communications policy is restricted to elites and those with serious financial stakes in the outcome. It does not reflect well onthe caliber of U.S. participatory democracy.

The effect of the Communications Act of 1995 is to assure that the market, and not public policy, will direct the course of both the Internet and the information highway. It is, in effect, a preemptive strike by corporate America to assure that there will be little public intervention in the communication system in coming years, and that government will exclusively serve the needs of the private sector. To answer the question of whither the Internet, one need only determine where the greatest profits are to be found. Indeed the commercialization of the Internet is growing at an exponential rate. More venture capital was invested in Internet companies in the first quarter of 1995 than in all of 1994 (Treese, 1995). "The rush to commercialize ... the Internet has created an investor frenzy not seen in the technology industry since the early days of the personal computer more than a decade ago," the New York Times reports (Zuckerman, 1995). Forrester Research reports that total annual Internet-related revenues will increase from $300 million in 1994 to $10 billion by 1999. Other estimates place Internet-related revenues as high as $200 billion by 2000. The revenues will come from Internet software, Internet access fees and on-line services, Internet-generated hardware sales, and Internet consulting and market research (Taylor, 1995). On-line direct selling and advertising are also vaulting into prominence (Goldman, 1995; Sandberg, 1995). The A. C. Nielsen Company now prepares a survey of Internet users to expedite Internet commerce and advertising even more (Caruso, 1995). Much of the commercial involvement with the Internet is still speculative and not generating a profit, much as it was with private radio station owners of the 1920s, who knew they had a potentially hot ticket, but did not yet know how to cash it in. Businesses are frightened of being outflanked in cyberspace, as suggested by the AT&T advertisement promoting the Internet as a business's "secret weapon against the other guys." Corporate media giants, in particular, are aggressively working to dominate the Internet. Levy (1995) contends that these corporate media ambitions in cyberspace will be foiled because of the antimonopolistic bias of the technology. If so, in the current political environment, that may well mean that the Internet will never fulfill its vast potential and will remain on the margins of the media culture. Aufderheide (1995b) concurs, arguing that the Internet will eventually be regarded as "a demonstration project on the electronic frontier" (p. 1). In any case, the Communications Act of 1995 guarantees that the eventual information highway based on the interactive telecomputer will be a thoroughly commercial enterprise with profit maximization as its founding principle (Baran, 1995; Besser, 1995). It is too early to predict where the nonprofit and noncommercial sector of cyberspace will fit into that picture, but its survival and growth will be based strictly on technology, not policy.

Those forces that benefit from this situation claim that the market is the only truly democratic policy-making mechanism because it rewards capitalists who "give the people what they want" and penalizes those who do not. When the state or labor unions or any other agency interferes with the workings of the marketplace, this reasoning goes, they produce outcomes hostile to the public interest. These were also the precise claims of the commercial broadcasters as they consolidated their hold over the radio spectrum in the 1930s. This ideology of the infallible marketplace in communication and elsewhere has become a virtual civic religion in the United States and globally in the 1990s.

This argument remains infallible only to the extent that it is a religion based on faith and not a political theory subject to inquiry and examination. Under careful examination, the market is a highly flawed regulatory mechanism. Let me provide three brief criticisms along these lines. First, the market is not predicated upononeperson, one-vote, as in democratic theory, but rather upon one-dollar, one-vote. The prosperous have many votes and the poor have none. Is it any surprise that the leading proponents of the market are predominantly well-to-do, and that markets invariably maintain and strengthen class divisions in society? Second, the market does not "give the people what they want" as much as it "gives the people what they want within the range of what is most profitable to produce." This is often a far narrower range than what people might ordinarily enjoy choosing from. Thus, in the case of broadcasting, many Americans may well have been willing to pay for an advertising-free system, but this was a choice that was not profitable for the dominant commercial interests, so it was not offered in the marketplace. As Barbara Ehrenreich (1995) puts it, "a consumer in a market can never be more than a stunted caricature of a citizen in a genuine democracy." Third, markets are driven solely by profit considerations and downplay long-term concerns or values not readily associated with profit maximization. One need think only of the global ecology to see the disastrous consequences of a blind embrace of the market. Yet, such an embrace is precisely what has occurred.

If not the market, what then would be a truly democratic manner to generate communication policy-making? The historical record points to two basic principles that should be made operational. First, in view of the revolutionary nature of the new communication technologies, citizens should convene to study what the technological possibilities are and to determine what the social goals should be. At this point, several alternative models of ownership and control should be proposed and debated, and the best model selected. In short, the structural basis of the communication system should be decided after the social aims are determined. The key factor is to exercise public participation before an unplanned commercial system becomes entrenched. This runs directly counter to the present U.S. experience, whereby the decisions are essentially made by self-interested parties whose goal is to entrench a commercial system before there is any possibility of public participation. Is such public participation an absurd idea? Hardly. In the late 1920s, Canada, noting the rapid commercialization of the U.S. and Canadian airwaves, convened precisely such a public debate over broadcasting that included public hearings in 25 cities in all nine provinces. The final decision to develop a nonprofit system was adopted after three years of active debate (Vipond, 1992). Is this a ridiculous extension of democracy? One hopes not. If the shape of the emerging communication system that stands to alter our lives radically for generations is not fair game for democratic debate, one must wonder just what is.

Second, if such a public debate determines that the communication system needs a significant nonprofit and noncommercial component, the dominant sector of the system must be nonprofit, noncommercial, and accountable to the public. The historical record in the United States and globally is emphatic in this regard. In addition, it is arguable that commercial interests, too, must always be held to carefully administered public service standards. There are legitimate reservations about government involvement with communication. The purpose of policy-making, in this case, should be to determine how to deploy these technologies to create a pluralistic, decentralized, accountable, nonprofit, and noncommercial sector that can provide a viable service to the entire population. Fortunately, communication technologies seem to be quite amenable to such an approach. One suspects that if our society would devote to this problem only a fraction of the time that it has devoted to commercializing communication, we could find some workable public service models. Perhaps these two principles seem entirely unfeasible for contemporary U.S. political culture, but is the only alternative to turn the entire coordination of and responsibility for the new communication system over to the private sector? The communication corporations "don't have our best interests, they have their best interests at heart," David Bunnell, a former Microsoft executive and trade publication publisher, warns. "They're supposed to create profit for their stockholders . . . this information highway is just too important to be left to the private companies" (Flores, 1995, p. D1). This sentiment is shared by many of the most creative minds in the communications industries, seemingly to no avail (Kapor, 1994). As this basic question is off—limits in contemporary U.S. political culture, most Americans do not even know that it is their right to entertain thoughts along these lines and act accordingly.

Nonetheless, there are numerous Americans currently working to generate a viable nonprofit and noncommercial sector in the information highway, preparing insightful proposals along these lines (Bollier, 1993; Chester, 1994; Chester & Montgomery, 1992; Guma, 1994; Kranich, 1994). These reformers find themselves ignored by the press and shunted aside by politicians. They face the classic dilemma that has haunted U.S. communication activists since the middle 1930s: To be taken seriously, one must acknowledge the primacy of corporate rule, that is, they must concede that theirs is a battle for the margins, not the heart, of the communication system. As gloomy as the situation may be, as long as the identity of the eventual corporate masters of communication is being fought over, there are possibilities for concessions that will not exist once the industry is stabilized. Prior to 1934, for example, commercial broadcasters devoted ample time to noncommercial programming in an attempt to persuade the public that they could be trusted with the control of broadcasting. Once the organized opposition disappeared, however, the commitment to noncommercial broadcasting did, as well. So, in this sense, there might be some hope to promote and protect a nonprofit sector, and in the current political culture that may well be the only immediate option. Nonetheless, by historical standards, there is little reason to believe the nonprofit sector could survive a sustained commercial assault, and any concessions gained now need to be written in such a way as to be protected from later attack.

If, indeed, this is to be the course of the Internet and the information highway, what will be the nature of the U.S. policy debates in the coming generation? By the logic of this argument, the legitimate policy issues will be tangential, the province of lobbyists, lawyers, bureaucrats, and academics, and will assume the role of the market as natural. When the contours of the eventual commercial system become clear, so, too, will the precise nature of the legitimate policy issues. Moreover, the distinct attributes of the Internet and the information highway, for example, interactivity, will create unanticipated policy issues. Clearly the past paradigm of commercial broadcasting policy-making cannot be imposed willy-nilly. At present, the issue of state censorship of the Internet is a reigning concern (Lewis, 1995; Plotkin, 1995), and it is crucial to protect free speech, especially since the record suggests that the impetus toward censorship will increase with pronounced Internet deviation from mainstream thought. At the same time, however, without a principled critique of the market and the types of censorship it systematically imposes, this blanket adoption of the First Amendment can also serve to provide the purely commercial aspirations of corporate America with a constitutional shield from justified public criticism. Such has been the case in commercial broadcasting and with advertising. In these cases, the First Amendment has been used to contract the arena of public debate, and not to expand it (Schiller, 1989).

The new super powerful democratic technology?

Even if the market is permitted to determine the course of the information highway and there is minimal public deliberation over fundamental communication policy issues, there is no evidence that the Internet, or the subsequent information highway, can possibly come under the same sort of monopoly corporate control as have broadcasting and traditional media. "The very architecture of the net," one scholar argues, "will work against the type of content control these folks have over mass media" (Newhagen, 1995). Others contend that, whereas the large commercial enterprises will develop their "cybermalls," the rest of cyberspace will be "unpaved," thereby opening the door to a genuine cultural and political renaissance (Flowers, 1995). The issue here is not whether a citizen-based, nonprofit sector of cyberspace can survive in the emerging regime. That seems guaranteed. Nor is the issue whether this sector can thrive in the emerging regime, because that, too, seems likely if the wildfire growth of the past few years is any indication of what is to follow. If nothing else, cyberspace may provide a supercharged, information packed, and psychedelic version of ham radio. Nor is the issue whether the nonprofit sector of cyberspace will be a significant part of a process that transforms our lives dramatically. That may well take place. Rather, the key issue is whether the nonprofit, noncommercial sector of cyberspace will be able to transform our societies radically for the better and to do so without fundamental policy intervention. In short, will this sector be able to create a 21st-century, Habermasian "public sphere," where informed interactive debate can flower independent of government or commercial control? This follows the critical strain of democratic theory that argues that the structural basis for genuine democratic communication lies with a media system free from the control of either the dominant political or economic powers of the day (Habermas, 1989; Meiklejohn, 1948).

I have framed the question from a critical perspective, where the market is not assumed ipso facto to be beyond reproach. In my view, the evidence indicates the market is far from a neutral or value-free arbiter of culture and ideas (Herman, 1993b; Herman, 1995; Murdock, 1992). This is also the perspective of the Internet's most articulate advocates. "The Internet represents the real information revolution," a member of Alternet argues, "the one that removes the governmental and corporate filters that have so long been in place with traditional mass media" (Beacham, 1995, p. 18). Mainstream observers who exult in the potential of the Internet would disagree with the notion that the market or capitalism is an impediment to the development of a democratic public sphere. Some of these analysts often see the Internet and the information highway as elevating existing capitalism to an even higher level of sheer perfection (Gilder, 1994; Gingrich, 1995). In this view, capitalism is synonymous with democracy; therefore, the more that social affairs can be turned over to private interests the better. The function of government is to protect private property and not much else. Indeed, some market-philes take a technological, deterministic stance, asserting that the new communication technologies, since they eliminate the monopolies on knowledge that large corporations have, will lead to a new global economic regime of small entrepreneurs and flexible production. The transnational corporations that presently dominate the global economy will eventually appear like so many clumsy dinosaurs on their way to rapid extinction. Market enthusiasts see this as especially true in communication industries, where size will prove to be a competitive disadvantage. In this perspective, the information highway will be the basis for a new golden age of high-growth, competitive capitalism and an accompanying renaissance in culture and politics (Broder, 1995). As appealing as this may be to some at an ideological level, though, there is no empirical evidence to support this view or to suggest it is on the horizon. In fact, the shift to digital technologies has produced convergence, meaning that the traditional distinctions among media types are disappearing. This in turn enhances synergy, meaning corporations can expand their profit-making abilities by building empires, thereby accelerating the momentum toward global corporate concentration (Murdoch, 1994). Contrary to the claims of the market-philes, the empirically verifiable consequence of the digital revolution is that the telecommunication, computer, media, and entertainment industries, which traditionally have been relatively independent of each other, are now merging and coalescing into grand combinations of unprecedented global scope (King, 1995).

Other mainstream observers may not revel to such a degree in capitalism, but they see the market as the natural order of things and pliable enough to permit the technological revolution to work its magic for both business and the public (Negroponte, 1995; Toffler & Toffler, 1994; Scheer, 1995). In either approach, the market is presupposed to be innately wonderful, or at least neutral, so it is not subjected to any further analysis. The markedly dominant role of corporations and the wealthy in the U.S. political economy goes unmentioned. If the information highway fails to deliver the goods, it will not be the fault of the market or of those who profit by the system.

In fact, the capitalism one finds described superficially in the literature on the Internet and the communication highway is an intoxicating one: It is composed of venture capitalists, daring entrepreneurs, and enterprising consumers. There are no cheap, exploited laborers; no environmental degradation; no graft or corruption; no ingrained classes; no economic depressions; no instances of social decay; and no consumer rip-offs. There are bold, open-minded winners and hardly any losers. It is capitalism at its best. Even to the extent there is a grain of truth in this sanitized version of capitalism, the notion that the communication system is a consequence of the free market is bogus. For example, many of the communication technologies associated with the revolution, particularly the Internet, grew directly out of government, usually military, subsidies. Indeed, at one point fully 85% of research and development in the U.S. electronics industry was subsidized by the federal government, although the eventual profits accrued to private firms (Chomsky, 1994).

I have spelled out my criticism of the market as a democratic regulator of communication and all else in the first section. If we are to accurately evaluate the potential of the Internet and the information highway, we need to replace this mythological portrayal of capitalism with one that is more theoretical, historical, and critical. We also need a more viable notion of the relationship of democracy to capitalism and the relationship of communication to each of them. Only then can we evaluate the claim that the Internet is a supremely powerful democratic force. The relationship of capitalism to democracy is a rocky one. It is true that historically capitalism has been instrumental in giving birth to modern democratic regimes, but it has also worked to limit the extent or viability of that democracy. On one hand, capitalism tends to generate a highly skewed class basis that permits a small section of society, the wealthy, to have inordinate power over political and economic decision-making to the detriment of the balance of society. On the other hand, capitalism encourages a culture that places a premium on commercial values and downplays communitarian ideals. Capitalism thereby undermines two prerequisites for genuine democracy.

Political democracy has always been a problem for a capitalist society like the United States, where a minuscule portion of the population makes fundamental economic decisions based upon its self-interest. This becomes an acute problem when a mature, corporate-dominated, capitalist society also grants near universal suffrage. There is the constant threat, inherent to democracy, that the dispossessed might unite, rise up, and demand greater control over basic economic decisions. In the minds of the powerful, therefore, the system works best when the crucial political and economic decisions are made by elites outside of the public eye, and the political culture concentrates upon superficial and tangential matters. Autonomous labor organizations, social movements, and political parties that oppose the rule of capital are discouraged through a variety of mechanisms, and, when necessary, they are sometimes repressed. Moreover, the tendency of capitalism to commercialize every nook and cranny of social life renders the development or survival of nonmarket political and cultural organizations far more difficult. It is these independent associations that form the bulwark of democracy, making it possible for individuals to come together and become informed political actors (Mills, 1956). In sum, fundamental political activity is discouraged, and, in this context, political apathy appears as rational behavior for those outside the inner circles. This has been, and remains, the reigning characteristic of U.S. politics (Macpherson, 1977).

As Chomsky (1987) notes, it is considered a "crisis of democracy" in conventional thinking when the long-dormant masses rise up and begin to pursue their own interests. Therefore, it is not surprising that a major development in the 20th century has been the rise of public relations—or what is often systematic corporate propaganda—to promote elite interests and to undermine ideas and groups that might oppose corporate rule (Carey, 1995; Stauber & Rampton, 1995). The role of the masses is to ratify elite decisions.

Communication is essential to meaningful participatory democracy. Although the record is certainly mixed, on balance U.S. commercial journalism and media have failed to provide the groundwork for an informed citizenry (Lasch, 1995). In Habermasian terms, the media became sources of great profitability in the 20th century and have been colonized by the corporate sector, thereby losing their capacity to provide the basis for the independent public sphere so necessary for meaningful democracy (Murdock & Golding, 1989). The upshot of most critical media research is that the commercial news media tend to serve elite interests and undermine the capacity for the bulk of the population to act as informed citizens (Herman & Chomsky, 1988). Recent scholarship suggests that increasingly concentrated corporate ownership and commercial support of the media have further destroyed the capacity of the press to fulfill a democratic mission (Bagdikian, 1992).

Communication is increasingly essential, too, to the market economy. That is why an analysis of global capitalism needs to be at the center of any study of communication systems in the coming years. It is no coincidence that the communication revolution appears at the same historic moment as the current globalization of capitalism. The tremendous desire by corporations and capitalists to expand globally has provided much of the spur to innovation in computers and telecommunications, with striking effect (Sullivan-Trainor, 1994). In the early 1970s, only 10% of global trade was financial, with the remaining 90% being trade—in goods and services. The percentages flip-flopped in the subsequent two decades and grew at a rate far greater than global economic activity (McChesney, 1995b). Communication and information-related industries are now, by near unanimous proclamation, at the very heart of investment and growth in the world economy, occupying a role once played by steel, railroads, and automobiles (Mosco, 1990).

So what are the observable, new, and important tendencies of this global capitalist order? Several related points are accepted by most observers, though how they are framed and their relative importance are subject to debate (Business Week, 1995; Foster, 1995). First, the ease of transborder capital flows has lessened the capacity of national governments to determine economic policies that might promote any interests apart from those of transnational business, as capitalists can quickly move to more profitable climes (Picciotto, 1991). John Maynard Keynes once noted that democracy would be impossible if capital could move beyond national borders (Bernstein, 1987); indeed, the immobility of capital is a core assumption of neoclassical economic theory. Next, the new global capitalism has also had the effect of giving the international business community far greater leverage in its dealings, not only with government regulations and policies, but with labor as well. As a result, the global trend is toward deregulation, in the hope of luring capital and reducing the power of labor and labor unions, since if they are too effective, business will invest elsewhere. Environmental regulation is an immediate casualty of globalization, as are most government services, which must be eliminated in order to reduce taxes on the well-to-do (capital flight) and reduce economic stagnation.

A third effect is that this process of globalization has been accompanied by decreasing economic growth in the United States and globally in each decade since the 1960s. In fact, globalization emphasizes one of capitalism's basic flaws: What is rational conduct for the individual capitalist is utterly irrational and counterproductive for the system as a whole. Rational investors seek out low-wage areas and use the threat to keep domestic wages low even if they do not move abroad (Albo, 1994; Panitch, 1994). The consequence is that there is a strong downward pressure on buying power (i.e., economic demand), which leads to a decline in profitable investment possibilities (i.e., continued economic stagnation; MacEwan, 1994). Moreover, governments are incapable of exercising the traditional Keynesian policies to stimulate economic growth, as these measures run directly counter to those policies necessary to attract and keep investment. Stimulative economic measures are no longer even a legitimate policy option; even if the World Bank and International Monetary Fund do not veto them, the global capital markets will (Tanzer, 1995). In addition, investment in information and communication tends to destroy existing jobs almost as well as it creates new ones. Unlike steel and automobiles, these new paradigm—identifying industries seem to be incapable of resolving the crisis of unemployment that afflicts the global working class. In this sense, the immediate consequence of the information revolution is not liberation from drudgery, but a sentencing to a life of sheer destitution (Noble, 1995). Finally, because of the wildfire growth of enormous transnational global financial markets that are well beyond the powers of any effective national or international regulation, there is an element of overall instability to the global economy unknown since the 1930s (Sweezy, 1994). In sum, the economic thrust of global capitalism is one of deteriorating public sectors, environmental recklessness, stagnation, instability, and widening economic stratification (Cowling & Sugden, 1994). For those lucky few who sit atop the global pyramid, the future never appeared brighter; for the bulk of humanity, the present is grim and the future is an abyss. Nothing on the horizon suggests any other course (Fitch, 1996; Henwood, 1995).

Salvaging political culture

The implications of the global order for political culture are mostly negative (Herman, 1993a). Capitalism's two inherent and negative traits for democracy-class stratification and the demise of civic virtue in the face of commercial values—are enhanced in the new global regime. There is nothing short of a wholesale assault on the very notion of democracy, as the concept of people gathering, debating, and devising policy has been supremely truncated. This is often presented as a crisis of national sovereignty; in fact, it is a crisis of sovereignty writ large. There is nothing really left to debate in the new world order since nations are required either to toe the global capitalist line or to face economic purgatory. Hence, the range of legitimate debate has shrunk considerably, with socialists and conservatives alike effectively pursuing the same policies. The great paradox of our age is that formal democracy extends to a greater percentage of humanity than ever in history; yet, concurrently, there may well be a more general sense of political powerlessness than ever before. Since the democratic system seems incapable of generating ideas that address the political economic crises of our times, the most dynamic political growth in this age is with antirationalist, fundamentalist, nationalistic movements that blame democracy for capitalism's flaws and threaten to reduce humanity to untold barbarism.

The communication revolution is implicated in these developments. On one hand, the transnational communication corporations—among the greatest beneficiaries of globalization—have been leading the fight for NAFTA, GATT, and other institutional arrangements advantageous to global capital (Glaberson, 1994). These firms have set their sights on dominating world communication, entertainment, and information (Oneal, 1995; Parkes, 1995; Schiller, 1995). Public sector broadcasting and communication across the planet have been dismantled and replaced by capitalist, often transnational, communication systems (National Telecommunications and Information Administration, 1993; Pendakur & Kapur, 1995). In particular, the great public service broadcasting systems of Europe, and their associative journalistic and cultural values, have been either eliminated or required to adopt commercial principles in order to survive in the global marketplace (Blumler, 1992). This new world order of communication tends to be uncritical of capitalism and commercialism and to be preoccupied with satisfying the needs of the relatively affluent, a minority of the world's population (Nordenstreng & Schiller, 1993). In short, the new world order of global communication, among the most profitable consequences of global capitalism, tends to reinforce the status quo.

In this gloomy scenario, what are the prospects that the Internet and the technological revolution in communication might break down oligarchy and lead to a revitalization of democratic political culture? Proponents emphasize the attributes of the Internet that make it so special: It is relatively cheap, easy to use, difficult to prevent access to, and almost impossible to censor. Gibson (Harris, 1995, p. 49) characterizes the Internet as "a last hope for democracy as we know it." The most thoughtful arguments, and the most concerted activity, on behalf of the Internet as a means for revitalizing democracy tend to emphasize how it can empower individuals and groups presently ignored or distorted by the existing media industries. In effect, the Internet, especially the bulletin boards and discussion groups, can provide democracy's much needed public sphere that has been so corrupted by the market. Moreover, given the instantaneous and global nature of the Internet, proponents of the "Internet as public sphere" argue that this permits the creation of a global public sphere, all the more necessary in light of the global political economy. In Mexico, for example, these computer networks may well have permitted the prodemocracy forces to bypass the atrocious media system and to survive and prosper, whereas in earlier times these forces would have been crushed (Frederick, 1995). As evidence to bolster the belief that this is a viable alternative to commercial media, supporters point to a Rand Corporation memorandum indicating considerable dissatisfaction with the existence of these uncontrolled networks of communication and suggesting state surveillance or regulation to keep them in line (Simon, 1995: Wehling, 1995). Although it is true that the prospects for computer networks are encouraging for activists, I believe the following qualifications are appropriate before we can extrapolate that the Internet will provide an unambiguous boon for democracy. First, assuring universal access and computer literacy is far from a certainty, and, without it, the democratic potential of the information highway seems supremely compromised. As of 1995, only a third of the nation's population owns computers, and many of them cannot get access to the Internet (Aufderheide, 1995b). Personal computers are still not affordable for a large number of people, and computer manufacturers favor producing the big ticket PCs with heftier profit margins (Baran, 1995). Although the extent of diffusion of PCs over the next decade can only be guessed, there is little reason to believe that it will approach the level of either indoor plumbing or television, if left to the market. Significant portions of the U.S. population do not have cable television, and in poor neighborhoods up to one third of the population goes without telephone service (Aufderheide, 1995b). Hence the only way to insure universal access and computer literacy will be to enact public policy to that effect, and in this era of fiscal constraint, that might prove to be a tall order. Schools and libraries are often pointed to as the key agents that will democratize computer usage, yet these institutions are in the throes of long-term cutbacks that seem to render absurd the notion that they could undertake this mission. And without universal access and computer literacy, as BYTE magazine contributing editor Nicholas Baran (1995) emphasizes, the PC may well "become a tool for further increasing the economic and educational disparity in our society" (p. 40).

Aside from the question of access, bulletin boards, and the information highway more generally, do not have the power to produce political culture when it does not exist in the society at large. Given the dominant patterns of global capitalism, it is far more likely that the Internet and the new technologies will adapt themselves to the existing political culture rather than create a new one. Thus, it seems a great stretch to think the Internet will politicize people; it may just as well keep them depoliticized. The New York Times cites Wired magazine approvingly for helping turn "mild-mannered computer nerds into a super-desirable consumer market," not into political activists (Keegan, 1995, pp. 38–39). In particular, having mass, interactive bulletin boards is a truly magnificent advance, but what if nobody knows what they are talking about? This problem could be partially addressed if scholars and academics shared their work with and tailored their analyses to the general public, thereby engaging in a public dialogue. Unfortunately, such behavior runs directly counter to the priorities, attitudes, and trajectory of academic life.

This is precisely where journalism (broadly construed) and communication policy-making enter the picture. Journalism provides the oxygen for democratic discussion; it provides the research and contextualization necessary to understand politics and to see behind the official proclamations of those in power. Journalism does not constitute the range of debate; rather, it provokes it, informs it, and responds to it. As a rule, it is not something that can be done piecemeal by amateurs. It is best done by people who make a living at it and who have training and experience. Although journalism per quo is justly criticized for its failures, mostly due to commercial constraints, journalism per se is indispensable to any notion of democracy worth the paper it is written on. A quality journalism seems mandatory if the "Internet as public sphere" is to be a viable concept, and current theories along these lines are at a loss to address this problem.

Moreover, journalism is presently in the midst of a deep and profound crisis. The corporate concentration of ownership and the reliance upon advertising have converted much of U.S. journalism into a travesty of entertainment, crime, and natural disaster stories. The professional autonomy of journalists—always an ambiguous notion, especially in a commercial environment—has suffered severe body blows. Journalism, real journalism, is not profitable, and resources dedicated to it have been cut back (Kimball, 1994). Without resources, journalists are unable to do any investigative work and must rely upon the public relations industry (generally corporate) and official sources (mostly politicians, corporate-sponsored think tanks, and government officials) for news stories. Morale for U.S. journalists is arguably at an all—time low (Mazzocco, 1994; McManus, 1994; Squires, 1993; Underwood, 1993). Michael Eisner, CEO of the Walt Disney Company, says his firm's prospective growth is based on a "nonpolitical" product that does not threaten political regimes around the world, yet Eisner is now leader of one of the world's largest journalistic organizations (Auletta, 1995b). In short, the market has little apparent interest in serious journalism, nor is such interest in the offing.

Some have described how the Internet will improve dramatically journalists' access to information, but none have come forth with ideas for how it will address the crisis noted above (Crichton, 1995; Gordon, 1995; Isaacs, 1995). The primary contribution of the Internet to journalism at present is ideological: Some mainstream scholars and industry public relations agents point to the vitality of cyberspace as an explanation for why there is no need for alarm at the concentrated corporate control of global communication or for political action to address the problem (Farrell, 1995; Levy, 1995). In the new mythology, the Internet joins the now battered notion of the professional autonomy of journalists as the public's protection from the negative consequences for democratic journalism of an oligopolistic, commercial media system. This argument evades the core point that journalism requires resources and institutional support. In this context, the battle for public and community broadcasting is crucial both in the United States and globally. It is not about the survival of Big Bird as much as it is about the survival of an structural basis for journalism and public affairs (McChesney, 1995a). In sum, the Internet can reproduce only part of the public sphere, and its part will not necessarily be worth much if there is not the institutional framework for a well-subsidized and independent journalism. Shapiro (1995) argues in this fashion that public policy must move aggressively to promote and protect and, by implication, subsidize a public forum in cyberspace. The third qualification to the "Internet as public sphere" hypothesis is that it often seems to exhibit an unchecked enthusiasm for these technologies, and technology in general, that is unwarranted. At its most extreme, some argue that the quantitative improvement in communication technology is leading to a truly qualitative shift in human consciousness. By this reasoning, the computer networks are liberating humanity from the material chains that have kept human imagination and creativity locked up (Rushkoff, 1994). Some argue that cyberspace has created genuine communities that offer a glimpse of how we might truly become a global human family (Rheingold, 1993). Both of these Utopian views recognize that commercial and government forces seek to undermine the transcendental potential of the Internet and the information highway, yet both emphasize the revolutionary power of technologies to liberate humanity. At its best, this perspective emphasizes cyberspace as a spawning ground for counterculture, and often harks back to the 1960s and other eras of communitarian ideals. Yet, as appealing as this line of reasoning may be, it really is a nonsensical notion of how history is going to unfold, and, at its worst, this argument degenerates, as Stallabrass (1995) puts it, into "business people and their camp followers (engineers and intellectuals) spinning universalist fantasies out of their desire to ride the next commercial wave" (p. 32).

Indeed, one could characterize the adoption of the Internet as public sphere as not so much a grand victory as it is a case of making the best of a bad situation. On one hand, the motor force behind the development of these technologies is business and business demand. Hamilton noted 60 years ago that "Business succeeds rather better than the state inimposing restraints upon individuals, because its imperatives are disguised as choices" (Rorty, 1934, p. 10). We did not elect to have these technologies, nor did we ever debate their merits. They have been presented either as some sort of product of inexorable natural evolution or as a democratic response to pent-up consumer demand, when, in fact, they are here because they are profitable and because a market was created for them. Now that they are here, people can ignore them only at the risk of jeopardizing their careers and their ability to participate in society. As Postman (1995) notes, "new technologies do not always increase people's options; just as often they do exactly the opposite" (p. 4). I am not advancing a Luddite argument; I merely point out that a central part of democratic communication policy-making is to evaluate the effects of a new technology before adopting it, to look before we leap. That has not been the case with the Internet or the information highway.

All communication technologies have unanticipated and unintended effects, and one function of policy-making is to understand them so we may avoid or minimize the undesirable ones. The digitalization and computerization of our society are going to transform us radically, yet even those closely associated with these developments express concern about the possibility of a severe deterioration of the human experience as a result of the information revolution (Deitch, 1994; Stoll, 1995; Talbott, 1995). As one observer notes, "Very few of us—only the high priests—really understand the new technologies, and these are surely the people least qualified to make policy decisions about them" (Charbeneau, 1994, pp. 28–29). For every argument extolling the "virtual community" and the liberatory aspects of cyberspace, it seems every bit as plausible to reach dystopian conclusions. Why not look at the information highway as a process that encourages the isolation, atomization, and marginalization of people in society? In fact, cannot the ability of people to create their own community in cyberspace have the effect of terminating a community in the general sense? In a class-stratified, commercially oriented society like the United States, cannot the information highway have the effect of simply making it possible for the well-to-do to bypass any contact with the balance of society altogether? These are precisely the types of questions that need to be addressed and answered in communication policy-making and precisely the types of questions in which the market has no interest (Chapman, 1995). At any rate, a healthy skepticism toward technology should be the order of the day.

Democracy, scholarship, and communication technology

The nature of contemporary communication policy-making in the United States is only superficially democratic, and, therefore, there is little reason to believe that the results of such a system will do much more than satisfy the interests of those responsible for the decisions. Communication policy-making follows the contours of political debate in general (Brenner, 1995). This is a business-run society, and the communication system is tailored to suit corporate interests. The role of the citizenry is to conform its ambitions and goals to satisfy the needs of business and profit maximization. It is not the responsibility of those directing the economy to make their activities meet the democratically determined aims of the citizenry or to be accountable for the social consequences of those actions, as democratic theory would suggest (Meiklejohn, 1948). In fact, the market is hardly a substitute for democracy. At most it is a tool, like technology, to be thoughtfully employed in a democracy. And the immediate consequence of the market for global communication is one of increasingly private concentration and commercialization, which are hardly the stuff of democracy.

It is also appealing to think that the new communication technologies can solve social problems, but they cannot. Only humans, acting consciously, can address and resolve problems like poverty, environmental degradation, racism, sexism, and militarism. As Singer (1995) notes, our task is to overcome "the contradiction between our technological genius and the absurdity of our social organization" (p. 533). We encounter the magnificent potential of the new technologies with the wet blanket of conventional wisdom draped over the fires of our social and political imaginations. Nor is the blanket there by accident: Those who benefit by the status quo have helped place it there and are holding it down. So, can the Internet and communication technologies save demo-cracy from capitalism? No, not unless they are explicitly deployed for public service principles. In the short term, that means struggling for universal access, for computer literacy, and for a well-subsidized and democratic noncommercial and nonprofit media sector. In the long term, that means working for explicit public planning and deliberation in crafting fundamental communications policy. Any hope of success will depend on linking and integrating communication concerns to larger efforts to bring heretofore underrepresented segments of the citizenry into the political arena, thereby reducing the power of business and working toward lessening inequality in our society.

Is that possible? Given my argument about the nature of the global economy and the demise of sovereignty, one might assume the situation to be nearly hopeless, and that the only rational course would be to try to eke out the best possible reforms from the existing regime. And since even minor public interest reforms within the existing corporate communication system have proven nearly impossible, some may therefore regard the overall situation as hopeless for the foreseeable future.

In fact, I believe the exact opposite is the case. The current promarket policies are going to be little short of disastrous for the quality of life for a majority of people both in the United States and globally. In the coming generation there will be a pressing need for alternative policies that place the needs of the bulk of the citizenry ahead of the demands of global capital. The Internet may possibly play a crucial role in expediting these developments. We are entering a critical juncture in which no social institutions, including corporations and the market, can remain exempt from public scrutiny. The challenge for those committed to democracy is, as Greider (1992) notes, "to refashion the global economy... so that it enhances democracy rather than crippling it, so that economic returns are widely distributed among all classes instead of narrowly at the top" (p. 403). The tension between democracy and capitalism is becoming increasingly evident, and communication—so necessary to both—can hardly serve two masters at once. From a critical perspective, where democracy is privileged over profit, this is the context for communication policy-making. Given the centrality of communication to global capitalism, the move to reform communication must be part and parcel of a movement to reform the global political economy, as Greider suggests. It is unthinkable otherwise. By this reasoning, there is a special role for communication scholars to play in debating and devising democratic communication policies, but the academic context for critical research is in turmoil. The rise of the Internet and the information highway places the future of communication research and education at U.S. universities in jeopardy. It demands a restructuring, or at least a rethinking, of the very field of communication, precisely at a time that many U.S. universities are downsizing as a consequence of the global economic trends outlined above, specifically stagnation and the collapse of the public sector. This is putting considerable pressure on universities to redirect their activities to elicit support from the corporate sector. In effect, there is increased pressure to move away from the traditional standard of intellectual and scholarly autonomy and link education and research explicitly to the needs o f business (Soley, 1995). This has clear implications for the nature of the scholarship that the new "lean and mean" university will produce, which perhaps explains why the promarket political right is most enthusiastic about the elimination of academic autonomy. The stars on campus are the departments and individuals who attract the most grant money, and departments and scholars who fail to do so face an uncertain future. Nowhere are these pressures more apparent than in communication. It is a paradox that precisely at the historic moment that communication is roundly deemed as central to global political economy and culture, those academic departments expressly committed to communication research are facing severe cutbacks or even elimination. This can be attributed to the historic weakness of communication on U.S. campuses. When cutbacks need be made, communication is easier to attack than more established disciplines. The pressures are doubly strong, therefore, to link up communication research and education to the masters of the corporate communication order, and to opt for what Paul Lazarsfeld (1941) termed the "administrative" rather than the "critical" path for scholarship.

Although cultivating ties to the capitalist communication sector may appear a logical management move, it will probably lead to the demise of communication as a viable discipline. On one hand, the administrative turn is morally deplorable. It takes communication away from what Innis (Carey, 1978) termed the "university tradition," a source of honest, independent inquiry in service to democratic values. At a practical level, too, business schools are far better suited to conduct research along these lines, especially as communication is now a central business activity. Who needs departments predicated upon public service and professional principles like journalism when the whole idea is to maximize profit? There is no alternative, then, but to do honest independent scholarship and instruction, with a commitment first and foremost to democratic values. Let the chips fall where they may. The field of communication needs to apply the full weight of its intellectual traditions and methodologies to the daunting questions before us. They desperately require scholarly attention. The lesson of the last 50 years on U.S. campuses is clear. If the field of communication does not do it, nobody else will. It will make for a rocky road, but what other choice is there?

Note

1 The author wishes to thank Leonard Rifas, Bill McKibben, Patricia Aufderheide, Robert "Lou" Torregrossa, Inger Stole, John Bellamy "Duke" Foster, Thomas Guback, Edward S. Herman, Greg Bates and Vivek Chibber for their helpful comments on earlier drafts of this article.

References

Albo, G. (1994). "Competitive austerity" and the impasse of capitalist employment policy. In R. Miliband & L. Panitch (Eds.), *Socialist Register 1994* (pp. 144–170). London: Merlin Press.

Andrews, E. (1995, June 14). On $700 billion data highway, persuasion has a polite frenzy. *New York Times*, pp. C1, C4.

Aufderheide, P. (1995a). Giving away the cyberstore. Unpublished paper.

Aufderheide, P. (1995b, April). Media wars in cyberspace. Presentation to Conference on Technology and Democracy, Case Western Reserve University, Cleveland, OH.

Auletta, K. (1995a, June 5). Pay per views. *The New Yorker*, pp. 52–56.

Auletta, K. (1995b, August 14). Awesome. *The New Yorker*, pp. 28, 30–32.

Avery, R. (Ed.). (1993). *Public service broadcasting in a multichannel environment.* New York: Longman.
Bagdikian, B. (1992). *The media monopoly*, 4th ed. Boston: Beacon Press.
Baran, N. (1995). Computers and capitalism: A tragic misuse of technology. *Monthly Review*, **47(4)**, 40–46.
Baughman, J. (1992). *The republic of mass culture.* Baltimore: Johns Hopkins University Press.
Beacham, F. (1995), Questioning technology: Tools for the revolution, *Media Culture Review*, **4(2)**, 6, 18.
Bernstein, M. (1987). *The great depression: Delayed recovery and economic change in America.* New York: Cambridge University Press.
Besser, H. (1995). From Internet to information superhighway. In J. Brook & I. Boal (Eds.), *Resisting the virtual life: The culture and politics of information* (pp. 59–70). San Francisco: City Lights.
Bien, C. (1995, July 6). Correspondence to Robert W. McChesney.
Blumler, J. (Ed.). (1992). *Television and the public interest: Vulnerable values in West European broadcasting.* London: Sage.
Bollier, D. (1993). *The information superhighway and the reinvention of television.* Washington, DC: Center for Media Education.
Brenner, R. (1995), Clinton's failure and the politics of U.S. decline, *Against the Current*, **10**, (3), 26–31.
Broder, D. (1995, June 27). Democrats in tug-of-war over view of Americans. *Wisconsin State Journal*, p. 7A.
Business Week. (1995, January 24). Twenty-first century capitalism. Special Ed.
Carey, A. (1995). *Taking the risk out of democracy.* Sydney: University of New South Wales Press.
Carey, J. (1978). A plea for the university tradition. *Journalism Quarterly*, **55**, 846–855.
Caruso, D. (1995, August 21). Digital commerce. *New York Times*, p. C3.
Chapman, G. (1995, June 2). Virtual communities. *Texas Observer*, pp. 22–23.
Charbeneau, T. (1994). Dangerous assumptions. *Toward Freedom*, **43(7)**, 28–29.
Chester, J. (1994). Statement before the subcommittee on telecommunications and finance, committee on energy and commerce, U. S. House of Representatives, on H.R. 3636, the "national communications competition and information infrastructure act". February 2.
Chester, J., & Montgomery, K. (1992). Media in transition: Independents and the future of television. NVR Reports #10, November.
Chomsky, N. (1987). *On power and ideology: The Managua lectures.* Boston: South End Press.
Chomsky, N. (1994). *World orders old and new.* New York: Columbia University Press.
Cowling, K., & Sugden, R. (1994). *Beyond capitalism: Towards a new world economic order.* New York: St. Martin's Press.
Crichton, M. (1995). Mediasaurus. In C. Jensen (ed.), *Censored: The news that didn't make the news—and why* (pp. 25–32). New York: Four Walls Eight Windows.
Deitch, J. (1994). Post human. *Adbusters Quarterly*, **3(1)**, 20–27.
Douglas, S. (1987). *Inventing American broadcasting, 1899–1922.* Baltimore: Johns Hopkins University Press.

Du Boff, R. (1984). The rise of communications regulation: The telegraph industry, 1844–1880, *Journal of Communication*, **34**(3), pp. 52–66.
Synergy
Ehrenreich, B. (1995, August 20). Global arches. *New York Times Book Review*, p. 8.
Farrell, C. (1995, August 14). Media control is narrowing, should we worry? *Business Week*, p. 37.
Feldman, A. (1996). Staking a place in the ether: The politics of public service broadcasting in Wisconsin, 1918–1940. Unpublished Ph.D. dissertation, University of Wisconsin-Madison.
Fitch, R. (1996). *Digital delusions: The promise of the information age and the return of Dickensian poverty.* Monroe, ME: Common Courage Press.
Flores, M. (1995, May 25). Show offers inside look at Microsoft, Gates. *Seattle Times*, p. D1.
Flowers, J. (1995, July 1). Idiot's guide to the. . . . , *New Scientist*, pp. 22–26.
Foster, J. (1995, July). Globalization – What is it? Presentation to workshop on Globalized Economy and Alternative Visions, Eugene, OR.
Frederick, H. (1995, January). North American NGO computer networking: Computer communications in the cross-border coalition-building. Research report for Rand Corporation/Ford Foundation, Program for Research on Immigration Policy.
Frost, Jr., S. (1937). *Education's own stations.* Chicago: University of Chicago Press.
Gilder, G. (1994). *Life after television*, 2nd ed. New York: W. W. Norton.
Gingrich, N. (1995). *To renew America.* New York: HarperCollins.
Glaberson, W. (1994, December 5). Press: A dispute over GATT highlights the complex links between newspapers and their corporate parents. *New York Times*, p. C8.
Godfried, N. (1996). *The rise and fall of labor radio: WCFL, Chicago's labor station, 1926–1978.* Urbana: University of Illinois Press.
Goldman, K. (1995, April 5). Now marketers can buy a service to track Internet customer usage. *Wall Street Journal*, p. B5.
Gordon, A. (1995), Journalism and the Internet, *Media Studies Journal*, **9**(3), pp. 173–176.
Gore, A. (1995, February). Remarks by Vice-President Al Gore to G-7 Ministers Meeting on the Global Information Initiative, Brussels, Belgium.
Greider, W. (1992). *Who will tell the people? The betrayal of American democracy.* New York: Simon & Schuster.
Guma, G. (1994, December). The road from here to media democracy. *Toward Freedom*, p. 2.
Habermas, J. (1989). The structural transformation of the public sphere, Thomas Burger with Frederick Lawrence, Trans. Cambridge: MIT Press. (Originally published in German in 1962).
Harris, B. (1995). The geopolitics of cyberspace. *Infobahn. Premiere issue*, pp. 48–53, 86–87.
Henwood, D. (1995). Info fetishism. In J. Brook & I. Bial (Eds), *Resisting the virtual life: The culture and politics of information* (pp. 163–171). San Francisco: City Lights.
Herman, E. (1993a, September). The end of democracy? *Z Magazine*, pp. 57–62.
Herman, E. (1993b). The externalities effects of commercial and public broadcasting. In K. Nordenstreng & H. Schiller (Eds.), *Beyond national sovereignty: International communication in the 1990s* (pp. 85–115). Norwood, NJ: Ablex.

Herman, E. (1995). *Triumph of the market: Essays on economics, politics, and the media.* Boston: South End Press.

Herman, E., & Chomsky, N. (1988). *Manufacturing consent: The political economy of the mass media.* New York: Pantheon.

Hickey, N. (1995). Revolution in cyberia. *Columbia Journalism Review*, July/August, pp. 40–47.

Isaacs, S. (1995). The Bill Gates factor. *Columbia Journalism Review*, July/August, pp. 53–54.

Kanaley, R. (1994, November 4). Internet passes quietly into private hands. *Philadelphia Inquirer.*

Kapor, M. (1994). Mitchell Kapor on dharma, democracy, and the information superhighway. Tricycle: *Buddhist Review*, **Summer**.

Keegan, P. (1995, May 21). The digerati! *New York Times Magazine*, pp. 38–44, 86–88.

Kimball, P. (1994). *Downsizing the news: Network cutbacks in the nation's capital.* Washington, DC: Woodrow Wilson Center Press.

King, T. (1995, September 15). What's intertainment? *Wall Street Journal*, pp. R1, R6.

Kranich, N. (1994). *Internet access & democracy: Ensuring public places on the info highway.* Westfield, NJ: Open Magazine Pamphlet Series.

Lasch, C. (1995). *The revolt of the elites and the betrayal of democracy.* New York: W. W. Norton.

Lazarsfeld, Paul F. (1941). Remarks on administrative and critical communications research, *Studies in Philosophy and Social Science*, **9(1)**, 2–16.

Levy, S. (1995, September 24). How the propeller heads stole the electronic future. *New York Times Magazine*, pp. 58–59.

Lewis, P. (1995, July 17). On the net. *New York Times*, p. C5.

Lipson, M. (1995, April). The organizational politics of a functioning anarchy: Governance of the Internet. Presentation to Midwest Political Science Association, Chicago.

MacEwan, A. (1994), Globalization and stagnation, *Monthly Review*, **45(11)**, pp. 1–16.

Macpherson, C. (1977). *The life and times of liberal democracy.* New York: Oxford University Press.

Mazzocco, D. (1994). *Networks of power: Corporate TV's threat to democracy.* Boston: South End Press.

McChesney, R. (1993). *Telecommunications, mass media, and democracy: The battle for the control of U.S. broadcasting, 1928–1935.* New York: Oxford University Press.

McChesney, R. (1995a). The attack on U.S. public broadcasting in historical perspective. *Monthly Review*, in press.

McChesney, R. (1995b). On media, politics, and the left, part 1: An interview with Noam Chomsky. *Against the Current*, **10(1)**, 27–32.

McManus, J. (1994). *Market-driven journalism: Let the citizen beware?* Thousand Oaks, CA: Sage.

Meiklejohn, A. (1948). *Political freedom.* New York: Harper.

Mills, C. (1956). *The power elite.* New York: Oxford University Press.

Mills, M. (1995, April 23). The new kings of Capitol Hill. *Washington Post.*

Mosco, V. (1990). Transforming telecommunications: Political economy and public policy. Presentation to Conference on Canadian Political Economy in the Era of Free Trade, Carleton University, Ottawa, Canada.

Murdock, G. (1992). Citizens, consumers, and public culture. In M. Skovmand & K. Schroder (Eds.), *Media Cultures: Reappraising Transnational Media* (pp. 17–41). London: Routledge.

Murdock, G. (1994). The new media empires: Media concentration and control in the age of convergence. *Media Development*, **41(4)**, 3–6.

Murdock, G. & Golding, P. (1989). Information poverty and political inequality: Citizenship in the age of privatized communications. *Journal of Communication*, **39(3)**, 180–195.

Synergy, ISI, CSA

National Telecommunications and Information Administration. (1991). *Telecommunications in the age of information.* Washington, DC: U.S. Department of Commerce.

National Telecommunications and Information Administration. (1993). *Globalization of the mass media.* Washington, DC: U.S. Department of Commerce.

Negroponte, N. (1995). *Being digital.* New York: Knopf.

Newhagen, J. (1995, July 10). Correspondence to Robert W. McChesney.

New York Times. (1995, April 12). Too fast on communications reform, p. A14.

Newslink. (1995). FCC commissioner Susan Ness: Regulating the Infobahn, **5(2)**, 1, 4.

Noble, D. (1995). The truth about the information highway. *Monthly Review*, **47(2)**, 47–52.

Nordenstreng, K. & Schiller, H. (Eds.). (1993). *Beyond national sovereignty: International communication in the 1990s.* Norwood, N.J.: Ablex.

Oneal, M. (1995, August 14). Disney's kingdom. *Business Week*, pp. 30–34.

Panitch, L. (1994). Globalization and the state. In R. Miliband & L. Panitch (Eds.), *Socialist Register 1994* (pp. 60–93). London: Merlin Press.

Parkes, C. (1995, August 21). FT guide to Hollywood. *Financial Times*, p. 6.

Pendakur, M. & Kapur, J. (1995, January). Think globally, program locally. Paper presented to Democratizing Communication conference.

Picciotto, S. (1991). The internationalisation of the state, *Capital & Class*, **43(Spring)**, 43–63.

Plotkin, H. (1995, July 27). Cleansing the net, *Isthmus (Madison, WI)*, **20(29)**, 10–12.

Postman, N. (1985). *Amusing ourselves to death.* New York: Penguin Books.

Postman, N. (1995, February). 1995 Russell Lecture. Presbyterian College, Clinton, SC.

Rheingold, H. (1993). *The virtual community: Homesteading on the electronic frontier.* Reading, MA: Addison-Wesley.

Rorty, J. (1934). *Order on the air!* New York: John Day.

Rushkoff, D. (1994). *Cyberia: Life in the trenches of hyperspace.* New York: HarperCollins.

Sandberg, J. (1995, April 10). Time Warner sells ads in cyberspace via its pathfinder service on internet. *Wall Street Journal*, p. B6.

Scheer, C. (1995). The pursuit of techno-happiness, *The Nation*, **260(18)**, 632–634.

Schiller, H. (1989). *Culture, Inc.* New York: Oxford University Press.

Schiller, H. (1995). The global information highway: Project for an ungovernable world. In J. Brook & I. Boal (Eds.), *Resisting the virtual life: The culture and politics of information* (pp. 17–33). San Francisco: City Lights.

Shapiro, A. (1995). Street corners in cyberspace, *The Nation*, **261(1)**, 10–12, 14.
Simon, J. (1995, March). Netwar could make Mexico ungovernable. Pacific News Service dispatch.
Singer, D. (1995). The sound and the furet. *The Nation*, **260(15)**, 531–534.
Smulyan, S. (1994). *Selling radio: The commercialization of American broadcasting, 1920–1934.* Washington, DC: Smithsonian Institution Press.
Soley, L. (1995). *Leasing the ivory tower: The corporate takeover of academia.* Boston: South End Press.
Spigel, L. (1992). *Make room for TV.* Chicago: University of Chicago Press.
Squires, J. (1993). *Read all about it: The corporate takeover of America's newspapers.* New York: Times Books.
Stallabrass, J. (1995). Empowering technology: The exploration of cyberspace. *New Left Review*, **211**, 3–32.
Stauber, J. & Rampton, S. (1995). *Toxic sludge is good for you: Lies, damn lies, and the public relations industry.* Monroe, ME: Common Courage Press.
Stille, A. (1995, August 28). Media moguls, united. *New York Times*, p. A13.
Stoll, C. (1995). *Silicon snake oil: Second thoughts on the information highway.* New York: Doubleday.
Sullivan-Trainor, M. (1994). *Detour: The truth about the information superhighway.* San Mateo, CA: IDG Books Worldwide.
Sweezy, P. (1994). The triumph of financial capital. *Monthly Review*, **46(2)**, 1–9.
Talbott, S. (1995). *The future does not compute: Transcending the machines in our midst.* Sebastopol, CA: O'Reilly.
Tanzer, M. (1995). Globalizing the economy: The influence of the International Monetary Fund and the World Bank. *Monthly Review*, **47 (4)**, 1–15.
Taylor, P. (1995, June 15). Revenues of $10bn forecast. *Financial Times*, p. IV.
Toffler, A., & Toffler, H. (1994). *Creating a new civilization: The politics of the third wave.* Atlanta: Turner Publishing.
Treese, W. (1995, June 29). The Internet index #8. Internet Post.
Underwood, D. (1993). *When MBA's rule the newsroom: How the marketers and managers are reshaping today's media.* New York: Columbia University Press.
Vipond, M. (1992). *Listening in: The first decade of Canadian broadcasting, 1922–1932.* Montreal: McGill-Queen's University Press.
Wehling, J. (1995). Netwars. *Z Magazine.* **8(7–8)**, 63–66.
Zuckerman, L. (1995, August 10). With Internet cachet, not profit, a new stock amazes Wall Street. *New York Times*, pp. Al, C5.

62

THE SECOND ENCLOSURE MOVEMENT AND THE CONSTRUCTION OF THE PUBLIC DOMAIN*

James Boyle

Source: *Law and Contemporary Problems* 66(1–2) (2003): 33–74.

> The law locks up the man or woman
> Who steals the goose from off the common
> But leaves the greater villain loose
> Who steals the common from off the goose.
>
> The law demands that we atone
> When we take things we do not own
> But leaves the lords and ladies fine
> Who take things that are yours and mine.
>
> The poor and wretched don't escape
> If they conspire the law to break;
> This must be so but they endure
> Those who conspire to make the law.
>
> The law locks up the man or woman
> Who steals the goose from off the common
> And geese will still a common lack
> Till they go and steal it back.
>
>   Anonymous

Part one: enclosure

I The first enclosure movement

This poem[1] is one of the pithiest condemnations of the English enclosure movement, the process of fencing off common land and turning it into private property.[2] In a few lines, the poem manages to criticize double standards, expose the artificial and controversial nature of property rights, and take a slap at the legitimacy of state power. And it does this all with humor, without jargon, and in rhyming couplets. Academics (including this one) should take note. Like most of the criticisms of the enclosure movement, the poem depicts a world of rapacious, state-aided "privatization," a conversion into private property of something that had formerly been common property or, perhaps, had been outside of the property system altogether. Sir Thomas More went further, though he used sheep rather than geese to make his point. He argued that enclosure was not merely unjust in itself, but harmful in its consequences—a cause of economic inequality, crime, and social dislocation:

> But yet this is not only the necessary cause of stealing. There is another, which, as I suppose, is proper and peculiar to you Englishmen alone. What is that, quoth the Cardinal? Forsooth my lord (quoth I) your sheep that were wont to be so meek and tame, and so small eaters, now, as I hear say, be become so great devourers and so wild, that they eat up, and swallow down the very men themselves. They consume, destroy, and devour whole fields, houses, and cities. For look in what parts of the realm doth grow the finest and therefore dearest wool, there noblemen and gentlemen ... leave no ground for tillage, they enclose all into pastures; they throw down houses; they pluck down towns, and leave nothing standing, but only the church to be made a sheep-house.... Therefore that one covetous and insatiable cormorant and very plague of his native country may compass about and enclose many thousand acres of ground together within one pale or hedge, the husbandmen be thrust out of their own.[3]

The enclosure movement continues to draw our attention. It offers irresistible ironies about the two-edged sword of "respect for property," and lessons about the way in which the state defines and enforces property rights to promote controversial social goals. The most strident critics of the enclosure movement argue that it imposed devastating costs on one segment of society.

> Enclosures have appropriately been called a revolution of the rich against the poor. The lords and nobles were upsetting the social

order, breaking down ancient law and custom, sometimes by means of violence, often by pressure and intimidation. They were literally robbing the poor of their share in the common, tearing down the houses which, by the hitherto unbreakable force of custom, the poor had long regarded as theirs and their heirs'. The fabric of society was being disrupted. Desolate villages and the ruins of human dwellings testified to the fierceness with which the revolution raged, endangering the defences of the country, wasting its towns, decimating its population, turning its overburdened soil into dust, harassing its people and turning them from decent husbandmen into a mob of beggars and thieves. Though this happened only in patches, the black spots threatened to melt into a uniform catastrophe.[4]

Some of these costs were brutally and relentlessly "material"—for example, the conversion of crofters and freeholders into debt-peons, seasonal wage-laborers, or simply, as More argued in *Utopia*, and Polanyi argues 400 years later, into beggars and thieves.[5] But other harms are harder to classify: the loss of a form of life; the relentless power of market logic to migrate to new areas, disrupting traditional social relationships and perhaps even views of the self or the relationship of human beings to the environment.

So much for the bad side of the enclosure movement. For many economic historians, everything I have said up to now is the worst kind of sentimental bunk, romanticizing a form of life that was neither comfortable nor noble, and certainly not very egalitarian. The big point about the enclosure movement is that it *worked*; this innovation in property systems allowed an unparalleled expansion of productive possibilities.[6] By transferring inefficiently managed common land into the hands of a single owner, enclosure escaped the aptly named "tragedy of the commons." It gave incentives for large-scale investment, allowed control over exploitation, and, in general, ensured that resources could be put to their most efficient use. Before the enclosure movement, the feudal lord would not invest in drainage systems, sheep purchases, or crop rotation that might increase yields from the common—he knew all too well that the fruits of his labor could be appropriated by others. The strong private property rights and single entity control that were introduced in the enclosure movement avoid the tragedies of overuse and underinvestment:[7] More grain will be grown, more sheep raised; consumers will benefit; and fewer people will starve in the long run. If the price of this social gain is a greater concentration of economic power, or the introduction of market forces into areas where they previously had not been so obvious, or the disruption of a *modus vivendi* with the environment—then, enclosure's defenders say, so be it. In their view, the agricultural surplus produced by enclosure helped to save a society devastated by the mass deaths of the sixteenth century. Those who weep tears about the terrible effects of private property should realize that it literally saves lives.

I am not going to concentrate on the first enclosure movement here. It is worth noting, however, that while earlier scholarship extolled enclosure's beneficial effects,[8] some more recent empirical work has indicated that it had few, if any, effects in increasing agricultural production.[9] The tragedies predicted in articles such as Hardin's *Tragedy of the Commons* did not occur.[10] In fact, the commons frequently may have been well-run, though the restraints on its depletion and the incentives for investment in it may have been "softer" than the hard-edged norms of private property.[11] Thus, while enclosure produced significant distributional changes of the kind that so incensed an earlier generation of critical historians, there are significant questions about whether it led to greater efficiency or innovation. These results are little known, however, outside of the world of economic historians. "Everyone" knows that a commons is by definition tragic, and that the logic of enclosure is as true today as it was in the fifteenth century. Private property saves lives.

II The second enclosure movement

This is all very well, but what does it have to do with intellectual property? We are in the middle of a second enclosure movement. It sounds grandiloquent to call it "the enclosure of the intangible commons of the mind," but in a very real sense that is just what it is.[12] True, the new state-created property rights may be "intellectual" rather than "real," but once again things that were formerly thought of as either common property or uncommodifiable are being covered with new, or newly extended, property rights.

Take the human genome as an example. Again, the supporters of enclosure have argued that the state was right to step in and extend the reach of property rights; that only in this way could we guarantee the kind of investment of time, ingenuity, and capital necessary to produce new drugs and gene therapies.[13] To the question, "Should there be patents over human genes?," the supporters of enclosure would answer that private property saves lives.[14] The opponents of enclosure have claimed that the human genome belongs to everyone, that it is literally the common heritage of humankind, that it should not and perhaps in some sense *cannot* be owned, and that the consequences of turning over the human genome to private property rights will be dreadful, as market logic invades areas which should be the farthest from the market. In stories about stem cell and gene sequence patents, critics have mused darkly about the way in which the state is handing over monopoly power to a few individuals and corporations, potentially introducing bottlenecks and coordination costs that slow down innovation.[15]

Alongside these accounts of the beneficiaries of the new property scheme run news stories about those who were not so fortunate, the commoners of the genetic enclosure. Law students across America read *Moore v. Regents of University of California*, a California Supreme Court case deciding that

Mr. Moore had no property interest in the cells derived from his spleen.[16] The court tells us that giving private property rights to "sources" would slow the free-wheeling practice researchers have of sharing their cell lines with all and sundry.[17] The doctors whose inventive genius created a billion-dollar cell line from Mr. Moore's "naturally occurring raw material," by contrast, are granted a patent. Private property rights here, by contrast, are a necessary incentive to research.[18] Economists on both sides of the enclosure debate concentrate on the efficient allocation of rights. Popular discussion, on the other hand, doubtless demonstrating a reprehensible lack of rigor, returns again and again to more naturalistic assumptions such as the "commonness" of the property involved or the idea that one owns one's own body.[19]

The genome is not the only area to be partially "enclosed" during this second enclosure movement. The expansion of intellectual property rights has been remarkable—from business method patents,[20] to the Digital Millennium Copyright Act,[21] to trademark antidilution rulings,[22] to the European Database Protection Directive.[23] The old limits to intellectual property rights—the anti-erosion walls around the public domain—are also under attack. The annual process of updating my syllabus for a basic Intellectual Property course provides a nice snapshot of what is going on. I can wax nostalgic looking back to a five-year-old text, with its confident list of subject matter that intellectual property rights *couldn't* cover, the privileges that circumscribed the rights that did exist, and the length of time before a work falls into the public domain. In each case, the limits have been eaten away.

To be sure, there is a danger of overstatement. The very fact that the changes have been so one-sided makes it hard to resist exaggerating their impact. In 1918, Brandeis confidently claimed that "[t]he general rule of law is, that the noblest of human productions—knowledge, truths ascertained, conceptions, and ideas—become, after voluntary communication to others, free as the air to common use."[24] That baseline—intellectual property rights are the exception rather than the norm; ideas and facts must always remain in the public domain—is still supposed to be our starting point.[25] It is, however, under attack. Both overtly and covertly, the commons of facts and ideas is being enclosed. Patents are increasingly stretched out to cover "ideas" that twenty years ago all scholars would have agreed were unpatentable.[26] Most troubling of all are the attempts to introduce intellectual property rights over mere compilations of facts.[27] If Anglo-American intellectual property law had an article of faith it was that unoriginal compilations of facts would remain in the public domain, that this protection of the raw material of science and speech was as important to the next generation of innovation as the intellectual property rights themselves.[28] The system would hand out monopolies in inventions and in original expression, while the facts below (and ideas above) would remain free for all to build upon. But this premise is being undermined. Some of the challenges are subtle: In patent law, stretched interpretations of novelty and non-obviousness allow intellectual property rights to move closer and closer to the underlying data-layer; gene sequence patents come very close to being rights over a particular discovered arrangement of data—Cs, Gs, As, and Ts.[29] Other challenges are overt: The European Database Directive does (and the various proposed bills in the United States would) create proprietary rights over compilations of facts, often without even the carefully framed exceptions of the copyright scheme, such as the usefully protean category of fair use.[30]

The older strategy of intellectual property law was a "braided" one: Thread a thin layer of intellectual property rights around a commons of material from which future creators would draw. Even that thin layer of intellectual property rights was limited to allow access to the material when the private property owner might charge too much. Fair use allows for parody, commentary and criticism, and also for "decompilation" of computer programs so that, for example, Microsoft's competitors can reverse engineer Word's features to make sure that their program can convert Word files.[31] It may sound paradoxical, but in a very real sense protection of the commons was one of the fundamental goals of intellectual property law. In the new vision of intellectual property, however, property should be extended everywhere —more is better. Expanding patentable and copyrightable subject matter, lengthening the copyright term, giving legal protection to "digital barbed wire" even if it is used in part to protect against fair use: Each of these can be understood as a vote of no-confidence in the productive powers of the commons. We seem to be shifting from Brandeis's assumption that the "noblest of human productions are free as the air to common use" to the assumption that any commons is inefficient, if not tragic.

The expansion is more than a formal one. It used to be relatively *hard* to violate an intellectual property right. The technologies of reproduction or the activities necessary to infringe were largely, though not entirely, industrial. The person with the printing press who chooses to reproduce a book is a lot different from the person who lends the book to a friend or takes a chapter into class. The photocopier makes that distinction fuzzy, and the networked computer erases it altogether. In a networked society, copying is not only easy, it is a *sine qua non* of transmission, storage, caching, and, some would claim, even reading.[32] As bioinformatics blurs the line between computer modeling and biological research, digital production techniques blur the line between listening, editing, and recreating. "Rip, mix, and burn," says the Apple advertisement. It marks a world in which the old regime of intellectual property, operating upstream as a form of industrial unfair competition policy, has been replaced. Intellectual property is now in and on the desktop and is implicated in routine creative, communicative, and just plain consumptive acts that each of us performs every day. The reach of the rights has been expanded at the same moment that their practical effect has been transformed.

III How much of the intangible commons must we enclose?

So far I have argued that there are profound similarities between the first enclosure movement and the contemporary expansion of intellectual property, which I call the second enclosure movement. Once again, the critics and proponents of enclosure are locked in battle, hurling at each other incommensurable claims about innovation, efficiency, traditional values, the boundaries of the market, the saving of lives, the loss of familiar liberties. Once again, opposition to enclosure is portrayed as economically illiterate; the beneficiaries of enclosure telling us that an expansion of property rights is needed in order to fuel progress. Indeed, the post-Cold War "Washington Consensus" is invoked to claim history teaches the only way one gets growth and efficiency is through markets; property rights, surely, are the *sine que non* of markets.[33]

But if there are similarities between our two enclosures, there are also profound dissimilarities; the networked commons of the mind has many different characteristics from the grassy commons of Old England.[34] I want to concentrate here on two key differences between the intellectual commons and the commons of the first enclosure movement: differences that should lead us to question whether this commons is truly tragic and to ask whether stronger intellectual property rights really are the solution to our problems. These differences are well known; indeed, they are the starting point for most intellectual property law. Nevertheless, reflection on them might help to explain both the problems and the stakes in the current wave of expansion.

Unlike the earthy commons, the commons of the mind is generally "non-rival." Many uses of land are mutually exclusive. If I am using the field for grazing, it may interfere with your plans to use it for growing crops. By contrast, a gene sequence, an MP3 file, or an image may be used by multiple parties; my use does not interfere with yours. To simplify a complicated analysis, this means that the threat of overuse of fields and fisheries is generally not a problem with the informational or innovational commons.[35] Thus, one type of tragedy of the commons is avoided. The concerns in the informational commons have to do with a different kind of collective action problem: the problem of incentives to create the resource in the first place. The difficulty comes because of the idea that information goods are not only non-rival (uses do not interfere with each other), they are also assumed to be non-excludable (it is impossible, or at least hard, to stop one unit of the good from satisfying an infinite number of users at zero marginal cost). Pirates will copy the song, the mousetrap, the drug formula. The rest of the argument is well known. Lacking an ability to exclude, creators will be unable to charge for their creations; there will be inadequate incentives to create. Thus, the law must step in and create a limited monopoly called an intellectual property right.

This is a well known argument, but it has recently acquired an historical dimension, a teleology of intellectual property maximalism. If the reason for intellectual property rights is the non-rival and non-excludable nature of the goods they protect, then surely the lowering of copying and transmission costs implies a corresponding need to *increase* the strength of intellectual property rights. Imagine a line. At one end sits a monk painstakingly transcribing Aristotle's *Poetics*. In the middle lies the Gutenberg printing press. Three-quarters of the way along the line is a photocopying machine. At the far end lies the Internet and the online version of the human genome. At each stage, copying costs are lowered and goods become both less rival and less excludable. My MP3 files are available to anyone in the world running Napster. Songs can be found and copied with ease. The symbolic end of rivalry comes when I am playing the song in Chapel Hill, North Carolina at the very moment that you are both downloading and listening to it in Kazakhstan—now *that's* non-rival. My point is that there seems to be an assumption that the strength of intellectual property rights must vary inversely with the cost of copying. To deal with the monk-copyist, we need no intellectual property right because physical control of the manuscript is enough. To deal with the Gutenberg press, we need the Statute of Anne.[36] To deal with the Internet, we need the Digital Millennium Copyright Act,[37] the No Electronic Theft Act,[38] the Sonny Bono Term Extension Act,[39] and perhaps even the Collections of Information Antipiracy Act.[40] As copying costs approach zero asymptotically, intellectual property rights must approach perfect control. If a greater proportion of product value and gross national product is now in the form of value-added information, then we have still another reason to need strengthened protection. A five-dollar padlock would do for a garden shed, but not for a vault.

Like any attractive but misleading argument, this one has a lot of truth. The Internet does lower the cost of copying and, thus, the cost of illicit copying. Of course, it also lowers the costs of production, distribution, and advertising, and dramatically increases the size of the potential market. Is the net result, then, a loss to rights-holders such that we need to increase protection to maintain a constant level of incentives? A large, leaky market may actually provide more revenue than a small one over which one's control is much stronger. What's more, the same technologies that allow for cheap copying also allow for swift and encyclopedic search engines—the best devices ever invented for detecting illicit copying. It would be impossible to say, on the basis of the evidence we have, that owners of protected content are better or worse off as a result of the Internet.[41] Thus, the idea that we must inevitably strengthen rights as copying costs decline doesn't hold water. And given the known static and dynamic costs of monopolies, and the constitutional injunction to encourage the progress of science and the useful arts,[42] the burden of proof should be on those requesting new rights to prove their necessity.

How about the argument that the increasing importance of information-value-added and information-intensive products to the world economy means that protection must increase? Must the information commons be enclosed because it is now a more important sector of economic activity?[43] This was certainly one of the arguments for the first enclosure movement. For example, during the Napoleonic War, enclosure was defended as a necessary method of increasing the efficiency of agricultural production, now a vital sector of a wartime economy. Here, we come to another big difference between the commons of the mind and the earthy commons. As has frequently been pointed out, information products are often made up of fragments of other information products; your information output is someone else's information input.[44] These inputs may be snippets of code, discoveries, prior research, images, genres of work, cultural references, or databases of single nucleotide polymorphisms—each is raw material for future innovation. Every potential increase of protection, however, also raises the cost of, or reduces access to, the raw material from which you might have built those products. The balance is a delicate one; one Nobel Prize-winning economist has claimed that it is actually impossible to strike that balance so as to produce an informationally efficient market.[45] Whether or not it is impossible in theory, it is surely a difficult problem in practice. In other words, even if enclosure of the arable commons always produced gains (itself a subject of debate), enclosure of the information commons clearly has the potential to harm innovation as well as to support it.[46] More property rights, even though they supposedly offer greater incentives, do not necessarily make for more and better production and innovation—sometimes just the opposite is true. It may be that intellectual property rights *slow down* innovation, by putting multiple roadblocks, multiple necessary licenses, in the way of subsequent innovation.[47] Using a nice inversion of the idea of the tragedy of the commons, Heller and Eisenberg referred to these effects—the transaction costs caused by myriad property rights over the necessary components of some subsequent innovation—as "The Tragedy of the Anticommons."[48]

IV Intellectual property and distributed creativity

My arguments so far have taken as a given the incentives/collective action problems to which intellectual property is a response. I have discussed the extent to which the logic of enclosure works for the commons of the mind as well as it did for the arable commons, taking into account the effects of an information society and a global Internet. What I have not done is asked whether a global network actually *transforms* our assumptions about creativity and innovation so as to reshape the debate about the need for incentives, at least in certain areas. This, however, is exactly the question that needs to be asked.

For anyone interested in the way that networks can enable new collaborative methods of production, the free software movement, or the broader but less vociferous movement that goes under the name of open-source software, provide interesting case studies.[49] Open-source software is released under a series of licenses, the most important being the General Public License ("GPL"). The GPL specifies that anyone may copy the software, provided the license remains attached and the source code for the software always remains available.[50] Users may add to or modify the code, may build on it and incorporate it into their own work, but if they do so, then the new program created is also covered by the GPL. Some people refer to this as the "viral" nature of the license; others find the term offensive.[51] The point, however, is that the open quality of the creative enterprise spreads. It is not simply a donation of a program or a work to the public domain, but a continual accretion in which all gain the benefits of the program on pain of agreeing to give their additions and innovations back to the communal project.

The free software and open-source software movements have produced software that rivals and, many would say, exceeds the capabilities of conventional proprietary, binary-only software.[52] Its adoption on the "enterprise level" is impressive, as is the number and enthusiasm of the various technical encomia to its strengths. The remarkable thing is not merely that the software works technically, but that it is an example of widespread, continued, high-quality innovation. The remarkable thing is that it works socially, as a continuing system, sustained only by a network consisting largely of volunteers. Here, it seems, we have a classic public good: code that can be copied freely and sold or redistributed without paying the creator or creators. This sounds like a tragedy of the commons of the kind that I described in the first section. Obviously, with a non-rival, non-excludable good like software, this method of production cannot be sustained; there are inadequate incentives to ensure continued production. *E pur si muove*, as Galileo is reputed to have said in the face of Cardinal Bellarmine's certainties, "And yet it moves."[53]

There is a broad debate on the reasons that the system works. Are the motivations those of the gift economy? Is this actually a form of potlatch, in which one gains prestige by the extravagance of the resources one "wastes?" Is open-source an implicit résumé builder that pays off in other ways? Is it driven by the species-being, the innate human love of creation that continually drives us to create new things even when *homo economicus* would be at home in bed, mumbling about public goods problems?[54]

Yochai Benkler and I would argue that these questions are fun to debate but ultimately irrelevant.[55] Assume a random distribution of incentive structures in different people, a global network: transmission, information sharing and copying costs that approach zero, and a modular creation process. With these assumptions, it just does not matter why they do it. In lots of cases, they *will* do it. One person works for love of the species, another in the hope of a better job, a third for the joy of solving puzzles, and so on. Each person has his own reserve price, the point at which he says, "Now I will turn off *Survivor* and go and create something." But on a global network, there are a *lot* of people, and with numbers that big and information overhead that small, even relatively hard projects will attract motivated and skilled people whose particular reserve price has been crossed. For the whole structure to work without large-scale centralized coordination, the creation process has to be modular, with units of different sizes and complexities, each requiring slightly different expertise, all of which can be added together to make a grand whole. I can work on the send-mail program; you on the search algorithms. More likely, *lots* of people try, their efforts are judged by the community, and the best ones are adopted. Under these conditions, this curious mix of Kropotkin and Adam Smith, Richard Dawkins and Richard Stallman, we *will* get distributed production without having to rely on the proprietary/exclusion model. The whole enterprise will be much, much, much greater than the sum of the parts.

What's more, and this is a truly fascinating twist, when the production process does need more centralized coordination, some governance that guides how the sticky modular bits are put together, it is at least theoretically possible that we can come up with the control system *in exactly the same way*. In this sense, distributed production is potentially recursive. Governance processes, too, can be assembled through distributed methods on a global network, by people with widely varying motivations, skills, and reserve prices.[56]

But in the language of computer programmers, does it "scale?" Can we generalize anything from this limited example? How many types of production, innovation, and research fit into the model I have just described? After all, for most innovations and inventions one needs hardware, capital investment, and large-scale real-world data collection—*stuff*, in its infinite recalcitrance and facticity. Maybe the open-source model has solved the individual incentives problem, but that's not the *only* problem. And how many types of innovation or cultural production are as modular as software? Is open-source software a paradigm case of collective innovation that helps us to understand open-source software and not much else?

Again, I think this is a good question, but it may be the wrong one. My own guess is that an open-source method of production is far more common than we realize. "Even before the Internet" (as some of my students have taken to saying portentously), science, law, education, and musical genres all developed in ways that are markedly similar to the model I have described. The marketplace of ideas, the continuous roiling development in thought and norm that our political culture spawns, is itself an idea that owes much more to the distributed, non-proprietary model than it does to the special case of commodified innovation that we think about in copyright and patent. Not that copyright and patent are unimportant in the process, but they may well be the exception rather than the norm. Commons-based production of ideas is hardly unfamiliar, after all.

In fact, all the mottoes of free software development have their counterparts in the theory of democracy and open society; "with enough eyeballs, all bugs are shallow" is merely the most obvious example. Karl Popper would have cheered.[57] The importance of open-source software is not that it introduces us to a wholly new idea; it is that it makes us see clearly a very old idea. With open source the technology was novel, the production process was transparent, and the result of that process was a "product" which out-competed other products in the marketplace. "How can this have happened? What about the tragedy of the commons?" we asked in puzzlement, coming only slowly to the realization that other examples of commons-based, non-proprietary production were all around us.

Still, this does not answer the question of whether the model can scale further. To answer that question we would need to think more about the modularity of other types of inventions—can they be broken down into chunks suitable for distribution among a widespread community? Which forms of innovation have some irreducible need for high capital investment in distinctly non-virtual components—a particle accelerator or a Phase III drug trial? Again, my guess is that the increasing migration of the sciences towards data- and processing-rich models makes more innovations and discoveries potential candidates for the distributed model. Bio-informatics and computational biology, the open-source genomics project,[58] the possibility of distributed data scrutiny by lay volunteers[59]—all of these offer intriguing glances into the potential for the future. Finally, of course, the Internet is one big experiment in, as Benkler puts it, peer-to-peer cultural production.[60]

If these questions are good ones, why are they also the wrong ones? I have given my guesses about the future of the distributed model of innovation; my own utopia has it flourishing alongside a scaled-down, but still powerful, intellectual property regime. Equally plausible scenarios see it as a dead end, or as the inevitable victor in the war of productive processes. These are all guesses, however. At the very least, there is some possibility, even hope, that we could have a world in which much more of intellectual and inventive production is free. "'Free' as in 'free speech,'" Richard Stallman says, not "'free' as in 'free beer.'"[61] But we could hope that much of it would be *both* free of centralized control *and* low cost or no cost. When the marginal cost of production is zero, the marginal cost of transmission and storage approaches zero, the process of creation is additive, and much of the labor doesn't charge—well, the world looks a little different.[62] This is at least a *possible* future, or part of a possible future, and one that we should not foreclose without thinking twice. Yet that is what we are doing. The Database Protection Bills and Directives, which extend intellectual property rights to the layer of facts;[63] the efflorescence of software patents;[64] the

UCITA-led validation of shrinkwrap licenses that bind third parties;[65] the Digital Millennium Copyright Act's anti-circumvention provisions[66]—the point of all of these developments is not merely that they make the peer-to-peer model difficult, but that in many cases they rule it out altogether. I will assert this point here, rather than argue for it, but I think it can be (and has been) demonstrated quite convincingly.[67]

The point is, then, that there is a chance that a new (or old, but under-recognized) method of production could flourish in ways that seem truly valuable—valuable to free speech, innovation, scientific discovery, the wallets of consumers, what William Fisher calls "semiotic democracy,"[68] and perhaps, valuable to the balance between joyful creation and drudgery for hire. True, it is only a chance. True, this theory's ambit of operation and its sustainability are uncertain. But why would we want to foreclose it? That is what the recent expansions of intellectual property threaten to do. And remember, these expansions were dubious even in a world where we saw little or no possibility of the distributed production model I have described, where discussion of network effects had yet to reach the pages of the *New Yorker*,[69] and where our concerns about the excesses of intellectual property were simply the ones that Jefferson, Madison, and Macaulay gave us so long ago.

V Beyond enclosure?

Thus, we have come full circle. Is this the second enclosure movement? As I have tried to show, in many ways it is. The opponents and proponents of enclosure remain locked in battle, each appealing to conflicting and sometimes incommensurable claims about efficiency, innovation, justice, and the limits of the market. But *should it be* the second enclosure movement? Do we know that property rights in this sphere will yield the same surge of productive energy that is claimed for the enclosure of arable land?[70] There, I think the answer is a resounding "No." We rush to enclose ever-larger stretches of the commons of the mind without convincing economic evidence that it will help our processes of innovation and with very good reason to believe it will actually hurt them.[71] As I have argued elsewhere, this second enclosure movement should bother people across the ideological spectrum, from civil libertarians to free marketeers; the world of the arts and sciences should be particularly interested in the process. The American system of science, for all its flaws, has worked astoundingly well. Changing some of its fundamental premises, such as by moving property rights into the data layer, is something not to be done lightly.

The dangers are particularly important at the moment for three reasons. First, propertization is a vicious circle. The argument is a little complex to lay out here,[72] but in essence the position is this: Once a new intellectual property right has been created over some informational good, the only way to ensure efficient allocation of that good is to give the rights holder still greater control over the user or consumer in the aftermarket so as to allow for price discrimination, since the only efficient monopoly is a monopoly with perfect price discrimination.[73] Yet, to achieve perfect price discrimination with digital intellectual property goods, whose marginal cost is zero, the rights holders will argue that they need even *more* changes of the rules in their favor: relaxed privacy standards so they can know more about our price points; enforceable shrink-wrap or clickwrap contracts of adhesion so that we can be held to the terms of our particular license, no matter how restrictive; and changes in antitrust rules to allow for a variety of practices that are currently illegal, such as resale price maintenance and various forms of tying. Rights holders will also claim that they need technical changes with legal backing, such as the creation of personalized digital objects surrounded by state-backed digital fences, objects that are tied to particular users and particular computers, so that reading my e-book on your machine is either technically impossible, a crime, or a tort—or possibly all three. The point of all this is that it is a slope that is much easier to go down than to come up. Thus, we ought to think clearly about the consequences of the decisions now being made in such a rush.

Second, in order to create the conditions for the kinds of price discrimination described above, the characteristics of the Internet that make it so attractive to civil libertarians—its distributed, anonymous character, its resistance to control or filtering by public or private entities, and its global nature—start to seem like bugs rather than features. The process of trying to make the Net safe for the price discrimination project has already begun; this, as Larry Lessig teaches us, is a fundamental public choice that ought to be made deliberately and openly, not brought about imperceptibly as a side-effect of an economically dubious digital enclosure movement.[74] Because of threats such as terrorism, we might choose to live in a pervasively monitored electronic environment in which identity, geography, and thus regulability, have been reintroduced, though in my own view the price would not be worth paying. But to do so on the basis of some bad microeconomic arguments about the needs of the entertainment industry, in the absence of good empirical evidence, and to foreclose some of the most interesting new productive possibilities in the process? Well, that would be really sad.

Third, the arguments in favor of the new enclosure movement depend heavily on the intellectually complacent, analytically unsound assumptions of the "neo-liberal orthodoxy," the "Washington Consensus."[75] The world of the Washington Consensus is divided into two parts. In one, growing smaller by the minute, are those portions of the economy where the government plays a major regulatory role. The job of neo-liberal economic thought is to push us toward the privatization of the few areas that remain; after all, we know that "state intervention in the economy" is a recipe for disaster. The second area of the Washington Consensus is an altogether happier place.

This is the realm of well-functioning free markets, where the state does not regulate, subsidize, or franchise, but instead defines and protects property rights. While unintended consequences are rife in the world of government regulation, no such dangers should be feared if the government is simply handing over a patent on gene sequences or stem cell lines, or creating a property right over compilations of facts. Property is good, and more property is better.[76] It would be ironic, to say the least, to maintain this view in the *information* commons, the one area where the delicate balance of the property system should be clearest and the political choices involved most obvious. It is doubly ironic to do so at a time when there are examples of modes of distributed production that stretch our sense of the economically possible, and that upset our complacency about the limited ways in which innovation and production can be managed.

But what is the alternative to the second enclosure movement? It is one thing to say, as I do, that we need more and better empirical information, and that our intellectual property system should be audited like any other government subsidy to make sure that we are getting what we pay for, and not paying too much for what we get. But the process I have described here is not entirely rational. In some cases, it is driven by industry capture of the levers of state power; in others, by a variety of alluring beliefs that dominate thought on the subject. The logic of enclosure ("Property saves lives! More incentives mean more production!") is the one I have concentrated on here. In other works, I have explored the impact of the ideal of original creation, creation *ex nihilo*, on our assumptions about the need to protect the public domain.[77] Who needs a public domain if you can create out of nothing? The point of this essay is that it is not enough merely to offer criticisms of the logic of enclosure. What is needed is deeper. We need a change in the way that these issues are understood, a change that transforms even our perceptions of self-interest, making possible coalitions where none existed before.

***

In the second half of this article, I try to develop the vocabulary and the analytic tools necessary to turn the tide of enclosure. I offer an historical sketch of various types of skepticism about intellectual property, from the antimonopolist criticisms of the Framers of the U.S. Constitution, through the emergence of affirmative arguments for the public domain, to the use of the language of the commons to defend the possibility of distributed methods of non-proprietary production. In many ways, it turns out, concepts of the public domain show the same variation in assumptions, and the same analytic differences, as the concept of property itself. I conclude by arguing that, for a number of reasons, the appropriate model for the change in thinking which I argue for comes from the history of the environmental movement. The invention of the concept of "the environment" pulls together a string of otherwise disconnected issues, offers analytical insight into the blindness implicit in prior ways of thinking, and leads to perception of common interest where none was seen before. Like the environment, the public domain must be "invented" before it is saved. Like the environment, like "nature," the public domain turns out to be a concept that is considerably more slippery than many of us realize. And, like the environment, the public domain nevertheless turns out to be useful, perhaps even necessary.

Part two: against enclosure

VI Anti-monopoly and a tax on reading

Intellectual property has always had its critics—brilliant ones, at that, whose writing puts contemporary academics to shame.[78] Thomas Jefferson leads off the list for American audiences. Writers from justices of the Supreme Court of the United States to John Perry Barlow quote Jefferson's 1813 letter to Isaac McPherson:

> If nature has made any one thing less susceptible than all others of exclusive property, it is the action of the thinking power called an idea, which an individual may exclusively possess as long as he keeps it to himself; but the moment it is divulged, it forces itself into the possession of every one, and the receiver cannot dispossess himself of it. Its peculiar character, too, is that no one possesses the less, because every other possesses the whole of it. He who receives an idea from me, receives instruction himself without lessening mine; as he who lights his taper at mine, receives light without darkening me. That ideas should freely spread from one to another over the globe, for the moral and mutual instruction of man, and improvement of his condition, seems to have been peculiarly and benevolently designed by nature, when she made them, like fire, expansible over all space, without lessening their density in any point, and like the air in which we breathe, move, and have our physical being, incapable of confinement or exclusive appropriation. Inventions then cannot, in nature, be a subject of property.[79]

Those who quote the passage sometimes stop here, which is a shame, because it leaves the impression that Jefferson was unequivocally against intellectual property rights. But that would be an overstatement. When Jefferson said that invention can never be a subject of property, he meant a permanent and exclusive property right which, as a matter of natural right, no just government could abridge. "Stable ownership is the gift of social law, and is given late in the progress of society. It would be curious then, if an idea, the fugitive fermentation of an individual brain, could, of natural right, be claimed in exclusive and stable property."[80] This did not mean, however, that inventions could not be covered by temporary state-created monopolies, instituted for the common good. In the lines immediately following the popularly quoted excerpt, Jefferson goes on:

> Society may give an exclusive right to the profits arising from [inventions], as an encouragement to men to pursue ideas which may produce utility, but this may or may not be done, according to the will and convenience of the society, without claim or complaint from any body. Accordingly, it is a fact, as far as I am informed, that England was, until we copied her, the only country on earth which ever, by a general law, gave a legal right to the exclusive use of an idea. In some other countries it is sometimes done, in a great case, and by a special and personal act, but, generally speaking, other nations have thought that these monopolies produce more embarrassment than advantage to society; and it may be observed that the nations which refuse monopolies of invention, are as fruitful as England in new and useful devices.[81]

Jefferson's message was a skeptical recognition that intellectual property rights *might* be necessary, a careful explanation that they should not be treated as natural rights, and a warning of the monopolistic dangers that they pose. This message was famously echoed thirty years later in Britain by Thomas Babington Macaulay. Macaulay's speeches to the British Parliament in 1841 on the subject of copyright term extension still express better than anything else the position that intellectual property rights are necessary evils which must be carefully circumscribed by law. In order for the supply of valuable books to be maintained, authors "must be remunerated for their literary labor. And there are only two ways in which they can be remunerated. One of those ways is patronage; the other is copyright."[82] Patronage is rejected out of hand:

> I can conceive no system more fatal to the integrity and independence of literary men than one under which they should be taught to look for their daily bread to the favour of ministers and nobles. . . . We have, then, only one resource left. We must betake ourselves to copyright, be the inconveniences of copyright what they may. Those inconveniences, in truth, are neither few nor small. Copyright is monopoly, and produces all the effects which the general voice of mankind attributes to monopoly. My honourable and learned friend talks very contemptuously of those who are led away by the theory that monopoly makes things dear. That monopoly makes things dear is certainly a theory, as all the great truths which have been established by the experience of all ages and nations, and which are

taken for granted in all reasonings, may be said to be theories. It is a theory in the same sense in which it is a theory that day and night follow each other, that lead is heavier than water, that bread nourishes, that arsenic poisons, that alcohol intoxicates. If, as my honourable and learned friend seems to think, the whole world is in the wrong on this point, if the real effect of monopoly is to make articles good and cheap, why does he stop short in his career of change? Why does he limit the operation of so salutary a principle to sixty years? Why does he consent to anything short of a perpetuity? He told us that in consenting to anything short of a perpetuity he was making a compromise between extreme right and expediency. But if his opinion about monopoly be correct, extreme right and expediency would coincide. Or rather, why should we not restore the monopoly of the East India trade to the East India Company? Why should we not revive all those old monopolies which, in Elizabeth's reign, galled our fathers so severely that, maddened by intolerable wrong, they opposed to their sovereign a resistance before which her haughty spirit quailed for the first and for the last time? Was it the cheapness and excellence of commodities that then so violently stirred the indignation of the English people? I believe, Sir, that I may with safety take it for granted that the effect of monopoly generally is to make articles scarce, to make them dear, and to make them bad. And I may with equal safety challenge my honourable friend to find out any distinction between copyright and other privileges of the same kind; any reason why a monopoly of books should produce an effect directly the reverse of that which was produced by the East India Company's monopoly of tea, or by Lord Essex's monopoly of sweet wines. Thus, then, stands the case. It is good that authors should be remunerated; and the least exceptionable way of remunerating them is by a monopoly. Yet monopoly is an evil. For the sake of the good we must submit to the evil; but the evil ought not to last a day longer than is necessary for the purpose of securing the good.[83]

These words from Jefferson and Macaulay encapsulate an eighteenth and nineteenth century free-trade skepticism about intellectual property. Jefferson himself believed that the Constitution should have definite limits on both the term and the scope of intellectual property rights[84] and spoke of the difficulty of "drawing a line between the things which are worth to the public the embarrassment of an exclusive patent, and those which are not."[85] Madison, too, stressed the costs of any intellectual property right and the need to limit its term,[86] as did Adam Smith.[87] Their key concern was an antimonopolistic one, though we should remember that for these men the concept of monopoly was a much richer one than the impoverished neo-classical economic concept we employ today. For them, monopoly involved not simply economic loss, though they certainly cared about that, but also the tendencies towards "corruption" that monopolies introduced. This corruption included the harm to the fabric of the republic caused by great concentrations of wealth and power as well as the perverse incentives given to the beneficiaries of state-granted monopolies to spend resources suborning the legislature on which their monopoly rent depended. Today, we call those incentives "campaign finance," "the participation of stakeholders in the legislative process," or just "business as usual."

The intellectual property skeptics had other concerns. Macaulay was particularly worried about the *power* that went with a transferable and inheritable monopoly.[88] It is not only that the effect of monopoly is "to make articles scarce, to make them dear, and to make them bad."[89] Macaulay also pointed out that those who controlled the monopoly, particularly after the death of the original author, might be given too great a control over our collective culture. Censorious heirs or purchasers of the copyright might prevent the reprinting of a great work because they disagreed with its morals.[90] From more recent examples, we can also see that heirs may keep policing the boundaries of the work, attempting to prevent parody or tarnishment, long after the original author is dead. One wonders what Macaulay would have thought about the attempt by Margaret Mitchell's estate to prevent the publication of *The Wind Done Gone*.[91]

There were certainly other concerns raised about intellectual property in the eighteenth and nineteenth centuries. For example, while Macaulay is the best remembered critic of copyright in the debates of the 1840s, there were other more radical opponents who saw copyright primarily as a "tax on literacy," identical in its effect to the newspaper stamp taxes.[92] At a time when mass literacy and mass education were the hotly debated corollaries to the enlargement of the franchise, reformers looked with hostility on anything that seemed likely to raise the cost of reading and thus continue to restrict political and social debate to the wealthier classes.[93]

Patent law, too, attracted its share of attacks in the mid-nineteenth century. A fusillade of criticism, often delivered by economists and cast in the language of free trade, portrayed the patent system as actively harmful.

> At the annual meeting of the Kongress deutscher Volkswirthe held in Dresden, September 1863, the following resolution was adopted "by an overwhelming majority:" "Considering that patents hinder rather than further the progress of invention; that they hamper the prompt general utilisation of useful inventions; that on balance they cause more harm than benefit to the inventors themselves and, thus, are a highly deceptive form of compensation; the Congress of German Economists resolves: that patents of invention are injurious to common welfare."[94]

In the Netherlands, the patent system was actually abolished in 1869 as a result of such criticisms.[95] Observers in a number of other countries, including Britain, concluded that their national patent systems were doomed.[96] Various proposals were made to replace patent, with state-provided prizes or bounties to particularly useful inventions being the most popular.[97]

These snippets are hardly sufficient to constitute any kind of a survey of critical reactions to intellectual property systems, but I believe that nevertheless they give a relatively fair sense of the debate. Three points could be made.

First, from the early days of intellectual property as we now know it, the main objections raised against it were framed in the language of free trade and anti-monopoly. In the United States, the founding generation of intellectuals had been nurtured on the philosophy of the Scottish Enlightenment and the history of the struggle against royal monopolies. They were not immune to the arguments in favor of intellectual property, but they repeatedly warned of the need to circumscribe both its term and its scope. What were their concerns? They worried about intellectual property producing artificial scarcity, high prices, and low quality. They worried about its justice; given that we all learn from and build on the past, do we have a right to carve out our own incremental innovations and protect them by intellectual property rights?[98] Price aside, they also worried that intellectual property (especially with a lengthy term) might give too much control to a single individual or corporation over some vital aspect of science and culture. In more muted fashion, they discussed the possible effects that intellectual property might have on future innovation. But the overwhelming theme was the promotion of free trade and a corresponding opposition to monopolies.

Second, it is important to look at the structure of these comments by Jefferson, Macaulay, and others; they are framed as criticisms of intellectual property rather than defenses of the public domain or the commons, terms that appear rarely, if at all, in the debates. There is no real discussion of the world *outside* of intellectual property, its opposite, whether in conceptual or economic terms.

Third, a linked point: Most of these critics take as their goal the prevention or limitation of an "artificial" monopoly. Without this monopoly, our goal is to have a world of . . . what? The assumption is that we will return to a norm of freedom, but of what kind? Free trade in expression and innovation, as opposed to monopoly? Free access to innovation and expression, as opposed to access for pay? Or free access to innovation and expression in the sense of not being subject to the right of another person to pick and choose who is given access, even if all have to pay some flat fee? Or is it common ownership and control that we seek, including the communal right to forbid certain kinds of uses of the shared resource? The eighteenth and nineteenth century critics brushed over these points, but to be fair, we continue to do so today.

VII Recognizing the public domain

In the last section, I discussed the anti-monopolist criticisms of intellectual property law, criticisms that were heard from the beginning of intellectual property in its modern form and which continue to the present day. At what point does the negative account of the ills of intellectual property turn into, or get added to, a defense of something called "the public domain?"

By a defense of the public domain, I do not mean mere usage of the word. Though "public domain" was a term widely used to describe public lands in the United States, the intellectual property usage of the term comes to us from the French *domaine public* which made its way into American law in the late nineteenth century via the language of the Berne Convention.[99] But at what point do we find a defense of the public domain, rather than merely a criticism of the costs of intellectual property?

Many different starting points are defensible. In the United States, the work of Ralph Brown and Ben Kaplan is sometimes mentioned as initiating this way of looking at things.[100] The Supreme Court itself can plausibly be given some credit.[101] In a 1966 patent case, repeatedly citing the work of Jefferson, the Court made it clear that the public domain has a constitutional dimension:

> The Congress in the exercise of the patent power may not overreach the restraints imposed by the stated constitutional purpose. Nor may it enlarge the patent monopoly without regard to the innovation, advancement or social benefit gained thereby. Moreover, Congress may not authorize the issuance of patents whose effects are to remove existent knowledge from the public domain, or to restrict free access to materials already available.[102]

This is a remarkable statement. It goes beyond a mere recitation of the Framers' attitude toward the dangers posed by monopoly, and makes an affirmative defense of the public domain. Notice how the limitations are stated as additive and not as mutually equivalent, or even as mere corollaries; the Court does not say that "the enlargement of the patent monopoly must promote innovation and *this limits* Congress's power to remove material from the public domain." Instead, it postulates an existent public domain and makes it unconstitutional under the patent clause for Congress to privatize any portion of that domain. There are echoes here of the "public trust doctrine," which restricts the state's ability to privatize public resources or waterways and turn them over to private parties.[103] Notice also that the Court gives the public domain both direct and indirect protection: Protection from measures which formally create patent rights over portions of the public domain, but also from those which merely "restrict free access to materials already available."[104]

Thus, there are a number of possible places where one could say, "the defense of the public domain begins here." But, like most people, I attribute central importance to the writing of my friend and colleague David Lange, whose article *Recognizing the Public Domain* really initiated contemporary study of the subject.[105] Lange's article was driven by indignation about, indeed eloquently sarcastic ridicule of, expansions of intellectual property protection in the 1960s and 1970s.[106] Lange claims that one major cause of this expansion was that intellectual property rights are intangible, abstract, and thus, imprecise.[107] He argues, in a way that would have been familiar to Macaulay or Jefferson, that we should cease the reckless expansion.[108] But he also argues that "recognition of new intellectual property interests should be offset today by equally deliberate recognition of individual rights in the public domain."[109]

Lange is not arguing:

> that intellectual property is undeserving of protection, but rather that such protection as it gets ought to reflect its unique susceptibility to conceptual imprecision and to infinite replication. These attributes seem to me to require the recognition of two fundamental principles. One is that intellectual property theory must always accept something akin to a "no-man's land" at the boundaries; doubtful cases of infringement ought always to be resolved in favor of the defendant. The other is that no exclusive interest should ever have affirmative recognition unless its conceptual opposite is also recognized. Each right ought to be marked off clearly against the public domain.[110]

But what does this *mean*? What is the nature of these "individual rights in the public domain?" Who holds them? Indeed, what *is* the public domain? Does it consist only of works that are completely unprotected, say books whose copyright term has lapsed? Does it include *aspects* of works that are unprotectable, such as the ideas or the facts on which an argument is based, even if the expression of that argument is protected? What about limitations on exclusive rights, privileges of users, or affirmative defenses—are those part of the public domain too? Is the parody-able aspect of your novel in the public domain? What about the short quote on which a critical argument is mounted? Earlier in this article, I discussed the "commons of the mind."[111] What is the relationship between the public domain—however defined—and the commons?[112] If the public domain is so great, why? What does it do for us? What is its role? These questions can be reduced to two: (1) What is the public domain?, and (2) Why should we focus on it? In the following pages, I will argue that the answer to the first question depends on the answer to the second.

Work that followed Lange's article offered various answers to the questions he had posed. For example, Lindberg and Patterson's book *The Nature of Copyright* reverses the polarity from the normal depiction, and portrays copyright as a law of users' rights.[113] The public domain is the figure and copyright the ground. The various privileges and defenses are not exceptions, they are at the heart of copyright, correctly understood. Copyright is, in fact, a system designed to feed the public domain providing temporary and narrowly limited rights, themselves subject to considerable restrictions even during their existence—all with the ultimate goal of promoting free access.

Jessica Litman's fine 1990 article, *The Public Domain*, portrays the public domain's primary function as allowing copyright law to continue to work notwithstanding the unrealistic, individualistic idea of creativity it depends on:

> The public domain rescues us from this dilemma. It permits us to continue to exalt originality without acknowledging that our claims to take originality seriously are mostly pretense. It furnishes a crucial device to an otherwise unworkable system by reserving the raw material of authorship to the commons, thus leaving that raw material available for other authors to use. The public domain thus permits the law of copyright to avoid a confrontation with the poverty of some of the assumptions on which it is based.[114]

Litman's definition of the public domain is both clear and terse: "[A] commons that includes those aspects of copyrighted works which copyright does not protect."[115] Precisely because she sees the function of the public domain as allowing the kinds of additive and interstitial creation that the language of individual originality fails to capture, her *definition* of the public domain includes the recyclable, unprotected elements in existing copyrighted works as well as those works that are not protected at all. Form follows function.

Yochai Benkler takes a slightly different approach. He follows Litman in rejecting the traditional, absolutist conception of the public domain, a conception which included only those things that are totally unprotected by copyright:

> The particular weakness of the traditional definition of the public domain is that it evokes an intuition about the baseline, while not in fact completely describing it. When one calls certain information "in the public domain," one means that it is information whose use, absent special reasons to think otherwise, is permissible to anyone. When information is properly subject to copyright, the assumption (again absent specific facts to the contrary) is that its use is not similarly allowed to anyone but the owner and his or her licensees. The limited, term-of-art "public domain" does not include some important instances that, as a descriptive matter, are assumed

> generally to be permissible. For example, the traditional definition of public domain would treat short quotes for purposes of critical review as a fair use—hence as an affirmative defense—and not as a use in the public domain. It would be odd, however, to describe our system of copyright law as one in which users assume that they may not include a brief quotation in a critical review of its source. I venture that the opposite is true: Such use generally is considered permissible, absent peculiar facts to the contrary.[116]

Benkler's alternative definition, however, does not include every privileged use—such as, for example, the fair use privilege that I am able to vindicate only after litigating an intensely complicated case that involves highly specific factual inquiries.

> The functional definition therefore would be: The public domain is the range of uses of information that any person is privileged to make absent individualized facts that make a particular use by a particular person unprivileged. Conversely, [t]he enclosed domain is the range of uses of information as to which someone has an exclusive right, and that no other person may make absent individualized facts that indicate permission from the holder of the right, or otherwise privilege the specific use under the stated facts. These definitions add to the legal rules traditionally thought of as the public domain, the range of privileged uses that are "easy cases."[117]

The key to Benkler's analysis is his focus on the public domain's role in information production and use by all of us in our roles as consumers, citizens, and future creators. We need to focus on those works, and aspects of works, that the public can know to be free without having to go through a highly individualized factual inquiry. "Free" meaning what? Earlier in this essay, I asked what we mean when we speak of the freedom that the public domain will allow.[118] Free trade in expression and innovation, as opposed to monopoly? Free access to expression and innovation, as opposed to access for pay? Or free access to innovation and expression, in the sense of not being subject to the right of another person to pick and choose who is given access, even if all have to pay some flat fee? Or is it common ownership and control that we seek, including the communal right to forbid certain kinds of uses of the shared resources? I *think* that Benkler is arguing that the most important question here is whether lay people would know that a particular piece or aspect of information is free—in the sense of being *both* uncontrolled by anyone else and costless.

The test case is simple to imagine: Do we count as part of the public domain songs that can be "covered" by subsequent artists upon payment of a defined fee under a compulsory license? To put it in the language of legal theory, is content that is covered only by "liability rules"[119] actually part of the public domain? Well, of course that depends on why we care about the public domain, on what vision of freedom or creativity we think the public domain stands for, and what danger it protects against. The public domain will change its shape according to the hopes it embodies, the fears it tries to lay to rest, and the implicit vision of creativity on which it rests. There is not one public domain, but many.

What is true for the public domain turns out to be true also for the third and final language that seeks to circumscribe and offer limits to the enclosure movement: the language of the commons. The "commons" is a term that has come to be used increasingly often over the last five years to refer to wellsprings of creation that are outside of, or different from, the world of intellectual property. The Internet was seen as such a commons. The Internet expanded so rapidly precisely because its core protocols, TCP/IP and HTML, are open; like languages, these systems allowed all to create by offering a common framework owned by no one. And that insight, coupled with the positive images of communal production that the Net offered and the negative images of network-effect leveraged monopolies that the Net also offered galvanized a related but different type of interest in "the outside of property." It is to the commons that I will now turn.

VIII Discovering the e-commons

Let us start with Larry Lessig's definition of a commons:

> It is commonplace to think about the Internet as a kind of commons. It is less commonplace to actually have an idea what a commons is. By a commons I mean a resource that is free. *Not necessarily zero cost, but if there is a cost, it is a neutrally imposed, or equally imposed cost.* Central Park is a commons: an extraordinary resource of peacefulness in the center of a city that is anything but; an escape and refuge, that anyone can take and use without the permission of anyone else. The public streets are a commons: on no one's schedule but your own, you enter the public streets, and go any direction you wish. You can turn off of Broadway onto Fifty-second Street at any time, without a certificate or authorization from the government. Fermat's last theorem is a commons: a challenge that anyone could pick up; and complete, as Andrew Wiles, after a lifetime of struggle, did. Open source, or free software, is a commons: the source code of Linux, for example, lies available for anyone to take, to use, to improve, to advance. No permission is necessary; no authorization may be required. These are commons because they are within the reach of members of the relevant community without the permission of anyone else. They are resources

that are protected by a liability rule rather than a property rule. Professor Reichman, for example, has suggested that some innovation be protected by a liability rule rather than a property rule. The point is not that no control is present; but rather that the kind of control is different from the control we grant to property.[120]

Note the difference in focus between Lessig and Benkler. If our concern is monopolistic control over choke-points imposed by the will of others, freedom from others "telling us what we can do," then the norm of freedom we will seek to instantiate in property's outside, whether we describe it as a public domain or a commons, is a norm of non-discriminatory access. Freedom in one powerful liberal tradition means freedom *from the will of another*, not freedom from the background constraints of the economic system.[121] Why pick this vision of freedom instead of the vision provided by Benkler's account of the public domain—content that is literally "free," both free from exclusive rights, and available at zero cost?[122] There are lots of reasons. In the world of "network effects," an intellectual property right over a widely used standard or network protocol can give an unprecedented amount of power to the rightholder; the power might even include the ability to leverage one's rights to stifle innovation that threatens one's business. The Microsoft case is an obvious example.[123] The complaint against the Microsofts of the world is not so much that they keep their prices high—though that is sometimes alleged. Instead it is the claim that their intellectual property rights over fundamental standards with strong positive network effects give them too much power to control the course of innovation.

As the dysfunctional side of property/monopoly comes to be seen as a restraint on innovation rather than a problem of price gouging, correspondingly, property's outside—"not property"—shifts its core characteristics. If one's main concern is maintaining innovation, one might think that the danger of monopoly here is not higher prices, but rather the power of control itself; access to the intellectual property in question on payment of a flat fee might seem to avoid those dangers and to allow for free competition in follow-on innovation. The world of monopoly and property comes to be seen as a world of restraint on innovation, more than a world of restricted output and high prices. In technical terms, an imagined commons of pure Hohfeldian privileges gives way to a commons partly constituted of resources protected by liability rules.[124] The "opposite of property" comes to be defined as "that which will cure monopoly control of standards with strong network effects" rather than that which is not owned, or is owned by all. In describing the possibility of open standards with which all can work, the language of the commons apparently resonates better than the language of the public domain.

But I suspect that there is a second reason for the way in which "commons" and "public domain" now jockey for position as the instantiation of intellectual property's "outside." Although we present our reasoning on these matters in neat chains of apparently logical argument, our doing so conceals the power of "the paradigm case,"[125] the core example, or irresistible counter-example, in shaping our ideas.

As I argued in the first part of this essay, most recent theorists of the public domain start with the irresistible example of the free and open-source software movements before their eyes.[126] Here was a real-world spur to rethink the public goods problem, the tragedy of the commons, on which the economic rationale for intellectual property rights was based. Here was a "comedy of the commons."[127] To be sure, the claim was not that open-source or free software would provide a model that rendered all intellectual property unnecessary. There would still be an enclosed domain; the open source model would not work everywhere.[128] *But now, the placement of the line between the two domains was everywhere up for grabs.* This is a point that cannot be stressed enough. There was one small problem, however. Though open-source software is of particular interest to those concerned about the worldwide expansion of intellectual property rights, it is by no means clear how it fits into the binary opposition between intellectual property on the one hand and the public domain on the other.

Though journalists frequently and mistakenly claim otherwise, neither "free software," nor most "open-source software" is in the public domain. After all, the thing that makes open-source software work is the General Public License.[129] All the things that seem so interesting about open-source —its model of distributed production, the way it grows, binding future innovators who make use of it to add to the store themselves—are built on this license.[130] That license, in turn, rests on an intellectual property right, the copyrights held by the Free Software Foundation and other entities.[131] The GPL says, in effect: Here is this copyrighted body of work; you may use it, add to it, modify it, or copy it—all of these uses are legal, but *only* if you comply with the terms of the GPL. Otherwise, your actions are infringements of the exclusive rights conferred by section 106 of the Copyright Act.[132] If, for example, you take the Linux kernel, fiddle with it, add your own material, and attempt to sell the result as proprietary, binary-only software, you have violated the GPL license which gives you permission to reproduce this copyrighted material in the first place. In legal terms, at least, the free software movement stands squarely on intellectual property.

Given that free software stands as the kind of "irresistible example" around which theories tend to form, how is it to be assimilated into the older criticisms of intellectual property and defenses of the public domain? The free software movement, at least, was formed explicitly around criticisms of the effects of intellectual property that would have been familiar to Jefferson and Macaulay.[133] The answer to the perceived negative effects of strong intellectual property rights on innovation and freedom, however, was not to write a lot of code and release it unprotected by copyright. Instead, the

331

free software movement attempted to build a living ecology of open code, where the price for admission was your commitment to make your own incremental innovation part of the ecology.[134] On the one hand, this fit poorly into the old model of the "total freedom" public domain; there were, after all, significant restraints on use of the software, restraints that were vital to the project. On the other hand, however, it fit very well into a new literature on governing the commons from Elinor Ostrom, Robert Keohane, Margaret McKean, and many others.[135] This literature was able to show that not every commons was a tragedy. But the literature also showed that successful commons were not *entirely* "free"—they ran on layers of norms that were frequently invisible to the legal system, but which nevertheless served to avoid the various paradoxes of collective action. Whether the examples were Japanese herdsmen or Silicon Valley programmers, the literature seeks to show just how the commons was, and should be, governed.[136]

Notice the differences in approach. The old dividing line in the literature on the public domain had been between the realm of property and the realm of the free.[137] The new dividing line, drawn on the palimpsest of the old, is between the realm of individual control and the realm of distributed creation, management, and enterprise. To be sure, the two projects share a great deal, but they are also different in important ways. To put it bluntly, some of the theorists of the e-commons do not see restraints on use as anathematic to the goal of freedom; indeed, they may see the successful commons as defined by its restraints.[138] Those restraints may be legal—Lessig's liability rules—or they may be built on community norms and prestige networks of various kinds. The point is that "property's outside," property's antonym, was now being conceived of differently, though frequently, and somewhat confusingly, using the same words and many of the same arguments.

IX Disaggregating freedom: a legal realism for the public domain

This has been very long way of answering a short question. (I am an academic after all.) What are the alternatives to, and the critiques of, the second enclosure movement? I have sketched out three projects here: an anti-monopolistic critique of intellectual property, a defense of "a free public domain," and an attempt to outline the rules for a commons of the mind on the global net. These three projects overlap, draw from similar philosophical and economic sources, and use the same vocabulary. They are also not necessarily consistent with each other, and each may use the same term in different ways. "Free," "public domain," "commons," "enclosure"—each term shifts its meaning as we move from one intellectual project to the next, in part because each project is built around a different set of hopes and fears.

The first stage of the story I outlined here was the attempt by Jefferson, Madison, Macaulay, and others to balance the arguments in favor of intellectual property with criticism of its monopolistic costs and dangers; the goal was to build an awareness of the need for limitations *into the grant itself*. The second stage was a little more complex. Here, an affirmative argument for the public domain was put forward, rather than a mere criticism of intellectual property. There was an existent public domain, whose value we should recognize and which should have protection—perhaps even constitutional protection—against the danger that knowledge would be removed from it, or access to existing material impeded. Fine and dandy, but what *was* this public domain that we were to protect? There the answers were less clear. What norm of freedom did the public domain instantiate? Free trade? Free beer? Freedom from monopolistic control? Free communal production? The early public domain theorists were enigmatic on this point; the later ones vocal, but not necessarily consistent. The final panel in my triptych still relies on the criticisms of enclosure and monopoly, but in the place of the public domain, we find the rhetoric of the commons, a commons that in some conceptions one might have to pay to use.

At first sight, this may all seem distressingly messy. Surely, conceptions of the public domain, or the commons, should be more consistent. Why so much variation, such different definitions? Look at the question from the other side of the looking glass. Is this little potted history so very different from the history of the concept of property? We know very well that concepts of property have varied enormously over time and that the assumptions of the legal system about the analytical details of property have also varied enormously. Does property include notions that we might describe as human rights, or individual liberty, as it probably did for Locke?[139] Is property the sole, absolute, and despotic dominion that Blackstone wrote about (even though that did not match the reality in his own legal system)?[140] Are property rights the impermeable wall conjured up by the majority in the *Leroy Fibre* case, inside which we can do what we will without having to think about the possible conduct of others?[141] Is property the bundle of rights that first year law students learn about—more accurately a grab bag of rights, powers, privileges and immunities held together by nothing stronger than nominalism? (We choose to call these things "property," and so they are.)

Each of these conceptions of property is linked in a complicated way to the structure of belief in the larger society and in the legal system from which the property right came. Some of these conceptions are Sunday suits, smart clothing for external consumption, while others are working clothes, the day-to-day approximations used by legal practitioners to solve the problems before them. Our conceptions of property and sovereignty overlap, as the legal realists famously taught us, and the ideas of property taught in a law school classroom are markedly different from the same concept in ordinary language. We do not generally, however, throw up our hands and conclude that the whole concept should be jettisoned.

And what is true for property is true for the public domain. Just as there are many "properties," so too there are many "public domains." To the simple vision of property rights as consisting only of the state of absolute, perfect dominion can be counterposed the simple vision of the public domain as that which exists only where total freedom reigns. Here the "public domain" consists only of complete works that are completely free: free for appropriation, transfer, redistribution, copying, performance, and even rebundling into a new creation, itself covered by intellectual property.[142] To the "bundle of rights" conception of property, on the other hand, can be counterposed the "bundle of privileges" vision of the public domain, where we assume, for example, that fair use over a copyrighted work is part of the public domain. And to the predictive, legal realist vision of property, "predictions of what the courts will protect in fact," to paraphrase Holmes,[143] can be counterposed a predictive, critical conception of the public domain, "predictions of what the public can do freely and nothing more pretentious," to paraphrase Benkler.[144] Lessig's vision of the commons even includes works for which one has to pay, so long as the legal interest is protected merely by a liability rule and the payment is non-discriminatory.[145]

Each of these definitions is driven by an explicit or implicit goal. It may be that the public domain consists of those aspects of works which must remain outside of property if copyright's misleading presumptions about creation are to be squared with reality. It may be that the commons is constructed around the twin notions of preventing monopoly control over network protocols in order to preserve innovation, while still allowing for the type of collective management that will avoid a tragedy of the commons. We have not one public domain, not one theory of the public domain, but many. My own point of view is that this is all to the good, though a little clarity is certainly in order. But not everyone agrees.

X Conclusion: reifying the negative?

What is gained by reifying the negative and imaging a "theory" of the public domain?

Edward Samuels.[146]

The process I have described was a gradual one. From having been the invisible Other, the unquestioned margin of intellectual property, the public domain began to attract increasing attention. (Some of it, I must admit, from me, though I have wisely omitted that work from the history in this essay, out of self-preservation if nothing else.)[147] Soon, this body of work began to receive the ultimate intellectual compliment—thoughtful skepticism from others about whether there was any *there*, there:

> After reviewing the various proposed arguments supporting a general theory of the public domain, by Patterson and Lindberg or by other authors, it would appear that there simply is no such

general theory. Instead, there are several discrete contexts in which arguments about the public domain are encountered, each context raising different considerations that may have little or nothing to do with each other, and that cumulatively constitute what remains after one examines all possible sources of legal protection for works of authorship.... *What is gained by reifying the negative, and imagining a "theory" of the public domain*? If one wants to encourage a presumption against new forms or areas of protection, then one can do so without having to invoke a magical "public domain." There are dozens of battlegrounds between those who want to expand intellectual property protection and those who want to limit it or narrow it in any given context. The arguments in each context should be kept separate, since they raise different policy issues. Nevertheless, the individual issues sometimes tend to be elusive, and one's attitude toward them tends to be flavored as often as not by one's general attitude toward copyright law. If those who find themselves continually on the side arguing for a limitation of protection need a rallying cry, perhaps it can be "the public domain." The invocation may seem to add a moral overtone to the argument, to counterbalance the morally charged principles invoked time and again by the protectionists. In the final analysis, however, "such vague rhetoric does little more than adorn the stage on which actual choices must be played out."[148]

What is gained by reifying the negative? Professor Samuels' question is a good one. He supplies part of the answer with his thought that perhaps the language of the public domain will be used to counter the language of sacred property. This is, indeed, an important point—*language matters*, and not just as rhetoric. Even if the limits of my language are not the limits of my world,[149] the limits of my language certainly influence my world in a deeper way than as "vague rhetoric" adorning a stage, "on which actual choices must be played out."

The analogy I have tried to develop in my writing is that of the environmental movement.[150] Why talk of "an environment" or "environmental harm?" Why not simply list the pros and cons of each particular piece of development, type of technology, aspect of land use? In each case, there will be issues to be thought about: clean water, beautiful vistas, biodiversity, raised sea levels, the morals of species preservation, skin cancers from thinned ozone layers, carbon sequestration, responsibilities to future generations, and so on. It is not clear that there is any Ariadne's thread that links these issues together. What's more, it is fairly clear that there is no coherent or consistent definition of "nature" or "the environment."[151] There are certainly lots of discrete contexts in which the idea of nature or the environment is raised, and many different arguments for and against a particular type of development or technology. Why not simply deal case-by-case with the harms to this river, that wetland, this species, or that way of life? Why reify these individual loci of potential harm into a single entity called "the environment?" Part of the answer, of course, *is* rhetorical. The idea of the environment seems to add a moral overtone to the discussion, to counterbalance the arguments about "progress" and "growth" and "modernity." And this is hardly an unimportant function.

But that is not all there is to it. The environmental movement also gained much of its persuasive power by pointing out that there were structural reasons for bad environmental decisions—a legal system based on a particular notion of what "private property" entailed, and a scientific system that treated the world as a simple, linearly-related set of causes and effects. In both of these conceptual systems, the environment actually disappeared; there was no place for it in the analysis. Small surprise, then, that we did not preserve it very well. In other work, I have argued that the same is true about the public domain.[152] The fundamental tensions in the economic analysis of information issues, the source-blindness of an original author-centered model of property rights, and the political blindness to the importance of the public domain as a whole (not "my lake," but "The Environment") all come together to make the public domain disappear, first in concept and then, increasingly, as a reality.[153]

Of equal importance is the power of a concept like the environment both to clarify and to reshape perceptions of self-interest. When we are talking about the particular costs of this development proposal or that, the duck hunter is less likely to make common cause with the bird-watcher in another region, let alone the person worried about genetic drift in salmon populations or the effect of CFCs on the ozone layer. The idea that there is "an environment" allows a coalition to be built around a reframed conception of common interest. In the narrowest sense, that common interest might be the realization, spurred by greater attention to environmental interrelationships, that wetlands are important to both the duck hunter and the bird-watcher, and that they provide all kinds of ecosystem services. Naming encourages study.

In the broader sense, though, it is not merely the word "environment" that catalyses attention. Rather, there were two very important ideas behind the environmental movement. The first was the idea of ecology—the fragile, complex, and unpredictable interconnections between living systems.[154] The second was the idea of welfare economics—the ways in which markets can fail to make activities internalize their full costs.[155] The combination of the two ideas yielded a powerful and disturbing conclusion: Markets would *routinely* fail to make activities internalize their own costs, particularly their environmental costs. This failure would routinely disrupt or destroy fragile ecological systems, with unpredictable, ugly, dangerous, and possibly irreparable consequences.

These two types of analysis pointed to a general interest in environmental protection, and thus helped to build a large constituency which supported governmental efforts to that end. They were coupled with a simple point from public choice theory—public decisions are particularly likely to be bad when concentrated and well-organized groups with stable, substantial, and well-identified interests face off against diffuse groups with high information costs whose interests, while enormous in the aggregate, are individually small. There are lots of people who might be affected by a decision to rely on a particular power source, say, a coal-burning power plant in the Northeast. There are people who see acid rain killing off the fish in their lake, there are others who worry about particulate emissions, and there are those whose houses will be swallowed up by the sea if global warming lives up to its billing. But in the decisions about energy purchase and planning, they are neither as well-informed, nor is it easy for them to be as well-organized, as the company which proposes to run the particular plant. The notion of "an environmental movement" helps to sustain a coalition that people join, give money to, and so forth, even when the particular issue being lobbied over *affects them not at all.* By coming to be convinced that they should give loyalty to "the protection of the environment" rather than "oppose the stuff that affects me badly," the diffuse group was able to overcome some collective action problems. Specialized organizations fitting particular niches in the movement (Greenpeace, the Audubon Society, the Environmental Defense Fund, the Nature Conservancy) fulfilled a variety of roles and allowed people to "subcontract" their information-gathering to experts whose norms and pedigree they trusted.[156]

And, what is true for the environment is—to a striking degree, though not completely—true for the public domain and for the commons. The idea of the public domain takes to a higher level of abstraction a set of individual fights—over this chunk of the genome, that aspect of computer programs, this claim about the meaning of parody, or the ownership of facts. Just as the duck hunter finds common cause with the bird-watcher and the salmon geneticist by coming to think about "the environment," so an emergent concept of the public domain could tie together the interests of groups currently engaged in individual struggles with no sense of the larger context. This notion, in turn, allows people to solve collective action problems in a number of different ways, including the creation of specialized organizations whose technical expertise and lobbying proficiency allows the diffuse interests of a wider public to be better articulated. Here, too, we can learn. The public domain should have its Greenpeace, its Environmental Defense Fund, its Nature Conservancy, its Environmentally Concerned Scientists. In fact, organizations paralleling each of these functions are currently being created.[157]

The analogy goes further. Just as "the environment," or "nature," takes on multiple shadings of meaning to respond to different hopes and fears—

biodiversity, the preservation of beauty, a particular relationship between human beings and the planet—so, too, the various images of the public domain and the commons each expresses a specific set of fears about the dangers of property and hopes about the creative process. Frequently, the concept is constructed as an antonym—mirroring the analytic structure of the dominant idea of property to which it is counterposed. Samuels' skepticism is useful here; more clarity about the contents of the public domain and the relationship between the concept of the commons and of the public domain would indeed be useful. The literature on governing the commons promises to be exceptionally useful here,[158] as does the sadly neglected tradition of Hohfeldian legal analysis.[159] Each can offer a different kind of clarity. But just as with the environment, with nature, we do not respond to the revelation that these words are used in multiple and overlapping ways with the conclusion that we should simply abandon them and deal individually with the pluses and minuses of each development proposal, each dam, each CFC emission. The concept of the environment allows, at its best, a kind of generalized reflection on the otherwise unquestionable presuppositions of a particular mode of life, economy, and industrial organization. At their best, the commons and the public domain can do the same in helping us to reimagine creation, innovation, and speech on a global network. And this seems particularly important today.

The poem with which I began this essay told us: "And geese will still a common lack / Till they go and steal it back." I can't match the terseness or the rhyme, but if we assume that the second enclosure movement will have the benign effects claimed for the first, well, we will look like very silly geese indeed.

Notes

* An earlier and considerably shorter version of this article appeared as *Fencing off Ideas*, DAEDALUS, Spring 2002, at 13. I wish to thank Yochai Benkler and Larry Lessig for comments, and Matt Jones, Greg Manter, and Victoria Von Portatius for their research.

1 Apart from being anonymous, the poem is extremely hard to date. It probably comes from the enclosure controversies of the eighteenth century. However, the earliest reference to it that I have been able to discover is from 1821. Edward Birch was moved to compose some (fairly poor) verses in response when he reported "seeing the following jeu d'esprit in a Handbill posted up in Plaistow, as a 'CAUTION' to prevent persons from supporting the intended inclosure of Hainault or Waltham Forest." He then quotes a version of the poem. Edward Birch, TICKLER MAG., Feb. 1821, at 45. In 1860, a staff writer for the journal *Notes and Queries* declares that "the animosity excited against the Inclosure Acts and their authors . . . was almost without precedent: though fifty years and more have passed, the subject is still a sore one in many parishes. . . . I remember some years ago, in hunting over an old library discovering a box full of printed squibs, satires and ballads of the time against the acts and those who

were supposed to favour them,—the library having belonged to a gentleman who played an active part on the opposition side." The author then quotes the first verse as a "naive epigram . . . which forcibly impressed itself on my memory." *"Exon" Ballads Against Inclosures*, 9 NOTES AND QUERIES, at 130–131 (2nd ser., Feb. 1860). The context makes it appear that the poem itself must date from the late 18th century. In other sources, the poem is sometimes dated at 1764 and said to be in response to Sir Charles Pratt's fencing of common land. *See, e.g.*, Dana A. Freiburger, John Thompson, English Philomath—A Question of Land Surveying and Astronomy, poster paper submitted to the History of Astronomy Workshop University of Notre Dame, (July 1–4, 1999), note 15, *available at* http://www.nd.edu/~histast4/exhibits/papers/Freiburger/index.html (last visited Dec. 19, 2002). This attribution is widespread and may well be true, but I have been able to discover no contemporary source material that sustains it. By the end of the nineteenth century, the poem was being quoted, sometimes with amusement and sometimes with agreement, on both sides of the Atlantic. *See* Ezra S. Carr, *Aids and Obstacles to Agriculture on the Pacific-Coast*, in THE PATRONS OF HUSBANDRY ON THE PACIFIC COAST 290, 291 (San Francisco, A. L. Bancroft and Co. 1875); EDWARD P. CHEYNEY, AN INTRODUCTION TO THE INDUSTRIAL AND SOCIAL HISTORY OF ENGLAND 219 (1901).

2 Although we refer to it as "*the* enclosure movement," it was actually a series of enclosures that started in the fifteenth century and went on, with differing means, ends, and varieties of state involvement, until the nineteenth century. *See, e.g.*, J. A. YELLING, COMMON FIELD AND ENCLOSURE IN ENGLAND, 1450–1850 (1977).

3 THOMAS MORE, UTOPIA 32 (Alfred A. Knopf 1992) (1947).

4 KARL POLANYI, THE GREAT TRANSFORMATION: THE POLITICAL AND ECONOMIC ORIGINS OF OUR TIME 35 (1957); *see also* E. P. THOMPSON, THE MAKING OF THE ENGLISH WORKING CLASS 218 (1963).

5 POLANYI, *supra* note 4 at 35.

6 *See generally* LORD ERNLE, ENGLISH FARMING PAST AND PRESENT (1961).

7 For an excellent summary of the views of Hobbes, Locke and Blackstone on these points, see Hannibal Travis, *Pirates of the Information Infrastructure: Blackstonian Copyright and the First Amendment*, 15 BERKELEY TECH. L.J. 777, 789–803 (2000).

8 *See* ERNLE, *supra* note 6.

9 The most notable work is that of Robert Allen. *See* Robert C. Allen, *The Efficiency and Distributional Consequences of Eighteenth Century Enclosures*, 92 ECON. J. 937 (1982) [hereinafter Allen, *Efficiency*]; ROBERT C. ALLEN, ENCLOSURE AND THE YEOMAN (1994). Allen argues that the enclosure movement produced major distributional consequences, but little observable efficiency gain. The pie was carved up differently, to the advantage of the landlords, but made no larger. In contrast, Michael Turner sees enclosure as one possible, though not necessary, route to productivity gains. *See* Michael Turner, *English Open Fields and Enclosures: Retardation or Productivity Improvements*, 46 J. ECON. HIST. 669, 688 (1986). Donald McCloskey's work also argues for efficiency gains from enclosure, largely from the evidence provided by rent increases. *See* Donald N. McCloskey, *The Enclosure of Open Fields: Preface to a Study of Its Impact on the Efficiency of English Agriculture in the Eighteenth Century*, 32 J. ECON. HIST. 15 (1972); Donald N. McCloskey, *The Prudent Peasant: New Findings on Open Fields*, 51 J. ECON. HIST. 343 (1991). In Allen's view, however, the change in rents was largely a measure of the way that changes in legal rights affected the bargaining power of the parties and the cultural context of rent negotiations; enclosure allowed landlords to capture more of the existing

surplus produced by the land, rather than dramatically expanding it. "[T]he enclosure movement itself might be regarded as the first state sponsored land reform. Like so many since, it was justified with efficiency arguments, while its main effect (according to the data analyzed here) was to redistribute income to already rich landowners." Allen, *Efficiency*, *supra* at 950–51. Those contemporary accounts which argue that enclosure led to productivity gains tend to be more qualified in their praise. Compare Turner, *supra*, ("Enclosure cannot be seen as the automatic open door to this cycle of agricultural improvement, but the foregoing estimates do suggest that perhaps it was a door which opened frequently, and with profit.") with the more positive account given in ERNLE, *supra* note 6.

10 Garrett Hardin, *The Tragedy of the Commons*, SCIENCE, Dec. 13, 1968, at 1243.

11 The possibility of producing "order without law" and, thus, sometimes governing the commons without tragedy, has also fascinated scholars of contemporary land use. See ROBERT C. ELLICKSON, ORDER WITHOUT LAW: HOW NEIGHBORS SETTLE DISPUTES (1991); ELINOR OSTROM, GOVERNING THE COMMONS: THE EVOLUTION OF INSTITUTIONS FOR COLLECTIVE ACTION (1991).

12 The analogy to the enclosure movement has been too succulent to resist. To my knowledge, Ben Kaplan, Pamela Samuelson, Yochai Benkler, David Lange, Chrisopher May, David Bollier and Keith Aoki have all employed the trope, as I myself have on previous occasions. For a particularly thoughtful and careful development of the parallel between the two enclosure movements, see generally Travis, *supra* note 7.

13 *See, e.g.*, William A. Haseltine, *The Case for Gene Patents*, TECH. REV., Sept./Oct. 2000, *available at* http://www.technologyreview.com/articles/haseltine 0900.asp (last visited Dec. 19, 2002); *cf.* Alexander K. Haas, *The Wellcome Trust's Disclosures of Gene Sequence Data into the Public Domain & the Potential for Proprietary Rights in the Human Genome*, 16 BERKELEY TECH. L.J. 145 (2001).

14 *See, e.g.*, Haseltine, *supra* note 13; Press Release, Biotechnology Industry Association, Genentech, Incyte Genomics Tell House Subcommittee Gene Patents Essential For Medical Progress (July 13, 2000), *available at* http://www.bio.org/genomics/genetech.html.

15 *See, e.g.*, Howard Markel, *Patents Could Block the Way to a Cure*, N.Y. TIMES, Aug. 24, 2001, at A19. For the general background to these arguments, see Rebecca S. Eisenberg, *Patenting the Human Genome*, 39 EMORY L.J. 721, 740–44 (1990).

16 793 P.2d 479, 488–97 (Cal. 1990).

17 *Id.* at 493–94. One imagines Styrofoam coolers criss-crossing the country by FedEx in an orgy of communistic flesh swapping.

18 *Id.* at 493.

19 I might be suspected of anti-economist irony here. In truth, neither side's arguments are fully satisfying. It is easy to agree with Richard Posner that the language of economics offers a "thin and unsatisfactory epistemology" through which to understand the world. RICHARD POSNER, THE PROBLEMS OF JURISPRUDENCE xiv (1990) (citing the words of Paul Bator). On the other hand, explaining what it means to "own one's own body," or specifying the non-commodifiable limits on the market turns out to be a remarkably tricky business, as Margaret Jane Radin has shown with great elegance. *See* MARGARET JANE RADIN, CONTESTED COMMODITIES (1996).

20 *See* State St. Bank & Trust Co. v. Signature Fin. Group, 149 F.3d 1368, 1373 (D.C. Cir. 1998).

21 Pub. L. No. 105-304, 112 Stat. 2860 (1998) (codified as amended in scattered sections of 5, 17, 28 and 35 U.S.C.).
22 *See, e.g.*, Mead Data Central, Inc. v. Toyota Motor Sales, U.S.A., Inc., 875 F.2d 1026, 1030 (2d Cir. 1989); Mutual of Omaha Insurance Co. v. Novak, 836 F. 2d 397 (8th Cir. 1987), *cert. denied* 109 S. Ct. 326 (1987); American Express Co. v. Vibra Approved Laboratories Corp., 10 U.S.P.Q. 2d (BNA) 2006 (S.D.N.Y. Apr. 17, 1989); Jordache Enters., Inc. v. Hogg Wyld, Ltd., 625 F. Supp. 48, 56 (D.N.M. 1985), *aff'd*, 828 F.2d 1482 (10th Cir. 1987); Pillsbury Co. v. Milky Way Prod., Inc., 215 U.S.P.Q. (BNA) 124 (N.D. Ga. Dec. 24, 1981); General Electric Co. v. Almpa Coal Co., 205 U.S.P.Q. (BNA) 1036 (D. Mass. Oct. 12, 1979); Reddy Communications, Inc. v. Environmental Action Found., Inc., 199 U.S.P.Q. (BNA) 630 (D.D.C. Nov. 11, 1977); Coca-Cola Co. v. Gemini Rising Inc., 346 F. Supp. 1183 (E.D.N.Y. 1972).
23 Directive 96/9/EC of the European Parliament and of the Council of 11 March 1996 on the Legal Protection of Databases, 1996 O.J. (L 77) 20, *available at* http://europa.eu.int/ISPO/infosoc/legreg/docs/969ec.html [hereinafter Directive] (last visited Dec. 19, 2002).
24 Int'l News Serv. v. Associated Press, 248 U.S. 215, 250 (1918) (Brandeis, J., dissenting).
25 Yochai Benkler, *Free as the Air to Common Use: First Amendment Constraints on Enclosure of the Public Domain*, 74 N.Y.U. L. Rev. 354, 361, 424 (1999) [hereinafter Benkler, *Free as the Air*].
26 The so-called "business method" patents, which cover such "inventions" as auctions or accounting methods, are an obvious example. *See, e.g.*, State St. Bank & Trust Co. v. Signature Fin. Group, Inc., 149 F.3d 1368, 1373 (Fed. Cir. 1998).
27 Collection of Information Antipiracy Act, S. 2291, 105th Cong. (1998); Database Investment and Intellectual Property Antipiracy Act of 1996, H.R. 3531, 104th Cong. (1996).
28 *See, e.g.*, Feist Publ'ns v. Rural Tel. Serv. Co., 499 U.S. 340, 350, 354 (1991) ("Copyright treats facts and factual compilations in a wholly consistent manner. Facts, whether alone or as part of a compilation, are not original and therefore may not be copyrighted." To hold otherwise would "'distort[]' basic copyright principles in that it creates a monopoly in public domain materials without the necessary justification of protecting and encouraging the creation of 'writings' by 'authors.'").
29 *See* Eisenberg, *supra* note 15; Haas, *supra* note 13.
30 *See* Directive, *supra* note 23.
31 Those who prefer topographical metaphors might imagine a quilted pattern of public and private land, with legal rules specifying that certain areas, beaches for example, can never be privately owned, and with accompanying rules giving public rights of way through private land if there is a danger that access to the commons might otherwise be blocked.
32 *See* James Boyle, Shamans, Software, & Spleens: Law and the Construction of the Information Society 135 (1996) [hereinafter Boyle, Shamans]; Jessica Litman, Digital Copyright 91 (2001).
33 The phrase "Washington Consensus" originated in John Williamson, *What Washington Means by Policy Reform*, in Latin American Adjustment: How Much Has Happened? 7-38 (John Williamson ed., 1990). Over time, it has come to be used as shorthand for a neo-liberal view of economic policy that puts its faith in deregulation, privatization, and the creation and defense of secure property rights as the cure for all ills. *See* Joseph Stiglitz, *The World Bank at the Millennium*,

109 ECON. J. 577, 577–97 (1999). It has thus become linked to the triumphalist neo-liberal account of the end of history and the victory of unregulated markets. *See* FRANCIS FUKUYAMA, THE END OF HISTORY AND THE LAST MAN (1992). Neither of these two results are, to be fair, what its creator intended. *See* John Williamson, *What Should The Bank Think About The Washington Consensus?*, Institute for International Economics, *available at* http://www.iie.com/papers/williamson0799.htm (last visited Sept. 20, 2002).

34 The differences are particularly strong in the arguments over "desert:" Are these property rights deserved or are they simply violations of the public trust and privatizations of the commons? For example, some would say that we never had the same *traditional* claims over the genetic commons that the victims of the first enclosure movement had over their commons; this is more like newly discovered frontier land, or perhaps even privately drained marshland, than it is like well-known common land that all have traditionally used. In this case, the enclosers can claim (though their claims are disputed) that they discovered or perhaps simply made usable the territory they seek to own. The opponents of gene patenting, on the other hand, turn to religious and ethical arguments about the sanctity of life and the incompatibility of property with living systems even more frequently than the farmers of the eighteenth century. These arguments, and the appeals to free speech that dominate debates over digital intellectual property, have no precise analogue in debates over hunting or pasturage, although there are common themes. For example, we are already seeing nostalgic laments of the loss of the immemorial rights of Internet users. At the same time, the old language of property law is turned to this more evanescent subject matter; my favorite title is *The Ancient Doctrine of Trespass to Web Sites*. I. Trotter Hardy, *The Ancient Doctrine of Trespass to Web Sites*, 1996 J. ONLINE L. art. 7, *available at* http://www.wm.edu/law/publications/jol/95_96/hardy.html (last visited Dec. 19, 2002).

35 The exceptions to this statement turn out to be fascinating. In the interest of brevity, however, I will ignore them entirely.

36 13 Ann., c. 15 (Eng.).

37 Pub. L. No. 105–304, 112 Stat. 2860 (1998) (codified as amended in scattered sections of 5, 17, 28, and 35 U.S.C.).

38 Pub. L. No. 105–147, 111 Stat. 2678 (1997) (codified as amended in scattered sections of 17 and 18 U.S.C.).

39 Pub. L. No. 105–298, 112 Stat. 2827 (1998) (codified as amended in scattered sections of 17 U.S.C.).

40 S. 2291, 105th Cong. (1998).

41 My intuitions—and historical experience with prior "dangerous" copying technologies such as the VCR—point strongly to the position that owners of protected content are better off; but there really isn't enough evidence either way.

42 U.S. CONST. art. I, § 8, cl. 8.

43 Remember, I am talking here about *increases* in the level of rights: protecting new subject matter for longer periods of time, criminalizing certain technologies, making it illegal to cut through digital fences even if they have the effect of foreclosing previously lawful uses, and so on. Each of these has the effect of diminishing the public domain in the name of national economic policy.

44 *E.g.*, BOYLE SHAMANS, *supra* note 32; William M. Landes & Richard A. Posner, *An Economic Analysis of Copyright Law*, 18 J. LEGAL STUD. 325, 348 (1989); Jessica Litman, *The Public Domain*, 39 EMORY L.J. 965, 1010–11 (1990); Pamela Samuelson & Suzanne Scotchmer, *The Law & Economics of Reverse Engineering*, 111 YALE L.J. 1575 (2002).

45 Sanford J. Grossman & Joseph E. Stiglitz, *On the Impossibility of Informationally Efficient Markets*, 70 AM. ECON. REV. 393, 404 (1980).
46 For a more technical account, see James Boyle, *Cruel, Mean, or Lavish?: Economic Analysis, Price Discrimination and Digital Intellectual Property*, 53 VAND. L. REV. 2007 (2000) [hereinafter Boyle, *Cruel*].
47 The most recent example of this phenomenon is the multiple legal roadblocks to bringing "Golden Rice" to market. For a fascinating study of the various issues involved and the strategies for working around them, see R. David Kryder et al., *The Intellectual and Technical Property Components of Pro-Vitamin A Rice (Golden Rice): A Preliminary Freedom-to-Operate Review*, available at http://www.isaaa.org/publications/briefs/Brief_20.htm (last visited Apr. 9, 2002). In assessing the economic effects of patents, one has to balance the delays and increased costs caused by the web of property rights against the benefits to society of the incentives to innovation, the requirement of disclosure, and the eventual access to the patented subject matter. When the qualification levels for patents are set too low, the benefits are minuscule and the costs very high —the web of property rights is particularly tangled, complicating follow-on innovation, the monopoly goes to "buy" a very low level of inventiveness, and the disclosure is of little value.
48 Michael A. Heller & Rebecca S. Eisenberg, *Can Patents Deter Innovation? The Anticommons in Biomedical Research*, SCIENCE, May 1, 1998, at 698.
49 *See* GLYN MOODY, REBEL CODE: LINUX AND THE OPEN SOURCE REVOLUTION (2001); PETER WAYNER, FREE FOR ALL: HOW LINUX AND THE FREE SOFTWARE MOVEMENT UNDERCUT THE HIGH-TECH-TITANS (2000); Eben Moglen, *Anarchism Triumphant: Free Software and the Death of Copyright*, 4 FIRST MONDAY 8 (Aug. 2, 1999), *at* http://firstmonday.org/issues/issue4_8/moglen/index.html.
50 Proprietary, or "binary only," software is generally released only after the source code has been compiled into machine-readable object code, a form that is impenetrable to the user. Even if you were a master programmer, and the provisions of the Copyright Act, the appropriate licenses, and the DMCA did not forbid you from doing so, you would be unable to modify commercial proprietary software to customize it for your needs, remove a bug, or add a feature. Open source programmers say, disdainfully, that it is like buying a car with the hood welded shut. *See, e.g.*, WAYNER, *supra* note 49, at 264.
51 *See* Brian Behlendorf, *Open Source as a Business Strategy*, in OPEN SOURCES: VOICES FROM THE OPEN SOURCE REVOLUTION, 149, 163 (Chris Dibona et al. eds., 1999).
52 *See* Bruce Brown, *Enterprise-Level Security Made Easy*, PC MAG., Jan. 15, 2002, at 28; Jim Rapoza, *Open-Source Fever Spreads*, PC WEEK, Dec. 13, 1999, at 1.
53 E. COBHAM BREWER, THE DICTIONARY OF PHRASE AND FABLE, 1111–12 (1894).
54 For a seminal statement, see Moglen, *supra* note 49:

> "[I]ncentives" is merely a metaphor, and as a metaphor to describe human creative activity it's pretty crummy. I have said this before, but the better metaphor arose on the day Michael Faraday first noticed what happened when he wrapped a coil of wire around a magnet and spun the magnet. Current flows in such a wire, but we don't ask what the incentive is for the electrons to leave home. We say that the current results from an emergent property of the system, which we call induction. The question we ask is "what's the resistance of the wire?"

So Moglen's Metaphorical Corollary to Faraday's Law says that if you wrap the Internet around every person on the planet and spin the planet, software flows in the network. It's an emergent property of connected human minds that they create things for one another's pleasure and to conquer their uneasy sense of being too alone. The only question to ask is, what's the resistance of the network? Moglen's Metaphorical Corollary to Ohm's Law states that the resistance of the network is directly proportional to the field strength of the "intellectual property" system. So the right answer to the econodwarf is, resist the resistance.

Id.

55 Benkler's explanation is characteristically elegant, even formal in its precision, while mine is clunkier. *See* Yochai Benkler, *Coase's Penguin, or, Linux and the Nature of the Firm*, 111 YALE L.J. 369 (2002) [hereinafter Benkler, *Coase's Penguin*].

56 One organization theorist to whom I mentioned the idea said, "Ugh, governance by food fight." Anyone who has ever been on an organizational listserv, a global production process run by people who are long on brains and short on social skills, knows how accurate that description is. *E pur si muove.*

57 *See* KARL POPPER, THE OPEN SOCIETY AND ITS ENEMIES (1945).

58 *See* http://www.ensembl.org (last visited Sept. 18, 2002).

59 For example, NASA's "Clickworkers" experiment, which used public volunteers to analyze Mars landing data. *See* http://clickworkers.arc.nasa.gov/top (last visited September 30, 2002).

60 Benkler, *Coase's Penguin*, *supra* note 55 *at* 397.

61 Stallman, founder of the Free Software Foundation, describes this distinction at Website of the Free Software Foundation, *at* http://www.gnu.ai.mit.edu/philosophy/free-sw.html (last visited Dec. 19, 2002).

62 Exhibit A: the Internet—from the software and protocols on which it runs to the multiple volunteer sources of content and information.

63 *See, e.g.*, The Consumer and Investor Access to Information Act of 1999, H.R. 1858, 106th Cong., § 101(1) (1999); Database Investment and Intellectual Property Antipiracy Act of 1996, H.R. 3531, 104th Cong. (1996); *see also* Directive, *supra* note 23.

64 *See generally* Julie E. Cohen & Mark A. Lemley, *Patent Scope and Innovation in the Software Industry*, 89 CAL. L. REV. 1 (2001). *See also* Pamela Samuelson et al., *A Manifesto Concerning the Legal Protection of Computer Programs*, 94 COLUM. L. REV. 2308 (1994).

65 UNIF. COMPUTER INFO. TRANSACTIONS ACT (UCITA) (2001), *available at* http://www.ucitaonline.com/ (last visited May 13, 2002).

66 17 U.S.C. § 1201 (2002).

67 This point has been ably made, *inter alia*, by Pamela Samuelson, Jessica Litman, Jerry Reichman, Larry Lessig, and Yochai Benkler. *See* LITMAN, *supra* note 32; Benkler, *Free as the Air*, *supra* note 25; Pamela Samuelson, *Intellectual Property and the Digital Economy: Why the Anti-Circumvention Regulations Need to be Revised*, 14 BERKELEY TECH. L.J. 519, 566 (1999); J. H. Reichman & Paul F. Uhlir, *Database Protection at the Crossroads: Recent Developments and Their Impact on Science and Technology*, 14 BERKELEY TECH. L.J. 793 (1999); Lawrence Lessig, *Jail Time in the Digital Age*, N.Y. TIMES, July 30, 2001, at A17. Each has a slightly different focus and emphasis on the problem, but each has pointed out the impediments now being erected to distributed, non-proprietary solutions. *See also* Boyle, *Cruel*, *supra* note 46.

68 William W. Fisher III, *Property and Contract on the Internet*, 73 CHI.-KENT L. REV. 1203, 1217–18 (1998).
69 *See* James Boyle, *Missing the Point on Microsoft*, SALON.COM, Apr. 7, 2000, *at* http://www.salon.com/tech/feature/2000/04/07/greenspan/index.html. [hereinafter Boyle, *Missing the Point*].
70 That is assuming that enclosure really *did* produce efficiency gains for arable land, though as I pointed out earlier, economic historians are now divided about that issue. *See* Allen, *Efficiency, supra* note 9. At best, one could say that the empirical evidence is equivocal. There are certainly reasons to believe that the commons, far from being tragic, was often relatively well managed. But the case for enclosure is at its strongest with arable land; even if one gives no weight at all to the contrary evidence there, the commons of the mind is very different and most of the differences cut strongly against the logic of enclosure—at least without considerably more evidence than we currently possess.
71 Some of the legislation involved is also constitutionally dubious under the First Amendment and Copyright Clause. *See* Yochai Benkler, *Through the Looking Glass: Alice and the Constitutional Foundations of the Public Domain*, 66 LAW & CONTEMP. PROBS. 173 (Winter/Spring 2003). This is particularly strange at a time when other government subsidies are subjected to relentless skepticism and demands for empirical support. Is it *really* worthwhile teaching poor pre-schoolers to read? Where is the data?
72 The full version is given in Boyle, *Cruel, supra* note 46.
73 Perfect price discrimination is the ability to charge every user the exact maximum of their ability and willingness to pay, so that the market can be perfectly segregated by price.
74 *See* LAWRENCE LESSIG, THE FUTURE OF IDEAS: THE FATE OF THE COMMONS IN A NETWORKED WORLD (2001).
75 *See supra* note 33.
76 *See* Boyle, *Missing the Point, supra* note 69.
77 BOYLE, SHAMANS, *supra* note 32; James Boyle, *A Theory of Law and Information: Copyright, Spleens, Blackmail, and Insider Trading*, 80 CAL. L. REV. 1413 (1992) [hereinafter Boyle, *Theory*].
78 To be fair, this is not hard to do.
79 Letter from Thomas Jefferson to Isaac McPherson (Aug. 13, 1813), *in* 13 THE WRITINGS OF THOMAS JEFFERSON 326, 333–34 (Albert Ellery Bergh ed., 1907) [hereinafter Jefferson/McPherson Letter].
80 *Id.* at 333.
81 *Id.* at 334.
82 Thomas B. Macaulay, A Speech Delivered in the House of Commons (Feb. 5, 1841), *in* VIII THE LIFE AND WORKS OF LORD MACAULAY 201 (London, Longmans, Green, and Co. 1897).
83 *Id.*
84 For example, in a letter to Madison commenting on the draft of the Constitution:

> I like it, as far as it goes; but I should have been for going further. For instance, the following alterations and additions would have pleased me ... Article 9. Monopolies may be allowed to persons for their own productions in literature, and their own inventions in the arts, for a term not exceeding ____ years, but for no longer term, and no other purpose.

Letter from Thomas Jefferson to James Madison (Aug. 28, 1789), *in* 7 THE WRITINGS OF THOMAS JEFFERSON 444, 450–51 (Albert Ellery Bergh ed., 1907).

85 Jefferson/McPherson Letter, *supra* note 79, at 355.
86 James Madison, *Monopolies, Perpetuities, Corporations, Ecclesiastical Endowments, in Aspects of Monopoly One Hundred Years Ago*, HARPER'S MAG., Mar. 1914, at 489–90.
87 Smith says:

> When a company of merchants undertake, at their own risk and expense, to establish a new trade with some remote and barbarous nation, it may not be unreasonable to incorporate them into a joint-stock company, and to grant them, in case of their success, a monopoly of the trade for a certain number of years. It is the easiest and most natural way in which the state can recompense them for hazarding a dangerous and expensive experiment, of which the public is afterwards to reap the benefit. A temporary monopoly of this kind may be vindicated, upon the same principles upon which a like monopoly of a new machine is granted to its inventor, and that of a new book to its author. But upon the expiration of the term, the monopoly ought certainly to determine; the forts and garrisons, if it was found necessary to establish any, to be taken into the hands of government, their value to be paid to the company, and the trade to be laid open to all the subjects of the state. By a perpetual monopoly, all the other subjects of the state are taxed very absurdly in two different ways: first, by the high price of goods, which, in the case of a free trade, they could buy much cheaper; and, secondly, by their total exclusion from a branch of business which it might be both convenient and profitable for many of them to carry on.

> Adam Smith, *Of the expenses of public works and public institutions*, in III THE WEALTH OF NATIONS, 339 (London, Dent 1937) (1880).

88 Macaulay, *supra* note 82.
89 *Id.*
90 In a speech to the house of commons, Macaulay said:

> These are strong cases. I have shown you that, if the law had been what you are now going to make it, the finest prose work of fiction in the language, the finest biographical work in the language, would very probably have been suppressed. But I have stated my case weakly. The books which I have mentioned are singularly inoffensive books, books not touching on any of those questions which drive even wise men beyond the bounds of wisdom. There are books of a very different kind, books which are the rallying points of great political and religious parties. What is likely to happen if the copyright of one of these books should by descent or transfer come into the possession of some hostile zealot?

> *Id.*

91 The Mitchell estate attempted to block publication of *The Wind Done Gone* by Alice Randall, a work which retold *Gone With the Wind* from the slaves' perspective. The Eleventh Circuit reversed a preliminary injunction blocking publication. SunTrust Bank v. Houghton Mifflin Co., 268 F.3d 1257 (11th Cir. 2001).
92 *See* CATHERINE SEVILLE, LITERARY COPYRIGHT REFORM IN EARLY VICTORIAN ENGLAND: THE FRAMING OF THE 1842 COPYRIGHT ACT 46–48 (1999).

93 *Id.* at 48.
94 Fritz Machlup & Edith Penrose, *The Patent Controversy in the Nineteenth Century*, 10 J. ECON. HIST. 1, 4 n.8 (1950).
95 *Id.* at 5.
96 *Id.* at 1.
97 CHRISTINE MACLEOD, INVENTING THE INDUSTRIAL REVOLUTION 191–96 (1988). Ironically, contemporary economists are rediscovering the attraction of patent alternatives. *See* Steven Shavell & Tanguy Van Ypersele, Rewards versus Intellectual Property Rights, Working Paper 6956, *available at* http://www.nber.org/papers/w6956 (last visited Jan. 14, 2003).
98 Benjamin Franklin recalled that:

> Gov'r. Thomas was so pleas'd with the construction of this stove ... that he offered to give me a patent for the sole vending of them for a term of years; but I declin'd it from a principle which has ever weighed with me on such occasions, viz.: *That, as we enjoy great advantages from the inventions of others, we should be glad of an opportunity to serve others by any invention of ours; and this we should do freely and generously.*

> Benjamin Franklin, *Autobiography* (1771), *in* THE WORKS OF BENJAMIN FRANKLIN 1, 237–238 (John Bigelow ed., 1904).

99 *See* Litman, *supra* note 44. The process is somewhat ironic, since the French copyright law, with its focus on author's rights, is in many ways among the least solicitous and protective of the public domain.
100 *See* LITMAN, *supra* note 32; Edward Samuels, *The Public Domain in Copyright Law*, 41 J. COPYRIGHT SOC. 137, 150 (1993).
101 I admit this is an unusual admission from a legal academic.
102 Graham v. John Deere Co., 383 U.S. 1, 5–6 (1966).
103 Carol Rose, *The Comedy of the Commons: Custom, Commerce, and Inherently Public Property*, 53 U. CHI. L. REV. 711, 727–28 (1986).
104 *Graham*, 383 U.S. at 6.
105 David Lange, *Recognizing the Public Domain*, 44 LAW & CONTEMP. PROBS. 147 (Autumn 1981).
106 *Id.* at 151–71.
107 For example, in one memorable discussion of a hypothetical drawn from Tom Wolfe: "I think it is useful to remember, however, that what we are talking about, insofar as our senses can perceive it, is still a wet spot on the dead wino's napkin. Everything else is hypothesis." *Id.* at 149.
108 *Id.* at 147.
109 *Id.*
110 *Id.*
111 *See supra* Part II.
112 Non-lawyers, who are (rightly) skeptical of definitional inquiries and doubly skeptical of lawyers engaged in definitional inquiries, might believe these points are at best semantic and at worst essentialist. They could be right. We might take what Felix Cohen said about definitions of law and apply them to definitions of the public domain.

> A definition of [the public domain] is useful or useless. It is not true or false, any more than a New Year's resolution or an insurance policy. A definition is in fact a type of insurance against certain risks of

confusion. It cannot, any more than can a commercial insurance policy, eliminate all risks.

> Felix Cohen, *Transcendental Nonsense and the Functional Approach*, 35 COLUM. L. REV. 809, 835–36 (1935). Wittgenstein is equally eloquent in pointing out the dangers of seeking the one true definition:
>
>> Naming appears as a queer connexion of a word with an object.—And you really get such a queer connexion when the philosopher tries to bring out the relation between name and thing by staring at an object in front of him and repeating a name or even the word "this" innumerable times. For philosophical problems arise when language goes on holiday.
>
> LUDWIG WITTGENSTEIN, PHILOSOPHICAL INVESTIGATIONS 19 (1958). I am asking for a ten-page suspension of disbelief while I pursue the question.

113 L. RAY PATTERSON & STANLEY W. LINDBERG, THE NATURE OF COPYRIGHT: A LAW OF USERS' RIGHTS (1991).
114 Litman, *supra* note 44, at 1023.
115 *Id.* at 968.
116 Benkler, *Free as the Air*, *supra* note 25, at 361–62.
117 *Id.*
118 *See supra* Part VI.
119 In particular, I refer to statutory liability rules with pre-specified payments.
120 Larry Lessig, *The Architecture of Innovation*, 51 DUKE L. J. 1783, 1788 (2002).
121 Which is not to say that this is Lessig's only concern. *See* LAWRENCE LESSIG, CODE AND OTHER LAWS OF CYBERSPACE (1999) (focusing particularly on "material," code-based restraints imposed by the architecture of communications networks, and arguing that choices within and among different potential architectures should be subject to more democratic and constitutional scrutiny); *see also* James Boyle, *Foucault in Cyberspace: Surveillance, Sovereignty and Hard-Wired Censors*, 66 U. CIN. L. REV. 177 (1997) [hereinafter Boyle, *Foucault*].
122 *See supra* Part VII.
123 It is only fair to point out, however, that both the particular claims and the general economic observations about strong network effects and "path dependency" have been hotly disputed by Microsoft and independent academics. For a marvelously readable example, see Stephan E. Margolis & Stan Liebovitz, *We Don't Know Why She Swallowed The Fly: Policy and Path Dependence*, *at* http://www.utdallas.edu/~liebowit/regulatn.html (last visited Jan. 14, 2003).
124 For the most important statement of the value of liability rules in promoting follow-on innovation, see J. H. Reichman, *Of Green Tulips and Legal Kudzu: Repackaging Rights in Subpatentable Innovation*, 53 VAND. L. REV. 1743 (2000). Reichman does not, however, take a position on whether to define the information goods protected by liability rules as part of the commons.
125 I owe this insight to Jed Rubenfeld, *The First Amendment's Purpose*, 53 STAN. L. REV. 767 (2001).
126 *See supra* Part IV.
127 I borrow the phrase from the title of Carol Rose's magnificently prescient article which discusses the occasional superiority of common property regimes to individual private property rights. *See* Rose, *supra* note 103; *see also* Carol Rose, *The Several Futures of Property: Of Cyberspace and Folk Tales, Emission Trades and Ecosystems*, 83 MINN. L. REV. 129, 155–56 (1998).

128 *See supra* Part IV.
129 GNU Library General Public License, *available at* http://www.gnu.org/copyleft/library.txt (last visited Jan. 14, 2003).
130 *Id.*
131 *Id.*
132 17 U.S.C. § 106 (1994).
133 *See supra* Part VI.
134 An alternative approach, the Free BSD License, is closer to a mainstream understanding of public domain software. BSD License, *available at* http://www.opensource.org/licenses/bsd-license.html (last visited Jan. 14, 2003). The user is free to do anything with software covered by this license, including adding to it and selling the resultant program in a proprietary, binary-only format.
135 *See, e.g.*, SUSAN BUCK & ELINOR OSTROM, THE GLOBAL COMMONS (1998); LOCAL COMMONS AND GLOBAL INTERDEPENDENCE: HETEROGENEITY AND COOPERATION IN TWO DOMAINS (Elinor Ostrom & Robert Keohane eds., 1994); MARGARET MCKEAN, MAKING THE COMMONS WORK: THEORETICAL, HISTORICAL, AND CONTEMPORARY STUDIES (David Bromley *et al.* eds., 1992); ELINOR OSTROM, GOVERNING THE COMMONS: THE EVOLUTION OF INSTITUTIONS FOR COLLECTIVE ACTION (1991); Margaret McKean, *Success on the Commons: A Comparative Examination of Institutions for Common Property Resource Management*, 4 J. OF THEORETICAL POL. 247 (1992); Elinor Ostrom, *Reformulating the Commons*, 6 SWISS POL. SCI. REV., Apr. 15, 1999, at 29.
136 One of the most interesting attempts to revive the notion of the commons and apply it to contemporary intellectual property policy issues comes from David Bollier. Bollier's concerns go well beyond using intellectual property to deal with many different types of public assets. *See, e.g.*, David Bollier, Public Assets, Private Profits, *available at* http://www.bollier.org/pdf/PA_Report.pdf (last visited Feb. 13, 2003). Nevertheless he also places a very strong emphasis on the public domain and the information commons. *See* David Bollier, Recent Works, *available at* http://www.bollier.org/recent.htm (last visited Feb. 13, 2003).
137 *See supra* Part VI, recognizing a lot of ambiguities in the term "free."
138 Yochai Benkler wrote:

> [B]y limiting implementation of information policy to focus on two institutional devices, privatization and direct regulation, we have limited the potential for decentralization of information production in our society. Introducing a third institutional device, the commons, is likely to increase the degree of decentralization that can be sustained within the institutional constraints our society imposes on information production and exchange. Two efforts are necessary in order to introduce commons as a stable element in our information environment. First, it is necessary to identify information and communications inputs that, like radio frequency spectrum and some information, can be used without being subject to the exclusive control of any governmental or non-governmental organization. *Second, it is necessary to undertake the design of the institutional constraints necessary to take advantage of the economic or technological attributes that make these inputs susceptible to being used on a commons model.* These tasks are important avenues to serving two commitments our society has traditionally located in the first amendment.

Yochai Benkler, The Commons As A Neglected Factor of Information Policy (1998), *available at* http://www.law.nyu.edu/benklery/commons.pdf (last visited Dec. 19, 2002) (emphasis added).

139 My colleague Laura Underkuffler has been particularly insightful in showing how Locke, or for that matter Madison, used "property" in ways that are unfamiliar to modern eyes. Laura Underkuffler, *On Property: An Essay*, 100 YALE L.J. 127, 132–139 (1990).

140 2 WILLIAM BLACKSTONE, COMMENTARIES *233.

141 Leroy Fibre Co. v. Chicago Milwaukee & St. Paul Ry., 232 U.S. 340, 350 (1914).

142 It is no surprise to find this vision of the public domain flourishing at the times and in the places where the concept of property is hailed as being absolute—even if that is far from the actual truth.

143 *See* Oliver Wendell Holmes, Jr., *The Path of the Law*, 10 HARV. L. REV. 457, 461 (1897).

144 Benkler, *Free as the Air*, *supra* note 25, at 361.

145 It is not exactly clear how Lessig uses the term "liability rule." He uses free software as an example, but under the classic definition, software under the GPL is actually protected by a property rule backed by injunctive remedies. Under a liability rule, you could incorporate free software into a proprietary, closed-source, program (itself not subject to the GPL) provided you paid the appropriate level of damages, normally set at "actual harm." This is not the interpretation of the GPL, or the Copyright Act, that the Free Software Foundation supports, and I would have to agree with them. Leaving aside the question of whether or not a commons that includes content protected by liability rules includes free software, is this a useful definition of the commons? The non-discriminatory liability rule does deal with certain problems of open access to networks, protocols, or choke points for innovation. Under a liability rule regime, payment would be disaggregated from control. The Internet Service Provider would, on payment of a fee, get access to the cable company's network to provide competition with the cable company itself. The researchers would be entitled to access the stem cell lines, on payment of a flat statutory access fee to the patent-holder. But some of the types of distributed innovation described later will flourish only under a system where material is available free—meaning at zero cost. *The Wind Done Gone* might get published under a liability rule regime; Margaret Mitchell's estate could not say "No." They could merely demand a fee, and the potential profits might more than justify the payment. But a system which required *pervasive* paying of license fees (the Copyright Clearance Center generalized to all forms of data) would surely fail to live up to the appellation of a "commons." It would deter both collective creation by the poor, and complicated, multi-source, incremental innovation even by relatively wealthy institutions. Personally, I would reserve the label "commons" for something closer to Benkler's definition of the public domain—material that an individual is legally privileged to use, absent a showing of individualized facts to the contrary. Nevertheless, Lessig has an important point. The successful commons will often have some form of governance, and liability rules have extraordinary advantages, mitigating one of the largest potential dangers of the intellectual property system. I am probably reading too much into all of this because Lessig's remarkable new book avoids the liability rule definition altogether, simply saying that resources can be "free even though a price must be paid (a park is 'free' in the sense that I mean even if an access fee is required—so long as the access fee is neutrally and consistently applied)." LESSIG, *supra* note 74 at 20.

146 Edward Samuels, *The Public Domain in Copyright Law*, 41 J. COPYRIGHT SOC'Y U.S.A. 137, 150 (1993).
147 *See* BOYLE, SHAMANS, *supra* note 32; Boyle, *Cruel, supra* note 46; James Boyle, *The First Amendment and Cyberspace: The Clinton Years*, 63 LAW & CONTEMP. PROBS. 337 (Winter/Spring 2000); Boyle, *Foucault, supra* note 121; James Boyle, *Intellectual Property Online, A Young Person's Guide*, 10 HARV. J. L. & TECH. 47 (1997); Boyle, *Missing the Point, supra* note 69; James Boyle, *A Politics of Intellectual Property: Environmentalism for the Net?*, 47 DUKE L.J. 87 (1997) [hereinafter Boyle, *Politics*]; Boyle, *Theory, supra* note 77.
148 Samuels, *supra* note 146.
149 LUDWIG WITTGENSTEIN, TRACTATUS LOGICUS PHILOSOPHICUS §5.6 ("*The limits of my language* mean the limits of my world. . . . We cannot think what we cannot think; so what we cannot think we cannot say either.") Gibbon made a simpler but related point in describing the role of language in politics: "Augustus was sensible that mankind is governed by names; nor was he deceived in his expectation that the senate and people would submit to slavery, provided they were respectfully assured that they still enjoyed their ancient freedom." THE PORTABLE GIBBON: THE DECLINE AND FALL OF THE ROMAN EMPIRE 99 (D. Saunders ed., Viking Press 1952) (1782).
150 Boyle, *Politics, supra* note 147.
151 As I put it in a previous work:

> [S]mall wonder, then, that faith in Nature is hard to reconcile with the rationalist philosophers' critique of the naturalistic fallacy. Environmental ideas of Nature are often based on a skepticism about the power of reason, and a willingness to put faith in spontaneous order precisely because one knows the limits of one's own knowledge about the working of the system. We reify and anthropomorphize Nature in part to express this "faith in the system." But if we would be suspicious of this anthropomorphism when it is applied to "the Market" or to "national tradition," shouldn't we try to apply the same skepticism and feeling for nuance to "Nature"? Which system, which Nature, is being venerated? Are we humans in it? In medicine, does anything organic count as Natural? Do we let aconite and malaria have their way, smiling indulgently? Or is it merely any plant or mineral "traditionally" used as medicine? In environmental terms, is it some imaginary world without the impact of human history, without landscapes transformed, species eradicated, plant varieties cultivated? Is it "Nature as scenery;" the world with the human interventions we like, whether they are English hedgerows, drystane dykes, the bleak beauty of a Scottish moor, deforested before Dr. Johnson passed it by? The trouble with declaring one's reverence for a system, be it a market, a culture or an ecosystem, is that people actually disagree strongly about what the "natural" state of that system is. Then they disagree further about the normative implications of that natural state. Both sets of disagreements could often benefit from some old-fashioned rationalist skepticism.

James Boyle, *Against Nature*, TIMES LITERARY SUPPLEMENT, July 24, 1998 (reviewing Phil Macnaghten & John Urry, *Contested Natures* (1998)), *available at* http://www.law.duke.edu/boylesite/tls98nat.htm. What all of this *doesn't* mean, of course, is that the concept of Nature, or the Environment, is useless.

152 Boyle, *Politics, supra* note 147.
153 *Id.*
154 *See id.*
155 *See* PETER BOHM, SOCIAL EFFICIENCY: A CONCISE INTRODUCTION TO WELFARE ECONOMICS (1973); *see also* Boyle, *Politics, supra* note 147.
156 Once I decide that the Environmental Defense Fund does good science and good legal research, I rely on their opinion—leveling the playing field a bit between the power company, with its hired scientists and lawyers, and me.
157 *See, e.g.*, Public Knowledge, http://www.publicknowledge.org (last visited Jan. 14, 2003); Electronic Frontier Foundation's Campaign for Audio Visual Free Expression, http://www.eff.org/cafe (last visited Jan. 14, 2003); Creative Commons, http://www.creativecommons.org (last visited Jan. 14, 2003); Duke Law School's Center for the Study of the Public Domain, http://www.law.duke.edu/news/current/20020905pdic.html (last visited Jan. 14, 2003). There are, of course, other efforts along these lines. Honesty requires the confession that I am involved with several of these organizations as progenitor, advisor, or board member, which doubtless prejudices my selection.
158 *See supra* Parts I–III.
159 *See supra* Part VII.

63

THE TELECOM CRISIS AND BEYOND

Restructuring of the global telecommunications system

Dal Yong Jin

Source: *Gazette: The International Journal for Communication Studies* 67(3) (2005): 289–304.

Abstract

The global telecom system has undergone dramatic change under neoliberal globalization. A swift restructuring of the telecom industries, which began in the early 1980s, was possible because governments around the world adopted neoliberal telecom polices, as they confronted intensifying pressure not only from corporations but also directly from international organizations and the US government. Telecom companies, however, have in recent years begun to present symptoms of what appears to be the same life-threatening disease. This in turn has expedited new strategies such as spin-off and/or split-off strategies as well as counter-deregulation. This article examines who set the agenda for telecom policy over the last two decades to analyze a long-term change in the global telecom system. It investigates how transnational corporations were involved in the reshaping of the global telecom system by exploring the consolidation through mergers and acquisitions. It also examines the relationship between national policies and institutions on the one hand and international organizations on the other. Then, it attempts to clarify whether the transformation of the global telecom system has influenced the telecom crisis in recent years, and to find new strategies and/or new business models.

> Overcapacity and destructive competition, old economic scourges, have come to haunt the frontier of twenty-first century capitalism.
>
> (Schiller, 2003: 66)

Over the last two decades, the global telecommunications system has undergone dramatic change. The number of telecom industries has soared, and the market size and investment increased enormously with deregulation in the sector. The swift restructuring of the telecom industries, which began in the early 1980s, was possible because governments around the world adopted neoliberal telecom polices such as deregulation, privatization and liberalization, as they confronted intensifying pressure not only from corporations but also directly from international organizations and the US government. The neoliberal telecom policy gained momentum in the US and the UK in the 1980s, and has finally become a driving force for consolidation and reform of the telecom industries toward a market-oriented system around the world (Jonquireres, 1997; Thussu, 2000).

Telecom companies, however, have begun to present symptoms of what appears to be the same life-threatening disease in recent years (Schiller, 2003). In the US, dozens of companies have gone bankrupt, and the situation is no better abroad. Canada, the UK, South Korea and Malaysia have shown severe financial difficulties in the telecom sector over the last few years due to over-competition and overinvestment. From western countries to developing countries, overcapacity and severe competition among telecom companies have led to bankruptcies and financial deficits. Consequently, many telecom companies in several countries have sought new survival strategies, such as spin-off and/or split-off strategies as well as counter-deregulation in the post-telecom crisis era.

This article examines what and who set the agenda for telecom policy over the last two decades to analyze a long-term change in the global telecom system. It investigates the role of transnational corporations (TNCs), mainly examining how they were involved in the reshaping of the global telecom system. In particular, I explore the changing structure of the global telecom industries by examining the consolidation through mergers and acquisitions (M&As) in the telecom industry. I also discuss the relationship between national policies and institutions, on the one hand, and international organizations, including the International Telecommunication Union (ITU) and the WTO, on the other. Then, I attempt to clarify whether the transformation of the global telecom system has influenced the telecom crisis in recent years, and I thereafter articulate how many telecom companies around the world are trying to find new strategies and/or new business models, differentiating them from neoliberal telecom restructuring. Through the discussion, I hope to shed light on current developments and place them in perspective that has relevance for future telecom policy directions.

Theoretical framework/methodology

The global telecom industry between the early 1980s and early 21st century was an exemplary case of the neoliberal transformation thesis. The restructuring of the telecom sector was conducted under the banner of deregulation and liberalization not only in western countries where this trend was most pronounced, but around the world, including the countries of the old socialist bloc as well as Latin American and Asian countries.

Several communication scholars, including Dan Schiller and Robert McChesney, point out that the global telecom system has become increasingly transnational with the rise of neoliberalism, which refers to the policies that maximize the role of markets and profit-making and minimize the role of non-market institutions through deregulation and privatization. Across the world, a majority of governments also introduced economic liberalization measures, including opening the domestic telecom market.

As Dan Schiller (1999: 2–3) points out, neoliberalism comes by its name because of its adherents' primary aim – paring unwanted state regulation of the economy to gain more freedom of action for private firms. For neoliberal theory proponents, 'markets should be left alone to obey their presumed natural logic: so goes the laissez-faire doctrine that was reenshrined as domestic orthodoxy during the 1980s and assumed global pre-eminence during the 1990s'. Robert McChesney (2001: 2) also argues that neoliberalism unleashed national and international politics maximally supportive of business domination of all social affairs. According to him, 'the centerpiece of neoliberal policies is invariably a call for commercial communication markets to be deregulated'. To take one documented case, after conducting a case study of the transformation of mass communication in Chile, Matt Davies (1999: 112–13) concluded that privatization, deregulation and reliance on foreign direct investment all removed the state from participation in economic activities and communication policies, which resulted in a series of rapid boom and bust cycles in the Chilean economy and communications industry over the last two decades. As these communication scholars emphasize, neoliberalism engineers the restructuring of national economies and boundaries, and this has consequences for telecom industries. The telecom industries in Latin America and Asia as well as in the US underwent a dramatic transformation commonly referred to as neoliberal reform.

This article is an investigation of the recent history of the global telecom industry, focusing on changing telecom policy worldwide and its impact on the global telecom system in the context of the broader social structure of society. I therefore examine the political economy of the global telecom industry by means of historical and institutional analyses.

Transformation of the telecom industry

Since about 1980, telecom has been regarded as an important infrastructure for economic development around the world not only because of its size, but also because of its indispensable role in communication and information dissemination. Telecom has become a key to socioeconomic development within a national, regional, or global context over the last two decades. Since telecom has functioned as the basic infrastructure for the emerging information technology as well as the major driving force in economic development, construction of telecom systems is taking place on a large scale throughout the world. Except in the US, telecom systems were operated almost entirely as national monopolies prior to the mid-1980s, but each state has transformed the state monopoly system into a profit-driven private system over the last two decades (Cabanda and Afiff, 2002).

The telecom sector has developed enormously in terms of telephone lines, market size, and investment with its transition to market-oriented private corporations. To begin with, the recent expansion of the telecom sector has been notable in both main telephone lines, referring to the telephone lines connecting a customer's equipment to the public switched telephone network (PSTN) and which have a dedicated port on a telephone exchange, and wireless lines. The number of main telephone lines reached over 1 billion for the first time ever in 2002. Main telephone lines had jumped from 142 million in 1960 and 272.7 million in 1970 to 689 million in 1995 and to 1.1 billion by the end of 2002 (ITU, 2003b; UN Statistical Office, 1972). The increase in the number of mobile phones is far steeper than that of main telephone lines because the expansion began from a tiny base of the development. The number of mobile phone subscribers increased 12.6 times from 90.6 million in 1995 to 1.14 billion in 2002 and exceeds the number of subscribers to fixed telephone lines (ITU, 2003a).

A few developed countries, including the US, Japan and several European countries, have dominated telecom businesses for a long time by the number of main telephone lines and mobile phones. However, the emerging market in the telecom sector in recent years is also showing remarkable growth in Africa, Asia and Latin America, while western countries' portion has shrunk, reflecting saturation of the market. For instance, in 1981 non-OECD countries (with 81 percent of the world's population in 1999) had only 7 percent of all phones (fixed and mobile), but this increased to 11 percent in 1988 and to 43 percent in 1999 (Wellenius *et al.*, 2000). This growth partly resulted from the addition in the last decade of 170 million mobile customers outside the OECD mainly in China, Brazil and India. In particular, China, due to the state's initiative for developing infrastructure for information technology, became the largest country, followed by the US, in terms of numbers of both main telephone lines and cellular mobile phone subscribers, with 214 million main telephone lines in 2002 and with 144 million cellular phone subscribers in 2001 (ITU, 2002, 2003b).

As a reflection of the rapid growth of the telecom sector, the telecom service market has also expanded. Telecom services has become one of the largest and most profitable economic fields in repent years. In 2000, total worldwide telecom revenues in constant dollars[1] in service markets were at more than US$925 billion, representing a 10 percent increase over 1999 (US$841 billion), as opposed to US$300 billion in 1990 (ITU, 2002). The global telecom equipment export market also witnessed substantial growth from US$62.5 billion in 1995 to US$141.7 billion in 2000 (ITU, 2002). As usual, several western countries enjoyed tremendous benefits from the growing telecom services market. For example, in 1999 revenues in telecom services markets in OECD countries accounted for as much as 89.8 percent of worldwide revenues (OECD, 2001).

Governments throughout the world and transnational capitals have invested an enormous amount of money in the telecom industry, including basic telecom services over the last decade because of its significance as infrastructure for IT as well as the economy. When governments around the world invested US$202 billion in telecom in 2000, Japan as one of the advanced technological nations invested US$32.8 billion, while the US invested US$28.8 billion (ITU, 2002). The importance of the telecom industry has also led to some very ambitious projects in developing countries. In 2000, for example, the total investment in telecom in China was as much as US$26.8 billion (ITU, 2002). India, with a per capita income of under US$400 in 1999, has devoted massive resources to developing satellite communications since the 1970s, and the last of its second-generation satellites was launched in 1999. 'Telecom system build-outs, at every scale from local loops to the global grid, are occurring on an unparalleled scale throughout the world, although examples such as these are rare in the developing countries' (Schiller, 2001: 52).

Dramatic growth and transition in the telecom sector over the last two decades have occurred since governments across the world began to transform telecom companies into a competitive market structure from a state-owned monopoly. In other words, transformation of the telecom sector has been expedited with the adoption of neoliberal economic policy, although several significant factors were considered major reasons for restructuring such as efficiency and performance of the firms. These forms of transformation in telecom are very significant because these strategies interact in determining the ownership of telecom firms and the industry structure of the whole sector, which result in concentrating the ownership structure to a few shareholders and board members as well as conglomerating the telecom industries (Trillas, 2002). As Dan Schiller (2001) points out, by elevating the precepts of privatization, liberalization of market entry and specialized services aimed at privileged groups, policy changes have resulted in enriching and empowering a few thousand giant companies and their affiliated strata.

Liberalization in the telecom industry

Liberalization is leading to a restructuring of global telecom. There has been a trend toward the liberalization of telecom services since the mid-1980s. As is well documented, the trigger for neoliberal reform in the telecom industry can be traced back to 1982 when the AT&T was restructured in the US, and British Telecom (BT) was privatized in the UK. During Margaret Thatcher's term, the UK privatized BT and allowed the authorization of a competitive carrier, Mercury, which became a part of Cable & Wireless in 1997. These measures permitted the UK to offer itself as a hospitable site for the information system operations of major US firms needing access to European markets (Schiller and Fregoso, 1993). In other words, telecom liberalization comprised a spur to foreign investment in the UK. At the same time, the wake of the continuing liberalization of the US market led to the AT&T divestiture of 1982–4.

Since then, a number of countries have made significant changes in their telecom regulatory structures and allowed for substantial liberalization of markets. The changes made in telecom market structures in the 1980s indicated that competition, once the exception in telecom, was quickly becoming the norm (OECD, 1990). As a result of a series of deregulating markets, transnational capitals were active in domestic telecom markets in the world. TNCs were intent on achieving access to an increasingly sophisticated, seamless communications network, enabling them to conduct business around the clock and around the world (Oh, 1996). Capital investment not only occurred in domestic markets in developed countries, but also occurred in developing countries because telecom giants extended their investment for high profits, reflecting their advanced technologies and saturation of domestic markets in developed countries, which resulted in the rapid growth of transnationalization of the telecom sector.

A process of alliances, mergers and acquisitions was an important part of the operators' answer to these changes beginning in the mid-1980s. Mergers and joint ventures – such as the deal struck by BT and AT&T – merely climaxed a trend that has been fermenting for more than a decade, a trend that was accompanied by a growing need for new markets. In particular, two main events, the Telecommunications Act of 1996 in the US and the WTO telecom agreement in 1997, have sent shock waves through the telecom sector around the world in recent years (Schiller, 2003).

In the US, the 1996 Telecommunications Act allowed for an unprecedented level of competition in the sector. The Act has eliminated market entry barriers for entrepreneurs and other small businesses in the provision and ownership of telecom services, and thereafter triggered a huge M&A

across the greater communications industry. Since the passage of the Telecommunications Act, companies in the long-haul fiber-optic, cable television, satellite, local telephone, wireless and other sectors of the industry have undertaken massive capital expenditures to develop and upgrade networks. For instance, the US$53 billion marriage of GTE and Bell Atlantic in 1998 resulted in the creation of Verizon, the largest provider of local phone services and wireless communications as well as one of the world's largest providers of telecom services, exemplifying the wave of telecom mergers designed to enable global players to expand their strategic, and geographic reach (Bradbury and Kasler, 2000).

On the global level, the drive for liberalization culminated in the 1997 WTO telecommunications agreement. Signed by 69 countries, the Agreement on Basic Telecommunications Services requires them to open their domestic markets to foreign competition and to allow foreign companies to buy stakes in domestic operators (Jonquireres, 1997). This agreement was not the first or the only such attempt. Over the years, communications have appeared on the agenda of almost every major negotiation concerned with international trade, including meetings of the Asia-Pacific Economic Council (APEC), the European Commission (EC) and agreements such as the Maastricht Treaty and the North American Free Trade Agreement (NAFTA). In Europe, the European Union (EU) decided as a general rule to liberalize the telecom sector in 1998, with each country implementing liberalization via different strategies. The IMF and the ITU also each enrolled in the liberalization effort in the 1990s. They have pressed governments to open markets to foreigners over the last decade. More importantly, 'as US power groups' confidence increased, bilateral negotiations, US trade law, and encompassing multilateral initiatives all were pursued, which resulted in transformation of the institutional basis of world telecom' (McChesney and Schiller, 2002: 15).

However, the launching of basic telecom negotiations at the WTO sent a strong message to the telecom officials and telecom companies across the country (McLarty, 1998). The WTO agreement on basic services attracted widespread attention because it succeeded, on a global scale, in establishing the free trade principle in an area previously closed to foreign intervention. The 1997 WTO telecommunications agreement finally ignited a wave of M&As because each of the giant telecom firms has moved aggressively into deregulated domestic telecom markets around the world, and transnational corporations have formed joint ventures with other global giants and local investors. Several major global M&As occurred beginning in 1998. In Canada, Bell Canada Enterprises (BCE) completed its purchase of Teleglobe for US$7.6 billion to broaden its reach beyond Canada in 1999 (Hamilton, 2002). In Japan, KDD, DDI and Ido merged to become KDDI in 2000, and became a main competitor to Nippon Telegraph and Telephone (NTT), the largest Japanese telecom company (OECD, 2001).

Consequently, telecom became one of the most active industries in the M&A market, which resulted in mega-transnational corporations, beginning in the late 1990s. For example, telecom was the second largest industry in the global M&A market at US$105.9 billion in 196 deals worldwide in 1998, only behind commercial banks.[2] The magnitude of M&A in telecom jumped exponentially from only US$4.4 billion in 1992 to US$10.5 billion in 1993. Telecom also became the largest industry in the M&A market by dollar value at US$213 billion with 245 deals in 1999, and US$235 billion in 319 deals in 2000, respectively. Those years were recorded as the golden age of telecom companies in the global M&A market. With the rapid growth of M&A, telecom was the second largest industry in the M&A market between 1990 and 1999, valued at $524.3 billion in 1293 deals, just behind commercial banks ($547.2 billion; 2663 deals). In addition, in the late 1990s, the world's largest telecom firms raced to put together global alliances. For instance, AT&T allied itself with Singapore Telecom and four major European national firms to form World Partners. Sprint, Deutsche Telekom and France Télécom also formed Global One in 1997 (Maney, 1997).

Privatization of telecom companies

Privatization of telecom companies has been noticeable over the last two decades. Privatization involves the change in legal status of an incumbent carrier from public to private ownership in telecom. Typically, but not always, privatization is also coupled with deregulation. The pace of privatization opportunities has increased, particularly because many states have made market access commitments, under the auspices of the WTO, which relax or eliminate foreign ownership and licensing restrictions in telecom.

The UK's BT in 1984 triggered privatization, as well as liberalization of the telecom sector, and during the 1980s a politics of neoliberal telecom reform took hold in dozens of nations following the US and UK. Before 1989, only nine countries had privatized an existing telecom system operator. With the collapse of the Soviet Union in 1991, however, the scale of the neoliberal privatization project in telecom rapidly expanded and gained devotees within scores of countries (Thussu, 2000).

Privatization occurred in such diverse nations as Argentina, Australia, Brazil, Canada, Japan, Mexico, Peru and Venezuela. Overall, between 1984 and July 1999, within a broader context of state-asset privatization, around US$244 billion worth of privatization of state-owned systems occurred (US Federal Communications Commission, 2000). No region of the world has embraced the privatization of telecom as enthusiastically as Latin America. Of the 89 incumbent public telephone operators worldwide that had been privatized by 1999, one-quarter of operators were in the Americas region. Even more impressive is the degree of private participation in the sector. More than two-thirds of the countries of the Americas region have either partially or fully privatized their telecom companies, while in other regions like Africa and the Middle East, the proportion drops to 28 percent and 33 percent, respectively (ITU, 2000).

In 2000, the number of ITU members states with partially or wholly privately owned operators outnumbered those with state-owned operators for the first time since the 19th century. And as of the end of 2001, some 106 ITU member states had privatized their incumbent operators, in part or in whole. In the Middle East and Africa, state-owned operators were in the majority, but in the other regions private operators were in the ascendancy (ITU, 2002).

Privatization in telecom industries resulted in massive investment in the global telecom market. Incumbents facing competition at home in mainly western countries strongly pursued foreign markets for investment opportunities as a form of a consortium or joint venture (Frieden, 2001). The privatization and liberalization of telecom have also been stimulated by the desire for profits by telecom firms and the investment bankers who coordinate the neoliberal reforms (Herman and McChesney, 1997). These private interests worked with the governments of the developed states and the institutions of global capitalism such as the World Bank and the IMF to push these policies.

However, many countries still maintain their managerial power over telecom industries as major stake-holders, e.g. the US, France and Japan do maintain some forms of restriction on foreign ownership in basic services. Many developing countries defended themselves on the grounds that they maintained their managerial power because even the powerful global players saw the need for restricting foreign investment in the communication sector. Therefore, several countries, including the US, Canada, France, Japan, Brazil, Korea and more recently China, have chosen to keep some form of restrictions on foreign ownership (OECD, 2001).

Several reasons provide some justification for restrictions on foreign ownership. Governments around the world clearly wish to retain some control over their public telecommunications operators (PTOs) for national security and to ensure the legal status of regulation (OECD, 1993). In addition, most countries maintaining some restrictions, with some exceptions like Ghana and Tunisia, have a sizeable domestic market with a population over 20 million (Wang, 2003). In such cases as India and China, there are also budding national industries that have the potential to compete in the global market. Regardless of the pressure from foreign forces, governments in many parts of the world play significant roles in domestic telecom markets as the major investors and regulators.

The telecom crisis: failure of neoliberal transformation

Telecom companies have experienced serious problems such as overcapacity and overcompetition as well as mismanagement, including accounting scandals, in the midst of the transformation of the global telecom sector. While telecom companies were expanding, they had taken on enormous amounts of debt; one firm after another began having difficulty repaying these obligations and went into bankruptcy. Throughout the telecom industry, demand has failed to match expectation, businesses are losing money, stock values have plummeted and a radical consolidation is in the offing (Starr, 2002). Indeed, as of 2000, the group with the worst performance in the US stock market was the telecom sector. While the entire S&P Super 1500 index declined 8 percent in 2000, the S&P Communication Services index dropped 39.3 percent, led by a 69.3 percent plunge in the market value of long-distance carriers (Standard & Poor's, 2002).

To begin with, overcapacity in the telecom sector throughout the world has been notable, but problematic. Again in the US, after the passage of the Telecommunications Act of 1996, companies in sectors of the industry such as long-haul fiber-optic, cable television, satellite, local telephone and wireless have undertaken massive capital expenditure to develop and upgrade networks. Cable companies (through cable modems) and telephone companies (through digital subscriber lines [DSL]) are both offering broadband access to their subscribers in most areas of the country. This competition has led to network expansion, but it has also led to huge overcapacity. Many companies have built networks and burned cash. 'Build networks and customers will come' was the business model of the day for long-haul carriers and many new entrants in the telecom business. However, fiber-optic networks costing billions of dollars remain unused because there is no prospective demand for them, and the companies that built them are broke. As telecom companies have dramatically scaled down their expenditure, equipment suppliers and manufacturers have felt the brutal effects, with their revenue and values falling dramatically.[3] The collapse has extended to the equipment sector in part because much of the investment was vendor-financed – that is, capital came from manufacturers such as Lucent, Nortel, Motorola, Alcatel and Cisco, anxious to sell their products (Starr, 2002).

Overcompetition has caused even more serious consequences than overcapacity throughout the world. With deregulation and liberalization of the telecom sector, new companies entered the market at a fast pace. In the US, as of early 2001, approximately 700 companies offered long-distance services, although a select few dominated the market (Standard & Poor's, 2003a). In 1999, 74 telecom carriers with revenues greater than US$1 billion were operating in OECD countries, as opposed to 40 carriers in 1992 (OECD, 2001). The increasing number of new entrants in the telecom sector, including telecom investment, was readily evident from their shares in the industry total. Most notably, new entrants were responsible for 35 percent of capital expenditure in 1999. Many telecom companies went on a buying spree for Internet or telecom and cable assets as new strategic sectors possibly to make huge profits. Their strategy has not worked and the consequences have been harsh.

While telecom was not the only industry that collapsed due to over-capacity and overcompetition in recent years, it made some of the biggest headlines in the media because of its magnitude and huge impact on people's everyday lives. Following a wave of bankruptcies among newer telecom start-ups in 2001, some of the larger, longer-established players came under the severe threat of bankruptcy in 2002 (Standard & Poor's, 2003b). In the US, 23 telecom companies had gone bankrupt in a wave in the same year. Among these, three major telecom companies, Global Crossing, WorldCom and 360 Networks, filed for bankruptcy protection in 2002. Global Crossing was staggering toward bankruptcy beginning in 2000. Its losses increased from US$2 billion in 2000 to US$2.7 billion in 2001, while its stock lost 90 percent of its value in 2001. The debt ballooned to US$7.6 billion in 2001 (Creswell, 2001). The long-distance giant WorldCom Inc. was accused of falsifying its books by US$11 billion in the largest accounting scandal in US history as well as the single largest bankruptcy in American history. Declining revenues in long-distance service were a principal factor in the bankruptcy of WorldCom, which owns MCI (Starr, 2002: 23). However, sizable accounting errors were the event that triggered WorldCom's filing for bankruptcy (Standard & Poor's, 2003b).[4]

In addition, several other telecom companies in the US have also suffered from decreasing revenues in long-distance service, although they are not bankrupt. For example, due to declines in long-distance voice revenue, the total revenues of AT&T decreased by about 10.4 percent in 2002, compared to 2001, from US$42.1 billion to US$37.8 billion (AT&T, 2002). A few other countries also witnessed similar crises. For instance, Teleglobe, which was sold to BCE in 1999, filed for bankruptcy protection in May 2002 in Canada. Teleglobe borrowed billions of dollars to build a fiber-optic network, but failed to generate enough revenue to repay debt. As Dan Schiller (2003: 66) points out, 'long viewed as leading the way into the information age of productivity and enlightenment, telecom companies suddenly are presenting symptoms of what appears to be the same life-threatening disease'.

The dimensions of the collapse in telecom industries in the 21st century have resulted in massive layoffs, of half a million people in the US. According to *The New York Times*, telecom companies exceeded any other industry in the number of publicly announced job cuts between the end of 2000 and June 2002 (Uchitelle, 2002). Most of this rapid job shrinkage in telecom came through layoffs, buyouts and forced retirements. The cuts came from the dozens of companies that build and operate the nation's networks for telephone service, cable television, the Internet, email and data transmission. Having wildly overexpanded in the 1990s, the companies have been rushing to shrink ever since, serving as a drag on the economic recovery. During this period, Lucent laid off 52.8 percent of its workers from 106,000 in 2000 to 50,000 in June 2002. WorldCom also lost 21 percent of its workers, followed by AT&T (16.7 percent), Quest (14.9 percent), SBC (14.1 percent), Sprint (7.3 percent) and Bell South (7 percent) (Uchitelle, 2002).

In the middle of the telecom crisis, M&As have also declined dramatically in recent years, which partially resulted in the weakness in the US deal market. Again in 2000, M&As in telecom ranked in first place, valued at US$235 billion in 319 deals, but it became the fourth most active industry in the M&A market at US$79.8 billion in 221 deals in 2001, and plummeted to 10th position, valued at US$19.8 billion in 142 deals in 2002 ('M&A Almanac', 2001, 2002, 2003 [see note 2]). Deals in telecom in 2002 could not reach one-tenth of those in 2000. Overall, M&A activity in all industries has been significantly down in the world in recent years due to the global economic recession, but M&As in telecom declined at a faster speed than other industries across the world.

The telecom crisis did not happen all by itself. Reforms conducted during the 1990s were supposed to create a deregulated telecom industry with large numbers of firms generating entrepreneurial innovations and economic growth. The policy has had some successes. But now the industry is imploding. By 2000, companies began to realize that there simply was not enough business to go around, and they raced to gain market share in an explosion of overcompetition and price wars that drove down revenues, as Michael Powell, Federal Communications Commission chairman, explained in his 30 July 2002 testimony before the Senate Commerce Committee. At that time, Powell stated that 'the hyper-competition and vicious price wars that precipitated today's burst stemmed from the exaggerated forecasts of demand from "the Internet gold rush"'.[5] Since Powell is a strong advocate of deregulation of the communication industry, his remarks in testimony would be considered significant with regard to the telecom crisis in recent years.

As explained, there is no doubt that the Telecommunications Act of 1996 in the US and the WTO Agreement on Basic Telecommunications Services of 1997 were the real culprits of the telecom crisis, together with the recession in the global economy in recent years. As noted, 'the Telecommunications Act continued the process of liberalization by setting down terms on which local and long-distance carriers could invade one another's markets' (Schiller, 2003). After Congress passed the Telecommunications Act of 1996, capital flooded into telecom, as existing firms and new ones began building networks over land, undersea and in the air. Meanwhile, the WTO Agreement on Basic Telecom Services opened further investment opportunities in the telecom sector, but the telecom industry was also taking on massive debts as in the case of the domestic market in the US (Schiller, 2003). Overcapacity and overcompetition became the major problems haunting the telecom industry in the world in the post-WTO system. In other words, overcapacity and overcompetition in telecom rendered the major telecom companies vulnerable.

After the telecom crisis: new strategies for the next generation

With the crisis in the telecom industry, a third phase of transformation has occurred in the 21st century: spin-off and/or split-off strategies as well as counter-deregulation. Restructuring, i.e. splitting-off, has become an important dimension in reshaping telecom industries as a result of the growing 'telecom crisis' in the 21st century. In response to weaknesses in the longdistance market and depressed telecom stock prices, leading telecom companies began to separate their units, primarily wireless phone, Internet, broadband and cable services from more mature business operations in an effort to obtain higher market valuations and better profit. In other words, major restructuring projects among telecom carriers in recent years were related to announcements entailing increased decentralization, unlike ever-growing concentration through M&A (OECD, 2001: 14–15). What major telecom companies worried about was the lack of investor confidence and capital markets closing to new investment. The significant trend is for some of the largest telecom carriers to restructure themselves mainly due to commercial imperatives.

Spin-offs in telecom were pioneered in the US, but European telecom has embraced them enthusiastically for the flexibility they bring. On 10 August 2001, AT&T completed the split-off of Liberty Media Corporation as an independent company. In November 2002, AT&T also spun-off AT&T Broadband to AT&T shareowners. Of course, M&As have not ended because AT&T Broadband simultaneously combined with Comcast Corporation (AT&T, 2002). Some non-US companies also continue to expand but with a specific focus; for example, Vodafone, a leading British mobile phone company, is expanding with the aim of focusing on wireless markets. Likewise, Cable & Wireless, while divesting traditional telephony operation, is focusing on Internet services for business users and other carriers ('Cable & Wireless Company Analysis', 2002).

Regulatory constraints are another force leading to reorganization of businesses and creating opportunities for companies to float units. For example, in April 2000, the UK's BT announced a restructuring of the company along its different lines of business (e.g. retail, Internet, wireless) rather than along geographical divisions (Sommerville, 2000: 7). BT planned to separate its highly regulated wholesale wireline business from the other business units that suffer fewer constraints (Standard & Poor's, 2002).

A common thread of this restructuring was the objective to build greater shareholder value. One conclusion that might be drawn is that the mega-mergers of recent years no longer impress investors unless they have targeted specific lines of business (OECD, 2001). As M&A entices investment in the new giant company, spin-off strategy also entices investments in telecom because new companies focus on profitable businesses such as the Internet and broadband. By all means, the factors driving restructuring in the largest firms will inevitably affect other telecom carriers that are still trying to be all things to all customers (OECD, 2001).

Finally, overcompetition and a high level of debt required several governments, for instance in Malaysia and the Philippines, to initiate counter-deregulation communication policy to encourage formation of alliances to share facilities and infrastructure, resulting in a new mega telecom industry in the region (Standard & Poor's, 2002: 11-12). In these countries, liberalization of the telecom industry was carried out too fast and too far, impairing the ability of competitors to establish viable business. In the case of the Philippines, the country suffers from an excess of wireline capacity, considering the population's purchasing power. The Philippine telecom market was opened to competition in 1993, stimulating 10 new companies to challenge incumbent Philippine Long Distance Telephone (PLDT). Due to overcompetition, the Philippines had 6.8 million lines in January 2000 but only 2.9 million subscribers. Therefore, the government is encouraging the merger of regional telecom companies to achieve economies of scale and bring down the price of service. After acquiring two of the new players in the fixed line market, PLDT has acquired control of two mobile operators, making it the largest operator in the country. The excesses ironically bring about new regulation to some governments in the market-oriented deregulation era. In early 2000, the Communications and Multimedia Commission, a regulatory body in Malaysia, also reduced the number of mobile telecom companies from eight to five to curb overcompetition (Standard & Poor's, 2002).

In sum, the liberalization and privatization process beginning in the mid-1980s has increased the supply of infrastructure and services; however, the overcompetition and overcapacity expedited by deregulation have become the real culprits behind the telecom crisis in recent years. Liberalization and privatization of telecom industries in many countries were carried out too fast and too far, impairing the ability of telecom firms to establish viable businesses. Consequently, in the post-crisis era many telecom companies have adopted new survival strategies, including spin-off and/or split-off activities as well as counter-deregulation. The neoliberal transition in telecom industries is still occurring around the country; however, current forms of transition, such as splitting-off and counter-deregulation, indicate a new policy for the next generation in the global telecom sector.

Conclusion

The focus of this article has been on the dimensions and implications of neoliberal restructuring of global telecom. The global telecom system has dramatically changed since the 1980s. The changing political-economic environment in the world caused the rapid transformation of global telecom. The introduction of neoliberal economic policy has changed the global telecom system primarily from a government-dominated sector to a profit-driven private sector. Adoption of deregulation, liberalization and privatization of telecom systems in the early 1980s in the US and UK allowed the inclusion of new commercial telecom companies around the world.

TNCs played an important role in the process of change in cooperation with international organizations and the US government. These international forces served as the driving force behind neoliberal reform in the domestic telecom sector around the world. As each government adopted deregulation, TNCs invested an enormous amount of money in the telecom industry in developed countries because it became a highly profitable sector of the world economy, which resulted in ever-increasing rates of growth in the telecom industry. In other words, commercialized telecom industries through M&As could control the global market, and ultimately acquire a larger share of and larger profit from the global information and telecom markets.

Governments around the world, however, had pivotal roles in the transformation of the telecom industry because the industry is a symbol of national infrastructure, unlike other economic and communication sectors. Telecom remains primarily a national phenomenon in many countries, and national governments played a significant part in transforming the telecom system through legislative powers. In other words, in the neoliberal globalization era, characterized by a time of market deregulation and reduced state intervention into economic and cultural affairs, several governments around the world were pursuing a proactive telecom policy. Indeed, many governments throughout the world played a key role in the telecom sector because unremitting political intervention was necessary to actualize something approaching such a free market regime in the telecom industry (Schiller, 1999). Governments in developing countries also began to acknowledge that the neoliberal reform has not been applied successfully in their specific domestic situation, and they take counter-deregulation measures. It is recognized that overcapacity and severe competition among telecom companies, which occurred through neoliberal reform, have brought about the telecom crisis, and this in turn has demanded that governments set the agenda in the telecom sector.

This implies the next decade will be different from the 1980s and 1990s, which were the decades of market deregulation and liberalization in the telecommunication industry worldwide. New strategies and new business models such as split-off and counter-deregulation measures will be applied to achieve growth and development of the telecom industry. International agencies and global TNCs will still play important roles as they have over the last two decades. However, national governments and domestic telecom companies will set the agenda for telecom policies to survive and to grow in the midst of changing global and domestic political-economic environments that emphasize the specific domestic situation in their countries. Therefore, the global telecom system will be transformed, influenced sometimes by cooperative and at other times conflicting relationships between national governments, domestic capital and TNCs.

Notes

1 Constant dollars are used to adjust for the effect of inflation while current dollar is a measure of spending or revenue in a given year that has not been adjusted for differences in prices between that year and a base year. In other words, current dollar does not reflect adjustment for inflation. Since the value of money changes over time, it is useful to convert current dollar to constant dollar to remove the effects of inflation, in particular to produce a more useful time series data of GNP or GDP.
2 To analyze the trend of M&As in the international telecom sector, I referred to the 'M&A Almanac' in issues 1991–2002 of *Mergers and Acquisitions*, which is the dealmakers' trade journal that Thompson Financial Company published every month.
3 Testimony of Michael Powell, before the Panel of a Hearing of the Senate Commerce, Science and Transportation Committee, on 'Financial Turmoil in the Telecom Marketplace: Maintaining the Operations of Essential Communications Facilities', 30 July 2002, 16–17.
4 WorldCom's problems began in 2000. A vicious price war in the long-distance market ravaged profit margins in the company's consumer and business divisions. Rather than report the bad news, the company relied on aggressive accounting practices, such as moving reserves around. By 2001, however, these actions were not enough to keep the carrier afloat. The company then took line costs (fees paid to lease portions of other companies' telephone networks) out of the operating expense account on the income statement, where they belonged, and tucked them into the capital spending accounts on the balance sheet and the statement of cash flows. These improper accounting practices led to a Securities and Exchange Commission (SEC) civil fraud suit, and along with the company's heavy debt load, caused depreciation of stock value.
5 Panel of a hearing of the Senate Commerce, Science and Transportation Committee, 'Financial Turmoil in the Telecom Marketplace', 30 July 2002, 16–17.

References

AT&T (2002) *Annual Report 2002*. Bedminster, NJ: AT&T.
Bradbury, S. and K. Kasler (2000) 'Verizon Communications: The Merger of Bell Atlantic and GTE'. *Corporate Finance* November: 47.
Cabanda, E. and M. Afiff (2002) 'Performance Gains Through Privatization and Competition of Asian Telecommunications', *ASEAN Economic Bulletin* 19(3): 255–6.

'Cable & Wireless Company Analysis' (2002) at: www.budde.com.au/FreeNews/NewsArticle3774.html (accessed 24 May 2003).
Creswell, J. (2001) 'Global Flameout', *Fortune* 144(13): 109.
Davies, M. (1999) *International Political Economy and Mass Communication in Chile.* New York: Macmillan.
Frieden, R. (2001) *Managing Internet-Driven Change in International Telecommunications.* Boston, MA: Artech House.
Hamilton, T. (2002) 'Teleglobe Reported Set to Axe 40 Percent of Staff', *Toronto Star* 10 May: E1.
Herman, E. and R. McChesney (1997) *The Global Media: The New Missionaries of Corporate Capitalism.* New York: Cassell.
ITU (International Telecommunication Union) (2000) *Americas Telecommunication Indicators 2000: Executive Summary.* Geneva: ITU.
ITU (International Telecommunication Union) (2002) *World Telecommunication Development Report.* Geneva: ITU.
ITU (International Telecommunication Union) (2003a) *Cellular Subscribers.* Geneva: ITU.
ITU (International Telecommunication Union) (2003b) *Main Telephone Lines.* Geneva: ITU.
Jonquireres, G. (1997) 'Template for Trade Tariffs', *Financial Times* 18 February: 6.
McChesney, R. (2001) 'Global Media, Neoliberalism, and Imperialism', *Monthly Review* 52(19): 1–19.
McChesney, R. and D. Schiller (2002) 'The Political Economy of International Communications: Foundations for the Emerging Global Debate over Media Ownership and Regulation', paper presented at the UNRISD Project on Information Technologies and Social Development, April.
McLarty, T. (1998) 'Liberalized Telecommunications Trade in the WTO: Implications for Universal Service Policy', *Federal Communications Law Journal* 5(1): 1–59.
Maney, K. (1997) 'American is Building British Phone Empire', *USA Today* 20 March: 4B.
OECD (Organization for Economic Cooperation and Development) (1990) *Communications Outlook 1990.* Paris: OECD.
OECD (Organization for Economic Cooperation and Development) (1993) *Communications Outlook 1993.* Paris: OECD.
OECD (Organization for Economic Cooperation and Development) (2001) *Communication Outlook 2001.* Paris: OECD.
Oh, J. G. (1996) 'Global Strategic Alliances in the Telecommunications Industry', *Telecommunications Policy* 20(9): 713–20.
Schiller, D. (1999) Digital Capitalism: *Networking the Global Marker System.* Cambridge: The MIT Press.
Schiller, D. (2001) 'World Communications in Today's Age of Capital', *Emergences* 11(1): 51–68.
Schiller, D. (2003) 'The Telecom Crisis', *Dissent* 50(1): 66–70.
Schiller, D. and R. Fregoso (1993) 'A Private View of the Digital World', pp. 210–34 in K. Nordenstreng and H. Schiller (eds) *Beyond National Sovereignty: International Communications in the 1990s.* Norwood, NJ: Ablex.
Sommerville, Q. (2000) 'BT Goes Its Own Separate Ways', *Scotland on Sunday* 16 April: 7.

Standard & Poor's (2002) 'A Year of Turmoil for US Long-Distance Carriers', *Industry Surveys* 13 (April).

Standard & Poor's (2003a) 'Telecom Industry Enters New Era', *Industry Surveys* 3 (April).

Standard & Poor's (2003b) 'Telecom Troubles Continue', *Industry Surveys* 3 (April).

Starr, P. (2002) 'The Great Telecom Implosion', *American Prospect* 13(16): 21–7.

Thussu, D. K. (2000) *International Communication: Continuity and Change*. New York: Oxford University Press.

Trillas, F. (2002) 'Mergers, Acquisitions and Control of Telecommunications Firms in Europe', *Telecommunications Policy* 26(5/6): 260–86.

Uchitelle, L. (2002) 'Turmoil at WorldCom: The Work Force; Job Cuts Take Heavy Toll on Telecom Industry', *New York Times* 29 June: C1.

UN Statistical Office (1972) *Statistical Yearbook*. New York: United Nations.

US Federal Communications Commission, International Bureau (2000) 'Report on International Telecommunications Markets 1999 Update', prepared for Senator Ernest F. Hollings, Committer on Commerce, Science and Transportation, US Senate.

Wang, G. (2003) 'Foreign Investment Policies, Sovereignty and Growth', *Telecommunications Policy* 27(1): 267–82.

Wellenius, B., C. Braga and C. Qiang (2000) 'Investment and Growth of the Information Infrastructure: Summary Results of a Global Survey', *Telecommunications Policy* 24(8/9): 639–43.

64

INTERNET CO-GOVERNANCE

Towards a Multilayer Multiplayer Mechanism of Consultation, Coordination and Cooperation (M_3C_3)

Wolfgang Kleinwächter

Source: *E-Learning* 3(3) (2006): 473–87.

The governance of the Internet, its regulation and in particular the management of its core resources, is one of the most controversial issues in the ongoing discussion on the future development of the global information society within the context of the Geneva World Summit (WSIS I).

While everybody agrees that there is a need for something like a global regulatory framework to guarantee the stability, flexibility und further development of the Internet, there is a broad range of different ideas, which kind of regulation should be developed and applied. Concepts of private sector led self-regulation stands versus governmental regulation with a broad variety of co-regulatory ideas in between.[1]

The myth of the unregulated internet

Part of the problem is an often repeated myth of the early days of the internet that the "network of networks" is a "virtual space" which is separated from the "real places" and does not need any kind of regulation.[2] When futuristic visions, developed for "virtual netizens of cyberspace" by William Gibson, John Perry Barlow and others, were applied directly to the practical new issues, which emerged from the use of the Internet by "real citizens of sovereign states", confusion grew. But confronted with the reality of life, it became also clear, that the myth of a "free and unregulated Internet" in its radical understanding was never true.

The Internet never escaped from the existing broader framework of national and international legislation. What was illegal offline became not legal online.

It is true that the development of the Internet in the 1980s and 1990s took place in a policy environment in the United States, which was dominated by concepts of "de-regulation" (under the Reagan Administration from 1980–1988) and "private sector leadership" (under the Clinton Administration from 1992–2000). And true is furthermore, that the regulatory mechanisms for the technical components of the Internet in a more narrow sense and the philosophy behind them were different from the traditional law making with regard to public policy issues: Neither national parliaments nor international diplomatic codification conferences were involved in the making of TCP/IP or the Domain Name System (DNS).[3] However, national governments, first the USA and later in Europe subsidized both the research and development and early implementation of the Internet.

The Internet standards, codes and guidelines, as described in the "Requests for Comments" (RFCs)[4] came not "top down" by "majority voting" of elected representatives, but drafted "bottom up" by the respected and competent key players of the global Internet community and their groups, the concerned and affected constituencies, mainly the technical developers, but also the providers and users of Internet services. The RFC procedure, which was used later also in other non-governmental standard making bodies, became a special form of legislation and broadened our understanding of regulation and governance in the Information Age.[5]

Growing interdependence between two different worlds

In the early days of the Internet these two different worlds – public policy legislation in real places and technical standard codification in the virtual space – had no or little interdependence. This changed with an ongoing "informatization" of nearly all areas of daily life in the second half of the 1990s. Step by step it became evident, that the technical Internet codes and standards had deep political, economic and social implications and that more and more policies became dependent on the technical environment under which they hade been developed. Technical and political aspects of "Internet Governance" became interwoven in a way which did not allow anymore a clear split of related issues into two different pieces: In Internet Governance, there is no "policy regulation here" and "technology freedom there".

In "Code and other Laws of Cyberspace" (1999) Lawrence Lessig argued, that "in real space we recognize, how laws regulate – through constitution, statutes and other legal codes. In cyberspace we must understand how code regulates – how the software and hardware that makes cyberspace what it is, regulate cyberspace as it is." And he continued: "This code presents the greatest threat to liberal or libertarian ideals, as well as their greatest promise. We can build, or architect, or code cyberspace to protect values that we believe are fundamental, or we can build, or architect, or code cyberspace to allow those values to disappear. There is no middle ground.

There is no choice that does not include some kind of building. Code is never found, it is only ever made, and only ever made by us."[6]

Lessig opens our eyes to the fact that traditional policy and law making, which frames public policy issues into national and international legislation, finds itself in a framework which is constituted by technical codes and standards. Like the natural laws of physics, the architecture of the Internet determines the spaces in which public policy can be developed and executed. But while the law of physics are not made by man, the architecture of the cyberspace is constructed by individuals and institutions.

As a consequences, we have two different, but interlinked problems:

1 how public policy is framed inside the global Internet architecture and
2 how the technical architecture of the Internet itself is designed.

Public internet policy: United Nations

For the first category – public policy regulation for eGovernment, eCommerce, eLearning, content distribution in the Internet, privacy protection in cyberspace, Spam etc. – the problem is not "Internet regulation" as such. The majority of countries have a national legislation for all these issues, which can be more or less easily adopted and/or adjusted to Internet based applications. The problem is whether the regulation is liberal or restrictive, that is promotes or blocks the development of the Internet and, how such policies and regulation can be executed in concrete cases if different jurisdictions are involved.

The global character of the Internet has not changed the existing legal system. But it has made simple regulatory issue more complex, a phenomenon which arises also (and is pushed further forward as a result of the opportunities offered by the Internet) in other areas like competition policy, the pharmaceutical market, air transport, etc.

With trans-border transactions, any kind of communication between two or more end-users can be legally treated by the jurisdiction of the state under which

a the sender lives,
b the service providers and the servers, which enable the communication between the end users, operate, and/or
c the receiver lives.

This leads unavoidably to collisions between national legislation in areas, where no "harmonized" global legal framework is available.

To take only one example: While the selling of Adolf Hitler's fascist book "Mein Kampf" is forbidden by law in Germany, it is allowed under the "First Amendment" of the US Constitution. US-online book shops like "amazon.com" offer it for 20.00 USD in a paperback version.[7] If it arrives via s-mail in Germany, German costumes will confiscate it. But what to do, when it comes as an attached file via e-Mail? Other cases like the political and legal controversies around "racism and yahoo.com" in France or "terrorism and batasuna.org" in Spain and the discussion on implementation of national data protection laws in the global cyberspace have demonstrated the complexity of the problem. And they have also shown the limits of the existing system of international law, based on the sovereign nation state and the jus cogens principles enshrined in the United Nations Charter.

This does not mean that the traditional system is broken. It works and it remains an achievement of history. Insofar "global harmonization" of all relevant national legislation via diplomatic codification conferences is and will remain an option, but it won't work in the traditional sense in a growing number of concrete cases for simple practical reasons:

- Number one is the time factor. Big codification projects like the "Law of the Sea Convention" or the "Rome Statute of the International Criminal Court" needed two or more decades of intergovernmental expert negotiations. If governments could agree on a mandate for an "International Internet Law Codification Conference" now, an "International Internet Convention" would probably – in an optimistic scenario – ready for signature in 2020 or 2030.[8] What will be the rule in between? The "Law of the Cyberjungle"?
- Number two is the universality factor. While an international convention does not need the ratification by all UN member states to become effective, an Internet treaty with only a limited number of signatories would make no sense. It would be like a permanent invitation for "country shopping" by cybercriminals. They would search for "Internet Paradises" in Pacific or Caribic islands with "liberal" Internet and ccTLD policies.

Technical internet policy: United constituencies[9]

For the second category – technical standard codification for Internet Protocols, IP addresses, Domain Names etc. – this is different. As shown above, the architecture of the Internet – which is constituted by these codes – has been developed neither within "national places", nor by sovereign "top down" governmental regulation. They emerged as a result of a "bottom up" policy development process in the "global space" on the basis of the principle "rough consensus and running code" by the concerned and affected constituencies.

The reality has proven that the norms and principles, which has been developed by non-governmental networks are as successful and workable globally, as traditional governmental regulation nationally. Even more, the innovative bottom up procedures – at least in the early days of the Internet – had introduced a high level of efficiency: Regulation was developed only, where needed, decisions could be achieved with high speed, the rough consensus principle guaranteed an effective implementation by all main stakeholders and produced the needed flexibility to adjust the set of rules according to technical innovations.[10]

The Internet Architecture is a non-material infrastructure. Although it uses physical networks and servers, which can be geographically localized and operate under special national legislation, the zone files of top level domains in the root server, the Internet protocols which enable the communication between networks and servers and the domain names, which constitute something like "the territory of cyberspace" on which whole companies like "ebay.com" or "google.com" have created their "empires", are virtual resources which should have no "nationality" and can not be directly linked to a "real place".[11]

Real places and virtual spaces

The two categories reflect the contrast between two different types of actors who represent two different forms of social organisations with different legal status: On the one side there are hierarchies, sovereign governments, organized in the "United Nations". On the other side there are networks,

Table 1 Comparison between United Nations and United Constituencies.

Issue	United Nations	United Constituencies
Actors	Governments	Private Industry/Civil Society
Structure	Hierachies	Networks
Codification	National Laws	Universal Codes
International Agreements	Legally Binding Treaties	Memorandum of Understanding
Mission	Broad	Narrow
Policy Development	Top Down	Bottom Up
Decision Making	Formally specified Majority Voting	Informally specified Rough Consensus
Representation	Elections by All	Delegation by competent Constituencies or via NomComs
Policy Making	Formallly Restricted Access and limited Participation	Formally Open Access and broad Participation
Negotiations	Mainly closed to outsiders,	Mainly transparent rather open for outsiders
Result	Stability and Predictability	Flexibility

competent non-governmental groups from private industry and civil society, organized in "United Constituencies".

A formal and rough comparison between "national hierarchies" of the "United Nations" and "global networks" of "United Constituencies" make visible, that they deal with similar issues but are rather different if it comes to organisational structures, procedures and objectives. United Nations represent more the culture of the "Industrial Society", "United Constituencies" can be linked more to the culture of the "Information Society".

It is a fact that both the "real places" and the "virtual spaces" cannot be separated in the information age. Without its virtual components, the real world would not be able to produce the extra value, which the Internet is offering. And the virtual world needs the real world to make use of its potential. Every virtual communication among netizens starts and ends with a real citizen.

Constructive co-existence

This approach brings us closer to the core of the challenge of "governance in the information age": the interdependence between the two different worlds of the "borderless cyberspace" and the "bordered real space". Governmental regulation – from data protection to taxation – is linked to a defined geographical territory. Technical standards and codes for the Internet – from the TCP/IP protocol to http-language and MPEGs – do not know the frontiers of a geographically defined territory, they are universal.

The subject here is not to have an "either-or approach". The question is not whether governmental top down regulation should be enlarged to the "technical world" or whether it should by substituted by non-governmental bottom up private sector and civil society self-regulation. The issue is not about "replacement". In cyberspace, the "United Nations" need the "United Constituencies" and the "United Constituencies" need the "United Nations". Governance in the information age needs co-regulatory models which take into consideration both the sovereignty of the nation state *and* the universality of global networks. There is a need both to raise the level of "global harmonization of legislation" by sovereign states *and* to improve the self-regulatory mechanisms of non-governmental networks and to bring the two procedurers into a productive interaction.

Decisive is not the formal legal status of an individual solution for a special issue, decisive is the substance: It has to be adequate, efficient, accountable, predictable, fair, balanced, inclusive, workable and it must avoid the emergence of "responsibility wholes" in important areas. What is needed is a constructive co-existence among the different stakeholders, the development of new and innovative models of "Co-Governance".

There is no "one size fits all" solution. Neither governmental top down regulation nor private sector or civil society bottom up self-regulation alone is able to manage the totality of issues raised by the global information society. The weakness of one partner in one area can be compensated by the strength of the other and vice versa.

Growing complexity: from the industrial society to the information society

We know from the theory of media, that "new media" does not substitute "old media" but changes the way in which old media operate in the new environment. Practically each new media adds a new layer to the whole media landscape and is regulated in a specific way.

This "layer theory" was used also by Alvin Toffler when he wrote his "Third Wave" three decades ago. He concluded that the "information revolution" added a new layer to the "industrial society" like the "industrial revolution" added a new "layer" to the "agrarian society".[12]

The information revolution of today does not remove the industrial economy of yesterday. But it has introduced a "new layer" – the "new (information) economy" – into the global economy.[13] Such an economic development has political consequences. It challenges the established governance mechanisms, which has been developed in the 19th and 20th century. The "new information economy" of the 21st century is organized around (global) networks. And this architecture is mirrored in the new governance mechanisms, which have been developed with the growth of the Internet and which are different from the traditional (national) power hierarchies.

While the hierarchical nation state will not disappear within the next 100 years, a number of issues which go beyond the national sovereignty of nation states, can be better managed, and governed by these new networks. The challenge is to find ways how the two different bodies with the different cultures can live and work together to the benefit of all, both citizens and netizens.

Nation states have to learn to share power with non-governmental actors, at least on the global level, while global networks have to accept that they operate in a political and legal environment defined by sovereign nation states. Governments have to understand, that the legitimacy they got from national democratic elections, includes today a greater international responsibility also for a global community. The global networks have still to proof their legitimacy and to demonstrate that they understand that the rights and freedoms they are calling for are linked to duties and responsibilities.

Global governance

The discussion around "Governance" or "Global Governance" in the information age is not new in political science. Daniel Bell in his "The Coming of

Table 2 The Diffusion of Governance.

Level	Private	Public	Third Sector
Supranational	Transnational Corporations	Intergovernmental Organisations	Nongovernmental Organisations
National	National Corporations	20th Century Model National Government	National Nonprofits
Subnational	Local Business	Local Government	Local Groups

Source: Joseph S. Nye Jr.; Information Technology and Democratic Government, in: democracy.com? Governance in a Networkd World, Hollins Publishing, 1999.

the Post-Industrial Society: A Venture in Social Forecasting" observed already in 1976, that "the nation state has to become too small for the big problems of life and too big for the small problems" and he concluded that a consequence would be that neither more centralization nor more decentralization should be the answer but a diffusion of governance activities in several directions at the same time. Some functions "may migrate to a supragovernmental or transnational level. Some may devolve to local units. Other aspects of governance may migrate to the private sector."

In "Powershift" (1990), Alvin Toffler, went one step further: "We live at a moment when the entire structure of power that held the world together is now disintegrating." And he argued, that the powershift, he describes, "does not merely transfer power, it transforms it."[14] Joseph Nye from Harvard's JFK School of Government mapped this later in a matrix which illustrated "the possible diffusion of activities away from central governments, vertically to other levels of government and horizontally to market and private non-market actors, the so-called third sector".

The discussion was pushed forward in the 1990s, when US President Clinton argued that "the era of big government is over" and that non-governmental actors, in particular from the private sector, have to take the lead in a growing number of global issues.[15]

The "United Nations Commission on Global Governance" adopted this idea in 1995 and tried to define in its report "Our Global Neighbourhood" the concept as follows: "Governance is the sum of the many ways individuals and institutions, public and private, manage their common affairs. It is the continuing process through which conflicting or diverse interests may be accomodated and cooperative action may be taken. It includes formal institutions and regimes empowered to enforce compliance, as well as informal arrangements that people and institutions either have agreed to or perceive to be their interest".[16]

Later, in 2001, the "OECD Forum for the Future" concluded after a series of conferences, that "first old forms of governance in both the public and private sectors are becoming increasingly ineffective; second the new forms of governance that are likely to be needed over the next few decades will involve a much broader angel of active players and third, two of the primary attributes to today's governance system – the usually fixed and permanent allocations of power that are engraved in the structures and constitutions of many organisations and the tendency to vest initiative exclusively in the hands of those in senior positions in the hierarchy – look set to undergo fundamental changes:"[17]

Internet governance

The coining of the term "Internet Governance" was neither the result of a serious academic discussion nor of an organized technical standardization process. There is no RFC which describes in detail what "Internet Governance" is. The term "Internet Governance" did not appear explicitly in the 1993 "National Information Infrastructure Initiative" (NII) of the US government, which can be seen as the first comprehensive policy framework for the information age. It was also not used in the "Bangemann Report" of the European Commission in 1994, the European answer to the NII, which underlined the leading role of the private sector. Even in the "Global Information Infrastructure: A Agenda for Cooperation" (GII), a global policy concept which was presented by US Vice President Al Gore to the ITU World Telecommunication Development Conference in Buenos Aires in 1994 and later to the G 7 Information Society Conference in Brussel, February 1995, "Internet Governance" was not singled out as a special problem.

"Internet Governance" was used as a "catchword" by some academicians, working mainly under the "Harvard Information Infrastructure Project" (HIIP) in the middle of the 1990s. It was seen as a "term of art" to describe some management functions related to the core resources of the Internet: the root server service, the adoption of Internet Protocols, the assignment of IP addresses and the management of the Internet Domain Name System.

With more than ten million registered domain names in 1995 it became clear that the management of these resources will go beyond a purely technical coordination. The consensus among the main players at this time was that Internet should not be "governed" by "governments". Insofar the term "Internet Governance" offered an opportunity to make a difference to "Internet Government" and to support a concept of "Self-Regulation" by the technical developers, providers and users of Internet services.[18]

In 1997, Done Heath, at this time president of the Internet Society (ISOC), said in a speech in Geneva: "We believe that for the Internet to reach its fullest potential, it will require self-governance. The Internet is without boundaries; it routes around barriers that are erected to thwart its reach – barriers of all kinds: technical, political, social, and, yes, even ethical, legal and economic. No single government can govern, regulate or otherwise control the internet, not should it. Most governments, the enlightened ones, will say that they endorse actions by responsible parties for efforts towards self-governance of the Internet. This does not mean that they should not be involved, they must be involved; they just need to exercise caution so that they don't control and dominate by virtue of their intrinsic power."[19]

This was echoed by ITU Secretary General Pekka Tarjanne as head of an intergovernmental organisation of the UN system when he used the term "Internet Governance" as a synonym for "multilateral voluntarism".[20]

The making of ICANN

After 1997 the term "Internet Governance" became more and more popular not only among academicians. It made its way also into the official language of the US government, the European Commission and the ITU. It became a not disputed "umbrella concept" for the management of the technical core resources of the Internet which were mandated in 1998 by the US government to the private "Internet Corporation for Assigned Names and Numbers" (ICANN).

ICANNs first bylaws reflected this idea of "Self-Governance" by a "network organisation". The "Board of Directors" as the highest decision making body of a whole mechanism of related organisations, representing different constituencies, included only representatives of non-governmental groups – technical developers, providers and users of Internet services – while the role of governments was described as "advisory".[21]

The Clinton administration wanted to avoid imposing on the Internet the burdensome governmental regulatory framework that had impeded the development of telecommunications in the USA; thus, it supported self-regulation by the private sector for Internet. ICANN got a rather limited technical mandate. Its governance structure reflected a mixture of the technical acrrhitecture of the Internet (a network of constituencies) and the power structure of the major commercial interests (big players with a privileged position) of the Internet at time.

The conceptual idea was, that the policy is developed bottom up via the various constituencies of supporting organisations (SO), which should try to find a rough consensus for policy recommendations to the Board of Directors. And the Board should represent a balance between providers and user of services: Under ICANN 1.0, nine directors should have come from the supporting organisations, representing the private industry, nine other directors should have come from the "At-Large Membership", representing civil society.[22]

Unfortunately the conceptual ideas became lost when ICANN started its business. The first ICANN Board acted more top down than bottom up, it behaved like a "governor", it never elected nine At Large directors, it became involved in a permanent discussion around "mission creep" and it did not get its full independence from the US government.[23] "In many ways", said EU Commissioner Erkki Liikanen in a speech in April 2004, "ICANN is a unique experiment in self-regulation. The expectation among governments at the outset was that ICANN would provide a neutral platform for consensus-building between the key actors who operate the naming and addressing infrastructure. It was also hoped that ICANN would provide a way for the US government to withdraw from its supervisory role. In this way, we could achieve a greater internationalisation and privatisation of certain key functions. While ICANN has had its successes, it has yet to fully deliver on either of these objectives."[24]

Different interpretations

Under such circumstances, the broader public perceived this new innovative corporation ICANN – which had no precedent in international policy – indeed as something like the "World Government of the Internet",[25] which was never true. ICANN had neither a mandate nor the power to adopt decisions, which would be in conflict with international conventions and which would call for changes in national legislation of a UN member state.

ICANN's Article of Incorporation stated (Article 4) clearly that "the Corporation shall operate for the benefit of the Internet community as a whole, carrying out its activities in conformity with relevant principles of international law and applicable international conventions and local law and, to the extent appropriate and consistent with these Articles and its Bylaws, through open and transparent processes that enable competition and open entry in Internet-related markets. To this effect, the Corporation shall cooperate as appropriate with relevant international organizations."[26]

To guarantee a channel of communication between the ICANN Board and national governments, a Governmental Advisory Committee (GAC) was established. While under ICANN 1.0 the GAC could make only non-binding recommendation to the Board, under ICANN 2.0 governments got something like a "political Veto-Right" for ICANN decisions which touch public policy issues. The problem with the GAC is, that de jure the GAC is an "advisory body" with no decision making capacity. And furthermore, although it has meanwhile about 90 members, it is not universal like the "United Nations", and, in practice most of the 90 members do not attend the meetings, which are tend to be dominated by OECD states.[27]

For a large number of governments, which have not been involved in the Internet development from its early days and which do not participate in the GAC, the Internet is not primarily a technical "network of networks" with virtual core resources, it is seen as a real political phenomenon, affecting their national economy and impinges substantially on their national policy and regulation. In the industrial age, governments could react against unwanted interference from outside with traditional means of stricter border control, protecting legislation and bi- or multilateral agreements. In the information age, these instruments are much less effective and harder to implement.

As a consequence, the vaguely defined concept of "Internet Governance" was given different interpretations by different groups of governments. While one group used it in a narrow sense, only marginally affecting "national sovereignty", the other one included everything related to the Internet and saw it as a major challenge to their national sovereign rights.

WSIS and WGIG

Before the World Summit on the Information Society (WSIS), the two conflicting "schools of thought" came only marginal in a practical political conflict.[28] While ICANN, with the support of the governments of the developed countries, claimed to represent the "United Constituencies", some countries claimed that the ITU, with a majority of developing countries in its membership, represented the "United Nations". Both organisations had different core businesses and only little interaction. ICANN was not a sector member of the ITU, ITU had no seat in the ICANN Board. On the other hand, ITU had always been a full member of the GAC and ITU's Standardization Sector had always been a member of ICANN's Protocol Supporting Organisation (PSO) under iCANN 1.0.

The ITU Secretariat had little to say about GAC recommendations until 2002, when it started to take reservations on topics for which there was no consensus in ITU. In October 2002, ITU's Plenipotentiary Conference in Marrakesh adopted two resolutions, which called for a greater role of national governments in public policy related internet governance issues.[29] After the conference it became clear, that a separation of the two camps or a "mutual ignorance" could no longer last. WSIS pushed the "United Nations" and the "United Constituencies" under one roof. But WSIS was unable to find a common language for the issue and postponed any decision to WSIS II.[30]

The complexity of the challenges was formulated by EU Commissioner Erkki Liikanen as follows: "It is not realistic to expect governments to take a back seat completely and leave the Internet solely to market forces. Whatever the relative merits of a government initiative might be, we will not be thanked by Internet users if any measure has the down-stream effect of destabilising the Internet's underlying architecture. The challenge for policy makers will be to find a policy approach that reinforces the Internet's reliability without hindering its potential for further growth."[31]

The "Geneva Compromise" established a "Working Group on Internet Governance" (WGIG) and gave it the mandate first to define what "Internet Governance" is and then to make recommendations for further actions. But additionally WSIS agreed also on some important principles like "Multistakeholderism", "Transparency", "Openess" and "Inclusion". Practically, the WGIG framework is based on an understanding that the "United Nations" and the "United Constituencies" have to work together in a spirit of "constructive co-existence". The problem is that no principles for such a constructive co-existence have been written so far. WGIG is pushed into new territory with a lot of troubled water.

The difficulty for WGIG is that the group can base their deliberations neither on a clear consensus on the concepts of "multistakeholderism", "bottom up" and "transparency" nor on an accepted definition of "Internet Governance". During the WSIS phase, there were two different ideas about what Internet Governance is. While the supporters of a non-governmental system preferred to use a "narrow definition", which concentrated on the technical core resources like root server, domain names, IP addresses and Internet Protocols, the supporter of an intergovernmental approach used a "broad definition" and included spam, content, cybercrime and eCommerce.

The situation was summarized by UN Secretary General Kofi Annan during the Global Governance Forum in in New York in March 2004: "The issues are numerous and complex. Even the definition of what mean by Internet governance is a subject of debate. But the world has a common interest in ensuring the security and the dependability of this new medium. Equally important, we need to develop inclusive and participatory models of governance. The medium must be made accessible and responsive to the needs of all the world's people". And he added that "in managing, promoting and protecting (the Internet's) presence in our lives, we need to be no less creative than those who invented it. Clearly, there is a need for governance, but that does not necessarily mean that it has to be done in the traditional way, for something that is so very different."[32]

But what the "innovative creation" could be is still an open question.

Many layers, many players, one mechanism (M_3)

The Internet is not a single body but a network of networks where end users communicate to each other via servers, linked together by the TCP/IP protocol. With other words: a technical non-material infrastructure – zone files in servers, protocols, domain names – enables the peer-to-peer communication and the delivery of different application services from providers to users.

Such an approach allows a distinction between two basic categories:

- basic services, which enable communication
- enhanced services, which deliver value

While the "basic service" is primarily a technical issue which has a public policy component in some of its elements, the "enhanced service" is primarily a political, economic and social issue which has a technical component. Both services are interlinked. Basic services make no sense without enhanced services while enhanced services do not work without the basic services. Such a distinction between different but interdependent layers is not new, but can be helpful in the process of problem identification, policy development and the creation of governance mechanisms. It enables (governmental and non-governmental) policy makers to to deal with the elements of a "big package" piese by piece. And it helps to build a matrix which brings more light into the options and scenarios for a differentiated approach.

"Basic Internet Governance" (BIG) on the lower level includes drafting Internet Protocols and allocating IP Addresses. On the higher level it includes primarily the management of the Domain Name System (DNS) with all its components like Root Servers, TLDs, Whois, Names Transfer, iDNs, Dispute Resolution etc. Basic Internet Governance deals mainly with enabling services. It is rather neutral, political and economic interests are more indirectly involved and it represents no real "content". It enables users to provide value – from eCommerce to eGovernment.

The public policy problems, which are identified by governments, concern both basic services (issues such as legal intercept, emergency services, access for the disabled, equal access, control of dominant market players) as well as enhanced services, related to its content (issues such as intellectual property, data privacy, content control). Since the issues are different, "Enhanced Internet Governance" (EIG)[33] is consequently different. It is not neutral, concrete political, economic and social interests are directly involved. It also can be divided into sub-categories. There is a need for general rules in a more constitutional sense, and there is a need for specific regulation for specific issues.

"United Constituencies" are often better equipped to manage the "Basic Internet Governance". But they need governmental help if the technical questions they are dealing with involve public policy components.

"United Nations" is often better equipped to deal with "Enhanced Internet Governance". But governments will also need the participation of non-governmental stakeholders – both from private industry and civil society – when it comes to frameworks or specific issues that have either a technical component or a policy component of importance to the general public.

In other words, all kinds of Internet Governance need the involvement of all stakeholders, but the concrete level of involvement of the individual stakeholders for a special issue is dependent on the nature of the question and the level of the layer.

It makes sense to go through the different layers issue by issue; to determine on a case by case basis the most adequate triangular stakeholder

Table 3 Multilayer Multiplayer Mechanism (M_3).

Category	Service	Regulatory level			
		Governmental	Non-Governmental		
			Private Sector	Technical Developers	Civil Society
Basic Internet Governance					
Technical Services	IP Adresses Internet Protocols	Medium	High	Very high	Medium
Enabling Services	Root Server DNS iDNs Whois	High	Very High	Medium	High
Enhanced Internet Governance					
Specific Services	eCommerce eContent eMusic eGovernment	High	High	High	High
General Services	Cybercrime Spam IPR Privacy	Very High	Medium	Medium	Medium

combination. As a general rule one can conclude that the options range from "dominant private sector leadership" on the lowest layer to "dominant governmental leadership" on the highest layer with different co-governance combinations on the layers in between, according to the specific nature of the service.

Each layer and each service would have a special governance model. Each player would remain "sovereign" and "independent" with an own decision making power according to its individual constitution and mandate. But all layers and players would have to work together to make the system as a whole functioning and efficient. Even more, all layers and players are becoming dependent from each other and constitute in their entirety a global Internet Governance model which could be described as a "Multilayer-Multiplayer Mechanism" (M_3).

- "multilayer" means to differentiate between different layers and to find adequate governance models for each individual layer;

- "multiplayer" means to identify for each layer the main (governmental and non-governmental) players who have to be involved for effective and workable solutions;
- "mechanism" means no single hierarchical central organisation but a network of different governmental and non-governmental institutions.

Communication, coordination and cooperation (C_3)

There is a high level of interdependence among the different layers and players which have to interact in various ways. The "Multilayer-Multiplayer Mechanism" (M_3) would have no central or final authority. The involved governmental and non-governmental organisations and institutions are not subordinated to each other. All institutions are "independent" in their "internal affairs", but "dependent" from the other institutions in their "external affairs".

Every institution has its own responsibility for the global Internet community. But this is only part of a general responsibility, which all players, regardless of their legal status, have to share. To make the system work a high level of communication, coordination and cooperation (C_3) among all members of the mechanism is needed. A system of "communication channels" and "liaisons" has to link the players together. To make the mechanism stable, a net of bilateral arrangements in this multilateral environment can be developed, where needed.

- "Communication" means that each member of the mechanism should establish permanent communication channels with other members of the mechanism so that everybody is "informed" what is going on inside the other individual organisations.
- "Coordination" means that if a communication signals that two or more members of the mechanism are doing similar things (with different priorities) they should enter into consultation and should, where needed, coordinate their activities. This could be done, where needed, via "liaisons".
- "Cooperation" means that if coordination signals, that there are overlapping or conflicting activities of different members of the mechanism, formal "cooperative agreements" (MoUs) among the affected and/or concerned members of the mechanism should be signed.

Communication channels, liaisons and agreements need a certain structure which brings an "order" into the C_3 processes. Here the technical Internet architecture itself can be a source of inspiration,

In the Internet, a query from one end user is send via an ISP and a name server to a root server which points the query back via name servers and ISPs to the wanted end user. While the root servers are essential for the communication, they have nothing to say to "content" and do not really have decision making power. The only thing they can say is "yes" or "no". What users expect from a root server is the knowledge in which domain the wanted e-mail or web address is located. And if one root server is not available, others will overtake the task of delivering the query from A to the final destination B.

In the context of the present Internet Governance debate, one could imagine a mechanism which is designed accordingly. A WGIG type of multistakeholder organisation – something like a "clearinghouse"[34] – which includes both "United Nations" and "United Constituencies", could function as a "governance root server": It would not need a decision making power, but all the knowledge about all "top level domains", it would have to know "who is doing what where with which capacity", and it have to guide queries to the right place for policy development and decision making.

Furthermore, ITU and ICANN, as the most qualified representatives of the "United Nations" and the "United Constituencies", could function like a name server. They have a special "domain" under their radar: ITU has its "study groups", ICANN has its "Supporting Organisations". All of them will become active, if issues under their competence will be raised or if they asked to develop recommendations for actions. Furthermore, other organisations like UNESCO, WIPO, OECD, GBDe, IETF, ISOC, ICC etc. can also function like a "name server": they manage their "own internet governance domains" under their own constitutions with their own constituencies. And in cases they need something from another "domain", they could go down the road to the root and ask who in the mechanism deals with the relevant issue.

Looking forward

Internet Governance, both on the basic and the enhanced layer, needs the participation of all affected and concerned governmental and non-governmental constituencies. There is no Internet for a single country or single group. The Internet is a global public resource, which is owned by nobody but brings benefits to everybody. But it is too big that it could be governed, managed and/or coordinated by somebody.

WGIG has a tremendous task but a great opportunity. WGIG is not for negotiations but for fact finding. This enables the group to produce as a first step a comprehensive map with options and scenarios which would allow all sides to see clearer the strengths and weaknesses, the opportunities and threats of different individual solutions. There is a long way to go. If such a "roadmap" could be produced by WSIS II, this would be a big step forward. And this would enable the coming Tunis summit to negotiate a mandate for another multistakeholder group, which could then – between WSIS II and WSIS III – produce a framework for a multilayer multiplayer mechanism which is based on communication, coordination and cooperation.

Notes

1 See, inter alia: Manuel Castells, The Internet Galaxy: Reflections on the Internet, Business and Society; Oxford University Press, 2001; Lawrence Lessig; The Future of Ideas: The Fate of the Commons in a Connected World; Vintage Books, New York 2002; Milton Mueller, Ruling the Root: Internet Governance and the Taming of Cyberspace, Cambridge, MIT Press, 2002; Brian D. Loader (Ed.), The Governance of Cyberspace; Routledge, 1997, Susan J. Drucker & Gary Gumpert; Real Law and Virtual Space: Regulation in Cyberspace; Hampton Press, 1999, Francis Cairncross, The Death of Distance: How the Communication Revolution is Changing our Lives; Harvard Business School Press, 1997; Wolfgang Kleinwächter; Governance in the Information Age, Aarhus, 2001
2 The ideas were widely popularized by John Perry Barlows "Declaration of the Independence of Cyberspace", where he declared "Governments of the Industrial world, you weary giants of flesh and steel, I come from Cyberspace, the new home of Mind. On behalf of the future, I ask you of the past to leave us alone. You are not welcome among us. You have no sovereignty where we gather". And he argued that for netizens, "identities have no bodies, so unlike you, we cannot obtain order by coercion. We believe that from ethics, enlightened self-interest and the commonweal, our governance will emerge". Published in: Cyber Right Electronic List, Davos, February, 8, 1996 http://www.eff.org/~barlow/Declaration-Final.html
3 see, inter alia: Christos J. P. Moschovitis, Hilary Poole, Tami Schuyler, Theresa M. Senft; History of the Internet: A Chronology;, ABC-Clio, Sanata Barbara, 1999, Barry M. Leiner, Vinton G. Cerf, David D. Clark, Robert E. Kahn, Leonard Kleinrock, Daniel C. Lynch, Jon Postel, Larry G. Roberts, Stephen Wolff; A Brief History of the Internet, in: http://www.isoc.org/internet/history/brief.shtml
4 the series was started by Steve Crocker in the 1970s, later managed by Jon Postel and now in the hands of the IETF
5 The RFC procedure differs from the traditional (intergovernmental) standards-makes process of, say ISO, IEC, or ITU, in that it is based on "rough consensus" rather than true consensus. Thus, the "bottoms up" approach is moderated by the fact that, at the end of the day, the IETF leadership makes decisions, which may not fully incorporate dissenting points of view.
6 Lawrence Lessig, Code and other Laws of Cyberspace, Basic Books, 1999, p. 6
7 see an offer by amazon.com under: http://www.amazon.com/exec/obidos/tg/detail/-/0395083621/qid=1092478384/sr=1-7/ref=sr_1_7/103-7687623-7247836?v=glance&s=books
8 Even the Budapest Cybercrime Convention of November, 23, 2001 is an illustration for the sceptical arguments. Negotiations on a "computer crime convention" among member states of the Council of Europe started in the middle of the 1980s. In 1996 the mandate of the negotiation group was enlarged to "Cybercrime". Five years there was no progress. It remains open, whether the convention would have been signed without the terrorist attacks of September, 11, 2001, which pushed a substantial number of governments across their "wait and see" line. 34 governments signed the treaty in Budapest in 2001, but until Fall 2004, only six countries (Albania, Croatia, Estonia, Hungary, Lithuania,

and Romania.) have ratified the convention. See: http://conventions.coe.int/Treaty/en/Treaties/Html/185.htm

9 I use the term "constituencies" in the sense of the different non-governmental groups which have constituted themselves within the process of the making of ICANN. "Constituencies" are networked groups of (competent and informed) individuals and institutions with different citizenships which have common interests, share responsibilities, organize themselves around certain values, speak a similar (technical) language, communicate online and offline and can not be linked to a special country. ICANN is constituted by six constituencies under the GNSO (Registries, Registrars, ISPs, IPR, Business, Non-Commercial), one constituencies with potentially 243 ccTLDs Registries under the emerging CNSO, five constituencies under the ASO (the Regional Internet Registries), five regional constituencies under the ALAC, and a number of other constituencies under the Technical Liaison Group, the Stability and Security Advisory Committee and the Root Server Advisory Committee. All these "constituencies" are independent and sovereign organisations and networks, but are "united" under the ICANN Bylaws.

10 While this procedure has made an innovative contribution on the application level it has also its limits. It worked well and fast for an Internet with one million users, but it is much slower for an Internet with one billion users.

11 In practice, the issue is more complex as long as all root servers obtain their data from one "hidden" authoritative server, operated by VeriSign under a contract with the US Department of Commerce (DoC) and DoC must approve any changes to the entries in that authoritative server and can control the entries in all root servers.

12 Alvin Toffler; The Third Wave, Bantam Books, 1980

13 see inter alia Marc Porat, The Information Economy, US Office of Telecommunication, Washington 1978, Dave Tapscott; The Digital Economy: Promise and Peril in the Age of Network Intelligence; McGraw Hill, 1996

14 Alvin Toffler, Powershift: Knowledge, Wealth, and Violence at the Edge of the 21st Century; Bantam Books, 1990, p. 3/4

15 But it remains the role of the state to (1) create an appropriate legal framework (2) ensure that companies don't break the law (3) use tax incentives and/or subsidies to achieve goals other than maximizing profits.

16 United Nations Commission on Global Governance; Our Global Neighborhood; New York 1995.

17 Governance in the 21st Century, Future Studies, OECD, Paris 2001

18 This did not work in other languages. In the German language, where "Government" means "Regierung", it is difficult to find an adequate word for "Governance". While some Germans proposed "Management" or "Administration", the majority of authors decided to use the English term "Governance" in the German language.

19 Don Heath; Beginnings: Internet Self-Governance a Requirement to Fulfill the Promise, Geneva, April 29, 1997, in: http://www.itu.int/newsarchive/projects/dns-meet/HeathAddress.html

20 Pekka Tarjanne, Internet Governance, Towards Multilateral Voluntarism, Geneva, April, 29, 1997; in: http://www.itu.int/newsarchive/projects/dns-meet/KeynoteAddress.html

21 see: Wolfgang Kleinwächter; The Silent Subversive: ICANN and the New Global Governance; in: Info: The Journal of Policy, Regulation and Strategy for Telecommunication, Vol 3, No. 4, Fall 2001

22 see ICANN's first bylaws from November, 6, 1998, in: http://www.icann.org/general/archive-bylaws/bylaws-06nov98.htm

23 see: Wolfgang Kleinwächter; ICANN between Technical Mandate and Political Challenge; in: Telecommunication Policy, Vol. 24, London 2000
24 Erkki Liikanen; Internet Governance: The Way Ahead; The Hague, April, 15, 2004; in: http://europa.eu.int/rapid/pressReleasesAction.do?reference=SPEECH/04/191&format=HTML&aged=0&language=EN&guiLanguage=en
25 When ICANN organized global public elections for five Board Directors, representing individual internet users, in summer 2000, the German news magazine "Der Spiegel", called its readers to participate in the election of the "World Government of the Internet".
26 ICANN's Article of Incorporation, November, 21, 1998, in: http://www.icann.org/general/articles.htm
27 see: Wolfgang Kleinwächter; From Self-Governance to Public Private Partnership: The Changing Role of Governments in the Management of the Internet's Core Ressources; in: Loyola Law Revies of Los Angeles; Vol, 36, No. 3, Spring 2003
28 There has been a controversial discussion during the ITU Plenipotentiary Conference in Minneapolis in October 1998 about principles for Internet Governance which ended with the compromise, that the DNS should be managed under "private sector leadership". This was revised partly during the ITU Plenipoentiary Conference in marrakesh, October 2002.
29 see in particular ITU Resolution 102, Management of Internet Domain Names and Addresses, Marrakesh, November 2002; The resolutions says, inter alia:" that the management of Internet domain names and addresses includes: a.technical and coordination tasks, for which technical private bodies can be responsible, and; b. public interest matters (for example, stability, security, freedom of use, protection of individual rights, sovereignty, competition rules and equal access for all), for which governments or intergovernmental organizations are responsible and to which qualified international organizations contribute; in: http://www.itu.int/osg/spu/resolutions/2002/res102.html
30 see Wolfgang Kleinwächter; Beyond ICANN vs. ITU? How WSIS Tries to Enter the New Territory of Internet Governance, in: Gazette: The Internationa Journal for Communication Studies, Sage Publications, Vol. 66/No. 3–4, 2004
31 Erkki Liikanen; Internet Governance: The Way Ahead; The Hague, April, 15, 2004; in: http://europa.eu.int/rapid/pressReleasesAction.do?reference=SPEECH/04/191&format=HTML&aged=0&language=EN&guiLanguage=en
32 Kofi Annan, Internet Governance Issues are Numerous and Complex, New York, March, 25, 2004, in: http://www.unicttaskforce.org/perl/showdoc.pl?id=1333
33 Enhanced Internet Governance could be also labeled as "Information Society Governance" or "Information and Communication Technology Governance" because it takes everything on board which is related also indirectly to the internet.
34 Such an institution could produce an annual report about the state of the art of the Internet development with a full directory of all old and new emerging members of the Multilayer Multiplayer Mechanism

65

COMMONS-BASED PEER PRODUCTION AND VIRTUE*

Yochai Benkler and Helen Nissenbaum

Source: *Journal of Political Philosophy* 14(4) (2006): 394–419.

Commons-based peer production is a socio-economic system of production that is emerging in the digitally networked environment. Facilitated by the technical infrastructure of the Internet, the hallmark of this socio-technical system is collaboration among large groups of individuals, sometimes in the order of tens or even hundreds of thousands, who cooperate effectively to provide information, knowledge or cultural goods without relying on either market pricing or managerial hierarchies to coordinate their common enterprise.[1] While there are many practical reasons to try to understand a novel system of production that has produced some of the finest software, the fastest supercomputer and some of the best web-based directories and news sites, here we focus on the ethical, rather than the functional dimension. What does it mean in ethical terms that many individuals can find themselves cooperating productively with strangers and acquaintances on a scope never before seen? How might it affect, or at least enable, human action and affection, and how would these effects or possibilities affect our capacities to be virtuous human beings? We suggest that the emergence of peer production offers an opportunity for more people to engage in practices that permit them to exhibit and experience virtuous behavior. We posit: (a) that a society that provides opportunities for virtuous behavior is one that is more conducive to virtuous individuals; and (b) that the practice of effective virtuous behavior may lead to more people adopting virtues as their own, or as attributes of what they see as their self-definition. The central thesis of this paper is that socio-technical systems of commons-based peer production offer not only a remarkable medium of production for various kinds of information goods but serve as a context for positive character formation. Exploring and substantiating these claims will be our quest, but we begin with a brief tour through this strange and exciting new landscape of commons-based peer production and conclude with recommendations for public policy.

I. Commons-based peer production – examples

The best-known examples of commons-based peer production are the tens of thousands of successful free software projects that have come to occupy the software development market. Free or open source software development is an approach to developing software that resembles nothing so much as an idealized barn raising—a collective effort of individuals contributing towards a common goal in a more-or-less informal and loosely structured way. No single entity "owns" the product or manages its direction. Instead, it emerges from the collaboration of groups of developers, ranging from a few individuals up to many thousands. Many of the participants are volunteers working in their spare time. Some are paid by corporations that do not themselves claim ownership in the product, but benefit from its development by selling services or equipment associated with the software. The flagship products of free or open source software development—the GNU/Linux operating system, the Apache web server, Perl and BIND—are the most famous. But at any given moment there are tens of thousands of free software development projects, and hundreds of thousands of software developers collaborate on them in various forms to produce some of the world's best software.[2] As Moglen pointed out, free software gains its salience from its functionality. One can compare the products of free software development communities with those of corporations, like Microsoft's. There is a technical answer to the question: is this software better or worse?[3] It is this measurable quality that has forced businesses and governments to take notice of free software. It is what caused the President's Technology Advisory Committee in 2000 to recommend U.S. adoption of open source software as a strategy for supplying mission critical software.[4] Measurable contributions to its machines and services caused IBM to invest over a billion dollars to support development of the Linux kernel and Apache Web Server software, without seeking ownership in the product.

While its functional success forces observers to take free software seriously as a sustainable form of production, what makes free software interesting from a social or moral perspective is its social and human structure. No one "owns" a free software project, though individuals own—in a formal sense—the software they contribute. Its touchstone is that all these individual contributors agree that none of them shall exclude anyone else from using it—whether they contributed to the development or not. No one is a formal manager who tells different people what they must do so that the project can succeed. Though leadership is present in many projects, it is based on no formal power to limit discussion, prevent subgroups from branching off if they are unhappy with a leadership decision, and in any event never involves the assignment of projects—no one can require or prohibit action by anyone. The effort is sustained by a combination of volunteerism and good will, technology, some law—mostly licensing like the GNU General Public License that governs most free software development—and a good bit of self-serving participation. But all these factors result in a model of production that avoids traditional price mechanisms or firm managers in organizing production or motivating its participants.

While the measurable efficacy of free software has captured wide attention, free software does not exhaust the universe of instances where one sees this emerging phenomenon of "barn raising"-like production on the Net. As one begins to look at information, knowledge and cultural production on the Internet, it becomes clear that free software is but one, particularly salient, instance of a more general phenomenon, the phenomenon of commons-based peer production. To provide something of a sense of this phenomenon and its human characteristics, we offer a few more examples. The first two capture the potential efficacy of widespread volunteer effort. The latter begin to give texture to the claim that these efforts offer a platform for qualitatively attractive human behavior.

The simplest example of large-scale volunteer production is distributed computing. Take SETI@home for example. The project is a scientific experiment that uses Internet-connected computers in a Search for Extraterrestrial Intelligence (SETI). The data sets collected from large radio telescope observations are immense. The project was organized to harness the computer processing cycles of millions of volunteers with computers connected to the Internet to process these vast data sets. Participants download a small free program that functions as a screen saver when they are not using their computers. At that point, it downloads and analyzes radio telescope data. According to statistics maintained on the SETI@home website, as of August, 2003, the project had absorbed over 4.5 million users from 226 countries, and provided an average computation speed almost twice that of the fastest "supercomputer" then in operation in the world. The approach, called distributed computing, has been similarly harnessed to simulate the process of protein folding (Folding@home), to model the evolution of drug resistance and design anti-HIV drugs (Fightaidsathome), and a host of other scientific and publicly minded projects.

A step up in human participation, but still fairly mechanical, was the NASA Clickworkers experiment. In this project, tens of thousands of individual volunteers collaborated in five-minute increments to map and classify Mars's craters, performing tasks that would normally require full-time PhDs working for months on end, freeing those scientists for more analytic tasks. In the first six months of the project's operation, over 85,000 users visited the site with many contributing to the effort, making over 1.9 million entries (including redundant entries of the same craters, used to average out errors). An analysis of the quality of markings up to that point showed "that the automatically-computed consensus of a large number of Clickworkers is virtually indistinguishable from the inputs of a geologist with years of experience in identifying Mars craters."[5]

Both Clickworkers and distributed computing on the model of SETI@home offer examples that are easy to comprehend and measure, but involve relatively mundane and small-scale contributions. They require relatively little of their participants. To outline the type of behaviors that one sees in these collaborations, we turn to three richer examples of large-scale collaboration, where contributions are larger and require more of the knowledge of the participants and their willingness to participate in a cohesive social process.

The first such project is the Wikipedia project, which involves some 30,000 volunteers who collaborate to write an encyclopedia. While they have not been able to generate a complete encyclopedia in their roughly three years of operation, they have made substantial progress, producing about 250,000 articles in English and many more articles in other languages. Readers are invited to test their own evaluation of the quality, but we would venture that Wikipedia holds its own by comparison to all other online encyclopedias, excluding, perhaps, Britannica. What Wikipedia provides, then, is a rich example of a medium sized collection of individuals, who collaborate to produce an information product of mid-brow quality and who are reasonably successful.

The Wikipedia project runs on a free software collaborative authorship tool, Wiki, which is a markup language similar in concept to HTML but optimized to permit multiple users to edit a single document and interlocking documents while generating archives of the changes made to each. Unlike the projects we will describe in the following few paragraphs, Wikipedia does not include elaborate software-controlled access and editing capabilities. On the contrary, its most interesting characteristic is the self-conscious use of open discourse, usually aimed at consensus, and heavy reliance on social norms and user-run quasi-formal mediation and arbitration, rather than on mechanical control of behavior. It begins with a statement of community intent—to produce an "encyclopedia"—rather than a series of opinion pieces. It continues with a technical architecture that allows anyone to contribute, edit and review the history of any document easily. These two characteristics account for the vast majority of document development. Someone starts a definition. Others update, contributing substance and editorial improvements. Occasionally, disagreements will arise. These are usually dealt with in a "Talk" page associated with every definition. On relatively rare occasions when disagreement persists, there are mechanisms for mediation, and ultimately arbitration, run by participants in the community who are chosen by other users for their sustained commitment to the project. For more decisions, such as determining the policies of Wikipedia, consensus rather than majority vote is the practice. In the cases of vandalism, which occurs on Wikipedia occasionally, the first line of defense is provided by the editors themselves, who have simple means of reverting to an earlier, clean version. The last line of defense is for system operators to block a user.

The important point is that Wikipedia requires much more than mere mechanical cooperation among participants. It requires a commitment to a particular approach to conceiving of one's task, and a style of writing and describing concepts, that are far from intuitive or natural. It requires self-discipline. It enforces the behavior it requires primarily through appeal to the common enterprise in which the participants are engaged, coupled with a thoroughly transparent platform that faithfully records and renders all individual interventions in the common project and facilitates discourse among participants about how their contributions do, or do not, contribute to this common enterprise. This combination of an explicit statement of common purpose, transparency, discourse and the ability of participants to identify each other's actions and counteract them—that is, edit out "bad" or "faithless" definitions—seems to have succeeded in keeping this community from devolving into inefficacy or worse. What is surprising from the perspective of established conceptions of social cooperation is that this success occurs not in a tightly knit community with many social relations to reinforce the sense of common purpose and the social norms embodying it, but in a large and geographically dispersed group of otherwise unrelated participants: there are as we write about 25,000 participants in the English language Wikipedia, and another 30,000 participants contributing to younger Wikipedia projects in many other languages.

Perhaps the most visible collective commentary project on the Internet as of the mid-2000s is Slashdot, a collaboration platform used by between 250,000 and 500,000 users. Users post links to technology stories they come across, together with comments on them. Others then join in a conversation about the technology-related events, with comments on the underlying stories as well as comments on comments. Comments are in turn "moderated" by other readers in small increments, for quality and relevance: To "moderate" in this system means to grade a comment—to mark whether it is relevant or not, high or low quality, etc. Users who are registered, rather than anonymous, and who have posted for a while, are given by the system limited moderation privileges. Each moderator has a single vote, positive or negative, on any given comment. Out of the collective judgment of the users who chose to moderate a given comment, a collective judgment is computed. The comment is then associated with a certain value, ranging from -1 to 5, indicating its quality and relevance to the topic of conversation, as judged by the moderators in the aggregate. Users can then set their browsers to read only comments above a certain threshold they choose to use, or they can organize their reading of the comments based on the quality judgments of their peers. Out of these mechanisms a newsletter emerges that is widely read as a highly informative source of information about computer software in particular, and information and communications technology more generally.

The relative roles of technology and social norms in Slashdot and Wikipedia are very different. The Slashdot software platform, Slash, is given a very active role in moderating the discussion and the peer review process. Rather than relying on self-discipline and a sense of common purpose, the software builds in limits on use that are designed to constrain anti-social behavior. For example, each user receives only five moderation points in any three day period. This severely limits the amount of influence any one person can have on the collective judgment of a group of hundreds of thousands of users. Users cannot post constantly and automatically—their submissions will be rejected if they try to post comments too often in any minute or hour. But the system also relies on collective judgment and mutual review. Every person who moderates comments is subject to peer review. Users who agree to perform this peer review, or "metamoderation," receive a series of anonymous moderations produced by other participants. They rank these moderations as fair or unfair. A moderator whose judgments are consistently considered by others to be unfair will no longer be permitted by the system to moderate comments. Because there is no ultimate single document, the conversation facilitated by Slashdot does not require the kinds of dispute resolution mechanisms that Wikipedia has employed. Disagreements persist in the record of the conversations, to be resolved by subsequent readers.

There are many other peer-production projects on the Net. Somewhat similar to Slashdot is Kuro5hin, designed to enable its users to share more substantial writing efforts than the usually brief comments produced for Slashdot. Scoop, the software that runs Kuro5hin, functions in many senses similarly to Slash. The most interesting difference is that in Kuro5hin, there is a substantial degree of pre-publication peer review in a "submissions" area, whereas in Slashdot all the discussion is public. Kuro5hin also involves editorial commentary, rather than simply substantive discussion and an up-or-down moderation. A more distinct, but no less impressive exercise, is the Open Directory Project. That site relies on tens of thousands of volunteer editors to determine which links should be included in a human-edited directory similar to Yahoo. Acceptance as a volunteer requires application. Not all are accepted, and quality relies on a peer review process based substantially on seniority and engagement as a volunteer. The site is hosted and administered by Netscape, which pays for server space and a small number of employees to administer the site and set up the initial guidelines, but licenses the database freely. The volunteers are not affiliated with Netscape. Out of the joy of doing so, or for other internal or external motivations, they spend time in relatively small increments selecting sites for inclusion in the directory. The result has been perhaps the most comprehensive, highest quality human-edited directory of the Web—competing with, and often outperforming, Yahoo in this category.

II. Commons-based peer production – principles

The phenomenon of large- and medium-scale collaborations among individuals, organized without markets or managerial hierarchies, is emerging everywhere in the information and cultural production system. Elsewhere, Benkler has provided a detailed analysis of the economics of this emerging phenomenon;[6] here we briefly recapitulate this analysis, with a particular focus on characteristics that are relevant to the specific arguments of this paper.

At its core, peer production is a model of social production, emerging alongside contract- and market-based, managerial-firm based and state-based production. These forms of production are typified by two core characteristics. The first is decentralization. Authority to act resides with individual agents faced with opportunities for action, rather than in the hands of a central organizer, like the manager of a firm or a bureaucrat. The second is that they use social cues and motivations, rather than prices or commands, to motivate and coordinate the action of participating agents. As a descriptive matter, the phenomenon is a product of the emergence of digital networks and the rising importance of information and cultural production. The wide distribution of low-cost processors, coupled with increasingly ubiquitous computation, changes the capital structure of information production. Physical capital is widely distributed and owned by those individuals who also are capable of contributing the other major input into information and cultural production—human effort and creativity. Because it obviates the need for centralized capital investment, this capital structure makes possible—though does not require—the reorganization of at least some information and cultural production along decentralized lines. In this technical-economic context, peer-production enterprises appear to be emerging as newly feasible social and technical systems that motivate and organize human collective contributions by means other than contracts and monetary compensation for the use of physical capital.

Commons-based peer-production relations regularly exhibit three structural attributes. First, the potential objects of peer production must be modular. That is, they must be divisible into components, or modules, each of which can be produced independently of the production of the others. This enables production to be incremental and asynchronous, pooling the individual discrete efforts of different people, with different capabilities, who are available at different times. Second, the granularity of the modules is important. Granularity refers to the sizes of the project's modules, and in order for a peer-production process successfully to pool a relatively large pool of contributors the modules should be predominantly fine-grained, or small in size. This allows the project to capture contributions from large numbers of contributors whose motivation level will not sustain anything more than quite small efforts towards the project. Novels, for example, at least those that look like our current conception of a novel, are likely to prove resistant to peer production. But as we have already suggested, encyclopedia entries, judgments about the worth of one or another website and components of software programs are commonly and effectively produced in this fashion. In addition, a project will likely be more efficient if it can accommodate variously sized contributions. Heterogeneous granularity will allow people with different levels of motivation to collaborate by contributing smaller or larger grained contributions, consistent with their level of motivation.

Finally, a successful peer-production enterprise must have low-cost integration—the mechanism by which the modules are integrated into a whole end product. Integration must include both quality controls over the modules and a mechanism for integrating the contributions into the finished product. First, the project must include an established, low-cost way of defending itself against both incompetent and malicious contributions. Given that peer production is dependent on self-identification of people for projects, each community must have a way of weeding out contributions from those who misidentify their talents. Second, the project must include a mechanism for integrating the competent modules into a finished product at sufficiently low cost. As one observes actual peer-production communities, a number of robust methods have emerged. First, one sees automated integration and iterative peer production of integration. For example, the use of free software mechanically to integrate modules of some other information good is a primary mechanism by which particular peer-production projects like Slashdot, Kuro5hin and Wikipedia have lowered the cost of integration to the point where they can succeed and sustain themselves. Second, one sees peer-production enterprises using a variety of approaches towards solving collective action problems that are relatively familiar from the offline commons literature.[7] These include various formal rules, like the GNU GPL (General Public License) that prevents defection from many free software projects, including most prominently the GNU/Linux operating system. They also include technical constraints that prevent or limit the effect of defection, as in the case of the limited voting power that Slash or Scoop give each individual editor on Slashdot or Kuro5hin, respectively. Social norms too play a role in sustaining some of these collaborations, both where there are small groups, and where there are larger groups and the platform allows for good monitoring and repair when individuals defect. This approach is particularly salient in the Wikipedia project. Finally, the NASA Clickworkers project suggests that the sheer size of some of these projects enables the collaboration platform to correct for defection by using redundancy of contributions and averaging out the contributions of outliers—be they malicious or incompetent.

When they succeed in motivating and organizing collaborations, peer-production enterprises have two primary advantages from a purely economic perspective over both markets and firm hierarchies. The first is an information gain. Because individuals have widely variable creativity, experience, insight, motivation and availability, human capital tends to be hard to specify for efficient contracting or formal organizational assignment. Firms and markets therefore simplify decision making by losing a lot of information about the tremendous variability of human creativity and motivation over time and context. Peer production, by contrast, allows individuals to self-identify for tasks that attract them and for which they are suited. As long as a peer-production enterprise institutes mechanisms for peer review of some sort to weed out mistakes, peer-production enterprises generate more textured and dynamically updated information about the capabilities and availability of agents for actions. Second, the variability in fit of people to projects and existing information resources is great. This leads to substantial increasing returns to scale to the number of people, resources and projects that may be pursued without need for a contract or other transaction permitting the use of the resource for a project. The larger the number of people who can potentially work on projects, the larger the number of resources with which they can work to pursue projects; and the larger the number of projects they can initiate and imagine, the higher the probability that the best set of persons will be able to work on the set of resources with which they would be most productive, towards the project most suitable from that combination. Peer production, by making information resources freely available to potentially huge collections of individuals, maximizes the effect.

Before turning to an analysis of the relationship between the emergence of peer production and virtue, it is important to underscore one further central characteristic of peer production. By definition, peer-production enterprises are non-price based, that is, they are devoid of marginal payments to contributors for contributions. While some contributors contribute because of an expectation of learning and earning a reputation that could translate into a job in the future, most of the participation cannot easily be explained by a relatively mechanistic reliance on economic incentives. Rather, it seems that peer-production enterprises thrive on, and give opportunity for, relatively large scale and effective scope for volunteerism, or behavior motivated by, and oriented towards, positive social relations. People contribute for a variety of reasons, ranging from the pure pleasure of creation, to a particular sense of purpose, through to the companionship and social relations that grow around a common enterprise. What makes peer-production enterprises work best has been the capacity to harness many people, with many and diverse motivations, towards common goals in concerted effort. While understudied and difficult to predict and manage by comparison to a more simple picture of human motivation as driven by personal wealth maximization, peer production begins to offer a rich texture in which to study the much more varied and multifarious nature of human motivation and effective human action.

The economic potential of the phenomenon of commons-based peer production may or may not be sufficient reason to support its growth and justify attention to factors or conditions needed for its flourishing. It certainly suggests the potential staying power and sustainability of this mode of production in an economy and society heavily attentive to economic performance. Here, however, we are interested in considerations beyond economic efficiency. Taking a moral perspective, we argue that the remarkable social and technical phenomenon of commons-based peer production fosters virtue by creating a context or setting that is conducive to virtuous engagement and practice, thereby offering a medium for inducing virtue itself in its participants.

III. Commons-based peer production and virtue

Before we are able to develop our claim about virtue and commons-based peer production, we need to say something about the notion of virtue that we will be using. Those of us educated in a Western, analytic school of philosophy tend to think of virtue as essentially an Aristotelian creation, passed down and elaborated along the way by just about every historically significant moral philosopher, including Kant, Nietzsche and Hume, falling into disfavor in the mainstream until roughly two decades ago and benefiting from a revival of interest through persuasive interventions of contemporary moral philosophers such as Phillipa Foot, Alasdair MacIntyre, Martha Nussbaum, Bernard Williams, Michael Slote, Rosalind Hursthouse and others. Yet the idea of virtue is far richer than even that pedigree would suggest, spanning centuries as well as cultures and religions. Robust notions of virtue have been recorded in commentaries on ancient Confucian philosophers, such as those by Xunzi, born circa 310 B.C.E. Not only has it been theorized by countless philosophers and theologians throughout ages and across continents, but it has a robust meaning in natural languages, regularly uttered in everyday speech.

We have tried not to tie our discussion to a specific theory or doctrine of the virtues and virtue ethics. By staying as close as possible to an intuitively plausible sense of virtue, remaining neutral on many of the most controversial theoretical questions, and plumbing only the most robust insights of scholarship where they are relevant to our arena of application, we have aimed for as broadly appealing a conceptual foundation as possible. This neutrality applies to three broad areas: We make no commitment to the specific number or particular catalog of the virtues but assume the existence and character of those that have enjoyed broad recognition. We are agnostic on the foundations of virtue, whether in ideals of human flourishing and the good life (Aristotle, MacIntyre), naturalism (Foot and Hursthouse) or utilitarianism (Hume, Driver).

Finally, we take no position on the meta-ethical question of whether virtue ethics is best understood as a rival to deontological and Utilitarian accounts of "the problems and phenomena of ethics."[8] As a working position, we prefer David Wiggins' ecumenical line:

> What a grown-up moral philosophy might attempt is an account of morality that embraces the full gamut of moral predications, seeing them as mutually irreducible and mutually indispensable, allowing no primacy to character traits or practices or states of affairs—or allowing primacy to all at once.[9]

Ideally, this stance will allow the primary focus of our discussion, and inevitable controversy, to settle on concrete claims rather than these much debated elements of the conceptual landscape.

At a minimum, however, we take virtue ethics to be an important approach to moral evaluation, which offers a framework for appraising people over time, in contrast with other dominant approaches that appraise actions, atomistically, in terms of consequences or compatibility with deontological rules. In other words, where the basic unit of moral evaluation for rival frameworks is individual actions (or action-types), the basic unit of moral evaluation for virtue ethics is the person (or soul or character), an entity persisting over time. Accordingly, Rosalind Hursthouse writes, "If you have the virtues of, say, generosity, honesty, and justice, generous, honest, and just is the sort of person you are."[10] Most contemporary virtue theorists and virtue ethicists consider the character to be the bearer of virtue, "an admirable character trait;"[11] that is, "those qualities of character the possession and exercise of which make human beings flourish."[12] Finally, most virtue theories allow that character, the bearer of virtues, is not immutable and its virtue may ebb and flow.

By most accounts, virtues are dispositional properties, though particularly with many of the most important virtues such as, honesty, justice, courage and benevolence they are not simple dispositions to act in narrowly specified ways. Being honest, for example, does not merely involve telling the truth, or never telling a lie, but a complex pattern of beliefs, desires, emotions, preferences, sensitivities, opinions and broadly related actions and practices, even as general as how one rears one's children. Equally clear is that particular instances of beliefs, actions, emotions and so forth need not imply the virtue of honesty, as, for example, the conman who happens to tell the truth in a court of law. This point, thoroughly discussed in contemporary writings such as those of Hursthouse and others, is also recognized in ancient works, such as in those of Xunzi, who holds that virtues are dispositions involving the faculties of choice, judgments, desire, emotion and action. Further, virtues can be manifested in a great variety of ways, depending on circumstances.[13]

Later in the paper, we will refer to other general features of virtues but, first, it will be useful to plunge directly into an analysis of systematic associations between particular virtues and characteristics inherent to commons-based peer production. To avoid quibbling over differences that may have more to do with contingencies of language than with substance, it makes sense to put forward these associations in terms of clusters of virtues associated with socio-technical systems of commons-based peer production rather than individually named virtues.

A. Cluster I: autonomy, independence, liberation

As noted above, an essential feature of commons-based peer production is volunteerism and self-selection. In the first place, individuals have chosen freely to participate and are free to continue or cease to participate as they please. Usually, they are able to contribute when and how much they want, and can select aspects of production according to their own criteria. In the typically decentralized, non-hierarchical settings, even if participants seek to please and impress peers, they need not cower to a boss or any other such authority. As volunteers, they exercise independence of will, initiative, even self-reliance, discretion and free-spiritedness. No matter what other demands constrain their lives, participation in peer production constitutes an arena of autonomy, an arena where they are free to act according to self-articulated goals and principles. In this arena, they manifest, in Charles Taylor's terms, the virtue of "liberation," manifest in bearers "directing their own lives, . . . deciding for themselves the conditions of their own existence, as against falling prey to the domination of others, and to impersonal, natural, or social mechanisms which they fail to understand, and therefore cannot control or transform."[14]

Note that when one is speaking of autonomy as a virtue, as an attribute of character, the ambiguity between autonomy as an instantiated property versus a human potentiality recedes as it is unlikely we would value in another the merely presumed capacity to be free. It is actual liberation, actual self-direction, that is admirable in a character. In the context of commons-based peer production, this may mean independence from the wide-ranging commercial entities influencing our actions and choices as well as from the typical array of institutional entities, whether employers, banks, agents of government, or whoever.

B. Cluster II: creativity, productivity, industry

Through their involvement in commons-based peer projects, participants are able to reach beyond the humdrum routines many of us experience in our workdays, including those of us privileged to live materially comfortable lives in industrialized and wealthy nations. Even our recreational choices tend to be passive and limiting, such as selecting among TV channels, watching movies and shopping in malls. While the industrially organized, mass market economy largely structures so many of our choices as comparatively passive consumption choices, or comparatively regimented production choices in fairly controlled work environments, peer production opens up new avenues for creative, productive practices. Few of us will write novels, create encyclopedias or works of art, or produce effective computer programs. Fewer still will do so in their spare time. But peer production offers a medium for contributing our thoughts, our knowledge, our know-how, or merely the spare cycles of our PCs toward a meaningful product.

Peer production offers the possibility of engagement in what MacIntyre terms a "practice," namely, a "socially established human activity through which goods internal to that form of activity are realized in the course of trying to achieve those standards of excellence which are appropriate to, and partially derivative of, that form of activity, with the result that human powers to achieve excellence, and human conceptions of the ends and goods involved, are systematically extended."[15]

In commenting on other forms of peer-based engagement, a broader category that includes commons-based peer production, others have highlighted their potential for active rather than passive intellectual and social participation online. Andy Oram, for example, has asserted that, "peer-to-peer technologies return the Internet to its original vision, in which everyone creates as well as consumes."[16] Those engaged in peer-to-peer activities "are active participants, not just passive 'browsers.'"[17] They are writing code, collaborating in community networks, commenting on the news, and so on.

C. Cluster III: benevolence, charity, generosity, altruism

If the previous two virtue clusters can be considered "self-regarding" virtues,[18] this cluster and the next can be considered "other-regarding," or in Hume's terms, "social virtues." Although each element of this cluster has a distinctive character and is favored in varying measure by theorists and scholars of virtue, their common core is the disposition to benefit others, "to seek the good of others as an end in itself, and in circumstances in which it is not required of us."[19] Among all the virtues, these are central to almost all theories of the virtues and virtue ethics, serving as in David Hume's work, as one of the bedrocks of a general moral theory. Benevolence and generosity require not only that the good of others be furthered, but that a cost be borne by the generous individual alone.

Participants in commons-based peer production benefit others by contributing time and effort that could, in principle, be spent in more directly self-serving pursuits. In helping others, in small ways such as donating spare cycles, or larger ways such as creating carefully researched encyclopedia entries without receiving conventional, tangible payments or favors in return, peers exercise kindness, benevolence, charity and generosity. In the specific case of free and open source software, the literature is ambiguous on the centrality of the role that this cluster of virtues plays. Some, like Richard Stallman, founder of the free software movement, seem more animated by the linkage with virtues in the autonomy and self-reliance cluster, though they also highlight themes of helping friends and neighbors through the sharing of software.[20] Some proponents of open source, trying to bring it into the business world's mainstream, have sought to depoliticize free software by explaining the motivations of participants in terms palatable to believers in *homo economicus*.[21] And yet, many who have worked hard to make open source tractable to economists and business people have lauded its underlying "gift culture."[22] Although it is entirely possible that the persistent and pervasive practice of spending time and effort producing something of value and giving it freely to be used by others for no compensation can be explained as self-serving behavior in pursuit of, say, reputation, a more efficient and direct explanation in many, if not most cases, is the pleasure or satisfaction of giving—generosity, kindness, benevolence.[23]

D. Cluster IV: sociability, camaraderie, friendship, cooperation, civic virtue

This cluster of virtues is thematically related to Cluster III, but not identical to it. Cluster III virtues involve giving to others, sometimes needy others, to benefit them—and if Hunt's thesis is to be believed—at a cost to the giver. In this cluster, the virtues also imply giving, but the open-hearted contribution is to a commons, a community, a public, a mission, or a fellowship of which the giver is a part, and the giving dimension might be only one aspect of it. Its core is a conception of the self as part of a collective and of one's efforts as a part of a collective effort, whether the collective or common search for extra-terrestrial life, the quest for a free encyclopedia for all, or for a balanced, popular vision of advanced technologies in society. The giving, therefore, does not merely involve agents parting with something of value, but agents working in cooperation with others to give or produce something of value to all.

Whereas generosity, benevolence, and so on are universally present in the explicit lists of virtues proposed by ethicists from Aristotle to Rosalind Hursthouse, from Xunzi to Martha Nussbaum, the virtues within this cluster are rarely encountered in explicit terms. Although, arguably, they are implicitly present in, for example, David Hume's list of the virtues of "humanity, benevolence, friendship, public spirit, and other social virtues of that stamp,"[24] Hume does not develop the notion of public spirit, nor say much about its relation to benevolence. MacIntyre, too, seems interested in the social contribution of virtues: "The catalogue of the virtues will therefore include the virtues required to sustain the kind of households and the kind of political communities in which men and women can seek for the good together and the virtues necessary to enable us to understand what more and what else the good life for man is."[25] But in extended discussion, he does not develop in detail the relation between political and other communities and specific virtues.

Among political theorists, however, these social, or civic virtues have had greater salience. Defenders of liberalism, for example, have sought to characterize "liberal virtues," including among them the dispositions to engage in voluntary associations and to promote common ends in social cooperation.[26] Michael Sandel, a renowned contemporary proponent of Republicanism, traces the commitment to these civic virtues in the United States back to the founders, who sought to nourish "public virtue" in the citizenry. A complex virtue, public virtue involved a commitment to the public good, or, in John Adams' words, "a positive passion for the public, the public interest, honour, power and glory."[27] According to Sandel, the Revolutionaries valued "public good" second only to liberty, meaning by public good, "more than the sum of individual interests. Accordingly, the practice of politics should be aimed not merely at brokering a compromise among competing interests but to transcend these interests by seeking the good of the community as a whole."[28] In Sandel's account, the founders believed "civic virtue" to be the bedrock of liberal democracy.[29]

In a similar way, participants in a commons-based peer effort cooperate, build upon the work of others, contribute time, effort and expertise to create and enhance a public good. The self-reliance, vaunted by Richard Stallman and other proponents of free software, is not in tension with fellowship—rather, it is only in tension with the incapacity to make do for oneself, and hence reliance on the commercial other to make do for one. The act of creating for oneself and one's fellows is an act both of self-reliance and of fellowship—like barn-raising or establishing a community watch.

IV. From structure to virtue

So far, our analysis has established a structural connection between key defining properties of commons-based peer production and the possibility of engagement in creative, autonomous, benevolent and public-spirited undertakings. This is a less ambitious claim than the one with which we set out, namely, that the practice of commons-based peer production is connected to virtue. The remaining sections of the paper will argue that a plausible causal connection can be drawn in two directions: first, that virtue leads people to participate in commons-based peer projects, and second, that participation may give rise to virtue. Based upon these observations, we conclude the paper with some prescriptions for public policy and design.

Even if participation in peer production yields benefits to others, contributes to the common good, is a setting for cooperative activity, has the capacity to engender autonomy and so forth, the claim of virtue requires that participants are, in fact, acting generously, exercising autonomy and so forth. Supporting this claim requires more than pointing out that the behaviors benefit others, promote the public good and so forth, but also that they are performed with the right kinds of attitudes and motives. (There is also the theoretical question of the role of motivation in defining particular virtues, which lies outside the scope of this paper.) This issue is not new for many admirers of open source and free software, who continuously seek to account for the motivations of project participants.[30] Establishing the strongest version of the claim, that *all* participants are motivated by benevolence, good-will, fellowship and so forth, is impossible and also unnecessary. Without a doubt, there are many reasons people participate. It will suffice if we are able to show that virtuous motivations are at least a substantial part of the picture.

Laudable actions, in general, may arise out of a variety of motives. We know, for example, that people give gifts for many reasons besides sheer generosity, including a wish to reciprocate, to win favor, to impress onlookers or recipients or to place recipients in the giver's debt.[31] People behave fairly or even-handedly as much out of fear of disapproval or selfish ambition— say, to promote their own professional status—as out of the virtue of justice. And likewise with other virtues and related behaviors. Moreover, it is likely that participants in the projects described above and others like them are motivated by many factors, which may also vary systematically across projects and people and within individuals, over time. Some may be lonely and seeking company, others may wish to promote their chances of a good job, still others may seek the benefits of learning the craft through participation in one of the peer-production projects. None of these reasons is morally reprehensible. But for purposes of drawing the connection between commons-based peer production and virtue, it is crucial that we discover a substantial set of participants whose motivations implicate the four clusters of virtue. Such knowledge is of empirical fact and not purely a matter of analysis.

Despite considerable interest in the issue of motivation, particularly regarding free and open source projects, we found no empirical studies that could rigorously confirm the causal connection between virtue and participation in commons-based systems of peer production. There are, nevertheless, suggestive findings—more than mere anecdotes—that lend systematic support to our thesis. One datum comes from the SETI@home website, where volunteers are asked by organizers to participate in a poll which includes a question about motivation: "What is your main reason for running SETI@home?" Participants are offered a set of multiple choice answers, including an option of "Other," which allows for free form answers as well.

With a number of 117,894 participants when the site was last visited the results were:

Find ET for the good of humanity	58.33%
Find ET to become famous	3.08%
Keep my computer productive	16.92%
Get my name on a top 100 list on the web site	2.29%
Other	19.37%[32]

The free-form responses stimulated by the "Other" category were even more telling. As illustrated below, respondents indicated a clear attraction to the opportunities SETI offered for contributing to the public good, for promoting welfare by helping with scientific research, and for the opportunity to be part of an interesting, possibly momentous project. For example:

- "Because the SETI is one of the greatest science programs running and I like to participate in this great search and, of course, for humanity."
- "Support a worthwhile cause. Participate in the largest parallel processing effort."
- "Find ET and it is just plain cool to help with the research."
- "Find ET and to be part of an exceptional distributed computing project."
- "Find ET for good of humanity and prove the net power."
- "Find ET for humanity. Keep my computer productive, and to just be a part of this great project!"
- "Helping out the Scientific Community."

In the context of free software and open source, the rhetoric of movement leaders like Richard Stallman, Linus Torvalds and Eric Raymond clearly endorses the relevance of values such as autonomy, self-reliance, gift-giving, collaboration, active participation, liberation and creativity in motivating participation.[33] These ideological and anecdotal accounts resonate with findings of the Free/Libre and Open Source Software (FLOSS): Survey and Study, the first large-scale study of the role and importance of open source and free software worldwide. Funded by the European Commission and carried out by Berlecon Research and the International Institute of Infonomics at the University of Maastricht, the FLOSS survey and study not only generated primary data on usage and development, indicators of value dissemination and distribution, business models and economic and regulatory implications. It also included a survey of 2,784 developers worldwide on a variety of topics with a section devoted to reasons (or motivations) for participating. A few of the questions drew noteworthy answers.

In commenting generally on the Open Source/Free Software (OS/FS) scene, the greatest percentage agreed that it enabled more freedom in software development. In significant numbers they also cited new forms of cooperation, opportunities to create more varieties of software and innovative breakthroughs. When asked what they thought other OS/FS developers expected from them, the majority said "share my knowledge and skill," a large percentage said "help in realizing ideas for software projects," and in relation to these and other responses a tiny fraction said "provide better job opportunities" and "make money." As to why they began, the highest proportion answered "to learn and develop new skills," closely followed by "to share my knowledge and skills," "to participate in new forms of cooperation" and "because I think that software should not be a proprietary product." As to why they continue, the first is still dominant, though with a smaller margin, while the other three, namely sharing, cooperating and objecting to proprietary control over software, all rise significantly as motivating forces. It is also striking that although a number of other non-moral reasons achieved mid-range scores, the ones that consistently earned lowest were, "to make money" and "to get a reputation in the OS/FS scene."

We admit that neither SETI@home nor FLOSS study results are conclusive. For one thing, they both suffer from the possibility of a self-reporting bias, people wanting to portray themselves as more altruistic than they in fact are. With SETI@home there is the additional problem of self-selected respondents. Indeed, no matter how many participants we survey, or how closely we observe them, we may never prove to the satisfaction of some (diehards) that these benevolent, independent, civic-minded and productive behaviors were performed with the right types of attitudes to qualify for virtue. We share this plight with a host of others, who somehow must prove to skeptics that true altruism or sympathy or generosity exists. Although the burden of so doing strikes us as absurd, it lies outside the scope of this paper to enter this larger debate. A limited conclusion, however, seems credible: insofar as any other-regarding action is possible, there is good reason to hold that a sizable proportion of peer participation is pro-social, or morally praiseworthy in the ways discussed.

The general question of what warrants the move from observed behaviors to assertions about virtue is a core component of most theories of virtue, but lies outside the scope of the paper. It is normally assumed that to assert the presence of an underlying disposition requires not only that the relevant actions are performed, or performed on a one-off basis, but that they are performed habitually. Pitching in, for example, is praiseworthy, but only one who pitches in regularly is seen as instantiating the virtue of good-fellowship. The projects described earlier and many more provide precisely this type of opportunity for repeated engagement in relevant actions over an extended period of time, so that we can say that those who participate are the kinds of people who give to others with no prospect of direct payoff or punitive sanctions. Such engagement may reasonably be seen by others, *as well as by participants themselves*, as expressions of the associated virtues.

Assuming we have shown that a significant number of participants in peer production are acting in ways that are morally and politically praiseworthy, not only producing utility but doing so for the right reasons and with the right motives, we would like to take our account one step further, suggesting not only that in many instances reliable and long-term participation constitutes evidence of virtue but that participation may also lead to virtue. This causal connection from behavior to virtue is arguably the more interesting one.

For those of us accustomed to conventional philosophical thinking about action as the upshot of beliefs, desires, emotions and so forth, the reverse direction of causation may seem odd. Nevertheless this is widely embraced by virtue theorists and ethicists, who agree that significant sources of virtue include good habits and practice. Grounded also in common sense ideas about the power of good habits, this idea is evident in Leon Festinger's notion of cognitive dissonance, which captures the paradoxical (but ultimately compelling) idea that people's attitudes and beliefs are frequently formed as a consequence of their actual choices and actions and not vice versa. Aristotle endorses the importance of practice in his account of the three sources of character formation: nature, explicit teaching and—most central to our discussion—habit. Virtuous action performed habitually could induce or contribute to the attainment of virtue itself. Because of this, Aristotle recommends that children, in addition to being taught explicitly about the virtues, should be trained to adopt certain habits because "it is our actions that determine our dispositions."[34] Moreover, "[i]t is the repeated performance of just and temperate actions that produces virtue.... It is therefore quite fair to say that a man becomes just by the performance of just actions, and temperate by the performance of temperate actions."[35]

Interpreters of Xunzi, the ancient Confucian philosopher, have attributed to him a similar account of the sources of virtuous character. Accordingly, virtuous practice, alongside learning and training in various rituals, is a crucial element contributing toward development of full virtue. Virtue is thus a product of correct practice; and the capacity to act correctly is a step toward virtue itself. Immanuel Kant affirms this principle: "Helping others to achieve their ends is a duty. If a man practices it often and succeeds in realizing his purpose, he eventually comes to feel love for those he has helped. Hence the saying: you ought to love your neighbor ... means do good to your fellow-man, and this will give rise to love of man in you."[36]

The Aristotelian ideal of a dedicated mentor to guide the character development and education of each child is no longer feasible in the contemporary landscape. We rely on a far more diverse and less systematic set of offerings, including the mass media, public education and other social institutions (such as museums, religious institutions and a myriad of others), which serve, directly and indirectly, as sources of learning, training and even character formation. If, as we have suggested, participation in commons-based peer production is an instance of an activity that not only enables the expression of virtuous character but serves as a training ground for virtue, it holds the potential to add to the stock of opportunities for pro-social engagement. With this in mind, we now turn to consider some implications of what we have said for public policy.

V. Public policy

In chapter fifteen of *After Virtue*, Alasdair MacIntyre remarks: "Only in fantasy do we live what story we please. In life, as Aristotle and Engels noted, we are always under certain constraints. We enter upon a stage which we did not design and we find ourselves part of an action that was not of our making."[37] MacIntyre means something quite general about the ways people's lives reflect their distinctive narratives mingled together with those of others, constrained by the stories and experiences of families, tribes, traditions, communities, social, political and cultural institutions and historical circumstances, which together shape choices and possibilities by exposing possibilities and defining good and bad behavior, vice and virtue.

A practical corollary of the observation that social and institutional arrangements have the power to shape human behavior and disposition is to strive for positively valued behaviors and dispositions through purposive interventions in these arrangements. This ambition is not unprecedented either in the actions of political leaders or in evaluations of leaders, policies and institutions by members of the academy.[38] Sandel cites noteworthy historical instances in which stances on critical policy issues, emerging during formative periods of the United States, turned on the potential effects on human character of the alternatives. As an example, Sandel cites George Mason's vehement opposition to the Port Bill to promote development of large commercial cities, which was grounded in the belief that development would undermine the moral virtue of residents, diminishing their "frugality, probity and strictness of morals."[39] According to Sandel, such arguments would not have been out of place for the environment in which there was general agreement regarding the principle that: "The public life of a republic must serve a formative role, aimed at cultivating citizens of a certain kind." The government was seen to have "a stake in cultivating citizens of a certain kind." The Constitution of 1787 was another vehicle designed to save "American republicanism from the deadly effects of [the] private pursuits of happiness," and "from the acquisitive preoccupations that so absorbed Americans and distracted them from the public good." In addition to policy and the Constitution, there would be other public institutions aimed at "improving" moral and civic character, from "education, to religion, and more broadly, to the social and economic arrangements that would define the character of the new nation."[40] It goes without saying that the argument supporting the role of social and political institutions in shaping character is separable from substantive beliefs about what counts as virtue.

In *Character and Culture*, the philosopher Lester Hunt shares insights into ways the design of social institutions may influence the development of virtues. He writes:

> [T]here are some virtues that it is comparatively easy to acquire and instill in the context of American institutions. At any rate, parents who are trying to get their children to respect the property of others or keep their promises probably do not so often have the feeling that they have the whole world working against them. Our institutions do seem to be arranged so that they facilitate the acquisition of some good traits of character. . . . We may find, for instance, that some of the limits to the powers that moral instructors possess are not due to the immutable facts of human nature but to institutions that we have the power to change. Perhaps people are no more generous or just than they are, no less envious and vengeful than they are, because of the institutions that influence their behavior, and not because the guardians of virtue—whoever they may be— have failed to be sufficiently vigilant or skillful.[41]

The institutions Hunt has in mind may be loosely construed as cultural rituals like gift-giving, or explicit regulatory vehicles as in the historical cases Sandel discusses, or contemporary counterparts such as tax-deductions for charitable gift-giving. As Hunt observes, the virtue-enhancing properties of any given social institution are complex and subject to a variety of contingencies:

> A theory of the origin of a trait of character does not state that from a specific concrete situation, in all its complexity and with all the features of it that individuals might perceive and to which they might respond, one specific result must emerge. Rather, it picks out certain features of many actual situations—as, for instance, that the people in them are taught a certain type of rule—and shows that these features support the formation of certain traits of character.[42]

Accordingly, the efficacy of the virtue-enhancing properties of commons-based peer production will, likewise, be tempered by contingencies of the highly variable background conditions in which participation takes place.

The past few decades of the philosophical and social study of technology (STS) has shown, however, that it is possible to give a more concrete interpretation of MacIntyre's remark by considering the stage not only as a social context but as the material context, designed by others, into which we must enter. For the philosophers and social scientists who study technology, this metaphor draws attention to a world in which we are constrained not only through the narratives and expectations of the self and other social agents and institutions, but by the material world which is constituted in increasing measure by technology. From Lewis Mumford's authoritarian and democratic technics to Marshall McLuhan's medium as a shaper of content, to Langdon Winner's artifacts with politics, to Bruno Latour's inscription of morality in machines—each of these expresses the common idea that technical systems and devices, in virtue of their properties, architecture or functionality, have the capacity both to limit and to facilitate what individuals and collectivities are able do.[43] Rejecting the view of technology as neutral, producing outcomes only as a result of the uses and applications chosen by people, these theorists of technology, and others, hold that technology embodies values. Values may be "built into" technical design characteristics of technologies, which, in interaction with the social, political, economic and cultural characteristics of the contexts in which they are embedded, produce outcomes skewed in one way or another. In drawing attention to the ways technologies enhance or suppress social, political and moral values, these philosophers, legal scholars and social scientists frequently see their work as continuous with social, political and moral commentary. Brian Pfaffenberger observes:

> All around us today are artifacts that were generated in the technological dramas of their time: railways, canals, aviation artifacts, radios, and more. And yet their meaning, together with their location in what was formerly a deeply felt grammar of political action, is utterly lost; in their place is what appears to be nothing more than a material record of "technological progress." What was once the conscious product of human cultural and political action, passionate and meaningful, is now a silent material reality within which we lead our daily lives, mutely acting out patterns of behavior that once had obvious connections to the root paradigms of our culture.... To become fully aware of the political circumstances of their lives, new generations of students, at every level of education, must be trained (as Hughes suggests) to 'fathom the depth of the technological society, to identify currents running more deeply than those conventionally associated with politics and economics.' Because STS offers a way to recontextualize technological artifacts, it is therefore the political philosophy of our time, and it deserves to stand at the center of any curriculum that teaches political awareness and civic responsibility.[44]

In other words, technical systems and devices are as much a part of political and moral life as practices, laws, regulations, institutions and norms that are more commonly seen as vehicles for moral and political values.

The political aim of this paper is similar to those pointing to social or political consequences of specific technical systems, for example, those warning of privacy threats posed by pervasive video and data surveillance and biometric measurement technologies, diminishment of autonomy and accountability due to automated command and control systems and alterations in hierarchies of power and authority due to design features of certain network infrastructures. Unlike many political analyses of technologies, however, ours does not warn of a direct threat of harm. Rather, it warns of a threat of omission. We might miss the chance to benefit from a distinctive socio-technical system that promotes not only cultural and intellectual production but constitutes a venue for human character development.

Some might challenge the underlying premise, arguing that "low-cost" contributions to the public good, such as those afforded by commons-based peer production, are not capable of training virtue. Because an inherent feature of these production schema is to facilitate contribution at relatively low personal cost, its virtue-enhancing capacities are questionable. This characterization misses the point. As noted above, commons-based peer production generates new modes of contributing to the public good by facilitating the collaborative engagement of thousands of ordinary individuals in the voluntary, creative, communal, regular, non-commercial production of intellectual and cultural goods, for a wide variety of reasons and motives. There are also many different *types* of projects, demanding highly variable degrees of effort. Whereas some, such as SETI@home, call for relatively low levels of engagement and effort, others such as Wikipedia[45] call for significant commitment, work, time, patience, dedication, fairness and civic-mindedness.

Effort (or cost) may be a requirement for moral action but it is surely not boundless; effort may be required, but not supererogation. Where to draw the line is not a question we need settle here, except to observe that moral action lies somewhere between the extremes of no-effort and supererogation, and is surely also a function of the good it engenders. There is no reason to appraise participation in peer production any differently. Accordingly, although what critics say may apply to a fraction of the cases, it certainly does not apply to all when we take into consideration the effort involved, the good produced and the widely shared intentionality and self-understanding as providing that public good. When a society endorses social policies that, for example, offer protection to whistle-blowers, provide tax-credits for charitable donations, or generate institutional safeguards against corruption, it is not shrinking the moral sphere, but structuring the environment to lessen the burden of valued practices. In a similar way, commons-based peer production opens a path previously restricted by economic cost and industrial organization to small numbers of professional producers of information, knowledge and culture to large numbers of ordinary people, enabling them to contribute to the public good in a particular domain. The path does not bypass virtuous action, but generates new opportunities for it.

Despite the positive potential of commons-based peer production, there is cause for concern over its future flourishing. The primary sources of resistance are rent-seeking behavior by incumbent firms of the industrial information economy and well-meaning, but ill-informed policies and judicial decisions. The former stems from the fact that commons-based peer production presents an alternative to, and therefore a form of competition with, the incumbents. The latter arises because policy makers and judges have been habituated by the twentieth-century economics of information production to think that market production, in particular established firms, are critical to growth, innovation and creativity. Relatively few have adjusted to the new economics of networks, and recognized the potential and value of peer production.

The most visible conflict between commons-based peer production and incumbent firms is in the area of free or open source software. Here, FLOSS is seen as a potential alternative, and is actively supported and used by major corporations and many governments. This has led Microsoft, in particular, to try to resist these developments.[46] More subtle is the way in which the incumbents of the cultural industries, in particular Hollywood and the recording industry, have successfully lobbied Congress and litigated in courts to expand copyright and to introduce new related technical requirements—like the Digital Millennium Copyright Act of 1998 and the persistent efforts to pass hardware regulation. While these efforts have mostly succeeded in allowing these firms to extract higher rents from their inventories, they impose higher entry barriers than is necessary to the public domain. Because all information production requires access to existing information inputs, these constraints on the public domain create barriers to effective pursuit of peer production. While not always aimed directly at peer production, these efforts raise the costs of maintaining information production activities and dampen the development of some technologies that can be useful to peer production, as well as to other peer-to-peer uses that are more legally controversial—like music file-sharing.

VI. Conclusion

We have argued that participation in commons-based peer production fosters important moral and political virtues. We have not made the case that it is therefore incumbent upon the state to support peer production. That would require a greater commitment to a perfectionist state agenda than we have stated or defended here, or are willing to defend. Nonetheless, we have offered new reasons to find peer production to be a morally attractive set of social, cultural and economic practices. There is a growing literature on the relative efficiency of peer production in many domains of information production, and some exploration of its attractiveness from the perspective of a variety of liberal commitments: to democracy, autonomy and social justice.[47] Here we have contributed additional reason to think that peer production is normatively attractive. For those who hold one of a broad range of conceptions of virtue, peer production can be said to provide a social context in which to act out, and a set of social practices through which to inculcate and develop, some quite basic human, social and political virtues. It is in light of the whole picture that we recommend vigorous support for this exceptional socio-technical phenomenon that serves not only as the source of knowledge and information but as a platform for virtuous practices and the development of virtue in its participants.

Notes

* We have benefited from the generous help and wisdom of others, particularly Julia Driver, Francis Grodzinsky, Gilbert Harman, George Kateb, participants at the Conference on Computer Ethics: Philosophical Enquiry 2003 and the valuable research assistance of Daniel J. Bloch. Arguments were improved by the careful and astute comments of reviewers for this Journal.

1 Yochai Benkler, "Coase's penguin, or Linux and the nature of the firm," *Yale Law Journal*, 112 (2002), 369–446; Benkler, "Sharing nicely: on sharable goods and the emergence of sharing as a modality of economic production," *Yale Law Journal*, 114 (2004), 273–358.
2 Josh Lerner and Jean Tirole, "Some simple economics of open source," *Journal of Industrial Economics*, 50 (2002), 197–234.
3 Eben Moglen, "Anarchism triumphant: free software and the death of copyright," *First Monday*, 4 (August 1999); Available at http://www.firstmonday.org/issues/issue4_8_mogden (accessed April 25, 2005).
4 President's Information Technology Advisory Committee, *Developing Open Source Software to Advance High End Computing* (Washington, D.C.: Government Printing Office, 2000).
5 "Clickworkers results: crater marking activity," July 3, 2001; available at http://clickworkers.arc.nasa.gov (accessed April 25, 2005).
6 Benkler, "Coase's penguin."
7 Charlotte Hess and Elinor Ostrom, "Artifacts, facilities, and content: information as a common-pool resource," *Journal of Law & Contemporary Problems*, 63 (2003), 111–145. See also Ostrom, *Governing the Commons: The Evolution of Institutions for Collective Action* (Cambridge, Mass: Cambridge University Press, 1992).
8 Michael Slote, *From Morality to Virtue* (New York: Oxford University Press, 1987). For further information on "human flourishing and the good life," see Aristotle, "Nichomachean ethics," *Moral Philosophy: Selected Readings*, ed. George Sher (San Diego: Harcourt Brace Jovanovich, 1987) and Alasdair McIntyre, *After Virtue* (Notre Dame, Ind.: University of Notre Dame Press, 1984). On "naturalism," see Philippa Foot, *Virtues and Vices and Other Essays in Moral Philosophy* (Berkeley: University of California Press, 1978) and Rosalind Hursthouse, *On Virtue Ethics* (Oxford: Oxford University Press, 1999). On "utilitarianism," see Julia Driver, *Uneasy Virtue* (Cambridge: Cambridge University Press, 2001) and David Hume, *Enquiry Concerning the Principles of Morals*, ed. P. H. Niddich, 3rd edn (Oxford: Clarendon Press, 1975; originally published 1751).

9 David Wiggins, "Natural and artificial virtues: a vindication of Hume's scheme," *How One Should Live: Essays on Virtue*, ed. Roger Crisp (Oxford: Clarendon Press, 1996), pp. 131–40.
10 Hursthouse, *On Virtue Ethics*, p. 11.
11 Slote, *From Morality to Virtue*, p. 10.
12 Peter Simpson, "Contemporary virtue ethics and Aristotle," *Virtue Ethics: A Critical Reader*, ed. Daniel Statman (Washington D.C.: Georgetown University Press), pp. 245–59 at p. 246.
13 Lester Hunt, *Character and Culture* (New York: Rowman & Littlefield, 1997).
14 Charles Taylor, "The diversity of goods," *Moral Philosophy: Selected Readings*, ed. George Sher, 2nd edn (New York: Harcourt Brace, 1996), pp. 581–93 at p. 589. Taylor adds, "I have integrity to the degree to which my actions and statements are true expressions of what is really important to me" (p. 589).
15 McIntyre, *After Virtue*, p. 175.
16 Andy Oram, *Peer-to-Peer: Harnessing the Power of Disruptive Technologies* (Sebastopol: O'Reilly & Associates, 2001), p. ix.
17 ibid., p. 51.
18 See Slote, *From Morality to Virtue*.
19 Hunt, *Character and Culture*, p. 63, for an extensive discussion of generosity and benevolence.
20 Richard Stallman, "Philosophy of the GNU project;" available at http://www.gnu.org/philosophy/ (accessed April 25, 2005).
21 Eric Raymond, "Homesteading the noosphere," *First Monday*, 3 (April 1998); available at http://www.firstmonday.org/issues/issue3_10_raymond (accessed April 25, 2005). See also Lerner and Tirole, "Some simple economics of open source."
22 Eric Raymond, *The Cathedral and the Bazaar: Musings on Linux and Open Source by an Accidental Revolutionary* (Cambridge, Mass.: O'Reilly Associates, 1999): "It is quite clear that the society of open source hackers is in fact a gift culture" (p. 81).
23 See Hunt, *Character and Culture*, p. 192 and fn 5, for interesting points on Aristotle and Nietzsche on productive work and gift giving as valuable both to us and to others.
24 Hume, *Enquiry Concerning the Principles of Morals*, Sec. I.ii, p. 204.
25 McIntyre, *After Virtue*, p. 543.
26 See, for example, William Galston, *Liberal Purposes: Goods, Virtues, and Diversity in the Liberal State* (New York: Cambridge University Press, 1991). In addition, see Stephen Macedo, *Liberal Virtues* (Oxford: Clarendon Press, 1990).
27 John Adams, "Letter to Mercy Warren, April 16, 1776," *Warren-Adams Letters*, ed. Worthington C. Ford (Boston: Massachusetts Historical Society, 1917), vol. 1, p. 222, as quoted by Michael J. Sandel, *Democracy's Discontent: America in Search of a Public Philosophy* (Cambridge, Mass.: Harvard University Press, 1996), p. 126.
28 Sandel, *Democracy's Discontent*, p. 127.
29 See discussion in ibid., p. 126.
30 See Lerner and Tirole, "Some simple economics of open source." See also Benkler, "Coase's penguin" and "Sharing Nicely."
31 See such key works on gift giving as: Bronislaw Malinowski, *Argonauts of the Western Pacific* (New York: Dutton, 1950; originally published 1922); Marcel Mauss, *The Gift: Forms and Functions of Exchange in Archaic Societies*, trans. Ian Cunnison (New York: Norton, 1967; originally published 1925); Maurice Godelier, *The Enigma of the Gift*, trans. Nora Scott (Chicago: University of Chicago Press, 1999; originally published 1997).

32 "Why people are running SETI@home;" available at http://setiathome.ssl.berkeley.edu/motivation.html (accessed December 20, 2002).
33 Pekka Himanem, *The Hacker Ethic, and the Spirit of the Information Age* (New York: Random House, 2001).
34 Sher, *Moral Philosophy*, p. 478.
35 ibid., p. 480.
36 Immanuel Kant, *The Doctrine of Virtue: Part II of the Metaphysic of Morals*, trans. Mary Gregor (New York: Harper & Row, 1969), as quoted by J. B. Schneewind, "The misfortune of virtue," *Ethics*, 101 (1990), 42–63 at p. 60.
37 McIntyre, *After Virtue*, p. 213.
38 Contemporary theorists who have explored links between political institutions and virtue include William Galston and Stephen Macedo, as well as Michael Sandel.
39 Sandel, *Democracy's Discontent*, pp. 125–126.
40 ibid., quotations from respectively, pp. 127, 131, 129 and 133.
41 Hunt, *Character and Culture*, p. 150.
42 ibid., p. 186.
43 Significant works that explicate related ideas include: Langdon Winner, "Do artifacts have politics?" in *The Whale and the Reactor* (Chicago: University of Chicago Press, 1986); Lawrence Lessig, *Codes and Other Laws of Cyberspace* (New York: Basic Books, 2000); Joel Reidenberg, "Lex informatica: the formulation of information policy rules through technology," *Texas Law Review*, 76 (1998), 553–93; Philip Brey, "Disclosive computer ethics," *ACM SIGCAS Computers and Society*, 30 (Dec. 2000), 10–16; Batya Friedman and Helen Nissenbaum, "Bias in computer systems," *Human Values and the Design of Computer Technology*, ed. Batya Friedman (New York: Cambridge University Press, 1997), pp. 21–40; Lucas Introna and Helen Nissenbaum, "Shaping the web: why the politics of search engines matters," *The Information Society*, 16 (2000), 1–17; Yochai Benkler, "Communications infrastructure regulation and the distribution of control over content," *Telecommunications Policy*, 22 (1998), 183–96; Bruno Latour, "Where are the missing masses: the sociology of a few mundane artifacts," *Shaping Technology/Building Society*. Eds. W. Bijker and J. Law (Cambridge, Mass.: MIT Press, 1992), pp. 225–58; Lewis Mumford, *Technics and Civilization* (New York: Harcourt, Brace and World, 1934); Marshall McLuhan, *Understanding Media: The Extensions of Man* (New York: McGraw-Hill, 1964); Neil Postman, *Amusing Ourselves to Death* (New York: Viking, 1985).
44 Brian Pfaffenberger, "Technological dramas," *Science, Technology and Human Values*, 17 (Summer 1992), 282–312, in part quoting Thomas P. Hughes, *American Genesis: A Century of Innovation and Technological Enthusiasm, 1870–1970* (New York: Penguin, 1989), p. 4.
45 Joseph M. Reagle Jr. "A case of mutual aid: Wikipedia, politeness, and perspective taking;" available at http://reagle.org.joseph/2004/agree/wikip-agree.html (accessed April 25, 2005).
46 Joe Wilcox and Stephen Shankland, "Why Microsoft is wary of open source," News.com, June 18, 2001; available at http://news.com.com/2100-1001-268520.html?legacy=cnet (accessed April 25, 2005).
47 Yochai Benkler, "Freedom in the commons: towards a political economy of information," *Duke Law Journal*, 52 (2003), 1245–76.